POLITICAL THEORY

IDEAS AND CONCEPTS

Second Edition

SUSHILA RAMASWAMY

Associate Professor
Department of Political Science
Jesus and Mary College
University of Delhi

PHI Learning Private Limited

Delhi-110092
2026

In fond memory of ***Shri Asoke K. Ghosh*** *(October 1942 – February 2024), Founder Chairman and Managing Director of PHI Learning, whose vision endlessly inspires.*

The Legacy Continues . . . .

Published by Pushpita Ghosh, PHI Learning Private Limited, Rimjhim House, 111, Patparganj Industrial Estate, Delhi-110092 and Printed by Multi Colour Services, 92, DSIDC Sheds, Okhla Industrial Area, Phase-I, New Delhi-110020

₹895.00

POLITICAL THEORY: Ideas and Concepts, Second Edition
Sushila Ramaswamy

ISBN-978-81-203-5048-9 (Print Book)
ISBN-978-93-90669-47-9 (e-Book)

The export rights of the book are vested solely with the publisher.

To the memory of
Sir Isaiah Berlin (1909–1997),
one of the finest and most formidable exponent of
freedom and pluralism in our times

Contents

Preface

This edition incorporates new interpretations and refinements, and also takes up a larger view in the context of the actual political processes and vindications or refutations of many well-established concepts, like multiculturalism.

As it is in the history of political thought, the major concepts in political theory is constantly put to test in the context of the evolution of knowledge, scientific inventions and discoveries and many questions that are constantly being formulated leading to further debates and exposition of new issues. In light of the same, following topics have been added to the book like: cosmopolitan citizenship, democratic peace, deliberative democracy, global justice, and Ostrom's governing the commons.

However, any exercise like the present volume remains incomplete and I will be grateful if there are suggestions for improvements which will be incorporated in the future editions.

My students have been greatly helpful in bringing to my notice the portions that needed greater clarity and elaboration and I would like to thank them all. I will like to express my gratitude to Sr. Marina John, Principal, Jesus and Mary College, for her continued encouragement and support of academic endeavours. I also wish to thank Ms. Sanghamitra Roy, Ms. Sudha Jha, Dr. Alka Marwaha and Ms. Renuka Subba for their manifold contributions to my academic and professional pursuits. However, I am solely responsible for the shortcomings in the book.

SUSHILA RAMASWAMY

Preface to the First Edition

Political theory and political philosophy are generally used interchangeably though sometimes a distinction is made between the two. Political theory deals with the study of political institutions and with theories of state, law, liberty, equality and representation. It is essentially comparative in its methodology. Political thought implies political writings that reflect on policy issues and political behaviour. It is a normative exercise in which *what ought to be* is an important component. In contrast, the ambit of political theory is restricted to *what it is*.

The very nature of the discipline of political theory leads to a continuous process of innovation, refinement, rejection and incorporation from other sources. The open-ended nature of political theory is reflected by the fact that one of the most distinguished liberal political thinkers of contemporary times, John Rawls is a philosopher by training and profession. The formidable influence of political economy and political sociology on concepts in political theory indicate its inter-disciplinary nature. Schumpter or Parsons are as familiar to students of political theory as Arendt or Oakeshott. This blurring of disciplinary boundaries does not allow for a differentiation like Schumpeter's distinction between Economics and Political Economy. It simultaneously contains the value-free with value-loaded concepts and ideas, and to seek a Kuhnian kind of consensus in political theory is a futile attempt. However, if this is a serious academic limitation it is at the same time a challenge as new theories and innovations emerge with alterations in the context and temper of politics.

The present work is a modest attempt to deal with the leading arguments, which are being examined within all the major concepts of political theory. It examines and analyzes key concepts like the state, authority, power, sovereignty, political obligation, civil disobedience, citizenship, rights, liberty, equality, justice, property, democracy, development and social change. These concepts are explained with reference to important thinkers from the ancient Greeks to contemporary times to understand their evolution in the context of significant changes in science, society and politics. The non-Western inputs—including Indian and Chinese—are incorporated to underline cultural plurality and shared values in an enterprise that tries to set universal standards. Moreover, the Western tradition is not as monolithic as is sometimes imagined. There are considerable variations even in that tradition and I have tried to deal with them. The different ideological standpoints with regard to various concepts are explained with the purpose of highlighting the differences in their perspectives. It is important to understand, as Sheldon Wolin rightly describes, that continuity and change characterize concepts and ideas in political theory. No idea becomes out of fashion and in our age with rich heritage of thousands of years they reappear in one form or another. Some ideas may go into cold storage for a while but they get resurrected and redefined in a new context and time. An effort is made to emphasize the continuing relevance of these concepts today and to understand how and why an idea of yesteryears gains prominence. It is for this reason, that Pitkin rightly remarks '... ideas like religion or prices are not by nature *a priori* either political or non-political. They are made political in certain times and places. And that means, in those times and places they are lifted out of unplanned drift and placed on the political agenda as conscious collective concerns.' As far as possible the latest reference material is used with the author's summing up at the end of each chapter.

I have incurred many debts while writing this book. Prof. Sunder Ramaswamy, my younger brother with whom I have had long discussions on many of the issues covered in this book has been instrumental in motivating me to write this book. Mrs Kausalya Ramaswamy, my mother has read all that I have written enthusiastically and appreciatively and has encouraged my academic pursuits. Mrs Dharmu and Dr Krishnamurthy and Mr S. Narasimhan have been supportive in my academic work and without their constant encouragement and help the book would not have seen the light of the day. Diya and Surinder helped me to sustain my academic interests by their constant involvement and positive attitude towards my work. But for the academic guidance and direction provided by Prof. Milton Fisk, Prof. Barbara Goodwin, Prof. David McLellan, Prof. Subrata Mukherjee, Prof. Jon Quah and Prof. M.P. Singh it would not have been possible for me to undertake such a big and challenging academic project. My students at Jesus and Mary College and at the University of Delhi, South Campus have responded heartily to my writings and I owe a great deal to them for being encouraging and appreciative. My principal and colleagues at the college have always been supportive and helpful in my various academic endeavours. Mrs Madhu Maini, librarian of Jesus and Mary College library and the other staff there have been extremely cooperative with books and resource material. I also wish to thank the librarians and staff of the University of Delhi South Campus Library, Central Library of the University of Delhi, British Council, New Delhi, American Center, New Delhi, Max Mueller Bhavan, New Delhi, Indian Council of World Affairs, New Delhi and American Studies Research Center, Hyderabad for their assistance. To my friends Alan Chong, Monica Chopra, Usha Chug, Ishtiaq Hossain, Ashima Kaul, Kiran Nanda, Suman Sharma, Farida Siddiqui, Bharathi and Asharam Sihag, and Kripa Sridharan, I am deeply grateful for their manifold contributions. However, any shortcoming in the book is entirely mine.

SUSHILA RAMASWAMY

Chapter 1

Nature of Political Theory

A political theorist is no Robinson Crusoe or a dispassionate observer of political events. A political theorist establishes an intricate link between the political process, the political actors and institutions with his belief structures. This extraordinary capacity leads to the emergence of an epic theory. A political theorist reflects on particular incidents with the purpose of understanding and analysing institutions and practices with the view to change them. Political theories are not manufactured in laboratories but are written with an eye fixed on the public forum. A political theorist analyses an event in its totality without ignoring the minute details. A political theorist is not a political pamphleteer or a strategist or a participant aspiring for power, but is a gifted analyst of contemporary events with a sense of the movements in history, for posterity.

A text in political theory contains three elements: (1) factual statements, (2) what is likely to happen and (3) what ought to happen. It has to describe the 'ought to' from an explanation of the 'is' and, hence, traditionally political theory is normative in content. It contains 'factors of three kinds—the factual, the causal and the valuational' (Sabine 1939: 6). It is a personal endeavour to understand and experience the present political reality with the view of evolving a mechanism in order to transcend the present imperfect society and to lead to a better and more perfect and just order. This includes a study of the evolution, nature, composition, necessity and purpose of the governmental apparatus and also an understanding of the human perception and nature, and its relationship with the larger community. Political theory usually flourishes during times of acute crises, when shifts from one set of values to another evoke intense debates and momentous transformations. Crises act as a stimulus, though all crises do not necessarily give rise to political theorising. It is usually the desire for a good life and a good society, optimism and hope, which are the major impetus for a worthwhile political theory. A sense of hopelessness and despair normally dissuades political theorising. Sabine identifies the two most important periods when political theory was rich and diverse—the fifth century BC in Greece and the seventeenth century AD in England. Both periods witnessed tumultuous and cataclysmic changes. In the former, the city-state was being eclipsed by a new political formation, the empire that Philip and his son Alexander had begun to establish. In the latter, the 'first constitutional state on national lines and the preparation of those intellectual or scientific changes that governed the Western World down at least until 1914' (Sabine 1939: 3) began to emerge. Political theory emerged primarily in Greece from the sixth to the fifth century BC, though India, China and Egypt also simultaneously developed their distinct philosophical world views.

POLITICAL THEORY AND OTHER INTERRELATED TERMS

Political theory is one of the core areas in political science. It is only in recent times that it emerges as an academic discipline. Earlier, those who were engaged in this enterprise styled themselves as philosophers or scientists. From ancient Greece to the present, the history of political theory has dealt with fundamental and perennial ideas of political science. The first modern usage of the term 'political science' is in the works of Charles-Louis de Secondat Montesquieu (1689–1755), Adam Smith (1723–1790), Adam Ferguson (1723–1816) and David Hume (1711–1776), where it means the 'science of the legislator'.

A distinction has to be made between political theory and the terms like political science, political philosophy and political ideology, though often these are treated interchangeably. The differentiation between political theory and political science arises because of the general shift in intellectual perceptions brought out by the modern science. **Political science** tries to provide plausible generalisations and laws about politics and political behaviour while **political theory** reflects upon political phenomenon, processes and institutions and on actual political behaviour by subjecting it to philosophical or ethical criterion. It considers the question of the best political order, which is a part of a larger and a more fundamental question, namely the ideal form of life that a human being ought to lead within a larger community. In the process of answering immediate and local questions, it addresses perennial issues, which is why a study of the classical texts forms an important component of the discipline. A classic in political theory has the essential ingredients of a great literary work, which in spite of its local setting, deals with the perennial problems of life and society. It contains the quintessence of eternal knowledge, and is an inheritance not of any one culture, place, people or time, but of the entire humankind.

> Political theory is the most appropriate term to employ in designating that intellectual tradition which affirms the possibility of transcending the sphere of immediate practical concerns and 'viewing' man's societal existence from a critical perspective (Germino 1967: 7).

Specific political theories cannot be considered as the correct or final understanding of an event. The meaning of an event is always open to future interpretations from new viewpoints, each explaining and analysing from a particular standpoint or concern in political life. Furthermore, political theory is critical in its endeavour, for it gives an account of politics that rises above those of ordinary people. There is no tension between political theory and political science, for they differ in terms of their boundaries and jurisdiction, and not in their aim. Political theory supplies ideas, concepts and theories for the purpose of analysis, description, explanation and criticism, which in turn are incorporated in political science.

> Political theory was political science in the full sense, and there could be no science without theory. Just as we may speak of theory as either the activity of theorizing or the recorded results of the theorizing, so political theory may legitimately and accurately be used as synonymous with political science (Germino 1967: 7).

Political philosophy provides general answers to the questions like what is justice, what is right, the distinction between '*is*' and '*ought*' and the larger concerns in politics. Political philosophy is part of normative political theory, for it attempts to establish inter-relationships between concepts. It is perhaps accurate to say that every political philosopher is a theorist, though every political theorist is not a political philosopher. Political philosophy is

> a complex activity, which is best, understood by analysing the many ways that the acknowledged masters have practiced it. No single philosopher and no one historical age can be said to have defined it conclusively, any more than any one painter or school of painting has practiced all that we mean by painting (Wolin 1960: 2).

There is an intimate and on-going relationship between political philosophy and philosophy. The credit for it goes to Plato (428/27–347 BC), who in the *Republic* (380–70 BC) shows that the good of the individual is inextricably linked with that of the community. Subsequently, well-known philosophers have 'contributed generously to the main stock of our political ideas, but they have given the political theorist many of his methods of analysis and criteria of judgment' (Wolin 1960: 2). The difference between philosophy and political philosophy is not with regard to method or mood but to the subject matter. Philosophy attempts to understand the 'truths publicly arrived at and publicly demonstrable' (ibid: 4), while a political theorist tries to explain the meaning of the political and its relationship to the public sphere.

Political thought is the thought of the whole community that includes the writings and speeches of the articulated sections such as professional politicians, political commentators, social reformers and ordinary persons of a community. Thought is in the form of political treatises, scholarly articles, speeches, government policies and decisions. It also includes poems and prose that capture the anguish of the people. Thought is time bound, as evident from titles like *A History of Twentieth Century Political Thought* or like Political Thought, which include theories that attempt to explain political behaviour and values to evaluate it and methods to control it. One notable example of the inclusion of the normative perspective in a political document is the *American Declaration of Independence* (1776) which spoke of 'life, liberty and the pursuit of happiness.' Similarly, the Preamble of the Indian Constitution is considered by Barker (1976: Preface) as the best possible articulation of a collective desire of *an entire nation*.

Political theory, unlike thought, refers to the speculation by a single individual, usually articulated in treatise(s) as models of explanation. It consists of the theories of the institutions, including that of the state, of law, of representation and of election. The mode of enquiry is comparative and explanatory.

> Political theory attempts to explain the attitudes and actions arising from ordinary political life and to generalize about them in a particular context: thus political theory is concerned about/with the relationships between concepts and circumstances. Political philosophy attempts to resolve or to understand conflicts between political theories, which might appear equally acceptable in given circumstances (Crick 1973: 5).

Political ideology, a systematic and an all-embracing doctrine, attempts to give a complete and universally applicable theory of human nature and society along with a detailed programme of attaining it. John Locke (1632–1704) is often described as the father of modern ideologies. Marxism is the classic example of an ideology summed up in the statement that the purpose of philosophy is to change and not merely to interpret the world. All political ideology is political philosophy, though the reverse is not true. Twentieth century has seen many ideologies like Fascism, Nazism Communism and Liberalism. A distinctive trait of political ideology is its dogmatism, which unlike political philosophy, precludes and discourages critical appraisal as it aims to realise a perfect society. According to Germino (1967) and Sabine (1939), political ideology is a negation of political theory because an ideology is of recent origin, and under the influence of positivism, is based on subjective, unverifiable value preferences. Germino furthermore distinguishes a political theorist from a publicist as the former has a profound understanding of issues while the latter is concerned with the immediate questions. By this distinction, Germino considers Aristotle (384–22 BC), St. Thomas Aquinas (1224–1274), Niccolo Machiavelli (1469–1527), Thomas Hobbes (1588–1679), Jean Jacques Rousseau (1712–1778) and George Wilhelm Friedrich Hegel (1770–1831) as theorists. Their contemporaries Phaleas of Chalcedon (4th century BC), Giles of Rome (d 1316), Giovanni Botero (1544–1617), Sir Robert Filmer (1588–1653), Marie Jean Marquis de Condorcet (1743–1794) and Joseph-Marie comte d' Maistre (1753–1821) are seen as publicists. The gap between a theorist and a publicist is wide and divergent, differing 'fundamentally in orientation, scope, emphasis, tone and terminological sophistication' (Germino 1967: 14). In this context, Germino rejects Karl Mannheim's (1893–1947) thesis of sociology of knowledge which contends that belief structures have a social origin and that social science knowledge is dependent on the class origin of a theorist thereby precluding objectivity.

> While the data offered by the 'sociology of knowledge' are of obvious relevance in explaining the thinking of some propagandists for mass movements they are of scant significance in helping us understand a Plato or Hegel (Germino ibid: 13–14).

Furthermore, Germino, like Plato, also distinguishes between mere opinion and knowledge, the latter being the starting point of a political theorist. Every political theorist has a dual role, that of a scientist and a philosopher, and the way he divides his roles depends on his temperament and interests. Only by combining the two roles can he contribute to human knowledge in a worthwhile manner. The scientific component of a theory can appear coherent and significant only if the author has a preconceived notion of the aims of political life. The philosophical basis is revealed in the manner in which reality is depicted (Hacker 1961: 2–3). Political theory is

> dispassionate and disinterested. As science, it describes political reality without trying to pass judgement on what is being depicted either implicitly or explicitly. As philosophy, it prescribes rules of conduct which will secure the good life for all of society and not simply for certain individuals or classes. The theorist, in theory, will not himself have a personal interest in the political arrangements of any one country or class or party. Devoid of such an interest, his vision of reality and his image of the good life will not be clouded, nor will his theory be special pleading. ... The intention of ideology is to justify a particular system of power in society. The ideologue is an interested party: his interest may be to defend things as they are or to criticize the status quo in the hope that a new distribution of power will come into being. ... Rather than disinterested prescription we have rationalization. ... Rather than dispassionate description we have a distorted picture of reality (Hacker 1961: 4–5).

MEANING OF THE POLITICAL AND DIFFERENT IDEOLOGIES

Political theorists, since Aristotle, try to define the term 'political' as understanding political practices and their application. Aristotle's remark that 'man is a political animal' takes note of the inherent human desire for society and the fact that human beings need and find fulfillment only through a political community. For Aristotle, the political is important as it stands for a common political space in which all citizens participate, thus limiting the ambit of the political. This notion resonates in Michael Joseph Oakeshott (1901–1990) and Hannah Arendt (1906–1975) for whom political life is a distinctive form of human organisation with special value, a place for freedom, honour and full human development. The political is autonomous and has to be safeguarded particularly from the onslaughts of social and economic issues. Remarkably similar to this view is that of David Easton (1965) for whom politics is an authoritative allocation of values, elaborating on Harold Lasswell (1936) famous phrase, "Who gets what, when and how? The subject matter of political theory is linked to a quest for a proper and legitimate form and scope of politics as a practical activity". At the other end of the spectrum is the view that regards politics as co-extensive with the entire extent of human activity. Accordingly, politics is described as a universal dimension of human life treating power with which human beings are able to sustain or alter their human and natural world as the appropriate subject matter.

The 'political' dimension of political theory concerns itself with the form, nature, organisation of the state or government and its relationship with the individual citizen. Though inter-linked, the political is treated as a specific area distinct, independent and different from the other spheres like the economy and culture. This is the primary focus of the liberal tradition. The liberal tradition also upholds the divide between the personal and political. On the contrary, Marxism categorically rejects the liberal distinction and considers political power as the hand-maiden of economic power. It identifies affinity between economic power and the state. However, such a view also raises certain problems. It tries to comprehend the political with reference to economic power, and thus precludes or ignores all those aspects that cannot be understood from the standpoint of class. For instance, questions relating to gender, nationality, minority rights, ecology, power of bureaucrats over their clients, form and nature of electoral systems are not addressed (Held 1991: 6). Further by projecting the socialist society as a stateless society, Marxism does not theorise about the law-governed state nor explains the relationship between the individual and the state, the issue of rights, political freedom and power and role of authority in the socialist society. As a result, it does not take into account the evils of concentrated, unrestrained and unlimited state power and the question of political accountability (Dahl 1986: 73; Djilas 1990: 7; Held 1991: 6). Germino considers Marxism to be an ideology rather than a political theory.

Early feminist writings provide a new definition of 'political' with their stress on the intimate link between the public space and the private domain. It deconstructs the private and public dichotomy in classical and contemporary political theory and calls for a rethinking of this distinction and its meaning for politics. Mary Wollstonecraft (1759–1797) and John Stuart Mill (1806–1873) point to the subjugation of women in the private domain, which is insulated from the ideals of freedom, equality and justice that dominate the public sphere. The aim of these first wave liberal feminists' emphasis is on equal rights, equal gain and access to the public sphere on the same terms as men. However, **radical feminism**, since the 1960s characterises as 'second wave feminism', questions this separation. It identifies men to be the cause for women's oppression by coining the phrase 'personal is political' to cogently and dramatically demand the extension of political analysis and controversy to the 'personal' spheres such as marital relationships, domestic violence, childcare and the like. It challenges the public-private divide from both ends: the devaluation of the public space because of its exclusion of women and private concerns from its purview and the bankruptcy of the private because of the exclusion of men from domestic responsibilities including childcare. It considers the public sphere as the structural expressions of the male gender values—non-nurturing ones—the basis of male-constructed politics. Since the 1980's, feminism coalesces with postmodernism by rejecting the modernism of the Enlightenment philosophy, namely the rational pursuit of truth, certainty and objectivity and drew attention to the 'maleness' of its central concepts. It believes that—

> it has not been until recently that debates about this form of 'slavery', and its entwinement with the public and the private have touched the centre of political theory. Indeed, recent debates have been broadened to include questions about the patriarchal construction of the central categories of political thought; the political meaning of sexual difference; the relation between the intimate, familial and domestic, and the economy and state; and the interconnections among nature, reason, politics and the sexes (Held 1991: 7–8).

In the first wave, the focus is on the omission of women by classical political theorists and the need to incorporate women's issues and concerns. In the second wave, the emphasis is—criticise, reject and start again—to bring to light the bankruptcy of the whole of Western thought in light of the contemporary concerns. In the third wave, emphasis is to deconstruct and transform in order to 'understand the sexual politics of our cultural and intellectual heritage' intending to 'comment and transform it' (Beasley 1994: 4–5).

To summarise, the meaning of the political is of crucial significance for political theory as the description of the details will define the boundary of the political map. There is no unanimity about this subject to what constitutes the political and this normative question continues to provoke diverse formulations and a Kuhnian consensus eludes us even today.

USAGES OF POLITICAL THEORY

As the History of Political Thought

Usually courses in political theory offer a detailed and elaborate study of books or particular political philosophies, from Plato to contemporary times, from a historical perspective. These books are studied for their normative statements about the desirability of certain types of institutions, governments and laws, which are usually accompanied by rational arguments. The classics are portrayed as timeless in quality, permanent in relevance and universal in its significance. The classical tradition demonstrates a great deal of unity in style and manner of argument, which is why it constitutes a common school of enquiry. However, in spite of this intrinsic unity, the classics offer divergent interpretations of politics and this makes their study useful for understanding contemporary politics. In course of analysing texts from a historical perspective, it is important to see how a particular idea or concept has evolved in course of time, and the different meanings and interpretations it has been subjected to. While it is important to know who said something for the first time, it is equally important to know the new ramifications of an idea or a concept. It is for this reason that Wolin (1960) rightly describes the history of political theory as marked by both continuity and innovation.

As Technique of Analysis

Aristotle's remark that the 'individual is a political animal' indicates the primacy of politics and the fact that political thinking takes place at various levels and in a variety of ways. The political in such a view becomes not only all pervasive but also the highest kind of activity. Politics symbolises a collective public life wherein people create institutions that regulate their common life. Even deceptively simple common sense questions and political opinion merit an answer, for instance, are individuals equal? Is the state more important than the individual? How to justify violence employed by the state? Is there an inherent tension between freedom and equality? Is the minority justified in dictating terms to the majority and vice-versa? One's response to these statements often reflects *what ought to be the case* rather than *what is the case*. At stake here is a choice between values and ideals. By exercising one's preferences, one also inadvertently subscribes to a political ideology which means that answers to questions not only will vary according to individual opinion but also would diverge depending on one's value preferences. It is because of this basic reason that political theory is to be a part of an open society, for there would always be liberals and conservatives. Training in political theory helps one to answer the aforesaid questions logically, speculatively and critically.

> Political theory is quite simply, man's attempts to consciously understand and solve the problems of his group life and organization. ... [It] is the disciplined investigation of political problems ... not only to show what a political practice is but also to show what it means. In showing what a practice means, or what it ought to mean, political theory can alter what it is (Sabine 1973: 3–5).

Political theory is used to either defend or question the status quo. Taking into cognisance of the facts and details, it explains and describes politics in abstract and general terms that allow space for critical imagination. As a discipline, the aim of political theory is to describe, explain, justify or criticise the existing institutional arrangements and power equations in society. Some commentators like Goodwin (1992) emphasise the centrality of the power paradigm, whereas others like Talcott Parsons (1902–1979) downgrade it comparing it to money in modern societies. Recent important works by

John Rawls (1921–2002) and Robert Nozick (1924–2002) do not emphasise at all on power. It is interesting that Rawls emphasises on a well-ordered society identifying justice, stability and efficiency as its main ingredients without any attempt to speak about the distribution of power.

As Conceptual Clarification

Political theory helps to understand the concepts and terms used in a political argument and analysis like freedom, equality, democracy, justice and rights. These terms are frequently used not only in daily conversation but also in political theory discourse. An understanding of these terms is important for it helps one to know the way these terms have been employed, the shifts in their definition and their usage in a structure of argument. Many, like Weldon (1953), stress on the need to scrutinise concepts in ordinary pre-theoretical language. Analyses of concepts also reveal the ideological commitment of a speaker or/and writer. Liberals define freedom as implying choice, absence of restraints while socialists link freedom with equality. Liberals define a state as an instrument of human welfare, while for a socialist a state is an instrument of oppression, domination and class privileges. Conceptual clarification is definitely possible but cannot be neutral. Those engaged in it overtly or covertly subscribe to value preference, and in this sense their task is not different from the authors of classics in political theory who help one to understand the underlying basis of human, political and moral actions.

As Formal Model Building

This perception is particularly popular in the United States for it considers political theory as an exercise in devising formal models of political processes, similar to the ones in theoretical economics. These models serve two purposes—first, they are explanatory, offering systematically the factors on which political processes are based, and second, they are normative, for they try to show the consequences that accrue from following a certain rule. A good example of such an exercise is Antony Downs' theory of electoral competition which perceives voters as trying to gain maximum utility from an election result and parties as teams trying to maximise their probability of winning. Downs then shows how parties, in order to win, devise ideological stances. Another important model is Kenneth Arrow's impossibility theorem, which states that, among other things, where a democratic choice has to be made between more than two alternatives, the outcome would very likely be an arbitrary one influenced by the procedure employed to exercise the choice. Josef Schumpeter's elitist theory of democracy is based on the assumption that a human being takes his economic life more seriously than the political one.

As Theoretical Political Science

The emergence of political science in the twentieth century has led some political scientists to look upon political theory as a mere theoretical branch of the discipline. An attempt is made to integrate empirical observations with a systematic explanation of one's everyday experiences in the world. This view dispenses with the normative consent of traditional political theory. Though mere explanation of political phenomena is possible but grounding it in empiricism is not adequate. Any attempt to formulate a political theory free of normative elements would inherently fail. This is because any explanation of political events would mean an interpretation of the intentions and motives of the participants and such an interpretation would bring forth normative issues.

KEY THEORETICAL CONCEPTS

A reader getting introduced to political theory for the first time may think it sufficient to study the institutions rather than abstract concepts in order to understand the character and nature of the society. While a study of institutions is possible, one has to realise that institutional arrangements vary from society to society because they are based on divergent sets of ideas. This realisation takes us to the heart of the matter as to what is more important, reality or ideas, facts or concepts. Do ideas reflect reality or is reality based on ideas?

It may be difficult to find satisfactory answers to these perennial questions that satisfy everybody. However, in trying to define them one comes across categorisations and labels that become useful tools for analysis. For instance, an idealist like Plato contends that there exist some permanent immutable ideas to which reality should approximate. On the contrary, there are those like Locke who believe that concepts are derived from our observation of the material reality, and are called *materialist* or *realist*. Usually, though not always, a materialist approach is *empirical* and *inductive* in nature. An inductive method of reasoning means that general statements are derived from observing particular facts. It is the opposite of *deductive* form of reasoning in which the conclusion of an argument is validly inferred from some premises. A *descriptive* theory is one that describes reality and constructs explanations on the facts collected. In contrast, an evaluative theory analyses ideas with reference to other concepts and values. The opposition between descriptive and evaluative theory is reflected in the distinction between *facts* and *values*. Facts are empirically verifiable while values cannot be substantiated or verified. A *deontology* is an ethical theory that considers certain moral duties as self evident and absolutely binding irrespective of their consequences. As opposed to this is *teleology* or *consequentialism*, which believes that the right or wrong actions are determined by the goodness or badness of their consequences. It also holds that events can be explained and evaluation is possible only by considering the ends towards which they are directed. The Kantian and, in recent times, the Rawlsian theory is deontological. Classical utilitarianism is teleological. An important distinction is made between *normative* and *empirical* theory. A normative political theory is prescriptive, for it sets standards or forms of conduct and does not describe facts or events. Normative statements include words like 'ought', 'should' and 'must'. An empirical social scientist observes reality and experience and then constructs a general theory based on a plethora of facts and data. He does not accept *a priori* knowledge.

Closely related to empiricism is *pragmatism*, a philosophical theory associated with American philosophers C.S. Peirce (1839–1914), William James (1842–1910) and John Dewey (1859–1952), which holds that beliefs have a meaning and justification because of their practical results. It also accepts the fact that the subject of knowledge is not merely a recipient of sensation but also an active inquirer. Some see experience as intelligible in isolation without any reference to the nature of its object or to the circumstances of its subject. This implies that there is no need to explain social condition of an experience. Such a view was implied in Hume's theory of the relation between 'idea' and 'impression' and in Bertrand Arthur William Russell's (1872–1970) *Logical Atomism*. Experience and fulfillment of desires as the basis of human nature is articulated by *utilitarianism*, which judges human actions in terms of the pleasure promoted/increased and the pain caused/decreased.

As opposed to empiricism, *rationalism* contends that the world can be known through the power of reason, and reason can correct experiences delivered by senses. Rationalism has its origins in Plato but it is popularly associated with modern theorists beginning with Rene Descartes (1596–1650) and culminating in the German academic philosophy of the Enlightenment. Other early modern exponents of rationalism were Baruch or Benedict Spinoza (1632–1677) and Gottfried Wilhelm Leibniz (1646–1716). Rationalism was critiqued by Immanuel Kant (1724–1804) but re-emerged in the writings of Hegel. Max Weber (1864–1920) understood rationalism in the sense of preferred legal-rational authority over others—traditional and charismatic. Rationalism that J.S. Mill used meant search for rational solutions other than prejudices, scientific explanations other than mysticism. It also meant favouring clear and explicit solutions based on principles. Rationalism is regarded as a political vice by theorists like Oakeshott who pointed out that a rationalist mind is skeptical of any authority other than reason, dismissing tradition, custom and habit and group experience as irrelevant.

A distinction is also made between *subjective* or personal/individual and *objective* or impersonal/impartial. Rousseau's General Will promotes the objective good of the community by attempting to transcend the narrow particularistic and selfish will of the individual. Rousseau considers anything collective to be inherently good and elevating. This is an idea that he borrows from Plato and transmits to the early socialists and Marx. Since the 1980s, the communitarians espouse a similar view.

Another term, *relativism* connotes that values and principles do not have universal or timeless validity and that there is no absolute criterion of truth. Values are valid within a social group or individual person or an age. It is commonly associated with *historicism*, which has two meanings. In the late nineteenth century, it meant uniqueness of all historical phenomena and that each age should be interpreted in terms of its own ideas and principles. The second meaning associated with Popper, means belief in large-scale laws of historical development on the basis of which prediction could be made.

CHANGING CONTEXT OF WORDS AND ITS IMPLICATION FOR POLITICAL THEORY

Like ideas, even words have a context. This proposition, Raymond Williams (1958) defends by contextualising five words in the English language, i.e., industry, democracy, class, art and culture. In the context of these words, the last few decades of the eighteenth century and the first fifty years of the nineteenth century is of crucial significance. All these words which were a part of the English vocabulary were used for a long time, but acquired a new and significant meaning at this aforesaid period. Williams argues that this change in words can be described as some kind of a map which reflects a larger change in life and thought and the subsequent changes in language itself. With drastic changes in the life itself in all its significant manifestations, social, political and economic, and the altered relationships of institutions and activities led to this sea change in the meaning and contextualisation of words.

In the context of the industrial revolution, the word 'industry' which was associated with particular human character meaning individual attributes became a description of a collective word for manufacturing and productive process. The earlier use continues even today but ever since Smith changed the context of the word 'industry' the latter use is more common. *Democracy* which had a Greek origin, meaning government by the people, came into the English language at the time of the American and French Revolutions as 'it was not until the French Revolution that democracy ceased to be a mere literary word and became part of the political vocabulary' (ibid: 14). The present use of the term 'democracy' till the eighteenth and the beginning of the nineteenth century was equated with mob-rule and was supposed to be both dangerous and subversive. But the connotation totally changed with the struggle, as expressed by Williams, as 'democratic representation'. The word 'class' in the modern sense began around 1740. Before this time, class had a connotation of describing division of a group in school and college taken from logic and philosophy. But towards the end of the eighteenth century, class in the modern social sense came into use with expressions like higher class, middle class and a middling class. The phrase 'working class' came into use around 1815 and upper class in 1820s. The important phrases like class prejudices, class legislation, class consciousness, class conflict and class war followed this early trend and the phrase 'upper middle class' was first used in the 1890s and the phrase 'lower middle class' only in the twentieth century. *Art* also reflected this process of change. Originally, it meant an individual skill but subsequently it came to refer an institution meaning 'activities of a certain kind' (ibid: 15). Earlier art was any kind of human skill but in the new context it means a specialised category of imaginative or creative arts. Similarly, culture which was understood as 'tending of natural growth' changed to something which is 'doing in itself', i.e., 'a general state or habit of the mind linked to human perfection, intellectual development within the entirety of society within a larger framework of general category of arts' (ibid). Later it encompassed the entirety of all arts and culture came to mean the whole society including the material, the intellectual and the spiritual. Williams considers that this changing connotation of *culture* is of striking importance as the change reflects the change in the other key words of industry, democracy and class. The importance for political theory in this changed contextualisation is two-fold: (a) the changes in society connote total alteration in the meaning of some key words and (b) the change reflects the new personal and social relationships that inevitability came out of the significant changes in this period of quick change. This means that the new idea of culture came as a response not only to the new industrial society but also to a new social and political phenomenon called democracy. Apart from this total transformation of older words, a lot of new words emerged to describe the new situation like ideology, intellectual, rationalism, scientist, humanitarian, utilitarian, romanticism, atomistic, bureaucracy, capitalism, collectivism, commercialism, communism, doctrinaire, equalitarian, liberalism, masses, medieval, medievalism, primitive, proletariat, socialism, unemployment, cranks, high-brow, isms and pretensions.

APPROACHES TO POLITICAL THEORY

There is the question about the approaches to analysing a text in political theory. Disagreements exist about whether to emphasise the historical contexts of a text or analyse texts without taking note of time and context from which they arise. The **textualist approach**, exemplified in the writings of Hacker (1961) and Plamentaz (1963), stresses that political theory texts can be studied without reference to their historical context. This approach has been dominant since 1945. Political theory is considered as a sub-category of philosophy and its central concerns are to clarify concepts used in political discourse and debate and second, to critically examine and evaluate political beliefs and principles (Raphael 1990, Heywood 1999). The textualists allege that while historical understanding of the milieu in which these texts have originate may give us some insights but they do not play a central role in interpreting them. On the other hand, there are contextualists like Skinner (1966), Pocock (1971), Dunn (1979) and Collini (1983), who contend that a mere textual approach is inherently weak as it overlooks the historical background, the purpose, motivation and the intention to write a text. Every text is the result of a conscious effort of the author(s). To ignore the historical context could lead to an error in interpreting and understanding the texts. Macpherson (1973) pays attention to the concerns of the author by situating him in the historical society in which the text was composed. This approach emphasises that political theory itself has a history (Ashcraft 1986, Dunn 1979 and Tully 1988).

The contextualists are skeptical about the claims of the textualists who assert that there are universal and timeless questions and problems that the great political texts of the past raise. Skinner maintains that to suggest that these writings provide answers to fundamental political questions that confront contemporary society is far-fetched. The political and moral assumptions and beliefs that underlie the great works of political theory are historically specific creation. The great works raise questions and provide answers that should be viewed as relative to the particular societies and cultures from which they emerged. The contextualists point out that to understand the formulations and theoretical statements about politics it is necessary to stress the interrelationship between political theory and practice. The texts are in response to specific events, controversies, debates and crises reinforcing Berki's observation that "political thought issues out of practical experience and not the other way around" (1977: 32). The historians of political thought also point out that the writers of the past intended to communicate with particular audiences. Only when we comprehend the writers' intentions, their use of language and the words that prevailed at that point of time can one understand the meaning of these texts. Merely reading it without any reference to time and social, economic and cultural milieu would be to approach the texts in the 'biblical' sense as if their meaning can be ascertained simply by reading it and reflecting on its universal message' (Berki ibid: 31).

In interpreting texts, its time period must be taken into consideration as it enables us to see the way a word is defined, assigned different meanings revealing the intent of the writer and relate it to the immediate social and political environment, the aims and purpose of writing the text, how well the author has tackled the problems vis-á-vis his contemporaries, and finally the meaning of the text today. It is through the consideration of these aspects that we can perhaps understand why, among a host of innumerable tracts, only some have been elevated to the status of classics. It also helps to see and appreciate the plurality of ideas that exists within a particular time-frame. For example, Rousseau's attempt to distinguish between government, democracy, state and sovereignty is a case in point. The word 'sovereignty' was used to describe the power of the people acting as lawmakers themselves and not through their representatives. Neither was sovereignty a characteristic of the state. It differed from the government, which administered and enforced the law but could not make the law. Sovereignty meant the exercise of power by the people directly. The diverse contributions of Rousseau make him a genius, in the opinion of Catlin.

Since political theory is by and large descriptive, a historical approach is important, for that would help us to see how political theory varies according to time and circumstances. It helps, as Dunning says, to know the 'successive transformation' of a particular idea or concept, or as Sabine says, the 're-interpretation and re-adaptation' of received beliefs and theories. Furthermore, as Sabine argues, an examination of the history of political theories reveals that its literature is not a product of a laboratory. The authors have an eye fixed on the public forum, and if political theories are produced in quantities, then it is a symptom that society itself is undergoing a period of stress and strain. This is because "theories of politics are themselves a part of politics. In other words, they do not refer to an external reality, but are produced as a normal part of the social *milieu* in which politics itself has its being. Reflection upon the ends of political action, upon the means of achieving them, upon the possibilities and necessities of political situations, and upon the obligations that political purposes impose is an intrinsic element of the whole political process. Thus, conceived, the theory of politics no more reaches an end than politics itself, and its history has no concluding chapter (Sabine 1973: Preface to the 1st edition). Dunn endorses this assertion by stating that 'the history of political theory is still a key aid in understanding politics' (cited in Tuck 1995: 2).

Another way of approaching texts is by placing them in the tradition of Western political theory or philosophy. Such an approach has been used by Strauss (1952) and Wolin (1960). They understand the tradition, not as a chronological sequence of books and writers, but as a narrative discourse in which the writer consciously articulates and elaborates a theme. Strauss argues that political philosophers from Plato to Hegel have grappled with the problem of natural right, namely stating and justifying trans-historical standards of right or justice. The Greeks defend this proposition, whereas modern theorists reject it. For both philosophical and political reasons, Strauss favours the Greek position and characterises modern political theory as degenerative, for it has given rise to ethical relativism resulting in the death of political theory. The moderns look to comfort, affluence and avoidance of death to mean good life, which could be secured not through rational understanding, but by gaining power over nature. The pre-moderns reject this view, for they consider human desires as insatiable, making it difficult to realise happiness. Moreover, mere scientific power without the knowledge of ends would only lead to crude hedonism. As a result, modern thought rejects divine revelation, eternal nature or inevitable history as contributing a yardstick for measurement leading to uncritical acceptance of liberal democracy without exploring alternatives. Strauss does not regard political philosophy as a historical discipline. Though knowledge of history is important for political philosophy, "it is only preliminary and auxiliary to political philosophy; it does not form an integral part of it" (Strauss 1949: 30). Furthermore, refuting the claim that a text is historically conditioned, Strauss observes that every political situation consists of elements that could be found in other political situations as well, and that explains why classics are evergreen.

Wolin contends that traditional political theory attempts to define the dignity, distinctiveness and the importance of the political, which disintegrates since the seventeenth century, leading eventually to the decline and sublimation of the political. Within this framework, he selects thinkers for whom the political is primary, general and integrative. It is imperative to discern the philosophical teachings of thinkers who try to clarify the meaning of the political, rather than focus on their historical backgrounds. The philosophical content should not be confused for historical understanding. Many, like Pocock (1962, 1971 and 1980), Dunn (1968a), Skinner (1969) and Gunnell (1978) reject the idea that it is possible to identify a unity in tradition, and that the great masters are engaged in a common activity, or addressed some common issues.

Many see the classics as addressing questions and elucidating themes that are of perennial interest. Such a perspective is offered by Hacker (1961), Plamentaz (1963) and Bluhm (1965). Viewed in this manner, political theory is perceived as a complex and comprehensive activity that deals with universal and eternal issues to convince readers that the classics are relevant to contemporary times. However, mere historical study is not sufficient. Care must be taken to see that the texts do not get submerged within the pages of history. As Iain Hampsher Monk (1992, x–xi) points out that such an approach would stifle their capacity 'to formulate statements with any reference beyond the historically parochial', thus, denying them any significance for contemporary times. Emphasis on the historical context of the text might result in the possibility of the writer and text getting fragmented and disappearing into context.

It is important to look for consistency, coherence, clarity, truth, reliability and certainty in the text, for that would enable us to see how best a text is in terms of providing a conceptual paradigm. Each text advances, defends and justifies a set of values or preferences, and it is important to see how best it does it. For this, one must look at the internal consistency of a text, and then compare it with that of others written in and during that time, for such a relative assessment will tell us why, out of a plethora of books, only some become great or immortal. Sabine feels that it is possible to enumerate the properties that political theories have actually had, and examine a variety of questions relating to the truth and validity of political theories.

There is moreover a need to recognise that there exists a broad Western political tradition to which diverse political thinkers, from different circumstances and concerns adhere to. Notwithstanding the wide variations there exists a history of political thought 'one broadly defined, yet coherent tradition of political discourse. We are not faced with a chaotic whirl of disembodied ideas and texts, but with a concrete world of interlacing and interweaving visions' (Berki 1977: 36–37). Some thinkers have treated 'the past as a treasure trove from which they can draw for their own purposes' (Morrow 1998: 5). Rawls says he is reviving and updating Kant and Nozick of Locke thus continuing 'with the ancient practice of pillaging the classics in search of ideas and styles to be revived for their own time' (Tuck 1993: 72). Aristotle in *Politics* refutes many of the formulations of Plato's *Republic*. Paine provides a liberal defense of the French Revolution in response to Burke's conservative critique. Wollstonecraft is critical of Burke and Rousseau in her formulations of the first principles of feminism.

A classic can be interpreted from a philosophical perspective, that is, by its efforts at developing a set of moral principles for the purpose of evaluating political events and guiding political choice. The important fact is that 'moral concepts are embodied in and are partly constitutive of forms of social life. One key way in which we may identify one form of social life as distinct from another is by identifying differences in moral concepts' (Maclntyre 1971: 1). The philosophical approach bestows upon the reader/scholar the role of a judge, for the idea is to evaluate the differing conceptions of moral principles and political theories. A noticeable fact that emerges while interpreting the classics is that the history of political theory is marked by both continuity and change. Concepts undergo a change in the course of their evolution, yet one can see a remarkable continuity. Originality lies in the course of their interpretation and redefinition. This explains the complexities and intricacies within the tradition. Classics are also reinterpreted following new frameworks of analysis. For example, feminism has enabled us to take a fresh look at the texts with certain questions in mind like the position accorded to women, perceptions regarding sexual relations, the home as a place of equality and justice. The republican view of politics has led to reinterpretation of thinkers like Machiavelli and Locke, the authors of the *Federalist Papers* from the standpoint of their analysis of the public space, civic virtues and the obligations of private citizens towards their states. Classics are an indispensable part of liberal arts, education, because their authors engage themselves and their readers in a discourse of the problems and issues of their time and place. Such an understanding heightens the appreciation of the possibilities and limits of political action and theorising. The importance of the classical tradition has been succinctly captured by Strauss. The return to classical political philosophy is both necessary and tentative or experimental. ... We cannot reasonably expect that a fresh understanding of classical political philosophy will supply us with recipes for today's use. For the relative success of modern political philosophy has brought into being a kind of society to which the classical principles as stated and elaborated by the classics are not immediately applicable. Only we living today can possibly find a solution to the problems of today. But an adequate understanding of the principles as elaborated by the classics may be the indispensable starting point for an adequate analysis, to be achieved by us, of the present day society in its peculiar character, and for the wise application, to be achieved by us, of these principles to our tasks (Strauss 1964: 11).

Hermenetuics assigns principal attention to the meaningfulness that permeates the social world. It rejects the thesis of unity of sciences. It is the art, skill or theory of interpretation, of understanding the significance of human actions, utterances and institutions. It "refers to an 'ability' we acquire to the extent to which we learn to 'master' a natural language: the art of understanding linguistically communicable meaning and to render it comprehensible in cases of distorted communication. The understanding of meaning is directed at the semantic content of speech as well as the meaning-content of written forms or even of non-linguistic symbolic systems, insofar as their meaning-content can, in principle, be expressed in words" (Habermas 1987: 175).

Wilhelm Dilthey (1833–1911) in the late nineteenth century brings the term from theology into philosophy to refer to the human form of understanding (*verstchen*) that is an idea, experience or understanding, in short human sciences. Every expression, he holds, must be understood in its social, historical and cultural contexts if its full meaning is to be revealed, which is why humane education is essential for the correct perception of the human world. Without that education, history and society will remain partly intelligible. Martin Heidegger (1889–1976) applies the term broadly to emphasise the general metaphysical meaning of his investigations into the nature of human existence.

CONCLUSION

To summarise the aim of political theory is to include the following diverse aspects: first, the philosophical—questions that are normative and conceptual; second, empirical and analytical and relating to explanation and understanding and third, assessment, from where one is to where one ought to be or might be. All these have to be undertaken within a historical framework by being conscious of our inheritance from the past and our legacy to the future. Political theorists analyse ideas, concepts and theories by understanding its evolution, change and continuity in a disciplined, systematic and rigorous manner knowing fully well that there is no finality as political theory will continue to develop reflecting on new issues and problems. Each age will bring with it its own particular evolution but within a larger context of total worldwide human development.

Further Readings

Dyke, V. Van, *Political Theory: A Philosophical Analysis*, Stanford University Press, Stanford, 1960.

Gunnell, J.G., *Political Theory: Tradition and Interpretation*, Winthrop, Cambridge, 1979.

Heywood, A., *Political Theory: An Introduction*, Macmillan, London, 1999.

Kateb, G., *Political Theory: Its Nature and Uses*, St. Martin's Press, New York, 1968.

Miller, D. and Siedentop, L. (Eds.), *The Nature of Political Theory*, Clarendon Press, Oxford, 1983.

Quinton, A. (Ed.), *Political Philosophy*, Oxford University Press, Oxford, 1967.

Sibley, M.Q., *Political Ideas and Ideologies*, Surjeet Publications, New Delhi, 1981.

Wolff, J., *An Introduction to Political Philosophy*, Oxford University Press, Oxford, 1996.

Endnotes

1. See Chapter on Politics.
2. See Chapters on Equality and Justice.

Chapter 2

Contemporary Political Theory

Since the time of Hegel, political theory has faced its severest challenge from two sources: ideology and positivism. When Marx proclaims that his intention is not to interpret the world but to change it, he obliterates the distinction between theory and practice. He produces an anti-theory offering to humankind, the most radical form of messianic and ideological thinking (Germino 1967: 57). For Marx, reality inheres in practical productive activity. Theory loses its critical dimension for it is described as the tool of the privileged class. This makes Marx an ideologue and not a political theorist (Germino 1967). Ideology, as defined by Antonio Louis Claude Graf Destutt de Tracy (1754–1836), means the science of deciphering the origin of ideas. According to Tracy, all thoughts are reflected and determined by sense experience as the world of sensation is the only reality. He points out that a truly scientific study of human beings helps in exposing illusions and abstractions, which has no roots in reality. All forms of abstract thought, for Tracy, including religion and philosophy, have to be discarded, thus rejecting all kinds of critical enquiry.

POSITIVISM

Positivism in social sciences emerged mainly out of the tremendous influences of Isidore Auguste Marie Francois Comte (1798–1857), who is regarded as the father of positivism. Determined to formulate 'sociology' as a new master science of human beings, he asserts that only experiences derived from senses is real. Metaphysical, ethical and theological theories have little or no use. Positivism emphasises precision, constructive power and relativism. In this context, political theory lacks meaning. Positivism contends that analytical statements about the physical or social world fall into three categories—first, such statements can be useful tautologies, meaning repeating the same things through different words, and purely definitional statements that give specific meaning to a particular concept or phenomenon, second, statements are to be empirically tested by observation to assess its truth or falsity and third, statements that do not fall into the aforesaid categories and lack analytic content have to be dropped. In short, the positivists understand meaningful analysis are possible only through useful tautologies and empirical statements. This precludes metaphysics, theology, aesthetics and ethics, for they merely introduce obscurity into the process of enquiry. Positivism aims to be 'value free' or 'ethically neutral' patterning itself after natural sciences in deciding about the right and the wrong of issues. Empiricism, which believes that observation and experience are sources of knowledge, is central to the many shades of positivism. Comte integrates this assumption with two more—first, he reviews the development of the sciences with a view to ascertaining the thesis of unity among sciences, natural and social, whereby they are integrated into a single system of knowledge and second, with the idea of a unified science, he finds sociology in the belief that scientific knowledge offers the requisite clues for control over both nature and society. With the help of these three tools of analysis—empiricism, unity of science and control—positivism in the nineteenth century focuses itself on society in general in the hope of overcoming the present malaise and realising a better future. In this enterprise, ironically though, while positivism rejects political theory, it continues with one of its major preoccupations, the concern with 'ought'.

LOGICAL POSITIVISM

Logical positivism, a revitalised form of positivism espoused by the Vienna Circle, consists of mathematicians, philosophers and scientists in the 1920s and 1930s. The members of this group are Moritz Sdick (1882–1936), Rudolf Carnap (1891–1970), Otto von Neurath (1882–1945), Victor Kraf and Herbert Feigl (1902–1988), and others who are associated with it are Ludwig Wittgenstein (1889–1951), Hans Kelsen (1881–1973) and Sir Karl Raimund Popper (1902–1994). Wittgenstein provides the intellectual link between the circle and the school of linguistic philosophy that thrives in Oxford and other English universities in the early quarter of the twentieth century.

Logical positivists reject traditional metaphysics' cognitive status. For them, scientific propositions are of two kinds: analytic and synthetic. An analytic statement is logical or mathematical in nature. It is synthetic when a 'proposition adds something to the meaning of a given term'. Verifiability is the criteria for synthetic or substantive and factual statements suggesting that a synthetic statement has meaning only if it is capable of empirical verification. The lack of empirical verification means that a statement cannot be proved to be true or false and so is meaningless. From this standpoint, traditional political theory is rejected as unverifiable and meaningless. Logical positivists espouse a more radical form of empiricism and phenomenalism, (a theory propounded by J.S. Mill stating that material things are 'permanent possibilities of sensation') restricting experience of sensations as the basis of science. They insist on logical analysis with the aim to unifying science with social science on the premise that experience supplied the knowledge and logic provided the formal language to link experience with theories and laws. The impact of logical positivism on political thought is twofold. First, by its principle of verification it views politics as metaphysical, beyond science, essentially non-rational and arbitrary. Science, on the contrary, instructs one as to what happens rather than what should happen. This distinguishes them from the positivists, who attempt to make politics scientific. Second, to be scientific means adopting those aspects of science that logical positivism identifies as science. The logical positivists consider physics as a paradigm of a unified science, for it proceeds inductively from observations to laws.

Popper suggests an amendment to the principle of verification with his principle of falsification, which he uses to solve the problem of induction, popular ever since **Francis Bacon** (1561–1626) invented it, known as 'Hume's problem'. Popper's seminal achievement has been to work out a reasonable solution to the problem of induction (Magee 1984: 22). **Hume** is the first to raise doubts about the inductive method as he convincingly argues that no number of singular observations, however large and fool-proof, really leads to a scientifically satisfactory general statement. For instance, if one particular *A* is exactly the same as another *B*, it is not logically defensible that all *A*s are *B*s. Even if a very large sample is taken to arrive at a definite conclusion, it merely remains a psychological fact and not a logical one. This is true of predictions as well, as past experience does not imply that the same continues to happen in future. An inherent limitation of observation is the impossibility to observe future events. The propensity to accept the validity of the inductive method is due to our psychological conditioning rather than any logical cause. Hume concludes that non-scientific law has really a rationally secure foundation.

Following Hume, Popper rejects the traditional view of science and replaces it with another by pointing out the logical asymmetry between verification and falsification. This means that no number of cases of *A* that brings *B* really establishes that all *A*s are *B*s. Such universal notions cannot be disproved or negated. Popper argues that even a large number of confirmations of a rule would never prove it. A scientist must seek to disprove his hypothesis. Popper advances the principle of falsification by arguing that no observations, however numerous, can prove the truth of a hypothesis. But only one is sufficient to falsify and disprove it. By the principle of falsification, a theory continues to hold until it is falsified, and therefore, falsification and not verification, is the most suitable method for scientific enquiry. All knowledge is provisional based on hypotheses. Such formulations are continuously scrutinised by negative instances of falsification. Knowledge develops in a process of conjectures and refutations open to searching and uncompromising tests. Arguments are always tentative and could be criticised as being valid. The basis of falsification is 'commonsense realism' and indeterminism considered as essential for the proper functioning of a critical method.

Theory formulation has to be rigorous, according to Popper, as it has to withstand refutation. Refutation of existing knowledge leads to the emergence of new problems and subsequently by a solution that advances knowledge. The challenge is to go beyond the existing evidence that enables one to face a new situation. The implication of this is that a theory, whether true or false, leads to further accumulation of knowledge by new discoveries and inventions, and better theories. Scientific discoveries are mostly accidental. All knowledge is incomplete and provisional. What one considers as the truth today may be falsified tomorrow. However, the new paradigm assumes the possibility of being refuted. As a result, no theory can claim finality. At best, it can claim that it is better than the preceding theory. Science as a body of well-established facts is incorrect, for in a scientific enquiry nothing is permanently established, and as such nothing is considered unalterable. Accuracy is also provisional, as all measurements of both time and space are within a certain level. The quest for knowledge arises because of the problems one faces and the attempts made to solve them. Exactness is an illusion and there is no point in trying to get it. However, this does not mean that, since one cannot get a final answer for anything, humankind cannot progress, as the quest for greater degree of accuracy will continue to expand the horizon of human knowledge. Advancement is always possible, but whether one has reached the goal or not is always open to question. Popper situates this argument with reference to two of the greatest scientists, Newton and Einstein—the former's laws of gravitation were superseded by the latter's theory of relativity.

Popper contends that scientific knowledge is conjectural and no theory can be relied upon as the final truth. At best, one can say that it is supported by every observation so far and is more precise in terms of predictions than the available alternative, but it is still possible to replace it with a better theory. He denies the traditional assertion that scientists look for the maximum degree of probability, given the evidence. Scientists look to falsify the information in statements and the falsification can then be tested. For Popper, falsification in whole, or in part, is the anticipated fate of all hypotheses. Therefore, one has to seek criticisms, for bigger the fault, the greater is the prospect for improvement. This, he considers to be applicable to both natural and social sciences. He dismisses the search for inherent laws that determine the course of history as contrary to reason, to morality and to religion. On the basis of this paradigm, he attacks the theories of Plato, Hegel and Marx.

Popper's arguments are very similar to that of the theory of relative truth propounded earlier by Protagoras (580–496 BC) and Mahatma Gandhi (1869–1948). Protagoras' *Truth, or the Rejection* (*of Science and Philosophy*) begins with a mammoth sentence 'man is the measure of all things, of those that are that they are, of those that are not that they are'. Since no human society is formed without a feeling for morality and justice, Protagoras regarded all morals and laws as relatively valid, that is binding only on the human community which formulates them and only so long as that community holds them to be good. He thereby rejects notions of absolute religion, absolute morality and absolute justice. It is for this reason that Popper regards Protagoras to be the first democrat, relativist, humanist and individualist. Gandhi, like Popper, concedes that it is practically impossible to know the truth though all of us are its seekers. At best, one knows one's version of it. Both also oppose all forms of dogmatism and determinism.

LINGUISTIC PHILOSOPHY

Linguistic philosophy criticises the traditional political theory by agreeing with logical positivism that metaphysical statements are value judgments, which have emotive and no cognitive value. Philosophy is described as 'second-order study' devoted to conceptual enquiry. Though the linguistic philosophy resembles the Vienna circle, yet it is more open towards metaphysical experiences due to the influence of Wittgenstein's *Tractatus Logico-Philosophicus* (1921) in which he contends that there may be truths that cannot be expressed through the language of sense experience. Weldon points out that the function of political philosophy is not to provide new information about politics and its conclusions, as they have no bearing on the decisions of practical politicians. Moreover, philosophers must refrain from suggesting reforms. Linguistic philosophy dismisses political/ philosophical thought as a misconceived enquiry, for it takes up the wrong questions. Weldon's thesis about the lack of influence of political thinkers on politicians can be challenged by pointing to the enormous influence Locke has exerted on the makers of the American constitution. Former US President Clinton's reference to Thomas Jefferson (1743–1826), the inspiration Gandhi derived from Henry David Thoreau (1817–1862), John Ruskin (1819–1900), and Leo Tolstoy (1828–1910) and the late Prime Minister Nehru's indebtedness to Fabian collectivism are other examples. Weber plays a crucial role in exposing the limitations within positivism by conceding to the 'value related' nature of social science enquiry. The human mind does not randomly observe reality. It makes a conscious choice depending on one's interest. He repeatedly stresses the relationship of science to values, which it may not be able to validate.

> An empirical science can teach no one what he ought to do, but only what he can do, and under certain circumstances, what he wants to do. The validation of values is an affair of faith, and besides this perhaps a task of speculative thinking about life, the world, and its meaning, but certainly never an object of a science that is based on experience (1958: 54–55).

Herbert Marcuse (1898–1979) accuses positivism for being non-critical, non-evaluative and superficial, serving as an ideological support for a repressive society. Its theory 'succumbs to helpless relativism, thus promoting the very powers whose reactionary thought (it) wants of combat' (1972: 45). Friedrich August von Hayek (1899–1992) attacks scientism (a theory that an investigational method used in natural sciences is *facto* applicable in all areas of human enquiry and knowledge) rather than science as an obstacle to proper thinking and inappropriate application of natural scientific methods to the social sciences. He points out that natural sciences study objective facts or phenomena perceptible to the senses, which social sciences cannot do, for its data is subjective or what people think about an event or a fact. Furthermore, the methodology of social sciences is also individualistic and composite. Since there is nothing as group minds for Hayek, it is important to take into account individual mind, its thoughts and purposes as the starting point of social theory. Complex phenomena are constructed from the concepts and views held by individuals. He asserts that it is individual phenomenon that is directly observable whereas references to social wholes are thought of as postulates or theories about the relations between individual phenomena. The existence of social wholes is a myth as the larger societal whole is a reflection of complex existence of the interplay of different segments and parts in their different and individual roles (1955: 55). For instance, the University of Delhi has a meaning only with reference to its various departments, libraries, research centres and student hostels. As such the title, the University of Delhi, is a description, which is devoid of any meaning unless its composition is made clear. This is known as methodological individualism that distinguishes between the ideas of individual, which constitute social phenomena and explanatory or theoretical ideas about the existence of larger collective whole. Hayek insists that mere postulation of a social whole does not guarantee its existence for it is only a theory about the relations between individuals. To suppose that social wholes exist is to commit the error of collectivism—an error as much in the methodology of social sciences as it is in political philosophy. Furthermore, though all social phenomena are the result of intentional actions of individuals, it does not follow that all social phenomena are intended by an individual(s). It is just the opposite. For Hayek, the task of social science is precisely to track the undesigned results of the intentional actions of many individuals and, in particular, to trace and explain undesigned social regularities and social order. He explains this with reference to the formation of footpaths in 'wild broken country'.

> At first, everyone will seek for himself what seems to him to be the best path. But the fact that such a path has been used once is likely to make it easier to traverse, and therefore, more likely to be used again; and thus more and more clearly defined tracks arise and come to be used to the exclusion of other possible ways. Human movements through the region come to conform to a definite pattern which, although the result of deliberate decisions of many people, has yet not been consciously designed by anyone (Ibid: 40).

Jurgen Habermas (1929–) considers positivism and, in particular, positivist social science as philosophically naive and politically harmful. Positivism naively assumes that science is straightforwardly the knowledge of the world as it actually is, that the scientific approach is the best or the only way to knowledge and should, therefore, be applied to the social world just as it has already been applied so successfully to nature—in order to produce a social science fundamentally similar to natural science. The positivist tenet that all knowledge is of facts, not of values is naive, for it neglects the relation between knowledge and human interest and the dependence of human knowledge on human interests, and thus on human purposes and values. Habermas, drawing from Peirce and Dilthey points out that 'the empirical sciences contain information about reality from the viewpoint of possible technical control' (1972: 162) and that may not be useful. Our interest in the natural world is fundamental because we wish to use it for our human purposes, and natural sciences answer to that interest. He agrees with Marx that it is through our work that we come to know the natural environment, but beyond this he parts company with Marx for extending this natural science to society. That is the flaw in positivism to which Marx inadvertently subscribes.

The later decades of the nineteenth century till the end of the Second World War, according to Germino, are a bleak period for political theory. However, this observation ignores the contributions of Bernard Bosanquet (1848–1923), Antonio Gramsci (1871–1937), Thomas Hill Green (1836–1882) and Leonard Trelawny Hobhouse (1864–1929). The challenge of positivism and ideology were largely countered by Soren Kierkagaard (1813–1855), Vilfredo Pareto (1848–1923), Gaetano Mosca (1858–1941), Henri Bergson (1859–1941), Alfred North Whitehead (1861–1947), Benedetto Croce (1870–1940), Max Scheler (1874–1928), Robert Michels (1876–1936), Karl Theodore Jaspers (1883–1969) and the theorists of the Frankfurt school.

With the emergence of political science as a professional discipline since 1903, political theory becomes one of the sub-fields. In the 1920s, Charles Merriam and the University of Chicago played a key role in attempting to make political science more scientific. Merriam along with Graham Wallas stresses on the need to incorporate methods and concepts from other fields like psychology and sociology and quantitative techniques to cope with the facts that the discipline needs to collect. In the 1920s, despite the increasing use of scientism, there is not much schism between empirical scientific theory and study of the history of ideas as the two are regarded as complementary. Science is used for practical reform and further rational public policy.

BEHAVIOURALISM

Behaviouralism emerges in the early years of the twentieth century though its full import became clear in the 1950s. Its philosophical roots lay in Comte's writings and logical positivism of the Vienna Circle. It reaffirms many of the basic ideas of American political science in spite of initiating significant changes in the research programmes within the discipline, and hence represents a conservative revolution (Gunnell 1987: 388). Behaviouralism, according to **Easton**, tries to organise research in political science on the model of natural sciences. It emphasises on the need to develop a pure science of politics giving a new orientation to research and theory-building exercises within the discipline. In the process, it rejects political theory as a merely chronological and intellectual history of ideas with no practical relevance in comprehending contemporary political reality. Throughout the fifties those who remain committed to evaluative and prescriptive analysis and the study of the classical tradition perceive scientism of behaviouralism as a threat to political theory. The behaviouralists, on the contrary, claim that normative political theory is a serious hindrance to scientific research.

> It was from these debates that many of the subsequent images of political theory—whether as a world-historical activity concerned with criticism and restructuring of political life or as a mode of cognitive science—would emerge (Gunnell 1987: 388).

Behaviouralism remains the dominant theme even in the 1960s in the United States. It focuses on the simple question 'Why do people behave the way they do?' It differs from other social sciences by its insistence that (a) observable behaviour at the level of both an individual and a group is the basic unit for analysis, and (b) that it is possible to empirically test any explanation of that behaviour. It rejects a priori reasoning about human beings and society and prefers factual and statistical enquiries. It believes that experience alone can be the basis of knowledge. Within this framework, behaviouralists analysed the reasons for mass political participation in democratic countries, elite behaviour in the context of leadership and decision-making process, and activities of non-state actors in the international arena like the multinational corporations, terrorist groups and supranational organisations.

Behaviouralism does not accept all the philosophical arguments of positivism and subjects the latter to a critical scrutiny. Behaviouralism like positivism ascertains the correctness of an explanatory theory and evaluates it in three ways: for its internal consistency, consistency with respect to other theories that seek to explain related phenomena, and the capacity to generate empirical predictions that can be tested against observation. Only empirical testing can decide between competing theories, for behaviouralism posits a 'value free' and 'scientific' theory steering clear of ethical and political bias. It is this stress on empirical observation and testing that characterises the behavioural approach. A behaviouralist systematically compiles all the relevant facts, quantitative and qualitative, for an evaluation of a theoretical statement. Furthermore, behavioural analysis asserts that all scientific theories and/or explanations in principle must be capable of being falsified. This reflects behaviouralism's commitment to Popper's revision of traditional positivism whereby he (a) substitutes the principle of falsification for that of verification and (b) simultaneously identifies falsification as the criterion for deciding a scientific from a non-scientific theory. A scientific theory will generate empirical predictions that are capable of being falsified. If not, then it is sophisticated tautology, which is elegant and detailed but fails to explain anything meaningfully. In the strict sense, the positivists and behaviouralists reject normative theories on the grounds that they do not contain empirical and definitional statements. For instance, Lasswell's and Kaplan's writing on the classics in political theory concludes:

> A rough classification of a sample of 300 sentences from each of the following yielded these proportions of political philosophy (demand statements and valuation) to political science (statements of facts and empirical hypotheses): Aristotle's *Politics*, 25 to 75; Rousseau's *Social Contract*, 45 to 55 ... Machiavelli's *Prince*, by contrast, consisted entirely (in the sample) of statements of political science in the present sense (1952: 118).

However, Germino severely criticises this assumption on the grounds that 'political theory is neither reductionist, behavioural science nor opinionated ideology. It is the critical study of the principles of right order in human social existence (1967: 6)'. In a similar vein Brecht observes:

> Research upon research can be done, and statement can be piled upon statement, on what Plato, Aristotle, St. Thomas, Locke, Rousseau, Kant, Hegel and a hundred others of the great philosophers have thought about values and about what science can do regarding them. There is no end of delight for the scholar, and no end of discovery or rediscovery of deep observations, penetrating arguments, and appealing speculations. No relativity need tune down our statements about what others said and what their theories were. Yet what we are dealing with is *history*—history of ideas, and history of science; it is not science unless we accept their ideas as still scientifically valid today; and if we do so, it is our responsibility to say how through the old ideas, and through which of them the present crisis in theory can be overcome. Otherwise we merely ignore the problem in a particularly sophisticated manner (1965: 11–12).

Furthermore, Germino argues that this exercise has a scientific basis with roots in internal human experience. It can also be tested and verified. It is based on Heraclitus' doctrine of deep knowing in contrast to much knowing. Sabine also echoes this view. Germino's emphasis, like Manabendra Nath Roy's (1887–1954) position, on radical humanism is on the centrality of human experience which includes the ethical, metaphysical and theological dimensions. Any other method for such an enquiry is inadequate, as the basis of political theory building is experiential and not strictly experimental. Gandhi's use of inner voice to defend an action would meet the approval of this kind of argument. The major tenets of the behavioural credo include:

1. *Regularities* or uniformities in political behaviour, which can be expressed in generalisations or theory.
2. *Verification* or the testing of the validity of such generalisations or theory.
3. *Techniques* for seeking and interpreting data.
4. *Quantification* and measurement in the recording of data.

5. *Values* as distinguished between propositions relating to ethical evaluation and those relating to empirical explanation.
6. *Systematisation* of research.
7. *Pure science* or the seeking of understanding and explanation of behaviour before utilisation of knowledge for solution of societal problems.
8. *Integration* of political research with that of other social sciences (Easton 1965: 7).

Criticisms of Behaviouralism

Behaviouralism like positivism is criticised for its mindless empiricism. Both Hempel and Popper reject the 'narrow inductivist view' of scientific enquiry by arguing that a proper enquiry is possible only if relevant facts are supported by clear minimum theoretical expectations. They dismiss enquiries based on the idea of 'all the facts up to now' as irrelevant, for every fact gathering can never accomplish much,

> for, a collection of *all* the facts would have to await the end of the world, so to speak; and even *all the facts up to now* cannot be collected since there are an infinite number and variety of them (Hempel 1966: 11).

Positivism has tried to move away from a narrow inductivist approach in the 1950s, but scholars working within the behavioural persuasion during the same time remained committed to the inductive method in research. Their emphasis on data and consequent downgrading of theory has led to two undesirable tendencies—first, the stress on what is measurable compared to what is theoretically important and second, concentration on phenomena that is readily observable than on studying the covert and profound structural boors, which contribute to change and stability within the political system. The other shortcomings as Easton (1997: 15) enumerates include:

1. A tendency where behaviouralism pursued fundamental rather than applied knowledge, to distance itself from immediate political reality and neglect the special responsibilities of an intellectual.
2. A conception of scientific method that seemed to direct attention away from human actors and their choices and towards the conditions that influence and constrain action, resulting it, was claimed in a subjectless, nonhumane discipline, one in which human intentions and purposes played little creative part.
3. The naive assumption that behavioural political science alone was free of ideological presuppositions that might shape its substantive concerns and its conception of its own methods of inquiry.
4. The uncritical acceptance of a pristine positivist interpretation of the

nature of science, despite many criticisms that had already gained credibility even among many of those who favoured the continued use of the scientific method in the pursuit of social understanding.

5. The entrapment in a degree of professionalisation that increasingly hampered communication not only with the general public but even with other disciplines that were no less specialised.
6. An apparent indifference to the resulting fragmentation of knowledge, even in the face of the need for the use of this knowledge to solve whole social problems that, by their nature, are undifferentiated to be confined to a discipline.
7. An acknowledged inability to deal with value concerns to describe the nature of the good society, and the denigration of values to a nonscientific and, therefore, nonconfirmable status.

Critics of behaviouralism point out that the movement is ill-conceived and flawed in its conception. They contend that it is not possible to establish regularities in human behaviour and this makes it difficult to explain human behaviour through the methods of science. According to Germino, the meaning of behaviouralism had become elusive. There are many differences within the group and that it is not monolithic. Many behaviouralists do not agree with Lasswell regarding the need to establish a closed society that can be scientifically controlled. They are reticent about their claims for political science and looks to classical political theory appreciatively. Conformity to behaviouralism in the strictest sense only leads to a closed society unless this could be changed by two considerations—first, the need to reject rigid reductionism and scientism and second, in case the first happens, political theory could be restored to its former glory. Germino charges behaviouralists like Cobban, Easton and Waldo for their inability to separate normative political theory from political and ideological doctrines and utopian constructions. He clarifies that in criticising behaviouralism he is not against empirical research, for the Great Masters like Aristotle, Machiavelli and Mosca undertake such an approach.

> What I object to is the tendency among the advocates of a so-called scientific as opposed to a philosophical political science to decapitate political science and to argue that only propositions purporting to refer to or describe 'empirical'—sensorially observable—facts may be considered part of political science. The neglect of critical standards in terms of which we order and evaluate our data is the principal defect of the new or behaviouralist political science. This neglect often leads to the adoption of uncritical standards, which do not hold up at all well to theoretical reflection. The rebirth of political theory would not lead to the neglect of empirical research ... but to the correction of claims that such studies constitute the whole of political science. Such a rebirth would focus again on the need for elaborating criteria in order to evaluate political behaviour, the importance of paradigm, the crucial question of the highest good and best society for man as

> man, the dilution of the paradigm for concrete historical conditions, etc. (Germino 1967: 192–193).

IS POLITICAL THEORY DEAD?

In the middle of the twentieth century, many observers readily wrote an obituary of political theory. Cobban (1953 and 1960) and Easton (1953) speak of its decline, while Laslett (1957) and Dahl (1958) proclaim its death. Reimer (1962: 1) refers to political theory being in the doghouse. This dismal view is because the classical tradition in political theory is by and large loaded with value judgments beyond the control of empirical testing. The logical positivists in the 1930s and later on the behaviouralists criticise normative theory. Easton contends that since political theory is concerned with some kind of historical form, it loses its constructive role. He blames William Dunning, Charles H. Mcllwain and George M. Sabine for historicism in political theory. This kind of political theory has dissuaded students from a serious study of value theory.

> In the past, theory was a vehicle whereby articulate and intelligent individuals conveyed their thoughts on actual direction of affairs and offered for serious consideration some ideas about the desirable course of events. In this way they revealed to us the full meaning of their moral frame of reference. Today, however, the kind of historical interpretation with which we are familiar in the study of political theory has driven from the latter its only unique function, that of constructively approaching a valuational frame of reference. ... In the past, theory was approached as an intellectual activity whereby the student could learn how he was to go about exploring the knowable consequences and, through them, the ultimate premises of his own moral outlook. ... Scrutiny of the works by American political theorists ... reveals that their authors have been motivated less by an interest in communicating such knowledge than in retailing information about the meaning, internal consistency, and historical development of past political values (Easton 1953: 234–235).

Dunning in his three volumes entitled *A History of Political Theories* (1902) sets the tone for research in political theory. His training as a historian enables him to approach political theory primarily as offering problems of historical change and to unfold the role of political ideas in this process. As a result, political theory, for Dunning, becomes a historical account of the conditions and consequences of political ideas. He seeks to uncover the cultural and political conceptions of an age and to isolate the influences of these ideas, in turn, on the social conditions (Easton 1953: 238).

Easton describes Dunning as a historicist, for he deflects political theory from moral consideration and consciously avoids dealing with moral issues in a purely historical context. Dunning perceives political theory as essentially historical research into issues that arise from observation of political facts and practices. He confines his study to the legal rather than the ethical dimensions of political life, though subsequently his students broadened it to encompass empirical theories of political activity. He considers moral views as a product of caprice, dogmas without justification, and hence, not worthy of analysis or interpretation. He neglects the meaning and logical consistency of ideas.

McIlwain's *The Growth of Political Thought in the West* (1932) uses historical research, for he regards political ideas as an 'effect rather than an influential interacting part of social activity. Being virtual ciphers in the changing patterns of actual life, ideas can have meaning only as a part of a history of theories in which ideas may condition subsequent ideas, but in which they leave no impact upon action' (Easton 1953: 241). The title of McIlwain's work reveals the historical nature of his study. It tries to show the evolution of ideas in the West on the premise that ideas have a history and justify behaviour though they influence political activity in a sense that motivate individuals to act. He considers ideas to be influential but confines their influence exclusively to the realm of thought. McIlwain believes in the sense of continuity of the history of ideas, which is why it makes sense to trace its evolution. Unlike Dunning, who considers ideas contributing causally to the process of history, McIlwain focuses on the historical contexts from which an idea emerged.

> Political theory is here construed as a branch of the sociology of knowledge, which deals primarily with the circumstances shaping knowledge as it has varied over time. The task of the political theorist is to show the way in which a social milieu molds and shapes political thought. It is concerned with the exclusively empirical task of uncovering the determinants of ideology (Easton 1953: 244).

Unlike Dunning, McIlwain's work shows respect for moral issues since a theory is more than mere propositions rooted in observation. He prefers an inclusive history of theory that pays attention to a political idea justifying political practices and institutions. The moral defense is important since his concern is to study the way human beings defined good political life. The impression that McIlwain's work gives is that moral issues are worth discussing and endorsing. The special role he assigned to ideas makes him a historicist, but he is not strongly influenced by moral judgments. The reason being, he considers moral standards as propositions that could not be proved. He contends that in the past some of the most important assertions remained unproved because by nature they could not be proved. This makes values a matter of personal opinion representing an emotional response to experience. McIlwain regards moral judgments as subjective and relative, and calls for affirming one's moral premises. However, that does not deter him from grappling with one of the issues of moral relativism; namely, that if all moral beliefs are a result of individual life experiences then can one claim one's belief to be better than that of the others. Such proposition renders any discussion of values meaningless, for each individual will regard one's values as being as good as that of the others. In that case, only a historical approach is useful to understanding moral problems. McIlwain does not agree to this reasoning, for he believes in the superiority of his own moral outlook. However, the fact that he does not go beyond the historical analysis proves that his 'historicism, in practice, indicates the firm grip that this interpretation of the consequences of moral relativism has upon his study of political theory. ... The fact that Mcllwain confines himself to historicism, however, indicates that he has not availed himself of this alternative conception of the meaning of moral relativism' (Easton 1953: 248).

Sabine's *A History of Political Theory* (1939) has singularly influenced studies in political theory more than any other book written during the thirties. Like Dunning and Mcllwain, Sabine considers the historical study of theory as an appropriate approach to the subject matter. The impression that one gets from the book and from a description of his method is 'that a historical study of theory provides its own self evident justification' (Easton 1953: 249). Sabine combines the approach of both Dunning and Mcllwain. Like Dunning he believes that political thought is a part of the political process which interacts and influences social action. He shares Mcllwain's belief that it is necessary to describe and analyse moral judgment in each theory as these are determining factors in history and not mere rationalisations of an activity. Moral judgments are not inferior to factual propositions as Dunning contends. Though Sabine reiterates Dunning in his interpretation of the relation between ideas and action, he differs in his conception of the nature of history of political theory by his emphasis on the role of ethical judgments.

For Sabine, every political theory can be scrutinised from two points of view: as social philosophy and as ideology. As an ideology, theories are psychological phenomena precluding truth or falsity. Theories are beliefs, 'events in people's minds and factors in their conduct' (1939: 6–7) irrespective of their validity or verifiability. Theories play an influential role in history and therefore the task of a historian is to ascertain the extent to which these theories help in shaping the course of history. A theory has to be examined for its meaning rather than for its impact on human actions. Viewed in this perspective a theory comprises of two kinds of propositions: factual and moral. Sabine focuses on factual rather than moral statements for the latter precludes descriptions of truth or false. He regards values as reflecting human preferences to 'some social and physical fact'. They are not deducible from facts nor can they be reduced to facts or rationally discovered as being expressions of emotions. Since political theory advances some statements of preference, value judgments form the core of theory and explain the reason for its existence. The moral element characterises political theory, which is why it is primarily a moral enterprise. In spite of factual propositions within a theory, a political theory on the whole can hardly be true in depicting a particular episode or period.

Easton examines the reasons for the decline of political theory in general and its decline into historicism in particular. First, and foremost, is the tendency among political scientists to conform to the moral propositions of their age leading to a loss of the constructive approach. The emphasis is to uncover and reveal one's values which imply that there is no longer the need to enquire into the merit of these moral values but merely understand their 'origins, development and social impact' (Easton 1953: 257). History is used to endorse existing values. Secondly, moral relativism is responsible for the attention a theory received with history.

> The vital fact about this meaning of relativism is that the description of the conditions surrounding the emergence of moral preference does not by itself necessarily imply any opinion about the merit or demerit of these preferences. It does not demonstrate values to be either equal or unequal in worth. It merely indicates that they are equal in their origins, in the sense that they are each a product of historical circumstances. If we wished, we could of course compare them with regard to other qualities such as their moral worth. This would however be a separate and independent task. To do so we would need first to establish an acceptable moral standard in terms of which varying preferences could be compared. But barring agreement on such a standard, two differing value judgments can be said to be neither better nor worse when each stands by the side of the other. They just differ and are incommensurable until some third standard of comparison is adopted (Easton 1953: 261–262).

Thirdly, since the latter half of the nineteenth and in the early twentieth centuries, there is, beyond doubt, considerable agreement on values in Western Europe. Sharp differences on ethical questions have got diffused. With greater unity in moral perceptions, the value theorists focus more on the history of moral ideas.

REVIVAL OF POLITICAL THEORY

In the 1930s, political theory begins studying the history of ideas with the purpose of defending liberal democratic theory in opposition to the totalitarian tenets of Communism, Fascism and Nazism. Lasswell tries to establish a scientific political theory with the eventual purpose of controlling human behaviour, furthering the aims and direction given by Merriam. Unlike the classical tradition, scientific political theory describes rather than prescribes. Political theory in the traditional sense is alive in the works of Arendt, Theodore Adorno (1903–1969), Marcuse, Leo Strauss (1899–1973), Oakeshott, Bertrand de Jouvenal and Eric Vogelin. Their views diametrically differ from the broad ideas within American political science for they believe in liberal democracy, science and historical progress. All of them reject political messianism and utopian politics. Arendt focuses mainly on the uniqueness and responsibility of the human being, with which she initiates her criticism of behaviouralism. She contends that the behavioural search for uniformities in human nature only contributes towards stereotyping the human being. In *The Human Condition* (1958) she observes:

> The unfortunate truth about behaviorism and the validity of its 'laws' is that the more people there are, the more likely they are to behave and the less likely to tolerate non-behaviour. Statistically, this will be shown in the levelling out of fluctuation. In reality, deeds will have less and less chance to stem the tide of behavior, and events will more and more lose their significance, that is, their capacity to illuminate historical time. Statistical uniformity is by no means a harmless scientific idea; it is no longer the secret political ideal of a society which, entirely submerged in the routine of everyday living, is at peace with the scientific outlook inherent in its very existence (1958: 40).

Arendt rejects the idea of hidden and anonymous forces in history. Like other leading figures in the revival of political theory, she points to the essential incompatibility between ideology and political theory. She is aware of the loss of human experience in the modern world and desires a need to recover a sense of dignity and responsible freedom in human action seeing it as a basis for the revival of political theory. Through the example of Eichmann, the transportation expert manning the trains to the Nazi concentration camp at Auschwitz, a 'perfectly normal man', she illustrates the difference between responsible action and efficient automatic behaviour.

Oakeshott's main theoretical achievement is his philosophical analysis of experience, which attempts to resurrect the multidimensionality that is denied to experience by positivism and ideology. Oakeshott understands experience to be a concrete whole with different kinds of 'modes'. The modes constitute 'arrests' in experience and the purpose of philosophy is to identify each mode and define its relationship with other aspects of experience. In *Experience and its Modes* (1933) he identifies four principal modes of, or 'arrests' in experience: history, science, practical and poetry. Science concerns itself with measurement and quantification, history with the past, practice with an act of desiring and obtaining and poetry with imagination and contemplation. Oakeshott does not define philosophy other than indicating it to be an activity undertaken in discoursing upon experience and its modes. When philosophising one leaves the tight model islands of incomplete experience and charters the 'open sea of experience'. He concedes that philosophy cannot serve as a guide for practical life, for it is not 'clear-sighted, not those who are fashioned for thought arid the arduous of thought, who can lead the world'. Great achievements are accomplished in the mental fog of practical experience. What is farthest from our needs is that kings should be philosophers' (Oakeshott, 1933: 320–321). Philosophy serves the truth and is not determined by its historical setting. Though its place and time are important, the key question remains 'can it maintain what it asserts?' Oakeshott does not distinguish between subject and object, fact and value. He distrusts any accepted route or pattern, which explains his skepticism of rationalism with its efforts at systematisation and categorisation. The process of politics and the very basis of rationalist enquiry are incompatible and mutually exclusive. He rejects the contention that philosophy can learn from the methods of science.

> The understanding of politics as an empirical activity is, then, inadequate because it fails to reveal a concrete manner of activity at all. And it has the incidental defect of seeming to encourage the thoughtless to pursue a style of attending to the arrangements of their society which is likely to have unfortunate results; to try to do something which is inherently impossible is always a corrupting enterprise (1956: 5).

Philosophy is not a practice and is pursued for its own sake by maintaining 'its independence from all extraneous interests, and in particular from the practical interest' (Oakeshott 1933: 3). Philosophy is not about preaching a doctrine—though every philosopher has a preacher within him—and is 'not in persuading others, but in making our own minds clear' (ibid). It cannot be popular and any attempt to popularise will only debase it. Nor is it a search for a universal system, which consists of knowledge about every aspect of reality. A philosopher seeks 'valid' and not 'universal' knowledge (ibid: 1). Like Arendt, Oakeshott regards political philosophy as philosophising about politics. Unlike ideology which he rejects, it does not promise salvation or a 'bogus eternity'.

> Political ideology purports to be an abstract principle, or set of related abstract principles, which has been independently premeditated. It supplies in advance of the activity of attending to the arrangements of a society a formulated end to be pursued, and in so doing it provides a means of distinguishing between those desires which ought to be encouraged and those which ought to be suppressed or redirected (1956: 5).

Oakeshott rules but political ideology and empiricism in an understanding of politics.

> Wherever else politics may begin, they cannot begin in ideological activity. Just as scientific hypothesis cannot appear, and is impossible to operate except within an already existing tradition of scientific investigation, so a scheme of ends for political activity appears within, and is valuable only when it is related to, an already existing tradition of how to attend to our arrangements (1956: 12).

As far as political philosophy is concerned, it cannot be called a 'progressive' science. The important thing is history. In fact, it has nothing but a history, which is a history of the problems philosophers detect and the manner of solution they propose, rather than a history of doctrines and systems. Political philosophy cannot be expected to increase our ability to be successful in the political activity. It will not help us to distinguish between good and bad political projects; it has no power to guide or direct us in the enterprise of pursuing the intimations of our tradition. But the patient analysis of the general ideas, which comes to be connected with political activity—ideas such as nature, artifice, reason, will, law, authority, obligation, etc.—insofar as it succeeds in removing some of the crookedness from our thinking and leads to a more economic use of concepts, is an activity neither to be overrated nor despised (1956: 20).

Jouvenal, like Arendt, opposes the modern trend of converting politics into administration depriving it of the potentiality for creativity in the public sphere. The modern trend conceives politics as a competitive process and is concerned about totalitarianism. It opposes ideological sloganeering and utopianism. Politics essentially involves moral choice with the purpose of building and consolidating individuals.

Strauss reaffirms the importance of classical political theory to remedy the crisis of the modern times. He does not agree with the proposition that all political theory is ideological in nature mirroring a given socio-economic interest, for most political thinkers are motivated by the possibility of discerning the principles of the right order in social existence. A political philosopher is primarily interested in truth (1959: 12). Past philosophies are studied with an eye on coherence and consistency. The authors of the classics in political theory are superior because they were geniuses and measured in their writings. Strauss scrutinises the methods and purposes of the 'new' political science and concludes that it was defective when compared with classical political theory, particularly that of Aristotle. For Aristotle, a political philosopher or a political scientist has to be impartial, for he possesses a more comprehensive and clearer understanding of human ends. Political science and political philosophy are identical because science consisting of theoretical and practical aspects is identical with philosophy. Aristotle's political science also evaluates the political things, defends autonomy of prudence in practical matters and views the political action as essentially ethical. These premises behaviouralism denies, for it separates political philosophy from political science and substitutes the distinction between theoretical and practical sciences. It perceives applied sciences to be derived from theoretical sciences but not in the same manner as the classical tradition visualises. Behaviouralism like positivism is disastrous, for it denies knowledge regarding ultimate principles. Their bankruptcy is evident, for they seem helpless, unable to distinguish the right from the wrong, the just from the unjust in view of the rise of totalitarianism. Strauss counters Easton's charge of historicism by alleging that the new science is responsible for the decline in political theory, for it pointed to and abetted the general political crisis of the West because of its overall neglect of normative issues.

> The habit of looking at social or human phenomena without making value judgments has a corroding influence on any preferences. The more serious we are as social scientists, the more completely we develop within ourselves a state of indifference to any goal, or of aimlessness and drifting, a state which may be called nihilism. The social scientist is not immune to preferences; his activity is a constant fight against the preferences he has as a human being and a citizen and which threaten to overcome his scientific detachment. He derives the power to counteract these dangerous influences by his dedication to one and only one value—to truth. ... (1) It is impossible to study social phenomena, i.e. all important social phenomena, without making value judgments ... a society cannot be defined without reference to its purpose. (2) The

> rejection of value judgments is based on the assumption that the conflicts between different values or value systems are essentially insoluble for human reason. The belief that value judgments are not subject, in the last analysis, to rational control, encourages the inclination to make irresponsible assertions regarding right and wrong or good and bad. One even creates the impression that all important human conflicts are value conflicts, whereas, to say the least, many of these conflicts arise out of men's very agreement regarding values. (3) The belief that scientific knowledge, Lethe kind of knowledge possessed or aspired to by modern science, is the highest form of human knowledge, implies a depreciation of pre-scientific knowledge (1959: 19, 21, 22–23).

Strauss equates behaviouralism's value-free approach with 'dogmatic atheism' arid 'permissive egalitarianism'. It is dogmatically atheistic because of its attitude of 'unreasoned unbelief. It is rooted in permissive egalitarianism because its proponents who distinguish facts and values believe that,

> Men can live without ideologue: they can adopt, posit, or proclaim values without making the illegitimate attempt to derive their values from facts or without relying on false or at least inevident assertions regarding what is. One thus arrived at the notion of the rational society or of the non-ideological regime: a society that is based on the understanding of the character of values. Since this understanding implied that before the tribunal of reason all values are equal, the rational society will be egalitarian or democratic and permissive and liberal; the rational doctrine regarding the difference between facts and values rationally justifies the preference for liberal democracy—contrary to what is intended by that distinction itself (1962: 324).

Vogelin regards political science and political theory as inseparable and that one is not possible without the other. Political theory is not ideology, utopia or scientific methodology but an experiential science of the right order in both the individual and the society. It has to dissect critically and empirically the problem of order.

> Theory is not just any opining about human existence in society; it rather is an attempt at formulating the meaning of existence by explicating the content of a definite class of experiences. Its argument is not arbitrary but derives its validity from the aggregate of experiences to which it must permanently refer for empirical control (1952: 64).

The Frankfurt school to which Adorno and Marcuse belong emerges in Germany in the 1920s, and has attracted some of the best minds of the contemporary German social sciences. Its origin can be traced back to a debate about the nature of Marxism that arises as a result of the defeat of the left-wing workers' movement in West Europe after the First World War; the collapse of the mass left-wing political parties in Germany, the rise of Stalinism and with its institutionalisation, the total degeneration of the Soviet Revolution, and the meteoric rise of Fascism and Nazism in Europe eclipsing Marxism. These bitter experiences shatter the School's faith in the inevitability of the historical march towards socialism. Reactions to these events are present in the writings of Antonio Gramsci (1891–1937) within Italy and from the Frankfurt school within Germany. The school is directly associated with 'an anti-Bolshevik radicalism and an open ended or critical Marxism' (Held 1983: 182). It is a 'para-Marxist movement' (Kolakowski 1981: 341). The school rejects both capitalism and Soviet socialism and like the Euro-communists tries to project a third alternative. However, a great deal of pessimism and anti-utopianism prevents them from projecting a bright future as attempted by Marx. With an emphasis on totality and rejection of crude determinism, the members of the school produce a large number of scholarly works in humanistic science, philosophy, empirical sociology, psychoanalysis, theory of literature, law and political theory. Though the works of the members of the school are recognised as a distinct category under the term critical theory, there is no attempt to form a core unity and the adherents differed widely in their approaches and emphasis. Their commitment ends with a general agreement of a necessity to provide a critical theory of Marxism. They oppose all forms of positivism and criticise the possibility of a value-free social science. They reject Marxist interpretations based on crude materialism or dogma. The most well-known political theorist Habermas belongs to this school. His famous theory of legitimisation crisis assesses advanced capitalism and communicative action. His commitment to the Enlightenment philosophy's faith in the power of reason and progress makes him a critic of the post modernism and makes him rooted in modernism.

Kolakowski (1981: 341–342) lists six basic characteristics of the Frankfurt school:

1. it does not treat Marxism as sacrosanct but as a helpful tool in analysing and criticising culture;
2. its programme is strictly non-party in orientation, for it never identifies with rather it is hostile towards any political movement, either with communism or social democracy;
3. it is profoundly influenced by the interpretation of Marxism developed by Georg Lukacs (1885–1971) and Karl Korsch (1886–1961) in the 1920s;
4. it is opposed to the concept of praxis and emphasizes the autonomy and independence of theory;
5. differing with Lukacs, it accepts the Marxian position on exploitation and alienation of the proletariat though it does not identify with the communist party. The school doubts the proletariat's revolutionary role of liberation and subsequently drops this part of Marx's teaching altogether;
6. in spite of its revisionist outlook, it considers itself a revolutionary intellectual movement rejecting the reformist plank, though it advocates a complete break with the past.

DEFENCE OF THE CLASSICAL TRADITION

Berlin and Wolin

Sir Isaiah Berlin (1909–1997) starts of as a logical positivist, but the First World War leads him to develop a critical response towards it. He is unconvinced about the anti-metaphysical claims of the logical positivists, and doubts their contention that problems of philosophy are problems that stem from linguistic confusion. He contends that 'our understanding of reality already includes the conception of it as existing independently of us and our understanding, so that our reflection of what we mean when we characterise that reality cannot accommodate the positivist idea that truths about reality should be equivalent to truths about us' (1980: xii). Berlin rejects Oakeshott's proposal that dilemmas insoluble by reason could be resolved by going back to tradition. He considers philosophy to be important, for it highlights the incoherence of practices though it could not resolve these inconsistencies. He opposes philosophy, proposing radical social reforms, for its role has to be humble, to straighten the crookedness in our thoughts.

> The goal of philosophy is always the same, to assist men to understand themselves and thus operate in the open, and not wildly, in the dark (1992: 49).

Berlin's conception of the role and function of philosophy is linked to his idea of freedom and pluralism, namely the existence of an indefinite number of competing and irreconcilable ultimate values from which a choice is made and that this choice cannot be forced on others. He accepts that it is the absence of a commanding work in the twentieth century that has led to the declaration that political theory is dead or is dying. The absence of critical dimension has nothing to do with the nature of political theory, which will survive in a society whose ends collide.

> In a society dominated by a single goal, there could, in principle, only be arguments about the best means to attain this end—and arguments about means are technical, that is, scientific and empirical in character: they can be settled by experience and observation or whatever other methods are used to discover causes and correlations; they can, at least in principle, be reduced to positive sciences. In such a society, no serious questions about political ends or values could arise, only empirical ones about the effective paths to the goal. It follows that the only society in which political philosophy in its traditional sense, that is, an inquiry concerned not solely with the elucidation of concepts, but with the critical examination of presuppositions and assumptions, and the questioning of the order of priorities and ultimate ends, is possible, is a society in which there is no total acceptance of any single end (1980: 149–50).

Berlin argues with conviction that political philosophy in the traditional sense can be pursued only in plural societies, for any kind of analysis involves a critical inquiry, which is not possible under rigid monism. Monists are Platonists, Aristotelians, Stoics, Thomists, Positivists and Marxists who understand political problems in scientific terms and see solutions to human problems as being technical, for human ends are objective in accordance with some discoverable laws. The pluralists do not see the possibility of human perfection and distrusted empirically, the possibility of attaining the final solution to the deepest human problems. Skeptics and relativists are pluralists. Berlin points out that philosophical analysis brings out the sharp differences that exist between concepts and value preferences. Political thinkers search for validity and truth in an attempt to understand whether a model distorts reality. Disputes and doubts can arise regarding values and the relationship between values.

These questions are not purely technical and empirical, nor merely problems about the best means to a given end, nor are they mere questions of logical consistency, that is formal and deductive; but properly philosophical (1980: 151).

Traditional political theory does not get marginalised under the dominance of behaviouralism. In the premier American universities, important works in political theory continued to emerge in the 1950s and the 1960s. An important critic of behaviouralism, Sheldon Wolin accuses behavioural political scientists of abdicating their true 'vocation' in their concern for method. He not only addresses the attack mounted on traditional political theory by behavioural social scientists but also explains the beauty and usefulness in the tradition of political theory from Plato to contemporary times. He comments on the substance and significance of political theory along with suggestions as to how to revitalise political theory or political philosophy. Wolin's masterpiece *Politics and Vision: Continuity and Innovation in Western Political Thought* (1960) conveys his view that political theory represents 'seeing' political phenomena in two senses: first and most obvious is that political theory provides a description of the politics, and second and more significantly, political theory constitutes a form of aesthetic or religious vision (1960: 18). In the second sense, political theory relates to the imaginative capacity of the theorist; 'an esemplastic' power that 'forms all into one graceful intelligent whole' (1960: 18). Through fanciful statements, a theorist exaggerates aspects of political phenomena in an abstract manner, the interconnections which are invisible, with the purpose of illuminating them. Imagination is necessary since no political theorist has the capacity to observe all political things directly (1960: 19). This imaginative element of 'seeing' is described as an architectonic vision, for political phenomena are portrayed and shaped in light of a vision of good which lies external to the political order. This ordering element has differed throughout the tradition from religious, historical and in recent times economic, but all of them possess one common trait—a 'futuristic quality, a projection of the political order into a time that is yet to be' (1960: 20). Besides, through an exaggerated portrayal of the political order, one can get an idea of the possibilities of political life that serves as 'a necessary complement to action' (1960: 20).

In his subsequent writings, Wolin classifies political visionaries as 'epic theorists' (1969: 1078–1081). An 'epic' theory differs from other kinds of theory and method by its structure of formal features and its 'structure of intentions' (1969: 1078). Comparing it to Kuhnian paradigms, an epic theory ushers in a new way of looking at the world by reassembling existing political institutions and relationships. All epic theories are governed by a public concern, a quality, which is important for any one engaged in the enterprise of political theory (1969: 1078–1079), By public concern, Wolin means two things: first, the object examined is common to the whole community and in this context, he mentions Marcus Tullius Cicero's (106–143 BC) description of the commonwealth as *a. res publica*, a public thing (1960: 4) and second, philosophy as pointed out at the outset is intrinsically public, for it gives knowledge that enables individuals to become wiser in their conduct of life. Epic theories surface mainly during times of crisis.

> The range of possibilities appears infinite, for now the political philosopher is not confined to criticism and interpretation; he must reconstruct a shattered world of meanings and their accompanying institutional expressions; he must in short, fashion a political cosmos out of political chaos (1960: 8).

However, Wolin does not say that epic theory emerges only in times of crisis though crisis brings forth epic theories. The possibility of political chaos during periods of tranquillity leads to a search for order and stability. Epic tradition is also inspired by the fact of immortality, the hope to achieve 'memorable deed through the medium of thought' (1970: 4). The purpose of great minds is not to merely state the 'logical or factual merits of the words but an attempt to compel admiration and awe for the magnitude of the achievement' (1970: 5). Wolin points out that 'political theorist, tried to understand and alter the whole of politics, but the whole was with reference to a particular context. Theorising about politics contained a paradox. A theorist aimed to provide an understanding about the whole of politics but was compelled by necessity to reduce the whole to manageable proportions, emphasising some aspects at the expense of others' (1968: 319).

> Every political philosophy... represents a necessarily limited perspective from which it views the phenomena of political nature (1960: 21).

Wolin points to another aspect of the relationship between the existing political order and political theory. He refers to the 'institutions (that) establish a previous coherence among political phenomena; hence, when the political philosophy reflects upon society, he is not confronted by a whirl of disconnected events or activities hurtling through a Democritean void but by phenomena already endowed with coherence and interrelationships' (1960: 7). The existing coherence is given by a continuous tradition of political thought and it is this tradition that poses as the biggest inhibitor for the theorist. Previous theorists had bequeathed a legacy, namely, the function of 'preserving the insights, experience, and refinements of the past, and compelling those who would participate in the Western political dialogue to abide by certain rules and usages' (1960: 22). Though the philosophical inheritance circumscribes the terms of the discourse, it also facilitates it by providing familiar vocabulary, concepts and terminology allowing for fresh insights and new interpretations. Each theorist confronts the fundamental issues of his time and place but in the process scrutinises insights of the past for the purpose of applying to the present. As a result,

> a political philosopher unavoidably infects his own thought with past ideas and situations. In this sense the past is never wholly superseded; it is constantly being recaptured at the very moment that human thought is seemingly preoccupied with the unique problems of its own time. The result is, to borrow Guthrie's phrase, a 'coexistence of diverse elements', partly new, partly inherited, with the old being distilled into the new, and the new being influenced by the old. Thus the Western tradition of political thought has exhibited two somewhat contradictory tendencies: a tendency towards an infinite regress to the past and a tendency towards accumulation ... or a tendency towards acquiring new dimensions of insight (1960: 26).

The combination of the insights from the past with those of the present gives to the Western political tradition not a 'fund of absolute political wisdom', but rather as a 'continuously evolving grammar and vocabulary to facilitate communication and to orient the understanding' (Wolin 1960: 26, 27). Viewed in this perspective, both an individual theorist and the Western political tradition are studied best in the light of historical development 'since the history of political philosophy is an intellectual development wherein successive thinkers have added new dimensions to the analysis and understanding of politics, an inquiry into that development is not so much a venture into antiquarianism as a form of political education' (Wolin 1960: 27). Through the example of Arendt's writings, Wolin shows how the great theories of the past 'might be used to illuminate the predicaments of the age' (1977: 92–93). He describes Arendt's theorising as 'an act of recovery, or reacquiring lost meanings of remembering' (1977: 96). Theories of the past are to be used for a better understanding of politics but they need not be judged in the light of contemporary standards alone. Echoing Germino, Wolin observes that in its concern for method, contemporary political theory abandons the critical dimension, which is one of its major characteristics. It no longer furnishes a radical critique of the basic principles of politics as,

> There has been an effort to imbue political scientists with what is understood to be the ethic of science: objectivity, detachment, fidelity to fact, and deference to intersubjective verification by a community of practitioners (1969: 1064).

Wolin distinguishes between a scientist and a theorist for both try to clarify an individual's view of the world but 'only the former attempts to change the world itself (1969: 1064). He (2000) criticises the reigning behaviouralism and methodism in American political science for its reductionist explanations of the political and its complicity with the status quo. Instead he stresses on the vocation of political theory, not only with its concern for *res publica* but also in the ability of theory to sharpen judgement, focus on the complexities of political life, appreciate the subtleties of implicit political knowledge and widen and sharpen political vision. He argues that theory has to be attuned to the fluctuating circumstances and vicissitudes of politics and is more than a method. Like Berlin and Oakeshott, Wolin argues that political theorists do not and cannot offer recipes for salvation nor can they confine themselves in self-absorbed intellectual activity or in that of others totally dissociated from the world of politics. The task of a political theorist is to offer a political education in the 'subtle complex interplay between political experience and thought'. The vocation for political theory is that it does not suppress, displace or overcome politics but that it attends to the ongoing challenges and provides thoughtful political action.

KUHN'S SEMINAL CONTRIBUTION

Thomas Kuhn's (1922–1996) observation that in every age a discipline solves some of its problems but in the process generates new ones is made with reference to natural sciences. However, this observation is equally valid in social sciences and could be seen as a critique of the behavioural quest for a standardised scientific theory and explanation. His notion of paradigm as 'research firmly based upon one or more past scientific achievements, achievements that some particular scientific community acknowledges for a time as supplying the foundation for its further practice' (1970: 10) has interested social scientists. A paradigm is a perspective, a set of beliefs and had ideals—conceptual, theoretical and methodological—of a scientific community helping the latter in selection of problems, evaluation of data and formulation of theory. In perceiving the nature of a paradigm, Kuhn concedes the difficulty of discovering rules that would help scientific traditions. The concepts, laws and theories of science are found historically in prior experience. They are not abstract and become the basis of scientific learning and research. A paradigm establishes limits of what is possible and states the boundary with regard to enquiry. A successful paradigm helps the scientific community in the selection of problems and finding a solution. A scientist working with the help of a successful paradigm normally does not see beyond his assumptions. Kuhn describes four phases—first, is the *pre-paradigmatic phase*, in which no single theoretical approach or school predominates within a scientific community although there may be a number of competing approaches; second, is the *paradigmatic phase*, one in which the scientific community follows a dominant paradigm; third, is the *crisis phase*, where the dominant paradigm faces challenges and revisions allowing for a new paradigm to evolve with a possibility of reviving an old one with appropriate modifications and fourth, is the *scientific revolution* phase, which occurs following the shift to different paradigms by the scientific community. The traditional, behavioural and post-behavioural approaches do not fit into the Kuhnian definition and analysis of paradigm (Chilcote 1981: 58–59).

Wolin (1968) observes that no scientific revolution has occurred, and as such, there exists no such dominant and new theory among political scientists, along the lines that Kuhn suggests. There is no significant theory like that of Newton except a framework of guiding assumptions, 'the ideological paradigm reflective of the same political community' (1969: 1064) that applies to political science. Kuhn's work and 'the new challenges in the philosophy of social science (such as those advanced by Peter Winch and Alfred Schutz) to the idea of positivistic social science, begins to spill over into political theory. Much of the discussion in the 1970s is devoted to meta-theoretical debates about the nature of social scientific theory and explanation. While the earlier critique of behaviouralism raises questions about the value of science as such and largely accepts the same positivist conception of science as behaviouralism, the new critique questions not only the idea of the methodological unity of science but the adequacy of the prevailing conception of natural science' (Gunnell 1987: 389). These debates weaken the claims of positivism. Political scientists begin to devote more time to policy and substantive issues than have a scientific image. Policy sciences and theories like rational choice and Prisoner's dilemma receive much attention.

POST BEHAVIOURALISM AND NEO-BEHAVIOURALISM

In 1969, Easton announces a new revolution in political science: post behaviouralism that emphasises less on the scientific method and empirical theory, and stresses on the public responsibilities of the discipline. The tenets of post behaviouralism include the following:

1. First, substance precedes technique, which means that the pressing problems of society have become tools of investigation.
2. Second, behaviouralism itself has become ideologically conservative and limited to abstraction rather than to the reality of the times in crisis.
3. Third, science could be neutral in the evaluative sense for facts are inseparable from values and value premises have to be related to knowledge.
4. Fourth, intellectuals have to shoulder responsibility of their society, defend human values of civilisation arid not become mere technicians insular to social problems.

5. Fifth, intellectuals have to put knowledge to work and engage in reshaping the society.
6. Sixth, intellectuals have to actively participate in the politicisation of the professions and academic institutions. The behaviouralists accept that theoretical analysis has to remain the starting point of any serious empirical research. In fact, while post behaviouralism accepts the pivotal role played by theory, it also accepts the possibility of different theories yielding different observations. This possibility makes the task of subjecting rival theories to empirical testing far more complex. For the post behaviouralists, a theory to be considered as an explanatory theory, in the first place, had to be evaluated. This implies empirical testing. Easton (1997: 16–17) points out that the dissatisfaction with behaviouralism has led to revisions in the method and content favouring a revival of interpretive understanding and historical analysis and a complete rejection of systematic, methodology while simultaneously emphasising the need for introducing formal modelling and rational actor deduction. Moreover, the emergence of new concerns like feminism, environmentalism, ethnicity, racial identity and equality and nuclear war has led to a general loss of central focus regarding the subject matter and consensus about methodologies. It is for this reason and to bring about a new unity in the theoretical focus of the discipline that Easton announced in the 1990s the beginning of neo behaviouralism.

CONCLUSION

Political theory since the time of Plato has been influenced by its time and place. Our own time is no different. The better part of the last one hundred years has seen a keen contest between liberal democracy, fascism and communism. The fascist challenge was short lived, ending with its defeat in the Second World War, but the communist challenge continued even after the War for another four decades. During this period there are fresh insights into the nature of totalitarianism by Arendt and Friedrich, defense of liberal democracy by Berlin, Hayek and Popper and Plamentaz's contrast between German Marxism and Soviet Communism. There are penetrating criticisms of Marxist theory and practice by Avineri, Berlin, Dahl, Popper and Tucker, Miliband and the East European dissidents who highlight the libertarian aspect of the socialist discourse. The post Second World War period sees the emergence of convergence theory and the end of ideology debate emphasising the commonalities between advanced capitalism and developed socialism. Thus, contemporary political theory becomes global with important contributions from practically every corner of the world. Colonialism and imperialism has led to an impressive flowering of non-Western input to political theory reflected by the denunciation of western materialistic civilisation in Gandhi's *Hind Swaraj*

(1908), refinement, rejection of Eurocentricism in the writings of Mao Zedong (1893–1976), Amilcar Lopes Cabral (1924–1973), Edward Said and in the concept of negritude and African identity of Leopald Senghor (1906–2000).

The most impressive contributions are by the twentieth century liberals inaugurated by Hobhouse's *Liberalism* (1911) and culminating in Rawls' grand theory. They clarify and refine earlier positions rather than initiate new paths of enquiry. This is because 'by Hegel's time all fundamental positions have been taken up; after Hegel they reappear in new guises and new variations but the reappearance is a testimony to the impossibility of fundamental innovation' (Maclntyre 1971: 199). The political theory of our times has stood over the rich tradition of theorising of the last two thousand years and the recent scholarly works in applied politics more than normative theory has dealt with the important aspects of our political life. Our age also differs from the ones that precede it in a fundamental manner. It is an age of technology, manifest in microchip revolution and satellite networks. With nation states becoming more porous and receptive to outside influences, political theory has to respond to the increasing sweep of globalisation and the role of technology. However, as Lord Maynard Keynes (1883–1946) points out, the influence of ideas will always be widespread and contemporary political theory dealing with complexities of our time within the framework of the rich heritage of political theory will have its rightful place in the history of political theory.

Further Readings

Barry, B., 'The Strange Death of Political Philosophy' in *Democracy, Power and Justice: Essays in Political Theory*, Clarendon Press, Oxford, 1989.

Berlin, Sir I., 'Does Political Theory Still Exist?' in P. Laslett and W.G. Runciman (Eds.), *Philosophy, Politics and Society*, 2nd series, Blackwell, Oxford, 1964.

Eulau, H., *The Behavioural Persuasion in Politics*, Random House, New York, 1964.

Chapter 3

Politics, Power and Authority

Aristotle considers the activity of politics to be the art of the possible, while for Gramsci it is activity *par excellence*. Politics is an activity universal to all societies, at all levels and all times—past, present and perhaps even the future. It is not only unique to the state, groups, institutions, political parties and trade unions but also exists in the family, clubs, schools, colleges, religious organisations, cultural bodies, civic association, sports organisations, international organisations, multinational companies and the workplace. In other words, it is not confined merely to the public sphere but also exists in the private domain. Not only is politics inevitable but even consequences are inescapable. However, the ambit of politics for one is related to issues of state power and its distribution of 'who gets what, when and how?' Politics is important considering the fact that political decisions and ideologies shape important issues of our lives. Not only can we say this intuitively but we can also understand it if we spend a day reading newspapers and watching television news programmes. Normally one understands politics as the arena for politicians, political parties, elections and institutions of the government. Beyond these are the pressure groups, the social-economic and cultural institutions that form the background of political activity, and the media. This is the scenario within a nation-state. Therefore, it becomes imperative to understand the meaning, nature and scope of politics.

POLITICS: AN ACTIVITY AND AN ACADEMIC DISCIPLINE

There is an important distinction between politics as an activity and politics, political studies and political science as a discipline. Political science covers various specialisations of political theory, political philosophy, comparative government, international politics and public administration. Political science studies and analyses the activity called politics. Its practitioners are not the same as politicians. The skills in analysing politics are different from the skills in practicing politics. It is not a science in the same way as physics or chemistry, but politics can be studied systematically as a social science. Politics is normally judged by the results it produces while political science is considered in terms of the methods it uses for its results to be valid. There are two definitions of political science—one, it is the study of politics and two, it is what political scientists do from 9:00–5:00 (Wasby 1970: 3). The first definition, because of its complexity and variety, is of little help unless one can come up with a proper working definition. The second definition does not tell one what political scientists are. Perhaps one way of explaining the second is that political scientists study politics and so we are back to where we began. This study of politics began with the beginning of politics in antiquity and continues to evoke considerable interest among political scientists even today.

Traditional Approach

Till 1900, history, law and philosophy dominated the study of politics. This is described as the traditional approach, which continues to play an important role although it is no longer the dominant approach. The study of political theories and thinkers still form an important component of the study of politics for the questions they raise and the solutions they prescribe. The historical dimension becomes evident when constitutions and their development are studied with reference to important historical events of a particular country. This is evident in the works of Sir Ivor Jennings or Samuel Beer. The study of constitutional law constitutes the third aspect of the traditional approach for it focuses on the major political institutions of the state. Dicey's *Law of the Constitution* (1885) is a good example of this approach. The descriptive and constitutional approach to analyse institutions that form the core of the traditional approach is still an important component of political science.

New Approaches

The publication of Wallas' *Human Nature in Politics* and Bentley's *The Process of Government* both in 1908 symbolises a significant change in political science. They place greater emphasis on the informal process of politics and less on the institutions of the state. Wallas begins by focusing on the study of human behaviour and political activity to find solutions to larger social problems. Political science freely borrows from other disciplines, in particular from economics, psychology and sociology. It also acquires a greater empirical orientation leading to examination of concepts as power, authority and political elites. After the First World War, the Americans tried to search for a science of politics and fashions new tools of analysis, like, the quantitative method. Merriam and Lasswell are two pioneers of this approach that rigorously and systematically studied communities and power in the 1950s. In the post-Second World War period, the study of governments, constitutions and political institutions constituted only a part of the search for political understanding.

Institutional Approach

The study of political institutions is central to the identity of the discipline of political science. Eckstein (1963) attributes the study to the tendency within political science to distance itself from philosophy, political economy and even sociology and considers it the exclusive subject matter of political science for it can be studied without tools of analysis and methods from other sister disciplines. The subject matter of the institutional approach is obvious for it focuses on the rules, procedures and formal organisations of the government but there is an 'ominous silence about the manner in which study is to be conducted' (Oakeshott 1967: 302). The traditional constitutional method to the study of constitutions is *descriptive-inductive* for it employs the techniques of the historian and inquires specific events, eras, people and institutions. It is inductive for it draws inferences from repeated observations. It is also *formal-legal* and *historical-comparative* for it studies public law and formal governmental bodies in a comparative perspective within a historical context. Herman Finer is considered to be a doyen of this approach. New institutional approach gives more importance to the social context of political behaviour and downsizes the role of the state. It differs from the earlier approach as it covers riot-only constitution and formal political practices but also 'less formal organisational networks'. The behavioural revolution associated with the American Political Science, is dissatisfied with the traditional normative approach to political theory. It shifts the focus to the study of the actual process of politics emphasising on the behaviour pattern of both elite and masses within a framework inspired by social sciences like economics and cybernetics. The kind of behaviour regarded as political is no longer associated only with the state or the government but with certain activities like what Easton calls the authoritative allocation of values within a society or as what Dahl (1963: 9) says with 'power, rule or authority'. Easton's *The Political System* in 1953 is a milestone for he attempts to study the whole political process in a framework of different and overlapping boundaries that differentiate the nature of political activity from the other within this framework of authoritative allocation of values.

WHAT IS POLITICS?

Is it about the government? Traditionally, the state and the government have been the subject matter of politics which tries to furnish the general principles on which organisation of the government should be based. Political science tries to improve the existing political life by reflecting on the aims of the government to realise a 'good life'. This is evident in Aristotle who treats the study of politics as a branch of practical knowledge, of knowing what political action to adopt to deal with a particular set of circumstances. At the same time, politics is a form of knowledge with a distinct subject matter. Aristotle considers politics as arising in organised states that is an aggregate of many members from different tribes, religion, interest and tradition. Politics arises from accepting the fact that different groups with different interests and traditions could co-exist simultaneously within a territory under common rule. This means the presence of different truths and a degree of tolerance towards recognising and accepting these, making governments possible and also necessary for mediating between rival interests through negotiation, accommodation and conciliation. Politics brings together, under the aegis of government, different groups each with their interests so that they can and will speak freely and thereby achieve order. Aristotle regards politics as natural but not spontaneous, for it depends on deliberate and continuous individual activity. It is a master science not in the sense that it explains or embraces all other sciences but in the sense that it provides order to the rival claims of different groups on the scarce resources of any given community. It is because of this crucial role of politics that Aristotle emphasises on the need for the right kind of institutions that follows the principle of 'Mean', avoiding extremities and staying at the middle. It is because of his perceptive and in-depth analysis of politics that Aristotle is considered as the Father of political science.

Like Aristotle and Arendt, Oakeshott describes 'politics as an activity of attending to the general arrangements of a collection of people, who in respect of their common recognition of a manner of attending to its arrangements compose a single community' (1956: 12). He regards political relationship as one between peers whose views are mutually important implying that politics is about persuasion rather than coercion. He rejects the idea of final solution or ultimate goal in politics, like human life, politics is a continuous process, involving endless adjustments. Like Aristotle, Arendt and Edmund Burke (1729–1797), he stresses on the importance but also on the limits in politics. Echoing Albert Camus (1913–1960), he emphasises that the present suffering can never be justified in the name of some abstract vision of the future. Politics does not arise from instant desires nor from general principles but from existing traditions of behaviour. Both political crises and their solutions stem from within a tradition of political activity.

> In political activity, then, men sail a boundless and bottomless sea; there is neither harbour for shelter nor floor for anchorage, neither starting-place nor appointed destination. The enterprise is to keep afloat on an even keel; the sea is both friend and enemy; and the seamanship consists in using the resources of a traditional manner of behaviour in order to make a friend of every hostile occasion (Oakeshott 1956: 15).

Crick, too, in this Aristotelian tradition, defines politics 'as the activity by which different interests within a given unit of rule are conciliated by giving them a share in power in proportion to their importance to the welfare and the survival of the whole community' (Crick 1963: 21). A political system is a kind of government 'where politics proves successful in ensuring reasonable stability and order'. Since an organised government is a civilised value in comparison to anarchy or arbitrary rule, political doctrines ought to attempt at procuring specific and viable solution to the question of conciliation. Politics involves discussion and genuine discussion requires a free government that tolerates opposition. 'Politics needs men who will act freely, but men cannot act freely without politics. Politics is a way of ruling divided societies without undue violence—and most societies are divided' (ibid 1963: 33).

Miller also points out that 'government is the arena of politics, the prize of politics' and, historically speaking, the residue of politics' (1962: 19). Politics is about disagreement and conflict and 'disagreements are due to differences, unevenness, variety or inequality in social conditions'. These disagreements need not always be violent but the government tries to resolve conflict by either pushing towards or preventing change. Moodie (1984) does not agree with Miller who considers many of the services that government rendered as uncontroversial whereas politics, according to Moodie, is much more than being a provider of services. This is because conflict is intrinsic to any society and conflict arises from two permanent characteristics of human life. The first is that most of us want the same things. The second is we also want different things and not all our wants are fully congruous. Politics becomes the regulatory mechanism of coordinating and managing such claims and counter-claims.

Power, Rule and Authority

Dahl points out that Aristotle is among the first to propound the intrinsic link between power, rule and authority for he considers authority or rule as an aspect of political association and classifies constitutions in terms of the location of final authority or rule. Weber and Lasswell share Aristotle's notions though they differ in identifying what is politics. Dahl, accepting the definition of politics provided by Aristotle and Weber, expands to include business firm or a trade union. He defines a political system as 'any persistent pattern of human relationships that involves, to a significant extent, control, influence, power or authority' (1963: 10). This definition is a broad one, for it covers almost all kinds of associations and organisations. However, the political dimension is just one aspect, for people also experience relationships other than those based on power and authority: love, respect, dedication, shared beliefs and so on. It totally leaves out human motives. However, such a definition helps to clarify the public nature of politics, that it involves public purposes or public good or public interest (1963: 11).

Authoritative Allocation of Values

Easton defines political system as the system of interactions in any society through which binding or authoritative allocations are made. He speaks of inputs from the various environments into the political system, which are converted into outputs, i.e., authoritative decisions. Feedback mechanisms put outputs back into the system of inputs, thus completing a complex, cyclical process. Many demands will be made or articulated but some are lost in the conversion process and do not reach the output stage. If there are too many demands, or particular types of demand, stress arises and the channels are then overloaded. There are various regulatory mechanisms to control demands and to minimise overloading—first, there are structural mechanisms that function as gatekeepers', i.e., pressure groups and political parties; second, the cultural mechanisms, the various norms which consider the appropriateness of the demands; third are the communication channels and fourth, demands may be controlled in the conversion process itself by legislators, executives and administrative bodies. For Easton, the social process represents an uninterrupted flow of different activities by which a limited number of valuable objects are transferred to and from interacting individuals whose principal interest is in adopting and enjoying such objects. These objects may extend from physical goods to abstract ones like power and the right to deference. The allocation process is not a haphazard one. It is to a large extent institutionalised if social life is to have any pattern and continuity. It must produce or validate the assignment to certain individuals of certain objects, devalued as well as valued. In three ways—custom, exchange and command—this allocation process is structured, which makes it relatively predictable and stable. Easton defines the whole ambit of politics with reference to command as the basis of allocation, for political allocation necessarily involves the submission of one party to another's will. Customary allocations reflect consensus among the participants, while parties to an exchange are equal and they agree rather than submit. Since objects in question are valued and scarce, political allocations cannot rest solely on someone's will and need binding. Submission to a command does not depend on a person's spontaneous goodwill or indifference, but could be enforced against his opposition. The command-giver should be able to support his statements with sanctions, which is punishment for noncompliance rather than reward for compliance. Politics then deals with the allocation and handling of a resource, which in turn, can be used for making further allocations of other valued objects. Understood in this way, politics seems a mundane business while one intuitively considers it to be important and pivotal to social business involving major players and occupying the centre-stage in the society. Easton tries to reconcile these views by stating that it is not proper to consider any command-based allocation as political; rather, only that which takes place within relatively broad and durable social contexts with broadly defined constituencies should be considered political. A parent's commands, the rulings of a club's chairperson or even the decisions of a corporation's executive are not in the proper sense political. Memberships in local groupings are often voluntary, and even if it is, it could be surrendered without much loss to oneself. However, such groupings form a part of a much wider one with membership that cannot be easily relinquished and such comprehensive grouping that is territorially bounded is 'society'. Easton applies the term 'political' only to those command-based allocations whose consequences are directly or indirectly valid for society as a whole. Political business involves in particular visible, diverse and demanding relations of superiority-inferiority, and ultimately it can sanction the uniquely compelling one of physical coercion. For Easton, politics necessarily takes place within bounded interaction contexts that can co-exist with other such contexts. It deals with a functional problem of allocating values among interacting units which can in principle be dealt by two other institutional methods of custom and exchange. This leads us to the question as to whether politics is a necessary feature and ingredient of social life. The answer is unequivocally in the affirmative except in the very simplest interaction contexts. It is clear that custom and exchange, singularly and collectively, can do all the allocation that has to be done. There are bound to be contingencies, which can be met only by command-based allocations. Custom-based allocation cannot, by its very nature, allow for the mobilisation of resources, the evasion of routines, the inquiry into new lines of action that becomes necessary from time to time for society to endure, to safeguard its values, to defend and maintain its boundaries with nature and with other societies. A wholly custom-controlled society can endure and meet new eventualities only if its customs empower some members to mobilise others in response to such contingencies, to devise new routines, to choose among alternative patterns of action and have their choices accepted. This implies the necessity of command. Regarding exchange, Durkheim has shown long ago the need for enforceable, policed rules for even the most sophisticated and flexible exchange system. Effective contracts depend on the existence of the institution to guide and implement contract, which is not merely and theoretically contractual, but is binding by a command. Easton contends that some allocations will take place through command, for that suggests the necessity of politics. The three modes of allocation do not exist in water-tight compartments and can be interchanged and combined.

Wasby notes that the 'authoritative allocation of values does not distinguish politics adequately from other means of social control. Values are authoritatively allocated within the family, church, and business corporations, as well as government, political parties and interest groups'. It is therefore imperative to distinguish between informal means of social control and those that are coercively enforced. A police officer using force in order to enforce a value is visible, while there are situations when the use of force is not visible and it is not easy to tell who is allocating values. Furthermore, consider a case when companies through their separate decisions have been able to establish a similar price and the government because of paucity of evidence, lack of investigative officers to probe into the case or some other reason ignores the action taken by the companies separately. Is this tantamount to authoritatively allocating values even if these are economic and not directly political (1970: 11)? The approach is criticised for its failure to cater to concepts such as political power or being unable to handle mass political behaviour, aspects like voting. However, Easton by his emphasis on different boundaries and by the input–output mechanism, may deal with such a situation when an economic issue becomes a political one. He constructs a theoretical model that can be modified and changed as he himself has done.

An offshoot of the general systems theories is structural-functionalism, which explains the basic functions performed by political structures within the political system. For instance, a political party is a structure within the political system that performs many functions including those of communicating the wishes of the electorate to the government, informing the electorate on important political issues and allowing for wider participation by more people in the political system. The party maintains the system since it performs these functions. Of course others like pressure groups or formal government institutions could also perform these functions. However, even in a non-party or a single party system, the political functions will be carried out differently. This is the reason that the structural-functionalists do not merely emphasise on structures but also on functions to deal effectively with the wide variety of political systems that prevailed in the 1950s and 1960s. This approach has been used extensively in the field of comparative politics as it provides a standard to study different political systems, mainly of the developing countries.

Collective Choice, Consensus or Conflict

Weale (1984) considers politics as a process of collective choice with a relatively formal method like voting for combining individual preferences into a collective decision. According to Leftwich (1984: 65), politics 'comprises the activities of co-operation and conflict, within and between societies, whereby the human species goes about organising the use, production and distribution of human, natural and other resources in the course of the production and reproduction of its biological and social life'. Hague, Harrop and Breslin (1994) concur with Leftwich. Another view of politics is that it involves both consensus and controversy or conflict. This happens because resources are scarce and political activity is conducted within generally agreed rules that enable people to achieve their goals. Politics involves resolution of disagreement and reaching collective decisions through persuasion, bargaining and a mechanism to reach the final decision. One dimension of politics is controversy as issues get debated, and out of this process of dialogue emerges consensus. It is the affirmation of the Classical Greek view that truth emerges out of discussion. It is appropriate to consider politics as a mechanism for bringing consensus and ending cleavages. Conflict, if managed well and handled by consensus or political compromise, sustains the political process giving it strength and vibrancy. Gandhi describes this as the beauty of compromise. Consensus plays a key role in liberal and pluralist politics while conflict is a crucial idea in Marxism.

Nicholson does not think that it is adequate to define politics just with reference to conflict. Acceptance of endemic conflict between social classes means that societies without class struggle are beyond politics. It would also imply that societies, which have classes, would have conflict, and once classes are abolished conflict will also be eliminated. Such a view also suggests that a classless society is free of politics while it is generally conceded that politics can be minimised but cannot be eliminated in any kind of human organisation. It is not enough to define politics in terms of undefined conflict and it is, worthwhile to consider a criterion that tells us the nature of conflicts. Nicholson (1984: 37) thinks that force is that criterion, for political action can be enforced, 'because the government can coerce people into obedience by the threat of physical force, and ultimately by using it' through its laws. Furthermore even if force is not actually used, the fact that it could be is what is distinctive about politics. Nicholson concedes that some like rebels, armed robbers or a parent chastising a child use force but this is private force and not public force. Endorsing Weber, Nicholson argues that 'a government can be said successfully to claim monopoly of the use of force, because it controls crime and represses rebellion; and it can be said to monopolise the legitimate use of physical force because private individuals may use force only with its permission and within specified limits' (1984: 40). He observes that within a territory only one political organisation can exercise force and that's what distinguishes it from other conflicts. In any given society, there can exist only one type of decision-making body whose decisions are backed by force and that's what makes them political.

NOTION OF POWER

Politics is understood as the study of power. This notion has a time honoured history. Machiavelli and Hobbes lay its foundation and Harrington, Pareto, Mosca and Michels try to uncover its dynamics. In recent times, this view finds extension in the writings of leading American political scientists like Dahl, Easton, Kaplan, Lasswell, Morgenthau and Parsons, who make notable contributions to this view. Power is understood in its different dimensions. Political power can be described as the power that the government and its organs—the police, bureaucracy and the law courts—exercise. It is the key concept in political science, for if politics is the resolution of conflict, the distribution of power within a political community determines how the conflict is to be resolved, and whether the resolution is to be effectively observed by all parties. For some politics involves 'influence and influential'. Power is the ability to influence people to do things that they may not want to do otherwise. Power and influence are closely related. In this context power may, but need not, have anything to do with the government. Since power is generally regarded as bringing about an action by someone against the will or desire of another, it is a relational concept, for it is exercised with respect to others. To be a leader, one has to have followers over whom he exercises power. Power is also bilateral in addition to being relational. A leader has to take into account the needs/desires/

demands of those over whom he commands. As Lasswell and Kaplan (1952: 74–75) note, 'those whose acts are affected also participate in decision-making: by conformity to or disregard of the policy they help determine whether it is or is not in fact a decision'. This makes it difficult to identify who is powerful and who is not. Power is situational. A teacher who has the power to discipline a student in a class has no power over the student's social life. Power is also inherent in certain specific situations or roles. All the Presidents of the United States are powerful compared to other government officials though some use their available skills more than others, which is why one speaks of presidents as 'strong' and 'weak'. Power is intrinsic to human agency for it is the capacity to affect another's behaviour. Power is also a form of relationship in the sense of who has the power in relation to what? In a subtle differentiation of power, it is said that the American President is powerful but the British Prime Minister is strong. This is because the most powerful elected head of the state is severely limited in authority and power because of the doctrine of checks and balances in the United States. The British Prime Minister, on the other hand, enjoying the confidence of the House of Commons is stronger because he has no such constraints. Authority usually accompanies power. Political authority is the recognition of the right to rule irrespective of the sanctions the ruler may possess.

Power needs to be distinguished from related notions like force, manipulation, persuasion and domination. Force exists wherever the exercise of power involves the use of sanctions that create obstacles which restrict the freedom of others. Manipulation involves concealment of intent on the part of the agent exercising power. Persuasion exists where power operates on the basis of an argument about right and wrong. Force, manipulation and persuasion are mechanisms of power that can operate in interpersonal contexts but they can also be involved in the establishment of stable institutionalised structures of power that are normally understood under the nomenclature of social power. This is also understood in the Weberian sense of domination, existing where power relations are structured into patterns of command and obedience. An individual or group exercises domination when it can issue a command to others and can be certain that this will result in obedience. Domination according to Wrong (1979) can be understood in five senses—coercive, induced, competent, personal and legitimate. Coercive domination is said to exist where institutionalised power rests on a threat of force. It is possible to establish a stable power relationship on the basis of coercion without resorting to the use of actual force. This form of domination is the basis of Machiavelli's understanding and finds expression in the elite theories of Pareto, Mosca and in some versions of conflict theory. Induced domination exists where power-holders offer rewards for compliance to a command and this is the view espoused by the social exchange theory. Coercive and induced domination are closely associated with one another, in fact, they are converse to one another. Coercive domination involves the threat of deprivation and is found particularly in the political sphere while induced domination involves promise of rewards and is found in the economic sphere. Competent domination refers to that form of domination that derives from the possession of specialised knowledge or expertise. The subordinates obey only because they recognise the technical competence of those above them. Personal domination is what Weber calls charismatic authority, where subordinates obey because they identify some personal trait in the superior. Legitimate domination is the other name of authority involving consent and a framework of shared norms, through which the subordinated see their superiors as possessing the right to command, what Weber termed as rational-legal authority.

Different ideologies theorise about the nature and limits of political power. **Liberalism** emphasises limits to power. Power has to be clearly and precisely defined with constitutional safeguards to prevent its misuse and abuse. **Marxism** regards political power as the power wielded by the dominant economic class based on the institution of private property. Pluralism believes in wide dispersal of power among different groups in a liberal democratic society with none in a position to monopolise. These groups interact to produce an overall consensus, and conflict resolution is non-violent through forms of bargaining within procedural devices like elections. **Elitism**, like Marxism, believes that a small group of people rule and control the majority but differ on the sources of elite power which could be psychological, organisational, economic or occupational.

Ideological Power

Ideological power is the power exerted by political ideas to legitimise political structures and attenuate political stability. An elected government is obeyed because it is believed that it is representative of the people. Ideas can also be used to attack and criticise the existing distribution of power. The ideas of liberty, equality and fraternity were used during the French Revolution to bring down an absolutist monarchy and replace it with a democracy. The idea of the free world was a powerful symbol that the US and its allies invoked against the Soviet Empire during the Cold War era symbolised by Churchill's famous description, the Iron Curtain. Studies in civic culture speak of attitudes, beliefs, emotions and values of society that relate to the political system. Almond and Verba (1963) refer to three pure types—parochial, subject and participatory political cultures. The process of establishing and developing attitudes to and beliefs about the political system is called political socialisation and is different from political indoctrination in which the government or the ruling class deliberately and intentionally influences the belief structures of its citizens. The agencies of political socialisation are the family, the schools and educational institutions, voluntary groups and mediating groups, religious institutions, the mass media and agencies of the government and political parties. **Economic power** is the power derived from wealth, money and control of material resources. It is identified as an important source of power and influence in any society and by all shades of opinion. Since Plato, political theorists have been concerned with containing the influence which wealth and money wield in the political arena. It is for this reason that Plato proposes abolition of private property for the rulers, a theme that is reiterated by the Marxists and Anarchists. Others like Aristotle are not willing to impose such harsh strictures but were aware of the debilitating effects that unequal property possessions exert in politics. Most political theories follow Aristotle and propose methods of controlling and harnessing economic power for the self interest of all or for the common good.

ANALYSIS OF POWER

There are two conceptions of power in the history of modern political thought. One is the idea of 'power as a simple quantitative phenomenon', 'a generalized capacity to act'. The other is more complex, for it involves 'not only a capacity but also the right to act, with both capacity and right being seen to rest on the consent of those over whom the power is exercised' (Hindess 1996: 1). The first conception understands **power as a means of domination** as evident in the works of Hobbes, Weber, behaviouralists and pluralists. The second view—**power based on consent**—is found in proponents like Arendt and Parsons. A distinction is also made between sectional and non-sectional type of power. Sectional power is asymmetrical involving zero-sum relations. It considers power as arising wherever *A* affects *B* in a manner that is contrary to *B*'s interests. This has been the view of many leading writings from Hobbes to Harrington, Pareto, Mosca, Michels and Weber to Dahl, Easton, Morgenthau, Kaplan and Lasswell. Non-sectional or non-zero sum concept views power as existing only in and through processes of the legitimate. It is seen as a collective capacity that arises from structures of harmonious communal organisation which can be traced from Plato and Aristotle. The leading exponents of this view are Arendt and Parsons. Lukes observes that the non-sectional concept is less valuable than the sectional concept because it systematically ignores the conflictual aspects of power. Mann (1986) defines social power as a matter of domination, on the one hand, and collective organisation on the other. In a similar vein, Giddens (1984: 14–15) refers to power as the 'capacity of one or more agents to make a difference, while on the other it is a structural property of society or the social community'. Giddens' view implies that there is more to the notion of power in any society than just the analysis of the distribution of power amongst its members. Russell (1938) defines power as the production of intended results: the unforeseen effects of our influence on others cannot be called power. This view regards power as an activity. Others like the elite theorists consider power as a possession.

Hobbes and Locke

Hobbes in his efforts to make politics and the study of power more scientific and rigorous defines power as a relation between cause and effect, between an active pushing 'agent' and a passive 'patient'. This differs from the ancient view as defined by the Romans as the capacity or ability of one person or thing to affect another. In the English language, the word 'power' is derived from the Latin word *potestas* or *potentia* meaning ability. According to Hobbes, all human beings desire and seek power presumably in view of the good that the agent perceives that it would bring about. Life is therefore a perpetual and relentless desire and pursuit of power, a prerequisite for felicity and this 'restless desire for power after power ceaseth only in death' (1991: 70). The fact that all individuals, and not just the political elite, seek power, distinguishes Hobbes from Machiavelli who too defines politics as the struggle for the acquisition, maintenance and consolidation of political power. This desire for power, according to Hobbes, is held in check with the institution of the sovereign, as the supreme constituted from combining the powers of the individuals. There is a two-fold significance of this description. First, it suggests that different political powers can be joined together to form a power greater than those who constitute it, thus being an early elaboration of the conception of power as simple quantitative capacity. The second implies that the power of the sovereign really is a power that is greater than the power of any single subject or group of subjects since it combines the power of all subjects. This suggests the right of the sovereign to make use of the powers of his subjects, which do not necessarily mean that he has an effective capacity to make use of those powers. Hobbes, and in fact much of the modern political theory, confuse the two notions of power as a capacity and power as a right (Hindess 1996: 14–15). Subsequent political theorists repeat Hobbes' understanding with variations. Weber identifies power with 'the chance of a man or a number of men to realise their own will in a communal action even against the resistance of others who are participating in the action' (1958: 926).

Locke understands the legitimacy and the complimentary nature of power in terms of rational consent of the governed thereby implying a definite obligation of the holder of power towards his subjects. Political power is 'the Right of making laws with penalties of Death and consequently all less Penalties, for regulating and Preserving of Property, and of employing the force of the Community, in the Execution of such Laws and in the defence of the Commonwealth from Foreign Inquiry and all this only for the Public Good' (Locke I960: 308). By defining political power as a trust of the general community, which specifies its purposes and limits, Locke rejects Filmer's claims of absolutism and patrarichalism based on the divine right of kings. He also rejects conquest as the legitimate foundation for political power. He regards political power as conventional while paternal power—the power of the parent over the child—is natural but temporary and limited till the child attains maturity. Paternal power cannot be invoked to uphold the claim to exercise power over those who have the use of their reason. Locke's definition of political power as a trust provides the basis for a radical critique of traditional view of political power that demands unconditional allegiance—an aspect evident in the *American Declaration of Independence* and in the anti-absolutist doctrines of the eighteenth century Europe.

Elitists and Pluralists

Lukes (1974) acknowledges that the concept of power is essentially a contested one as different commentators have assigned different meanings and defined power, following Hobbes and Weber, as the idea of bringing about consequences. Lukes surveys the different debates on the subject that dominates American academic discussions in the 1960s and 1970s. On one side are the elite theorists who argue that power is concentrated in the hands of the elite both at the local and national level of American politics. On the other side are the pluralists led by Dahl contending that the distribution of power may be unequal but that does not suggest that it is concentrated in the hands of the unified elite. The elite theorists contend that the history of politics is the history of elite domination though they concede that the nature of the elite changes from time to time. They challenge the core premises of most Western liberal postulates about politics, the organisation of the government and the appropriate relationship between the state and the civil society.

> In all societies—from societies that are very meagrely developed and have barely attained the dawnings of civilisation, down to the most advanced and powerful societies—two classes of people appear—a class that rules and a class that is ruled. The first class, always the less numerous, performs all political functions, monopolises power and enjoys the advantages that power brings, whereas the second, the more numerous class, is directed and controlled by the first (Mosca 1939: 50).

Elite domination is a fact of all societies—consensual or authoritarian, dynamic or static, pacifist or totalitarian, legitimate or illegitimate. The nature of every society is determined by the nature of its elite, which in the context of the spirit of the time sets the parameters of human action and movement. Plato and Machiavelli support the idea that a small group shall manage and control the government, but elitism as a social theory is associated with the works of Pareto, Mosca and Michels, which arise in reaction to the spread of democratic ideals and the increasing people's participation in the political process. It rejects the contentions of a majority rule of both the liberal democratic theory and a classless society of Marxism, and considers the elite rule as inevitable in all societies. **Pareto** argues that oligarchy and elite circulation between the governing and the non-governing are borne by historical experiences. In every field of human endeavour, the elite is distinct from the masses. He borrows Machiavelli's two types of elite—foxes and lions—to explain the nature of governing elite structures. These two elites represent two different methods of governance. The foxes govern by consent since they are intelligent, cunning, enterprising, artistic and innovative while the lions are persons of strength, stability, integrity and unimaginative capacity to use force to achieve and maintain their position. Lions are defenders of the status quo with a commitment to public order, religion and political orthodoxy. The qualities of lion and fox are mutually exclusive and history is a process of circulation between them. The ideal for Pareto is a balance between the two types, which rarely happens. This ceaseless process of elite renewal, circulation and substitution highlights the fact that an elite rules in all organised societies. Pareto rejects the Marxist proposition of the state as a mere tool of the dominant economic class and that 'the history of all hitherto existing society is the history of class struggle'. He also rejects the pluralist's contention of the state as a coordinator of the national interest in a plural society. In **Mosca**'s formulations, there are historical and sociological reasons for elite rule. The elite as compared to the masses are organised with a certain unity. In the modern society consisting of leaders, trained administrators and technicians, rule is because of wealth, knowledge and bureaucratic skills. **Michels**, drawing from his own experiences within the German Social Democratic Party (SPD), argues that the basis of elite rule is organisational skills and capacity. He points out, extending the existing elite critique against pluralism and Marxism, that the direct government by the masses is impossible. Applying this argument to political parties, he points to the inevitability of bureaucracy first and then of oligarchy due to its technical and administrative functions. He poignantly observes, 'Who says organisation, says oligarchy' (1962: 364). His theory of 'iron law of oligarchy' explains the nature of elite structures. Elite control over rank and file in any organisation is due to its control of organisation. Michels' novelty lies in the fact that he vindicates his theory by instances of the working of a socialist party, which was ideologically against any kind of elitist control. **James Burnham** (1907–1987) in the *Managerial Revolution* (1941) suggests that the rise of professional managers would create a new class to replace the old ruling class of capitalists. The managerial class is in the process of establishing control across all capitalist states implying that the manager and the technocrat will gain prominence over the owner of capital. A theory very different from Burnham emerges in **C. Wright Mills**' (1916–1962) *The Power Elite* (1956). Mills criticises the American pluralism by arguing that far from being an independent arbiter of national interest, the state is dominated by the power elite of politicians, military and corporate bosses who shape the public policy to suit their own ends. Mills' theory involves a three level gradation of the distribution of power. At the top level are those in command of the major institutional hierarchies of the modern society—the executive branch of the national government, the large business corporations and the military establishment controlling political power, means of production and death, respectively reinforcing Eisenhower's conception of the military-industrial complex. The pluralist model of competing interests, according to Mills, applies to the middle level—the semi-organised interplay between interest groups and legislative politics that the plural is mistakenly assumed as the feature of the whole power structure of capitalist state. At the bottom exists the politically fragmented masses (1956: 167–168). Mills' account explains the close nexus between economic elites and governmental elites—the corporate rich and 'the political directorate'. He asserts that the growing centralisation of power in the federal executive branch of the government is attended by a declining role for professional politicians and a growing number for 'political outsiders' from the corporate world (1956: 235). Notwithstanding this, Mills declares that it is misleading to consider that 'the political apparatus is merely an extension of the corporate world, or that it had been taken over by the representatives of the corporate rich' (1956: 170). He tries to distinguish his position from that of what he terms as 'simple Marxian view' that holds economic elite to be the real holders of power and therefore uses the term power elite rather than the 'ruling class' for that implies too much economic determinism (1956: 276–277). He also asserts that his analysis is compatible with the Marxist view. Furthermore, he also maintains that the political, military and economic elites are considerably autonomous, often in conflict and rarely act in unity.

Critics of Mills

Miliband thinks that there is no room for debate about details in Mills' account, but the background thesis is reasonably satisfactory. Robert Dahl (1915–2014) criticises the analysis on the grounds of insufficient data. He notes that a theory, which cannot be converted to empirical evidence, could not claim to be a scientific theory. The burden of such a proof has to be provided by the theorist and not by his critics. The argument that 'A is more powerful than B' is both ambiguous and meaningless without specificity. No comparison is actually possible when two actors are performing different and not identical functions. Any ideal of political equality is utopian and the absence of political equality does not mean that there is a ruling elite.

Parsons praises the copious data of Mills and agrees that Mills has put it to good use but rejects Mills' claim as the data is not enough for sufficient empirical grounding. He argues that Mills ignored two very important developments—first, the dynamics of a maturing industrial society and second, the altered position of the United States in the world in the context of the relative decline of Western Europe, rise of the Soviet power and independence of colonies. The combination of all these factors has led to enormous enhancement of the American power in a short time and with their profound repercussions old political institutions have disappeared. In an essentially non-political society and localism, this increase in relative importance of government and its power, has created a great degree of tension in a society where Jeffersonian individualism places primacy in economic values of production. Ignoring these important developments, Mills makes large generalisations on the basis of short-term experience. Parsons argues that the structure of American political leadership is far from settled. Mills provides for a very selective treatment of a complex problem. Without dismissing power to be illegitimate, one should accept it as essential and a desirable component in a highly organised society. However, it is clear that power can be abused and needs many safeguards and controls. In Mills, there is no explicit position except that he is partly pre-liberal, anti-capitalist and pro-socialist within the Jeffersonian tradition, but such loose identities are no longer enough for serious model building.

Sweezy finds the greatest merit in the book in its graphic description of those who ruled America. He considers it to be an authentic voice of American radicalism. However, he also criticises Mills for blurring class relationships in the light of the dynamics of the class system in areas of the process of co-option and the loss of high-class status. In short, even the admirers on the left like Miliband and Sweezy do not consider Mills' account to be rigorously worked out and an empirically verifiable thesis of power in the contemporary United States.

The pluralists view politics as an arena of resolving conflict between different groups, who represent all the dominant interests of the society. They concede that some marginal groups may be left out, but assert that all the major streams are represented. They also argue that certain groups try to establish close links with particular departments in the government and that may lead to a neglect of other interests. For instance, Truman (1951: 10) acknowledges that institutionalised relationships between an agency and its attendant interest groups can develop and this leads to other interests being ignored. However, Wilson (1977: 45) points out that there is **Whitehall pluralism**, meaning that if even one department ignores the interest of a particular group, their views are taken up 'by the fact that other departments have checks and have different departmental views accordingly'. The pluralists perceive the state as a balancing factor between departments that represent a range of interest groups. Authority is distributed within the government (Eckstein 1963: 392), meaning that the state is not controlled and dominated by any single interest. Yet the state is seldom neutral but mirrors the range of group pressures it faces as 'policy arises from the interaction of various social elements' (Easton 1965: 172). The state attempts to make policy by bargaining between a range of conflicting interests and the government takes into consideration the interests of 'unorganised and potential groups' and, therefore, they do not need 'organised expression except when these needs are flagrantly violated' (Truman 1951: 448). Politics is a constant process of negotiation that ensures that conflicts are resolved peacefully (Dahl 1967: 24). It is thus contended that an explanation of politics is an analysis of groups. Policy emerges as a result of a constant method of conflict and exchange between different groups with the government being regarded as just another group. Only by organising themselves into groups can individuals get their interests represented in government. The state is a distinct organisation that makes policies in response to the innumerable groups exerting pressure on the government. It is accepted that conflict between groups is persuasive within liberal democracy and this conflict rarely threatens the stability of the system. Consensus defining the limits of political action and the framework of policy outcomes ensures political stability.

The pluralists understand power as the capacity to achieve one's aims despite opposition from others. Power is 'the capacity of one actor to do something affecting another action, which changes the probable pattern of specified future events' (Polsby 1963: 5). Dahl (1957: 23) defines power as 'a realistic relationship, such as *A*'s capacity for acting in such a manner as to control *B*'s responses'. It is also 'power as a successful attempt by *A* to get *B* to do something he would not otherwise do' (Dahl 1957: 201–215). Whether power is capacity as Dahl's first definition suggests or the actual behavioural outcomes that his second definition emphasised the pluralist definition of power rests on the exercise of control over immediate events: the issue of overcoming *B*'s immediate resistance to *A*'s will or command (Lukes 1974: Ch. 2). The pluralists concede that there are many dimensions of inequalities in the society and that not all the groups have an equal access to all types of resources, let alone equal resources. However, nearly every group has some advantage that can be utilised in the democratic process to make an impact. Since different groups have access to different kinds of resources, the influence of any particular group will generally depend on the issue at hand. The pluralists perceive power as non-hierarchical and competitively arranged and embroiled in an 'endless process of bargaining' between many groups representing different interests. These groups in the long run change their concerns and shift their positions. Both at the local and at the national level political decisions are not a reflection of a unified public opinion on basic issues that Locke, Rousseau and Bentham have presumed. The details of policy-making in the complex world of today emerge out of intense lobbying by different interested groups and ultimately the policy reflects the inputs of all such divergent groups. Political outcomes are the consequence of mediation and adjudication between competing demands of groups. There is no powerful decision-making centre in the pluralist model. Since power is dispersed throughout the society, there is plurality of pressure points, a variety of competing policy-formulating and decision-making centres. Equilibrium in society is achieved, according to Truman (1951: 503–516), because of the existence of diversity of interests and overlapping membership, which unleashes competing forces without any one force wielding excessive influence. The existence of these varied groups sustains democratic goals and helps citizens to advance their goals.

The key questions for the pluralists are: who are involved in the decision-making process; and who is successful in getting their preferences accepted as decisions; who is it who could be seen to influence outcomes? Polsby advises that researcher has to study the actual behaviour either first hand or from documents, informants, newspapers and other appropriate sources. The pluralists point out to the actual process of decision-making. By ignoring untested concepts like false consciousness, hegemony and dominant ideology they are able to develop a theory of power that is empirically verifiable. Their notion of 'modern society and polity as fragmented, diverse and democratic' is 'more accurate about the distribution of power than found in monolithic Marxist and elitist theories' (Smith 1995: 214). Owing to their equal emphasis on both democracy and pluralism, it is called **democratic-pluralist** view.

Criticism

Bachrach and Baratz (1962) criticise the pluralist analysis for focusing only on one of the two sides of power—the public face. The other, the private side, namely the interests of particular individuals or groups, which affect the entire community, remains hidden and excluded from scrutiny. The critics maintain that the hidden side of power makes it possible to project the benign political representation of power as serving the general interest. Lukes observes that these disputes indicate a conflict between two views—the elitist and the pluralists—of the one underlying concept of power, which he terms as one-dimensional and two-dimensional. The one-dimensional approach is associated with the pluralists and in particular Dahl. This is the liberal view. The two-dimensional view—the reformist view presented by the critics of pluralism—takes into account behind the scene manoeuvring which can prevent issues from becoming matters of open public discussion. The one-dimensional view sees interests in exclusively subjective terms—power as related directly to individual wants. The two-dimensional view perceives the existence of wants that get deflected, submerged or concealed alongside those that get politically recognised. The three-dimensional view that Lukes suggests as an alternative to one-dimensional and two-dimensional views holds that wants are social constructs which socialisation and structural constraints shape and that interests can be seen as involving 'what they would want, are they able to make the choice'. Lukes introduces the notion of 'latent conflict' as a necessary corollary to the ideal of objective interests. It seems that people are unaware of their 'real' interests and the absence of conflict in a society may be seen as reflecting false or manipulated consensus. The fact that there exists a contradiction between the interests of those who wield power and the interests of those on whom this power is wielded means the potentiality for conflict behind the facade of consensus. According to Lukes, the one-dimensional and two-dimensional views of power fail to recognise the systemic aspects of power. These systemic phenomena cannot be analysed for they are seen as a function of collective forces and social arrangements. He considers collective agencies like political parties, trade unions and business enterprises as true agents of power, thereby, combating methodological individualism by its emphasis on collective agencies.

His second essay—'Three-Dimensional Power' (2006) tries to locate the sense of freedom or autonomy in relationship to the patterns of power that exist. His third dimension occurs not only where there is domination, but where the dominated acquiesce in their domination. Pluralism is far more subtle and complex than many of its critics have suggested. Pluralists are aware of inequalities in society and between groups and accept them because of institutional relationships, which mean that some groups have privileged access to the government. However, they continue to see power as scattered and non-cumulative—success in one area does not mean an increase in power in other policy matters. They do not see a link between economic and political power. They regard the political system as benevolent and do not entertain the possibility that some groups are deliberately left out for a long period of time (Smith 1995: 215). Furthermore, by concentrating on the observable, they miss the real reasons for policy. They fail to examine the ideological and the structural context of policy decisions (Smith 1990).

Reformed and Neo-pluralism

In response to the critics, the reformed pluralism accepts that relationships between groups and the state can be structured and institutionalised but argues that structured relationships are disintegrating and becoming confused and increasingly open to groups (Jordan and Richardson 1987: 117–118). However, like the classical pluralists, they fail 'to contextualise the decision-making process. They confuse a large number of groups being involved in decision-making with a large number of groups being influential' (Smith 1995: 221). Neo-pluralism, a radical response to the criticisms of pluralism that developed in the United States, recognises the superior position business groups enjoy over others. The importance of business means that the government will automatically respond to its interests. Lindbolm observes that business has two advantages—first, the government depends on a successful economy and therefore tries to offer incentives to perform better. This gives business 'a privileged position in government' (1977: 175) and second, in a market economy most of the decisions taken are for inducing investments and employment and despite the impact these decisions have on other people's lives they are not subject to democratic controls (1977: 172). Neo-pluralism shares with pluralism certain basic traits, for it stresses the importance of groups and the existence of competitive policy areas. It accepts the privileged position of business but argues that it does not dominate the policy process completely. However, neo-pluralism fails to take into consideration that business is not as unified as it presumes.

Class and Power—The Marxists

Lukes' three-dimensional view resonates in other views like Marx's claim in the *German Ideology* (1845–1846), that the ideas of the ruling class are in every historical period. The ruling ideas and that the class which is the ruling material force in society becomes at the same time its ruling intellectual force. For Marx, politics is to be understood in the context of a process of historical change and therefore the concept of class is of pivotal importance, though neither Marx nor Engels offers a systematic exposition of it. In one sense, it is the starting point in Marx's theory between 1843–1844, for his discovery of the proletariat as a new force engaged in a struggle for emancipation lead him to analyse the economic structures of modern societies and its process of development. Subsequently, the idea of class conflict as the driving force of history becomes evident in the famous sentence in the *Communist Manifesto* (1848) that 'the history of all hitherto existing society is the history of class struggle' (Marx 1977b: 109).

Marx and Engels even suggest in the *German Ideology* that 'class itself is a product of the bourgeoisie' and that class is a uniquely conspicuous characteristic of the capitalist society. Class, for Marx, symbolises collective unity in the same manner as the nation in Hegel's theory. Each class produces its own ideas and beliefs and operates within a particular economic and social system with a theory of ownership and control. The individual is important with respect to his membership within a class that determines his moral conviction, aesthetic preferences and reason. For the Marxist, the principal theoretical classifications are those of master and slave, patrician and plebian, lord and serf (in feudalism) and bourgeois and proletariat (in capitalism). Class struggles intensifies under capitalism to the point of a revolution when the whole society is overturned in the interest of the rising class—the proletariat. Classes cease to exist once capitalism is destroyed by the worldwide proletarian revolution, since socialism abolishes private property there is no rationale for classes and hence class struggle. Marx defines classes in terms of their position tending to dramatise history by speaking of whole classes as if they move up and down through the social and economic hierarchy. However, Marx is imprecise in his theory of the upward and downward movement of classes, as within the class itself there are several differentiation and specialisation of functions. One puzzling inadequacy of the Marxist explanation of the dynamics of power in the modern society is its stubborn resistance to any plausible acceptance of division of power and the tacit pillars on which modern societies are established.

According to Marx, the dominant economic class, based on the institution of private property, controls and wields political power. He believes that it is a mistake to start from human consciousness and to proceed from this to an explanation of the material reality. The correct approach is the other way around. The origin of the problem is not mistaken ideas but the distorted nature of social reality that generates mistaken ideas: 'It is not consciousness of men that determines their existence but, on the contrary their social existence determines their existence' (Marx 1977: 242). According to the materialist conception of history, the way human beings respond to their material needs determine the rest of the society. For Marx, the class that controls the means of production also controls the means of mental production. A person's vision of the world is determined by his mode of life, specifically by his position in a system of production relations and hence a person's class, thought alone cannot change one's vision of reality and therefore, there is no purely intellectual pursuit of truth, at least in matters concerning social and political perceptions. This false consciousness can only be altered by revolutionary action. This active move towards a mode of consciousness that is true is called *praxis*, a happy combination of theory and practice.

For Gramsci, the basic idea is that in a modern democratic state people are not ruled by force but by control of the ideological apparatus, which operates through civil society. He provides fresh insights into the role of intellectuals and the ideological apparatuses (education, media, church, etc.) in social and political consciousness and in the production of ideology. The intellectuals play an important role in the civil society by creating hegemony. **Hegemony**, a key word for Gramsci denotes the ascendancy of a class not only in the economic sphere but also through all social, political and ideological spheres, and its ability thereby to persuade other classes to see the world in terms favourable to its own ascendancy. It refers to the way class domination is based not simply upon coercion but upon the cultural and ideological consent of the subordinate classes. The political issues cannot therefore be understood as either consent or force, for they consist of both the elements. Consent, however, does not indicate a permanent state of affairs but conveys a struggle between competing ideological positions that are shifting constantly to 'accommodate the changing nature of historical circumstances and the demands and reflexive actions of human beings' (Carnoy 1984: 70). If the intellectuals can successfully create hegemony then the ruling class rules by controlling the apparatuses of the civil society and if they fail then the rule is through coercion. Gramsci points out that an advanced state rules by perfecting the ideological apparatus rather than through repressive measures like force and repression and on this basis criticises the Leninist state in which the 'state was everything and civil society nothing'. In developing the concept of hegemony, Gramsci deviates from the positions held by Marx and Engels in two important ways. First, he emphasises the importance of the ideological superstructures vis-á-vis the economic structure. He considers private ownership of the means of production as a necessary but not the sufficient basis of capitalist domination, thereby implying the need to take into account political, cultural and ideological dimensions of class struggle. Second, his views emphasise the importance of consent within the civil society as opposed to the use of pure force by the state (Carnoy 1984: 69). Gramsci extends the concept of power to include the vast array of institutions—education, mass media, parliaments and courts—that mediate power relations in the society.

The structuralists, beginning with Louis Althusser (1918–1985) challenge this view by beginning with Gramsci's assertion of the relative autonomy of the state, which explores not only the economic dimension but also the various other components—political, legal and ideological segments—of the society. The repressive apparatus of the state works out the mechanism of domination of the working class by the ruling class with its apparatuses like the bureaucracy, police, courts, prisons and the army. Besides these, there are the ideological and structural dimensions like the church, family, schools, political parties, trade unions, communications and cultural organisations. Althusser (1969) argues that in advanced capitalism the ruling class maintains itself in power by using both the repressive and the ideological apparatuses. In mature capitalism, education is a mechanism of ideological domination, similar to the role that the church performed in the pre-capitalist phase. Education was the real mechanism of control behind the formal parliamentary set-up with universal suffrage and competing party system. Nicos Poulantaz (1936–1979) defines power as a property of impersonal social structure and not of individual agents, their aims and aspirations. He (1973) establishes the relative autonomy of the capitalist state that is institutionally separate from capitalist production. Since capitalist exploitation does not require extra economic coercion, the capitalist state can be organised as a national popular state. The struggle among political forces to win hegemony in this context is the means through which a capitalist power bloc is organised, disorganising in the process the dominated classes. In maintaining social cohesion of a class-divided society, the capitalist class helps to promote continued accumulation.

Group[1] and Power: The Subaltern View

One very important development in the human history is the European domination of the non-European world that ultimately led to imperialism and colonialism. The discovery of America and Vasco de Gama's arrival in India and subsequent control of the entire world by European nations has permanently distorted the natural evolution of a cooperative and mutually beneficial human history. Terms like civilised and the 'barbarians' and the 'white man's burden' reflect this Eurocentric bias, which took for granted the superiority of Europe over the rest. To a large extent, the classical political theory has endorsed this view, which has been challenged only recently by a new post-colonial narrative popularly called the subaltern perspective.

An important source of subaltern theorising is Gramsci's notion of hegemony. A subaltern group is not simply an oppressed group or a category that lacks autonomy and is influenced and controlled by the hegemonic spell of another dominant social group, but is dispossessed because it lacks its own hegemonic position, unable to articulate its own identity and aspiration. There is a striking similarity between subaltern and feminist perspectives, for both reject the traditional liberalism and Marxism as being unable to capture the complexity, diversity and the irresolution of the numerous scattered voiceless subaltern groups. The post-colonial societies exhibit a strange multiplicity where the liberal idea of citizenship, modern state and bourgeois privacy, civil society and negative freedom have little meaning for the subalterns who are submerged in their savagery, traditionalism and abject poverty. Because of this underdevelopment, a subaltern is more of a spectator than a participant in the public political space, created by the civil society. The diversity that liberalism accepts is narrow, unable to comprehend the heterogeneity of the subaltern desire expressed in very different idioms which even centuries of colonial domination could not eliminate. It is this autonomous space that is the concern of the subaltern theorists. Few, if any, will deny that colonialism has led to a gross distortion in the historical evolution of human kind and in pointing this out the subaltern discourse is a contemporary revival of a negative tradition in the political theory that begins with the Cynics, Stoics and the Epicureans, the critics of Plato and Aristotle. Like these early critics, the major shortcoming of this discourse is that it is imprecise and though it is critical of the dominant contemporary ideologies which have claims of universal application as being inappropriate to post-colonial societies it has not been able to provide an alternative grand narrative.

Such a grand narrative eludes the subaltern theorists because colonialism in its worldwide application had no core argument. The European interaction with the two Americas, Australia and New Zealand, on the one side, as settler colonies and their interaction in Asia and Africa which have reflected a variety of exploitative mechanisms, on the other, denies the possibility of developing a unified colonial heritage, making a global post-colonial discourse virtually impossible. The problems of aborigines in Australia and New Zealand, the American Indian in North and South America are very different from the problems of post-colonial societies of Asia and Africa. Any plausible narrative is only possible if it accepts, as Laski says, the mood rather than the doctrine of liberalism by broadening the narrow diversity, as subalterns allege, of liberalism and incorporate claims of all post-colonial societies. A worthwhile starting point for the subalterns can be Berlin's value and cultural pluralism that is rooted in historical communities.

Gender, Patriarchy and Power—Feminist View

Feminism explains the process of male domination of women in reality and symbolically. It asserts that social and political structures of society symbolise the power of men over women resulting in the latter's oppression and subjugation. It highlights the causes for women's disadvantage and seeks to remedy it. It emerges in the modern period adopting its foundational ideas of equality, rational individualism, universal rights and abstract rights while objecting to their inconsistent application, which marked women as an oppressed class. Gender is to the feminist theory what class is to Marxism. Gender is the *differentia specified* between feminist and 'male stream' theory. Feminism has developed in three distinctive waves—the first wave of liberal and socialist feminism (eighteenth century to the 1920s), the second wave of radical feminism (1960–1980) and the third wave of postmodernist feminism (1980s onwards). Liberal feminism and Marxist/socialist feminism, which continue to subscribe to their parent philosophies, apply the assumptions of their respective parent doctrines to the woman's question. However, radical feminism differs from both liberal and Marxist/socialist feminism in the hope of modifying it to include exclusively women's interests and perceptions. It dismisses liberal initiatives of changing existing laws as cosmetic that conceal and sometimes perpetuate the injustice that exists within the structure of the family itself, about which liberalism and liberal-feminism are silent. Similarly, the socialist and Marxist stress on the economic basis of women's oppression ignores the non-economic aspects, especially the sexual forms (Benhahib and Cornell 1987: 3, 5, 16–30). It criticises traditional political philosophy, as it legitimises male power. In claiming 'personal is political', it wants to deny the existence of a separate political realm and insists that the concept of political is itself 'male'. The public sphere is the product of male imagination reflecting its competitive and inegalitarian values. This is with regard to its regulation of the private sphere (through laws and customs and the personal power men exert in their families) and in the hierarchical structuring of the political, social and economic status among men. Sexism and the assumption of male superiority permeate the dominant culture and patriarchal power embodied in the political arena (Pateman 1988, Okin 1989). The first wave feminists define patriarchy as a situation of inequality which excludes women from citizenship. However, the second wave feminists understand patriarchy to denote male power and politics, because it establishes the complete link between the domination of women by men and the domination of men by other men (Randall 1987).

Patriarchy, according to Mitchell (1974), is an ideological phenomenon that underpins the cultural construction of masculinity and femininity and it is only with the psychic transformation of patriarchy that women will secure liberation. Radical feminism accepts gender difference and criticises the earlier generation of egalitarian feminists for demanding women's equality with men by devaluing the feminine identity as something imposed by patriarchy and not something that patriarchy justifies. Both Wollstonecraft and J.S. Mill contend that if women appear irrational, it is due to inadequate education and training. In conformity with the liberal presumption of human equality, they contend that women are as rational as men and they ought to be equal participants in the political process. In their view, women's identity is submerged under the weight of this general equality. The womanly identity is confined to a powerless and ineffectual domestic sphere placing women in an impossible situation. For, in patriarchal societies where sex and gender are rigidly aligned, they have only two choices—to acquire masculine qualities consonant with humanity and citizenship but to be derided as aberrant because unfeminine, or to accede to the feminine norm patriarchy decrees for women, only to be judged unsuited for public life' (Coole 1993: 201).

Radical feminism considers women's oppression as a distinctive form of oppression transcending other forms of oppression, which can be combated if women unite with women against men as oppressors. Its importance to political philosophy lies in its novel deconstruction of what constitutes the political arena. Since the public space has left out female gender values both men and women have to pay a heavy price in a distorted decision-making process. However, their aim is not to emphasise only the public sphere, for that is tantamount to reinforcing its dominance with the attendant danger of turning women into yet another of its many 'out-groups' on the one hand and excluding the female values that are linked to and devalued in the private sphere on the other. Instead the women's liberation movement tries to liberate women from male oppression and their gender socialisation and also to overcome the barriers between the public and private spheres by recreating society, culture and politics in new non-patriarchal forms. Women's disadvantages at the work place and the problems associated with the status of domestic work are indicative of a wider problem of their sexual subordination to men. Radical feminism tries to disclose the whole gender-based system of sexism and patriarchal power, explicit in social, political and economic structures, in language and cultural images of men and women; in the alienation of women from their bodies, the repression of their sexuality and the male control of women's reproduction; and in the male violence against women. It considers politics to be a much broader phenomenon to be encompassed in the state, government or in any centralised demand for distributive justice. The radical feminists reject existing politics by providing a new definition of politics that emphasises the need to build a new political world of non-hierarchical, unstructured political forms and relationships which would reflect the complex network of particular relationships and personal responsibilities in women's nurturing role. Radical feminism, a critique of political philosophy than being a political philosophy itself, severely criticises both the male dominated classical political discourse and the early feminism's concern with women's lack of political power rather than issues affecting women.

If the stress is on women's traditional roles as alternatives to male politics, then radical feminism perpetuates a male constructed difference. If the feminists believe female alternatives as better, they construct another model of gender dominance of women over men. Besides confusion about goals, there are anxieties about how far they can go in projecting a separate sphere in which women can act and interact autonomously outside the male-dominated structures. For some this represents an organisational strategy, either as a temporary measure till a more androgynous society emerges or one that allows participation of both the sexes. For others who view men as enemy, separatism is not the means but the end, which is as final and total as it could be.

Feminists have faced divisions from within their ranks. In 1970s, the Marxist feminists contend that feminism must be subordinated to the socialist movement, while the radicals espouse the reverse point of view, emphasising that a real change in the nature of relations with men is impossible unless there is a fundamental change in the attitude of the society towards women's values. The rise of black feminism identifying racism as yet another distinct oppressive system also added to the problem. It raises objections to the over-generalisations due to the dominance of well-off white women in the women's movement. It forges links with the Third-World feminists and provides new views of women's experience and aims to Western feminism, revealing the ethnocentricity of some of its assumptions. The assumption of black feminism that racism makes the experience of black women unique and that only they could articulate them made them see white feminism as a form of racism. As a consequence, black feminists insist that racism, like class relations for socialists, must be treated as a separate system of oppression from that of gender and that black women must organise separately from the white. This happens because of two divisive influences that the new waves of feminism exert on the women's movement. One is guilt, the result of which is to create a hierarchy of oppression that judges the most oppressed as the most valued. The second is that of relativism and 'difference'.

Most feminists readily admit and concede the uniqueness of every group that needs to be expressed in view of 'deconstructionism', the central concern of Women's Studies in the 1980s. The only way to liberation is deconstructing a discourse and 'privileging' one's own oppressed identity. For a feminist, deconstruction of the dominant masculine discourse mean not only to expose its hidden misogynist agenda but also to liberate all the women's voices and the experiences they have been denied. The problem with relativism, if pushed to the extreme, is fragmentation. This is the same with deconstruction: no identity is free from deconstruction. The consequence for feminism is a movement of diverse and overlapping oppressed groups for whom feminism is the only common factor but not the primary one. Furthermore, the removal of patriarchy requires that women think as women and for women to think they need a language and that in itself, is man-made. Therefore, the question as to whether there is any such thing as 'thinking as a woman' or just different subjectivities and no unified category of woman has arisen. If there is no certainty then what is the status of women's oppression? By denying objectivity, postmodernism robs feminism of its central axiom—its claim that women as a group suffer systematic political disadvantage.

These contradictions have led Elshtain (1981) to criticise radical feminism for failing to develop a theory of public-private relationship that is to be integrated to the political process. Against the dreary interpretations of the 'personal is political', she wants to capture both the centrality of family and the importance of politics. She objects to the over-politicisation of childrearing that understates the importance of a permanent relationship between the child and the caring adult. She also objects to the de-politicisation of 'politics' that discourages feminists from addressing issues of citizenship or political authority. Pateman (1983) and Okin (1991) have distanced themselves from the literal interpretation of 'the personal is political' that radical feminism espouses. Many contemporary feminists have begun to stress the fresh insights feminism can bring to the political process by giving their input into it. Increasing attention is paid to women's under-representation in decision-making bodies, to developing legislations for sexual equality and re-theorising the notion of citizenship. The political campaigns that women espouse are (a) gender free and equal education, (b) equal employment opportunities with equal pay and conditions along with the role of housework in the economy, the idea of women's double burden, safety measures and special care for working mothers, like day care centres and flexible hours of work; (c) safe maternity, abortion, importance of mothering, child care and safe contraceptives; (d) sexual equality and steps to contain sexual violence and sexual harassment and (e) portrayal of women and men in art, cinema, literature, theatre, etc. in a dignified manner.

Power as Consent

Arendt and Parsons, unlike the earlier view, conceptualise power with reference to conflict, and define it as fundamentally dependent on the consent of those over whom it is exercised. While some use power in a general sense, Arendt insists on it being public power and that it should be exclusively referred to the government, for it is an important feature of the modern state. She regards power as that which 'corresponds to the human ability not just to act but to act in concert. Power is never the property of an individual; it belongs to a group and remains in existence only so long as the group keeps together' (Arendt 1973: 113). She clarifies that power should not be confused with strength or violence. Similar thoughts underpin Parsons' idea that power is a 'generalised medium of mobilising commitments or obligation for effective collective action, a generalised facility of resource that rests on accepted forms of legitimacy' (1967: 332). Parsons is concerned with the nature of power and not with its specific effects. He is unwilling to treat power as anything connected with compliance; power is a specific mechanism that operates to bring about changes in the action of other units, individual or collective, in the processes of social interaction. Power is analogous to money in the economy as a generalised capacity to secure common goals of a social system. Money facilitates economic transactions and power facilitates political transactions. With money one could procure goods and services and with power one could secure the performance of political obligations.

More recently **Foucault** proposes a radical re-conceptualisation of power. Till date, major concern of political thinkers has been to treat power in the context of sovereignty and legitimacy. As long as such power is derived from actual or tacit consent of the people it was considered legitimate. Foucault departs from this tradition since he thinks the attributes of power are to be based on foundations very different from sovereignty and legitimacy. He wishes 'to cut off the king's head in political theory that has still to be done' (1980: 21). To arrive at a new basis of power, he makes a distinction between power in general, on the one hand, and domination and government, on the other. His theory of power is based on 'structure of actions' which has an impact on the actions of free people. In such a conception, the power relationship will mostly be unstable and reversible. His concern is not with governmental legitimacy but with the ways and means by which the effect of power is felt. He follows the Weberian tradition in claiming that the governmental function is much more than just making and enforcing laws. In Weber, there is no total subordination of the specialised and the trained bureaucracy by the political top brass. Foucault develops this argument by stating that governmental activity extends beyond the ambit of state bureaucracy in a variety of ways, like specialised knowledge of accountancy, finance, science and psychiatry. According to Foucault, particular reforms are always incompatible with power because in practice such reforms substitute one set of powers by another, rather than putting into motion a process of universalistic emancipation from the effects of power itself. However, such a theory that resembles Friedrich Wilhelm Nietzsche's (1844–1900) conception of power is inherently problematic as Foucault categorically avoids providing for a universalistic discourse of emancipation free from effects of power.

AUTHORITY

Authority is the right to exercise the power and influence of a particular position that comes from having been placed in that position according to regular, known and widely accepted procedures. It is the legitimisation process of the acts and commands exercised in the name of those in authority. In short, it is the legitimate power based on law, which in a democracy is derived from the constitution, which expresses the sovereignty of the people and guarantees the legality of laws. It is derived from notions of *auctor* and *auctoritas* which mean producing, inventing or influencing the sphere of opinion, counsel or command (Benn and Peters 1959: 18). Besides being understood as the right to rule, it also means expertise. The first one means to be in authority while the second usage refers to the theoretical knowledge (to be an authority). In both the meanings, there is an acceptance of the fact that an individual subordinates his will or judgement to that of another person in a manner that is binding, independent of the particular content of what that person says or requires. If a person's authority is justified then it is *de jure* authority, and if it is recognised then it is *de facto* authority. Authority is different from power, being a relation, *de jure* and not necessarily *de facto*: authority is a right to act rather than the power (not coercive or naked) to act. Hobbes fuses the two together, for their separation, in his view, is fatal. A tyrant or a despot is authoritarian, but cannot be considered authority, for the latter in the true sense is derived from rules and must be limited and restrained. Authoritarianism demands absolute obedience of the individual as against individual freedom. Therefore, authority is used in both *de jure* and *de facto* senses. Hobbes uses authority in the *de jure* sense meaning a set of procedural rules which determines who shall be the '*auctor*' or 'in authority', 'the authorities' or 'an authority'. In its *de facto* sense as used by de Jouvenel authority involves reference to a man whose word in fact goes in some sphere—as when one says, 'He exercised authority over his men' (Benn and Peters 1959: 19). *De facto* authority can secure obedience without a rule or entitlement and yet without threats, for obedience in many such instances is out of fear of reappraisal. As long as the rule is generally respected *de jure* authority will also be *de facto*. This means that people will abide 'by official's suggestions because they recognise in him a person appointed and entitled to give orders; though they might not respect the man, they might yet respect his office' (Benn and Peters: 1959: 297).

Weber tries to provide a sociological explanation of people's compliance to authority rather than philosophically analysing the concept of authority. He classifies authority into traditional, that rests on customs and prescription; charismatic or a leader's personality; and rational-legal as exercised by the modern-day industrial bureaucratic state. Traditional authority commands obedience of the people on the basis of unwritten, but internally binding rules that are customary, religious or historical. The authority of the tribal chief is an example of this. The Divine Right of Kings is a sophisticated approach to traditional authority. Charismatic authority seems unrelated to rules but is explained in terms of personal quality that an individual may have that entitles a person to obedience. Political theorists like Plato and Machiavelli are profoundly impressed by the role of leadership in societies while **Locke**, **Bentham** and **Popper** recognise the importance of political institutions for there can never be perfect rulers (Benh and Peters 1959: 306–307). From this stems the **rational-legal** authority. Rational-legal authority rests on rules that are impersonal and is normally attached to offices. In most societies, one can find these three types, though one amongst them is likely to be predominant.

When one uses the term political authority, one usually means the states, and this notion has three distinguishing features. First, the state claims and enforces compulsory jurisdiction over everyone within its territory. While the authority of the state is supreme, it is subject to constitutional limits. Second, it regulates the most essential interests of everyone within its territory. Third, it can impose obligations of obedience. Authority accompanies political power. Political authority is the recognition of the right to rule irrespective of the sanctions the ruler may possess. In certain situations, the two may be separate. Some political leaders may have the authority but are unable or reluctant to translate it into political power. For instance, General de Gaulle's authority was recognised in German occupied France in the 1940s, but the coercive powers of the German and pro-German French governments prevented the conversion of that authority into political power. Political authority is supported and perpetuated by the use of symbols, such as the national flag or a coronation ceremony and most importantly, by political idioms that people recognise and respect.

Most political philosophers understand political authority as the authority that demands obedience for securing order. The basis of a government's authority rests on its legal validity and on people acknowledging their political obligations underlining their loyalty to the government and the laws. Thus, authority has two aspects—objective and subjective—and is incomplete and uncertain till both are achieved. Authority, when properly established and accepted commands people's obedience more easily and with little violence than coercion. Authority is usually based on law. In a democracy, it emanates from the constitutions that express people's sovereignty and guarantees legality of the laws. Furthermore, authority does not simply imply command and obedience but also involves the ideas of rationality and criticism. Friedrich (1973: 172) emphasises the importance of reasoning, and argues that a social system communicates through opinions, beliefs and values and that constitutes the basis of authority. Arendt (1968) emphasising the complementary nature of authority and its acceptance rejects the modern concept of authority that identifies authority with the legitimate power to rule another. Generally, political theorists regard authority as a distinctive type of social control or influence without employing overtly the use of coercion. She is concerned with the specific relationship between the ruler and the ruled that symbolises the nature of the modern state. She understands authority with reference to its contrasting qualities of coercion by force and persuasion by argument. Scrutinising the Roman experience, she points out that those in authority do not wield authority by virtue of force or by virtue of persuasion but by virtue of relationship between themselves and their origin. They do not assert authority by posing themselves as its originators but instead assert their authority on behalf of men or principles from the past, to claim their right to rule. This is evident from the etymology of *auctoritas*, the Latin word for authority meaning to augment. The Romans maintain authority by accepting change with continuity. Arendt insists that authority is crucial to stability. She holds the collapse of authority in the modern world as responsible for the rise of totalitarianism.

Only with the advent of the modern period, authority becomes secular, limited, accountable and responsible. Prior to that, authority was seen as derived from God, and hence, absolute and beyond doubt. The liberals reject absolute authority and accept authority to be a product of human reason and will and it can be judged and disobeyed when the need arises. Conservatives have a deferential attitude towards authority, seeing it as necessary for guidance, support and security. Libertarians and anarchists reject authority, except those aspects which are self-regulating, for authority imposed from above and outside curtails and undermines individual liberty. The Marxists like the anarchists reject authority and conceive of a society without political authority.

CONCLUSION

A very influential section of political theorists led by de Bonald and de Maistre of the eighteenth century and later in the post-Second World War period by Shils, Janowitz, Almond, Verba, Lazasfield, Mayo and Eckstein have contended that a well-built consensus leads to the disappearance of both conflict and power, as they are indicators of disruption and strife. A consensual order will be one of minor contradictions which reflect a great deal of agreement on major issues and consequently the exercise of power increases or decreases in the context of polarisation or basic agreement in politics. Marshall's assertion of the qualitative change in the nature of politics and power by the introduction of one person, one vote is the beginning of this process of reduction of the conflict and suspicion between the ruler and the ruled. Parsons even goes to the extent of using this right to vote to resolve serious problems of the modern society, the resolution of the contradiction between equality and inequality. Legitimacy of power and office comes out of this selective principle. Election is the mechanism by which the solidarity of the entire political system is achieved. Parsons put it categorically, 'voting is an exercise of power' (1969: 337). By this exercise, three important objectives—trust, obligation and legitimacy in conformity with citizenship choice—are achieved. Dahl disagrees with this theory of political consensus and considers it a 'dogma that democracy would not work if citizens were not concerned with public affairs' (1963: 58–59). He rejects the thesis that conflict is at the centre of the political system, for he places a great deal of emphasis on people's apathy. He stresses on harmony because lack of controversies strengthens the existing power mechanisms by various processes of socialisation and existence of different value systems. The exponents of general system theory and cybernetics like Easton and Deutsch emphasise on the larger whole at the expense of the smaller parts justifying the arrangement for a smooth functioning of a political system. Authorities, for them, are functionalist categories performing different functions. In that kind of a situation, democratic participation is relegated to be of secondary importance since the total system functions without participatory individuals because rational consensus is replaced by communication. Easton agrees that this process of communication involves different sections of population unevenly, that is the marginalised groups do not become part of the political process and decisions are thrust on them from above which means there is an element of compulsion. This, according to Easton, may create a

> … class, status or caste differences between authorities and sections of membership may give birth to divergent psychological sets characterised by different ideological, ethical and perceptual predispositions. Authorities may be relatively incapable of becoming aware of and responsive to cues fed back from members other than those who resemble their own class, status or caste categories or with whom they identify (1965: 438).

In the 1950s, liberal social scientists like Bell, Aron and Lipset advance the notion of the 'end of ideology'. They contend that because of important changes in capitalism, democratic participation of workers in politics and the growth and development of welfare state, the old ideologies of right and left have run out of steam and become ineffectual. Furthermore, western societies, having solved their social problems, are in a state of consensus and a near equilibrium. This is also reinforced by the belief that advanced capitalism and developed socialism is fundamentally alike, moving towards a convergence relegating ideological debates to the third world. The convergence thesis is hinged on the belief that the process of industrialisation produces common and uniform political, social and cultural features in societies, which prior to industrialisation has very different historical backgrounds and social structures. This convergence is possible because industrialisation needs certain characteristics for its effective functioning. These are (1) an extended social and technical division of labour; (2) the separation of the family from the enterprise and the workplace; (3) a mobile, urbanised and disciplined workforce; and (4) some form of rational organisation of the economic calculation, planning and investment. The convergence thesis reinforces the 'end of ideology' debate as both contend that there exists a level of consensus in the highly industrialised society. As a result of this consensus, politics today, according to Lipset, has become boring because there is an absence of debates and policy alternatives as it is only a 'nickel here and nickel there and nothing more'. This seems to be a gross simplification and trivialising of the importance of politics. This is because the nature of the state and its institutions that reflect the dynamics of power in the society do not deal with just a nickel here or a nickel there but with policy prescriptions and alternatives that affect millions of people. For instance, the debates on environment, hunger, quality of life, inequalities between countries and among people, are live issues today, as they are in earlier times and politics will always play an important role and will not be just a matter of routine or boredom.

The prime importance of politics has increased and not diminished in this age of democracy and technology. The eclipse of the strong regimes, both of the right and the left, has brought to the centre-stage of the debate, issues of participation and equity without actualising the ideals of direct democracy in today's indirect mass democracies. The issues that are raised now have no easy universal acceptance and have led to an intense debate amongst the proponents of democratic theory. It is because politics is the most important activity and that political decisions affect all of us as no other decision do. De Gaulle said that politics is too serious a matter to be left to politicians alone and the continuing concern of the political theorists in dealing with various aspects of political power, legitimacy and authority is a reflection of its seminal importance.

Further Readings

Andrain, A.F. and Apter, D.E. (Eds.), *Political Protest and Social Change: Analyzing Politics*, Macmillan, London, 1995.

Bottomore, T., *Elites and Society*, Penguins, Harmondsworth, 1966.

Elstain, J.B. (Ed.), *The Family in Political Thought*, Harvester, Brighton, 1982.

Evans, J., *Feminism and Political Theory*, Alfred A. Knopf, New York, 1986.

Friedrich, B.J. (Ed.), *NOMOS I: Authority*, Harvard University Press, Cambridge MA, 1958.

Gatens, M., *Feminism and Philosophy: Perspectives on Difference and Equality*, Polity Press, Cambridge, 1991.

Green, L., *The Authority of the State*, Oxford University Press, Oxford, 1988.

Laski, H.J., *Authority in the Modern State*, Yale University Press, New Haven Connecticut, 1919.

Laswell, H.D. and Kaplan, A., *Power and Society: A Framework for Political Inquiry*, Yale University Press, New Haven, 1952.

Parry, G., *Political Elites*, Allen and Unwin, London, 1969.

Pennock, J.R. and Chapman, J.W. (Eds.), *NOMOS: XXIX. Authority Revisited*, New York University Press, New York, 1987.

Raz, J. (Ed.), *Authority*, Blackwell, Oxford, 1990.

Udoidem, S.I., *Authority and the Common Good in Social and Political Philosophy*, University Press of America, New York, 1988. E.D. Watt, *Authority*, Croom Helm, London, 1982.

Watt, E.D., *Authority*, Croom Helm, London, 1982.

Endnote

1. Group view of power includes the views of the subalterns and pluralists.

Chapter 4
State
Different Perspectives

The State is the pivot of political theory and politics, as the latter is derived from the Greek word *polis*, which means city-state or organised community. Its correct meaning, however, is city-community rather than city-state. The word 'State' is derived from the Latin past participle *status*, which means a situation or state of being (Sartori 1987: 278). Machiavelli is the earliest to use the term state as an impersonal entity but does not define it. In political theory, the concept of state is used to convey a historical or philosophical idea, an eternal form of political community, which is a specifically modern phenomenon (Forsyth 1987: 503). A basic divide exists between those who comply with right based theory of politics as espoused by Aristotle, Locke and Hegel that use concepts like rights, obligation, law and justice to describe and explain the political system from those who subscribe to the **power theory** as delineated by Machiavelli and Weber (Scrunton 1982: 367, 410). Both accept the distinction between **state** and **society** and consider law as fundamental to the state but not so in case of society. However, beyond the differences in the descriptions about the nature and role of the state, it is possible to define the state with reference to its basic components. A state is defined as a political entity that possesses people, territory, a government and sovereignty. A government is a concrete reality of the state, which is an abstraction. Governments change structurally and can be removed without entailing a change in states. A government is the policy deciding body that makes, declares and enforces a law. It can exist without a state as history and anthropology reveal. An administration is a set of persons and bodies that work under the direction of government to discharge the ordinary public services. A government is the political executive while administration is the permanent executive. The state is 'the political organisation of a society, its government, the agent through which it acts, and the law, the vehicle through which much of its power is exercised' (Raz 1986: 70).

Furthermore, the modern state is highly differentiated, specialised and complex upholding the difference between the private and the public space. As a modern phenomenon, the state develops with sovereignty as its distinguishing trait. The concept of sovereignty reinforces the public-private divide and also between one body politic and another. Concurrently with the idea of sovereignty—and partly in opposition to it—grows another idea that distinguishes the state as a modern phenomenon, namely the idea that it is the people as a single entity who rightly decide and constitute the form of rule within the body-politic. This idea was carried further by the American and French Revolutions that established representative institutions and also developed the idea that the proper end of the state is primarily protection of individual rights. The emphasis on 'pursuit of happiness' as proclaimed by the American Revolution and the notions of liberty, equality and fraternity as declared by the French Revolution answer the willing obedience of citizens to political authority. 'The state as a modern phenomenon may, thus, be defined as the institutional representation of the people's will, enabling it to act effectively in both the normal and extreme situation to secure the defence and welfare of the whole and the rights of the parts—together with this very activity itself (Forsyth 1987: 506)'.

A distinction is made between state and some interrelated terms like society, community, association and nation. A society, like the state, consists of people within a given territory engaged in cooperative activity but a society concerns itself with the social order while the state with the legal order. Society is a whole made up of many voluntary associations, each with specific tasks and purposes and includes the family right up to an international forum. Like society, the idea of a community stands for fellowship, personal intimacy and wholeness and is characterised by common ends or feelings. The state is bureaucratic and a government body of institutions and officials with a special purpose of maintaining a compulsory scheme of legal action and acting through laws enforced by direct and positive sanctions. The state, like society is national in its scope but differs from society in two respects—(a) it consists of all people who inhabit a particular territory and has the power to use legal coercion, the power of enforcing obedience through sanction of punishment, to decree rules of behaviour and (b) other associations because of their being voluntary in nature can enforce social discipline, expect voluntary obedience of its conventions and rules and only in the last resort may expel a deviant member. The state is an association like other associations in the sense that it is a union of human beings that would act as partners to realise the common purpose. However, it is an association with a difference, for it can exercise an all-embracing compulsory jurisdiction within a given territory and is in position to act competently as an umpire to decide between conflicting claims, whether that of individuals or of associations. Michael Walzer (1935–) characterises the state as a primary association. People who live in a country may differ in religion, race, language and ethnic composition. When people identify with others who live within the state, they constitute a nation. Nationalism supplies the reasons for people to set aside the internal divisions within a state, a process that have been going on since the sixteenth century. A state can exist as a juridical entity while a nation needs emotional props. A nation state means political institutions that combine the concepts of nation (an anthropological idea) with state (a legal notion). All modern states are nation-states. Its political apparatuses are distinct from both rulers and ruled, with supreme jurisdiction over a demarcated territorial area, backed by a claim to a monopoly of coercive power and enjoying a minimum level of support or loyalty from their citizens (Skinner 1978: 349–358, Giddens 1985: 17–31, 116–121).

STATE AND SOCIETY THROUGH AGES: NOTION OF CIVIL SOCIETY

A common assumption has been to equate the body politic or political community with the state that has some universal characteristics. The Greek view as exemplified in Aristotle's writings uses the term *koinōnia* that includes the notions of association, community and society, and there is no evidence of separate terms for each of these words. Aristotle's main concern is not 'between society and the State but between the private or familial and the political-cum-social (Runciman 1965: 25). However, in the context of developing a philosophy of what constitutes the political, Aristotle provides a series of distinctions that indicates the difference between political society and the society of citizens. Aristotle points out that a number of natural associations are formed for some good purpose and the highest of them all is the state. A state is distinct from the household which arises naturally out of a union of male and female for the satisfaction of daily needs. Within the household there is natural hierarchy of the husband over the wife, parents over children and master over the slave. A cluster of households forms a village and several villages together constitute the state that ensures economic and political independence. The state comes into being for the sake of life but continues for the sake of good life. It is established as a teleological end of other associations. The state exists by nature since 'man by nature is a political animal', for human beings alone have perceptions of good and evil, just and unjust. 'A person who does not feel the need for a state is either an angel or a beast'. It is this commonality that makes possible for a household and a state. However, this unity between a household and the state does not imply that the two associations are equal, for the 'state has priority over the household and over any individual among us, as the whole must be prior to the part'. The household satisfies the basic needs and necessities while the state tries to secure good life. The quality of life within a state depends on those who constitute it and the ends they wish to pursue. Aristotle answers this question by defining a constitution not just as a form of government or a set of norms but as a way of life, as that determines the moral character of a state. Furthermore, criticising Plato for conflating the household into a state, he points out that household differs from a state in a fundamental sense. In the former, relationships are between the superior (husband and master) over the inferior (wife, children and slaves) whereas in the state, the relationship between the ruler and the ruled is one of equality, a point that Locke subsequently develops in his critique of political absolutism and patriarchal authority. A *polis*, for Aristotle, is an association of free and equal men bound together by friendship and a common search for justice secured in law; leaving women out as they have domestic responsibilities. Aristotle also believes that stability of the state is achieved only by balancing the oligarchic (principle of quality relating to exclusive category of birth, wealth, property, social position and education) with democratic (quantity or numbers, the claims of the mass of people) elements. This is the polity or the state that is governed by the middle-class which Euripides (480–06 BC) describes as the 'save states'. It fulfils two important political ideals—equality and consensus. The idea of mixed constitution advocated by Aristotle is reiterated by Polybius, Cicero, St. Aquinas, Machiavelli, Smith and the English classical economists. The 1787 US Constitution is based on the idea of mixed constitution.

In the post Aristotelian phase, the Stoics developed a conception of world citizenship and the Roman Empire tried to unite all human beings under it. The development of Christianity snaps the unity that Aristotle emphasises by separating the *polis* or *civitas* and the church or *ecclesia* creating in St. Augustine's (354–430) doctrine a dual citizenship of *civitas Dei* and *civitas terrna*. Christianity infuses social unity by appealing to a divine inspired and commonly shared spiritual fellowship. Augustine, like Cicero, defines the *civitas* as a group of men joined in their agreement about the meaning of *ius* or *right*. However, while Cicero considers the Roman Republic as the expression of *ius* or *right*, Augustine believes that a community unified by the love of God or *civitas de* expresses *ius*. Augustine contends that only a Christian political community could be a true commonwealth, as it fully implements the indispensable requirement of justice.

Later Christian tradition, exemplified in Aquinas' writings, revives Aristotle's notion of political life in the polis, by viewing the state as natural and the highest form of organisation but existing within and subordinate to the general frame of divine direction of the world. The community and society is synonymous even in Aquinas just as it is in Aristotle. Alighieri Dante (1265–1321) makes a break with the old ideal of a unified Christian commonwealth and substitutes a carefully balanced and complete dualism in which the state and the church are independent of each other, though necessarily co-operative. The ultimate political unit is no longer unity Christen states but a world state. In the feudal society, there exists, in a narrower sense, a division of society into estates, communities and guilds but the traditional notions of community and society continues to refer to both the political society of the state and the units within it. The concept of civil society as distinct from the state emerges only with the disintegration of feudal societies. The distinction between a political community and a spiritual community comes under sharp focus in the wake of religious strife unleashed by the reformation.

Hobbes demonstrates that ecclesiastical power is not a form of rule, command or coercion but a form of teaching and persuasion. It cannot claim power over the state while on the contrary only through acts of state can religious doctrines acquire a political status. However, he still identifies political and civil society. Locke reiterates Aristotle and points out that the political community is not an extended family and that political rule is not paternal. Both Hobbes and Locke interchange features of the existing civil society back into the state of nature in order to demonstrate the natural and rational grounds for establishing a social contract.

The end of the eighteenth and the beginning of the nineteenth centuries, after the French and the Industrial Revolutions, brought about another distinction between the state and the society. A distinct concept of civil society emerges in Western political theorising from the middle of the seventeenth century. Till 1750, civil society (*koinōnia*, *politikē*, *civilis*, *sociētē*, *civile*, *bürgerliche*, *Gesellschaft*, *Civill Society*, *societā civile*) as used synonymously with that of the state (*polis*, *civitas*, *état*, *Staat*, *state*, *stato*). But from 1750, society no longer meant the fundamental union between human beings that the state established but a network of interaction and exchange formed by individuals exercising the right to pursue the satisfaction of their particular needs in their own way. A member of the civil society is also expected to be a citizen of the state and under obligation to act in accordance with its laws and without harming other citizens. The concern till the middle of the eighteenth century is with the nature of civil society and the limits of state action. Civil society as a concept originates with liberalism with an attempt to undermine liberalism.

Civil society emerges as a network of interaction and exchange formed by individuals exercising the right to pursue the satisfaction of their particular needs in their own way. Montesquieu points out that commercialism cures human beings of their prejudices that conceal their true needs. Once human beings realise their true needs, they will discover their sense of 'humanity' which would supersede the previous religious, ethnic and national sectarianism. They will look with disgust at military exploits and risks of war once they understand the attraction of peaceful trade leading to overall prosperity. They will also begin to appreciate national diversity and individual singularity. Commerce brings about frugality, economy, moderation, work, prudence, tranquillity, order and rule and more importantly, the spirit of proper juridical remedies that will make a balance between outright robbery and neglect of one's interest for the sake of others. Hume considers interest rather than the contract as the factor that cements individual to the society.

Smith and others of the Scottish Enlightenment describe the civil society as the expanding material sphere of trade and manufacture making a break with the traditional conception of the economy and the political notion of the civil society as adhered to by the social contractualists. For Smith and his followers, the economy is no longer limited, as it is for Aristotle, to the household but an essential element of the civil society and of the civilised society that benefits from trade and exchange, extension of the division of labour and the market. Its roots can be traced to the writings of Marsilius of Padua (1275/80–1342) for whom material tranquility makes possible for the smooth interchange of economic and social benefits constituting the essence of peace in a political community. He traces the development from family to state as a result of growing specialisation and differentiation of activities, all aiming at a common end, namely the acquisition of those things necessary 'for life and even the good life'.

Smith shares with his contemporaries like Hume, Ferguson, John Millar (1735–1801) and others the perception that advantages secured by commerce and mutual support are the bases for forming society. Not only self-interest but also development of emotions (in particular, Smith mentioned sympathy), rational character and conflicts, which arise between individuals have to be taken into consideration. Civil society is shaped not merely by material desire for exchange but also by contract which requires trust and justice. Ferguson's *An Essay on the History of Civil Society* (1767), within the general framework of the Scottish Enlightenment, provides the most succinct analysis of civil society. According to Ferguson, civil society is not a sphere of life that is distinct from the state; the two are in fact identical. "A civil society is a kind of political order which protects and 'polishes' its mechanical and commercial arts, as well as its cultural achievements and sense of public spirit, by means of regular government, the rule of law and strong military defences" (1792: vol. 1: 252). He considers modern division of law as a corrupting public spirit, a view that unites him with the old tradition of civic humanism. The loss of public spirit defuses the citizens' suspicion of power and thus prepares the way for despotic government. The destruction of public spirit by civil society augments the ambit and power of the state and habituates its subjects to the civil order and tranquility. Civil society also institutes a professional army increasing the dangers of formation of the government by military force. However, Ferguson does not say how the corrupted citizens of the civil society can get rid of corruption or even entrenched despotism. To the dilemma that the modern civil society requires a sovereign centralised constitutional state, which together with commerce and manufacturing 'breaks the bands of society (ibid: 218) and threatens civil liberties and capacity for independent associations of citizens, thus undercutting the rationale for life in the civil society, Ferguson proposes strengthening citizens, associations, whether in juries, militias or in civil society at large. Echoing Aristotle, Ferguson points out that human beings act best when they are in social groups. 'Under the influence of the animated spirit of society', human life is the happiest and freest (ibid, 30). Interestingly, he presumes public spirited constitutional monarchy as the best. This formulation emphasises the different realms of the state and the civil society, but the realms are complementary and not antagonistic. However, the subsequent formulation reflects a total negation of this formulation.

In the context of the modern evolution, Ferguson's formulation is the first phase whereas, the second phase begins with Thomas Paine's (1737–1809) polemic against Edmund Burke (1729–1797) in the *Rights of Man* (1791–1792).

Writing in the background of the American Revolution with its innovative principles, that of natural rights of man, popular sovereignty, right to resist unlawful government, and republican and federal political structure, Paine points out to the utmost need to restrict the power of the state in favour of the civil society, as the state is a necessary evil while the civil society is unqualified good. The more perfect the civil society is, the more it would regulate its own affairs leaving very little for government. With the exception of the United States, according to Paine, states everywhere crush and barbarise their people. Despotic governments stifle individual initiative, support patriarchal forms of power within households and institute class divisions win society through excessive rates of taxation. Paine thinks that reduction of the state power to a minimum would encourage the formation of an international confederation of nationally independent and peacefully interacting civil societies. This is the beginning of a new idea of 'a government being the best which governs the least'. The nationally sovereign state would be a mere elected manager and guarantor of 'universal peace, civilisation and commerce (1977: 183). He is convinced that limited states guided by civil societies cemented by ties of reciprocal interests and mutual affection make it possible for global order and harmony. Civil society thrives on common interest which is more powerful than the positive law enacted and administered by governments. Individuals interact with others spontaneously enabling them to form interlocking self sufficient social whole free from conflict and if states everywhere were built upon this natural social bases then the existing inequality, aggression and bondage among individuals and group would disappear. A 'cordial union' (Ibid: 189) of civilised society would replace social divisions and political unrest.

Paine, pointing to the positive aspects of the American Revolution, repeatedly emphasises on the need for deliberately resisting excesses of the state power, underlined by two related, but quite different set of arguments, resulting in conclusions different from that of Ferguson. In the first place, the principle of natural right and active consent of the governed guides a legitimate state. Individuals delegate power to the state held as trust, one that could be legitimately withdrawn at any time. No particular political group or institution has the right to bind and control how, and by whom, the world is to be governed, as all individual are born equal and with equal natural rights. These rights are god-given and incline individuals to act freely and reasonably for their own comfort and happiness without injuring the natural rights of others. Natural rights measure the legitimacy of states and cannot be annihilated, transferred or divided and no generation can deny them to their heirs. This rights-based argument lead Paine to insist that states are legitimate and civilised only when they are formed by the explicit consent of the individuals and when this active consent is formulated constitutionally and articulated continuously through parliamentary and representatives mechanisms. These governments have only duties and no rights towards their citizens. Government is the product of an individual contracting with one another and is subject to its constitution which specifies such matters as the duration of parliament, the frequency of elections, the mode of representation, the powers of the judiciary, the conditions under which war can be declared and the levying and spending of public monies. Government without a constitution is comparable to power without right—"A constitution … is to a government, what the laws made afterwards by that government are to a court of judicature. The court of judicature does not make the laws, neither can it alter them; it only asks in conformity to the laws made: and the government is in like manner governed by the constitution" (Ibid).

According to Alexis de Tocqueville (1805–1859), the problem of state despotism is the new problem that confronts modern nations which could be checkmated only by the growth and development of civil associations that lie beyond the control of state institutions. The plurality of civil associations is necessary for consolidating the democratic revolution. Civil associations, according to Tocqueville, are permanent open schools of public spirit within which citizens learn their rights and obligations, and press their claims and become familiar with others. He considers civil associations as arenas in which individuals can direct their attention to more than their selfish, narrow private and conflicting goals and also realise that they are dependent on one another and hence must work for cooperation. He acknowledges that central state institutions ensure the survival and coordination among civil associations but he also insists, like Hegel, that freedom and equality among individuals and groups depend upon preserving types of associations that nurture local freedoms and provide for the active expression of particular interests. He is categorical that the right of association within the civil society is inalienable. For democracy to flourish, a pluralistic and self-organising civil society, independent of the state, is absolutely necessary. He observes that 'no legislator can destroy it without attacking the foundations of society itself' (1981: 279). Tocqueville has a three part model that differentiates, although unsystematically between a civil society of economic and cultural associations and publics, a political society of local, provincial and national assemblies and the administrative apparatus of the state.

Hegel stresses that the state proper and the civil society are two different things. Civil society embodies a 'system of needs' and totality of private individuals. With gradual freeing of the Third Estate, the civil society comes to be regarded as bourgeois society; a society of private, free and equal individuals with property but without the domination of one group by another. Civil society for Hegel represents conflict of interests that can be resolved by the state representing all interests of the society. Civil society embodies a 'system of needs' and totality of private individuals. With gradual freeing of the Third Estate, the civil society came to be regarded as bourgeois society; a society of private, free and equal individuals with property but without the domination of one group by another. Civil society, for Hegel, represents conflict of interests that can be resolved only by the state representing all interests of society. Hegel sees the civil society as crippling and in constant need of state supervision and control. Unlike Paine, Hegel does not consider the civil society (*bürgerliche*

Gesellschaft) as a natural condition of freedom but as a 'historically produced sphere of ethical life' that lies in between the simple patriarchal household and the universal state. It includes the market economy, social classes, corporations and institutions concerned with the administration of welfare and civil law. The creation of civil society is the achievement of the modern world (1976: 339) and is made possible because it develops the 'system of needs'.

Hegel, reiterating Ferguson, points out that the bourgeois economy generates commodities that make a level of specialisation and mechanisation of human labour necessary, thus transforming the nature of human needs, which no longer remain natural, and become social. There is no possibility of harmony within the civil society. Harmony derived from unadulterated love is possible only within a family. Relationships within civil society are tenuous and, at times, bordering on serious conflict due to class division leading to restlessness. Hegel recognises a variety of classes or class fragments—civil servants, landowners, peasantry, intellectuals, lawyers, doctors and clergymen—but the moving principle of the civil society, is primarily in the *Bürgerstand*. Much of Hegel's analysis is similar to that of Ferguson. The class of burghers, in which Hegel includes the workers, also is defined by its selfish individualism. The burgher class depends on the corporations—municipal, trade, educational, religious, professional and other state-authorised forms of collective associations—and is less public spirited than a self-serving bourgeois. Hegel agrees with Ferguson and Paine that the modern civil society is a complex system of transacting individuals, whose livelihoods, legal status and happiness are interwoven but it is this universal selfishness, and on this point, rejects Ferguson's trust in citizenship and Paine's belief in natural sociability, that turns the civil society into a 'blind and unstable field of economic competition among private non citizens'. Hence, the civil society is unable to resolve its inherent conflicts and overcome particularity and can remain civil only, if ordered politically, by the state. The state may intervene in the society to remedy its injustices and inequalities, for instance, the domination of one or more classes by another, the pauperisation of whole groups or the establishment of oligarchies. It could also intervene in order to protect and attenuate the universal interests of the people, one that the state itself defines. Keane (1988) points out that Hegel's analysis represents the third phase in the evolution of the concept of civil society.

The **Young Hegelians**[1] and **Marx** criticise this relationship between the state and the civil society. In writings like *On the Jewish Question*, *Contribution to the Critique of Hegel's Philosophy of Right: Introduction and Economic and Philosophical Manuscripts*, Marx uses the term 'civil society' to make a critique of Hegel and German Idealism. The term disappears in the later writings. For Marx, the civil society is the site of crass materialism, of modern property relations, the struggle of each against all, and egotism. Civil society, he stresses, arises from the destruction of the medieval society. In the medieval society, the individual was a part of different societies, like guilds or estates, each of which had a political role and hence there was no need for a civil realm. With the breakdown of these partial societies, individual becomes all important, thus giving an impetus to the rise of the civil society. The old bonds were replaced by selfish needs of atomistic individuals, distinct and separate from one another and from the community. Law provides the links between individuals but it arises not from human will, and dominates them by the threat of punishment. The fragmented and conflictual nature of the civil society determines the nature of the modern state.

Antonio Gramsci (1871–1937) writes extensively on the civil society and uses the term in a manner different from that of Marx. It is not simply a sphere of individual needs but of organisations that has the potential for rational self regulation and freedom. While Marx stresses the separation between the state and civil society, for Gramsci, the two are inter-related. The civil society consists of private institutions like schools, churches, clubs, journals and parties which are instrumental in crystallising social and the political consciousness and the political society consists of public institutions like the government, courts, police and the army, the instruments of direct domination. It is in the civil society that the intellectuals play an important role by creating hegemony. If hegemony is successfully created by intellectuals, then the ruling class rules by controlling the apparatus of the civil society and if they fail then the rule is through coercion. Unlike Marx who places total emphasis on economic relations, for Gramsci, it is the superstructure that is important. The hegemony of the dominant class is exercised through the civil society, culturally and not through coercion. But this hegemony of the civil society does not exist equally in all societies. Writing about the former USSR, Gramsci observes "in Russia, the state was everything, civil society was primordial and galantines; in the West, there was a proper relationship between the state and the civil society, and when the state trembled, a sturdy structure of the civil society was at once revealed. The state was only an outer ditch, behind which there stood a powerful system of fortresses and earth works".

The concept of civil society reappears in the neo-Marxist critics, Kolakowski, Mlynar, Vajda, Michnik, Habermas, Lefort, Touraine, Bobbio, Weffort, Cardoso, and O'Donnell of socialist authoritarianism locating the conceptual origins of the communist totalitarianism in the young Marx's demand to overcome the distinction between the state and the civil society. The separation of the civil society from the state makes a decisive break from the Graeco-Roman conception that regards civil society as bound up with the state. The unity between the particular and the general in Hegel's account of the civil society and the state is also rejected by August Marie Francois Comte (1798–1957), seeking to establish a separate discipline of sociology as positive science of society. Sociology analyses social dynamics and social static with the first deliberating on general law of social development and the second, on the 'anatomy' of society and the mutual interaction between its constituents. Comte's view of interconnectedness of elements of the social system anticipates functionalism.

Most conceptions on the state accept this distinction except for totalitarianism in the twentieth century that negates the distinctions between the state and the society, between the private and the public and between the state and the nation. Totalitarianism conflates nation in the state and makes the state the sole and complete expression of the nation. It subordinates the state to a party and a paternalistic leader. Philosophically, some ideologies like Marxism and anarchism feel strongly that the state will ultimately wither away. Radical versions of liberalism, as in **Hayek**, contend that society represents spontaneity while the state stands for coercion and hence its ambit ought to be reduced to the minimum.

A brief overview of the writings of thinkers, other than Marx and Engels, reveals of their awareness of the importance of market competition, commodity production and exchange and the growth of the bourgeoisie, hostility to aristocracy and its inherited wealth, corrupt manner and political privileges, to the modernisation of the concept of civil society. These thinkers are profoundly aware of the heterogeneity and complexity of civil society and 'rarely reduced the complex patterns of stratification, organisation, conflicts and movements of civil society to the logic and contradictions of a mode of production, the emerging capitalist economy … they usually noted the patterns of harmony or (potential) conflict between civil society's privately controlled commerce and manufacturing and its other organisations, including patriarchal households, churches, municipal governments, publishers, scientific and literary associations and such policing authorities as charitable relief organisations, schools and hospitals' (Keane 1988; 64). The early thinkers on the civil society were aware of the inequalities within capitalism and the possible losses of freedom that commodity production and exchange would bring out. Above all, they were profoundly sensitive to the dangers of concentration of political power. It was the fear of despotism, attenuated by the experiences of the French Revolution that made them think of ways and means of limiting state power and in strengthening the civil society. This view originated when liberal individualism was consolidating itself and becoming an integral component of the modern political discourse. The modern democratic age comes of age first in the post fascist period and then in the post communist era with the roll back of the state leviathan and the triumph of the civil society.

LAW AND THE STATE

Law is central to the constitutional state unlike the arbitrary rule in the police state. Law is a body of widely recognised social rules and compulsory regulations that govern the behaviour of both the ruled and rulers and among citizens. Law is theorised in two distinct ways. The first is the **Natural Law Theory** that views all laws as attempts by human reason to approximate to those rules of natural law that enshrine an ideal of good conduct and are universal property of rational beings. These laws have been seen either as God's commands or derived from human reason. The second is the Positive Law notion, enunciated by Bentham and Austin, that views law as human convention or stipulation whose authority is derived from the legislature that makes these laws, derived from what Kelsen calls *Grundnorm* or the rules of recognition that H.L.A. Hart uses. Kelsen advances a legalistic conception of the state as a system of positive law. Each system of positive law consists of norms imposed and enforced by the state. Its validity is derived from law, the basic norm (*Grundnorm*); the proposition that the constitution is supreme. The *Grundnorm* is the essence of the state. Law, for Kelsen, is a rationalised and systematised convention through which political power exerts itself. Hart distinguishes between law and morality and treats any command from a *de jure* power as lawful and legally binding. Non-enforceable rules like those recognised as constituting a body of conventions and expectations known as 'international law' do not have the status of the law. Law is seen as being universal in character. Law and order refers to a state or society in which there is a regular process of the criminal and civil law and maintained by agencies like the police. It is seen by most conservatives and many liberals as the basic requirement of a state and without it, civil society, political freedom and civil liberties are impossible.

Rule of law refers to the procedures, principles and constraints contained in the law and in which the citizen can find redress against another, however powerful and/or influential, and against the officers of the state itself, for any act which involves a breach of the law. It is not merely important to declare that the constitution is supreme. It is equally important, for the citizen, that the law is enforced. This, at the minimum, suggests independence of the judiciary if the law is to be enforced against the state. However, it ought to be remembered that it is the state that makes and revises the law and it is the state that controls the appointment and dismissal of judges. Rule of law is opposed to 'rule of persons' which is normally equated with unfettered and arbitrary exercise of power. As far as arbitrariness is concerned, there are three related concerns—first is the danger that rulers will simply govern willfully and capriciously and this would result in inconsistency or incoherence of policy leaving people confused, second, people will feel dominated by the rulers and third arbitrariness could result in oppression leading to overriding of people's legitimate expectations and needs. Aristotle, writing about the merits of constitutional rule, as opposed to personal rule has this to say: first it is a rule in the general or common interest of the people rather than one or few as is with personal rule; second, it is lawful as government is carried on in accordance with general regulations and not by arbitrary decrees. A government cannot act contrary to the constitution and third, constitutional government signifies rule by consent of the people rather than by force. Rule of law in the international arena is the generally agreed rules by nation states, applied by international courts or adjudicators whose decisions are generally accepted and obeyed by those subject to their jurisdiction.

Aristotle's *Politics* is the first to recognise that individual human judgment on each and every case of social conflict that comes before a judge is not likely to produce fairness and equity, and thus, recommends that the judge should be no more than appliers of previously fixed rules to factual cases. Following this idea, the rule of law is seen as a major contribution to equality and liberty. It requires legislatures to look only at the abstract feature of a problem and to lay down a general rule, and judges to look only at relevant characteristics, under the immediate rule, in deciding cases. The gist being that the judge should decide according to the rule laid down and not according to their own sense of justice or personal preferences. This can at times lead to largely similar cases being judged very differently due to marginal circumstantial variations.

The phrase is associated in England with Dicey's three-fold description of the English constitution. First, and foremost, it means that the law excludes the exercise of arbitrary power. This means that an Englishman could be punished for breaches of law and nothing else. Arbitrary punishments caused by prerogative power or by uncontrolled bureaucratic discretion are inconsistent with the rule of regular law. Second, the rule of law means equality of persons before the law and the equal subjection of the ruled and the ruler to the ordinary law administered by ordinary law courts. Third, the rule of law in England stands for the idea that citizens' rights is not derived from the constitution but the result of the benefits and liberties conferred on the individuals by the remedies provided by the ordinary law of the land.

The rule of law in the wider sense is associated with the notion of limited government, procedural guarantees of the due process of law, fair legal procedures, fair trials, natural justice, judicial independence and access to courts for the enforcement of rights conferred by the law. This means that laws have to be drafted with precision, not retrospectively in operation, at least in criminal matters and that they should not impose penalties on named individuals, or delegate ill defined or unduly broad discretionary powers. Raz, in 1977, identifies principles that ought to be associated with the rule of law, as requirements of guiding individual's behaviour and minimising the danger that results from the exercise of discretionary power in an arbitrary manner. Raz's principles are as follows:

1. Laws should be prospective rather than retroactive;
2. Laws ought to be settled and not changed too often. Frequent changes result in confusion and prevents the law from guiding human behaviour;
3. Clear rules and procedures should be there for making laws;
4. Guarantee of an independent judiciary;
5. Observance of the principles of natural justice, particularly in matters concerning the right to a fair hearing;
6. The courts must have the power of judicial review;
7. The courts should be accessible to all and that no one may be denied justice and
8. The discretion of law enforcement and crime prevention agencies should not be allowed to pervert the law.

Hayek gives pivotal role to the notion of the rule of law in his constitutional theory. He develops his account out of his critique of economic planning. He believes that there is an intimate connection between interventionist economic policies and totalitarian politics: the one entails an incremental increase in arbitrary interferences with individual liberty that ultimately leads to the other. The true role of law is to provide stable conditions in which individuals could choose for themselves the ends that they wish to pursue without the government or other individuals intervening arbitrarily. As he observes, the law should operate like a Highway Code: it provides those rules of the road needed for the people to drive about with a reduced risk of accidents, not a set of orders directing people where to go when and how' (Hayek 1944: 55–56). Hayek is categorical that it is impossible to frame an ideal legal code aimed at achieving certain ends. Rules arise spontaneously through individuals trying to adapt to each other and their environment. Much of law is based on custom rather than a priori reasoning. However, laws have certain formal features so as to preclude it from becoming instruments of arbitrary power. They have to be universal, expressed in general terms and apply equally to all, taking into account relevant differences, be prospective (only invoking retroactivity as a curative measure), public, clear and stable. Legislators must ensure legal rules and procedures that are as fair as possible and enacted solely for securing collective agreements that are in public interests. He considers judicial independence and review as essential to maintain integrity of law, preventing its arbitrary use or abuse by the authorities, but rejects judicial activism that promotes certain policies. Courts ought to ensure conformity to the law. He also proposes constitutional checks on legislature since the chief cause of the expansion of command like the law is popular sovereignty. He also recommends separation of powers, and also the need to separate laws needed to run the public administration from law making for the wider society, and the latter is assigned to a representative body that is free from some of the perverse electoral pressures that afflict modern parliaments.

Republicanism attributes arbitrariness and domination to asymmetries of power. Within the polity, there must be balance between different social groups to prevent any one dominating another. For this, the standard devices like bicameral legislatures with different kinds of representation, various types of federalism, mixed form of popular government and the process of negotiation that safeguards against arbitrary exercise of power. The political system must allow the people, through their representatives, to ensure the laws show them equal concern and respect. In order to prevent tyrannous powers of electoral majorities an equitable dispersal of power is necessary and to ensure that law is framed for public good and not for factional interests of particular persons.

CENTRAL PERSPECTIVES ON THE STATE

A technical definition of the state refers to its four components—population, territory, government and sovereignty. However, different ideologies provide different descriptions about the origin, nature, role, purpose and functions of the state. Wayper (1977) groups them into three broad classifications—state as a machine (Hobbes and Locke), state as a class (Marx and Lenin) and state as an organism (Rousseau, Hegel and Green). Goodwin (1992: 267–268) identifies four alternative views—the contractual view (Hobbes, Locke and Rousseau), the state as arbiter and nightwatchman (early liberals and utilitarians), state as organism (Hegel) and state as oppressor (the Marxists). All these classifications can also be understood as the central perspectives within which this chapter discusses the state.

Liberal–Democratic State

There are two distinct and yet interrelated ideas within the notion of the liberal-democratic state. The liberal component signifies the limits to state power by rejecting political absolutism backed by the notion of Divine Right of Kings, the dominant idea in the late sixteenth and early seventeenth centuries, the time when liberal ideas crystallise and begin to evolve. The democratic component signifies people's rule, participation and representative institutions. The liberal state gradually becomes a democratic state with the extension of franchise and by improving on the institutions and procedures that exemplify people's will. In spite of the differences among the liberals about how the state comes into being and its ends, it is possible to identify the core elements that constitute the liberal theory of the state. All liberals agree that the state exists for the people and not vice-versa. They accept a constitutional state with well-defined powers based on the consent of the ruled and by observing the public–private divide of 'things that are Caesars' and 'things that are not Caesars'. A liberal state, by definition, is a limited state, for it confers upon persons, rights and claims of justice, which governments must acknowledge, and respect and which can be invoked against the government. Limited state refers to the way power is exercised rather than the form of the government. A liberal state has constitutional restraints on its exercise of power. It can assume the form of constitutional monarchy as in Britain or a republic as in the US. The former is a unitary system with a largely unwritten constitution, while the latter is a federal system with a written constitution but both are classic liberal states. Britain is an exception. Most liberal states follow the American practice of acknowledging written constitution, federalism and separation of powers and bicameralism as constraints.

Hobbes lays the foundations of a liberal state, though he is not a thorough-going liberal and his philosophy contains illiberal features (Dunn 1979: 42–43; Held 1989: 14). The liberal aspect of his theory pertains to his conception of the state and society as constituted by free and equal individuals while the illiberal feature is the all-powerful self-perpetuating sovereign. He rejects Aristotle's belief that the state is a natural institution which is needed for a good life and considers security and safety as the reason for the state that was artificially created for specific ends. His goal, like Bodin, is to restore order through an all-powerful sovereign. Writing in the background of the English Civil War, his choice was between total order and total chaos. He differs from Bodin, and, like Galileo, seeks precision in politics, and thereby, defines human being as a machine, mere matter acted upon by the motion of various bodies that trigger off this reaction or that. Hobbes divides bodies into two kinds, i.e. 'natural' (human being himself) and 'feigned' or 'artificial' ones. The state, according to him, is an artificial body, a third party, and a consequence of each individual contracting with others agreeing to surrender their total powers, except the right of self-preservation. Hobbes deserves credit for inventing the state as an abstract entity separate from both the sovereign and the ruled, 'that great Leviathan, or rather (to speak more reverently) of that Mortall God, to which we owe under the Immortall God, our peace and defence' (Hobbes 1991: 120). It exercises public power as a permanent sovereign which comes into existence by two methods—acquisition and institution. Acquisition is when individuals are threatened into submission while institution is when individuals, of their impulse, unite and agree to transfer all natural powers through a contract to a third party of one, few or many. Hobbes prefers a monarchy for three reasons—first, there is identity of interests between the king and his subjects, second, the self-indulgence of one is cheaper than that of the many and third, there will be less intrigues and plots that normally arise due to personal ambitions and envy of the members of the ruling elite. His defense of an absolute state, in reality, is a justification of absolute government or absolute monarchy, a conclusion similar to the Divine Right theory that he set to dislodge, since he does not distinguish between the state and the government. The all-powerful sovereign is a product of a contract, but Hobbes fails to carry the contractarian argument to its logical conclusion by not providing for a renewal of consent or a periodic assessment by the people.

From absolutist to a limited state

The features of a liberal state emerge properly in Locke's writings. His *First Treatise* is entirely devoted to showing that parental and political power are not the same and distinguished between the state and the ruler. He also distinguishes between the civil society and the state; not only does Locke proclaim that the former precedes the latter, but it actually creates the state in a deliberate attempt as a legitimate political power that is derived and based on consent. Locke explains in length, the point that Bodin raises first that subjects are emphatically not members of their ruler's household as the principles applying to their government are different from that of household. He regards all human authority and relationships as based on trust, as derived from the moral relationship that individuals share with God. He rejects Sir Robert Filmer's (1588–1653) biblical account of the origins of political power without abandoning its religious foundations. The state, for Locke, comes into being to fulfil three important wants—the want of an established settled known law, the want of a known indifferent judge and the want of an executive power to enforce just decisions that the state of nature or the pre-political order lacks. The contract creates the civil society with majority rule (though the ideal is unanimity) as the basis for arriving at decisions. The individuals surrender their powers partially, namely the aforesaid three specific powers that constitute the natural right to enforce the laws of nature. Locke astutely observes that people at any given time will not surrender all their powers to an outside body including their own government. He insists that all true states are established by consent and assumes that a minority will consent to all things in the rule by the majority. Through express and tacit consent, he circumvents Filmer's critique by insisting that legitimate power combines power with right, as a government cannot be arbitrary: the general laws, which are public and not subject to individual decrees, bind it. All individuals have to be governed by the same rules as everyone else; otherwise it will violate individuals' natural moral equality. Once a civil society is formed, the individuals then establish a government to act as a judge in the nature of a 'fiduciary' power or a trust for promoting certain ends. Within the government, it is the legislature that is supreme as the people's representative with the power to make laws. Besides the legislature, there is an executive that includes judicial power and is always in session. The legislative and executive power has to be separate, thus, anticipating Montesquieu's theory of separation of powers. The third wing of the government is federative power, the power to make treatises and conduct external relations. Locke advocates a limited sovereign state, as political absolutism is untenable by both reason and experience. Absolute power is illegitimate and wicked, for people will never give up all the powers and rights to another to exercise them on their behalf. Furthermore, it does not provide safety measures against potential violence and oppression of an absolute ruler. He describes a good state as one that exists for the people who form it and not vice-versa. It is based on the consent of the people subject to the constitution and the rule of law. It is limited since its powers are derived from the people and held in trust. Natural rights and laws of nature also limit it. It is a tolerant state, pluralistic in nature which means that the state would remain neutral to the conceptions of good life that individuals wish to pursue but creates the framework for individuals wishing to pursue their ends as they deem fit. Locke stresses that the state deals with matters strictly political in nature with no warrant to interfere in domains that are outside the political. The state cannot demand more power on the pretext of public safety or welfare. Since supreme power resides in the people, the people as a community have the inalienable right to institute and dismiss a government. Once a government is dismissed, there is no return to the state of nature as Hobbes insists. Moreover, a government is assessed periodically and its sanctions scrutinised meticulously. Locke rules out anarchy and insists on the need for a just authority to uphold a decent and civilised life.

Institutional safeguards for a limited state

Montesquieu's main accomplishment has been the enunciation of ways to protect the civil society against the arbitrary power of the sovereign, for absence of protection leads to despotism and any kind of civilised life becomes difficult if not impossible. He takes into consideration Hume's critique of the philosophical foundations of the natural law but relegates it to the background. Hume argues that reason is subjective and, in the last resort, a mere servant of passion that dictated the ends towards which it shall be directed. There is no such thing as objective reason that all people share and, if such a connection exists between it and the intentions of nature, it cannot be completely demonstrable. Montesquieu agrees and argues that to avoid tyranny it is still necessary that the government is based on law—not such law as has been laid down once and for all by some external force or authority, but by a legislator. In this manner, he completes the process that has been going on since the Middle Ages, in which the forces of law, other than those made first by the ruler and then by the state, are whittled away and finally abolished. Like Hobbes, the law is what the state enacts but not arbitrarily, but by taking into consideration varying climatic and geographical circumstances of each community. In each community, sovereignty is divided among three authorities to ensure the liberty of the people. Besides Locke's legislature, there is an executive and judiciary and all three are in separate hands, each balancing and checking the other, which the US Constitution embodies.

The blow to social contract that Hume delivers, needed a new principle to explain the origins and justification of the state which Bentham provides with his idea of utility. The rejection of the social contract and with it its attendant ideas of natural law and natural rights means a new conception of a state that is legal with rights enacted and enforced by a duly constituted political authority. Bentham preserves the notion of moral autonomy embedded in the doctrine of individualism and makes it the basis of his state as a legal entity. He stipulates happiness and not liberty as the end of the state, a contrivance created for fulfilling the needs of the individual. He categorically argues that a government and state have to be judged by their usefulness to the individual and insists on the need for a watchful and interested government that readily and willingly acts for the individuals' happiness. Reiterating Montesquieu, he instructs a legislator to take into cognizance factors like people's customs, prejudices, religion and traditions while codifying laws.

From limited to an interventionist state

For J.S. Mill, the goal of the utilitarian state is liberty rather than happiness. He pleads for respect of individuality in an age of democracy that encourages egalitarianism and social conformity. Mill warns that the threat to individual freedom comes from not only arbitrary power of the state but also a tyrannical and intolerant majority that seek to act as a moral police officer. He also insists on the need for a liberal state and society to be more responsive to the interests of the working-class and women. He prescribes 'optional' areas of state interference in fields of education, care of children and insane, planned colonisation, relief for poor, public utilities like water and regulation of hours of work. Mill desires general *embourgeoisement* so that everyone works for a living and enjoys a decent standard of living with sufficient leisure to cultivate one's mind. The liberal doctrine undergoes a revision in the hands of Green, who incorporates Hegelianism and integrates it with liberal individualism. Green argues that the state is neither a will nor an artifice but an institution whose purpose is to ensure common good. He attempts to reconcile Rousseau's theory of the general will with Austin's theory of sovereignty, for he agrees with the latter that supreme coercive power indicates the visible presence of the state, but like Rousseau the question of legitimacy is a moral one for him. His focus on the state arises from his concern for a moral order that synthesises individual identity with common good. The notion of common good, though predominantly associated with Green, has this illustrious ancestry in the Aristotelian-Thomistic theory that identifies common good as the object of law. Green argues that individual goodness has to be judged by its contribution to the goodness of the community; 'since a man is part of the city, it is impossible for any man to be good, unless he is properly in conformity with the common good'. The common good is not merely the sum total of the individual goods of those composing the community that Bentham advocates. The difference between individual and common good is one of quantity and also of kind.

The function of a state for Green is not the maintenance of law and order but removal of hindrances in the person's moral development. The state is moral because it creates conditions that enable its members to fulfil their basic potentialities. A state cannot survive for long through use of coercive power alone. Force by itself cannot be the legitimate basis of a state, but Green is discerning while conceding that some amount of force may be legitimate when it is used to achieve specific ends sanctioned by the common good of the community. A state does not enjoy unlimited power of compulsion by its superior authority but by its capacity to recognise general interests in the society. A society that recognises common good acknowledges individual rights and this very synthesis indicates the willing consent of the individual. Hence, Green proclaims will, not force, to be the basis of the state. He and Bosanquet rejected the conception of negative liberty in favour of freedom as ability.

Laissez faire but not a minimal state

It is often argued that the early liberal emphasis on a police or nightwatchman state is because they distrust any extension of state activity as essentially restricting individual liberty. Furthermore, functions of the state are limited to guaranteeing life and property. This is because Europe in the seventeenth and early eighteenth centuries was ravaged by intense religious and civil conflicts and everything else had to wait till peace was restored. This explains why, in spite of England having a relatively well developed parliamentary tradition, Locke, Montesquieu and his eighteenth century successors do not share Hobbes' conclusion of an irrevocable sovereign but agree with Hobbes that the state has to be an instrument for making people civilised. Even as late as 1790, Bentham continues to consider the state as a machine in a strictly utilitarian sense with the sole aim of maximising happiness of the largest number of people (Creveld 1999: 189). In spite of the commitment of early liberals to *laissez faire*, free trade and the motto that the 'best state is one that governs the least', they, like Smith, support large number of government programmes: universal public education, public health measures against contagious diseases and safety regulations for labour protecting them against fraudulent practices of the employers. Smith stresses on the need for government action in six key areas: moderate taxes as incentive to growth, finance of public works which shall come from those whom it benefits, private organisations to be given public responsibilities, programmes benefitting a locality to the local authorities, for that ensures accountability and efficiency and accountability of the market to the government. Bentham, a supporter of *laissez faire* insists that the government maximises happiness, which means security, abundance, subsistence and equality. Of these four, security and subsistence are most important. Bentham thus proposes free education, guaranteed employment, minimum wages, sickness benefit and old age insurance (Mack 1955: 85).

Bentham proposes a system of agricultural communes and industry houses to take care of the indigent as distinguished from the working poor. The indigent would be encouraged to become part of the normal labour market as soon as possible. Care shall be taken to ensure that the lot of the indigent is not more beneficial than those who are poor for that means rewarding shirkers, thus becoming a positive disincentive to the industrious poor, a point that Rawls subsequently develops. Bentham recommends an interventionist state in a backward country but prefers private enterprise in advanced ones. He justifies intervention on the grounds that if its advantages outweigh the costs then it is good rather than bad.

In the nineteenth century, the expanding economy, both internally (due to maturity of capitalism) and externally (overseas trade and colonial empires) demanded extension of state activity. Equally important are the criticisms of capitalism and the liberal state by the socialists, conservatives and other radicals, which the liberals like Mill confront. He realises the need to change capitalism by incorporating an ethic of social welfare and supports local workers and retail cooperatives, workers' participation in management, schemes of profit sharing between workers and managers and other workers' savings. A larger community should not 'dispense with the inducements of private interests in social affairs'. He supports trade unions and the right to strike but rejects compulsory membership of the unions. While aware of the exploitation under capitalism, he is more perturbed by the uniformity that socialism/communism enforces. Capitalism according to Mill would decrease misery and injustice in the long run and that socialism would succeed only if it remains true to its liberal heritage, otherwise it would run into a dead end. He dislikes the inherent statism of the socialist doctrine fearing submersion of individuality, a point that Bernstein develops in great detail. Green transforms the very basic character of English liberalism by defining the state not as the aggregate of individuals pursuing private good but as a device for realising common good and positive freedom. Conscious of the great inequalities in his society, he suggests remedies like compulsory education, universal suffrage, active participation in the affairs of the state by all, change in the character of the parliament, so that it is no longer a club of the rich and also prescribes limitations on the right of property.

He was the most influential thinker in Britain from the 1870s to the 1920s. MacIntyre commenting on Green's profound impact says that his pupils from Balliol carried into the bureaucracy, the church and in politics (including into the cabinet itself, which includes a Prime Minister) 'a belief that liberal individualism could be overcome within a liberal framework. Green is the apostle of state intervention in matters of social welfare and of education; he is able to be so because he could see in the state an embodiment of that higher self the realisation of which is our moral aim' (1971: 247).

Towards a welfare state

Green's revisionary liberalism finds its systematic exposition in the writings of Hobhouse, who attempts to synthesise the philosophies of Mill and Green. Hobhouse supplants the older conception of natural liberty with ideals of distributive justice and social harmony to shape progressive opinion in England that is not outright socialist. He accepts the need for government intervention not on paternalistic grounds, but to ensure some level of well-being for all, an essential precondition for a liberal society. The idea of liberty shall not prevent the general will from acting, where it must, for the common good. He stresses on the contribution of welfare measures to the realisation of the liberal value of equality of opportunity.

The welfare measures of Lloyd George's reforming budget of 1909 are explained not as an intrusion into the working of the market and individual freedom, but as justified extension of public control on humane grounds. It is clear that the old liberal order is waning and during the inter-war years, Keynes, Sir William H. Beveridge (1879–1963) and other revisionist liberals tried to steer the middle way between the old capitalist order and the new socialist ideals. The post-Second World War Keynesian consensus in England and Roosevelt's New Deal in the United States led to the revival of economies and ushered in an era of prosperity and full employment by the mid-1950s. Equally important is the fact that it marshals the support of the socialists both in Europe and in Britain and that furthers the wedge between Western Marxism and Soviet Communism. Public opinion is not overtly socialist, but favours an activist state and mixed economy rather than free market. However, there are those who swam against the current, claiming allegiance to classical liberalism, and its most noteworthy exponent is Hayek who rejects central planning and collectivism as leading to totalitarianism and pleads a return to free market and spontaneous social order. In his view, these spontaneous or undesigned social patterns and orders exist and serve human purposes. The 'footpath example' demonstrates that useful social institutions could arise and function without any overall organisation, without exercise of power or authority, without coercion and thus without compromising individual liberty. The other important exponent of liberal outlook is Popper who rejects wholesale transformation of society that Marx advocates and justifies piecemeal reform of social institutions as the path of reason. Talmon develops a powerful critique of totalitarianism. Berlin offers an eloquent defence of the importance of negative liberty. The most extraordinary revival of liberalism comes in the writings of Rawls. Nozick (it would be appropriate to regard him as a libertarian) criticising Rawls provided a powerful defense of the minimal state.

Communitarian State

While the liberal state tries to enhance right, freedom and equality without interfering with the individual's construction of his life plans and conception of good, the communitarian state's primary role is to ensure the health and well-being of the community life that enables human flourishing. The state must define both right and good. Like Plato, communitarians believe that human beings can achieve a good life only if they live within a well-functioning society, which the government must help to create, though unlike Plato, they are committed to a democratic form of government. In order to achieve this end, the state must articulate a conception of good to which all people conform. They reject the liberal idea of pursuing autonomously, a conception of good independent of cultural traditions and social roles. While a liberal state is responsible to individual citizens, a communitarian state is responsive to the society that is constituted by individual citizens. For communitarians, politics starts with the community since it is the community that determines and shapes individuals' natures. The role of the state is to help protect practices that encourage the development of human excellence. If individuals are left to realise their autonomy as desired by the liberals, it will result in social disintegration and moral disaster. They further criticise the liberal emphasis on 'reason' as a tool with which the liberal state governs on the grounds that the liberals define reason disconnected from social traditions and hence de-linked from real concerns, aspirations and goals. Conversely, they insist that social harmony and health is only possible through a discourse derived from the culture of the community. An ideal state is one that is closely associated with social practices that constitute and define the goals of the culture of the community.

Libertarian State

Libertarianism considers the state to originate in plunder and persist, because the groups who control and support it believe that they can do better for themselves by forcibly extracting resources than by the exchange in the market. The original political class consists of bandits who exhort tributes from defenseless people, in return for some kind of protection against other gangs of bandits. Their position is regularised through legislation, thus, giving rise to the state. The state tries to gain support from the financiers, landowners, merchants and industrialists by giving them economic favours. The libertarian regards the market, other than the state, to perform the economic functions including the defense of person and property, through a private form, which will supply protection for a fee. It is a radical form of *laissez faire* that rejects state intervention, for the system is capable of generating true prosperity. However, libertarians are deeply divided over the issue of the moral justification of a night-watchman state. Rothbard rejects it, even if it is sanctioned through free and informed consent of all members of a society. Libertarians strongly oppose the welfare state. Nozick is a staunch advocate of such a state as it respects individual rights.

Nozick justifies a minimal state as 'inspiring as well as right' and that 'any more extensive state will violate people's rights and is unjustified' (1974: ix). The functions of the state are limited to protection against force, theft, fraud and enforcement of contracts. It follows from this emphatic assertion that the coercive state apparatus cannot be used for the purpose of getting some citizens to aid others and to prohibit activities of people for their own good or protection. He agrees with the anarchist assertion that the state is intrinsically immoral, for in course of maintaining its monopoly on the use of force and protecting everyone within its territory, it violates individual rights. However, he believes that he could explain the minimal state and justify it against the anarchist objections by showing that it arises from a situation of anarchy without violating anyone's rights. He begins with Locke's position about inconveniences in the state of nature and relies on the 'invisible hand' to show the purely voluntary nature of its emergence and transactions, without any predetermined objective. Groups of individuals form mutual protection associations which function like insurance companies ensuring protection and enforcing their clients' rights. This leads to the formation of a Dominant Protective Agency of preeminent power within a territory. It is not a 'state', for protection and enforcement of people's rights is determined by the market and treated as an economic good like food and clothing. Different individuals may pay for different levels of protection. Some may not pay at all. The ultra minimal state, which is the next step, guarantees protection and also enjoys a monopoly of force. Eventually a minimal state evolves, which combines the two functions with a third, namely redistribution. The minimal state monopolises of protective services within a territory, and makes it available to all as a moral requirement. This prevents private enforcement of justice. Nozick categorically rejects the right of the state that the state has no right to force anyone to pay for protection or insist on anyone to become its client. He rejects the idea of a society as a cooperative enterprise based on mutual benefit and reciprocity. The minimal state is shielded by the entitlement theory of justice that states that if the procedures and processes were just, then the outcome is also just.

Idealist/Organic State

This conception is critical of liberal instrumentalism and rejects the contention that the state is an artificial machine which the individuals create deliberately to fulfil their interests and desires, and that the state is a product of human will. By the end of the eighteenth century and throughout the nineteenth century, this 'will and artifice' tradition gets dismissed as unsatisfactory and is replaced by the organic view which views the state as an organism, a person (Wayper 1977: 130–132). The Greeks adheres to this view but it flourishes in the nineteenth century with three assumptions—first, the intrinsic relationship between the parts (individuals) and the whole (state), with the parts having significance in context of the whole, second, the development of the organism takes place within itself and third, its ends lie within itself. All these three characteristics exist in a state. This view is best exemplified in the writings of Hegel. The idealist doctrine restores to political thought, the most characteristic idea of ancient Greek philosophy as articulated by Plato and Aristotle. The state is crucial to the realisation of good life and its ethical importance surpasses its economic, legal and political aspects.

Rousseau, in the *Social Contract* (1762), amalgamates the cohesiveness and solidarity of the ancient Greek *polis* with modern voluntarism and individual freedom through his notion of the General Will, a will of all individuals thinking of public interest. He amalgamates together the contractarian and organic traditions, using the former to explain the origins of the state and the latter in describing its nature. The general will does not represent the will of all nor is it the will of the majority. It is the 'Common Me' aiming and promoting the general interests of its members.

> The body politic, therefore, is also a moral being which possesses a will; and this general will, *which always tend towards the conservation and well being of the whole and of each part*, and which is the source of all laws, is for members of the state in their relations both to one another and to the state, the rile of what is just and what is unjust (Rousseau 1958: 146).

The general will emerges in an assembly of equal lawmakers and it cannot be alienated. The 'executive will' cannot be the general will, for only the legislative will, by virtue of being sovereign, will be the general will. Both Locke and Rousseau regard the legislature as supreme, but Locke advocates representative majoritarian democracy, while Rousseau supports direct participatory democracy. The government for Rousseau is an agent of the general will, which is the sovereign entity in the body politic. It is the source of laws and liberty and that reconciles liberty with authority and law.

For Hegel, the state represents universal altruism synthesising dialectically the elements within the family and the civil society. As in case of the family, the state functions in a manner that the interests of everyone are furthered and enhanced. It represents the universal tendencies within the civil society, thus giving rise to the notion of citizenship. It has 'its reality in the particular self-consciousness raised to the place of the universal'. It is 'absolutely rational' with a 'substantive will' realising itself through history and is, therefore, eternal. 'This substantive unity was its own motive and absolute end. In this end freedom attained its highest right. This end had the highest right over the individual, whose highest duty in turn is to be a member of the state' (Hegel cited in Bondurant 1967: 212–213). Hegel perceives the state as an end in itself; it is Mind realising itself through history. He emphasises the public nature of the state, but does not distinguish between the private and the public spheres. The indispensability of the state is demonstrated by the fact that the individual qualities and potentialities of good life could be realised only through the state. It is divine will, 'in the sense that it is mind present on earth, unfolding itself to be the actual shape and organisation of a world'. It is the most sublime of all human institutions, the final culmination which embodies both mind and spirit deriving its strength from a synthesis of the individual interest with that of the state. If there is a conflict between the two, the citizen would identify with those of the state rather than pursue one's own interests. The state is the individual writ large. Hegel examines the different components of the state like the rule of law, the bureaucracy and the monarchy.

Rule of Law is one of the key formulations in the *Philosophy of Right* (1821). Hegel does not see law as a hindrance to freedom but as a characteristic of freedom. He espouses a broad and a narrow conception of law. In the wide sense, it is one of the instruments for realising social cohesion with law not as a code but one that reflects ethical values which governed the cultural life. In this holistic concept, justice is linked to the institutional ordering of the entire society. In the narrow sense, law is linked to positive legal justice. The emphasis on the conventional principles of law made him reject a conception of higher or natural law, for modern civil codes were becoming more rational and public. Laws must be universally applied based on impersonal and universal values recognising every person as a legal entity entitled to dispose the objects, which are his property. The quantity of that property is a question of legal indifference, for what matters is the legal authority to acquire, use and exchange property with others based on the principle 'be a person and respect others as persons'.

An interesting aspect of the Hegelian legal system is its lack of the idea of 'command' normally associated with Hobbes. The determining characteristic of a legal norm is its form, which has its basis on practical rationality. The embodiment of a rule is more important than command, for that gives meaning and shape to the rule of law, distinguishing itself from arbitrary power. In an important distinction between command and law, Hegel asserts that commands and orders are specified purposes for identified people, whereas the ambit of law is wider as it addresses a larger and unknown audience and is equally applicable to all within its jurisdiction.

Command is from a superior to an inferior while the sanction of law is its rational authority. He rejects the ancient notion, as exemplified by Aristotle, of the purpose of law, being the realisation of human excellence or full development of human capacities and leaves it to the individual's private discretion. In contrast, the modern rule of law consists of a few necessary features that are common to all and is established by the rationality of free individuals. Laws have to be impersonal, rational, intelligent and written for people to conform and consent. He rejects Burke's appeal to tradition and customs, as it creates attitudes that result in ill-feeling and hatred for all laws and legislation.

The universal class is the bureaucracy, an important component of the Hegelian state, because of its commitment to impartiality. Unlike the other groups of the civil society, who are primarily interested in their own progression or business, the civil service performs the stupendous service of supervising the entire societal apparatus, which Hegel calls the public business. This class of people will not be recruited from the nobility but from the modern middle class symbolising 'the consciousness of right and the developed intelligence of the mass of people'. For this reason, it becomes 'the pillar of the state so far as honesty and intelligence are concerned' (Hegel 1969: 190). It is 'knowledge and proof of ability' and not hereditary that is the criterion for recruitment (Hegel 1969: 190). Hegel in developing this philosophy of the civil service differentiates the modern constitutional state from oriental despotism because of the relative impersonality of the bureaucracy. The constitutional state retains its independence from its ruling groups by mechanisms of free institutions and a civil service. The state is not the personal property of an individual or a group, and institutional constraints define and limit the power of governments which do not depend on the virtues of statesmen or citizens. This is because modern constitutionalism is suspicious of the abilities of persons in power to control their passions and prevent abuse of power by the rulers. The rule of law and not rule of men reflect the concern of modern societies enabling the modern constitutional state to act impartially. The civil service, like Plato's Guardians, has the interests of the commonwealth in mind. Hegel is categorical that the bureaucracy shall be open to all citizens on the basis of ability and citizenship. They shall have fixed salaries so that they can resist the temptations of civil society. Unlike Plato's guardians, the universal class functions within a framework where the special interests expressed themselves legitimately within the Assembly of Estates and autonomous corporations.

The monarchy, for Hegel, is a functional requirement of the modern constitution based on separation and division of powers. He goes to the extent of saying that the division of power guarantees freedom. Hegel differentiates between the doctrine of the separation of powers from his own innovative theory of inward differentiation of constitutional powers, dismissing the former as a false doctrine as it supports total autonomy and independence of each functioning category. His model portrays all these categories as mutually supporting aspects of the same totality. His supreme concern is to find a method that secures the unity and integrity of the state. Absolute separation of powers either leads to a stalemate or causes self-destruction of the state. To avoid this, Hegel prescribes legally differentiated spheres for the crown, the executive and the legislative body, each cooperating with the other to guarantee freedom to its citizens. Interdependence and harmony of the three important branches are the precondition of continuance of the sovereign state with the monarchy at the apex, signifying this unity. Hegel opposes the idea of an elected monarchy or the American-style President, for, even though it may express the popular will as that will still represent a small portion of the constitution, while the monarch embodies, in his view, the whole constitution. Hegel's defense of monarchy has to be understood on the basis of his philosophical framework to find out rational arrangements within the existing institutions. It does not descent into mysticism as Marx thought. He is not interested in finding a philosophic ruler as Plato nor is he trying to depict a future based on human emancipation within a framework of true democracy like Marx. Such ideas are a negation of the entire approach of Hegel, which is based on the assumption that the *real is rational* and that the *immediate present* and not the future is the concern.

The Hegelian conception influences the British idealist school in the later part of the nineteenth century, especially in the writings of Bosanquet who exalts state authority. The state, in his theory, expresses the general will which is constituted by a person's real will, the characteristic of his true individuality. The essence of being human is being moral and as a moral being a person must will the conditions that make possible a moral life. Moral life is possible only in society and therefore, the state shall maintain social conditions necessary for the 'good life' by realising the will of every truly moral individual. A person's supreme duty is the development of his social capacities. Each person's morality and real happiness consists in satisfactorily fulfilling his appointed place in the society. This is similar to Plato's conception. Hegel considers the state as a supreme community because of its comprehensive membership and competence as compared to other associations. It is not only physically supreme but also morally preeminent among the social institutions! It is necessarily right and its opinion will prevail when there is a conflict between its opinion and that of a citizen. **Bradley** echoes many of these ideas.

The **British idealist** philosophy arises as a reaction to empirical utilitarianism and economic individualism dominant in Britain, in the early part of the nineteenth century. It tries to assimilate Kant and Hegel with liberalism. It regards the state as a product of deliberate negotiation among individuals who establish the political society to serve their conscious needs and it represents the individual as the source of rights. According to this philosophy, the state is created by the individual to protect his original rights, and the political will of the community is simply a summation of the wills of the individual citizens. The German idealist philosophy inspired by Hegel, describes the state as original and organic in nature, the source of individual rights and the embodiment of a general community will, that may be very different from, and even substantially independent of, the wills of a majority of the citizens. The exaltation of the state takes its extreme form under Fascism that arises in Europe, in the early part of the twentieth century, negating the dominant ideas of the enlightenment, liberalism, conservatism and communism.

Fascist State

Fascism considers individuals as a means to the ends of society, which is understood as a nation based on unity of language, custom and religion. The state is the organic structure of the nation, supreme and all-inclusive. This concept is summed up best by Giovanni Gentile (1875–1944) who, like Croce,[2] identifies with an Italian school of Hegelian philosophy. The fascists use the Hegelian argument, but that does not mean they are well-versed with Hegel's philosophy. Like Hegel, they criticise individualism and parliamentarism. However, for Hegel, unlike the fascists, the state means a theory of constitutional government with a fair amount of civil liberty and orderly legal procedure. The motto of the fascist state is 'Everything for the state; nothing against the state; nothing outside the state'. The state is an ethical idea representing lofty ideals as opposed to the materialism of the Marxists and the selfish anti-social individualist ethic of political liberalism. The fascists espouse absolute sovereignty, moral and legal, of the national state. The interest of the latter is at times in conformity, and at times in conflict, with that of the interests of the citizens but will always enjoy precedence. The preservation and expansion of the state through war is justified. The fascists defend a nation that is organically and hierarchically constituted dismissing claims of equality and rights as essentially feeble creeds. Their slogan 'Responsibility, Discipline and Hierarchy' substitutes the democratic slogan of 'Liberty, Equality and Fraternity' with a view to encouraging the individual to garner all his resources and employ them for an efficacious participation in the national life. They stress on the need for law, order and efficiency rather than liberty, which they thought is possible only under a strong and progressive state. The individual fulfil his true personality and freedom not by safeguarding his private interests but by merging with the larger unions—his family, church and the state. Gentile declares that the 'maximum of liberty coincides with the maximum of state power'. The individual derives his rights from the state and his will counts in political decisions only when it coincides with that of the state. For the fascists, political authority is aristocratic and also autocratic, representing the essential groups and not the individuals within the state. Sovereignty resides with the state and not the people and only the elites are competent to speak, thereby repudiating democracy.

The German philosophers of nationalist socialism or Nazism ignore and reject Hegel. Nazism does not formulate a theory of the state. In the *Mein Kampf*, Hitler proposes that the state is a means to the end, namely the well-being of the *Volk* or the folk, the organic people. *Volk* represents culture that is learned and cannot be inherited and cannot be equated with the nation, for it is biological. It is not people for it is collective. Nazism speaks of the masses, the elite and the leader. The elites lead the masses and in turn are led by the leader. Hitler and Mussolini are contemptuous of the masses and advocate the selection of the elite. The elites are selected through the natural process that represents the folk and its inner will. The leader is the head of the elite, responsible for all and is served with unquestioning obedience. He symbolises what Weber called the charismatic authority. Hitler describes the leader as 'neither a scholar nor a theorist but a practical psychologist and an organiser—a psychologist in order that he master the methods by which he can gain the largest number of passive adherents, an organiser in order that he may build up a compact body of followers to consolidate his gains'. The idea of the leader and folk is supported by a general theory of race, specifically the myth of the Aryan race invented to uphold political chauvinism. It depends for effect on racial prejudice, particularly anti-Semitism. The *Mein Kampf* states clearly, but not systematically, the basic assumptions of the race theory and can be summarised as follows.

- First, the struggle for survival in which the fittest survive eliminating the weak, ensures social progress. When this struggle takes place within a race, it gives rise to a natural elite and also between races and cultures that bring out the differences between different races and cultures.
- Second, intermingling of two races leads to the degeneration of the higher race and causes political, social and cultural decay but a race can become pure when its hybrid character tends to die out.
- Third, though the creative powers of race is expressed in the social and cultural institutions, all great civilisations or important cultures are the product of one race or at least of a few. There are three types of races—the culture-creating Aryan race; the culture-bearing races that adopts and adjusts but cannot create and the culture-destroying race, namely the Jews. The culture-creating race requires the services of races that are inferior.
- Fourth, in the culture-creating race, self-preservation is transformed from egoism into care for the community.

Conservative State

The conservatives too, like the idealists, adhere to an organic and hierarchical conception of the society rejecting the ideas of contract and consent. They dismiss the mechanistic interpretation that views the state as an entity which can be replaced or destroyed any time. They reject the atomistic view of society though they see society as an aggregate of individuals pursuing their self-interest. They conceive the individuals in the context of groups and stress the importance of family and neighbourhood communities for the security and meaning they provide. They regard society as natural for the fulfillment of human needs with each part—family, church, work and government—playing a particular role in sustaining and maintaining the health of the social fabric. Each part understands its role and perceives society as a whole that is continuously evolving and changing. They understand authority as a hierarchy with each level playing a major role in the society. **Burke** categorically identifies the state with everything which is truly and properly public—public peace, public safety, public order and public property—precluding the private. Here Burke echoes the sentiments of the early liberals like Smith whom he greatly admired. **Louis Gabriel de Bonald** (1754–1840) reiterating Aquinas categorically asserts that authority and power is derived directly from god.

The conservatives emphasise on the social importance of religion as not only a spiritual phenomenon but also a cementing force that provides a set of shared moral values which hold the society together. They regard the nation with great respect, for it is a product of affinity among people who share the same language, history, culture and traditions and are skeptical of multi-cultural, multi-racial and socially plural societies. The conservatives do not favour a weak central government. **Tocqueville's** distinction between government and administration in *Democracy in America* is implicitly present in almost all shades of Conservative thought. Tocqueville advocates a strong and unified government while administration, in the interests of liberty and order, should be as decentralised and localised and generally inconspicuous as possible. **Joseph de Maistre** (1753–1821) considers the public executioner as the very cornerstone of proper governmental power over people. The executioner prevents as well as punishes crime but that does not mean that he is omni-competent, responsible for daily existence and the worst of all 'pretended moral teacher, guide to virtue and mother of spirit'. Burke warns that the price of erosion of all natural authorities in society is the increasing military domination of government. This stress on state, family, authority, religion, order and tradition finds resonance in **Neo-conservatism** that arises since the mid-1960s in the US, obliterating the distinction that exists in conservative thought between the tradition in the US[3] and that of Europe. The Neo-conservatives stress on intermediary institutions like ethnic groups, churches, labour unions, universities, family and community as an integral part of a decent society and the absence of these, in their view, led to alienation and spiritual vacuum resulting in totalitarianism and a secular rootless mass society (Nisbet 1962 and 1975).

Marxist State

Unlike Hegel who had worked out the details of a modern state by his distinction between the realm of the state and the realm of the civil society, Marx's account is sketchy. This is in spite of his professed aim to provide an alternative to the Hegelian paradigm as outlined in his *Critique of Hegel's Philosophy of Right* (1844). His views on the state are largely determined by his perceptions and analyses of the French state, the Revolution of 1848 and the *coup d'etat* of Napoleon III and that his ideas are the result of an elaborate misunderstanding of the 1789 French Revolution, of the role of classes and of the very nature of the revolution. The Bolsheviks in Russia imitated France as seen through the prism of the writings of Marx, which seems to them more real than the actual French history (Wolfe 1969: 7–8). Keeping the French experience in mind, Marx advocates a violent revolutionary seizure of power and the establishment of the dictatorship of the proletariat. Interestingly, he accepts the possibility of peaceful and parliamentary transfer in 1872 in England, America and Holland where the state is not that highly centralised and bureaucratic as in France. However, by and large, he remains committed to the idea of a violent revolution.

For Marx, the state belongs to the superstructure. So in course of history, each mode of production gives rise to its own specific political organisation to further the interests of the economically dominant class. The *Manifesto* declares 'the executive of the modern State is but a committee for managing the common affairs of the whole bourgeoisie' (1975: 44). For Marx and Engels, the state expresses human alienation. It is an instrument of class exploitation and class oppression. In the *Eighteenth Brumaire of Louis Bonaparte* (1852), Marx denounces the bureaucratic and the all-powerful state and advises its destruction. Bonapartism is a regime in a capitalist society in which the executive branch of the state, under the rule of one individual, attains dictatorial power over all other parts of the state and the society. Examples of such regimes during Marx's lifetime were that of Louis Bonaparte, the nephew of Napoleon I, who came to be known as Napoleon III after his *coup d'etat* of 2 December 1851. Engels finds a similar parallel with Bismarck's rule in Germany. Bonapartism is the result of a situation when the ruling class in the capitalist society is no longer in a position to maintain its rule through constitutional and parliamentary means, and the working class is also not able to wrest control. It is a situation of temporary equilibrium between the rival warring classes. The independence of a Bonapartist state and its role as the 'ostensible mediator' between the rival classes does not mean that it is in a position of suspended animation. In reality, it ensures the safety and stability of the bourgeois society and guarantees its rapid development. The relative autonomy of the state is based on cancelling out the forces in a situation of temporary equilibrium. Marx provides the outline of relative autonomy which Gramsci subsequently develops fully into a systematic theory.

For Marx and Engels, the communist society eliminates all forms of alienation for the human individual, from nature, from society and from humanity. It will be a true democracy with the majority ruling for all intent and purpose for the first time. The transitional state—the dictatorship of the proletariat—lies between the destruction of capitalism and attainment of communism. Interestingly, one of the well-known utopias is least delineated. Marx's own epistemological premises caution him about what the future will be like. To describe an object that exists in the consciousness of a thinking subject is philosophical idealism. Moreover, Marx did not rival with those socialists whom he had branded as 'utopian' by constructing detailed blueprints since the communist society was determined by the specific conditions under which it was established (Avineri 1976: 221). Marx projected an image of the future society from the internal tensions of the existing capitalist society, implying that, at the outset itself the communist society would perfect and universalise all the elements of the bourgeois society that could be universalised.

Dictatorship of the Proletariat

This controversial and ambiguous concept emerges in the writings of Marx and Engels as a result of a debate with the German Social Democrats, the Anarchists and more significantly from the practical experiences of the Paris Commune of 1871. Their observations on the subject have to be pieced together from remarks made solely *enpassant* and from different sources. The two major texts, however, are the *Civil War in France* (1871) and the *Critique of the Gotha Programe* (1875). This concept holds the key to the understanding of Marx's theory on the nature of the communist society and the role of the proletarian state. It is a concept that divides the Marxists and the Leninists from the Anarchists, on the one hand, and from the Social Democrats, on the other. Neither the phrase 'Dictatorship of the proletariat' nor the idea of eliminating state power is mentioned in the *Manifesto*. Instead, Marx and Engels speak of the 'political rule of the proletariat' advising the workers to capture the state, destroy the privileges of the old class and prepare the basis for the eventual disappearance of the state. They are convinced that existing states, whether as instruments of class domination and oppression or bureaucratic parasites on the whole of the society grow inherently strong and remain minority states, representing the interests of the small but dominant and powerful possessing class. Bearing in mind the experiences of the French Revolution of 1789, Marx advises the proletariat to seize the state and make it democratic and majoritarian. Irrespective of the form, the state machinery was powerful which the proletariat has to contend with. The initial 'capture' thesis of the state, however, yields to the 'smash' thesis subsequently. In a book-review written around 1848–1849, Marx observes that the destruction of the state has only one implication for the communists, namely the cessation of an organised power of one class for the suppression of another class (Draper 1977: 288). In the *Manifesto*, Marx describes the nature of the communist society as classless and 'an association, in which the free development of each is the condition for the free development of all' (1975: 76). For the purpose of socialising the means of production a list of ten measures are outlined that includes:

1. Abolition of property in land and application of all rents of land to public purpose;
2. A heavy progressive or graduated income tax;
3. Abolition of all rights of inheritance;
4. Confiscation of the property of all emigrants and rebels;
5. Centralisation of credit in the hands of the state;
6. Centralisation of the means of transport in the hands of the state;
7. Extension of factories and instruments of production owned by the state;
8. Equal liability of all to labour;
9. Combination of agriculture and industries; gradual abolition of the distinction between town and country; and
10. Free education for all children in public schools (1975: 74).

Marx modified his views on the state between the period of 1848–1852, as a result of events in France and more significantly, after 1871. Until 1850, March, Marx and Engels did not apply the word 'dictatorship' to the rule of the proletariat. Prior to that, they did not mention nor discussed the **Babouvist-Blanquist** conception of educational dictatorship for it contravened their vision of a proletarian revolution, which was based on the faith they had in the masses to emancipate themselves. They did not feel the need for a period of educational rule by an enlightened minority or the postponement of democratic elections. The phrase is used as a tactical compromise slogan with the Blanquists and then as a polemical device against the Anarchists and assorted reformists (Hunt 1975: 334). It is not Louis Auguste Blanqui (1805–1851), but Louis Eugene Cavaignac, a General and Blanqui's arch antagonist, who helps Marx and Engels to incorporate the word dictatorship into their vocabulary. Engels clarifies that dictatorship is necessary to fill the vacuum as a result of the destruction of the old order and till the creation of the new order. Marx accepts this formulation and like Engels is confident that it does not mean the permanent rule of one person or group. In March 1850, the phrase 'dictatorship of the proletariat' replaced the habitually used phrase 'rule of the proletariat'. Marx and Engels stress on the notion of extraordinary power during an emergency for a limited period of time. It is a constitutional dictatorship like the one suggested by Francois Noel 'Gracchus' Babeuf (1760–1797) and Blanqui, but differ from their conception insofar as it is not educational. It does not mean the rule of a self-appointed committee on behalf of the masses. Marx and Engels do not envisage the need for mass terror and liquidation. However, Marx does not define in any specific way as to what the dictatorship of the proletariat entails and as to what its relationship is to the state. It refers to 'a social description is a statement of the class character of the political power. It is not a statement about the forms of government authority' (Draper 1977: 94). Miliband (1965: 289–290) disagrees and considers the concept to be a statement of the class character of political power and a description of political power itself. Marx and Engels regard the dictatorship of the proletariat of the entire working class. In a series of articles written in *Neue Rheinische Zeitung*, later on compiled under the title *The Class Struggles in France* (1848–1850), Marx conceptualises the dictatorship of the proletariat as that of the whole class. He writes,

> the declaration of the permanence of the revolution, the class dictatorship of the proletariat as the necessary transit point to the abolition of class distinctions generally to the abolition of all relations of production on which they rest, to the abolition of all social relations that correspond to these relations of production, to the revolutionizing of all the ideas that result from these social relations (Marx 1977a: 282).

The phrase dictatorship of the proletariat is incorporated into the first of the six statutes of the Universal Society. In a letter to Otta Luning, co-editor of *Neue Rheinische Zeitung*, Marx clarifies that he does not find any significant departure to the idea of the dictatorship of the proletariat as articulated in the *Class Struggles* to the one formulated in the *Manifesto*. The ambiguous compromise slogan 'dictatorship of the proletariat' would have died a natural death had the Marxists and the Blanquists not renewed their contacts in the aftermath of the Paris Commune (Hunt 1975: 305–306). Meanwhile, an important event that helped in the clarification of the concept was the Paris Commune, which led to an amendment of the *Manifesto* in 1872:

> One thing especially was proved by the Commune viz. that the working class cannot simply lay hold of the ready-made state machinery and wield it for its own purpose (Marx 1975: 8).

Marx is enthused about the Commune regarding it as the 'glorious harbinger of a new society' and observes in his letter to Kugelman in April 1871 that,

> If you look at the last chapter of my Eighteenth Brumaire, you will find that I say that the next attempt of the French Revolution will no longer, be as before, to transfer the bureaucratic-military machine from one hand to another but to smash it and this is the precondition for every real people's revolution on the continent. And this is what our heroic Party comrades in Paris are attempting (Marx 1977 Vol. I: 240).

Marx views the Paris Commune as the first major rebellion of the modern industrial proletariat and is in consonance with his belief that France set the example in the struggle between capital and labour. In his address to the General Council of the International Workingmen's Association or the First International (1864–1876) in London, he outlines the importance of the Commune and the lessons in participatory democracy it held for the future socialist movements.

Criticisms by the Anarchists and Social Democrats

Michael Bakunin (1815–1876) in the *Statism and Anarchy* (1873) contends that the Marxist political order could turn out to be a rigid oligarchy of technocrats and officials. If such a state controls all capital and the means of production it would eventually lead to bureaucratisation and to a government by the intelligentsia, 'It will be the reign of scientific intelligence, the most aristocratic, despotic, arrogant and elitists of all regimes' (Bakunin cited in Dolgoff 1973: 19). The task of the proletarian revolution is not to transform but to abolish the state as it symbolises power and authority. He perceives that, to Marx, the abolition of the state plays no vital role for he merely wants to capture the state and not destroy it in its entirety. Marx desires to 'liberate from above' through the state. For Bakunin, true liberation comes only 'from below' through the individual. If, for Marx, the proletarian state represents the entire people then,

> ...why eliminate it? And if the State is needed to emancipate the workers, then the workers are not yet free, so why call it a People's state' (Bakunin cited in Dolgoff 1973: 331).

Marx points out that Bakunin's perception of all states as evil, since they are products of class-divided societies is a complete abstention from all politics. In *On Authority* (1872–1873), Engels clarifies that Anarchism is not the goal of Marxism. The impending social revolution abolishes all forms of authority but not the state. In a classless society, the state ceases to be an evil and eventually 'wither' away. To this, Bakunin contends that power corrupts all those who wield it. The clash of the titans took place in the First International. Here, Marx is involved in his polemics with Bakunin, Pierre Joseph Proudhon (1809–1865) and Ferdinand Lassalle (1825–1864), and in particular with the first two. Bakunin joins the International in 1868 with a short speech, which set the tone of the Anarchist critique of the Marxist notion of the dictatorship of the proletariat. He observes:

> I detest Communism because it is the negation of liberty and I cannot conceive anything human without liberty. I am not a communist because communism concentrates all the powers of society and absorbs them into the hands of the state while I want to see the state abolished. I want the complete liberation of the authoritarian principle of state tutelage which has always subjected, oppressed, exploited and depraved men while claiming to moralize and civilize them. I want society and collective or social property to be organized from the bottom up through free associations and not from the top down by authority of any kind ... in that sense I am a collectivist and not at all a communist (Bakunin cited in Woodcock 1944: 41).

The German Social Democrats, following the views of Lassalle, articulate the possibilities of using the existing state for the realisation of socialism and enhancement of human freedom. They favour reforms as opposed to a revolution and believe that the spread of suffrage would enable the workers to have a decisive role in the parliament and the institutions of the state. These demands are incorporated in the Gotha programme adopted by the SPD in 1875. In response to both the Anarchists and the German Social Democrats, Marx writes the *Critique of the Gotha Programme* emphasising the transitional nature of the dictatorship of the proletariat, thus outlining the attainment of full communism following a revolutionary transformation of society through a two-tier process.

> between the capitalist society and communist society lies the period of the revolutionary transformation of the one into another. There corresponds to this also a political transition period in which the state can be nothing but the revolutionary dictatorship of the proletariat (Marx 1977, Vol. III).

Marx contrasts the higher form of communism with primitive or crude communism, the first stage in the process of historical materialism. The latter is signified by the necessity of all to labour, a levelling down of all individual talents and communal ownership of women, essentially indicating a negation of the human personality. All these features are absent in the final communist society. Marx does not specify the mechanisms of change from stage I to stage II in the post-revolutionary phase of human history, casting serious doubts as to how stage I develops into stage II and whether it develops as intended (Avineri 1976: 329). Since this process is not explained, the ultimate aim of 'free development of each will lead to the free development of all' might not be realised (Wilson 1941: 335–336). In the *Anti Duhring*, Engels introduces the notion of the 'withering away' of the state in which the 'government of persons' is replaced by 'administration of things'. Both he and Marx accept the central planning and direction without force and coercion as a feature of the proletarian state but they fail to resolve the possible conflict between centralised planning and individual freedom in the Communist society.

Thus, Marx and Engels react sharply to Bakunin's criticism about the statist implications of their conception and Lassalle's conception of 'free state'. By 1875, it becomes clear that the German Social Democrats have begun to think of using the existing state apparatus and are settling down for reformist socialism. Marx continues to advocate the revolutionary overthrow of the existing bureaucratic-military state and replace it with the dictatorship of the proletariat a more truly democratic and majoritarian. Bakunin insists on the immediate elimination of all forms of political authority and replaces it with spontaneous and voluntary organisations. Marx accepts the anarchist demand on the abolition of the state but emphasises on the majoritarian content of the transitional state purely as a temporary measure hoping to counter both his critics.

In exploring the possibilities of a world proletarian revolution, Marx and Engels begin to show interest in the non-European world and set forth the idea of the **Asiatic Mode of Production**. Unlike the state in the European context that is an instrument of class domination and exploitation, the state in Asiatic societies controls all classes. It does not belong to the superstructure but is decisive in the entire economic arena, building and managing water supply as the life breadth of agriculture in arid areas. It performs economic and social functions for the entire society. Social privileges emanate from service to the state and not from the institution of private property as it is in Europe. Asiatic societies have an overdeveloped state and an underdeveloped civil society. Military conquests and dynastic tussles usher in changes periodically without affecting the economic organisation because the state continues to be the real landlord. The self-sufficient autarchic villages sustained by common property, agriculture and handicrafts buttresses social unity in the Asiatic societies. In Europe, cities rise independently helping with the growth of the production of exchange values which in turn determines the development of a bourgeois class and industrial capitalism. In the East, the city is created artificially by the state and superimposed on the economic structure remaining therefore a 'princely camp' subordinate to the countryside. The state appropriates the surplus in the form of taxes and this centralised state prevents the rise of free markets, private property and guilds, and bourgeois law.

For Marx and Engels, socialism represents the zenith of capitalism with the possibility of a proletarian revolution only in the advanced industrialised societies. However, they explore the possibilities of a revolution in semi-developed and backward areas with the view to fomenting a revolution in the developed areas. In this context, in 1882, they express the view that if a revolution breaks out in Tsarist Russia it may complement the efforts of the proletariat in the advanced West. Russia's backwardness and the lack of a coherent theory of post-revolutionary society in Marx attenuate the Blanquism in Leninism and Stalinism.

If Stalinism is an offshoot of Leninism, Marxism inspires Leninism. An examination of the development of the idea of the dictatorship of the proletariat reveals a tension between the concept's organisational necessities even though it may be of a transitory kind with the larger Marxist hypothesis of enlargement of human freedom. Marx's handling of the crucial role of the theory of the state remains inadequate, 'Marx sketched but never developed a systematic theory of the state and hence the idea of a political economy remained overdetermined and undescribed politically' (Wolin 1987: 469). His aversion to utopian blueprinting makes him ignore the details that are necessary for managing a society based on equity, just reward and freedom. The concept of the 'class struggle', which is central in the thinking of all Marxists have become largely irrelevant in America and Western Europe (Berlin 1939: xi). Berlin's last observation about the obsolesce of class struggle in advanced industrialised countries can now be extended to the developing world. There is no more any talk of revolutionary transformation of the society or that 'East is Red'. Moreover, the possibility of using democracy as a means of realising socialism never moves to the centre stage of his analysis of the future society. This is where the Social Democrats score over Marx. They, and in particular Bernstein, emphasise on the need to combine democracy (representative parliamentary institutions with universal suffrage) with socialism bringing about a permanent breach between German Marxism and Russian Communism (Plamentaz 1969).

The Leninist State

Vladimir Ilyich Ulyanov Lenin (1870–1924) regards the dictatorship of the proletariat as the core of the Marxist thought. In his 1916 tract, *State and Revolution* Lenin reviews the ideas of Marx and Engels on the state by examining the views of other contemporary Marxist scholars on the subject. The *State and Revolution* has been regarded as the most substantive contribution of Lenin to political theory (Colletti 1969). Using the model of the Paris Commune, he argues that the proletarian revolution destroys the bourgeois state and establishes the dictatorship of the proletariat, for that is the most appropriate political form during the transitional phase. Lenin argues that since the bourgeois class controls the bourgeois state with all its democratic instruments and its primary function is the direct coercion, it has to be destroyed totally. He clarifies that Engels' notion of the withering away of the state means that the proletarian state withers away while the bourgeois state is abolished. This differs from the anarchist notion of the abolition of the state. Lenin defines the state as a special organisation of force, an instrument of violence for the suppression of one class namely the bourgeoisie. He emphasises that the socialist revolution will lead to the political rule of the proletariat, and its dictatorship. The proletarian state wields coercive force but of a different kind; the majority exercises coercion over the minority, a reversal of the bourgeois state. Its *raison d'etre* is to crush the resistance of the exploiters and build up a socialist democracy for all, which he believes only the proletariat could accomplish. Reiterating Marx, he outlines the two-stage development to the attainment of the Communist society. The first or the lower stage—the socialist phase—retains the vestiges of the old bourgeois order in which, exploitation continues since the state as a coercive force continues but it is a 'bourgeois state without the bourgeoisie'. The second phase dawns when the imperative need for the state machinery completely disappears after the society adopts the rule of 'from each according to his ability to each according to his needs' and when the 'Government is replaced by the administration of things'. The antithesis between mental and physical labour also disappears. The proletarian state, like the Paris Commune, is one where the workers directly participate and manage the state affairs without a bureaucracy and a standing army. In *Left Wing Communism* (1920), he describes the tactics that the dictatorship of the proletariat was to employ. Lenin christens the first and the second phases as 'socialism' and 'communism', respectively, and since then the two phrases are used in common parlance. He faithfully reproduces the observations of Marx and Engels on the dictatorship of the proletariat and the Communist society and in the process adds a 'permanent ideology to Marxism, namely, that the attainment of the Communist society would be two phased'

(Sabine 1973: 762). For Lenin, the dictatorship of the proletariat is a political concept, 'a rule won and maintained by violence by the proletariat against the bourgeois rule unrestricted by any laws' (Lenin 1977: 117). It is viable only through the **Vanguard of the Proletariat**, the Workers' Party, for he had very little faith in the industrial proletariat as a mass.

Miliband (1977: 179–180) correctly comments that the Leninist model is illusory, for the revolution to properly succeed in Russia a 'state proper', that is strong enough to organise the process of transition from capitalism to communism, is needed. Unlike Marx, who conceives of a majoritarian revolution, Lenin speaks of a minority revolution made by the Vanguard Party on behalf of the proletarian mass. Therefore, given the scheme of minority revolution a majoritarian popular government in the meaning that is assigned to it is not feasible. Moreover, the proletarian state, for Lenin continues to be the state. The revolution ends the bourgeois state but not the state as such, for the bourgeois state is one that protects the interests of the bourgeois minority. The proletarian state promotes and furthers the interests of the proletarian majority representing the quintessence of true democracy. The *State and Revolution*, however, neglects the problem of political articulation and political organisation as a matter of avoidance rather than the resolution of the question. The tricky part is Lenin's emphasis on the need and role of the Vanguard Party (Miliband 1977: 182), for he remains skeptical of the role of the Soviets and workers' councils, which represents the spontaneity of the people till the eve of the revolution. The *State and Revolution* does not examine the relationship between the Soviets and the Vanguard Party. It is when Kautsky accuses the Bolshevik regime of violating democracy that Lenin describes the role of the Soviets as evolving from local bodies to national organisations directly organising the workers. However, within a short period of time, after the revolution, the regime in the Soviet Union becomes the dictatorship of the Bolshevik Party as the Party comes to enjoy an irretrievable and an irrevocable position, largely because of the failure to distinguish 'between the dictatorship of the proletariat and the dictatorship of the party' and Lenin's declaration 'that dictatorship of the proletariat is impossible except through the Communist Party' (Carr 1979: 230).

Lenin's critics

The Leninist experiment is severely criticised both within and outside Russia. Most of his critics unanimously point to the absence of democracy and the lack of sufficient institutional checks against abuse of power. From a social democratic standpoint, **Bernstein** dubs the Revolution as a counter-revolution and regards Bolshevism as a 'brutalised' version of Marxism, for it relies on terror and violence and abhors civilised behaviour as he believes that socialism ought to eschew all forms of dictatorship and violence. Julius Martov (1873–1923) and the Mensheviks are skeptical of the Bolshevik methods and tactics and argue that Russia is not yet ready for a socialist revolution in view of its backwardness. Martov rejects the Leninist conception of a minority revolution led by disciplined well-organised workers' Party with covert or overt mass support on the grounds that it institutionalise dictatorship or 'Commissarocracy'. He regards the Leninist model as a flagrant departure from the majoritarian perceptions of Marx and Engels and accuses Lenin of imposing the will of a 'conscious revolutionary minority' on an unconscious majority reducing the latter to a position of passive object of social experimentation. The Social Democrats, on the other hand, remain committed to realising both socialism and democracy. Martov's position coincides with that of Karl Johann Kautsky (1854–1938). Lenin's reply to Martov in *Will the Bolsheviks Retain State Power* is weak as he writes that if 130,000 landowners are able to govern Russia in the past why could not 240,000 members of the Bolsheviks party govern it now? To this, Martov and others reply, 'Yes, you may be able to stay in power with your 240,000 members but only insofar as you approach and then exceed the repressive measures of the 130,000 landowners'. In response Lenin retreats partially and launches the New Economy Policy (NEP) acknowledging the need for more time to build socialism and liberalise the economy without introducing political democracy and civil liberties. Later, the lack of political liberalisation only strengthens the autocracy under Josif Vissarionovich Stalin (1879–1953) who introduces forced collectivism, industrialisation, nationalisation and also simultaneously increases mass terror, mass murders and purges, thus, confirming the worst fears that Martov harbours.

The suspension of the Constituent Assembly and the suppression of universal suffrage provoke both Kautsky and Rosa Luxemburg (1871–1919) to virulently denounce the Revolution and Leninism and castigate Lenin for disregarding democratic norms and procedures and that the minority revolution would lead to militarisation and bureaucratisation. Kautsky points out that dictatorship of the proletariat means power of the workers through a majority in parliament and for Luxemburg the abandonment of spontaneity would encourage centralisation and personal dictatorship. Lenin in his reply *Proletarian Revolution and Renegade Kautsky* (1918) points out that the contrast between the Bolshevik and the non-Bolshevik socialist movements is a contrast between two diametrically opposite methods, dictatorial and democratic. For Lenin, the question of the dictatorship of the proletariat has to be understood with reference to the relationship of the proletarian state to the bourgeois states, of the proletarian democracy to the bourgeois democracy, a fact that Kautsky overlooks. Lenin clarifies that dictatorship does not mean the absence of democracy and for a Marxist, the class connotation of a regime is crucially important. Leon Trotsky (1879–1940) justifies the use of violence and terror to combat reactionary forces to enable the workers to transform society. Subsequently, he too concedes that backwardness and socialism are incompatible and the measures that he advocates as temporary means become permanent ones and the ends of the regime. He blames poverty for the bureaucratisation of the former Soviet Union for it becomes a 'caste' depriving the proletariat of its political right and by introducing brutal despotism.

Prince Peter Kropotkin (1842–1921), Bakunin's successor anticipates the establishment of the Marxist State in Russia and the fact that in Marxism an embryonic form of Leninism and its malignant form of Stalinism exist. Like Luxemburg, Bakunin also is confident that party dictatorship would eventually deaden spontaneous creativity of the masses, destroys the Soviets and the popular revolution and impresses upon Lenin the need for local initiative by local forces. He contends that the Bolsheviks have replicated a centralised state closely resembling the one with full dictatorial power proposed by Babeuf. Such a state in his opinion paralyses the reconstruction work of the people, undermining success totally.

The important gaps left by Marx in his theory of the state create controversies and generates debates in the first two decades of the twentieth century. As far as the basic principles are concerned there is considerable disagreement between Bernstein, Kautsky, Lenin and Luxemburg. Within the camp of the Russian Marxists too there are significant differences as the opposing views of Russian Marxists led by Lenin and the Western Marxists reflect two very different situations. In Germany, with its single largest following of Marx and the influential SPD, the lot of working class actually improves a fact that is totally at variance to what Marx had predicted. The collapse of capitalism was not imminent. The British Labour Party was also working towards that direction. The situation in France was similar.

The concept of the dictatorship of the proletariat would have ceased to be controversial had not Lenin resurrected it in his campaign against **Bukharin** who advocated the need to smash, rather than capture, as Lenin did, the existing state apparatus in a situation of revolutionary seizure of power. In 1917, on the eve of the October Revolution, he was confident of the spontaneous role of the workers and the rise of the Soviets which explained his libertarian outlook in the *State and Revolution* as opposed to the authoritarian tone of *What is to be done*? (1903). In view of the imminence of a proletarian revolution it became imperative to define the post-revolutionary state and the nature and form of socialist democracy and set the rules for dealing with problems of real politics. Marx was hardly helpful on this issue.

As Milovan Djilas (1911–1995) aptly points out Marxism lacks a theory of political liberty. Having visualised his classless communist society as a non-conflictive and a harmonious one, Marx never comprehends the dynamics of the democratic functioning of a modern society. The fact is that individuals function rarely as isolated creatures but very often through group(s), which serve to articulate and represent the plural and diverse interests in society. Marx's mistake has been to assume that a classless society necessarily means a homogenous and Unitarian one.

This fallacy coupled with the Leninist emphasis on a Vanguard Party led to the emergence of a monolithic party system in the erstwhile USSR, straddling and terrorising all aspects of civil society. The monopolistic position that the Communist Party held, as given to it by Article 6 of the Soviet Constitution, was never really examined at any point when political reforms were contemplated and initiated. It was finally revoked in 1989–1990 in the wake of de-Leninisation that led to the mushrooming of diverse political groups. In the absence of a philosophy for the post-revolutionary phase coupled with the backwardness of Russia and the lack of a democratic culture both within Tsarist Russia and the Leninist model, the minority nature of the Bolshevik Revolution reconstructed the state with total power under the guidance of the Vanguard party. This was inevitable since the revolution had to succeed and given its essential minority character, it was impossible to conceive of a majoritarian government.

Debate on the Advanced Capitalist State

Gramsci rightly points out that an advanced state rules by perfecting the ideological apparatus rather than through repressive measures like force and terror. The state consists of two elements—the coercive apparatus comprising of the police, army and judiciary that uphold the authority of the ruling class through force and the other includes various institutions of civil society like media, church, schools, clubs, parties and trade unions, the instruments of hegemony which are the means by which the ruling class secures spontaneous adherence of the rest of the society to comply with its rule. Hegemony allows a ruling group to hold on to power long after it has ceased to be the dominant class. For Gramsci, the tenacity and strength of societal forces within advanced capitalism make it possible for the capitalist class to assert its hegemony. In the process it renders a genuine communist revolution as a virtual impossibility unless carried out in the Leninist manner.

The democratic pluralist view provides the most popular defense of advanced capitalism as a viable and relatively just system. Its major emphasis is that within advanced capitalism there is equality of opportunity, for most, if not all the people, and because of this crucial factor, the concepts of a ruling class, power elite and class politics are largely irrelevant. In these systems 'all the active and legitimate groups in the population can make themselves heard at some crucial stage in the process of decision' (Dahl 1965: 137–138). Since 'the fundamental political problems of the industrial and political citizenship have been solved, conservatives have accepted the welfare state; and the democratic left has recognised that an increase in overall state power carries with it more dangers to freedom than solution to economic problems' (Lipset 1963: 443). This theory of classlessness within advanced capitalism has obvious limitations. Though it is generally conceded that the welfare state has lessened inequalities to a considerable degree by improving living standards of the poorer sections, it is acknowledged that far from any indication of withering away of classes, it continues with inbuilt cleavages. In other words, the Marxist analysis of these societies still retains validity to a very considerable degree.

In recent times, one of the most penetrating class analyses of the welfare state has come from Ralph Miliband, who in his *The State in Capitalist Society* (1969) makes a detailed critique of the pluralist view by asserting the superiority of the Marxist analysis. He begins by examining the concepts of ruling class or the power elite, which the pluralists totally ignore. Advanced capitalist countries are highly industrialised and a large portion of their activity is under private ownership and control. Miliband points out that there is state intervention, of varying degrees, in the economic life. Their economic base is identical, resulting in notable similarities within their social structure and class distribution. A relatively small number of people continue to own a very large and disproportionate share of wealth deriving their incomes from ownership. This class is the ruling class in the Marxist sense. Despite 'all the instances of growing or achieved 'classlessness' ... the proletarian condition remains a hard and basic fact in these societies, in the work process, in the levels of income, in opportunities or the lack of them, in the whole social definition of existence' (Miliband 1969: 16).

These affluent societies also carry with them large sections of people who live in misery. Managerial capitalism is not a selfless neutral institution but maintains definite class interests. They appear social in character but exist largely for private purposes. The social origins of this managerial class are similar to people with large incomes and ownership of property. The elite recruitment is mostly hereditary. Education is very important to rise in the ladder, though the elite institutions are usually accessible to upper and middle classes. The working class students do not get better jobs. The differences among the dominant classes are confined within a given ideological framework. The property owners control the state system. For instance, a very small percentage of the American army officers come from the working class background. It is the same case in Sweden and Japan. The main purpose of the government is to further the interests of capitalism for it, 'genuinely believed in the virtues of capitalism, and, have accepted it as far superior to any possible alternative economic and social system' (Miliband 1969: 70). Contrary to the general belief, the higher civil service is also not neutral. The military maintains close relationships with large-scale business houses. The government appoints judges who in turn appoint conservative judges. All these factors combine to create an imperfect competition. In different ways this process is legitimised. For instance, the bourgeois political parties are in a position to spend more money than the working class ones. Miliband also points out that the most significant political fact of advanced capitalism 'is the continued existence in them of private and ever more concentrated economic power. As a result of that power, the owners and controllers in whose hands it lies, enjoy a massive preponderance in society, in the political system, and in the determination of the state's policies and actions' (Miliband 1969: 265). The basic fact in these societies is that unequal economic power produces unequal political power.

> It is the capitalist context of generalized inequality in which the state operates which basically determines its policies and actions. The prevalent view is that the state in these societies can be and indeed mostly is the agent of a 'democratic' social order, with no inherent bias towards any class or group; and that its occasional lapse from 'impartiality' must be ascribed to some accidental factor external to its 'real' nature. But this too is a fundamental misconception; the state in these class societies is primarily and inevitably the guardian and protector of the economic interests which are dominant in them. Its 'real' purpose and mission is to ensure their continued predominance, not to prevent it (Miliband 1969: 265–266).

The instrumentalist view of Miliband argues that the capitalists use the state as a means for domination in society. The Structuralists like Althusser (1969) stressed the ideological and structural mechanisms that help the ruling class maintain itself in power using both force and consent. Elaborating on Althusser's basic formulations, **Poulantaz** (1973) relates it to the major function of capitalism, namely the reproduction of the capitalist society in its totality. The state along with maintaining the political interest of the ruling class also performs the functions of ensuring cohesion and equilibrium in society in a manner that blurs class divisions. As a result, social relations appear competitive and individual based. Any notion of class and class struggle disappears in that situation. The competitive party system conceals the contradictions, factions and disunity. It does not allow hegemony of any particular class, including the bourgeoisie. Since the state is not the instrument, as Miliband assumes, of a dominant class, it is a relatively autonomous and a stabilising factor. The Structuralist view like the instrumentalist one does not deal with the mechanism of change or the essential reasons for the continuance of the capitalist state.

Anarchist State

The abolition of the state is the goal of both Marxism and Anarchism. However, for the Marxists it is the ultimate end while for the Anarchists the immediate goal. Both regard the state as an end but to the anarchists the state is the basic source of social injustice while to the Marxists its nature is conditioned and determined by the superstructure; it is a tool wielded by the economically dominant class. The state withers away once society becomes classless in the transitional phase, of the dictatorship of the proletariat. The anarchists reject the notion of the dictatorship of the proletariat as it is just another form of state with all its privileges and inequalities. The anarchists not only criticise and reject the capitalist state and parliamentary institutions but also the Communist state. To the Anarchists, the proletarian revolution will end all forms of coercive and superimposed organisations. They reject the Marxist Utopia—the dictatorship of the proletariat—and rightly so on the grounds that it will give rise to fresh set of inequities, privileges, oppression, terror and injustices. The dictatorship of the proletariat will become a dictatorship on the proletariat. They reject statism altogether for it stifles the initiative of the masses and their immediate organs of self government—factory committees and local communes. Not only it undermines the libertarian and emancipatory elements of the revolution but is also inefficient for the central authorities can never ever gauge the pulse of the people at the local level.

Godwin is the first to formulate the economic and political principles of anarchism and the subsequent thinkers reiterate it by refining and adding to it. First and foremost is the rejection of government as it is illegitimate and evil, destructive of individual's moral self-direction. Since it is the major source of corruption in society, it has to be removed to end most of the wrongs in the society. In its place Godwin proposes federalism and localism as principles of political arrangement. **Proudhon** looks to the state, as an evil, for it is coercive, punitive, exploitative and destructive. He locates the origin of the state in human nature and family. His ideal is anarchy reducing political functions to industrial ones with the social order resembling nothing more than transactions and exchanges. Proudhon repudiates class war and opposes trade unionism and does not advocate sudden expropriation of the bourgeoisie and the abolition of the state. He looks to socialism as primarily a solution to a moral problem, namely the deliverance of the individuals from the fetters imposed by the industrial system. He describes communism as police despotism. He visualises society based on equality, law, liberty and independence. The state does not ensure justice, which was ensured only through a series of free contracts between free individuals as producers, who through freely negotiated contracts will produce goods and commodities and would have a right to the entire product of their labour.

Bakunin views the state as the complete manifestation of domination, an unconditional enemy of freedom since he considers history as the 'free inevitable development of the free spirit'. It does not create any precondition of freedom nor does it secure liberty. It destroys human solidarity and denies humanity. Bakunin, contrary to the arguments of the Liberal democrats, believes that local associations, communes and individuals and not the state represents and preserves the common interests in society. The idea of equality of political rights or a democratic state is dismissed as baseless as long a minority rules and oppresses the majority. He describes universal suffrage as a 'fraud' a 'great illusion' for it only consolidates oligarchic rule. The state negates the two basic human needs, namely material well-being and individual liberty. Along with the church and capitalism, it is detrimental to human freedom for it supports violence, conquest, enslavement and brutal suppression of the real people. While the feudal state tries to defend the use of force with the help of the church and god to justify its aristocratic power, the bourgeois state, in addition to church and god uses terms like popular sovereignty and general will to legitimate its power to rule. In spite of the libertarian outlook of the Anarchist doctrine, Bakunin supports the need for a secret organisation of revolutionaries on the Babeuvist model (perhaps inspiring Lenin) and not in masses. The Secret society[4] will inspire and lead spontaneous insurrections of peasants and workers and watch against the revival of any form of state authority. Regarding its role, Bakunin mentions that its members will prevent the re-establishment of the political ruling, and the emergence of a 'guardian state' by helping people to realise complete equality and fullest human freedom. Its members would not aspire for official power and act as 'watchdogs' to prevent the betrayal of the aims and ideals of the revolution. Bakunin like Marx envisages his future anarchist society to be one of abundance. Political power disappears completely for it is an equal society and any kind of inequality virtually amounts to slavery for the proletariat. He demands the complete and immediate abolition of the state and not merely the capture of political power by the victorious revolutionary forces. Bakunin considers federalism as the basis of organising political power in the new society. The basic unit, the small neighbourhood group can be geographical or functional (economic, intellectual or artistic). Agricultural associations and capital and the means of production will appropriate land of industrial associations. Every human being will have the material and moral means to develop his humanity with the right to work, to receive education and lead a life without exploitation. Autonomous communes with men and women enjoying equal rights will represent the majority of the votes of all the adult inhabitants. Political rights will be deprived to those who do not earn their own living. All officials will be elected and their mandates revoked any time with the view to prevent bureaucratisation. Women will be completely emancipated and will enjoy social equality with men. With the abolition of the patriarchal family, marriage law and the right of inheritance, men and women will live in closely united free unions. Women will still be responsible for the upbringing and education of their children with the help of the society. Children thereby will imbibe socialist morality of class and gender equality. For Bakunin, power would be organised from local provinces to the national level and finally at the international level. He prescribes conditions for the realisation of such a federation and advocates the abolition of existing states and their replacement by a new federal structure. Beyond this he does not offer much, for he believes that spontaneity could never be imprisoned in set forms. The principle of 'from the bottom up' is the organising principle of the federation with federating units enjoying the right of succession. Bakunin believes that such a right nullifies the possibility of succession. He favours not only the abolition of private ownership but opposes its expropriation by the whole society, i.e., by the new proletarian society. He fears that the popular government in the transitional period in Marx's conception is in reality, the domination of an educated minority. The anarchist ideal is the Paris Commune of 1871 hailed by Bakunin as a 'bold and outspoken negation of the state'.

Both the Anarchists and the Communists survive the end of the First International. The Anarchist–Marxist duel does not end with the death of Bakunin in 1876 and Marx in 1883. Both Bakunin and Marx recognise that the future society is not the end but the beginning and how it develops depended greatly on the character and decisions taken by the revolutionary movement itself and its organisation. The First International is significant as it highlights the views of the Marxists and the Anarchists, diametrically opposed on the strategy and on the subject of the working class, revolution, state and socialism. Anarchism continues as a critique and as a challenge to Marxism. Lenin faces the Anarchist challenge posed by the German Left and subsequently Bukharin.

As a philosophical anarchist, Gandhi's ultimate aim is the establishment of a stateless society meaning that the state will exist outside the daily life of the ordinary person. Instead of a centralised state power he wants a loose decentralised structure that will provide ample opportunity for the individual's self-development. His ideal is a polity based on equality, self-sufficiency and non-violence, free of conflict between capital and labour. This he characterises as *Swaraj* meaning self-rule and self-control and not just political independence. It means positive freedom or participation of the ordinary person in the process of politics. Real *swaraj* for him does not mean 'acquisition of authority by a few but the acquisition of the capacity by all to resist authority when it is abused. In other words, *Swaraj* is to be obtained by educating the masses to a sense of their capacity to regulate and control authority' (Gandhi 1947: 14). *Swaraj* for him means both political and economic independence, for the first without the second just amounts to replacing an exploitative foreign power by an Indian counterpart. He desires the welfare of the masses, particularly the poor person. He conceives of realising the individual's fullest potential only within a community, thereby sharing Green's idea of the common good. This means abolishing the gap between urban and rural areas, as visualised by Marx and Engels. Gandhi is conscious of the enormous differences that exist between the rural and urban areas in education, culture, medicine, recreation and employment opportunities. Like Marx, Gandhi desires a society free of conflict and strife, which he hopes to achieve through nonviolence rather than as Marx visualises through revolutionary class struggle. Gandhi also distinguishes between the state and society. He opposes the notion of the absolute state sovereignty in the Austianian sense and believes in limited sovereignty. His essential faith in the individual makes him fear an all-powerful state, for most states, in his view, undermine individuality that is necessary for progress. His preference for individual initiative and voluntary efforts makes him accept limited state. At any rate, he never desires complete state control.

Social Democratic State

Unlike Marxism and Anarchism, social democracy emphasises transforming the capitalist state and using it for the benefit and welfare of the workers. Lassalle, following Jean J.C. Louis Blanc (1811–1882), views the state as representing the will of the people as a whole which is why he supports the demand for suffrage, for that enables the people, including the workers to advance their cause. He describes the state as the highest form of human organisation with the purpose of enabling the individuals to maximise and realise their freedom and not merely, as liberals argues, to protect individual freedom and property interests. For Lassalle, socialism means political democracy, universal suffrage, and freedom of press and of association, referendum and trial by jury. He believes that the state provides the framework for the individuals to attain freedom. Therefore, he advocates the need to establish autonomous organisations independent of the bourgeoisie; representation of the working class in the German legislative bodies through universal direct and equal suffrage; establishment of state-aided producers' cooperatives to counter balance capitalism, will to freedom of the majority and appeal to the sense of equity. He remains, however, ambivalent as to whether the state will assume the form of parliamentary democracy or a democratic order based on spontaneous popular will guided by the revolutionary act of the leader, an idea that he borrows from Johann Gottlieb Fichte (1762–1814). Unlike Marx who defends proletarian internationalism, Lassalle's support for German nationalism is on the hope of organising the German working class on a national scale with universal franchise. The Gotha Programme of 1875 incorporates most of his ideas—universal, direct and equal suffrage, state-aided producers' cooperatives under the democratic control of the workers and a democratic republic to be realised through reforms. Lassalle rejects the conception of a night-watchman state and seeks to reform the existing state to become reflective and responsive towards workers' interests. **Eduard Bernstein** (1850–1932) accepts these arguments of Lassalle and emphasises that socialism must not unduly worship the state. Instead, following the arguments of Eugene von Duhring (1833–1921), he points out that the liberal element in socialism must never be sacrificed. He categorically states the need to realise socialism and democracy together. He acknowledges the need to use the existing state for improving the social and economic conditions of the working class.

The Erfurt programme of 1891, that Bernstein helps to frame, demands universal suffrage, equal rights for women, proportional representation, freedom of expression and of association, free and secular schools, local self-government, free legal assistance and medical care, election of magistrates, eight-hour day and prohibition of employment for women and children. The notable point was his assertion that revolutionary violence is not the means to achieve these ends. It was as late as 1959 that the SPD through its 'Bad Godesberg' programme finally renounced revolutionary goals at the level of theory. This programme identified five criteria that formed the core of social democracy: political liberalism, mixed economy, welfare state, Keynesian economics and a belief in equality. Besides the German SPD, even Austrian and Scandinavian social democratic parties have incorporated these ideas. This became the broad consensus between social democracy and liberalism in the post second world war era. It remained dominant till the 1980s when the New Right arose to challenge and revoke the consensus.

Fabian State

Fabianism, distinctively English in origin and nature is the third socialist movement in 1889, the other two being, Continental social democracy (Marxist and quasi-Marxist) and Anarchism or Anarcho-syndicalism. Fabianism represents the form in which the Benthamite tradition accommodates itself to the socialist movement, to become, in due course, the intellectual inspiration of the British Labour Party (Lichtheim 1975: 185). The Fabians, especially Sydney Webb (1859–1947) advocates state socialism by which they mean the extension of existing regulatory and protective functions of the state for the benefit of the working class and the community as a whole, besides envisaging direct transfer of services to social control. From the 1890s, they claim that it is the duty of the state to preserve certain standards below which no citizen shall be allowed to fall. They emphasise on a balance between complete decentralisation in local government and a rigidly centralised state. They hope for the gradual spread of socialism through the state and its institutions, particularly the civil service. They want nationalisation without socialisation, which means transforming state capitalism into state socialism undermining individual initiative. George Douglas Howard Cole (1889–1959) rejects the Fabian identification of collectivism with socialism, for he refuses to agree with their assumption that efficiency of production and justice of distribution are the two most important foundations of a socialist society. For Cole, this means replacing the capitalist state with a bureaucratic one, which can harm society as the individual in this scheme will become a passive recipient rather than remain an active participant in policy formulation and execution.

Weber's Analysis

Weber disagrees with the Marxist premise of the state as part of the superstructure that is determined and conditioned by the economic base. He contends that even if it is possible to transform class relations, the modern state and its bureaucracy cannot be replaced by institutions of direct democracy. This is because only the bureaucracy can resolve the massive task of coordination and regulation. He considers the problems posed by the liberal pursuit of a balance between might and right, power and law as inescapable elements of modernity. He develops one of the most significant definitions of modern state, placing emphasis upon two distinctive elements of its history—territoriality and violence. The modern state, unlike its predecessors, which is distressed by constantly warring factions, has the capability of monopolising the legitimate use of violence within a given territory; it is the nation-state in embattled relations with other nation-states rather than with armed segments of its population. Of course, 'force is certainly not the normal or only means of the state—nobody says that—but force is a means specific to the State ... The state is a relation of men dominating men, a relation supported by means of legitimate (i.e. considered to be legitimate) violence' (Weber 1958:178). The state maintains compliance or order within a given territory; in individual capitalist societies this involves crucially the defense of property and the enhancement of domestic economic interests overseas, although all the problems of order cannot be reduced merely to these. The state's network of agencies and institutions finds its ultimate sanction in the claim to the monopoly of coercion, and only when there is an erosion of this monopoly that a political order becomes vulnerable to crises. Weber's definition brings into focus the third element—legitimacy. The state enjoys monopoly of physical coercion that is legitimised by a belief in the justifiability and/or legality of this monopoly. Today, people do not obey authority as it was earlier when it was obeyed out of habit, tradition or the charisma of individual leaders. Rather there was general compliance by 'virtue of legality, by virtue of the belief in the validity of legal statute and functional competence based on rationally created rules' (Weber 1958: 79). The legitimacy of the modern state is primarily on legal authority, that is, commitment to a code of legal regulations. Weber's foremost concern among the state's institutions is the administrative setup or the bureaucracy consisting of appointed officials representing the rational legal authority. He supports power of private capital, the competitive party system and strong political leadership as countervailing forces against the bureaucracy.

Totalitarian State

The term 'totalitarianism' is first used by **Gentile** in 1916 to describe a seamless identification predicated on a Hegelian universalism that absorbs the elements of society into the totality of the state. It becomes a political term and a theoretical concept after the First World War, to apply to the three radical dictatorial regimes of the inter-war period—Italian Fascism, German National Socialism and Soviet Stalinism. It differs from the earlier absolutist states for it has the capacity to control politically, socially, economically and technologically the mass of their subjects. Hence in this sense, it is a twentieth century phenomenon. **Arendt** (1951) identifies four conditions that form the foundations of the totalitarian state. Firstly, during and after the two world wars, Arendt believes that the class and community breakdown occurs because of rapid industrialisation and the spread of individualistic liberal doctrine. Second, even though the non-politicised mass suddenly become enfranchised then political apathy about democratic procedure(s) makes them vulnerable to demagogic leaders who are able to manipulate them easily. Third, because of the chaos and havoc that the first two conditions cause, a 'negative solidarity' is created. After the confusion that is caused by the war, directionless individuals search desperately for an identity to link themselves back with society. In order to fight against isolation, individuals begin to participate in mass activities like political rallies, membership in political parties or other elements of the political machinery of the party. Fourth, a large population is an essential prerequisite because such states habitually generate internal cohesion and stir up misplaced nationalistic fervour by creating scapegoats on a massive scale. For instance, there was genocide and persecution of the Jews by the Nazis and the **kulaks** (peasants) by the Russians. For **Talmon** (1960), the conditions for totalitarian thinking are—

1. A dominant ideology that offers an explicit vision of the ideal society subordinating everything.
2. A pessimistic conception of human nature as being wicked, weak, selfish, anti-social and irresponsible and in need of guidance.
3. A belief that human beings are incapable of knowing their good because of their imperfections while the leader with the vision of ideal society is acting for its realisation.
4. As a result of this conception of human nature, personal freedom is diminished for greater material security.
5. The whole society is politicised obliterating the distinction between the public and private.
6. Finally, treating the individuals as ciphers with identical wants and needs—enforced homogeneity—and subordinating them to the greater whole, the state that is the locus of supreme political value.

Friedrich and **Brzezinski** (1965: 21–22) list a 'six-point syndrome' that best characterises a totalitarian state, namely (1) an elaborate holistic ideology, (2) single mass party with a leader, (3) system of terror, (4) total control of mass media, (5) monopoly of weapons and (6) control of economy. Ideology forms the most powerful means of perpetuating totalitarianism since it is a tool of persuasion and indoctrination. It appeals to the deep intuitive beliefs of the masses, to their traditions and culture, their fears, hatred and hopes. Despite the varying degrees of differences within the three totalitarian ideologies there are similarities among them with respect to one namely the manipulation of mass hysteria to the extreme.

All the aforesaid three totalitarian states possessed a bureaucratic and hierarchical party led by a single person. Each of these parties emerged after successful revolutionary movements and once in power became the only party to rule ruthlessly suppressing all competition from other parties and groups. The party was crucial, for it was the foundation of ideology through which the legitimacy of the regime flowed from and was a tool that was subjugated to the authority of the leader. Weber classified such a leader as charismatic with supernatural or superhuman qualities subjugating all institutions like the legislature, bureaucracy and their own party to their control. These totalitarian regimes used terror and force to maintain law and order, had a monopoly over communications and invaded the individuals' private space. It exercised total control over defence weapons and the economy with the view to mobilising resources. In Italy, the corporate state; in Germany the attacks on labour and on the property and financial investments of Jews; and in the former Soviet

Union the centrally directed economy, had one common aim, of extracting the maximum surplus value out of the economic mix of labour and capital. Of the three totalitarian regimes, Fascism and Nazism were defeated by the Allied powers during the Second World War. Communism collapsed in the 1990s due to its internal contradictions.

Feminist Critique

Feminists do not have a theory of state but their statements about what constitutes the political has been regarded as a statement on the notion of the state. They do not regard the state to be neutral; instead it not only 'treats women unequally in relation to men' but also 'constructs men and women differently' (Yuval Davis and Anthias 1989: 6). In their view, the state power has been used to enforce control over women in many ways. For instance, one was the policies followed by governments during the two world wars that pressed women into factories, offices and other forms of war work, as men were mobilised for military service. Once the war was over, women were persuaded to return to domestic life for the fear of social unrest caused by male unemployment. Equally important are the welfare policies relating to the grant or withholding of certain child benefits from single mothers. In most countries, the proper role for women in national life is as mothers and as the carriers of their country's unique cultural heritage. Another important aspect is biological, relating to the childbearing capacities that enable them to produce the next generation of male warriors for future wars. Towards this end, population policies have been crucial in encouraging women to have more children as in the nineteenth century France and the erstwhile Soviet Union after 1917.

Fox-Genovese criticises absolutist individualism of feminism on the grounds for failing to 'develop a notion of individual right as a product of collective life' (Ibid 1991: 241). The 'right to choice', according to her, misleadingly accepts 'women's absolute right to their own bodies' (Ibid 1991: 256–257). **Petchesky** (1990) argues for a need to enlarge the right of privacy to include social changes and public efforts that will make choices real for all women. Within individualist rights there is a need to incorporate social rights that will assign the state the responsibility for creating access to medical care, pre-natal care, drug treatment programmes, abortion and other necessities. Eisenstein draws attention to the notion of privacy rights and the equality of needs and the vision of an affirmative and activist and yet non-interventionist state. Such a 'state has to be willing to provide equal access to enable women's bodily integrity. Ensuring this integrity entailed a notion of privacy that is underwritten by sexual and radical equality' (Ibid 1996: 181–182). She desires a non-interventionist state in the realm of private choice but an activist and affirmative one multitude of options. The liberal democratic-patriarchal state, according to her, restricts women's privacy 'which is not defined as a right to reproductive freedom' (ibid 1996: 185). Crucial to the right of privacy are the reproductive issues that involve issues of bodily integrity intimately linked to a person's individual autonomy. Privacy demands that a woman shall have the right to choose the circumstances of her reproductive life that remain elusive to most women, especially the coloured and poor woman. She insists on the need to 'reinventing the liberal individualist language of privacy so that it challenges the inequalities of access women experience in accordance with their race, economic class, geographical location, age, and so on' (ibid 1996: 190). By focusing on reproductive rights it enlarges the issue of abortion to the related concerns—affordable and good health care; a decrease in infant mortality and teenage pregnancy, reproductive health, health services for infertility and access to appropriate contraceptives. Furthermore, such a view situates the question of abortion and privacy rights of women in a realm beyond race and economic class.

Post Colonial State

States that have emerged in the third world after the completion of the decolonisation process differ, both in evolution and nature, from their counterparts in the West. The fundamental difference has been that, in Europe, the nations created the state whereas in the third world it is the state that has supposedly created the nation. With wide social, cultural and economic cleavages this has been a stupendous task, compelling many to turn increasingly to authoritarianism to create the nation-state. With lack of proper institutions and an over-developed colonial state apparatus, the rulers by and large have advanced their own personal interests rather than of the society. Against the backdrop of lack of entrepreneurship, which has consolidated the parasitical bourgeoisie and the middle class as its junior partner, a new clientalism, with a mutually beneficial and reinforcing relationship between the patrons and the clients, has emerged. Legitimate authority in such circumstances has been further eroded by the co-existence of segmented groups of culturally divided people, who in the absence of a well-formulated formula of power sharing, do not consider the state as their primary identity, as it has happened earlier in Europe. This makes majority of the third world states weak, mostly because of continuing with the legacy and instruments of a repressive colonial administration. However, the recent third wave of democratisation, according to Huntington (1992), has created a new climate of optimism and with the overall acceptance of the multi-party democracy, there are indications that the third world states with more elite accommodation and power sharing will move towards the direction of becoming nations.

CONCLUSION

The wide diversity that is reflected in the various theories and practices of the state indicate the extreme complexity of dealing with this important concept. Even after the relegation of fascist and communist states, the debate about the state continues. However, there is a big difference between the arguments now and the ones articulated in earlier times. Today, the debate is within the framework of liberal democracy, between the individualists and communitarians. Owing to a larger consensus between the pluralists and the Marxists, a convergence in broad terms is also visible in the theories of the state, with emphasis both on structure (Marxist-elitist preference) and agency (the pluralist emphasis). However, one major inadequacy of the theories of the state, more in the case of pluralists and less in that of the Marxists, has been its lack of comprehension of the international impact of globalisation, which makes these theories locally dated. In this age of globalisation, a theory of the state must reflect both, on its relative autonomy and subordination in a world where most of the decisions are emerging from centre beyond the jurisdictions and control of the individual nation state.

Further Readings

Block, F., *Revising State Theory: Essays in Politics and Postindustrialism*, Temple University Press, Philadelphia, 1987.

Dunleavy, P. and Leary, B.O., *Theories of the State*, Macmillan, London, 1987.

Entreves, A.P.D., *The Notion of the State*, Clarendon Press, Oxford, 1967.

Hoffman, J., *Beyond the State: An Introductory Critique*, Polity Press, Cambridge, 1995.

Jessop, B., *The Capitalist State*, New York University Press, New York, 1982.

Levine, A. (Ed.), *The State and its Critics*, Edward Elgar, England, 1992.

Oppenheimer, F., *The State*, Free Life Editions, New York, 1975.

Vincent, A., *Theories of the State*, Basil Blackwell, Oxford, 1987.

Endnotes

1. The Young Hegelians were disciples of Hegel in the 1830s or 1840s. The leading members of the group were David Friedrich Strauss (1808–1874), Ludwig Feuerbach (1804–1872), Bruno Bauer (1809–1882) and his brother Edgar (1820–1886), Arnold Ruge (1803–1880), Max Stirner (1806–1856) and Moss Hess (1872–1875). They were republican, democratic, anti theological and revolutionary in their outlook. They tried to dilute Hegelian philosophy from its uncompromising metaphysical idealism. They insisted on the need to overcome alienation and divisiveness and particularity of social life.
2. Croce, the most important opponent of Fascism, points out that long before Fascism Gentile's metaphysics contained Neitzsche's irrationalism rather than Hegelianism.

3. Conservatism in the US has traditionally defended individualism, natural rights, property institutions, limited state and laissez faire, reinforcing Hartz's thesis that the American ideology was predominantly liberal in general and Lockean in particular.
4. Bakunin formed a secret society of his own called the Secret Alliance of Socialist Democracy. This fact was revealed only to his close associates. When the news became public he was expelled from the International Workingmen's Association in 1872 considering its activities as detrimental to the International.

Chapter 5

State
Origins and Developments

The origin and the development of the state have attracted a great deal of attention of practically all the important political thinkers. Like the other concepts in the political theory, important changes are reflected in the understanding of the nature of the state with the changes in political order and the advancement in other areas of human knowledge. The social contract theory in the seventeenth century introduces a radical departure in analysing the relationship between the ruler and the ruled challenging the traditional divine right of kings theory, by arguing that the ruler and ruled are two parties to the agreement and as such, essentially equal. The evolutionary theory provides a more plausible account of the gradual consolidation of the state in its present form.

SOCIAL CONTRACT THEORY

The distinction that the Greeks made between nature and convention is considered by many as the source of the social contract theory. One can find in the writings of the Sophists, **Antiphon**, **Hippias**, **Thrasymachus** and **Glaucon**, the idea of an agreement as the beginning of the origin and organisation of political society. Socrates (469–399 BC) in the *Crito*, illustrates the idea that implies contract and its concomitant obligations between the citizen and the state. Having remained and having enjoyed the benefits of Athens as an adult, he thereby implicitly enters into an agreement with the state to abide by with its laws and thereby accept its authority over him in exchange for those benefits. To the ancient Chinese, political authority is not supernatural and the Emperor is not divine. They justify and defend revolution. Government according to **Confucius** (K'sung Fu Tzu, 551–479 BC) is not a divine institution but a product of human reason and sound virtue. **Mencius** (Meng Tzu, 372–289 BC) even declares that a ruler who departs from reason and virtue could be executed and that a ruler is responsible for the quality of governance and is accountable to his subordinates. Throughout Chinese thought runs an ideal of a ruler who has to ensure the safety and the prosperity of his people. For the Hebrews, the monarch is both an agent of god and a symbol of the people and implies that, besides divine sanction, the monarch needs the support of his people. Hebrew thinkers repudiate the idea that the same person exercise both priestly and kingly functions. They advocate separation, so that the priest checks and criticise the king, if and whenever necessary.

The idea of voluntarism, a crucial idea in the social contract tradition comes to the western social thought with Augustine, who borrows Cicero and Seneca, L. Annaeus' (c. 4 BC–65 AD) *bona voluntas* and broadens it into a pivotal moral concept. Though not a voluntarist or a contractarian, Augustine stresses on a strong nexus between consent and will, thus paving the way for the social contract theory. An Alsatian Monk, **Manegold** of Lautenbach, wrote in 1080, 'If in any way the king transgresses the contract by virtue of which he is chosen, he absolves the people from the obligation of submission'. For Manegold, political authority exists for meeting certain needs of the people. **Aquinas** in whose writings the 'theory of Contract is finally hatched' (Barker 1960: viii) also speaks of artificial relationships, like agreements among a group of individuals to certain legal, economic and political standards. He explains the origin of the state as being a 'kind of pact between king and people'. **Marsilius** argues that people constitute the only legitimate source of all political authority and make laws either by themselves or through elected representatives, and it is the people who elect, correct and, if necessary, depose the government, an idea that Locke subsequently develops elegantly and cogently. **Engelbert** of Volersdorf (1250–1311) is the first to state the idea of what comes to be referred to as an original contract or *pactum subiectionis*, that implies the existence of a pre-political phase in human history. William of **Ockham** (1280/5–1349) and Nicholas of Cusa (1401–64) explicitly highlight the fact that a legitimate political authority depends on the free consent of subjects. Later writers refer to this as the **state of nature**. **Salamonio** in *De Principatu* (1511–1513) like Manegold uses contractarian arguments to place limits on the power of princes. He claims that god and nature create all individuals as equals and the latter finds it necessary to establish kingdoms by an agreement between persons. Salamonio's importance lay in his conception of the political community or state (*civitas*) in Roman law which he terms as a *civilis societas* to mean a partnership made by free contract among individuals. The civil society is a partnership among individual citizens made possible by a contract between them. He considers political society and its laws prior to the creation of the prince. The original contract is between the individual citizens and not between the ruler and people. George Buchanan (1506–1582), during the Reformation, endorses the idea of the contract. Franciso Suarez (1548–1617) argues that free will and consent are the cause of the state; that people will form one political body only on common consent that is voluntary. Richard Hooker (1554–1600) argues that the monarchs and bishops derive their authority from the consent of the community rather than from the divine right. Junius Brutus', (a pseudonymous French Huguenot) *Vindiciae Contra Tyrannos*, written in 1570s, reiterates the existence in all domains of a mutually obligatory contract between the king and his subjects that requires the people to obey faithfully and the king to govern lawfully. A transgression of faith by the prince frees people from their obligation of obedience. Prior to this is also another contract(s) that focusses on the role of the individuals and the government in the divine plan of the universe, as visualised by the Calvinists. This is a covenant between god and the ruler and the people in which the people undertake to honour and serve god, according to His will, revealed in His word. A ruler who destroys true religion shall be resisted for the breach of the fundamental authorising covenant. Johannes Althusius (1557–1638) establishes the authority of all princes and kings on an original contract between each people and its first ruler with a prior contract, the covenant of god that obliges the ruler to establish true religion and the people to resist him, if he does not do so. This is also preceded by a contract by which the political community itself—the people, commonwealth or realm—is first established. Like Salamonio, Althusius argues that these laws bound the ruler, being a part of the original contract between ruler and people. For Althusius, the parties to the commonwealth-forming contract are not individuals but provinces and cities, lesser political units with their government and laws. These are formed prior to the commonwealth by private associations and eventually contracting individuals. Through this hierarchy of contracts, Althusius makes the authority of the commonwealth and in particular its ruler, the supreme magistrate a conditional delegation from its component units and their representatives. This leads to the derivation of the Calvinist doctrine that the lesser magistrates have a duty to resist a tyrannical and ungodly king. Till the time of Althusius, the 'contract theory in politics was mainly invoked in order to justify resistance to rulers' (Lessnoff 1990: 10). The exception to this is Hobbes.

CONTRACT DOCTRINE IN MODERN TIMES

Hugo Grotius (1583–1654), Hobbes, Samuel Pufendorf (1632–1694), Locke, Rousseau and Immanuel Kant (1724-1804) in the seventeenth and eighteenth centuries, use the idea of the social contract to explain the origins and nature of the state and search for philosophical basis to moral and political obligation. Some like **Kant**[1] use the idea of contract to characterise a form of political association and regard it as a rational criterion of the just polity. The crux of the social contract theory is the idea that legitimate government is artificially and voluntarily agreed upon by free moral agents and it rejects the argument that there is something like natural political authority. Wayper calls it the 'Will and the Artifice Tradition'. Hobbes, Locke and Rousseau, the classical exponents of the doctrine of the social contract, produce political prescriptions that are profoundly at variance with one another. **Hobbes** places premium on order and through the contract justifies an all-powerful absolute state. Locke considers consent as the basis of a legitimate political authority and defends a limited constitutional state. Rousseau regards freedom as supreme, which is possible in community based on common interest and, thus, he advances the notion of a moral state. However, common to their perceptions is the idea that an agreement made by all individuals, who compose a state is the true foundation of the body politic. It is not a pact between ruled and rulers but one that establishes rule explained with reference to a transition from the state of nature to a civil state.

The idea of the social contract advances the notion of human equality as a result of the Protestant Reformation,[2] the civil wars that rages in Europe between 1560 and 1660 and the rapid expansion of the commercial economy and market relations. This idea of equality implies that all rule—just and legitimate—are constituted by the ruled, free and equal, and thus rejecting the notion of the rule by right of birth, by divine right, by charisma and by physical force. Most importantly, it rejects the contention, which can be traced back to Plato, that only certain people are qualified to rule over the rest because they have an access to 'truth' whether religious revelation or scientific truth of ideology. Through an agreement between or by a multitude of individuals embedded in the notion of the social contract, isolated individuals voluntarily incorporate themselves into an acting unity, by creating a permanent union between the present contractors and with the successors of the original contractors (Forsyth 1994: 37–39). The classic contractualists also contrast the pre-political—the state of nature—from the political order, to explain the rationale for political society.

The contract theory in the seventeenth century criticise and provide a democratic alternative challenging absolutism and traditional dictatorship, part of the then dominant theory—**Divine Right of Kings**. This theory accepts the proposition that the sovereign rules by divine ordinance or that he is divinity himself. **Augustus** consciously promotes the idea to the government of Rome to legitimise his newfound absolutism. In 1610, in a speech that James I the British monarch delivers, he argued that 'Kings are not only God's lieutenants upon earth and sit upon God's throne, but even by God himself they are called gods' adding that kings 'exercise a manner or resemblance of divine power on earth'. Since the authority of the monarchs is ordained by god himself for the benefit of humankind, the ruler has unlimited and indivisible sovereignty, though they are morally bound to follow the divine law. The theory is popular during the English Civil War in 1640 subsequently. Filmer defends and modifies its arguments in course of the events leading to the Glorious Revolution of 1688.

Grotius stresses that the contract that establishes the civil society constitutes a legal community compatible with individual's natural sociability and conforms to mutual recognition and protection of his moral rights. He believes that the contract actually takes place prior to the state in every community governed by law. Like Grotius, Hobbes considers self-preservation as a basic right. Through the state of nature, he portrays the dismal human existence since it prohibits the possibilities of commodious living that makes life meaningful and worthwhile. In the absence of a common power to keep individuals in awe, there are no legal or moral rules, no notions of right and wrong, justice and injustice. There is no property and each can take whatever he can get and so long as he can keep it. This state of nature is a state of war, 'a war of every man against every man'. Natural freedom and natural equality of individuals in the state of nature are the reasons for this intolerable and insecure life.

> In such condition there is no place for Industry, ... no Culture of the Earth; no Navigation, nor use of the commodities that may be imported by Sea; no commodious Building; no Instruments of moving such things as require much force, no knowledge of the face of the earth; no account of Time, no Arts; no Letters, no Society; and which is worst of all, continual fear, and danger of violent death; And the life of man, solitary, poor, nasty, brutish and short (Hobbes 1991: 89).

The contract between one individual and the others enables them to come out of the state of nature, which is made possible due to the presence of natural laws. These natural laws are nineteen in all. Of these nineteen, three are most important. These are (a) seek peace and follow it; (b) abandon the natural right to things and (c) that individuals must honour contracts. There is just one contract, perpetual and irrevocable, that creates both the civil society and an absolute political authority. The sovereign power, the third party, is a consequence and not a party to the contract. There is no question of individuals first contracting amongst themselves and then with the ruler thereby circumscribing his powers. Hobbes considers it the power of the sovereign to enforce contracts and make them binding.

Pufendorf criticises Hobbes and goes back to the older notions of 'two contracts' for he argues that individuals establish a sovereign without obtaining in return a promise of protection. Therefore, there must first be a contract to establish a political community, followed by a second one, between the community and its ruler. Interestingly, he does not concede the right of resistance, sharing Hobbes' perception that the pre-political state of nature is intolerable and the supreme political authority is by definition not accountable to or punishable by any person. The social contract creates the 'person of the state', demanding almost complete obedience. The state has a personality that is distinct from the people who institute it. The state is a moral person with a will and capacity to bear rights and duties that none of the individual comprising it could claim in their own right. The aim of the state was to ensure the security of its citizens.

Locke develops Pufendorf's arguments convincingly. He restores the traditional role of the contract theory as a justification of resistance to government. However, he does not follow Pufendorf's multiple contracts and his tasks are twofold—first, to refute Filmer's criticisms of contractualism and second, to explain the origins of legitimate political authority. The *First Treatise* rejects the central arguments of Filmer,[3] which are reiterated in the *Second Treatise* and these four arguments are discussed as follows:

1. God does not give the relevant power to Adam.
2. Assuming Adam had been granted this power does not mean that his heirs would also have a right to it.
3. Even if Adam's heirs do have such a right, there are no clear rules of succession according to which the rightful heirs could be named.
4. Even if there were such rules, it would be impossible to identify Adam's actual heirs, considering the time span since God's original grant of power to him (Locke 1960: 307).

Through the technique of the social contract, Locke explains that consent is the basis of a legitimate political authority. Like Hobbes, he too begins with the idea of the state of nature. He rejects Filmer's biblical account of the origins of political power, without abandoning its religious foundations and acknowledges an explicit moral relationship between an individual and god. To preserve oneself and the well-being of others is a duty that an individual owed to god as part of god's creation as the basic of moral law of nature, that exists in the pre-political state of nature. Like Grotius and Pufendorf, Locke views the state of nature as a social condition regulated by god's moral law. Political authority, like all moral claims for Locke, is ultimately based on religious obligations, the source of all morality. He uses the contract as a means to create a body politic but concurrently as a device, to subordinate the body politic to the 'Kingdom of God'. This is in sharp contrast to the rigid secularism of Hobbes, who refuses to begin from absolute moral presumptions, seeing the social contract as creating a temporal political power for fulfilling external peace, security and earthly felicity (Forsyth 1994: 39–40). Locke makes a cogent case for the need of contract in two stages and for two types of consent. The first contract creates the civil society from the state of nature, to which the individual contract directly consents and agrees to submit to the majority rule principle as the basis of decision-making. Unlike Hobbes, who considers the civil society as uniting otherwise morally unrelated individuals, Grotius, Pufendorf, Locke and Emmerich de Vattel (1714–1767), regard the civil society with its ensuing obligations as superimposed upon a universal moral community, thus, resulting in potential conflicts between one's duties as a citizen and a human being. While for Grotius, the universal moral community of humankind is declared as a real constraint upon the activities of the state, Locke, Pufendorf and Vattel gradually place the state at the centre of international relations. They endorse a process that attains formal recognition and is greatly made easy by the Peace of Westphalia of 1648. The state becomes the principal moral entity through which the interests of individuals are expressed in the international society of states.

The provision for an explicit consent as declaration of one's allegiance at becoming an adult exists in the constitution of Carolina in the United States, one that Locke helps to draft. The second contract creates political authority with all its institutions—legislature, courts and socially authorised property arrangements—in the nature of a 'fiduciary' power, a trust. Tacit consent enables successor generations to consent to the arrangement upheld by the original contractors, thus, circumventing Filmer's criticism. Three indicators demonstrate tacit consent—the first is when a person possesses and enjoys property and transmits it to his heirs, which means he is obliged to the laws of that government, the second is when a person lodges for a week and third, when he is travelling freely on the highway. Thus, unlike Hobbes, who in spite of providing a contractual and consensual basis to his sovereign power, accepts not only political absolutism but also the fact that this absolute sovereign is self-perpetuating, Locke is a thoroughgoing contractualist. Hobbes rejects the premise but not the conclusion of the divine right theory, thus being midway precariously perched between a tradition that he does not thoroughly reject and the new, which he does not completely embrace. Locke, on the other hand, rejects political absolutism, the divine right theory and patriarchialism. He provides for a two-staged process to create the government with two types of consent, to counter Filmer's defense of the divine basis of royal absolutism.

Rousseau uses the contract as a hypothesis to throw light on the human condition. He praises and dismisses the idea of social contract simultaneously. He criticises Grotius, Hobbes, Locke and Pufendorf for reading back into the natural condition of attributes and desires peculiar to civil society. Having identified inequality as the malaise of modern society, he uses the contract in the *Social Contract* (1762) to design the right society to transform it into a just body politic from the one that is corrupted by self-interest. He tries to instill a strong sense of the community of ancient Sparta and thus dilutes individualism. He retains the voluntarist theory of political obligation to legitimise sovereign authority by basing it on consent. Individuals would have both liberty and law if they are able to construct a society where they rule themselves through a contract of association that is not a pact of submission. Through the contract, the individual expresses his reciprocal commitment to his fellow contractors and also as a member of the state in relation to the sovereign that is deemed to possess a moral personality. The contract is between a collectivity that is a single moral person and each of its members taken individually. This collectivity is always right and always tends to the public good. Rousseau, like Hobbes, maintains that the individuals of the two contracting parties are responsible for upholding the terms of the contract, thus, arriving at the same conclusion as Hobbes but through a different route. Unlike Locke, for Rousseau the foundational contract is a mechanism that regulates the required balance between rights bearing individuals and government, or of obtaining the liberal functioning of institutions. For Rousseau, just like Hobbes, the contract is constitutive of society itself, with a difference in the ends that it envisages. For Hobbes, the ends are civil peace and commodious living, while for Rousseau it is to ensure that individuals unite without renouncing their liberty and the moral advancement of the components of civil society. The individual lost, through the social contract, his 'natural liberty and the absolute right to anything that tempts him and that he can take: what he gains by the social contract is civil liberty and the legal right of property in what he possess' (Rousseau 1958: 42). The contract replaces arbitrary relation that exists between persons with obedience of the citizen to the law and for this purpose, atomistic individuals with different wills transform themselves into a community with a common will or interest. For Rousseau, consent is the basis of society but emphasises the importance of the community along with the need to protect individual freedom. He attempts to reconcile the claims of the individual with that of the community through the notion of the general will that emerges in an assembly of equal lawmakers. He categorically asserts that each person is free only if he obeys his own will that finds expression in the laws of the state of which he is the lawmaker. He visualises a free state as a consensual and also the existence of participatory democracy. Rousseau is a critic of 'the fraudulent liberal social contract' (Pateman 1985: 142–162). The liberal contract, argued Carole Pateman (1940–), served to justify social relationships and political institutions that already existed, while Rousseau's contract provides 'an actual foundation for a participatory political order of the future'. It is one of associations based on self-assumed obligation and of substantive equality between 'active citizens who are political decision-makers'.

CRITICS OF THE CONTRACT DOCTRINE

The use of the contract along with its attendant idea of consent has its criticisms and limits. Many critics find its language inappropriate because it suggests that the obligation to obey authority, and even its very legitimacy, depends upon an original agreement by which succeeding generations are bound or a continuously renewed agreement that can be revoked if its conditions are not met. The contract doctrine has been criticised for its historical ambiguity, unfeasibility and defective logic. Filmer's long forgotten *Patriarcha or the Natural Power of the King* written in 1653–1654 but published in 1680 is important, for it forms part of the context in which the social contract doctrine emerges in the sixteenth and seventeenth centuries. Locke and his fellow revolutionaries Tyrrell and Sidney criticise Filmer's theory. Many of Filmer's arguments resonate in the contemporary feminist critiques of contractarianism and that of Pateman. Modern contractarians like Rawls, attempt to resurrect Kant while simultaneously responding to Hegel's criticisms of Kant. Most of the recent liberal/communitarian debate has labouriously tried to stress how neo-Kantianism can avoid the Hegelian inspired communitarian debate.

Filmer contends that patriarchal authority is absolute and analogous to political authority. Having created Adam, god gives him authority over his family, the earth and its product. Adam is the first king and the present kings derive their rightful authority from this grant. Adam is thus the first king and the first father and the subsequent generations of men are not born free, but subjects to Adam and his successors with the powers of the father derived from

God. Fathers, or patriarchs and their successors, exercise a natural authority that is inherent in the family, and command a natural obligation, that of children to their father. Fatherly authority for Filmer is both real and abstract. It inheres in natural fathers but it is not necessarily congenital: it is the authority that is natural, not the line of its decent. Filmer argues that kings are not now as they once were, the natural fathers of the families over which they rule, but 'they all either are, or are reputed to be, the next heirs to the first progenitors' (1991: 10). Sons who are not themselves fathers, but who become heads of households or states, exercise the authority attached to the office. Hence queens, in the absence of kings, exercise paternal rather than maternal authority. Since God's original grant to Adam is unconditional, monarchial rule is also unlimited. Any attempt to restrain absolutism results in a limited or mixed monarchy. Divided sovereignty weakens authority. Filmer does not support the idea of divided sovereignty though he makes the monarch obey God's laws.

Filmer criticises contractualism, contending that if contractual arguments are true, then it results in two unacceptable consequences, which its advocates find hard to explain. First, it is not possible to provide for a continuing valid political authority. If all authority is vested on consent, then an individual who has not consented is not bound by the laws, implying that minorities, dissenters, non-voters (women and children) need not obey the law and the new ruler, since one has not consented to them. If the original contractors who establish society are free, then each generation (unless it consents) is not bound to obey the laws. This makes the society unstable. If, on the contrary, one contends that succeeding generations have to obey because their father and forefathers had expressed their consent, then such argument is no different from the one championed by the patriarchists. Filmer argues, contrary to the contractualists, that men are not born free but into families, and hence subject to the authority of their fathers. There is nothing like natural liberty and equality. Individuals confer their authority upon a ruler, because they have none. Natural rights exist but they are not universal for 'there is, and always shall be continued to the end of the world, natural right of a supreme father over every multitude' (Filmer 1991: 11). Fathers have natural rights and the power to consent to the transfer of their authority to another party. Such transfers are however unconditional because the power exercised is not derived from consenting heads of families, but is merely substituted by God and acknowledged by them. Moreover, relationships of subordination are natural and that individuals are not equal for a son is subject to the authority of his father. The second argument is related to property rights. Filmer thinks that those who explain the origin of government with reference to consent of free individuals find it difficult to establish either feasible or morally acceptable political authority or rightful private possession of goods. Filmer, like many of his contemporaries, adheres to the view that each individual is God's property and does not have a right to take his own life. It is therefore absurd to harbour the idea that consenting individuals confer a power that they do not themselves have, namely that of life and death, upon a sovereign. Only God has this power and it is He who confers it upon kings. Locke not merely refutes Filmer's patriarchal theory but also rejects his critique of contractualism as absurd by providing an explanation about the origins of political power and private property.

In the eighteenth century, many try to explore 'the true foundation of society' but without using the social contract theory and its attendant idea that society is a mere collection of individuals whose psychological ends conclude in social institutions. Montesquieu insists that human beings need to be reminded that they live in society and are 'governed by many factors: climate, religion, law, the precepts of government, the examples of the past, customs, manners; and from the combination of such influences there arises a general spirit'. The individual is shaped by the particular social associations in which he lives. Political and moral systems are to be judged in terms of the social context in which they exist.

Maistre provides a more extreme defense for natural authority by rejecting the contractarian conception of the individual as a free and equal subject. He directs his arguments against European Enlightenment and French revolutionaries in general, and against Rousseau's conception of natural equality and popular sovereignty, in particular. Like Filmer, he regards human being's natural condition as social. Unlike the former's subtle charges against the contract doctrine, Maistre's arguments are a more virulent attack on the presumption of human beings to challenge a divine injunction and god's authoritative will. The contract theory's attempt to justify political authority and political obligation are seen as examples of human beings' sinful pride. It is precisely because of this that there is a need for unquestionable political authority in the person of the monarch. Any attempt to establish equal civil or political authority only results in barbarism and chaos. Maistre perceives human nature and human condition to be similar to that of Hobbes but does not consider it necessary to derive political authority from contractarian arguments. Instead it is the divinely instituted and authoritative will of god. He does not merely reject contractarianism but any effort to question, legitimise or circumscribe political authority, thus, forming an important source for extreme anti-rationalist conservatism. Lamennais too rejects Rousseau's contract theory, dismissing it as absurd for no society visualised as a random collection of individuals coming together by chance has ever originated in this manner. Furthermore, any pact has sanctions to ensure its implementation but Rousseau's has none that will stop the people from reclaiming their sovereignty. The social contract according to Lamennais reduces society into one vast realm where private interests dominate, for governments act purely for self-preservation and aggrandisement. Having dethroned God and kings, it has also dethroned human beings, reducing them to animals with consequences like turmoil and revolution. For Constant, the fact that Rousseau does not acknowledge any limits is the most serious threat to liberty. Proudhon perceives Rousseau's contract to be one of hatred, 'an offensive and defensive alliance of those who possess against those who do not possess'. Proudhon proposes a 'free contract' that leads to the dissolution and eventual disappearance of the state, which he thinks is possible if one moves away from politics to economics. A proper contract is not between the ruled and ruler, as Rousseau contends, but between individuals, as individuals for equal exchange of goods and services of equal value and that each individual is perfectly independent. This is possible when there is perfect equilibrium. Reacting to the excesses of the French Revolution and fearing its adverse effects on England, **Burke** points out that the overall structure of society cannot be reduced to a mere contract between two or more parties similar to a trade agreement, that is more transient and which can be dissolved by the parties involved. Society, in his memorable words,

> is a partnership in all science, a partnership in all art, a partnership in every virtue and in all perfection. As the ends of such a partnership cannot be obtained in many generations, it becomes a partnership not only between those who are living, but between those who are living, those who are dead and those who are to be born. Each contract of a particular state is but a clause in the great primeval contract of eternal natures, connecting the visible and invisible world, according to a fixed compact sanctioned by the inviolable oath which holds all physical and all moral natures, each in their appointed place (Burke cited in Curtis 1961b: 59).

Paine criticises Burke by reiterating Locke, that government is an outcome of a social contract between the people themselves. He criticises the British constitution for being unwritten and hence unhelpful as a reference point. Its precedents are all arbitrary, contrary to reason and common sense. Hume is the most virulent critic of the social contract theory and in his criticisms there is no reference to either the theory of Divine Right or that of patriarchy. In *A Treatise of Human Nature* (1739–1740), he submits that societies are prior to governments and the most likely reason why governments come into existence is not because of disagreement between members of the same society but external threats and conflicts. The sudden dangers to which societies are vulnerable necessitate retaliatory and immediate authoritative responses and a single individual assumes charge. Hume argues that this natural origin of monarchy is perhaps more convincing than the argument that it is derived from the natural right of patriarchy. He points out that most of the present governments, except for some stray cases, are not established through consent or contract, so there is no universal acceptance of the theory, a point that influences Bentham. Even if it is assumed that some kind of contact has taken place at an earlier time, the old contract cannot bind future generations. Authority in the long run is based on necessities of circumstances and not on consent. Not only in Persia and China but even in Holland and England, where consent is proclaimed as the basis of authority most people do not remember when they gave their consent. Nor is there any record of their ancestors giving their consent. As far as tacit consent is concerned, Hume points out that even if this is a criterion of consent, it is one that can never be applied. Most places fall under some jurisdiction and those that do not are without the necessary conveniences and comforts of the existing system, whatever the basis of its legitimacy. He concludes that the social contract doctrine is superfluous and unnecessary. He accepts the contention of Grotius and Pufendorf that the civil society is formed because of self interest but regrets their conclusion to base political obligation in the natural law of keeping faith with one's promises. He concedes that while consent is the basis of legitimising the origins of government it is the interest that ensures the continuing existence of its authority. As governments secure peace and commodious living, it is not direct or tacit consent, but one's interests that obligate one to render obedience. Hume's defense of authority and obedience is akin to Burke but, unlike the latter, he does not exalt virtues of tradition and convention but regards self interest as the basis of obligation. Bentham rejects the social contract as pure fiction and points out that the binding force of a contract comes from a government and from the habit of enforcement and not vice-versa. This habit of obedience will continue as long as the ruler(s) acts in the interest of the ruled or more precisely if it is possible to maximise the greatest happiness of the greatest number.

Hegel rejects the contract doctrine, for it assumes separateness and autonomy of the individuals rather than their unity. Paradoxically, he accepts voluntarism, a core idea of the contract doctrine. He points out that in modern times claims are made for private judgement, private will and private conscience whereas in pre-modern times individual wills coincided with the will of the state. The contract doctrine, according to Hegel, conceives the state as a voluntary association with obligations freely chosen and accords priority to private over public right, ignoring the fact that the former is dependent on the latter and not the other way around as the contract theory claims. The state is not a contractual institute for the protection of property rights of the individuals nor is it a private property of the monarch. The state is an ethical arrangement in which individuals realise their capacities. They are born into it with the capacity to acquire rights and duties that have originated as a result of human practices and which the state can sustain and do not choose it with natural rights. Hegelians and post-Hegelian German philosophers stress the organic unity, individuality and moral autonomy of the state and reject the contractarian arguments for its legitimacy. Bluntschili criticises Pufendorf and Locke, and to a lesser extent Kant, for not considering the will of the person of the state as composed of the wills of each individual. Bluntschili considers the social contract theory as historically and logically absurd. Marx accepts Hegel's contention that the individual was a social creation and criticises abstract individualism espoused by the contract doctrine. However, unlike Hegel for whom the state fulfils a person's rational nature, Marx believes in the emergence of a genuine community after the withering away of the state following a revolutionary transformation of society. Interestingly, recent communitarianism deriving inspiration from Hegel's anti-contractarianism accepts the community as a moral ideal and rejects Rawls' Kantian contractarianism. The feminists focus on the contract doctrine for its conception of the natural condition of the individual as being one of freedom and equality. Pateman considers the whole conception of society as a contractual association between free and equal citizens as part of the problem that needs to be addressed if women are to free themselves from the male dominance of modern societies. Locke, Kant and Rousseau are criticised because they explicitly exclude women from the class of rational subjects who consent to political rule. Moreover, the idea of the individual as a free and equal subject is a male classification because it accepts the pre-existing sexual division of labour that entrusts women with the tasks and responsibilities of the domestic sphere thereby freeing the man to concentrate on the public or political realm. Pateman (1988) points out that with few exceptions most contractarians conceived of women as subordinates of men with the establishment of the civil society. She does not agree with the claim of the contractualists that they have defeated patriarchy for what they have done is to replace fraternity with patriarchalism—father's right to rule. The sexual dominance of men over women replaces the dominance of the fathers over women. By maintaining relations between sexes as private, the liberal theorists remove the subject from political enquiry, thus doing little to alter the status of women. By disregarding women as individuals in the same way as men, even reforms that grant them contractual opportunities as similar as men cannot alter the sexual basis of the social contract. She concedes that identifying the sources of women's subordination is only the beginning of reconstructing politics and institutions free from sex inequality. Coole (1993), agreeing with Pateman, points out that the idea of social contract, both in its individualism and a theory of justice, operates with masculinity as its norm.

EVOLUTIONARY THEORY

The evolutionary theory contends that the state is a product of historical growth and gradual evolution and that a variety of factors have contributed to its emergence. Among these the main factors that have helped in the formation of the state are kinship, religion and political consciousness. The first of the earliest societies is the family. The desire to reproduce motivates the adolescent to move outside the old family and form a new one. Each new family is a union of two families. The kin comes into existence when consanguinity is recognised and grows into an order of society. The kin-relationship, according to **MacIver**, is a time-bracket while the political structure that binds the families and individuals that it includes is space-bracket. An ordering of society is not possible if human beings are merely conscious of their common descent through time; rather they have to be conscious of their present common interest and common nature. Kinship is reinforced by social relationship.

In the early kin-relationships, maternity is a far more definitive guide than paternity and the bond between the mother and her children is stronger and lasting than that of fatherhood, thereby, making it easy to trace descent through the mother and giving the family the misnomer of a matriarchal family. Sometimes, custom ordains that the bridegroom must leave his home and his people and enter the family group to which his bride belongs. In certain cases, the chief or king owed his office to the right that marriage grants and which he stands to lose in the event of the death of his spouse. However, all these do not mean that the female wields any power or exalted position, for, in reality, she is only a representative of transference. On closer examination, it also reveals that the wife and the mother have a social rather a personal status that offset man's natural dominance. With development of authority and growth of organisations, men gain dominance of groups mainly because of their physical superiority. Domestication of wild animals, increased wealth and control of property, pursuit of pastoral industry and the institution of slavery reinforced this dominance. Of these factors, control of wealth and property is the most important for that give social dominance to the male.

The early patriarchal society is organised on the basis of kinship through males. Women are regarded as a form of property and polygamy is common. The patriarch has complete control of the home and with his death the eldest male descendant carries forward the authority. From the original patriarchal group probably there are groups and sub-groups, each headed by a male who forms the council of elders and assists the patriarch. The patriarch later becomes the tribal chieftain and acquires military, judicial and religious authority. The patriarchal society is governed with the help of customs that play a more important role than law in the absence of definite sense of morality or legality. The patriarch enforces customs becoming both the judge and executioner simultaneously. In the course of time, custom develops into law. The state arises when authority becomes government and custom is translated into law. The patriarchal society differs from the modern society in being personal rather than territorial. Since kinship is the cementing factor, the entire group migrates with its organisation intact. The early kings are kings of their people and not of their land. The patriarchal society is exclusive, confining its membership to its people and it keeps strangers out. It is non-competitive and communal where the group, their freedom and rights are all that matters.

The next important factor in the rise and growth of social consciousness and state is religion. According to Gettel, kinship and religion are considered to be identical. Common worship reinforces kinship by disciplining the early man to authority. Patriarchal religion is universally ancestor worship, for that ensures a sense of continuity and immortality and therefore, enforces strictly within the group. Rituals, like annual offering to the dead, create a sense of bond among the descendents. When the patriarch becomes the tribal chief, he also assumes the role of high priest interpreting customs and often the magic-man or the medicine man. The combination of earthly authority with religious authority gives the chief a sense of aura and that instills reverence and awe in his followers. When the patriarchal tribe begins to expand by incorporation or conquest, nature worship arises to reinforce patriarchal religion. Religion and political rule are so intertwined that it is difficult to differentiate the two. Obedience to law and authority rests largely on the divine power of the ruler and in the sacredness of immemorial institution.

Another important factor that explains the rise of the state is political consciousness. Once the early man settles down in a territory and took to cultivating the land and domesticating cattle, population begins to increase, wealth accumulates and the idea of property develops. Economic life becomes complex and diverse necessitating an organisation that ensures order, security and protection to person and property. The state steadily grows with help of war and conquest, for more land is needed for the growing population and its needs. War and conquest help in not only extending the area of government but also consolidating political power. The victors in war become kings and nobles giving rise to stratification in the society. Once the state comes into existence, it develops from simple forms to complex forms. The modern state, the now familiar entity, goes back to the sixteenth century.

RISE AND DEVELOPMENT OF THE MODERN NATION STATE

This section examines the factors about the rise of the nation states in Europe and as to why the nation state became the supreme form of the modern state. The creation of nation states in Europe has contributed to the distinct identity that Europe has. The state system of Europe has exerted exceptional influence in the world beyond Europe, for European colonisation has positively drawn the political map of the modern world.[4] It is interesting, for a larger part of human history, human beings have lived without states but not without governments. States are historical phenomena emerging under particular conditions changing and quite fluid, without actually being fixed. The pre-state political communities were enormously divergent—all the more so since they often developed out of each other, interacted with each other, conquered each other and merged with each other to produce infinite varied forms, most of them hybrid. It may be possible to classify these into (1) tribes without rulers (2) tribes with rulers, (chiefdoms) and (3) city-states.

Tribes without Rulers

There are no states where human beings lived in hunting and gathering communities, small agrarian units and the regions inhabited by sparsely populated nomadic and semi-nomadic people. Even today anthropologists point out to communities that have no states, for example, the Jale Pale of the New Guinea highlands, the pastoral Anuak, Dinka, Masai and Nuer of the South Sudan, the M'dendeuile and Arusha of East Africa and some pre-Columbian Amerindian tribes in North and South America. In all these, government is the extended family, lineage or clan. None is superior except for men, elders, parents and no one is inferior except for women, young and children. The kin defines social relations and its rights and obligations. Within the kin, one's sex, age and marital status determine an individual's position. In the absence of institutional authority, except for what operates within an extended family, these societies are egalitarian and democratic. All adult males are equal. Public tasks are performed not by rulers and ruled but by leaders and followers. The absence of centralised authority also means the absence of permanent, specialised war-making armed forces or even popular militias. None of these societies have a system of rent, tribute or taxation that redistributes wealth, or a class of individuals with leisure. Institutional religion hardly plays any role and every household chief is also his own priest. However, the priest does not have the right to command obedience, levy taxes, have an organised following to enforce their wishes and do not exercise command in war and their methods are persuasion and mediation but not coercion.

Chiefdoms

These existed in many societies in Southeast, West and South Africa, as well as over Southeast Asia, Polynesia, Hawaii and New Zealand. History tells us of tribes that destroyed the Mycenean civilisation and ruled Greece between 1000 and 750 BC. These tribes were the various Gothic, Frankish and other Germanic tribes as they were from the later centuries of the Roman empire and the Scandinavian tribes during the tenth century just before they became Christianised and turned towards more centralised forms of government. In chiefdoms, the chief had an elevated position over other people with the right to command them. This right claimed as divine became the basis of succession from father to son. This led to frequent clashes and warfare. Most of these societies were polygamous. Women for their looks or their noble lineages were status symbols for their owners. Their labour was also a source of wealth. The natural result of polygyny was a large number of sons, candidates for succession when the time came, resulting in potential conflicts. Normally, the chief's first or principal wife was descended from an eminent family and her offspring(s) enjoyed precedence over the rest. Next to the chief, the society was divided into two different layers or classes—privileged group, small and consisting of the chief's extended family, lineage or clan. They enjoyed special rights like access to the chief, a higher compensation in case of injury or death and immunity from certain kinds of punishment that were considered degrading. They wore special insignia and clothing and, in areas with moderate climate, they were distinguished by tattoos. Their position in the society depended exactly on their relationship with the chief. From these people, the chief selected the provincial rulers and since they had some claim to succession, they were rarely appointed to senior court positions. Below the royal lineage or clan is the numerous classes of commoners: like the ancient Greek labourers or *thetes*, subject to different kinds of discrimination, like not being allowed to own cattle (the Hutu in Burundi and Rwanda), ride stallions (the bonders in pre-Christian Scandinavia), wear feather headgear (the Americas) or bear arms. In an event of injury or death, they got very little compensation and their punishment was savage. They were not blood relations of the chief. In parts of Africa, the chief and the commoners belonged to different ethnic groups and did not share the same customs or speak the same language. The commoners owed allegiance to the chief. The chief had extensive powers, especially, in large territories, he stood at the apex of a pyramid consisting of regional sub-chiefs. The chiefdoms became the first political entities to institute rent, tribute and taxation, forms of compulsory unilateral payments from the ruled to the rulers leading to concentration of wealth in the ruling few. The precise nature of the wealth paid depended on the resources made possible by the environment and also on custom. Everywhere it consisted of staple crop like rice and grain. There could be prestigious objects also, like the fine domestic animals, clothes in various forms and in some societies, women. Some of the tributes paid to the chief's storehouses were directly by his tenants. The rest of the population made payments to the sub-chiefs who, having collected them, took their cut which was not fixed, and depended on how much they could get away without inviting the wrath of the chief and passed the rest on. Both the chiefs and sub-chiefs possessed additional sources of revenue originating in their right to exercise justice, like fees, fines, the belongings of condemned persons and often bribes. There also existed some form of licensing system under which chiefs of all ranks demanded and received payment for granting their subjects certain privileges like the right to hold markets, engage in long-distance trade, go on raiding expeditions against other tribes (part of the booty went to the chief) and so on. In short, there was hardly any economic activity in which the chief was not involved and from which he did not get his share.

City States

These were overwhelmingly rural with a livelihood that was hunting, gathering, cattle-raising, fishing and agriculture practiced at the subsistence level. Most of these people were nomadic or semi-nomadic. There were three types of cities initially. The majority were ruled by petty chiefs, known as *lugal* in ancient Middle East, wanax in the Mycenean world and *kshatriya* in India. This type differed from the chiefdoms, mainly by their more sophisticated administrative system and a more complex social structure. The second type of cities were not independent communities but served as either capitals or as provincial centres like Mesopotamia in 235 BC, China from the time of the first imperial dynasties; India during the periods of centralised empire (320–185 BC, AD 320–500 and AD 1526–1707) and pre-Columbian Latin America. The third type comprised the self-governing cities that existed in pre-dynastic Mesopotamia confined to the Mediterranean littoral. Only in such self-governing cities were Greeks,

Romans and possibly also Etruscans and Phoenicians (Carthage) able to come up with a new principle of government.

> The earliest important political organization was the *polis* or the city-state in Greece that began as a common association for the security and for the satisfaction of daily needs but gradually became the pivot around which all human activity—moral, intellectual, social, cultural, aesthetic and practical life revolved. The Greek archipelago consisted of many islands among which Athens, Crete and Sparta were well-known. Mountainous terrain, valleys and rivers physically separated these islands. In spite of their territorial and political separateness, the Greeks shared cultural and social unity due to one language, common religious rituals and Olympic festivals. The Greeks never called themselves Greeks but Hellas. Most of the city-states were small and compact in size and population. Athens between 750–550 BC had 40,000 square miles of territory and 40,000 citizens and 400,000 mixed populations. The limit on size was important, for the Greeks were convinced that good order could be sustained only in small cohesive communities. The city state was both self-sufficient and self-governing and a cradle to the ideas of democracy, constitutional government and the due process of law, which were transmitted through Rome to the modern Europe. Rome also put into practice the Stoic idea of a universal society and the need for a uniform system of law. A number of textbooks, case books and codes of law were devised by a group of trained lawyers at the level of theory and for practical use of officials. The Romans established a system of jurisprudence as a system of general rules by which actions could be classified clearly with definitions. Gaius', Paulus' and Ulpian's treatises were systematic delineations of constitutional and political institutions. In order to unify the divergent peoples within the empire, to deal with the colonies it had conquered, to deal with aliens, to advance the idea of common citisenship and to settle commercial cases with foreign traders, a system of law was needed and that was provided by the formulation of a law of nations (*jus gentium*). This worked alongside the Stoic law of nature (*jus naturale*), the law common to all nations and the law common to all human beings. Roman lawyers also attempted to distinguish between public law—in essence constitutional law—and private law that which concerned private individuals and the institution of private property. Roman law is still a monumental achievement in its clarity and practicality. The Roman concept of a scientific jurisprudence has influenced the whole of Western thought (Curtis 1961 Vol. 1: 117).

Approximately sixteen hundred years ago, Roman Empire under Theodosius I (379–395 AD) was the last sole ruler and that split after his death in to Western and Eastern Roman Empires. In comparison to the East, the western side of the Empire sustained recurring attacks and thus became weak. In AD 410, the city of Rome was attacked by roaming Germanic tribes and fell in 476 AD following the dethroning of the last Roman Emperor of the West.

The Eastern portion was economically safer than the West because the export trade in spices and other commodities continued through the Middle Ages until the Islamic Ottoman Empire challenged it in 1453. The centuries following the disintegration of the Roman Empire saw no another imperial power in Europe, which continued to be ravaged by wars. The political map continued to be drawn and redrawn, as was evident from the presence of five hundred, more or less independent political units, with ill-defined boundaries in the late fifteenth century. This process continued till 1900 (Tilly 1975: 15). Five types of states can be distinguished since the fall of Rome in the fifth century—(1) traditional tribute-taking empires; (2) system of divided authority characterised by feudal relations, city-states and urban alliances, with the Church (Papacy) playing a leading role from the eighth to sixteenth centuries; (3) the polity of estates from the fourteenth to sixteenth centuries; (4) absolutist states from the fifteenth to eighteenth centuries and (5) the modern nation-states with constitutional, liberal democratic or single party polities locked progressively into a system of nation states (Held 1992: 78).

Empires

Imperial systems or empires of varying sizes and grandeur have dominated the history of states over the centuries. Some, like Rome and China, retained institutional forms for considerable period of time. Empires have sustained themselves through focus on coercive means and the ability to make money and through accumulation and when this ability decreased, they disintegrated. All empires were expansionists, which was the main cause for their development. Empires having long distance trading routes met their economic requirements through the exaction of tribute that sustained the emperor, his administrative and military apparatuses. Paradoxically, in spite of being powerful, their administrative authority was limited since they lacked the institutions, organisations, personnel and information to provide for regular administration in their territories. Most empires contained a plethora of communities that were culturally diverse and heterogeneous. Ruling rather than governing, was intrinsic to empires for their dominance in social and geographical space was restrictive. The polities of empires busied themselves with conflicts and intrigue within dominant groups and classes and within local urban centres; and beyond that, the use of military force was to knit peoples and territories together.

Feudalism

Feudalism was a political system with an overlapping and divided authority. It took different forms between the eighth and fourteenth centuries. Its distinguishing feature was a 'network of interlocking ties and obligations with system of rule fragmented into many small autonomous parts' (Poggi 1978: 27). Political power was local and personal in nature producing a 'social world of overlapping claims and powers' (Anderson 1974: 149). There was no one ruler or state sovereign in the sense of being supreme over a given territory and people (Bull 1977: 254). War was frequent and tensions endemic. The early roots of feudalism date back to the remnants of the Roman Empire and to the militaristic culture and institutions of Germanic tribal peoples (Poggi 1990: 35–37). There was a special relationship between a ruler or lord or king generally recognised or 'nominated' by followers on the basis of his military and strategic skills. The warriors swore faithfulness and obeisance to their lord and secured in return protection and privileges. In the late seventh century, rulers bestowed vassals with the rights of land, later called *feudum* ('fief') in the hope of securing continued loyalty, military service and flows of income. As a consequence, a hierarchy of lord, vassal and peasants, distinguished by a great chain of relations and obligations as major vassals sub-contracted parts of their lands to others. The vast majority of people were at the bottom of the hierarchy but they constituted the subject of a political relationship (Poggi 1978: 23). While the feudal kings were *primus inter pares* or the first among equals, they, with the exception of England and France, had diverse privileges and duties that included the need to consult and negotiate with the most powerful lords or barons, when taxes or armies were to be raised. The autonomous military capability that the lord was expected to maintain was for supporting their kings but this provided them with an independent power base which they at times used to promote their own interests. While some political forces pushed for centralisation, other sought local autonomy, thus, leading to disintegrative tendencies. In medieval Europe, agriculture was the basis of the feudal economy and its surplus were diverted for competing claims and the one that succeeded, constituted a basis to create and sustain political power. The complex network of kingdoms, principalities, duchies and other centres of power were challenged by the emergence of alternative powers in the towns and cities that depended on trade, manufacture and high capital accumulation. Different social and political structures emerged as independent centres like Florence, Venice and Sienna in Italy. Europe in the Middle Ages meant 'Christendom' securing overarching unity from the Holy Roman Empire and the Papacy. The Holy Roman Empire existed in some form from the eighth to the early nineteenth century. Under the patronage of the Catholic Church, the Empire represented an attempt at its zenith, to unite and centralise the fragmented power centres of western Christendom into a politically unified Christian empire. Countries from Germany to Spain and from northern France to Italy federated under the Empire. However, the complex power structures of feudal Europe, on the one hand, and the Catholic Church, on the other, circumscribed the actual secular power of the empire. The Catholic Church was the main rival power to the medieval feudal and city networks and the Church, throughout the Middle Age, subordinated the secular to spiritual authority. It emphasised that good lay in the submission to God's will. In the absence of any theoretical alternative to the theocratic positions of Pope and Holy Roman Empire, this order was described as the order of 'international Christian society' (Bull 1977: 27). It was first Christian, regarding God as the arbiter of disputes and conflicts with reference to religious doctrine and was coated with presumptions about the universal nature of human community. The rise of national states 'and Reformation gave rise to the idea of the modern state that challenged western Christendom. Its basis was prepared by the development of a new form of political identity—national identity.

Polity of Estates

This can be traced to the crisis within feudalism that is understood to have begun around 1300. The decline of feudalism began with the emergence of new concepts and ideas, for example, the claims of different social groups or estates (nobility, clergy and leading townsmen or burghers) to political prerogatives, specifically to rights of representation. Though these were extensions of existing feudal relations, they had some distinctive and new qualities.

> In the first place, in the polity of estates the rulers present themselves primarily not as feudal superiors, but as the holders of higher, public prerogatives of non—and often pre-feudal origins, surrounded by the halo of a higher majesty; often imparted by means of sacred ceremonies (for example, the *sacre du roi*, consecration of a king). In the second place, the counterpart to the ruler is typically represented not by individuals but by constituted bodies of various kinds: local assemblies of aristocrats, cities, ecclesiastical bodies, corporate associations. Taken singly, each of these bodies—the 'estates' represents a different collective entity: a region's noblemen of a given rank, the residents of a town, the faithfulness of a parish or the practitioners of a trade. Taken together, these bodies claim to represent a wider, more abstract, territorial entity—country, *Land*, *terra*, *pays*—which, they assert, the ruler is entitled to rule only to the extent that he upholds its distinctive customs and serve its interests.
>
> In turn, however, these interests are largely identified with those of the estates; and even the customs of the country or the region in question have as their major components the different claims of the various estates. Thus, the ruler can rule legitimately only to the extent that periodically he convenes the estates of a given region or of the whole territory into a constituted, public gathering (Poggi 1990: 40–41).

In these situations, the rulers had to deal with estates and estates had to deal with rulers resulting in the emergence of a variety of estate-based assemblies, parliaments, diets and councils, which sought to legitimate and enjoy autonomous faculties of rule. The polity of estates meant dual power, the power split between rulers and estates, which did not last long. It was threatened by the estates seeking more power and by the monarchy hoping to undermine the assemblies in order to centralise power in their own hands.

With the loosening of feudal traditions and customs, notions like nature and limits of political authority, rights, law and obedience began to engage political theorists.

Absolutist States

From the fifteenth to the eighteenth centuries, Europe had two types of regimes: the 'absolute' monarchies of France, Prussia, Austria, Spain, Sweden and Russia and 'constitutional' monarchies and republics in England and Holland. These two regimes differed in conceptual and institutional sense but some of these differences were more apparent than real. Absolutism was made possible by the absorption of smaller and weaker political units into larger and stronger political systems; an invigorated ability to rule over a united territorial space; a tightened system of law and order enforced throughout a territory; the application of a 'more unitary, continuous, calculable and effective' rule by a single sovereign head; and the development of a relatively small number of states engaged in an 'open-ended, competitive, and risk-laden power struggle' (Poggi 1978: 60–61). The absolutist rulers claimed that they alone had the legitimate right of decision over state affairs as evident from the statement attributed to Louis XV, King of France from 1715 to 1774:

> In my person alone resides the sovereign power, and it is from me alone that the courts hold their existence and their authority. That ... authority can only be exercised in my name ... For it is to me exclusively that the legislative power belongs. ... The whole public order emanates from me since I am its supreme guardian. ... The rights and interests of the nation ... are necessarily united with my own and can only rest in my hands (cited in Held 1992: 83).

The absolute king claimed to be the supreme source of human law although he justified his writ rule as being derived from the law of God, backed by the divine right theory. He stood at the pinnacle of a new system of rule that was progressively centralised and his sovereign authority to be supreme and indivisible. All qualities were visible in the rituals and routines of courtly life. There were developments, six in all that are crucial to the history of state system—uniform system of rule within a territory, creation of new mechanisms of law-making and law-enforcement; the centralisation of administrative power; extension of fiscal management; the formalisation of relations among states through the development of diplomacy and diplomatic institutions and the introduction of a standing army. Absolutism accelerated the process of state-making that began to decrease social, economic and cultural disparity within states and expand the variation among them (Tilly 1975: 19).

One reason for the expansion of state administrative power was because of its ability to collect and store information about its subjects and use that for supervising them (Giddens 1985: 14–15). This meant the need to rely more on cooperative forms of social relations, for force alone could not be the basis of managing its affairs and sustaining its offices and activities. As a consequence, there was an increased mutuality between the rulers and ruled, and since more reciprocity was involved. There were more opportunities for subordinate groups to influence their rulers (Giddens 1985: 198). Briefly absolutism encouraged the development of new forms and limits on state power—constitutionalism and for the eventual participation of powerful groups in the process of government itself. Absolute regimes in comparison to ancient emperor were limited despotisms, for they were not the sole source of law, of coinages, weights and measures, of economic monopolies and could not impose compulsory cooperation. The absolutist ruler owned only his own estates (Mann 1986: 478) and was weak in relation to powerful groups in society, for example, the nobility, merchants and urban bourgeoisie. Like its constitutional counterparts, the absolutist state tried to coordinate the activities of these groups and build up the state's infrastructural strength. A complex set of factors are responsible for the historical changes that changed the medieval notion of politics. Struggle between the monarch and barons over the domain of rightful authority; peasant's rebellion against excessive taxes and weighing social obligations; the spread of trade, commerce and market relations; the prospering of Renaissance culture with renewed interest in classical political ideas that included Athenian democracy and Roman law; changes in technology particularly with regard to military skills; the consolidation of national monarchies particularly in England, France and Spain; religious conflicts and the challenge to Catholicism's universal claims and the struggle between the Church and State were all contributory factors. By the end of the seventeenth century, Europe was no longer a mosaic of states. The claim of each state to supreme authority and control also meant the recognition of such a claim by other states as equally entitled to autonomy and respect within their own borders. In international context, sovereignty signified the independence of the state, namely an acknowledgement of its sole rights to jurisdiction over a particular group and territory, acceptance of a similar right of other states and equal rights to self-determination. In international relations, the principle of sovereign equality of all states was to become pre-eminent in the formal conduct of states with one another. With the emergence of international society, there also emerged international law as exemplified by the Westphalian[5] model covering a period from 1648 to 1945 and its features are:

1. The world consists of, and is divided by, sovereign states, which recognise no superior authority.
2. The processes of law-making, the settlement of disputes and law-enforcement are largely in the hands of individual states subject to the logic of 'the competitive struggle for power'.
3. Differences among states are often settled by force: the principle of effective power holds sway. Virtually no legal fetters exist to curb the resort to force; international legal standards afford minimal protection.

4. Responsibility for cross-border, wrongful acts are a private matter concerning only those affected; no collective interest in compliance with international law is recognised.
5. All states are regarded as equal before the law; legal rules do not take into account asymmetries of power.
6. International law is oriented to the establishment of minimal rules of co-existence; the creation of enduring relationship among states and peoples is an aim only to the extent that it allows military objectives to be met.
7. The minimisation of impediments on the state freedom is the 'collective' priority (Cassese 1986: 396, Falk 1969).

The era of absolutist states and their constitutional counterpart ushered in a new international order, which had an enduring and contradictory quality rich in implications: an increasingly integrated states system simultaneously endorsed the right of each state to autonomous and independent action. As a result the states were 'not subject to international moral requirements because they represent separate and discrete political orders with no common authority among them' (Beitz 1979: 25). According to this model, the world comprises separate political powers pursuing their own interests, and backed ultimately by their organisation of coercive powers.

Modern State

Absolutism, by concentrating political power in its own hands and in seeking to create a central system of rule, paved the way for a secular and national system of power. The English (1640–1688) and French (1789) Revolutions marked the transition from absolutism to modern state with the following features of fixed territory, control of the means of violence, impersonal power structure and legitimacy. The nation-state or national state does not essentially mean that a state's people 'share a strong linguistic, religious and symbolic identity' (Tilly 1990: 2–3). Though important, it is necessary to separate the nation-state from nationalism, 'What makes the "nation" integral to the nation-state ... is not the existence of sentiments of nationalism but the unification of an administrative apparatus over precisely defined territorial boundaries' (Giddens 1987: 172). The modern state can be understood with reference to its forms: constitutional state, the liberal state, the liberal-democratic state and the single-party polity. **Constitutionalism** refers to explicit and/or implicit limits on political or state decision-making. These limits can be procedural as to how decisions and changes can be made or substantive preventing certain changes altogether. Constitutionalism stipulates the proper limits and forms of state action. The state exists to safeguard the rights and liberties of individuals viewed as best judges of their own interests.

The state's scope and practice have to be restrained to ensure the maximum possible freedom of the individual. The **liberal state** is the effort to create a private space independent of the state and freeing the civil society—personal, family and business life—from unnecessary political interference and thereby limiting the state's authority. The components of liberal state are constitutionalism, private property, the competitive market economy and the patriarchal family. The Western state, at first is a liberal constitutional state which subsequently becomes a liberal constitutional democratic state with the extension of franchise to the working class and women. The third type is **representative democracy** or a system of elected rulers, who profess to represent the interests and views of the citizens within a framework of the rule of law. Election through two or multiparty system constitutes the life breath of representative governments. There is the one party or single party system that existed in erstwhile communist societies of East Europe and the Soviet Union and some Third world countries, on the basis that a single party can legitimately express the overall will of the society. The collapse of communism has ended the single party system. Even some third world countries, like Tanzania, have moved towards a multi-party system.

An important factor in the emergence of the modern state is the capacity of the states to organise the means of coercion (armies, navies and other types of military might) and to deploy them when necessary. Modern states spend considerable amount of their finances in acquiring military equipment and technology. Another crucial factor in the creation of the democratic nation-state is nationalism. The attempt to construct a national identity to bring people together within a framework of delimited territory gives the state a heightened power and status. National identity has been used to bring about mobilisation and legitimacy though state-building and nation-building have never overlapped. In certain cases, nationalism has become a means to challenge the existing nation-state boundaries, e.g., Northern Ireland. The economic factor for the rise of the modern state is trade and commerce. The main features of the modern states system—the centralisation of the political power, the expansion of administrative rule, the emergence of massed standing armies, the deployment of force—that existed in the sixteenth century Europe in nascent form becomes part of the entire global system.

It all began with the European states' capacity for overseas operations by means of naval and military force for the purpose of long range navigation. The Spanish and Portuguese were the early explorers followed by the Dutch and the English. By the middle of the eighteenth century, English power was on the ascendancy and had become dominant by the nineteenth century, so much so that England, the first industrial power also became the first world power. London became the centre of world trade and finance. The expansion of Europe across the globe, in turn, became a major source for expansion of state activity and efficiency. All the core organisation types of the modern society—the modern state, modern corporate enterprise and modern science—were shaped by it and benefited greatly from it (Modelski 1972: 37). While the European state systems developed and expanded the non-European civilisations, the

Chinese, Indian and Middle East progressively declined, and in this, capitalism played a crucial role with its origins in the sixteenth century. Capitalism penetrated and integrated the different and distant corners of the world, for its aspirations were never determined by national boundaries. The earliest political units that could be properly called states were France, Spain, Portugal, Britain, the countries comprising the Holy Roman Empire (Germany, Italy, Balkans, Austria Hungary) and Scandinavia and the Netherlands. This was in the seventeenth and eighteenth century occupying 1,450,000 square miles out of a global mass of 57,000,0000 (Crevald 1999: 263).

According to Wallerstein (1980), capitalism from the beginning has been 'an affair of the world economy and not of nation states'. He distinguishes between two types of world systems that have existed historically—world-empires and world economies. The former are political units characterised by imperial bureaucracies with substantial armies to exact tax and tribute from territorially dispersed populations, their capacity for success depends on political and military achievements. World empires are inflexible and eventually displaced by the world economy that emerged in the sixteenth and seventeenth centuries because of its gargantuan appetite for endless accumulation of wealth. This world economy is an economic unit that crosses boundaries of any given state and any constraint is on the state and not on the process of economic expansion. Wallerstein divides the modern world system into three components—the core (initially the northwest and central Europe); the semi-periphery (the Mediterranean zone) and the periphery (colonies). Each zone of the world-economy is characterised, according to Wallerstein, by a particular kind of economic activity, state structure, class formation and mechanism of labour control. The world capitalist economy creates a new form of worldwide division of labour. Colonialism in its original form has practically disappeared. However, the world capitalist economy continues to create and reproduce massive imbalances of economic and political power among the different constituent areas. Initially, the world capitalist economy took the form of expansion of market relations compelled by a growing need for raw materials and other factors of production. Capitalism invigorated this drive and was invigorated by it.

The development of capitalism can be explained partly due to the long-drawn changes in 'European' agriculture from as early as the twelfth century: changes resulting in part from the drainage and utilisation of wet soils, which increased agricultural yields and created a sustainable surplus for trade. Connected to this was the establishment of long-distance trade routes in which the northern shores of the Mediterranean were initially prominent. A combination of agricultural and navigational opportunities helped invigorate the European economic dynamic and the constant competition for resources, territory and trade. Accordingly, the objectives of war gradually became more economic: military endeavour and conquest became more closely connected to the pursuit of economic advantage (Mann 1986: 511). There is a direct connection between the success of military conquest and the triumphant pursuit of economic gain. As capitalism develops and matures, the state gradually gets more entangled with the interests of the civil society partly for its own sake. To be able to pursue and implement policy of its choice, it needs financial resources and for this reason it begins to steadily coordinate the activities of the civil society. The other side of the process also means that the civil society with its powerful groups and classes begins to shape the state action to suit their own interests. Weber analyses the relationship between modern capitalism and the emerging modern state. He points out that the Marxist analysis is based on a deficient understanding of the nature of the modern state and of the complexity of political life. The history of the state and the history of political struggle cannot in any way be reduced to class relations: the origins and functions of the state imply that it is far more than a 'superstructure' on an economic 'base'.

MARXISM, ANARCHISM AND THE NATIONAL QUESTION

Class and not nationality is the key factor for Marx and Engels. Their vision of proletarian internationalism is an advancement of the French Revolution's declaration of human brotherhood. The phrase 'workers of the world unite' is the consequence of the belief that while the bourgeoisie in each nation has its own vested interest, the proletarians in all the countries have the same interest and the same enemy. On the basis of this view, they divide the world into advanced and backward civilisations and supported the British imperialist expansion. They perceive the non-European societies as static without a sense of history and maintain that these societies will change from the outside. Writing on India, Marx points out that England had to fulfil a double mission, one destructive and the other regenerative; 'the annihilation of the old Asiatic society and laying the material foundations of Western society in Asia' (cited in Avineri 1969: 132–133). Furthermore, Marx and Engels oppose the right of nations to self-determination. On the contrary, Bakunin uncompromisingly supports the national self-determination for all including the great or small, weak or strong, civilised and non-civilised. He asserts,

> because a certain country constitutes a part of some state, even if it joined the state of its own free will, it does not follow that it is under obligation to remain for ever attached to that state. No perpetual obligation can be admitted by human justice, the only justice which we recognise any duties that are not founded upon freedom. The right of free reunion as well as the right of secession is the first and most important of all political rights; lacking that right, a confederation would simply be disguised centralisation (cited in Maximoff 1953: 274–275).

During the First World War, Lenin's plan was the conversion of the imperialist war into an international class-based civil war. He pleaded for self-determination of the oppressed nationalities of Tsarist Russia and other such empires. He understood proletarian internationalism to mean two things—first, proletarian struggle in any particular area of nation has to be subordinated to the strategy and planning of the larger socialist movement and second, any proletarian struggle, which wins its battle over the local bourgeoisie, must be capable and willing to direct all its energies for the overthrow of the international capital. Lenin was convinced that the socialist revolution in Tsarist Russia would be a catalyst for international socialist revolution for socialism in one country was unthinkable. He was more enthused about the right of self-determination than the other Bolsheviks, like Nikolai Ivanovich Bukharin (1888–1938). However, he also categorically stated that the right of self-determination cannot be higher than that of the interest of socialism itself, implying that once the Bolsheviks capture power it would be relegated to a secondary position. Therefore, in spite of the constitutional provision of the right to secede in the former Soviet Constitution, the question of autonomy was never to become an issue within the highly centralised Communist Party structure.

NATION STATES IN THE DEVELOPING WORLD

There has been a proliferation of new states after the Second World War mainly because of decolonisation. For the first time since the emergence of the modern state system, the Third World nations have become full members of the world community. The great disparity in wealth and other indicators of human development between the older nations and these newly emerging ones are enormous, but asserting their national identity and continuing as independent states have been an important aspect of world history for the last five decades. This new phase of nation-building process completes the process of the emergence of new nations that began with the British withdrawal from North America at the end of the eighteenth century, the freedom of the Spanish and Portuguese colonies in South America in the nineteenth century and subsequent acceptance of European settled states in Canada, Australia and New Zealand. This process in the context of Asia and Africa that began after 1945 was acknowledged in January 1960, by the then British Prime Minister Harold Macmillan. He considered the emergence of new states as a notable historical development and, though they have assumed different forms, all of them are inspired by a profound sense of nationalism. Commenting on momentous changes in Africa, he remarked 'the wind of change was blowing throughout the Continent'.

GLOBALISATION AND THE FUTURE OF THE STATE

In the recent times, the structures and processes of the world state system have been facing large-scale changes because of the force of globalisation.

The political foundation of the modern western style state has been undercut by five factors—moral, economic, military, cultural and political, representing different segments of one general trend, globalisation.

Revolution in transportation, communications and information has led to the shrinkage of the territorial space. Inventions like telephone, internet, radio, television, satellite television and jet planes have resulted in a situation, where the state no longer wields monopoly over information and communications and controls the access of its citizens to information. Migration, increase in international tourism, greater dependence on foreign companies at home and abroad for jobs or contracts, greater exposure and access to other cultures through the media have also led to changes in lifestyles and personal tastes and interests. This increasingly brings into focus notions like national identity and national culture. Held (1995) pointed out that globalisation of information far from creating a common human purpose establishes the significance of identity and difference. This encourages people without their own states to demand for one giving rise to new nation states.

The advent of nuclear weapons and intercontinental missiles has virtually made every state including the powerful and mighty, defenseless. The former US President Ronald Reagan's confession about the impossibility of winning a nuclear war has removed one of the most important props of the state since the mid-eighteenth century that the state protects its citizens from foreign threats. The emergence of global markets, greater imports and multinational corporations has weakened its economic supremacy. Though Aristotle taught us that a state ensures justice yet this is not entirely correct. Ever since the Nuremberg and Tokyo trials (1945–1946), it has been seen that states do inflict injuries and harm on its citizens, driving them to committing genocide. More recently, a fact has come to prominence that some groups, aided and abetted by the state power indulge in ethnic cleansing. Besides, there are international organisations, human rights groups and self-appointed spokesperson for democracy. All these undermine the claim that the state is the moral arbiter of its citizen's lives. In the context of globalisation of national politics, hi-tech and emergence of the world economy 'the national state has become too small for big problems and too big for small problems' (Bell 1990a: 14). The process of integration in Europe and the creation of NAFTA in America have drastically curtailed the earlier notions of state sovereignty and total domination. In the world village of today, nations co-exist as interdependent neighbours with a great degree of interaction and commonality. The problem today is that there exists a global economy but the political arrangements are still rooted in the sovereignty of states. The key task now is to reconcile global society with the sovereignty of states. The sovereign states often abuse power and the powerful ones do not want to strengthen international institutions. One argument of the stronger states is that international institutions do not work well because states in the international arena have no principles but only interests to protect. Coupled with this weakness there is yet another inadequacy, namely national bureaucracies that multiply into international bureaucracy. It is also a fact that international institutions like the United Nations have not been very successful in protecting and promoting universal principles like human rights. If globalisation is to succeed then international institutions have to perform better and that is only possible if there is an emergence of a responsive international civil society. As within the nation, the state power is restricted by the forces of civil society, which successfully monitor the process of globalisation there is to be an alliance of the democratic states with a commitment to principles and not merely interests with active intervention of the civil society.

Further Readings

Anderson, P., *Lineages of the Absolutist State*, New Left Books, London, 1974.

Anderson, P., *Passages from Antiquity to Feudalism*, New Left Books, London, 1974.

Gough, J., *The Social Contract*, Clarendon Press, Oxford, 1957.

Hall, J.A. and Ikenberry, G.J., *The State*, World View, Delhi, 1997.

McLennan, G., Held, D. and Hall, S. (Eds.), *The Idea of the Modern State,* Open University Press, Buckingham, 1984.

Schwarzmantel, J., *The State in Contemporary Society: An Introduction*, Harvester, New York, 1994.

Endnotes

1. The noteworthy features of Kant's theory of the social contract are—first, he does not accept the supposition that the citizens of a particular state have actually concluded a social contract; it is an idea that should influence a person's motives and intentions in acting rather than one which arises in observing the world. Second, it is connected with a programme of political reform that the ruler and ruled of a state try to implement. Third, he tries to work out the idea at an international level, the relations among states as well as relations among individuals. Fourth, the notion of a social contract is in moral terms constructive of civil society because a civil society comes into being for Kant only insofar as we act as moral (or rational) agents (Williams 1994: 132–146).
2. The freedom to comply voluntarily has been the part of the Christian doctrine but the Reformation reinforced the idea of individual choice and responsibility. This perception naturally came into politics and became the intellectual basis for the social contract theory. All the classic social contract exponents were Protestants.
3. Filmer and not Hobbes is Locke's main antagonist. According to Strauss, Locke is not a disguised and moderate version of Hobbes (Laslett 1960: 60).

4. The four waves of state creation that creates the present world's political map are (a) the nineteenth century withdrawal of Spanish and Portuguese colonialism from Latin America (b) the fall of dynastic empires at the end of the First World War in 1918 (c) the collapse of European overseas empires in Asia, Africa, Caribbean and the Pacific regions after the Second World War and (d) the emergence of nations in Eastern and Central Europe after the collapse of the former USSR in 1989.
5. This came about after the Peace of Westphalia of 1648 that brought to an end the eighty years wars between Spain and the Dutch and the German phase of the thirty years war.

Chapter 6

Sovereignty

Sovereignty distinguishes the state from all other associations. The word is derived from the Latin word *superanus* meaning supreme. It means that in every full-fledged or independent state there is an ultimate authority that is final and the highest, beyond which there is no appeal. It is 'the power or authority which comprises the attributes of an ultimate arbitral agent—whether a person or a body of persons—entitled to make decisions and settle disputes within a political hierarchy with some degree of finality' (King 1987: 493). The ability to take this decision implies that such an authority has to be independent from external powers and supreme over groups within its territorial jurisdiction. There are four characteristics of sovereignty. The first attribute is location. It is the highest power in the political and legal hierarchy for resolving conflicts. The second is sequence, meaning the final or the ultimate power to decide in that hierarchy. The third attribute is generality or the influence exerted on the overall flow of action, and the final one is autonomy or independence in its relations with others agents, both domestic and foreign (ibid: 1987: 493).

The distinguishing aspect of the modern state is sovereignty. This is in sharp contrast to the feudal times, when the state law was subordinated to the universal and eternal order. This law subordinated even political authority that was legal in nature and was backed by coercive power. The ancient Greeks did not differentiate between state and society and the 'ruled were citizen-governors ... who were simultaneously subject of state authority and creators of public rules and regulations' (Held 1989: 216). Rome under the rule, by a single central authority, signified ultimate power, but that was the will of the people. However, this notion got buried with the consolidation of the Empire itself. The Middle Ages did not distinguish between 'ideal and positive law, between public and private rights, between legality and religious morality' (ibid: 1989: 217). It conceived of society as a part of a larger whole that was divinely ordained and hierarchically organised. The Protestant Reformation revealed the bitter religious conflicts and highlighted the divisive nature of religion. The division between the spiritual and temporal power led to the establishment of state sovereignty. However, the claim to a universal framework was restored in the seventeenth century, in general, by Locke in particular when natural law as the yardstick for measuring existing human laws was advocated.

Sovereignty can be titular, legal, political, popular, *de jure* and *de facto*. **Titular** sovereignty is normally used with reference to a king or a monarch who was in the past the real sovereign, but now a constitutional head of the state. The British or the Dutch Monarchy is an example of titular sovereignty. Even today the Monarch is officially the sovereign, but without any real power of the government. He enjoys only ceremonial powers. **Legal** sovereignty is the supreme law-making body in the state. It is the determinate sovereign that Austin spoke of, and this view was shared by Hobbes and Bentham. It is the sovereign which the lawyer also acknowledges. In modern states, the constitution is the legal sovereign. **Political** sovereignty, a conception in Locke's theory, is a term associated with democratic systems of government to symbolise the will of the people, which is recognised as the ultimate and final source of all authority. It is a sovereign which, as Dicey pointed out, is recognised by the lawyer as one to whom the legal sovereign must bow. Raphael (1990: 158) points out that the state's coercive power is not always a necessary condition for substantiating its claim to supreme legal authority. Power alone is not enough. It must be accompanied, as Hobbes stresses, by people's acknowledgement of the legal and political authority of the state, of its right to make laws and political decisions. Weber too accepts this viewpoint for he held the essence of sovereignty to be right or entitlement and hence authority, rather than force or power. Internal sovereignty refers to the source and location of the supreme legal and political authority as well as the sovereign coercive power to make laws and take political decisions within the confines of a state's territory. Hobbes develops this conception of internal sovereignty. In reality, the issue is more complex. In Britain, for instance, the parliament is sovereign but in practice this has been diluted with the rise of executive government in the twentieth century and especially after 1945. This has been furthered weakened ever since Britain became a member of the European Community/Union in 1973, for in certain areas, the laws of the European Union take precedence over domestic law in an event of a clash between them. In federal states, it is the federal constitution that distributes power between the different tiers of government that is sovereign. Sovereignty in a federal system is polycentric because of the decentralised nature of power distribution, unlike unitary systems where sovereignty is monolithic. External sovereignty refers to the state's existence as an independent political entity in relations to other states in the inter-state system and also with regard to international organisations. **Popular** sovereignty which is associated with direct democracies, like Rousseau's plebscitarian model, argues that it is the people who are the ultimate authority. Both the concepts of political and popular sovereignty consider the legislature to symbolise supreme power, for it is the law-making institution. However, the difference as it develops historically, has been the association of political sovereignty with indirect representative democracies and popular sovereignty with direct democracy. *De jure* sovereignty is the legal sovereign, while *de facto* sovereignty is the actual sovereign. The former has a legal right to command obedience while the latter may rest on purely physical force, personal charisma or religious authority. The distinction between the two becomes clear during times of revolution. Austin refuses to accept this distinction as lawful and unlawful because, in his view, the two terms are inapplicable as far as sovereignty is concerned. It is the governments and not sovereignty which are *de jure* and *de facto*.

LEGAL OR MONIST THEORY OF SOVEREIGNTY OF THE STATE

This is a distinctively modern doctrine (Coker 1966: 498). In ancient Greece, the state enjoyed an exalted position, but was never considered to be above the law. In general, the Greeks considered the authority of the customary law consisting of the dictates of gods or human reason to be higher than the decrees of any political ruler, differentiating it with modern pluralism that accepts all authority as federal. Ancient Greeks regarded the state as the supreme social institution unique among the many associations that were essential to a person's existence. This is summarised in Aristotle's observation that the state is the highest of all associations. The pluralists find support for their views in the political situation of the Middle Ages where authority within a given region was widely distributed among a number of rival associations. For a large part of the Middle Ages, the state was not the dominant organisation of the community. The state as it existed in Greek and Roman periods hardly survived during the Middle Ages as during this period there was hardly an identifiable authority. In most areas, the organised control over a person was shared and exercised by different authorities—Roman Church, Holy Roman Emperor, king, feudal lord, chartered town, guild and many of them competed with one another in their efforts to extend their spheres of control over the individual. The laws that were 'civic'—secular and territorial in nature—were customary rather than national, differing often from one fief to another. Between the eleventh to thirteenth centuries, the Church began to control social authority fairly extensively not only with regard to moral conduct and religious doctrines but also in matters pertaining to education and learning, trade and commerce, war and peace. However, by the later Middle Ages, conditions changed and many factors led to the increase in the power of the state, dwarfing other rivals. The authority of the Roman Church began to loosen leading to the ascendancy of political authority as it had been in ancient Greece and Rome. In most parts of Europe, strong monarchies began to appear. The emergence of the nation-state led to the conceptualisation of state sovereignty. During the sixteenth and seventeenth centuries, the concept of state sovereignty became the foundation stone of Western political thought. It was embryonic in the political thought of Machiavelli, who made a decisive break from the assumptions of medieval Catholic thought, rejecting, in particular, the idea of a limited state, subordinate in status to the Catholic Church. Machiavelli formulates the idea of a state as a secular, independent and morally neutral entity. Bodin, in the sixteenth century and, subsequently, Hobbes, in the seventeenth century, explicitly delineates the concept of state sovereignty. Both, writing in the background of civil war and religious persecution, considered sovereignty as the highest and ultimate power of the state. **Jean Bodin's** (1529/30–96) *The Six Books of a Commonweal* (1596) is acknowledged as the primer of the notion of legal sovereignty (*maiestas*), which is defined as 'the highest power over citizens and subjects unrestrained by laws' (*legibus soluta*), a feature of the commonwealth or state. The state, in turn, is described as an 'association of families and their common affairs, governed by a highest power' (*suprema potestas*). The main feature of sovereignty 'is the power to give law to all citizens, generally and singly'. Bodin considers sovereign authority to be properly established, if the body politic is regarded as being composed of both the ruler and ruled and, if the governing power respects legal and moral rules. The authority that is sovereign must not only be truly supreme but also perpetual. Without sovereignty, a state does not exist in the proper sense. The focal point of this supreme legislative power determines the nature of the state as to whether it is a monarchy, aristocracy or a democracy, rejecting Aristotle's mixed constitution. In a significant manner, it departs from the traditional perception of the king as the judge and administrator of justice. Sovereignty, for Bodin, is the power to make laws regardless of whether these laws are just or not. He defines law as the command of the sovereign in the exercise of his sovereign power. The sovereign has the capacity to make and alter the law and is not subject to the command of another. He does not permit his subjects the right of consent or resistance to the laws of the sovereign power, thus providing the ideological props for monarchical absolutism that culminated in the reign of Louis XIV, in France. Bodin develops the idea found in **Machiavelli** into a statement of sovereignty by an ordered commonwealth, as one that depends on the creation of a central authority, which wields unlimited and effective power, which is represented by most, if not all the inhabitants.

Bodin identifies limits to sovereignty exercised by natural and divine laws and advances specific examples that demonstrated restrain upon sovereignty. The sovereign under the terms of natural and divine law cannot violate private property or break contracts to which he is a party, unless the upholding of the contract threatened his sovereignty. The prince or the princes, the term that Bodin frequently uses and as a result causes confusion that he equates sovereign with monarchy. The prince is the repository of sovereignty and cannot abrogate or modify them since they are a part of the very sovereignty that adorns him.

> The legislator is the legislator of the jurist, not of the theologian or of the moral philosopher. He assumes, but nowhere closely defines, the *legas divinoz naturae et gentium*. Those are conceptions beyond his precise field, always controlling, indeed, but from a higher plane, the phenomena with which he wishes specifically to deal. The sovereign like the subject, is bound by the law of God and of nature, but his

obligation in this respect is to God, by whom it will be enforced (Dunning 1966: 98).

With regard to civil law—the law of the land—the sovereign's will is the ultimate source of its every precept and the will is free. He considers the French type as a 'just monarchy' for the absolute power of the monarchy is tempered by the need to recognise both natural and divine law. The king has to combine power with justice. The fact that the king has the right to make laws without consent, can overrule custom and existing laws but he should not, for he must take into consideration the welfare of his subjects. The sovereign cannot be subject to his own laws just because they express his will, but he must respect the institutions of civil society, of which, particular importance is given to family and property. Bodin's defense of absolute monarchy does not justify autocracy, for he considered it to be the proper arrangement to reconcile and provide a balance between the various interests, since civil strife and factionalism were the major causes of injustice. He advocates rights for the minority in religious matters, judicial independence and restrictions on taxation. He also gave one of the first accounts of international law, regarded as specifying the rights of a sovereign over his subjects but against other sovereigns. His aim was to uphold the privileges of the French king at a time of factional insurrection and religious dissent that were encouraged by the Huguenot rebellions.

In view of the apparently contradictory statements, Hearnshaw (1924) points out that Bodin's advocacy of the limits to sovereignty indicates what the sovereign should not do. McIlwain (1932) and Shepard (1930) argue that Bodin upholds the legal limitation to sovereignty in the sense that, if the sovereign tread upon the divine and the natural laws and the laws of the realm, then the courts of the state can disregard his act. Bodin tries to establish, on the one hand, the idea that civil laws become laws only by command of the political sovereign and which do not bind the sovereign himself, and, on the other hand, reiterates the older notion that every political ruler is bound by customary laws which he cannot lawfully change. Subsequently, other theorists—Hobbes, Rousseau, Blackstone, Bentham and the analytical jurists of the nineteenth and twentieth centuries—have elaborated the content of the doctrine of legal sovereignty. The three social contractualists spoke of not only the origins of the state but also the nature and location of the sovereign power: Hobbes (legal), Locke (political) and Rousseau (popular).

For Hobbes, laws are nothing but the commands of a political sovereign, which means that there are no legal restraints on sovereignty by the divine or natural laws, except when they are adopted and interpreted by the political sovereign. The sovereign, the beneficiary, the third party, the mortal god under the immortal god is created through the contract in which the individuals surrender all their powers for peace and defense. Commonwealths differ not due to the nature of the sovereign powers but in the numbers who wield and exercise this power. Sovereignty, for Hobbes, is undivided, unlimited, inalienable and permanent. The sovereign power is authorised to enact laws since it is the sole source and interpreter of laws. It is the interpreter of divine and natural laws. Unlike Bodin, Hobbes does not circumscribe the sovereign power by placing it under divine and natural laws. In fact, the sovereign is not bound by the civil laws since he is their sole source and interpreter and is bound by them as long as he does not repel. He defines law as the command of the sovereign, reiterated by Bentham. Since the law is the sovereign's command, it is right, just and moral. Francois-Marie Arouet Voltaire (1694–1778), like Hobbes, favours an absolute undivided sovereign power, which, however, is not despotic. Since, like Locke, he is passionate about liberty, he believes a strong, centralised monarchy, totally modern and unhindered by medievalism ensures a good, just and progressive government. Hobbes conceptualises an absolute sovereign power only because of his thoroughgoing individualism. The absolute sovereign represents the individuals and is constituted by them for providing order and commodious living and to avert the worst of all evils, civil war (Plamentaz 1963: 116–154).

Hobbes, unlike Bodin, creates order and stability by subordinating non-political association, including the Church and universities. He does not recognise any pre-political order of society based on kinship, religion and other associations, which normally contributes to sociability in the individual. He rejects customs, traditions and moralities as these exist outside the purview of the sovereign. Hence, 'law is the command of the sovereign'. By making the sovereign above law, he deals a deathblow to one of the most cherished legal doctrines of the medieval period. He dismisses private beliefs, for he considers them a source of all sedition and dissension. He stipulates that, for ensuring civil peace, lesser associations should exist and only with the permission of the sovereign. He does not trust the motives of the private associations and factions, for he regards them as a seedbed for subversion. He subordinates the church to the sovereign and accepts its teachings as lawful only when authorised by the state. He rejects divisions and multiplicity of authority as that is an anathema to a stable political order. Authority is either unitary or nothing.

The sovereign has the right and the duty to govern and conduct policy, protect civil society from dissolution, limit or restrict freedom of expression, opinions and doctrines, control subjects' property, resolve all conflicts through the right of judicature—of hearing and deciding all controversies, right to make war and peace with the other nations, choose ministers, counsellors, magistrates, officers both in peace and war, confer honours and privileges, name the right to determine religion and forms of its worship, and prevent access to subversive literature. The subjects have no appeal against the will of the sovereign. Hobbes rejects division of sovereign authority as advocated by the parliamentarians in England of his time. The subjects will never have the right to change the form of their government because they are bound to obey a particular sovereign and acknowledge his public acts as their own. Moreover, since the individuals entered into a contract with one another and not with the sovereign power, they are not free from the subjection of the sovereign. The subjects have a duty and an obligation to obey the sovereign since the sovereign is the result of their social contract.

Hobbes is the first philosopher to comprehend the nature of public power, which he defines as a permanent, sovereign, rightful, and as an authorised representative to exercise powers 'giving life and motion to society and the body politic' (1991: 81). Sovereignty characterises the position rather than the person who wields it. The sovereign will unite all in one voice 'one will' to ensure unity. To Machiavelli's emphasis on interests, Hobbes adds the dimension of fear and provides a comprehensive theory of political absolutism that reconciles legitimate political authority with conflicting yet justified human demands. Hobbes' sovereign stands outside the society and with fear and interest are the reasons for its existence. However, his analysis of power is over simplistic, for power requires not only the elimination of hindrances but also getting the citizens to actively participate. Hobbes separates community and public will and it is Rousseau who subsequently 'revived the older notion of a community as a corporate fellowship and then endowed it with the unity of will associated with the Hobbesian sovereign' (Wolin 1960: 277). The authorised sovereign has its limits, bound by the laws of nature to ensure peace and safety. The sovereign has duties to protect his subjects and, for this, Hobbes lays down seven injunctions: first is the patriotic commitment to the status quo; second is to resist demagogues; third is to respect the established government; fourth, there is a specific need for civic education; fifth is the importance of discipline that is inculcated at home; sixth, people will be taught about law and order, to abstain from violence, private revenge, dishonour to person and violation of property; seventh, right attitudes would bring right behaviour. Hobbes has faith in the universities to train and educate the citizen-elite.

Rousseau's sovereignty resides in the 'body politic' or the 'General Will', with no legal limitations. The sovereign is the outcome of the individuals who compose it with interests identical to that of the other individuals. It is the sole judge of what is important since both in its origins and object it is general, without any particular interest. He rejects the idea of total surrender of powers, which makes the individual submissive to the sovereign, for that ensures social peace but without liberty. In response to Hobbes, he states 'tranquility is also found in dungeons; but is that enough to make them desirable places to live in?' Rousseau's concept of sovereignty differs from that of Hobbes and Locke. Like Hobbes, he supports total surrender of powers by the individuals, but unlike Hobbes, does not vest the transferred power in a third party, distinct from the people, but in people themselves, resulting in a sovereign similar to Hobbes' but with its head chopped off (Vaughan 1962). Hobbes' conception of a personalised sovereign power is missing in Rousseau. Sovereignty for Rousseau is inalienable and indivisible but vested in the body politic thereby expounding the concept of popular sovereignty. He is original, for he rules out the transfer of sovereignty and accepts the idea that sovereignty originates and stays with the people (Cranston 1986: 30). Unlike Hobbes for whom the sovereign is the ruler, the legal state, Rousseau distinguishes sovereignty of the people, the political community from that of the government and provides the foundation of public right. Locke, on the other hand, rejects the idea of sovereignty, for it suggests political absolutism. His conception of limited state and individual rights leads him to the idea that people are sovereign, an inalienable right but their sovereignty is held in abeyance when the government is in power and within the government it is the legislature that is supreme. For Locke, government's supremacy is a delegated supremacy that it exercises as a trust; it lasts as long as the trust existed and could be withdrawn any time if the ends of society and the rights of the individual are violated.

There is a difference between Locke's and Rousseau's conceptions because the French political thought, in the eighteenth century, believed that concentrated power provides more effective protection for all the members of the community. The Anglo-American liberal tradition accepts that the power must be checked and divided to prevent its abuse and for the protection of individual rights (Keohane 1980). Rousseau's authoritarian pronouncements relating to the General Will 'were restatements of hoary arguments in French absolutist thought' (Keohane 1980: 442), though his innovation lay in not identifying the sovereign will with any one individual. By doing so, he transforms the theory of absolute monarchy into 'the radically democratic alternative of absolute popular sovereignty' (Jennings 1994: 117). Furthermore, unlike his predecessors, he considers active sovereignty as something that is a permanent possession of the people. Derathe (1950) rightly points out that Rousseau's contribution has been to attribute not only the origin but also the exercise of sovereignty to the people.

Bentham recognises, as opposed to natural law and natural rights, legal laws and rights that are enacted and enforced by a duly constituted political authority or the state. A state is sovereign being, primarily a law-making body consisting of 'a number of persons (whom we may style subjects) are supposed to be in the habit of paying obedience to a person, or an assemblage of persons, of a known and certain description (whom we may call governor or governors) such persons altogether (subjects and governed) are said to be in a state of political society' (1977: 140). He defines law as the command of the sovereign and considers sovereignty as indivisible, unlimited, inalienable and permanent. **Austin** reiterates his views with greater rigidity and in a more legalistic way than the one that Bentham provides (Plamentaz 1966: 65). Bentham's theory, unlike that of Austin, is more sophisticated, for it takes into account factors like federalism and written constitutions (Barry, N.P. 1995: 43). Bentham, unlike Hobbes and Austin, does not consider the sovereign's powers as unlimited or illimitable. Instead, he dismisses talk of illegality of actions of government as absurd unless it is possible to limit these actions by conventions. He does not define law in terms of statute and accepts the division of sovereignty as in federal systems. He also envisages the possibility of constitutional law in place of morality and religion binds the sovereign power.

Monarchy is an important institution for **Hegel**, as it solves the problem of identifying national sovereignty. He rejects the concept of popular sovereign, since people represent a mere abstraction. Following Hobbes and Austin, Hegel argues that since the manifestation of the state is one, its head should also be an identifiable one. However, this guarantee cannot be provided by any single person but by the institution of monarchy. The monarchy is 'in essence characterised as the individual in abstraction from all his other characteristics, and this individual is raised to the dignity of monarchy in an immediate natural fashion, that is, by accident of birth' (Hegel 1969: 155). For holding this symbolic office of unity, physical power or intellectual gift is not necessary. Sovereignty, both in the *de jure* and *de facto* senses rested with the state. However, sovereignty, which stipulates that all functions are ultimately rooted in the state is not to be found in despotic rule or in a feudal state. His little faith in popular sovereignty leads him to conceive of a democratically elected legislature of an Assembly of Estates that represents the different interests with some link in matters of public concern.

It is with **John Austin's** (1790–1859) *Lectures on Jurisprudence* written in 1832 (1873) that the concept of legal sovereignty and the command theory of law are associated. He derives the idea from Hobbes, its first rigorously exponent, 'that the judge-made law in the common law system is subordinate to statute law and owes its validity ultimately to the sovereign' (Barry, N.P. 1995: 37). For Austin, laws in the positive sense as distinguished from divine laws and from rules of customs and morality are commands emanating directly or indirectly from a determinate legal sovereign in an independent society. The law is the command of the sovereign, expressing his wish and backed by sanctions. Austin and Hans Kelsen (1887–1973) are leading exponents of logical positivism, which advocates the study of actual legal systems and avoids the search for independent justifications in terms of the natural law. It assumes that all law is positive law—a law that the sovereign makes through legislative enactment or through the accumulation of customary rights. Laws are a system of rules, backed by coercion, which does not owe its status as law to any independent criterion, such as natural law and thereby it is difficult to explain the laws of contract or trust. Austin considers law to emanate from an ultimate sovereign in an independent political society that is defined as follows:

> If a determinate human superior, not in the habit of obedience to a like superior, receive habitual obedience from the bulk of a given society, that determinate superior is sovereign in that society and the society (including the sovereign) is a society political and independent (1873: 226).

Austin considers that in every civil society where law exists, such a sovereign is to be found. In Great Britain, the sovereign body consists of the crown, members of the House of Lords and the electorate and in the United States the sovereign is the aggregate body of the electorate of all the states.

He permits that a command may be explicit (as in the case of legislation) or tacit that allows laws which an earlier sovereign had introduced or were of customary origin which his subordinates enforced. It follows from Austin's definition of law that international law or customary law may be properly called law prior to enforcement in specific cases (Hart 1968: 471).

Austin insists on opposition to natural law theorists that law has no connection with morals and that a legal system, however morally wrong, is still valid if it is enacted in due form. He does not think that individuals are morally obliged to obey all valid laws, although they should always consider, before disobeying a law, whether under all the circumstances the consequences of disobedience are worse than obedience. He understands the realm of morality as consisting of 'positive morality', i.e., the actually accepted or conventional morality of a particular social group and the 'laws of God', of which the greatest happiness of the greatest number is the criteria. These laws of God are the absolute test of the rules of both positive law and positive morality, for it decides not what they are but what they ought to be. Austin uses positive morality to include all human-made rules of conduct—moral rules in the ordinary sense, codes of manners and international law—except positive law. Austin like Bentham makes a distinction, using different terms to the ones employed by Bentham, between science of legislation that criticises and reforms law and the science of jurisprudence which expounds, analyses the orderly organisation of systems of law. He believes that there are basic differences and conceptions common to all well-developed systems of law, which general jurisprudence clarifies and analyses. These include distinctions as between written and unwritten law, and between torts and crimes and such notions as rights, obligations, injuries, persons, things and acts. General jurisprudence is solely an analytical study that clarifies meanings and is not concerned with the history or the evaluation of law.

The analytical school to which Austin belongs argues that sovereignty rests in a determinate person or body of persons and law emanates from this body. The primary reason for obeying law is force and restraint. It distinguishes, while applying this theory to contemporary constitutional state, between sovereignty involving the power to make and change the fundamental law of the state and the ordinary government authority that is supreme only within the limits stipulated by the fundamental law of constitution, which only the sovereign, not the government can change. In the US, for instance, the Constitution prescribes limits to the law making powers that the Congress has, but two-thirds of each House of Congress with the concurrence of legislatures of three-fourths of the states, can change the Constitution and thereby exercise sovereign or legally unlimited powers. A distinction is also made between legal and political or physical sovereignty. Political sovereignty rests wherever the actual power is located—the power that is ultimately obeyed. The analytical jurist describes this as a political, not a legal fact. Their concern is only with the law (Coker 1966: 502).

CRITICISMS OF AUSTIN'S THEORY

Sir Henry Sumner Maine (1822–1888) censures Bentham and Austin for oversimplifying law and social behaviour and failing to consider them historically. He denounces the natural rights doctrine as resting on false factual claims about an initial state of equality and individualism. He visualises human society as developing from a corporate form of social existence, in which status in the kin-group determines all relations to modern individualism based on free individual ownership of property. He describes this movement in his famous phrase, 'from status to contract'. 'Customs, thus, are the result of years of evolution and do not emanate from any determinate person or body of persons'. He questions the basic assumptions of the analytical school and points out that law is the result of a long historical process. In the *Early History of Institutions* (1875), he shows that in many of the Empires of East there was nothing to correspond with Austin's determinate superior. Maharaja Ranjit Singh, the Sikh ruler of Punjab, exercised despotic powers over his subjects and disobedience meant death or mutilation but even he was subject to the customary laws of the community and never issued a command in the Austinian sense. Customs, thus, are the result of years of evolution and do not emanate from any 'determinate person or body of persons'.

Hart (1968: 472) observes that Austin's definition of law has been assailed on the grounds that despite the resemblance between criminal statutes and commands there are numerous types of law that are misconstrued by assimilation to a command. His conception of sovereignty has been criticised as being inapplicable to those societies in which the supreme legislature is subject to legal limitations imposed by a constitution. Furthermore, it applies to societies which are rudimentary in nature. His insistence on separating law and morals has been condemned, particularly in the United States, for concealing the true nature of the judicial process that was demonstrated at times where judges have a creative choice thrown open by legal rules and thereby relying on standards of morality and justice. His views on analytical jurisprudence have been criticised for abstracting law from its social setting and function. He has been accused for being blind to bad laws and encouraging subservience to tyranny. In view of these criticisms, Hart and other positivists have 'dropped the voluntarist thesis of laws as commands, restoring customary social norms to the category law, and focusing on facultative as well as imperative aspects of law' (MacCormick 1987: 28).

Green attempts to reconcile Rousseau's theory of the general will with Austin's theory of a determinate sovereign power. He agrees with Austin's view that the outward manifestation of the state is the visible presence of a coercive power and concedes that this authority may be exercised in a way that undermines the general well-being or the common good. However, significantly he also points out that such a power is incapable of maintaining supremacy in the long run, and echoing Rousseau's sentiments, he considers that ultimately sovereignty resides in the individual's quest for the common good. He considers Hobbes and Austin's explanation of obedience to the state as a matter of necessity arising out of the desire to survive as inadequate for they do not distinguish authority from legitimacy. Like Rousseau, he regards legitimacy as a moral issue and views the state sovereignty as a moral question that synthesises individual identity with common good.

Hayek argues that the Austinian (and Hobbesian) concept of sovereignty is incompatible with the rule of law and contrary to Austin (and Hobbes), law cannot be defined as the command of the sovereign. This definition equates law with the command-like rules of social organisation, rather than the abstract rules of conduct that characterise a free society. To define it in the former sense suggests that the society as a whole shall be an organisation, which can lead ultimately to totalitarianism. Hayek admits rather reluctantly, that it is normal to apply the term 'law' to command-type rules of one specific organisation, namely the government, but these are more in the nature of rules that a government requires to carry on its business. Only in totalitarian systems, government and society are co-extensive. Society's laws are different, for these are in the nature of 'enforceable rules of conduct' and the rule of law suggests that the government like everyone else is subject to these enforceable rules of conduct. In a free society, the rule of law does not originate from the sovereign, because there is no such sovereign, as understood by Austin and Hobbes. There are two possibilities for the origin of the rule of law. One is through legislation but that is not the only source, a mistake presumed by the legal positivists. The second, more important and historically prior, is the spontaneous evolution of a society's rules of conduct.

PLURALIST THEORY OF SOVEREIGNTY

The pluralist theory of sovereignty has been fully developed by J. Neville Figgis, Harold J. Laski, A.D. Lindsay and Leon Duguit and endorsed by Ernest Barker and Mary Follett. They object to the legal theory of sovereignty as pernicious, wherein the state habitually exercises any sort of authority and insist on the need to properly distribute social authority among the various groups. It is erroneous to assume that the state creates all non-political associations, which in turn, owe their existence to the will of the state and exercises only powers that the state concedes. The notion of state sovereignty undermines autonomous associations and treats the state as if it is a single agent with a single will. The pluralists point out that the interdependence of states in the modern world and the internal complexity of advanced industrial states makes the issue of state sovereignty untenable. This is because no state is so homogenous that a single sovereign will can prevail within it and without a complex process of mediation that dilutes and even perhaps destroys that will. A pluralist state is a minimal state whose primary task is to create the conditions for associations and through these enable individual citizens to freely pursue their purposes and objectives. Lindsay observes, 'If we look at the facts it is clear enough that the theory of the sovereign state has broken down' (1914: 136). **Laski**, its most persistent and vociferous critic, points out that monism is indefensible and also the benefits of abandoning it. Pluralists believe, following **Gierke's** and **Maitland's** legal and historical theory of corporations, that it is untenable to assert the state's sovereignty vis-á-vis associations which arise naturally, possess personalities that are real and function spontaneously and often act independent of state control. These associations are neither hypothetical nor fictitious and possess a collective will and consciousness which is distinct from the will and consciousness of the individuals comprising it. Each is an original agency in the explanation of law. It is prior to the state. The role of the state in this legal elaboration is primary but not exclusive.

Both Gierke and Maitland try to establish a basis for the recognition of the corporate privileges, obligations and liabilities of these associations. They contend that the state should accept the commonly held perception that permanent associations have rights and duties as groups, even if it does not recognise them as corporations. **Paul-Boncour** pays attention to the professional and economic groupings in society that arise spontaneously to further the interests of their vocations. Their relations with their own members and with the outsiders, albeit initially contractual, acquire an obligatory character that is derived from the law of associations. The free right of association and privileges that the law confers make these associations mandatory as well as sovereign. This development has not been incidental but integral to the very nature of economic society. Like Paul-Boncour, **Durkheim** pleads for the restoration and recognition of ancient occupational association as public institutions for the group that is involved with an occupation is aware of its needs and functions and is in a position to regulate its activities. The state cannot do that, for the economic life is too complex and highly specialised. It is, therefore, necessary that groups become bases for political representation and as a source of economic regulation. Vocational division will reflect social interests more accurately and would replace geographical divisions as those have lost their economic, social and political relevance. **Figgis** criticises the attempts of the modern state to invade into the terrain that strictly belonged to social groups such as churches, trade unions, local communities and the family. He demands a policy that treats these groups as public associations with discretion and initiative to control their respective spheres. The state is 'the society of societies' with the function of coordination and adjustment. Since smaller groups exist and command greater loyalty than the state, while the latter exists with its coercive power only 'to regulate such groups and to insure that they do not outstep the bounds of justice' (Figgis 1913: 49). **Barker** rejects the conception of Grieke and Maitland that groups have 'real personality' but accepts their basic premise that the existence of these groups precedes that of the state. Each of these groups is a legal person, for its members create it, and are convinced of its corporate character and function. This view requires a revision of the general theory regarding the nature of the state and its relations to the other associations. Lindsay points out that 'there are any number of corporate personalities in society and many of them are more homogeneous and symbolise a closer community of interests, attract deeper loyalties than the state and if permitted to act autonomously, prove themselves to be more effective agencies of social coordination'. Laski and others contend that the doctrine of sovereignty is practically untenable and powerless when faced with the resolute resistance by groups within the nation. Laski mentions three important ecclesiastical groups, in the nineteenth century, that successfully exert far-reaching rights of self-control against the opposition of the British Government. He also cites other examples of pressure exerted by private groups, like the Welsh miners and the Ulsterites, on the government. He categorically asserts that the state has no right to the allegiance of an individual, save insofar as his conscience assents. Political obligation is essentially moral and the state is not morally superior in its claims to regulate conduct and enforce obedience. He dismisses the idea of absolute sovereignty as a myth and a legal fiction. Follet considers the state to be a unifying agency but it could not be all absorptive. MacIver views the state as one association among many within the community with 'definite limits, definite powers and definite responsibilities' (1926: 473).

Duguit and **Krabbe** approach pluralism from the perspective of law. The former rejects the contention of monism that law is a command of an absolute and unlimited sovereign. Duguit considers law as, 'independent of, superior and anterior to political organisation, and is objective and not subjective'. Laws are conditions of social solidarity indicating human interdependence, for human beings could fulfil their diverse needs only through the exchange of services. They are obligatory not because a determinate human superior lays them down but because they pronounce rules and are obeyed, for that helps to attain social solidarity. If rules would not be observed, society would disintegrate. Law emanates from various sources and this plurality demands legal decentralisation. Duguit's interest is to stipulate a theory of state responsibility and place judicial limitations on administrative action (Gettel 1924). The sanction of law is psychological, for individuals know of the need to conform to social rules in order to preserve and promote the benefits derived from social life. He distinguishes between the authority of the state from that of law. Though both apply to individuals in society and are sustained by sanctions that secure their habitual obedience but they are different. The state as such has no connection with law and its authority has no legal or moral justification. It is merely a body of persons inhabiting a definite territory, in which the strong impose their will on the weak. It acts as an agency of law.

> Krabbe like Duguit willingly concedes only to the sovereignty of law, which is independent and superior to the state and is an outcome of a sense of right of the majority of the community constituting the state. The sense of right, he defines as, 'a universal human impulse, which

> calls forth a specific reaction with respect to our own behaviour and that of other men'. The purpose of law is to adjust conflicting interests among human beings. The distinguishing mark of the state is that it is a legal community and therefore performs only those functions that are of legal value. Krabbe, like Duguit, defends legal decentralisation but, unlike Duguit, he carries the idea of law into the realm of international relations. No nation has a natural right to lead an independent legal life. For Krabbe the sense of right should extend to the international affairs as well.

Pluralism is anti-statist, for it recognises groups in social life and demands functional representation, which constitutes a limitation on the state power. It differs from Mussolini's functional representation or corporatism for that compulsorily mobilises social interests to provide legitimacy for a centralised sovereign state. It is similar to Cole's proposal for functional and specific representation rather than general and inclusive representation. Cole rejects the theory of state sovereignty by stressing on the associational and functional nature of organisations. Pluralism is anti-collectivism, which enhances the state power as a compulsory organisation and thereby diminishes the wellsprings of true collective action through the freely associated activities of citizens. It considers centralisation of power as the absence of liberty. It rejects liberal individualism, for its atomism and regards group life as the basis of society. A good state is one that maximised liberty, which is only possible through diverse social groups. Common to all these arguments is the acceptance of the fact that individuals exist and develop through groups each with its select membership, special forms of organisation and action for serving various social needs. Pluralism owes a great deal to the constructive side of English idealism for the social nature of a person and the importance of freedom in conjunction with the common good. It claims that there is no single entity 'society' or a single common good. Persons develop through contributing to associations in order to fulfil definite purposes.

Pluralism's essential emphasis is the importance and role that by diverse groups, which arise spontaneously and voluntarily within society, play. The state has compulsory jurisdiction and comprehensive authority but that does not imply that it cannot undermine the autonomy of groups. The pluralists argue that the state cannot define common good since the diverse ends and goals that the various groups espouse are a reflection of an underlying moral consensus. They only reject the theory of absolute state sovereignty but, 'do not expunge from their theory the principle of either compulsory taxation or of a compulsory citizenship ...; and most of them assign to the comprehensive and coercive political community very extensive duties in directing the economic and social life of the nation' (Coker 1966: 515). The pluralists do not advocate the total abandonment of sovereignty but only propose its radical redefinition by emphasising the decentralised and multi-cellular nature of society.

SOVEREIGNTY AND GLOBALISATION

Held (1989: 228–237) identifies five gaps with regard to the concept of sovereignty in the global context. In the economic realm, there are forces that actually undermine the power and scope of national states. In the context of world markets, the role of multinationals, increased social and workforce mobility and the decisive role of technology and communications, to claim that the nation state is sovereign in its economic policies is not correct. Internationalisation of production has eroded the state's capacity to control its own economic future. The sovereign states continue to place their national interest, in the forefront while taking decisions concerning their economic policies but clearly their autonomy to do so is circumscribed. Economically weak states are under greater pressure than before, from both outside and inside, to set their economic house in order. For example, the International Monetary Fund with its structural adjustment programmes, insists on certain conditions on its loans to a government, namely cut in public expenditure, subsidised welfare programmes and currency devaluation thereby monitoring the policies or performance of the economically weak states. Global markets imply greater competitiveness and increased dependence among states, making the idea of splendid economic isolation redundant.

Till the Second World War the state was the primary military actor which, however, got undermined with the emergence of power blocs, one led by the US and the other by the former USSR, through their respective alliances NATO and the Warsaw Pact. The disintegration of the former USSR and the collapse of communism, has led to the dissolution of the Warsaw Pact. Though the US is the world's only superpower, its dominance within the NATO has diminished, primarily due to the rise of European Union. Furthermore, there has been a decisive shift in the world mindset, which sees economic domination to be more important than military strength. The proliferation of international and regional organisations has also moderated the idea of state sovereignty. Since the Nuremberg trial, following the end of the Second World War, there is an increasing emphasis on human rights as a yardstick in assessing the conduct of states. International law subjects individuals, governments and non-governmental organisations to a new set of regulations (Vincent 1986). 'The International tribunal at Nuremberg laid down for the first time in history, that when *international rules* that protect basic humanitarian values are in conflict with *state laws*, every individual must transgress the state laws (except where there is no room for moral choice)' (Cassese 1988: 132). This is in the spirit of the suggestion made by Grotius, who while confronting the main problem of seventeenth century Europe of how to cope with radical moral conflict and its derivative armed warfare, asserts the possibility of universal moral standards to adjudicate questions of international conflict. Grotius defends it as long as it is based on two principles—first, that self-preservation must always be legitimate and second, any reckless injury of another, not for reasons for self-preservation must always be illegitimate. On this basis of self-preservation, it is possible to establish rules for reconciling conflict. Finally, domestic autonomy gets limited, with the larger security concerns of the power blocs undermining the traditional concerns of sovereignty which conceives the state as the primary spokesman of its citizens by determining domestic public policy and protecting their foreign interests.

CONCLUSION

The concept of sovereignty remains the most important distinguishing mark of the state even today. The process of globalisation, the operation of international law during both peace and war, the international organisations and the non-governmental organisations redefine its meaning by making it more legitimate and accountable without, however, replacing it. The nation state still plays the role of both *de jure* and *de facto* sovereign and the citizen's identity is linked with it though there is a distinction between legitimate and illegitimate sovereign authority and also what is considered as just and unjust wars. These developments successfully question the Hegelian hypothesis of a conflict between two sovereign nations as reflecting two different notions of rights. The actualisation of human rights with a doctrine of some basic inalienable rights to every single individual has completely transformed the entire concept of sovereignty analogous to the change from the divine right theory to the emergence of the constitutional and accountable political authority. Nations, like individuals, have rights but again, like individuals these rights are not absolute and as a consequence no sovereign state, as no individual, is above the law of nations.

Further Readings

Bartelson, J., *A Genealogy of Sovereignty*, Cambridge University Press, Cambridge, 1995.

Camilleri, J.A. and Falk, J., *The End of Sovereignty: The Politics of a Shrinking and Fragmentary World*, Edward Elgar, England, 1992.

Hinsely, F.H., *Sovereignty*, 2nd ed., Cambridge University Press, Cambridge, 1986.

Hirst, P.Q., *The Pluralist Theory of the State*, Routledge, London, 1989.

James, A., *Sovereign Statehood: The Basis of International Society*, Allen and Unwin, London, 1986.

Jouvenal, B. de, *Sovereignty: An Inquiry into the Political Good*, Cambridge University Press, Cambridge, 1957.

Lyons, G. and Mastandumo, M. (Eds.), *Beyond Westphalia? Sovereignty and International Intervention*, Johns Hopkins University Press, Baltimore, 1995.

Chapter 7

Political Obligation

Berlin regards political obligation as the most fundamental of all political questions since there has to be a justification as to why one should willingly obey the state and the law. It is the duty incumbent on any person(s) to consensually submit to a legitimate political authority. Every human being is a member of a state and subject to political obligation due to the omnipresence of the modern nation state. However, a small number of stateless persons, refugees, diplomats and officials of international organisations enjoy different schedules of entitlements, immunities and responsibilities and are free of political obligation of the State, where they may be residing temporarily. However, this freedom also means that they cannot participate in the political process of the country where they are living as a special category.

Political obligation involves three aspects—(1) the identifiable authority to which political obligation is rendered, (2) the extent of political obligation and (3) the basis of political obligation. The first question concerns the origins of political authority with which political obligation corresponds. If a person has an obligation to do or abstain from performing an action, there must be somebody who possesses authority over the person with respect to his action. Characteristically, political authority is taken to mean the state or the government and its representatives. However, a person's political obligation is linked to citizenship of a state, which means a foreigner will have legal obligation and protection but no political rights. As far as the extent of political obligation is concerned, the state has a sole right to make and enforce laws and demand minimum political obligation. This implies that all laws have to be obeyed and one cannot be selective about obeying of laws. Besides obligation to obedience, a person also has an obligation of civility, namely to support and sustain the basic institutions of the state by participation, e.g., voting, jury service and military duty. In some countries, voting and military service are compulsory.

Liberal political theorists contend that a person's political obligations are decisively circumscribed in several ways. Political obligation is just one among the many others that include familial, professional and religious obligations. With regard to the third question, it is only since the sixteenth century that the issue of political obligation becomes central to political theory. Prior to that, a person's political obligation is explained as something that is inherited or as the will of god. However, modern political theory differs in its rejection of the certainty of political authority and by accepting that all citizens voluntarily assume what they consider to be valid obligations. The reasons for incurring such obligations are two fold—first, self-interest, the state is the necessary means to provide few essential services like physical safety, security of property or commodious living and second, the realisation that certain basic moral duties like securing justice or maximising happiness may not be possible without political authority. Liberal theory that regards obligation to be self-assumed is reinforced by a powerful, consistent and clear tendency towards the ideal of radical voluntarism—that authority to be legitimate must not be simply accepted but must be created by the individuals who will it. This forms the basis of the doctrine of the social contract and in its response arises utilitarian, idealist, democratic, socialist and anarchist alternatives detailing different views and basis of political obligation. The meaning and the content of political obligation, like citizenship, has changed drastically during the last few centuries. With larger citizen participation and increasing democratisation, there has been an increase in citizen demand for state action, which correspondingly altered the meaning of political obligation for people.

DIFFERENT NOTIONS OF POLITICAL OBLIGATION

Unconditional Obligation

As long as it is accepted that political authority is inevitable, natural or divine, the question of whether a person has an obligation or not is quite redundant. Deliberative defense of unconditional obligation arises only when the source of state's claims to authority are questionable. During the turmoil following the religious Reformation Martin Luther (1483–1546), in response to those who argued that individuals have the right to follow their conscience in all things including their political responsibilities, reiterates St. Paul's injunction of obeying the authority in power. In the sixteenth and seventeenth centuries, the **Divine Right of Kings** is used to explain authority and obligation. 'Authority and political obligation to it was not a matter of human will or choice, but was divinely ordained through the King' (Allen 1941: 122–123). In the seventeenth century, Filmer, in response to a constitutional crisis in England between the Royalists and the parliamentarians, maintains that the power of the Monarch is a type of paternal authority or rather all kings are the direct descendants of Adam. He contends that the kings inherit Adam's original authority as the father of humankind. In the process, he makes an appeal to the traditional veneration for the 'natural' hierarchy of the family to support the absolutist pretensions of the Stuart Monarchy. Obedience to the king means obedience to God, who appoints and delegates divine authority to the king.

In the theories of Bossuet and James I, the Divine Right of Kings claims special appointment or grace or charisma that distinguishes kings from the other men. It has secular parallels in theories that visualise a leader as a person marked out by Fate or History with a special mission, attributing to him, unique intuitions or insights, or identifying him with the progressive forces that shape the future. As **Weber** has shown that charismatic authority rests on devotion to his 'particular and exceptional sanctity, heroism or exemplary character'. Obligation, in such a case is automatic and is not based either on self-interest or on the basis of individual reasoning but on the total allegiance to the leader. The appeal to 'historic mission' adds to the appeal. History is not a mere record of past events but working and proceeding towards its inevitable goal that could be comprehended through intuition (as in Fascism) or scientific method (as in communism). The leader's insights into these historic laws justified his authority. **Popper** has shown the fallacy of such statements, for there are no historical laws and no scientific insights. Therefore, these are no different from the religious and metaphysical claims embedded in the Divine Right theory. The Nuremberg and Tokyo trials after the Second World War have started the process of doing away with such theories of total allegiance as human rights and laws of war cannot be subordinated to any single head of the state.

Conditional Obligation

The contractualists—Grotius, Hobbes, Pufendorf, Locke, Rousseau and Kant—espouse the idea of conditional obligation by using the device of the contract to explain the origins of the state and the basis of political obligation. In a nutshell, they explain that a political authority is legitimate only if it is conditional upon the will or the consent of its subjects and only as long as its scope is restrictive. The contract tradition fuses the two strands together, that human beings, in order to live well need conveniences and for this the state must be designed to advance a particular task (the deficiencies in the state of nature); and second is that political authority has to be confined to whatever is necessary in order to achieve this end. However, individual reserves his right to withdraw obligation if the state appropriates more shares than is originally intended. Locke even grants a right to rebellion under extreme circumstances. The supremacy of the individual and the civil society over the state is manifested in this theory of political obligation. Grotius considers the obligation to keep our agreements not merely as a consequence of living in civil society but sustaining its authority from the natural law of human rationality and sociability. Since the natural law is based on an instinct of human nature, it enjoys an independent status that even God cannot change by himself. This law derives its authority from all rational beings and hence commands consent at all times and places. Natural laws are distinct from positive laws and provides the criterion for validating or invalidating the latter. An important principle of the natural law is *pacta sunt servanda* meaning adherence to treatises and promises and forms the basis of political obligation. For Pufendorf, individuals in the state of nature have natural obligations, some congenital and other adventitious or incurred by agreement. These obligations are, however, imperfect since their performance is uncertain. The civil sovereign is created through an elaborate three-tier compact, comprising of two contracts and one decree, which converts imperfect into perfect obligation reinforcing it with civil law and authority. Among the social contract theorists there are variations about the agency towards which the contract creates obligation. In Locke's theory, obligation is with all the members of society individually, while for Rousseau it is with society which expresses itself through the general will, but for Bodin obligation is established towards the sovereign. Hobbes offers a number of practical reasons as to why the sovereign had to be obeyed. First, there is a purely **physical** consideration that if individuals disobey they will be punished. Second, there is a **moral** consideration that they must honour their contracts provided others do so, as ordained by the first three laws of nature, laws which are most significantly God's commands. It is human vulnerability and the ability of the state to provide security that provides the basis of obedience. The sovereign ensures that all parties adhere to the terms of the covenant. Third, there is a **political** consideration that the sovereign is their duly authorised representative, created consensually by the citizens authorising him to act on their behalf. For Hobbes, obligation stems from human nature and the laws of nature. Interpreting Hobbes' theory, Strauss (1936) stresses on the physical nature of obligation that the sovereign by virtue of his overwhelming power and authority can ultimately command his subjects to obey. The subjects obey out of fear of punishment. Taylor (1938) and Warrender (1957) observe that the laws of nature ultimately bound the individual to render obligations to the sovereign. These laws existed even in the lawless state of nature thereby enjoining the individual to enter into a contract and establish the sovereign. These laws are also moral in nature, prescribing duties. Pitkin (1967) points out that Hobbes tries to explain and defend political obligation arising out of the laws of nature that dictate the primacy of self-preservation so as to preclude acts of rebellion, revolt, anarchy and civil war. Oakeshott (1975) interprets Hobbes' theory as a theory of mixed obligation consisting of physical, rational and moral obligations. Since Hobbes maintains that civil society is a complex system of authority and power, each element has its own appropriate obligation. There was a *moral obligation* to obey the authorised will of the sovereign, which was not based on self-interest. Moral obligation arises from obedience to the sovereign authority whose basis was the consent of the governed. There is a *physical obligation* that is derived from the fact that the sovereign represents power, compelling the individual to eventually obey or face the consequences of disobedience. Last, there is a *rational obligation* based on self-interest. 'Each of these obligations provides a separate motive for observing the order of the commonwealth and each is necessary for the preservation of that order' (1975: 66–67). Macpherson (1973) interpreting it differently argues that Hobbes' analysis of human nature within a bourgeois society governed by the market, enables him to understand obligation as a result of two basic assumptions—materialism and market. The former enables him to assume that individuals have an equal need to be in continuous motion and thus establishes an equal right and a moral obligation. The market assumption allows Hobbes to contend that individuals are equal in their insecurity. Goodwin discovers a logical fallacy in Hobbes that, in spite of using the premise of contractarianism, his powerful sovereign is self-perpetuating and creates 'unconditional moral obligation in perpetuity' (Goodwin 1992: 305).

Locke explains consent of one with all, conceived as free and equal creatures of God, subject to the laws of nature, as the basis of legitimate government. There are two types of consent—direct and tacit—to explain the intent of the original contractors and their succeeding generations. By providing for tacit consent, he furnishes a more satisfactory answer than Hobbes, for the descendents of the original contractors to owe allegiance to the government. However, the doctrine of tacit consent creates some serious problems. It ascribes obligation to those who have not expressly consented, contrary to the model of self-imposed obligation (Pitkin 1972). The obligation to obey the government depends on the fact that public power has to be used for 'peace, safety and public good of the people'. Furthermore, Locke categorically states that individuals would not yield to the government more power than they actually possess in the state of nature meaning that there can be an absolute arbitrary power over their lives and fortunes, thus ruling out unconditional obligation. The contract is rational and limited that assures obedience for the preservation and enhancement of life, liberty and property. The validity of the contract is conditional and depends on the continuation of these benefits. A government can be arbitrary, for it is bound by the general laws that are public, and not subject to individual decrees. Though he grants the right to rebellion yet he is not categorical about what actually happens when people find themselves at liberty to entrust new hands with the government. He distinguishes between the dissolution of the government and the dissolution of the society but is imprecise about the dissolution of government (Laslett 1960: 128–129). People can use force only against unjust and unlawful authority in extreme cases. It is noteworthy that Locke identifies the reasons for disobedience including the right to revolt, which he insists would be exercised with utmost caution. People had the right to judge and assess authority that was no longer sacred or supernatural. Thus, Locke is a more thoroughgoing contractarian than Hobbes.

Hobbes' premises are contractual but not his conclusions, though like Locke, he too rejects the divine right theory. Unlike Filmer who interprets the right of rulers as a personal gift from God, where God gives them ownership over human beings and material goods, Locke makes a clear distinction between the duties of subjects to obey and the rights of rulers to command. In most societies, most of the time, the subjects have a duty to obey because civil order and peace are necessary prerequisites for a decent and civilised human existence. If they threaten civil peace and order, then the subjects have every right to judge the degree and immediacy of that threat and could resist it, if they thought it to be serious. Political authority is a matter of trust and rulers have the legitimate right to command if they provide practical services to their subjects. For Locke, the ruler is a trustee rather than the owner of the subject, thus turns Filmer on his own head. The modern notion of constitutional and limited political authority is the dominant idea in Locke's theory and, as such, like liberalism the modern basis of political obligation begins with him.

Hume, Rousseau and Paine point out that existing governments are not based on contract but established through force, fraud and deception. While Hume reject contract altogether, Rousseau and Paine argue that a just government should act on egalitarian contracts. For Hobbes and Locke, the contract mechanism is concerned not so much with the mode of consent but rather in portraying the nature of the state. For both of them, the obligation to obey the state would be spontaneous, voluntary and willing from people who are both rational and moral. This perception alters the entire process of analysing obligation and subsequently leads to the broadening of the concept in a number of ways. From Rousseau to contemporary times, efforts have been to democratise the system and to link consent to the actual process of participatory democracy. From Hume, the utilitarian tradition of maximising the individual's benefit as the cornerstone of political obligation began. Both these traditions raise a number of vexed problems. Democratic theories of consent encounter the problem of obligations of dissenting minorities or of estranged individuals. Utilitarian theories are based on both, the practice of promising, and the practice of political allegiance upon general utility. However, it flounders not only regarding the problem of particularity but also regarding the fact that the distinguishing aspect of political authority is the state's claim upon its citizens to obey the law not because it maximises utility but simply because it is the law. Riley (1982) rightly states that while the contract theorists wish to show government as a product of free will of the individuals but they do not explain what that 'will' actually means.

Modern contract theories try to avoid these shortcomings by concentrating on the ongoing process of the government and are not concerned with the origin of government. It is exemplified in **Plamentaz's** (1968: 154) argument that voting represents consent to obey whoever is elected. This implies concurrence with the rules of the democratic game and that a vote is a promise to the next government. This view can be criticised. First, it may hardly be rational to give prior consent to whatever the government might do, unless it strictly follows what has been stated in its manifesto, but that rarely happens. Voting normally is a passive acquiescent process and only a strong positive choice really qualifies as consent. Governments often enact policies by inaction or non-decision-making, in which case, it is not possible for the governed to democratically demonstrate their consent to, or dissent from such intangible decisions. To presume that there is consent of the people is to stretch the argument too far beyond recognition. Plamentaz does not tell us the grounds on which people could express their dissent. There are many who never exercise their franchise and yet are subjects of political obligation presumably on the basis of tacit consent (Goodwin 1992: 308–309). Actually many like Verba and Powell welcome citizen's passivity as they argue that too much of political involvement and participation may be destabilising.

Political Obligation to a Just Government

Pitkin (1972) improvises the argument of the legal positivists that the law by definition has to be obeyed, which means that there exists a political obligation to obey a despot just as much as a democratic government and that one is self-evidently obliged to obey a just government whether or not one consents to it. She develops a theory about the nature of government based on 'hypothetical consent'. A just government is to be hypothetically consented to and given obedience. A legitimate and just government is one that exudes justice of political institutions and procedures and justice in its measures, a view that **Rawls** (1972: 111–112) advances. A principle of fairness, according to Rawls, has two parts, to demonstrate how obligations arise—first, when the institutions are just and second, when one voluntarily accepts its benefits to further one's interest. The second stipulation is a kind of gratitude argument, for co-operation requires some restriction of one's liberty. It is illegitimate—a form of cheating—for anyone to act as a free rider without some special justification. Nozick disagrees with this argument, as benefits, which are an accidental result of one's activities, impose no obligation on others. Regarding the first, Rawls states that when the constitution and its social structure are reasonably just, one is obliged to comply even with unjust laws (1972: 351). Injustice may be tolerable if it is fairly distributed amongst all the groups and would disappear by the dynamics of the democratic process in the long run. However, this is no justification to comply with laws that deny our basic liberties (1972: 355). Besides obligation, Rawls also stipulates natural duties and considers the most important duty to support and further just institutions. This consists of two parts—first is where one has to comply with and contribute one's share to just institutions when they exist and second is to assist in the establishment of just arrangements when they do not exist. Rawls mixes moral obligation (gratitude) with consent, as the whole point behind the appeal of the principle of fairness is that obligation is generated by voluntary acceptance of certain benefits of cooperative political enterprise. Rawls builds into his theory of just government, a notion of democracy whereas Pitkin's argument implies that a just but non-democratic government is still legitimate. The argument of just government steers clear of some of the conceptual problems of the consent theory and the problem of those who do not agree to it because it considers a person's obligation to pursue justice as moral and unconditional, unless of course the government deviates from the course of providing justice. It also helps one to, 'distinguish between general obligation to a just regime and a modified—or annulled—obligation to particular unjust laws, and allows a theory of disobedience to be formulated without too much inconsistency' (Goodwin 1992: 312).

Political Obligation due to Self-interest and Gratitude

For the utilitarians, obligations arise due to the benefits that state provides. For Hume the bases of obligation are the advantages of a dependable system of political authority that surpasses the disadvantages of displacing it. He points out that keeping one's promises leads to reciprocal confidence building and trust in social practices. Governments provide authority to sustain a society, in which, promises are made and fulfilled with confidence. If it is to the contrary, appropriate punitive action is enforced. For Hume, political obligation is derived from a commitment, a point that Rawls elaborates. The principle of fidelity, according to Rawls, is a principle of fairness applicable to the social practice of promising and action defined by the public system of rules. These rules are, as in the case of institutions, generally a set of constitutive conventions. It is not a moral principle. Promising, in order to be binding, must be made with a rational frame of mind, conscious of the meaning of the phrase 'I promise'. It must be given freely and voluntarily without coercion and in a situation where the bargaining power is fair. According to Rawls, bonafide promise is one, which arises in accordance with the rule of promising when the practice it represents is just. While promising is a constitutive principle, the principle of fidelity is a moral principle, a consequence of the principle of fairness. Promising is an act done with the public intention of deliberately incurring an obligation, the existence of which in circumstances will further one's ends. Promise is fulfilled through reciprocal recognition and mutual confidence. He also explores the extent of the limits of compliance with unjust arrangements. The injustice of a law alone is not a sufficient reason. There is normally a duty and an obligation for some to comply with unjust laws provided these do not exceed certain bounds of injustice. The duty of civility imposes a due acceptance of the defects of institutions and certain restraint on taking advantage of them (Rawls 1972: 355).

Bentham, like Hume, asserts while assailing Sir William Blackstone's (1723–1780) use of the idea of the original contract that the doctrine of social contract is unnecessary in explaining political obligation for the institution of enforcing contracts is not only moral but also conventional. An appeal to the original promise cannot work unless there is a prior reason to keep one's promises. When a social contract theorist is asked as to why individuals must keep their promises, the answer very likely is utilitarian reasons. First, the individual who breaks his promise will have to face the disapproval of others and this will make it more difficult to enjoy the benefits of social cooperation. Second, to adhere to promise made is a useful social practice for that will be to the advantage of all in the long run. In that case, it is better to appeal to the general interest rather than promise or contract as the basis of political obligation. There are loopholes in the gratitude argument. It does not explain the origins of the state's legitimacy nor does it tell one when obligation ceases if the state decreases or does away with benefits or protection. It justifies any government as long as it provides protection; and what about the disenchanted unemployed people and their reason for gratitude. (Goodwin 1992: 314) Nozick argues that benefits which are an incidental result of one's activities impose no obligations on others and that in both large and small-scale situations, individual actions do not add up to become joint voluntary actions. Nozick espouses an individualism that is totally devoid of a sense of solidarity and fellow feeling.

POLITICAL OBEDIENCE AS SELF-DETERMINISM

Rousseau's position in the development of political obligation though influential and novel is complicated and ambivalent. He uses the contract arguments of Hobbes and Locke but develops a theory that is more in line with the idealists, thus representing the sharpest and the most thoroughgoing criticism of liberal individualism. Rousseau redefines political obligation, since his body politic bestowed with the general will morally transforms itself. With the individual will being identical with the general will, the obligation in reality is to oneself. The central question then becomes one of identifying the proper realm of individual rights and that of political authority and stating the conditions under which the individual may achieve true self-determination and freedom by synthesising one's own will with that of the general will. **Hegel** and subsequent idealists develop this point and provide a systematic philosophical critique of the individualist and empirical basis of liberal political thought. Liberal theory, as restated by **Green** makes a total break with the social contract and utilitarianism. Green argues that obedience to a state emerges from a source other than fear, which is never an adequate basis for obedience. To represent it as a basis of civil subjection is to confound the citizen with slave. Meaningful obedience is always the willing obedience of citizens and thus distinguishes legal from moral obligation. Legal obligations are those that arise from a given code of law and which, if necessary, can be enforced by the government by using its coercive power. Moral obligations are duties to act with certain dispositions and from certain motives which can be enforced. They belong to a rational agent as a social being which must be performed as a member of a society freely, voluntarily and responsibly, and if the rational agent neglects it then he may not be contributing to his society. Green criticises the theories of Spinoza, Hobbes, Locke, Rousseau and Austin as these advocate a political obligation as a conflict between the rights of the individual and the authority of society. He emphasises that as a social being a person has a moral duty to limit the exercise of his powers and cannot do what he likes without references to his social responsibilities. Laws shall create and maintain conditions necessary for the individuals to exercise will and reason. He points out that in civilised states there is habitual obedience to an established authority on the basis of common interests and sympathy, which harmonises and secures the rights of life and liberty. Green conceives of a partnership of freedom, rights and the state to form a theory of common citizenship based on parity in which all can claim a share in common economic and political rights. The ethical basis of political obligation is common good, which is sustained by individual rights and law. State action is essential in upholding these rights. It is not an antithesis of freedom but a co-operative enterprise bestowing benefit to all and gaining their political obligation.

NON-CONSENSUAL OBLIGATION

This explains political obligation as arising independently from any choice of the subject, say from piety, as in **Burke** and **Hegel** or from sovereign's right to obedience as in Hobbes. Piety basically means a recognition and acting upon obligations that are not based on contract or on any other voluntary choice of the agent. 'The duty I owe to my parent (whom I neither chose nor chose to be related to, nor chose to be obliged towards)' is one of piety as is, on some views like those of Burke and Hegel, my duty towards the state. Piety is connected to justice, in that it involves an inclination to grant and to acknowledge obligations and rights but is distinct from justice as it is not concerned with the regulation of contract, exchange or distribution, or with the derivation of rights from free transactions. This provides a model for theories of political obligation that deny the social contract or the tacit consent, constituting an important idea to anti-individualistic doctrines of legitimacy.

Burke rejects the idea of the social contract and accepts the privileged position of the aristocracy because of its contribution to the common good. He questions the proposition of reason alone as the basis of a stable political order and repeatedly stresses that societies need awe, superstition, ritual and honour for their stability and to secure the loyalty and support of those on whom it depends. A person renders obedience not because it benefits him or that he has promised to obey it but because he sees himself as an integral part of it. He rejects the divine right theory but affirms, like Cicero, that nothing is more pleasing to god than the existence of human *civitates*. He accuses the natural rights theorists of not merely 'imprudence and intellectual arrogance but of blasphemy and impiety as well' (Waldron 1987a: 95).

Hegel points out that the state as the highest expression of an individual's freedom results from the transcendence of the conditions of the family and the civil society. The bond of the family is piety and not contract, and it is an indispensable part of political existence without which no free being can emerge. Civil society is the realm of justice in which individuals freely secure and contract away their rights. The contracting parties possess autonomy made possible by the family and one that the state protects. The state transcends and resolves in a new, self-conscious piety, the conflict between particularised loyalty to the family and universal loyalty to all beings. The state represents the highest expression of individual's freedom, and allegiance to it as a necessary condition for full self-realised individuality. A contractual relationship he argues 'is a casual tie arising from the subjective need and choice of the parties', whereas the political relationship is qualitatively different, in that it is absolutely necessary, objective and above choice and caprice.

Unconditional Freedom from Obligation

This view is exemplified in the philosophies of anarchism and revolutionary socialism. The Marxists advance two distinct arguments about political obligation. The first, they consider that in a capitalist state—the instrument of a dominant economic class—the majority do not have political obligations, though the workers have an obligation to change the form of the state and then have political obligation to a just state. The second is more radical. Moral principles including political obligation have no independent and objective basis. They represent ideological expressions of economic interests and are transient and, once there is a change in the economic base, the new basis of political obligation emerges. Beyond this there is no theory of political obligation in the socialist and communist states. Anarchism concedes that in a just society individuals have a moral duty to act justly and to work towards an order that enlists the voluntary cooperation of all members according to principles of justice. However, anarchism does not develop a convincing description of a non-political form of social authority. Philosophical anarchism as exemplified in the writings of **Gandhi**, **Godwin** and **Paul Wolff** develop a more radical version by contending that it is the primary duty of the individual to maintain his moral autonomy, that is, not to make his judgment subservient to that of others. Moral autonomy and political obligation are irreconcilable but its importance lies in reminding one of serious dangers of blind and mechanical conformity to political authority.

In conclusion, political obligation is a contested concept. The terms 'legitimacy' and 'authority', which are often used to justify or oppose political obligation, have also an ideological connotation and the subjectivity of the individual may not match the objective legitimacy of the state. Moreover, in the large indirect democracies of the contemporary world where people have multiple identities, a theory of political obligation has to reflect the complexities of diversity rather than the unity of yesteryears, making the task more daunting. However, in spite of such difficulties in arriving at a consensus, the fact remains that no worthwhile political theory can ignore the questions of political obligation and legitimacy, as both of them are key components in judging obedience or disobedience to a particular regime.

Further Readings

Beran, H., *The Consent Theory of Political Obligation*, Croom Helm, London, 1987.

Delue, S.M., *Political Obligation in a Liberal State*, State University of New York Press, New York, 1989.

Flathman, R., *Political Obligation*, New York, Athenuen, 1972.

Harris, P. (Ed.), *On Political Obligation*, Macmillan, London, 1990.

Horton, J., *Political Obligation*, Macmillan, London, 1992.

Pennock, J.R. and Chapman, J.W., *Political and Legal Obligation*, Atherton Press, New York, 1970.

Simmons, A.J., *Moral Principles and Political Obligation*, Princeton University Press, Princeton, NJ, 1978.

Chapter 8

Civil Disobedience

Civil disobedience is a concept that may not be distinctly modern in political theory, but what makes it unique to the contemporary times is the context in which it has evolved. History in pre-modern times has examples of civil disobedients like Socrates (470–399 BC) and Sir Thomas More (1478–1535). Individuals have singularly defied authority in their times on the belief that their temporal rulers have acted contrary to higher law. However, civil disobedience assumes significance as a civilised form of protest ever since political authority became accountable and secular. The emergence of liberal constitutional democracy has established the idea of limited and secular government, popular sovereignty, and the rule of law and individual rights. The public-private divide unambiguously defines the scope of state's activity. As political authority is a trust and accountable, the individual citizen is seen both a participant and its custodian.

Civil disobedience is a principled, purposeful and public disobedience to law (Goodwin 1992: 319). It is a principled act, not undertaken for any selfish or personal gain or for the furtherance of private interests but for a reasonable and a just cause or objective. Its purpose is to question a law or policy from the standpoint of certain universal principles, which could be political, moral, cultural, economic or religious. It is justified by an appeal to one's conscience, inner voice or to a higher common moral or natural law or principles, or to human rights. This distinguishes a civil disobedient from a moral innovator or a conscientious refuser. A civil disobedient does not, like a moral innovator, 'invoke standards of a higher morality or of a special religious dispensation. He is no Zarathustra proposing a transvaluation of all values, and he does not ask the public to act on principles that it plainly rejects' (Cohen 1972: 284). When the civil disobedient appeals to conscience he tries to arouse that of the others as well and whenever principles are invoked they usually are those that are commonly agreed upon and cherished. A civil disobedient appeals to the sense of justice in the community among equals. By protesting against an unjust principle or policy, he differs from a conscientious refuser. Disobedience is to the law, as a mark of protest, with the view to influencing and awakening the public. It is a civic and a political act and by its very nature is performed in public or at least engages the attention of the public.

Civil disobedience accepts the primacy of the individual as moral and rational person capable of acting autonomously with a sense of social commitment. It recognises the individual as the key player in the political process, since it is a political act involving concerted efforts that are undertaken against a policy or law seen as unjust. However, the individual is not a knight in his shining armour. Through his acts based on common and universal rather than on divisive principles, he demonstrates his willingness to undergo punishment including jail sentence. His readiness to suffer and sacrifice helps to convert a minority perception into a majority viewpoint and arouses the conscience of the people. The willingness to accept punishment proves his commitment to the law and this demonstration is all the more imperative in a democratic society. This contrasts a civil disobedient from a rebel and a revolutionary, for protest against an unjust law is not out of mere defiance as the former does, nor is there a zeal, as in the case of the latter to have a new set of laws altogether since the present order is usually seen as imperfect. The civil disobedient tries to undo the unjust law or policy in the Popperian sense of piece-meal social engineering or in the Gandhian sense 'one step at a time'. There is no grand and holistic design in his mind on the basis of which change is to be effected.

From the examples of those—Thoreau, Gandhi, Rev. Martin Luther King Jr. (1929–1968) and Russell—who have successfully essayed out civil disobedience, one can see that they appealed to certain universal principles and commonly cherished values. Thoreau viewed slavery in Southern United States as morally wrong. Gandhi regarded colonialism as morally untenable and by the end of the Second World War, was able to convince the majority of the English speaking world about its injustice. His unique and unparalleled success was in the fact that he was able to liberate his fellow countrymen and, in the process, the majority of oppressed living in various other colonies. This was perhaps the greatest event of the twentieth century. King fought against racism and demanded equal rights and opportunities for the Blacks. Russell considered nuclear arms as a threat to the survival of the human race and supported campaigns for nuclear disarmament. Thoreau perceived civil disobedience as an individual act but it was Gandhi who made it an instrument of mass social and political change. 'In Thoreau the idea of civil disobedience was not clearly disengaged from the ideas of conscientious refusal and of revolution and it is only with Gandhi that civil disobedience is clearly articulated' (Cohen 1972: 306). This was Gandhi's original contribution to contemporary times, both at the theoretical and at the practical level. Subsequent theoreticians and practitioners of civil disobedience have worked within the framework that he provided.

Civil disobedience is a public act carried out in the open implying the willingness of the dissenter to accept punishment for breaking the law. A disobedient accepts personal responsibility publicly. He must inform the concerned government official(s) about the time and place of the act, the reason(s) for protest and if possible the law or the policy that is being protested against. For Russell the publicity that the act evokes more than the actual act would bring about the desired change in the law, policy or attitudes of the government. Disobedience is to a particular law without undermining the fabric of law. The civil disobedient is basically a law abiding citizen who adopts the technique of breaking the law with utmost respect for the law. He resorts to it only as a last recourse after exhausting other modes of protest and uses it sparingly and with utmost caution. It is the public and open nature of the act, based on universal principles and is clearly disinterested in motives. This distinguishes civil disobedient from the revolutionaries and criminals. A revolutionary seeks to overthrow the existing order in favour of a better alternative. Usually revolutionary activity is violent but civil disobedience, as developed and conceptualised by Gandhi, solves conflict in a non-violent manner. Since then most practitioners of civil disobedience insist on the need to adhere to non-violence in order to avoid it being misunderstood as threats. A criminal breaks the law secretly to avoid punishment and for an unfair gain but civil disobedience is an open, public and collective action.

Civil disobedience allows the possibility of an individual act to eventually develop into a mass action. As an open and a public act, it is inherently democratic and majoritarian. Any individual can resort to it if he feels that a law or a policy has no moral or rational justification. It rules out a Leninist Vanguard Party of professional revolutionaries and it is also not an elitist proposition. Civil disobedience is a midway path between constitutional forms of political action, on the one hand, and revolutionary activity, on the other hand. It accepts, as Russell did, that in a democratic society the normal procedure of elections and other procedures may be too slow to effect the desired change in law or policy, in which case civil disobedience is the only course of action. It legitimises such actions even in the well-established liberal democracies. Civil disobedience is not 'systemic', for it does not reject the legal system totally. It shuns anarchy and conspiracy. It does not defend infidelity to the law nor does it merely represent the frustration of a disgruntled individual, for it aims to bring about a change in the said law for the overall betterment of the society. It is different from resistance, which normally is the pattern of protest in authoritarian systems, where, in the absence of open, constitutional and organised modes of protest and change, secret operations are generally the accepted form. It also differs from insurrection where collective violence is used for attaining a specific goal. Unlike revolution, civil disobedience attempts to persuade through symbolic acts for limited specific changes within a given political and legal system. It is not like anarchism, which believes that government is an unnecessary evil since it restricts and coerces individual freedom. Unlike dissent, it is a protest that entails a breach of law or policy. Conscientious objectors disobey the law only if the privilege they demand is not granted, while civil disobedience demands a general change of laws or policies.

In summation, civil disobedience is a legal form of protest against a law or policy which contravenes with a strongly held and deeply cherished conviction or principle. It is usually occasioned by a major grievance that calls for immediate protest when the sense of justice in a community is infracted. A civil disobedient is not seeking to overthrow the existing social order for that will require a critique and an alternative. The purpose is to change an unjust law or policy or practice and not the entire legal system. It is usually non-violent and tries to minimise the use of force, for it seeks to avoid threats and intimidation. As popularised by Gandhi, the idea is to hate the sin and not the sinner so a civil disobedient through self-suffering and sacrifice tries to convince the wrongdoer of the wrongs of the act. It is not to embarrass or morally coerce but to subdue the opponent. It aims at compromise or solution with honour, on the premise that society would benefit and would become more just and harmonious.

ACTIVIST-THEORETICIAN: THOREAU, GANDHI, KING AND RUSSELL

Sophocles (496–406 BC) in the tragedy *Antigone* suggests that no ruler, however powerful, has the right to demand acts or omissions contrary to divinely ordained norms such as those of familial piety. Plato's *Apologia* and *Crito* depict Socrates, one of the earliest civil disobedient, as being torn between the dictates of his own individual conscience and the requirements of social authority. Socrates pleads innocence to the accusation of corrupting the young and was eventually convicted. He contends that even if the court found his discourses unlawful he will nevertheless continue, for that is the right thing to do. It is not an act of disobedience though he proposes civil disobedience in case the law actually prevents him from doing what he considers to be his moral duty. On hearing of his death sentence, Crito advises him to escape but Socrates refuses, for as an Athenian citizen he has been law abiding and considers it to be his moral duty to abide by the verdict pronounced in conformity with the law.

A general reading of *Crito* reveals that civil disobedience requires fulfillment of certain conditions. Its underlying assumption being the imperative obedience to the city, if one is reasonably satisfied with its laws. For Socrates, the entitlement of the state to obedience is because it confers benefits. Anticipating Locke, he argues that Athenian citizens were obliged to obey the laws of their city since they had freely consented to do so and obedience to the state was for three reasons—gratitude, consent and morality. However, he does not acknowledge any limits to an individual's duty. He does not consider the fact that person(s) accepts benefits with certain assumptions and in the hope of certain reasonable expectations. If these are not fulfilled then obedience to the state is no longer tenable, though breaking or defying the law may undermine and eventually destroy the state, a proposition that is valid if the state is just. In case there are unjust laws, it is better to rectify it, making the state stronger and just. Furthermore, the fear of disrupting the state is misplaced, as civil disobedience only succeeds if it has the support of the majority.

Socrates and Crito never discuss the justification of disobedience but rather the reasons for citizens' obedience to a city. Their answer is that if anybody remains in the city willingly that demonstrates his readiness to comply with its laws. Disobedience is only permissible if vocalised by a superior authority, in that case, the latter's command overrides that of the city. A modern day civil disobedient sees this question differently. He looks to the duty of a just citizen to disobey when an unjust law exists. He does not accept the proposition that being just is to obey the city. Justice is an independent criterion by which the laws of the city are evaluated and judged. This standard can be natural law, human rights or a belief of an honest conscience and if violated, then there is the duty to disobey. In such a situation, disobedience is the just course of action. However, the Socratic dilemma, one shared by those who believe that on certain occasions one's moral principles may compel them to disobey political authority or some specific law, while they still recognise authority and its rule making function as legal and therefore binding. One can find statements in Cicero, St. Augustine and St. Aquinas to the effect that when laws do not conform to nature, they can be overridden. There is no obligation to obey an unjust law and that no ruler can make an unjust law. However, none of them specify explicitly as to when an individual can decide to disobey the law of the government. Early Christians disobeyed Roman laws for they considered them to be contrary to their beliefs, evident in More's assertion of being 'the king's good servant, but God's first'.

Thoreau's passionate and eloquent lecture *On the Relation of the Individual to the State* (1848) inspires many to resist unjust laws. The lecture is published as *Resistance to Civil Government* (1849). It does not mention civil disobedience. The title is inserted subsequently after his death but, nonetheless, his name has been associated with the term. In 1848, he refuses to pay taxes in Massachusetts, in order to protest against the two policies of the government of the United States, the War in the Mexico and Slavery in the South, as these violated individual rights. Like Gandhi, he also does not consider the government to be important in the day-to-day activities of the individual. His disinterest and lack of enthusiasm towards government is because all states including the democratic ones are the embodiment of force and physical strength, concerned with functions related to law and order, and protection of property. Laws, policies and associations are essentially coercive, stifling and hindering individuality and spontaneity. Thoreau insists on the persons with conscience should disassociate from the state, for that enables them to lead lives untainted by the evils that the state sponsors and promotes. Since the government releases diabolical forces which it is unable to control, he suggests that the individual should withdraw from supporting the government and instead, rely on his inner resources. Thoreau is neither a rebel nor an anarchist. He is a liberal for whom individual conscience is inseparable from common sense standards of right and wrong and humane sensibilities. It is the true criteria of what is politically just and right since conscience is above the state. It is important that individuals perceive themselves primarily as individuals and only subsequently as citizens or subjects. Conscience, which he calls the inner voice and the 'genius', is an exclusive and purely personal thing and civil disobedience is a form of inspired self-expression. Law for Thoreau remains a form of control, hardly different from any kind of coercion. He insists that the citizen shall not surrender his conscience to the legislator. He declares 'the law will never make men free. It is men who have got to make the law free'. For Thoreau conscience is secular, the ability to do what one thinks to be right. He does not acknowledge the existence of general principles or universal standards of right. His notion of morality and politics is essentially subjective and anti-legalistic. This is evident from Thoreau's protest against slavery which he justified not with reference to any principles but only that his inner voice had convinced him of its evil. He accepted non-conformity and even eccentricity as a proof of the existence of a conscience. He never acknowledges consensus in morals and rejects every universally accepted standard of right, including the *Bible* and the constitution. Thoreau's conscience has three implications for politics. First, it becomes clear as to why he does not restrict conscientious action to non-violence and passive disobedience as conscience may demand more than non-complicity or withdrawal. He does not rule out the use of violence and force if conscience demands. In fact, he views conflict as the gist of life itself and any action that flows from one's convictions is good and if for this reason violence is necessary it is to be used. Second, intolerance is the nature of a militant conscience. Belief in one's convictions makes tolerance impossible. Third, in light of his anti-institutionalism he contends that solitary actions rather than collective ones are good (Rosenblum 1981: 101–103).

Thoreau's views on civil disobedience are important for two reasons. First, he does not complain against taxation as such, for he paid his highway taxes but objects to the state poll tax, for it finances an unjust government. Cohen suggests that Thoreau should be regarded more as a conscientious refuser than a civil disobedient since he withholds paying taxes for many years after his imprisonment. Moreover, he does not seem keen to arouse his fellow-beings for supporting his act. Instead, he merely desires to disassociate himself from a wicked and an unjust government. In the process, he hopes to convince his fellow-beings of his act and bring changes that are necessary and desirable. He tries to set an example of personal purity and impose his conscience on others. It is this characteristic rather than a concern with reform, according to Arendt, that set Thoreau apart from other civil disobedients.

> Thoreau's fundamental object is not to confront the state but to keep his hands clean or, if they are to be stained, then only by the huckleberry that he finds 'on one of our highest hills, two miles off, where the state is nowhere to be seen' (Cohen 1972: 306–307).

Second, Thoreau does not want to be guilty of aiding and abetting injustices that he condemns. He regards going to jail as a proof of his incorruptible integrity. He argues that every person individually, without waiting for the majority to take the initiative, could disobey an unjust law, for it offends his moral sensibilities. In his lecture he states, 'the only obligation which I have a right to assume is to do at any time what I think right.' He considers civil disobedience as a moral act by a moral individual. Thoreau never discusses the occasions and limits of civil disobedience or obedience, the likely or desired effects of either, nor the means and techniques of resistance to law. He considers disobedience to be persuasive but never explicitly rules out violence and subsequently and willingly supports John Brown's bloody anti-slavery raid. He invokes the rhetoric of revolution at times and states that 'this is a time to revolutionise and rebel, and if a little blood is spilled, it is spilled too, when conscience is violated.'

Gandhi's Views

Gandhi is primarily an activist-theoretician who refines Thoreau's concept of civil disobedience and incorporates ideas from Ruskin and Tolstoy to build a case for mass *satyagraha*. He read Thoreau for the first time in 1907, while he was held as a prisoner in a South African jail.

> He chose no more than was needed to vitalise his own beliefs, returned to find again, with the help of western insights, the resources of his own tradition, out of which he drew the strength that made him so responsive to the aspirations of the Indian poor and so imaginative as a leader in the fight for liberation. Yet, even if the strategy Gandhi evolved was fed by Indian traditions and adapted constantly to Indian circumstances, it was never exclusively Asian (Woodcock 1971: 13).

Gandhi integrates the concept of civil disobedience with his overall commitment to non-violence and *satyagraha* and dignity of labour. He regards truth (*satya*) and non-violence (*ahimsa*) as universal principles with an inseparable link between them. This omnipresence of truth and non-violence is derived from another basic foundation of his edifice that human beings are amenable to moral persuasion. The individual, a moral and a social person, follows the paths of truth and non-violence since it is the best possible way of leading a good and satisfactory life. It enhances human dignity, relative equality and human perfectibility, for it allows individual initiative and recognition and provides a mechanism for resolving conflicts in the complex modern world. It is the logical culmination of democratic principles based on active citizen's participation, civility and non-violence, as that leads to self-realisation, social awareness and responsibility, which are necessary for total fulfillment. Gandhi, like Green, accepts common good, without denying a pivotal role to the individual, endowed with moral law and duty (*dharma*). As a bearer of moral authority, he has the right and even the duty to judge the state and its laws, by the standards of *dharma*, which in turn combines the essentials of *satya* and *ahimsa*. The individual can challenge and even disobey the state, for all states violate satya and ahimsa. According to Gandhi, 'Every citizen renders majority to take the initiative, could disobey an unjust law, for it offended his moral sensibilities. In his lecture he states, 'the only obligation which I have a right to assume is to do at any time what I think right.' He considers civil disobedience as a moral act by a moral individual. 'Every citizen renders something more than a method of resistance to particular legal norms; it became an instrument of struggle for positive objectives and fundamental change (cited in Bondurant 1967: 3–4).

Gandhi regards women as the best messengers of peace and as soldiers of non-violence for they are inherently tolerant and peaceful. The woman, as a mother epitomises self-suffering and sacrifices, qualities, which he considers to be vitally important for a *satyagrahi*. He acknowledges the influence of his wife Kasturba and the black women in South Africa as his role-models and teachers in the art and technique of non-violent *Satyagraha*. Gandhian *Satyagraha* also demonstrates the intricate relationship between means and ends through a philosophy of action. In his approach to conflict, Gandhi does not seek compromise but a synthesis, in the sense that a *satyagrahi* never yields his position which he regards as truth but he is prepared to accept the opponent's position, if it is true. By sacrificing one's position he does not make any concessions to the opponent but only to a mutually agreeable adjustment. Both parties are satisfied without feeling triumphant or defeated for no one compromised in order to settle the conflict. This technique was tried out in colonial India, ruled by the British, known for their sense of justice and fair play, which perhaps explained the success of his actions. George Orwell (1903–1948) doubts the efficacy of the success of Gandhi's strategy in brutal totalitarian systems. Orwell's observations are to a large extent right but that does not belittle Gandhi's unparalleled and tremendous achievement. His supreme importance is in making non-violent mass action a potent force and by his commitment to open mass non-violent action with interludes of civil disobedience, Gandhi is able to convince the world that colonial subjugation is ethically wrong.

> Gandhi's greatest achievement was that virtual conversion of the British, which gradually and imperceptibly weakened to the vanishing point their will to rule as imperialists (Woodcock 1971: 13).

For Gandhi, civil disobedience is a tactic for social change, a weapon of the powerless and the oppressed. It is the Gandhian model that subsequent practitioners of civil disobedience employ. Moreover, Gandhi also demonstrates that the success of civil disobedience depends on whether it has a universal rather than a local appeal. This is best exemplified in the Civil Rights movement in the United States, which tried out his techniques to prove that it was 'appropriate to no single time and place; they can be used as effectively in a modern technological society as in a world, like the India of the 1930s, that was barely emerging from the medievalism of the Moghul Empire' (Woodcock 1971: 13).

In 1957, Harris Wofford points out that the Blacks in the United States use Gandhian techniques in their fight for racial equality and equal opportunities. He contends that every individual is responsible for preventing injustice and that law is not a command in the Austinian sense but a question. Subsequently, King distinguishes between the just and the unjust laws and argues that the law enacted and administered by individuals can be wholly disharmonious with the moral or natural law. If that happens then the said law become unjust. Any law that degrades human personality is unjust and all segregation laws distort the soul and damage the human personality, giving the segregator a false sense of superiority and the segregated, a false sense of inferiority. King rightly believes that injustice anywhere is a threat to justice everywhere, for human relationships are mutually interdependent. Whatever affects one directly, affects all indirectly. He does not develop a theory of justice and natural law but bases his case for breaking the law on Gandhian injunctions. King considers non-violent civil disobedience as supplementing and not replacing the process of change that law initiates. In the initial phase, he accepts civil disobedience as the logical and righteous response to the laws and practices that institutionalise racial discrimination. Breaking a law remains a subsidiary aspect of his programme of non-violent resistance.

Later on in his life, King gives a new perspective to civil disobedience, one that would end not only discrimination and humiliation but also poverty, for he wanted to 'to dramatise the whole economic problem of the poor'. King considers mass civil disobedience as a new stage of struggle and explores its prospects of becoming a viable alternative to the revolutionary and quasi-revolutionary activity. This means not only scrutinising the institutional arrangements and social priorities of the whole country but also continuing to retain the essential features of non-violent civil disobedience. The main objective was to 'interrupt the functioning of the larger society' with the view to compelling the United States Congress to act with the purpose of bringing about fundamental and lasting changes in the lives of the poor. For King, a true revolutionary is one who has nothing to loose and he personally identifies himself with the dispossessed of the nation. The poor, both white and black, had to organise a revolution against the system and not against their fellow-beings who perpetuated poverty. This does not mean mere job opportunities but a whole new life, a 'new economic deal for the poor'. He denounces capitalism and demands a guaranteed minimum income.

Russell was active in the Committee of Nuclear Disarmament (CND) which justified non-violent, civil disobedience against nuclear weapons. He believed the act would compel governments to reconsider and change their policies, since public opinion generated by the democratic and electoral processes are not adequate. He is convinced that a vigilant public opinion is the best method of ensuring that the state made laws that are in public interest. Laws make civilisation possible and that in a democracy as compared to dictatorships power is abused less, for it allows dissent and if necessary even disobedience.

The involvement of the United States in the Vietnam War resumes the debate on civil disobedience from different ideological commitments. **Irving Kristol** (1920–2006) the intellectual godfather of neo-conservatism felt that the Vietnam War did not justify civil disobedience but supported the war demonstrators. The neoconservative reaction towards the Vietnam War formed a part of their overall critique and opposition to World Communism, in which the United States was the bastion of the free world. Kristol contends that civil disobedience is not right, though it may be under certain circumstances an obligation. It is justified if there is an unjust action by a regime that is otherwise just and legitimate. Kristol, like Gandhi and King, describes civil disobedience as an open violation of the law with the hope of mobilising public opinion through a demonstration of exemplary self-sacrifice and a readiness to accept penalty. Clearly he visualises civil disobedience as a mass action, and rejects covert action by a small group, thus dismissing the idea of a 'Leninist Thoreau' as an 'intellectual and moral absurdity'.

Noam Chomsky (1928–) advocates non-payment of war tax and supports those who evade draft. He defends civil disobedience in a situation when one is confronted with intolerable evil. For instance, the horrors of Auschwitz and Dachau convince a person of conscience that political authority need not be obeyed all the time. A distinction between when to obey and disobey has to be drawn. Civil disobedience must be passive and its limits determined by the extent of evil that one confronts and by the considerations of tactical efficacy and moral principle. Both as a strategy and as a principle, civil disobedience must be non-violent. Chomsky also points out those unjust and evil laws and practices continue because various individuals obey and conform to them out of fear rather than out of a wish of wanting the evil to continue.

Arendt initially characterises civil disobedience as the politics of conscience, the ultimate commitment to be able to live with oneself, to tend one's spiritual upliftment. However, an article written in 1970, she abandons this view and describes civil disobedience as a truly political action free of self-regardiness or selfish motives. As the latest form of voluntary association, it revives the traditional American idea of free contractual fellowship for the sake of common action. It enjoins the government to abide by the Constitution. Arendt considers civil disobedience an American invention, though she does not explain why it begins in America and not elsewhere. This is perhaps because she regards the United States as the most fully developed form of representative democracy with a great deal of consensus in the public realm. Arendt welcomes spontaneous political action and distrusts those that threaten private concerns. She emphatically declares that political institutions must be independent of economic forces. On this basis, she opposes the Vietnam War and the involvement of universities in wars. She defends the citizen's right of civil disobedience and supports any action that is purely political devoid of any economic and social objectives.

RAWLS' ANALYSIS

Rawls articulates a fully developed theory of civil disobedience within a liberal constitutional democracy. Till date this is the most in-depth philosophical analysis on the subject so far. The liberals within the tradition who preceded him offered insights, which he incorporates in his analyses. Hobbes' arguments anticipates the recent discussions on civil disobedience, for he argues the need for a civil disobedient to willingly accept penalties and prove that he is breaking a law for a political reason and is otherwise an allegiant citizen, who has faith in the rule of law. Locke acknowledges the right of the people to resist an unjust government. In America, Jefferson extends the Lockean theory of consent by emphasising the majority needs to be conscious about minority rights and opinions. He regards the government as the main violator of individual thought and opinion but does not rule out the possibility of an over enthusiastic press and public opinion hindering independence of mind and conscientious judgement. Tocqueville regards unlimited power wherever lodged as a threat to justice and individual liberty and recommends disobedience when there is a transgression of those limits. Hegel allows justified disobedience, if the state is not rational by which he means its ethical substance. If the state fails to provide welfare and is inadequate in serving as means to the satisfaction of the citizen, then the basis of the state becomes insecure. He recognises the possibility of justified disobedience and acknowledges that the inequalities of civil society in his day brought into focus the validity of obligations for a large number of poor people but does not outline the concrete measures that disobedience should take. Moreover, he does not grant this right convincing legal form (Tunick 1998: 529–530). For Green, the majority and the minority have the right of resistance provided they demonstrate that it is for common good. Each citizen has the right to judge whether a particular law conforms to common good but has no right to break the law as long as there are legal methods for changing or abolishing the disputed law. Whenever there is resistance, common good suffers. It is only within non-democratic systems or where the law-making authority is itself obscure that individuals have a right of resistance provided there is a guarantee that authority would qualitatively change and the general social order would remain intact with its set of rights. This distinction between democratic and non-democratic system is set aside when Green discusses slavery in the context of the American Civil War. He defends the duty of the slaves to reject state laws since these deny basic rights. Even those who supported the cause of the slaves must disobey legitimately the laws upholding slavery provided they ensure that if they violated these laws there will be no anarchy and loss of general freedom. Green does not distinguish between disobedience to a particular law or policy from the issue of overthrowing government. He regards disobedience as a revolutionary activity.

Rawls accepts that even in a well-ordered society serious violations of justice do occur. He limits his enquiry to the role of civil disobedience in a democratic society since a state of near justice requires a democratic regime. In such a state, it is the conflict of duties that gives rise to the problem of civil disobedience. It involves the extent to which citizens feel that it is their duty to obey the laws enacted by the legislative majority, in order to defend their liberties and their duty to oppose injustice. A constitutional theory of disobedience has three aspects. First, it defines the possible reasons for dissent and distinguishes it from other forms of opposition in a democratic authority. This may range from protests and demonstrations to militancy and organised resistance. Second, the reasons for civil disobedience and the conditions under which such an action is justified in a democratic regime which is more or less just. Third, it should explain the role of civil disobedience within a constitutional system as an appropriate mode of protest (Rawls 1972: 363–364).

Rawls considers civil disobedience as a public, non-violent and conscientious act contrary to law, usually done with the intention of bringing about a change in the policies and laws of the government. It is a political act, which is justified by the moral principles that define a conception of civil society and public good. It is based on a political conviction as opposed to self or group interests. In the context of constitutional democracy, this involves a conception of justice which acts as a point of reference to the citizens to regulate their political affairs and interpret the constitution. It is a political act within the limits of the allegiance to the rule of law with the purpose of restoring democratic norms and processes that has been ignored or overthrown. It is addressed to the majority that wields political power. It is guided and justified by the principles of justice that regulate the constitution and its social institutions. It is a public act since it addresses to the sense of justice of the majority giving them an opportunity to reconsider the measures that are being protested against. It is a warning, which the dissenters give for not honouring the conditions of social co-operation for they are undermined when basic liberties are persistently violated. He specifically rules out appeal to, 'principles of personal morality or to religious doctrines' although he accepts, 'these may coincide with and support one's claims' (1972: 365).

Rawls grants to the minority the right to draw the 'attention of the majority to acknowledge their legitimate claims' (1972: 366). He considers the possibility of injustice being meted out on a minority and in this context he mentions religious minorities. He is not explicit as to whether the minority seeks justice, recognition, status and rights as individual members for themselves, or as a group. Civil disobedience is an expression of one's conviction, it has to be based on principles that regulate civic life, public life and also has to be non-violent, for in a situation where civil disobedience becomes necessary, only a law is broken but not the fidelity to the system of law. Rawls insists that social arrangements, however, efficient can be unjust. He grants the right to disobey in case the principle of equal liberty and fair equality of opportunity are violated and if a minority has been suffering for a long time and if avenues for legal redress are not available. Arendt confines acts of civil disobedience to redress political grievances excluding social and economic ones. This is evident from his decision to prohibit civil disobedience if there are violations of the difference principle.

Rawls rules out the possibility of anarchy as long as there is sufficient working agreement in the individuals' conception of political justice. What is required is an understanding of its meaning as embodied in the ethos of the democratic institutions. 'If legitimate civil disobedience seem to threaten civil peace the responsibility falls not so much on those who protest as upon those, whose abuse of authority and power justified such opposition' (1969: 255). For him, civil disobedience is distinct from conscientious refusal, which is non-compliance with a more or less direct legal injunction or administrative order. Civil disobedience unlike conscientious refusal is addressed to the sense of justice in the majority. In the latter, the conviction of the community cannot be invoked nor is it based on political principles. It may be founded on religious or other principles that are found in variance of the constitution. However, in reality this distinction does not exist.

OTHER VIEWS

Walzer contends that the right to resist is inherent in the pluralist nature of democratic societies. Society consists of innumerable intermediary associations voluntary in nature fulfilling the diverse social needs of the individual. The membership to these bodies is voluntary, unlike that of the state and the individual's commitment to them will be greater than that of the state since the individual opts for it willingly and knowingly. This commitment may clash with that of the state, in which case there is an obligation to disobey. Citizens also have the right to protest against anti-democratic institutions with all the necessary force.

Habermas, in his rejection of the new social movements and critique of post modernity, regards civil disobedience as a legitimate response only under certain conditions. In the early 1980's, on the occasion of the Pershing missile protests in the then Federal Republic of Germany, Habermas claims that civil disobedience is, 'among the indispensable necessities of mature political culture' (1985: 106). As a category civil disobedience 'must remain suspended between legitimacy and legality' since the citizen's obedience to political authority of a democratic constitutional state cannot be reduced to the positive law's sanctioning of such authority. Instead, it has to be reducible to the legitimacy of the law. Habermas clearly adopts Rawls' necessary conditions for a successful claim to civil disobedience. The acts must be public, symbolic and non-violent amounting to a 'premeditated transgression of individual legal norms' with the sole 'intention of appealing to the capacity for insight and the sense of justice of the relevant majority' (1985: 100–102). Furthermore, Habermas testifies that the disputed policy has to be one which will have relatively irreversible consequences or which involves, as in the context of missile protests, a 'confrontation of different forms of lives' (1985: 110–111), making an exception to the generally accepted liberal democratic principle of the majority rule. Pleading for a reflexive application of this rule, Habermas contends that in the case of civil disobedience the majority must limit itself in exercising its majoritarian rights against civil dissidents.

In conclusion, in the era of globalisation of liberal democracy, in the late twentieth century, any discourse on democracy will have to accept a theory of civil disobedience. This is because it is the most civilised and dignified form of protest in a non-violent manner, that is available to a citizen to bring about a revolution by consent. In the mass indirect democracies of today with most governments elected on the basis of minority popular votes, the right or the obligation of civil disobedience reinforces the libertarian aspect of early liberalism of Locke and Jefferson.

Further Readings

Bedau, H.A. (Ed.), *Civil Disobedience: Theory and Practice*, Bobbs-Merrill, Indianapolis, 1979.

Bedau, H.A. (Ed.), *Civil Disobedience in Focus*, Routledge, London, 1991.

Gandhi, M.K., *Non-violent Resistance*, Schocken, New York, 1961.

Haksar, V., Rights, *Communities and Disobedience: Liberalism and Gandhi*, Oxford University Press, New Delhi, 2000.

Milne, A.J.M., *The Right to Dissent*, Avebury Publishing Company, London, 1983.

Singer, P., *Democracy and Disobedience*, Claredon Press, Oxford, 1973.

Walzer, M., *Obligations: Essays on Disobedience, War and Citizenship*, Harvard University Press, Cambridge MA, 1973.

Zashin, E.M., *Civil Disobedience and Democracy*, Macmillan, London, 1971.

Chapter 9
Citizenship

In political theory, citizenship refers to not only a legal status as a member of a particular country but also a normative ideal—the ruled are full and equal participants in the political process. Citizenship is a distinctively democratic ideal, for people as in a monarchy or a dictatorship is subjects and not citizens. Often democracy and citizenship are indistinguishable, though the former focuses on the institutions and procedures—political parties, electoral systems and the rule of law and constitutional provision that enable citizens' active and full participation. Theories of citizenship focus on the attributes of individual citizens. Citizens have certain rights and duties, which vary from one country to another.

In ancient Athens, citizenship was perceived mainly with reference to duties, while the modern connotation of citizenship involves a set of rights besides duties. In modern times, citizens have a right to participate in politics and also a right to pursue their private commitments, besides their political commitment. In the modern period, citizenship connotes a status defined with reference to a set of particular rights and duties. It is also an identity, indicating one's membership in a political community. This identity is shared in common by different groups in society and thus is integrative in nature. It conveys equal status and equal rights before the law. Expansion of citizenship rights helps to incorporate previously excluded groups, like the working class and women in society. Citizenship signifies membership and the participation of citizens in the collective affairs of their government.

The ancients regarded citizenship a privilege to select a few. For the moderns, the spread of democracy and with it universal suffrage, has made citizenship universal. It signifies common identity as it makes each person proud of the whole nation to which he belongs. However, in both the conceptions, citizenship implies that citizens are equals under the law, even if one is richer or more gifted than other or occupies office for the moment. This democratic notion of citizenship differs from the pre-modern conceptions that determine people's status by their ethnicity, gender, religion or class. Citizens are classified as natural and naturalised citizens. The former are citizens by virtue of birth in a particular place, while the latter acquire citizenship. *Jus soli* and *jus sanguineous* are the two ways of determining citizenship. The crucial equalitarian impulse of modern citizenship is based on the principle of one person, one vote.

CITIZENSHIP THROUGH THE AGES

Citizenship and the City-state

Citizenship was an important theme in ancient Greek and Roman Republics but disappeared from feudal systems, to be revived as the most desirable aspect of civic humanism during the Renaissance. In ancient Athens, citizenship was primarily perceived in terms of participation duties. Citizens were legally required to take their turn in public office. In ancient Athens, citizens actively participated in the institutions of government—assembly, council and courts—and in public debates. The Athenian model is known as active citizenship. A man who had no interest in politics or in the administration of his state was described as an 'idiot'. Pericles praising the Athenian citizen in the Funeral Oration Speech (429 BC), delivered after the first casualties of the long-drawn Peloponnesian Wars (431–404 BC), describes the virtues of citizenship.

Here each individual is interested not only in his own affairs but in the affairs of state as well: even those who are mostly occupied with their own business are extremely well-informed on general politics—this is a peculiarity of ours: we do not say that a man who takes no interest in politics is a man who minds his own business; we say has no business here at all (Thucydides 1954: 118–119).

Citizenship during Pericles' time meant common good and common endeavours among the citizens. The constitution was not a legal document but a way of life, with every Athenian participating with total commitment. In the process, each individual acquired a civic personality and a sense of responsibility. There was general commitment to the idea of civic virtue, for private interests were subordinated to the public welfare and common good. With a civilisation based on slavery and commerce restricted to resident aliens who enjoyed the legal status of free individuals but no citizenship rights, there was not much of a disparity between citizens as what they valued was not affluence but leisure. It was a society of equals with rough parity that enabled them to pursue common goals. Though an ardent democrat, Pericles in 451 BC restricted the franchise to the legitimate offspring(s) of Athenian parents, in order to ensure that the rewards of citizenship were confined to the Athenian middle class.

As in many other areas of political enquiry, **Aristotle** provides the earliest discussion of citizenship. Citizenship is of pivotal importance to him, as with his practical sense, he easily perceives that ideal governance is possible only by a law-based state, in which citizens abide by laws. This is contrary to Plato's belief structure in the *Republic* wherein he does not consider participation by the average person as crucial to the process of government and places greater faith on the rule by the philosopher king. This changes in the *Laws*, for he defends a law-governed state as the best. Aristotle characterises political authority as constitutional between equals and since an individual is a political animal who finds fulfillment only within a *polis*, it is natural for people to aspire for political positions. Constitutional government with respect to citizenship rights allows people to compete for political office without civil chaos. Aristotle defines a state as a collective body of citizens. He rules out citizenship on the basis of residence since resident aliens and slaves also share a common residence with citizens but are not equipped to be citizens. Citizenship does not refer to the share that one has in civic rights, to the extent of being entitled to sue and to be sued in the courts of law, for this right belongs to aliens as well. A citizen is one who enjoys the right to share in the deliberative or judicial offices, is able to exercise his political rights effectively and enjoys constitutional rights under the system of public law.

For Aristotle, a citizen is one who shares power in the *polis*. He does not, like Plato, distinguish between, 'an active ruling group and a politically passive community' (Wolin 1960: 57). He stipulates that the young and the old could not be citizens for the former is immature and the latter infirm. He does not regard women as citizens since they lack the deliberative faculty and the leisure to understand the working of politics. As far as working class is concerned, though some states had made them citizens, they clearly do not have the aptitude or the leisure to display the true excellence to shoulder civic responsibilities. A good citizen has the intelligence and the ability to rule and to be ruled. He, however, shares with Plato the perception that citizenship is a privilege and a status to be inherited. Aristotle points out that in order to discharge the functions effectively citizens need to inhabit a *polis* that is compact and close-knit. He is critical of Plato's prescription of a citizen body of five thousand as the ideal, for that is too large requiring unlimited space, such as the sprawling lands of Babylon, rendering impossible functions like military command, public communications and judicial judgements. A cohesive citizen body where everybody knows one another intimately, can settle disputes effectively and satisfactorily, and distribute political offices according to the merit of the candidates. The quality of citizenship suffers in a larger political community due to lack of intimacy. This eulogy of the *polis* comes at a time when Alexander, Aristotle's pupil, was already establishing an empire and the city-state was on the throes of extinction.

Aristotle considers a good citizen as someone who could live in harmony with the constitution and has sufficient leisure time to devote himself to the tasks and responsibilities of citizenship. He regards the existence of diversity of interests within a citizen-body, as essential to the practice of citizenship for a good government could be attained only through a balance of these interests. A good citizen would possess virtue or moral goodness that would help in realising a selfless and co-operative civic life. Aristotle regards citizenship as a bond forged by the intimacy of participation in public affairs. The bond is moreover a relationship which is guarded with some jealousy by those privileged to enjoy it. It is neither a right to be claimed by nor a status to be conferred on anybody outside the established ranks of the class, no matter how worthy such an outsider might be. Indeed, Greek citizenship depended not so much on rights, which could be claimed as on responsibilities, which had with pride to be shouldered (Heater 1990: 4).

Rome developed a pragmatic, flexible and legalistic notion of citizenship. Full citizenship carried with it six privileges. Of these, four were public rights, service in the army, voting in the assembly, eligibility to public office and the legal right of action and appeal. The other two pertained to the rights of intermarriage and trade with other Roman citizens. In the fourth century, Rome's basic concept of citizenship underwent three historically significant adaptations. In 381 BC, Rome conferred full citizenship on the male members of the city of Tusculum in the region of Latium. The distinction between 'Latin' and 'Roman' citizenship was also introduced so that a person could simultaneously be a citizen of his own city and of Rome. Five decades later, the inhabitants of the other Latin towns were offered partial citizenship—*civitas sine suffragio* (citizenship without franchise) that allowed enjoyment of private privileges. Roman citizenship was conferred to the inhabitants of the territories that Rome annexed, quite contrary to the practice of the Greeks, who continued to treat the citizens of neighbouring Greek cities as aliens. Roman citizenship provided total equality before the law. Just as in Greece, in Rome too, citizenship meant virtue—the willingness to serve one's state. Service to the state meant military rather than juridical-political. Cicero reiterates the Aristotelian conception of an active and virtuous citizen, as one who uses his gift of speech and rational thought for the benefit of the community and such a person fulfils his nature as a social animal. Rome, reiterating Aristotle, bequeathes to the West the idea of active life of strict republican virtue and participatory citizenship of the economically independent and the belief that empire destroys *virtu*, even civic and political life. The theme of citizenship so prominent and so arduously worked out during Greek and Roman period disappears from medieval thought only to be revived during the Renaissance with the rebirth of republicanism. Rome in course of time with the expansion of its empire, unlike Greece, comes to accept a more inclusive notion. At the height of Rome's imperial power, citizenship becomes a tool of social control and pacification (Faulks 2003: 19).

During the middle ages with the predominance of Christianity, the emphasis was on simplicity and sacrifice. It was essentially other-worldly with little attention on earthly matters. Men were primarily citizens of the whole world or of the city of god. Earthly citizenship was not that important for a good life. Aquinas, however, revives Aristotle's notion of citizenship by reiterating the key distinction of being a good citizen without possessing the qualities of a good man. Though he says very little about constitutional mechanisms and political institutions yet, his resuscitation of Aristotle's concepts of the state and citizenship has a revolutionary impact on political theory. It becomes possible once again to conceive of a state as an abstract entity with which the individual *qua* citizen has a vital relationship in both senses of the word. It thus becomes possible in theory for the political man to be judged by criteria different from those used in judgement of the Christian soul; and for the active citizen of the state to supersede the passive subject of the prince (Heater 1990: 21). Marsilius severs the connection between the human law and god's natural law, as he regards the state as a self-sufficient entity, which is determined by the citizenry; and that no government is good and stable without the consent of the citizens. He also proposes representation to overcome the difficulties of direct participation by a large body of citizens. The first principles of indirect democracy crystallise under his vision.

Renaissance Republicanism

Machiavelli, for whom the *virtù* of the citizens is the greatest input to Rome's greatness, revives the classical argument of citizenship in the Roman, rather than the Aristotelian sense. Reflecting on the instability and vulnerability of his native city Florence and comparing it with the power and stability that Rome achieved, Machiavelli concludes that the key factor is citizen *virtù*, which means patriotism, self-discipline, simple piety and the willingness to subordinate private gain for public good. He also emphasises on the need for a citizen-army as the quintessence of citizenship, for a citizen, as opposed to a mercenary soldier is reliable enough to sacrifice his life for the unity of his state. Held (1996, 36–39) describes Machiavelli's notion as protective republicanism as he views citizenship as a method for asserting citizens' interest. This is in contrast to Aristotle's developmental republicanism that underlines the performance of citizenship as a core element of what it means to be human. Bodin's concern is with the legal and social dimensions of citizenship, for he states that birth, adoption or enfranchisement can be the basis for acquiring citizenship. He also points to the cohesive quality of citizenship when the whole body of citizens submits to a single sovereign despite the existence of diverse laws, customs, language, religion and race. He rejects the idea of equal citizenship for all as no state ever recognises its citizens to be equal in rights and privileges.

Hobbes and Locke ignore the ideals of classical republicanism and citizen virtue. For both Hobbes and Locke, consent plays a crucial role. However, Locke underlines the importance of continuous consent, in the form of tacit consent and individual rights as the basis of legitimate political authority. Hobbes' model is termed as 'subject-citizenship' because it had as its aim, the securing of order rather than the performance of civic virtue, or the protection of individual rights (Faulks 2003, 22). Rousseau resurrects the ideals of public spirit, simplicity of life and desire for self-government of ancient Athens and Sparta and incorporates it with the modern notion of voluntarism and consent. Modern citizenship's stress on universality and equality is derived from

Stoicism which asserts the moral equality of human beings. Another important input is the universalistic tradition of Roman natural law (ibid: 15). Modern citizenship unlike ancient notion is not exclusive; the primary difference between pre-modern and modern citizenship is the acceptance of inequality of status unquestioningly.

MARSHALL'S ANALYSIS

Marshall, a liberal-social democrat representing the post-Second World War Keynesian consensus, links citizenship to social class in the context of the rise of capitalism and its most important by-product, the market. His formulation is similar to the Marxist critique of inequality, deprivation and polarisation of classes that inevitably follows the institutionalisation of a market economy. However, what differentiates his analysis from the Marxist analysis is his assertion that citizenship, which is based on the principle of equality, blunts many of the sharp edges that the market induces that are based on inequality. The class structure gets significantly modified with the advancements of citizenship. The process of modification in the capitalistic market does not mean abolition of classes. The class structure remains but the rise of citizenship minimises its disadvantages. Marshall's essential example is the post-Second World War evolution of the welfare state in Britain. It is within this context that he examines the development of capitalism and the consequent social system and the class structure. Market relationship and citizenship are antagonistic because citizenship accepts that every individual is entitled to the full membership of the community enjoying equal rights and duties, whereas market inevitably leads to wide differentiation in status, power and attitude. Marshall's emphasis on the British experience follows from his understanding that there are no universal principles determining the rights and duties of citizenship, for these evolve in a specific context.

According to Marshall, citizenship has three essential divisions—civil, political and social. The civil component consists of rights necessary for individual freedom and in this the most essential ingredient is the rule of law and the legal system. The political basis of citizenship is reflected in the right to participate in the political decision-making process. The realisation of such rights is associated with representative parliamentary institutions. The social basis of citizenship accrues out of a right or the capacity to enjoy the fruits of prevailing standard of living and thereby providing the larger societal basis of community. Here Marshall's emphasis is on the social services and the educational system. In the British context, these different dimensions of citizenship evolved gradually in the eighteenth, nineteenth and twentieth centuries. However, he is careful to mention that these broad periods are not watertight compartments since these different components overlap. The important argument is that the different components of citizenship require different institutional supports and emerge at different historical periods.

In the feudal setup, the source of citizenship is the restricted basis of a society full of cleavages and visible hierarchies. Subsequently, the nature of citizenship changes with conflict between different social institutions and also social groups. The relationship and the interplay between citizenship and social class is Marshall's most important contribution to the theory of citizenship and here, in the British context, he notes the coincidence of the rise of modern citizenship with the rise of capitalism. Since the basis of citizenship is very different from the capitalistic ethos, it is 'reasonable to expect that the impact of citizenship on social class should take the form of conflict between opposing principles' (Marshall 1950: 84). What is striking is that the opposite evolution takes place without being contradictory and mutually exclusive. It is accepted that, in the initial phase of the development of capitalism, citizenship undermines the privileges of the feudal elite while consolidating the capitalist class relations and divisions based on commodity production and exchange. Modern citizenship evolves out of a limited formal basis of legal equality doing away with the feudal societal setup permitting the actualisation of a new class system with the institution of private property. Paradoxically, citizenship initially does away with a particular class system and promotes another. However, in the eighteenth and nineteenth centuries, citizenship rights co-existed harmoniously with the inequalities of the capitalistic system as these rights are the basic requirements to maintain a particular kind of inequality. During this period, citizenship rights are exclusively civil rights, which is the basic requirement of a competitive market economy. For entering the market, both the capitalist and the workers have the same perception of civil rights. To enter into the market for exchange and contracts with each other, Marshall argues that, if such rights are the basis of citizenship, then inevitably citizenship strengthens and stratifies class inequalities. However, when citizenship incorporates political and social rights as well, then the conflict with the unequal class system actualised by civil rights leads to a situation of conflict. However, the danger to the capitalist class by the working class after gaining political power does not materialise mainly because of its inexperience to effectively use political power for its benefit in the nineteenth century. So the potential of the reform acts to create a more egalitarian society remains unfulfilled. This inadequacy, however, is largely met by the creation of trade unions as 'a secondary system of industrial citizenship parallel with and supplementary to the system of political citizenship' (1950: 94).

The novel method of collective bargaining, which trade unionism facilitates, leads to the enhancement of the economic and social status of the organised workers. Trade unionism has established the claim of social rights of the workers. This incorporation of social rights in the charter of citizenship leads Marshall to comment that 'citizenship and the capitalist class system are at war' (1950: 84). In situations of fundamental shifts like the Second World War, social citizenship does not destroy class nor does it eliminate class inequality but leads to new inequalities. What social citizenship achieves is to reduce the number of social inequalities that are an inevitable outcome of market operations. Citizenship performs an integrative function, as by promoting equality of status of each individual it combats the disruptive inequalities of a market economy. Equality of citizenship allows the acceptance of economic inequalities. Marshall agrees that even if citizenship can really overcome market inequality totally, tension will always persist and integration will remain incomplete. However, this act of integration is not only a situation of equalising rights for all but also a feeling of actual membership of the community. It is a common possession of a civilisation with sharing of national and societal values. This realisation, impossible in a feudal set up with total stratification, is now possible because of acquisition of civil rights by all the citizens and, as a result, different and visible cultures of various classes have disappeared. A common citizenship bond creates a new national identity and consciousness. This common civilisation has a material base as mass production for the home market and a growing interest on the part of industry in the needs and tastes of the common people enables the less well-to-do to enjoy a material civilisation which differs less markedly in quality from that of the rich than it has ever done before. All this profoundly alters the setting in which the progress of citizenship takes place. Social integration spreads from the sphere of sentiment and patriotism into that of material enjoyment. The components of a civilised and cultured life, formerly the monopoly of the few, are brought progressively within the reach of the many (1950: 96).

Mass production in the twentieth century, brought by Fordism[1] has enabled an overall improvement in the standard of living for everybody. This Marshall calls 'concrete substance of civilised life' (1950: 102) for it reduces risk and insecurity and perhaps more importantly equalises the entire societal pattern of behaviour. Real satisfaction and money income gets increasingly distant as mass production is actualised with the destruction of distinctive and divisive class cultures by the realisation of civil rights. This assertion of Marshall in *Citizenship and Social Class* reiterates his stance in his earlier book, *Work and Wealth* (1945).

> There has been going on, especially in the last fifty years or so, a steady fusion of class civilisations into a single national civilisation. ... There was a time when the culture of each class was, as it were, unique species. ... Mass production destroyed this isolation. ... There has been a progressive equalisation of the quality of material culture so that, even though great differences remain between the top and the bottom, they are variations on a single theme and are linked in a continuous scale. ... (Among other things it follows that) as higher quality goods move down the social scale, so hands reach up towards them from below and voices are lifted demanding a speedier rise in the standard of living (1945: 216–17).

This common material civilisation promotes social integration by percolation of economic well-being to lower classes within a uniform pattern and standard. Integration is achieved more by economic well-being rather than by political citizenship. Marshall's theory of integration has three distinctive parts—first, civil rights creates a citizenship in which distinct and particularistic class cultures decline, as graphically described by Shaw in *Pygmalion*, immortalised and popularised by its theatrical and cinematic versions called *My Fair Lady*, second, social rights drastically reduce class inequalities, with the majority of people identifying themselves as middle class and third, mass production provides the basis of a common material civilisation, which in turn develops into an integrative citizenship. However, in spite of these integrative tendencies the conflict and contradiction between the egalitarian impulse of citizenship and the in-egalitarian thrust of the market is a continuous process and therefore there is no final resolution of them. In this perennial conflict, class inequalities are blunted only by the egalitarianism that is created by a material culture and a common civilisation. However, since the very basis of this social equilibrium does not have a consensual basis the endemic conflict between citizenship and social class will continue forever. Social integration is never final and as such, integration will always remain problematic, as the basic contradiction between citizenship rights and the market forces can never be done away with. The historical specificity of the British Welfare state resting on the Beveridge Report and the National Service arises under certain specific social and economic conditions, which emerges out of the war years. However, the subsequent rise of an affluent society and inflation, in the 1990s creates a different situation which is less conducive to the welfare state. Like civil rights, social movements are also important in Marshall's account of citizenship. Civil rights create groups, associations and movements of a wide variety and in the situation of a conspicuous absence of civil rights; social movements can be a source of power capacitating a group for effective action. Marshall's examples are the Black power movement in the United States and the Student Movement of the 1960s. As such, social movements play a dual role as contributing and facilitating citizenship.

CRITICS OF MARSHALL

Many commentators have made important criticisms of Marshall's theory of citizenship. Dahrendorf (1959) finds it as slightly odd that though Marshall mentions industrial rights and counts it in the development of citizenship yet he does not include it as one of the basic essential ingredients of citizenship along with civil, political and social rights. Dahrendorf also finds Marshall's emphasis on the egalitarian impulse of social citizenship irrelevant for comprehending the problem of class as it exclusively deals with social stratification and completely ignores the economic function of wealth and personal property. Marshall claims that citizenship reduces class conflict but does not answer the question of the basis and source of tension and conflict. He also does not provide an account of the dynamics of class and distributional relationship and because of this limitation, his conception of citizenship is fundamentally weak.

Turner (1986: 64) questions Marshall's entire developmental logic and asserts that there is 'no necessary historical logic or upholding process'. The development is more contingent than following a regular pattern. Turner, reiterated by Barbalet (1977), asserts that the extension of citizenship rights takes place when groups, which are previously excluded, specially the working class, get accommodated. Turner observes that 'Marshall can be interpreted as saying that social violence has the potential for expanding the universalistic definition of the citizen', but Marshall fails 'to emphasise that citizenship rights have been achieved in substantial degree only through struggle' (1982: 171). Turner's position has more support amongst sociologists. Lipset (1963: xx) categorically states that Marshall, 'kept alive the perspective that society requires conflict'.

Turner finds that Marshall's overemphasis and preoccupation with class leads to the neglect of other important factors of modern social change, mainly war and migration, a criticism which Gallie (1983: 225–227) rejects and points out that Marshall insists on the importance of class conflict in order to understand how the state tries to manipulate popular sentiment by the extension of citizenship rights. Turner emphasises the role of egalitarian ideologies, along with migration, as wielding crucial influence on moulding modern democratic citizenship. Migration from traditional rural cultures leads to secularisation of society, which intensifies the struggle for citizenship rights. The evolution of citizenship in essentially migrant nations like America, Australia, Canada and New Zealand has to be understood in view of the nature of this mass migration and its effects. Barbalet (1997: 41–42) contends that 'it is misleading to assume that migration will continue to play a positive role in the development of democratic citizenship without regard to the class context in which it operates'. Turner is critical of Marshall for accepting the present British nation-state. He mentions four waves of modern citizenship as an alternative to the historical evolution that Marshall suggests. These are (a) consequences of the removal of property connotation from definition of citizenship, (b) removal of sex as a category, (c) redistribution of age, kinship and family for citizenship rights and (d) expansion of citizenship rights by including nature and environment. Barbalet (ibid: 102) points out that though Turner's framework is refreshing and novel its 'role in understanding the development of citizenship is not clear and somewhat limited'. Moreover, as a guide to historical evolution it 'fails to adequately reflect the history of social movements'. Nor can this scheme 'replace nor usefully supplement Marshall's distinction between civil, political and social rights in the development of citizenship' (Barbalet, ibid). Miller (2000: 44) observes that 'Marshall's view runs into difficulties, once the idea of a common civilisation is challenged by the emergence of radical cultural pluralism. If there is no longer a shared "common heritage" or "way of life" by reference to which citizens' rights have been defined, how are we to arrive at the conception of social justice that defines citizenship?'

Giddens' alternative theory of citizenship begins by rejecting Marshall's theory. He is critical of Marshall's theory of industrial rights, which for him means forming trade unions, collective bargaining and right to strike. Giddens argues that rights are distinguishable by class bias. For instance, the rights of personal freedom and equality have been fought and won by the emerging capitalist class opposing feudal privileges for these hindered trade and commerce. From the point of the bourgeoisie, these rights imply strengthening of their control over the employees and other factors of production. As such, the struggle to form trade unions and the right to strike are not merely extension of civil liberties but a reflection of the working class movement against the employers and the state. Giddens claims that industrial rights can form a part of civil rights as Marshall acknowledges them to be. However, even his argument is inadequate as contrary to his separate categorisation one must not forget that civil and political liberties have been won, as pointed out by Miliband after centuries of struggle and as a precondition to the enjoyment of industrial rights that form a part of the latter rights. Giddens (1982: 171) also says that what Marshall claims to be conflict or struggles are actually contradictions and that 'extension of citizenship rights in Britain as in other societies, is in substantial degree the result of the efforts of the underprivileged to improve their lot'. Barbalet observes that Giddens' basic criticism of Marshall's three-stage theory of citizenship development in Britain flows from a basic error of confusing between power and rights. He says 'political citizenship, being rights of political participation without limitation by economic status, could only be added to the general status of citizenship when a class emerged in the social structure which was prepared and able to fight for such rights. This of course is Giddens' more general point, but it too requires qualification' (1997: 34).

Giddens acknowledges the importance of Marshall's analysis of citizenship but makes a number of critical remarks and provides a transformative criticism of his entire thesis. The historical account of Marshall is not acceptable to Giddens. The teleological and evolutionary theory of Marshall is based on a flawed logic of modern historical process. The three-fold classification is a gross overstatement and that Marshall simplifies the role of politics and the state in his theory. He acknowledges the support and approval of the state in consolidating citizenship but ignores the struggle of the people in achieving it. Moreover, Marshall ignores the unequal exchange between the privileged and the underprivileged in which the favourable balance for the latter was limited and rare, reflected only during the times of war, mainly the world wars. Halsey (1984: 11) says, 'Giddens' criticism cannot be fully sustained' because Marshall points out that class and citizenship and social forces 'at war in the twentieth century'. The basis of this conflict 'springs from the very roots of our social order'. As such, even amongst the critics there is no unanimity about Marshall's basic formulations.

Held (1989) considers all these criticisms as misleading for a number of reasons. There is very little evidence to prove that Marshall's contention is based on a logic that is teleological and evolutionary, for he is aware of the role of institutions and is conscious of the complexities in determining the speed of the movement of citizenship. There is no linear movement and Marshall is conscious of the ups and downs of this struggle, which is a struggle in the feudal state against hierarchy, and inequality that inevitably characterises a market and also against social injustice, which is perpetrated by the institutions of the state. This struggle has various phases, phases to fight for and the phases to protect and broaden it. The entire process reflects a fine balance between social and market forces. The intensity of the struggle is reflected by his description of a war situation between citizenship and class. His theory is based on the assumption of severe conflict, which Giddens ignores. Giddens also charges Marshall for conceiving citizenship as one-way traffic or a process that can be reversed. However, this criticism does not stand a close scrutiny of Marshall's work. He mentions the prevalence of primitive social rights, preceding the eighteenth century, and their disappearance in the latter half of the eighteenth and the early part of the nineteenth century Britain. Their reappearance begins with the spread of public elementary education but the subsequent development is heavily dependent on the relative strength or weakness of the various social movements supporting reform. A modern national consciousness accelerates for citizenship based on equal social worth of every single individual. A sense of community develops leading towards a feeling of oneness and rough parity. The international situation does not play an important part in his theory but it is equally true that he is conscious of nationalism and war in realising social rights. Even the present balance between class and citizenship does not mean that this equilibrium will continue into the foreseeable future as well. He even concedes that the durability of this balance is very difficult to determine. With regard to the factors that led to the actualisation of rights, Giddens thinks that though Marshall does not place due emphasis on conflict, the fact remains that conflict plays a very important role in his means of actualising rights.

Giddens' own model begins with the consolidation and expansion of state sovereignty and development of administrative power in the late sixteenth century. It begins with the capacity of the state to collect information about members of society and to supervise and create a governmental apparatus of surveillance. With the expansion of state's sovereign powers, the administrative centres become more powerful and the capacity of the state to enforce its writ by force got progressively reduced. A cooperative form of social relationship becomes increasingly necessary, which leads to a greater reciprocity between the governor and the governed and as this reciprocity increased the capacity of the subordinate groups to influence their rulers also increases. This double path expansion of power for Giddens was 'the dialectic of control' (Giddens 1985: 201).

The entire struggle for rights has to be analysed in this perspective. The identity of the subject population blossoms under the expanding sphere of state sovereignty. 'The expansion of state sovereignty means that those subject to it as in some sense—initially vague, but growing more and more definite and precise—aware of their membership in a political community and of the rights and obligations such membership confers' (Giddens 1985: 210). Nationalism also grows under similar circumstances. The administrative unity of the state is closely associated with nationalism and the mediation of this process is provided by citizenship. In this struggle for equal citizenship rights, there are many factors but the most important is class conflict, which at first takes the shape of the bourgeoisie against the feudal privileges, and subsequently the working class against the bourgeoisie. These struggles lead to important changes, first the delinking of the state from the economy, which is a consequence of the institutionalisation of civil and political rights. This enables the civil society to be free from the state's political interference. The institutions of the state and the economy gets remoulded with the separation of state from the economy creating new sets of rights and privileges which should not be seen as being created 'outside' the sphere of the state, but as part and parcel of the emergence of the 'public domain', separated from 'privately' organised economic activity. Civil rights thus have been, from the early phases of capitalist development, bound up with the very definition of what counts as 'political'. Civil and political citizenship rights develop together and remain, thereafter, open to a range of divergent interpretations which may directly affect the distribution of power (Giddens 1985: 207).

The rule by many or polyarchy develops in this background. The public-private divide also arises in this setting. Another historic change occurs after the right to vote is granted to gain 'social rights' or 'economic rights'. The struggle has been a long-drawn one for these rights ultimately led to the emergence of the welfare state. Giddens argues that the economic rights are not an extension of civil and political rights as they try to formalise the workers' control of the workplace. The entire extension of the ambit of citizenship is primarily due to class conflict. However, the achievements of the working class are still fragile and erosion is still possible in various political and economic situations. His conclusion is substantially similar to Marshall's formulations.

Held finds a number of weaknesses in Giddens' formulation, which emerges from his endorsement of many of Marshall's basic premises and due to lack of precision. 'The upshot of these problems is a fundamental underestimation of the complexity of citizenship: its multidimensional roots and the way the struggle for different types of rights is inscribed into, or embedded in, changing conception of citizenship' (Held 1989: 198). Giddens is critical of Marshall from a Marxist point of view, but also uses Marshall's arguments to criticise Marx. Giddens thinks that Marx is correct in ascribing many new rights as, 'bourgeois freedom' However, by using Marshall against Marx, he points to Marx's failure to take note of and see the possibility of actualisation of certain important citizenship rights to be realised within the ambit of liberal capitalism.

Among the industrialised societies, at least, capitalism is by now a very different phenomenon from what it was in the nineteenth century and labour movements have played a prime role in changing it. In most capitalist countries, we now have to speak of the existence of 'welfare capitalism', a system in which the labour movement has achieved a considerable stake and in which economic (social) citizenship rights brook large (Giddens 1985: 325).

However, as Macpherson (1966) points out, freedom of choice is the key to the basis of the individual as a citizen and this choice can be regarding religion, marriage, economic and political issues. Following Macpherson, Held (1989: 206) argues that Giddens', 'terms of reference are narrowly conceived' and do not permit the adequate specification of the diverse range of rights that emerge with the development of modern citizenship. He goes on to argue that a plausible theory of rights, taking note of the various range of rights which were a pre-requisite in creating the modern world, 'will require an analysis which goes far beyond that provided by Marx, Marshall and Giddens' (Held 1989: 206).

COSMOPOLITAN CITIZENSHIP

While Aristotle defines citizenship with reference to the city-state, a contemporary school, the Stoics put forward the notion of **cosmopolitan citizenship**. Despite Socrates drinking the hemlock without hesitation to prove his duty to obey the laws of his city, Athens, he speaks of allegiance to large humankind. It is in the fifth century BC Greece that the idea of cosmopolis or universal state emerges. Democritus (460–370 BC) and most **Sophists**, in general, and **Antiphon**, in particular, supported the idea. Antiphon was perhaps the first to speak of the existence of a universal law above local laws. Diogenes (d 324 BC), the Cynic, takes up the idea of cosmopolis or the 'city of the universe' as the community of the wise, the real community of human beings who pursue wisdom through reason. This community knows no geographical boundaries nor is it committed to any man made laws or constitutions. In the fourth century BC, the Cyrenaics, predecessors to Epicureans, defended cosmopolitanism as opposed to the city-state culture. The idea of world citizenship came into vogue and 'the ideal of Greek citizenship associated with the city-state was under question. At the same time, the city-state as an autonomous institution was itself being undermined in practice" (Heater 1990: 9). Ironically, Alexander, pupil of Aristotle, advocated positive and creative cosmopolitan notion of citizenship than Diogenes. He did away with the distinction between Greek and barbarian and "did not, as Aristotle advised him, treat the Greeks in the spirit of a leader and the barbarians in that of a master… rather he believed that he had a mission from God to be the reconciler of the world. … He wished to show that all things on earth were subject to one principle and included in one polity, and that all men were one people; and he demeaned himself accordingly. If the power that sent the world the soul of Alexander had not quickly recalled it, one law would have governed all men, and they would have turned their gaze to one system of justice as though to a common light' (Plutarch cited in Heater, ibid: 9–10).

Zeno (334/33–262/61 BC) of the Stoic school is another exponent of cosmopolitanism. Stoicism stresses on the rationality of men, and being children of god, because of this common attribute of reason, all men, of whatever race or social status, slave or free, equal resonates subsequently, in St. Paul's conception of the universal Church. Echoing Diogenes', the Stoics too believe wisdom to be an essential qualification for citizenship and point out that all men, world over and without distinction, are capable of attaining this status by developing their rational faculties. A citizen of the world will obey the 'law of nature', a code consisting of fundamental principles of justice derived from divine reason, and comprehended by man through the exercise of his reason. In case there is a clash between local, man-made laws with that of the law of nature, the laws of the world-city would prevail over those of the city-state. Two aspects of Stoicism exerts in-depth, perhaps lasting influence—one, the sacred relationship between god and man, absorbed by Christianity and the other, the conflation of law and nature, that subsequently becomes the basis of the doctrine of natural law. Cicero transmits the basic Stoic idea of human equality and brotherhood underpinning universal law of nature to Seneca, who writing a century later, believes that good life pursued in the interests of humanity at large is different and higher from the low life of the citizen in a state. During Seneca's time, the tussle between the two loyalties, the Christian loyalty to their 'heavenly kingdom' and the loyalty to the Emperor surfaced. The dilemma was that of men being loyal not only to mankind in general but to a spiritual belief and to the Roman Emperor. By the end of the first century, Marcus Aurelius became sensitive to this dilemma which eased off with Rome embracing Christianity and Christianity accepting Roman Stoicism. The Stoic universal city of men and gods metamorphoses into the Christian City of God and the fundamental tension remains. However, the Christian adapts the concept of cosmopolis and renders it mystical detaching it from earthly reality. The City of God would be attained only in heaven, or on earth, possibly, with the Second Coming. During the Middle Ages, Christian teaching dominates and the cosmopolitan ideas of Cynics and Stoics go into background. In the non-Western tradition, **Confucius** emphasised on the concept of *ta t'ung*, the greater unity and called for the restoration of the world commonwealth in which everyone worked for general welfare and harmony. A similar view existed in **India** too, which considered it petty to understand a person sans his humanity as exemplified in the popular phrase, *Vasudeva Kutumbakum.*

In the Middle Ages, the ideal of human unity on earth remains alive in the writings of **Ockham** and **Dante**. The latter argues for a global monarch as the ultimate source of authority in a world confederation of states and cities believing as he did in the full exercise of human reason, an idea that Kant subsequently borrows, and in existence of hierarchies in the nature of pyramid with the universal monarch at the top. Dante spoke of world government but not world citizenship as there was any individual participation.

In the seventeenth century, there is considerable thinking about the nature of international society and international law and thinkers of this period grapple with the universalist, natural law and Christian assumptions of the Middle Ages on the one hand, and with the emerging consolidated authority of the sovereign state on the other hand. Along with the consolidation of European state system, the notion of cosmopolitan citizenship gets consolidated in the seventeenth century. The Treaty of Westphalia accepts the principle of sovereignty and that each state as a self sufficient entity is the basis of international law and behaviour.

In the eighteenth century, the two revolutions—the American and the French—saw the consolidation of constitutional state and along with it the notion of popular sovereignty. The thinkers of the French Enlightenment's belief in human reason led them to believe that national, racial or religious distinctions as basically superficial. There was also a realisation that states inevitably led to oppression and war rather than human freedom and peace. Paine rejects the regimes of the eighteenth century and supports the ideal of world citizenship. Schiller too felt that he was the citizen of the world. Similar sentiments were expressed by Franklin, Beccaria, Priestly, Diderot and Condorcet. Franklin insisted on recognising 'Common Rights of Mankind, hundred years before the UDHR.

Cosmopolitan citizenship receives a fillip in the notion of Cosmopolitan Law formulated by Kant wherein he argues that man's rational nature will ultimately triumph over the agonies of struggle and violence and enable him to draft and obey an overarching world or cosmopolitan law which will ensure peace. He foresees the evolution of a loose confederation of states as the end-product of historical evolution. A citizen obeys the local law of his state but at the same time, in due course, also obeys the co regarded as citizen of cosmopolitan law, convinced that if citizens participate in the making of laws in his state then it is possible to reach the end. He accepts that the process would be slow. The conflict between the local law and the cosmopolitan law will ultimately cease and citizenship would acquire a universal status: 'the individuals who compose the state whose constitution is formed in accordance with cosmopolitan law … may be regarded as citizens of one world-state'… the highest purpose of Nature will be at last realised in the establishment of a universal Cosmo-political Institution, in the bosom of which all the original capacities and endowments of the human species will be unfolded and developed' (cited in Linklater 1982: 115). Kant does not however advocate world government. Like most of the thinkers of the eighteenth century, he too suspects concentration of powers in one authority and believes in the beneficence of individual human reason and wisdom. These two ideas are clearly manifest in Bentham who was 'personally the complete cosmopolitan in his outlook' (Heater 1990: 55). Believing as he does in the efficacy of public opinion, he is confident that international contacts on a personal level, rather than between governments, would result in a happier world.

The period between 1899 and 1914 saw a number of peace initiatives, primarily to reduce the power of arms manufacturers and the tendency on part of governments to go to war. In 1910, William James pleaded for substituting warlike tendencies with creative social ones and defended this as a new civic duty related to the global community. During the inter-war years, the League of Nations and the Kellogg-Briand Pact tried to restrain the absolute right of the state to wage war. H.G. Wells popularises the idea of world citizenship and calls upon the saner and abler persons of the world to establish a new World Order based on broadly socialist principles. He is however unclear about the structure of this new order except reposing faith in global-functional administration rather than world government. Angell is convinced of the usefulness of political wars once European community becomes interdependent due to economic reasons.

In more recent times, Held argues for cosmopolitan ideal for realising world peace and universal equality of individuals, but concedes that these cannot be achieved by relying on the democratic capacities of states alone. He pleads for internationalising democratic law if it has to be effective. Other than respecting reciprocal sovereignty between states, there is a need to agree on commonly shared norms to which states subscribe and institutionalising these principles through the establishment of inter-governmental organisations. For Held and Archibugi (1998), cosmopolitan ideal moves beyond the ethical parameters and emphasises the institutional aspects. Falk (1995) considers national citizenship to be exclusive and divisive; it legitimates unequal protection of rights and is responsible for the unequal distribution of global wealth. He pleads for the co-existence of national and global citizenship. Miller rejects the idea of cosmopolitan citizenship and points out that international peace, international justice and global environmental protection are important objectives but these 'cannot be achieved by inventing in theory cosmopolitan forms of citizenship which undercut the basis of citizenship proper' (Miller 2000: 96)

IDEOLOGIES AND CITIZENSHIP

Liberalism's emphasis is on the importance of the citizen's ability to engage in public discussion believing that good policy emerges out of filtering of such articulations. This does not merely mean an articulation of their point of view but also provides reasons for their political demands in a reasonable manner, avoiding threats as far as possible. These reasons must be of general interest and not sectarian or divisive, in the sense that others from different faiths and nationalities could empathise with them. It is not enough to rely on tradition or scripture but a conscious effort has to be made to distance merely from those beliefs that are private, different from those that can be publicly defended. Liberals, point to the socialisation process in schools that teach the young to understand others' standpoint besides their own cultural traditions. This viewpoint has been questioned by some traditionalists, who fear that liberal pluralistic education will undermine parental and religious authority in the private life. Some religious groups object to liberal education as an act of intolerance, even if it is carried out in the name of teaching the virtue of tolerance. Besides rationality, liberalism also emphasises universality, meaning equal rights for all before the law. Rights are important as they protect the individual from the growing power of the state. **Civic republicanism** supports active, responsible and virtuous citizenship by subordinating private concerns and interests to public good. It accepts the liberal conception of citizenship as a set of rights and adds to it the fact that a citizen is one who identifies with the political community to which he belongs, and is committed to promoting the common good through active participation in its political life. The contrast between republicanism and liberalism is not that the liberal recognises the value of entrenched rights whereas the republican does not, but that the liberal regards these rights as having a pre-political justification while the republican grounds them in public discussion. One institutional corollary is that liberals seek to make the judiciary the supreme arbiters of constitutional rights—in effect the interpretation of liberal citizenship is entrusted to them—while the republican gives this role to the citizen body as a whole (Miller 2000: 59–60). It differs from Aristotle and Arendt for whom political participation is intrinsically worthwhile, being the supreme and highest kind of activity. For Aristotle, this means the political life in a state is superior to private pleasures of the family and profession. For Arendt, this signifies the importance of the political, devoid of social and economic issues.

Burke reinforces the conservative desire to limit citizenship to a segment of adults with property, for they have the leisure for discussion and information. It is in Aristotle's writings that we find the notion of citizens as a leisurely class, men of property, who have the time to discuss the affairs of the state and participate in the formulations of law and policy of his state. This sentiment is best captured by Pericles. Burke considers the rule by the enlightened and aristocratic elite as the best, for the masses are not only incapable of governing themselves but can neither think nor act without guidance. For Burke, government is based not on general will but wisdom that has passed on from one generation to another. He desires representation of the interests and not as we believe in the representation of the people, for they are an objective, impersonal and unattached reality (Pitkin 1967: 10). He advocates restricted suffrage, so that the selection of the natural aristocratic group of parliament becomes foolproof. He distinguishes between actual representation and virtual representation. The latter is based on common interest and since an area will have one dominant interest virtual representation is preferred to actual representation. This also ensures that even those who did not vote are represented. Pitkin (1967: 169–170) points out that this is essentially a seventeenth century notion of representation with little relevance to the contemporary times. Conservatism fears democratic despotism or the tyranny of the majority the most, while considering issues involving representative democracy. Burke is disturbed by the democratic aspirations of the French Revolution and in particular, by the doctrines of popular sovereignty and general will. He blames the democratic forces of the Revolution for the vast increase in government bureaucracy. He is generally skeptical about the political ability of the ordinary people and regards democracy as the 'most shameless thing in the world' (Pitkin 1967: 190). The New Right and Neo liberals reject social citizenship[1] and emphasise on self-reliance and criticise the welfare state as promoting passivity and dependence among the poor. To promote active citizenship, they want reduction in welfare entitlements and therefore, stress the importance of responsibility to earn a living, which is seen as the key to self-respect and social acceptance. Their critics point out that withdrawal or reduction of welfare benefits further marginalises the underclass. Marxism observes that the idea of equal citizenship rights in a class divided society is a sham, for it is always the interests, privileges, rights and powers of the dominant economic class that are protected. It is part of the bourgeois legal ideology of individualism. For Marx, political emancipation through citizenship becomes meaningful with human emancipation. Conversely, only in a classless society, with collective ownership of the means of production and with the end of oppression, citizenship can transcend class distinctions and class divisions. Even here there is certain ambivalence. Since the socialist society embodies the idea of proletarian internationalism, there is no question of considering citizenship, which refers, in particular, to the nation state. However, the liberating vision of the society after the revolution remains incomplete, for the Marxists emphasise on economic freedom but not political freedom, a society of autonomous and materially satisfied social beings but not a polity of citizens. As a result, they ignore the complex question of institutions that actualise political freedom and citizen participation.

Feminism contends that the emphasis on self-reliance is based on the view that men should financially support the family, while the women would look after the household and care for the young, old and the sick and the elderly. This disallows women's full participation in the society. Since Wollstonecraft feminism has been concerned with how women can be treated as equal citizens along with men. Liberal feminism stresses on equal rights and equal access but ignores human interdependence that is integral to both families and polities. Marxist/socialist feminism accepts the idea of equal rights and equal access but stresses more on the need to transcend class societies through revolutionary struggle, thus, subordinating the women's question to realisation of socialism. Some recent feminists like Elshtain, whom Dietz (1985) labels as maternal feminists, draw attention to the conception of female political consciousness that is grounded in the virtues of woman in the private sphere, primarily, in mothering. They claim the need and importance to perceive women as mothers and not merely as 'reproducers'. Furthermore, while for the liberals and Marxists, men and women are the same and hence deserving equal treatment, postmodernist feminists, like Young, emphasise on the differences that separated men from women and the way these differences ought to be reconciled with claims of justice and equality. Young argues that the liberals and republicans are committed to an ideal of impartiality and reason, which acts to the disadvantage of certain groups in society and she identified the women and ethnic minorities as oppressed categories. She claims that the ideal of the civic public excludes women and other groups defined as different, because its rational and universal status derived only from its opposition to affectivity, particularity and the body. Republican theorists insisted on the unity of the civic public: insofar as he is a citizen, every man leaves behind his particularity and difference, to adopt a universal standpoint identical for all citizens, the standpoint of the common good or general will. In practice, republican politicians enforced homogeneity by excluding from citizenship all those defined as different and associated with the body, desire or need influence that might veer citizens say from the standpoint of pure reason (1990: 117).

Furthermore, Young argues that the republican ideal adheres to the private-public dichotomy, which discriminates against those whose concerns are conventionally perceived as, essentially, private ones. Though there is no *a priori* way of demarcating the private from the public but nevertheless, the distinction can be upheld between a person acting in a private capacity and as a citizen. Moreover, the divide will emerge in the course of public discussion for certain matters will be inevitably relegated to the private sphere. For instance, it may be difficult to obtain a consensus on an issue so the fairest way is to allow citizens to pursue their own preferences voluntarily, or it may be considered illegitimate for the state to interfere in a citizen's private life. Young ignores the fact that a distinction between private and public will always be maintained though some groups will differ on the issue, but that does not suggest that these groups will automatically lose out.

Lloyd in her *The Man of Reason* (1984) illustrates how concepts in liberal theory are constructed in masculine terms with the idea of citizen, identified with military service, which is still a male preserve. 'The masculinity of war is what it is precisely by leaving the feminine behind. It consists in the capacity to rise above what femaleness symbolically represents: attachment to private concerns, to "mere life". In leaving all that behind, the soldier becomes a real man, but he also emerges into the glories of selfhood, citizenship and truly ethical, universal concerns. Womankind is constructed so as to be what has to be transcended to be a citizen' (1984: 75). The liberal theory of universal citizenship is rooted in the public sphere permeated with the male gender values and women confined to the private domestic sphere do not qualify as citizen (Saxonhouse 1985, Phillips 1993).

Elshtain (1981) and Ruddick (1983) propose a **maternalist conception of citizenship** which is informal, particularist and communitarian as against the individualist, rights-based notion of citizenship that liberals propose. It draws substantially on an ethic of care and prioritises, like the communitarians, the community not only of shared final ends but also as Sandel (1996) calls a common vocabulary of discourse, as the basis of politics. Maternal citizenship is based on the values of the private sphere, emotional rather than rational, the recognition of difference rather than the aspiration to equality.

Dietz criticises the maternal feminists for ignoring the fact that citizenship involves virtues, relations and practices that are expressly political and more specifically, participatory and democratic. As long as feminists focus exclusively on social and economic questions relating to children, family, schools, work, wages, abortion, abuse, pornography, they do not articulate a political vision or address the problem of citizenship. It is only when they will emphasise on the intrinsic value of citizenship, rather than undertake active citizenship for the pursuit of social and economic concerns, that feminists can hope to achieve a truly distinctive politics of their own. This means considering citizenship as a continuous activity and good in itself. Dietz also argues against universalism and abstractions for these are at variance with the notion of citizenship as a relationship between equals. She points out that citizenship is about getting beyond one's immediate sphere and dealing as a citizen with other citizens, thus, emphasising on universalism and abstraction, of which Young is so suspicious. Dietz correctly warns against 'womanism' and points that a truly democratic defense of citizenship could not proceed from the assumption of woman's traditional neglect or superiority, for that suggests that one group is better or deserves more attention. Furthermore, a point that Dietz overlooks is the inherent divisiveness of maternal feminism, which seems to ignore those women who are not mothers, either by choice or circumstances. While most women marry and raise children, there are women who remain single by choice and also because of circumstances. One role common to all women is being a daughter, a suggestion made by Victorian feminists in their critique of J.S. Mill and one worthy of reconsideration in this context. The argument that women are different should not be stressed to the point of it becoming vacuous and divisive. In reality, Dietz's conception is similar to that of Elshtain, though "Elshtain speaks of women's moral insights Dietz speaks of feminists' political practices (Squires 1999: 178–179).

Chantal Mouffe, like Dietz agrees on the need to replace the liberal male conception of citizenship with a radical democratic conception of citizenship which would entail the rejection of the notion of **gender-differentiated citizenship**. She argues that sexual difference is a product of particular social discourses and finds no reason as to why all social discourses should draw distinctions of sexual identity. She favours a citizenship in which sexual difference is non-pertinent (1992: 376). Neither gendered nor gender neutral, her conception of citizenship is based on real equality and liberty for all citizens. She stresses on political issues and claims, and observes that the public-private distinction needs to be redefined from case to case, according to the type of political demands, and not in a fixed and permanent way.

To Marshall's three-tier citizenship rights, has been added a fourth one, namely environmental rights which are labelled as third generation rights. The first being tier of rights are civil and political and the second tier are social and economic rights. Environmental citizenship refers to quality of life which stands threatened by air, water and noise pollution, meteorological disasters like global warming and depletion of ozone layer, climatic change, industrial and population increase and its effect on resource-use.

CITIZENSHIP AND EDUCATION

Ever since Aristotle, the problem of reconciling the good man with the good citizen has been a recurring theme in political thought. Aristotle contends that while the qualities of a good man are universal and constant, the qualities of a good citizen depend on the constitution under which a citizen lives. He considers three qualities as necessary for a good citizen—loyalty to the established constitution, high degree of capacity for the duties of the office and quality of goodness and justice. For instance, in an oligarchy, a citizen has to preserve the dominance of the ruling wealthy class, while in a democracy a citizen upholds political and economic equality. Only under special circumstances is there an identity between the good man and the good citizen.

Aristotle, following **Plato**, pleads for responsible and effective forms of education for citizenship. This, they consider as a cure for corruption and political instability of their times. They are equally critical of the casual manner in which the Athenian State regarded the tasks of citizenship, which stood in sharp contrast to the disciplined citizenry of Sparta. As a corrective measure, both prescribe state-managed and state-controlled education, as practiced in Sparta. In the *Laws*, Plato makes it clear that the guardian of laws controls the educational system by selecting teachers only from among those who are willing to teach about the laws and traditions of the state in a manner determined by the Guardians. Both Plato and Aristotle 'believed that different styles of civic education should be used for different purposes. Plato emphasised training in self-sacrifice for rulers and obedience for the ruled; Aristotle emphasised the need to match the educational objectives to the form of government' (Heater 1990: 7).

Rousseau perceives the problem in the same manner as Aristotle and recommends the need to educate the man rather than educate the citizen. From Locke onwards, English political thinkers emphasise the importance of public opinion. Hume agrees that good citizenship requires education and knowledge. The citizen needs not merely a general education but specifically a political education that involves 'knowing how' and 'knowing what' with regard to the principles of justice. Aristotle, Rousseau and Hume point out that the citizen will need knowledge of the attitudes and the expectations of fellow citizens. He must learn to adjust with others and win their esteem. Both Aristotle and Rousseau emphasise on the fact that a citizen must learn to rule and to be ruled. This has become a constant theme in democratic thought.

J.S. Mill and **Tocqueville** reiterate Rousseau's stress on political knowledge and observe that participation in local government, voluntary association and jury service and management of one's work is also a form of education in how to make decisions. However, they differ from Rousseau in stressing the importance of plurality of life's experiments as that enhances freedom, creativity and independence. Mill accepts, what Aristotle had recognised, that the many could become effective citizens and surpass the experts only when their separate sources of knowledge 'meet together'. Oakeshott discusses extensively the importance of political education as that involves learning the political traditions and customs of one's country.

DIFFERENTIATED CITIZENSHIP[3]

It is recognised that unitary citizenship normally integrates diverse groups through a shared identity, the most important development as Marshall observes of one person, one vote. However, despite common citizenship rights, some groups, like African-American, indigenous people, ethnic and religious minorities and women, feel excluded. Differentiated citizenship requires mechanisms of group representation. Women as a social group, according to Young, face four of the five types of oppression (exploitation, powerlessness, cultural, imperialism and violence) and therefore require group representation. As a remedy, cultural pluralists propose that citizenship must reflect their distinct and different social and cultural identity. Young (1989) observes that these marginalised groups can be fully integrated through 'differentiated citizenship', that is the members of certain groups shall be incorporated into the political community not only as individuals but also through the group. That is, their rights shall depend, in part, to their group membership. This view challenges the conventional perception of defining citizenship in terms of treating people as individuals with equal rights under law.

It is important to distinguish between the two broad types of differentiated citizenship. There are groups like the poor, women, ethnic minorities and immigrants whose demand for group rights is a demand for greater inclusion and participation in the mainstream society. They may feel underrepresented in the political process due to historical reasons and therefore seek group-based representation. Or, they may seek exemption from laws that disadvantage them economically or they want school curriculum to recognise their contributions to society's culture and history. These groups accept the goal of national integration, for they desire to be part of the mainstream society as full and equal members but only insist that recognition and accommodation of their difference is needed to bring about national integration. The other group that seeks differentiated citizenship rejects the goal of national integration. They wish to be self-governing, to freely develop their culture and are usually national minorities or distinct historical communities occupying their own territory with a distinct language and history. They do not want greater representation in the central government but transfer of power from the central government to their communities, often through some kind of federalism or local autonomy.

They do not desire greater inclusion into the larger society but autonomy from it. However, this is primarily related to the issues of self-determination rather than citizenship. The latter is based on the expression of a common for each individual. Marion Young (1998: 401) accuses both the liberal and civic republican tradition of espousing 'an ideal of universal citizenship' and excludes groups that undermine the unity of the polity (ibid: 404–405). Modern citizenship emphasises homogeneity and university and that relegates differences to the private sphere. She defends a conception of differentiated citizenship one that understands not only the different needs and interests but also the different values and modes of expression. 'Each social group affirms the presence of the others and affirms the specificity of its experience and perspective on social issues' (ibid: 416–417).[4]

CONCLUSION

Citizenship focussing on certain common features of rough parity and identity like nationalism is of recent origin, making a beginning with the end of feudalism and completing the process with the emergence of the welfare state after the Second World War in Western Europe. Marshall portrays this sketch of citizenship at the inception of the welfare state with a favourable endorsement and clear approval within a liberal-social democratic paradigm. However, what makes him a seminal theorist is his acknowledgement of a permanent conflict between citizenship and the market, which has been reflected by the upsurge of New Right in, both the United States and Britain, questioning the entire thesis of social citizenship. The essential local basis of citizenship rights within the nation-states has also come under severe criticism because of globalisation and triumph of world capitalism. This has brought to the fore the questions of productivity, competitiveness, order and efficiency, relegating the issue of citizenship to the background. However, the post-Cold War resurgence in emphasising the centrality of social and economic issues have indirectly made citizenship rights as a prime concern of contemporary political theory. The difference between the citizenship rights discourse of yester years and now, is that, like other issues of political theory, it has assumed a global connotation and a modern theory of citizenship can be viable only if it deals with the primary rights of a world citizen.

Further Readings

Andrews, G., *Citizenship*, Lawrence and Wishart, London, 1991.

Beiner, R., *Theorizing Citizenship*, State University of New York Press, Albany, NY, 1994.

Clarke, P.B., *Citizenship*, Pluto Press, London, 1994.

Demaine, J. and Entwistle, H. (Eds.), *Beyond Communitarianism: Citizenship, Politics and Education*, Macmillan, Basingstoke, 1996.

Heater, D., *What is Citizenship?* Polity Press, Cambridge, 1999.

Oldfield, A., *Citizenship and Community: Civic Republicanism and the Modern World*, Routledge, London, 1990.

Riesenberg, P., *Citizenship in the Western Tradition: Plato to Rousseau*, Chapel Hill, NC and London, University of North Carolina Press, 1992.

Turner, G. and Hamilton, P. (Eds.), *Citizenship: Critical Concepts*, 2 Vols. Routledge, London, 1994.

Endnotes

1. Fordism is named after its founder Henry Ford, the car-maker. It refers to an industrial system that involves mass production of standardised goods by huge integrated companies. Each company was composed of many different specialised departments, each producing component and parts that were eventually directed towards the moving line for final assembly.
2. In the nineteenth century, citizenship meant the extension and consolidation of legal and political rights. However, by the end of the century and more so, the beginning of the twentieth century there is a realisation that a state must protect its citizens against poverty. Citizenship came to mean social welfare (see chapter on Welfare State).
3. See section on Multiculturalism in chapter on Recent Developments in Political Theory.
4. For criticisms of differentiated citizenship refer to the section on Multiculturalism in chapter on Recent Developments in Political Theory.

Chapter 10
Rights

The language of rights permeates and dominates our contemporary political, social and economic life. Rights figure in all current discussions, especially in liberal theory on the subject relating to the individual and the state. It is generally recognised that rights secure liberty by protecting the individual against the state and other persons. Even a majority gives a person the shield against arbitrariness and tyranny. It safeguards the individual's private space ensuring that neither the state nor others can morally interfere without justification. It is recognised that the rights that individuals enjoy are by virtue of being human rather than by being members of a political community. Embedded in the concept of right is the acceptance of ideas of personal autonomy, individuality, liberty and human equality and any denial and discrimination has to have sufficient reasons. The concept quintessentially is anti-statist in orientation. Since the middle of the twentieth century, there have been increasing concerns about human rights, in general, and, particularly, of certain segments of human beings, such as, the elderly, children, the handicapped, the unborn and the future generations. There are designated institutions to promote and monitor human rights. What then is a right?

In political theory, the concept of right has been broadly used in three different ways:

1. To describe a type of institutional arrangement in which interests are guaranteed legal protection, choices are guaranteed legal effect, or goods and opportunities are provided to individuals on a guaranteed basis.
2. To express the justified demand that such institutional arrangements should be set up, maintained and respected.
3. To characterise a particular sort of justification for this demand, namely a fundamental moral principle that accords importance to certain basic individual values such as equality, autonomy or moral agency (Waldron 1987b: 443).

The first usage is understood as **legal** right, while the other two as **moral** or **natural** right (Cranston 1973: 9–17). A legal right is a claim that is recognised by law and enforced by a court; a positivist maintains that any other explanation of rights, other than the legal rights is wholly subjective and metaphysical. It is a privilege granted and upheld by the sovereign power of the state, which a citizen enjoys. All legal rights are positive rights based on social recognition. Moral rights cannot be enforced by the legal system but depend for their validity on they being consistent with social and moral practices and their moral justifiability. The societal framework of the accepted behaviour pattern changes from time to time and according to place and that gets translated in the realisation of particular rights. However, in this age of globalisation and swift communication such a particularistic connotation of the sources of rights has diminished, and correspondingly universal component in matters such as human rights has increased.

The legal relations embedded in rights are succinctly elaborated by **Hohfeld's** (1919) highly influential analysis, which has left a permanent imprint on Anglo-American theory. According to Hohfeld, any one of four elements could constitute a legal right: a claim; a liberty; a power; or immunity. He divides them into four categories of relationships between right-bearer *a* and right-addressee *b*, and explains them by their corresponding correlatives.

1. A **claim right** depends for its existence on there being *a* duty on some else. Here *a* claims *Z* from *b*—and b has a duty towards *a* to do Z. For example, a person has a right not to be attacked.
2. A **liberty** or **privilege-right** is a right that imposes no specific duties on anyone else. Here *a* has a liberty or privilege to do *Z*—when *a* has no duty towards *b* not to do *Z*, and *b* has 'no right' towards *a*. For example, if a person is attacked, he has a right to defend himself.
3. **Immunity** is a specific exemption from a law granted to persons. Here *a* has immunity—when *b* lacks the authority to bring about a certain consequence for *a* and is, thus, under a disability. For instance, the elderly are immune from being drafted into the army.
4. A power is an ability to change people's claim—right and duties. Here *a* has a power to bring about a certain consequence for *b*. A person could alter the legal relationship between him and other people—for example, an owner has a right to bequeath his property to anyone he chooses in his will. An officer of the law could fine or demand to see licence of a speeding driver thus placing him under a liability.

Legal or human rights may be scrutinised as composite bunch of any or all of these basic legal relations. Political theory predominantly focuses on claim-rights, and on the relation between rights of a person and the duties they impose on other people, and particularly on the state. Rights correlate with duties for one person's right is another person's duty to enable the right-holder to enjoy his right. Regarding the co-relationship between rights and duties, Benn and Peters (1959: 89) make an interesting observation that while such a co-relationship does exist in most cases, but there are certain exceptions to the rule. All including children, animals and imbecile enjoy rights but to attribute duties to them is absurd.

Rights are also used in a variety of ways indicating differences in ideological position and philosophical perceptions. For some, rights are 'normative attributes' that belong to a self-conscious person who perceives himself as an agent of purposive creative action (Benn 1978: 66; Gewirth 1984: 31). For others, rights are entitlements to choose from (Beitz 1984: 172). McCloskey (1976: 99) describes rights positively, as entitlements, to do, have, enjoy or have done. For MacCormick (1982: 143), rights 'always and necessarily concern human goods', that is, concern with what it is good, at least in normal circumstances, for a person to have. Feinberg (1980: 239) and White (1984: 17) asserted that rights can be 'possessed, enjoyed, exercised and claimed, demanded and asserted'.

Hart (1967: 60–64) distinguishes special rights from general rights. Special rights arise out of specific undertakings and agreements between individuals who assume the existence of general rights, for, if one needs a special right to defend a restriction on another's freedom, and in the absence of such a right, everyone has the general right not to be constrained. Rights are categorised as **political**, **civil**, **social** and **economic** rights suggesting that these rights deal with that particular aspect of human endeavour and existence. Unlike the ancient times, where rights and liberties linked to citizenship were restrictive since large segments of society did not enjoy them, modern society based on the notions of primacy of the individual and equality of persons accepts universality of rights. Initially, rights were restricted to the propertied and the educated men but subsequently they were extended to the working class and women. Furthermore, initially political and civil rights received recognition but by the beginning of the twentieth century the content of rights has changed to include economic and social rights.

The origins of the notion of rights can be traced to late medieval thought and the natural rights tradition to the natural law doctrine in Greek philosophy. In the twelfth century, the concept of rights emerges in European thought and is fully developed by the end of fourteenth century into a coherent theoretical construct in the writings of Gerson. It forms the most prominent idea in the thought of the thirteenth century, Italian philosopher and theologian Aquinas, for whom there exists god-given natural law as an underlying force in the universe. This means a set of moral principles laid down by god as the basis for proper human conduct. However, Aquinas stresses moral duties of human beings—rulers and ruled alike, more than the rights of the individual citizens. Nonetheless this forms the theoretical background for the emergence of theories of natural law after AD 1500 associated with the gradual development of modern secular territorial state. Two different schools of thought appear in the seventeenth century, one the more conservative of these in the writings of Selden and Hobbes who speak of unlimited right to freedom to men in the natural condition which are surrendered once men enter civil society, the second and the more radical one, contends that while some natural rights are surrendered to government for social peace, others are not and could be appealed to by people against an oppressive government. The natural rights are asserted in defense of both the English Revolutions of 1640s and 1689 and this radical theory becomes more dominant theory of natural rights. The most influential exponents of this view is in the writings of Locke, the Levellers and the Diggers.

It is misleading though correct to perceive, as Shapiro (1986: 41) does, to regard Hobbes as the starting point for the modern analysis of natural rights. Though Hobbes develops the important aspects of the concept of rights he does not place the discourse of rights firmly within the emerging liberal tradition. Furthermore, his theory though individualistic par excellence (Macpherson 1973) contains liberal and illiberal features (Dunn 1979: 42–43; Held 1989: 14). Hobbes (1991: 110–111) defines the notion of right as 'the Liberty of each man ... to use his own power, as he will himself, for the preservation of his own Nature; that is to say, of his own Life'. There are certain distinctive features in the definition that Hobbes provides. First, a right is related to one particular end—self-preservation—offered as an independent value. Second, the right of nature is attached to individuals, who solely judge about the means needed to attain the end it preserves. Third, it is within a person's right to pursue anything that is conducive to self-preservation,[1] implying that such a right is unlimited and inconsiderate of other individuals, especially when an independent criterion to assess the relative value of rights-oriented actions conflicting with one another is absent. Fourth, if a right is a liberty, and a liberty signifies the absence of external impediments then it denotes a condition whereby one is able to use one's power, this being a descriptive rather than a normative term. Fifth, if a person can either choose to exercise that liberty or to forbear, then a right may be waived. In spite of using traditional terms, 'Hobbes detaches the concept of natural right from that of natural law: Law, and Right, differ as much, as Obligation, and Liberty; which in one and the same matter are inconsistent' (Freeden 1998: 12–13). His negative identification of liberties is similar to that of Hohfeld's notion of privileges, for it lacks correlative no-rights of others. Thus, it is inadequate in the contemporary understanding of rights.

THEORIES RIGHTS

Natural Rights Theory

The theory of natural rights originates in the seventeenth century and remains the dominant theory in the eighteenth century, rejects the idea of natural hierarchy and the notion of absolute authority. It found its ramifications in the writings of Locke who rejects the idea of divine right of kings and natural arrangement of political authority, and instead advances the notion of human equality. Locke's theory rests on a firm and explicit moral relationship between the individual and god. Since life is a gift that god has given, as a basic moral law of nature, no one has the right to kill himself nor destroy, rob or enslave others, for all are equal before the Almighty. The natural condition is a state of equality and the pre-political state of nature, regulated by the laws of nature is one of perfect freedom and perfect equality. Not only does Locke consider the individual more sociable than Hobbes but also more rational, capable of action and creativity. This capacity for free action allows human choice but the rational choice has to be in conformity with the morality of god's law. Within this sphere, each has a right of self-preservation and to preserve humankind in general.

From the laws of nature, individuals derive and enjoy the natural rights to life, liberty and property. Everyone has an equal right to one's natural freedom. Locke, unlike Hobbes, regards natural rights as derived from natural law. Besides rights, an individual has duties derived from the laws of nature, the most important being the right to hold others responsible for the breach of law and to punish offenders. Since the state of nature lacks a known settled law, a known indifferent judge and an executive, these rights were not secured and therefore a civil society was created through a contract and decided on issues on majority rule principle. In Locke's theory, natural rights have three political implications. First, since human beings derive and enjoy equal rights under the law of nature, none are under the political authority of another without his consent. Second, the maintenance and protection of these rights is the primary function of the government. Third, rights set and define the limits of the government authority.

Locke also shows that parental authority like political authority has its limits. Accepting the Christian dictum that children have to obey their parents, Locke argues that this obedience is temporary, till the child becomes morally responsible. The rights of parents are natural not because they have given birth to their children as the patriarchists contended but because it is their right to take care of them and educate them till they become independent; a right that could be revoked in case parents neglect their duties. What is due to parents is honour and not obedience and this honour is due to both fathers and mothers and not only to fathers. Children have a virtual right of inheritance, as that ensures conveniences and comforts to lead a reasonable life thereby rejecting the then prevailing practice whereby parents demand total obedience in exchange of bequeaths. Furthermore, Locke concedes that in spite of the physical differences between men and women, women are politically equal to men. The wife agrees to be subordinate to her husband, stronger and physically abler of the two, through the marriage contract but this is only if she has freely given her consent. As in the public domain, even family life is based on the premise that individuals are free and equal under the laws of nature.

The natural rights theory provides a powerful case for the existence of rights. First, it simply assumes that human beings are born with these rights which are as intrinsic as the colour of one's skin or our innate, inalienable and inviolable features. McCloskey (1976: 127–128) attempts to identify the human features—rational, autonomous, emotional, imaginative and creative—

to support the contention that human rights are self-evident. Finnis (1980) categorically claims that it is not possible to empirically demonstrate or verify self-evidence but recommends that it should be seen as an attribute of rationally acquired knowledge. Some like Gewirth (1982) deny the existence of right if it is not socially recognised, for recognition is not only a necessary and also a sufficient condition for a right to exist. The reference is not to legal recognition or majority support but its acceptance by people who are morally and intellectually conscious and that make way for legal or majority acceptance. One can reasonably assume that without recognition no right can exist. Gewirth is correct in stating that if someone denies the existence of a right this does not establish its non-existence. However, the following is equally true that for a right to exist, besides the claimant, somebody else also must recognise it and this must be combined with protection. The assertion that rights are inalienable is done so as to protect the characteristic of human rationality. It acknowledges that a person is the best judge of his own interests, important at a time when an idea of individuality, autonomy, personal choice and equality has to gain prominence to dilute and eliminate the hierarchical feudal mindset. It is for this reason that rights are described as indefensible in order to restrain the individual from harming others. Second, natural rights are absolute and non-negotiable. Third, natural rights are pre-social and are not an outcome of any social organisation, historical growth or political authority. The reverse is true since political society is created to recognise, protect and enforce them.

Criticisms

Many critics like Burke, Bentham, Hegel and Marx object to atomistic conception of the individual and abstract egoism that the natural rights theory propounds. They contend that human life involves substantial social commitment and that a community cannot be based on principles of self-interests and egoism. They attack the doctrine of natural rights on the premise that it tries to provide instant and unconditional satisfaction of purely selfish individual desires (Waldron 1987a). In fact, these criticisms help to clarify the social side of the theory as evident in the revisions of Paine, J.S. Mill and Green. However, these criticisms overlook the social dimension even in Locke's conception, for implicit in the defense of self-preservation is also the general preservation of the community at large. The proclamation by the French Assembly of the *Rights of Man* in 1791, elicits varied and diverse responses: Conservative Burke, Liberal Paine, Utilitarian Bentham and Feminist Wollstonecraft. These responses also form the basis for different theories of rights. Burke and Bentham reject the idea of natural rights while Paine reiterate and reaffirm the liberal position. Wollstonecraft and other feminists point out the male bias in the natural rights doctrine.

Historical Theory

Burke, the classic exponent of liberal theory, accepts Locke's theological premises but denies the linkage between natural rights and natural law as individual reason and interests would never be an adequate basis of political legitimacy. Like Locke, he regards political authority as a trust but emphasises on the importance of traditions, history, stability, customs and intergenerational wisdom as society cannot be reduced to a mere contract between two or more parties. He rejects the *Declaration of the Rights of Man* on grounds of expediency and not because it is inadequate as the basis of government. He is convinced that the doctrine of sovereignty of the people could not be allowed to make the same mistake that the divine right of kings makes. The individual's right to choose his representatives does not give him the power to destroy the social fabric. Burke supports the cause of American colonies and had a liberal attitude towards India but his response to the revolutionary events in France shows his conservative side.

Burke points out that in view of the intricacies of human nature and complexities of society no simple analysis is possible. He rejects claims of economic and political equality and provides a theory of rights within the overall framework of his philosophy of change without undermining the constitution and disrupting the social fabric. On this basis, he rejects the rationalist and untested theory of *The Rights of Man* as it attempts to create a new order by making a total break with the past. Burke does not reject the argument of human rights except that he tries to rescue the real rights from the imagined ones. He shares with Locke the view that political philosophy has roots in theology but rejects the derivative argument of political and juridical equality of human beings. He also dismisses the idea of creating order with the help of human reason. The doctrine of natural rights is nothing but 'metaphysical abstraction', contrasting it with the real right of men. He does not deny natural rights but asserts that they cannot be translated into civil and political rights. Unlike Locke, for whom these rights are innate, Burke views them as a product of convention, which is why they cannot be challenged on grounds of rationality, individuality and equality. It fails to take into account the differences that exist between societies. Following Montesquieu, he insists that different countries merit different legal and political systems in the light of differences in climate, geography and history. The universality of the doctrine overlooks the national, geographical and cultural distinctions. He emphasises that there are no simple answers in politics and that nothing can be stated as axioms, valid for all times and places as envisaged by the *Declaration*. He also points out that the theory of natural rights, based on the new ideas of liberty and equality is not conducive to the establishment of order. It creates a consciousness of rights but not of duties of order, discipline and obedience to authority. Bentham echoes Burke's criticisms of natural rights but these are significant differences. Burke, unlike Bentham, does not perceive the human being to be hedonistic. His view resembles Aristotle's idea of *eudaimonia*, linking moral virtue and duty with that of political morality and duty. Maximisation for Burke is moral rather than mathematical, bringing him closer to Aristotle's *phronesis*, for he rejects the utilitarian idea of trade-offs. Unlike Bentham, Burke's attitude to the new scheme has been one of caution.

Restatement of natural rights

Paine in the *Rights of Man* rebuts Burke's views by reiterating Locke's premises, which found expression in the *Declarations* and *Bill of Rights* of the eighteenth century. The individual is created as equal and rational, with natural and imprescriptible rights by virtue of being a human being. These rights include Locke's rights to liberty, property and security, and a derivative right of resistance to oppression. Paine argues that a government comes into existence as a result of a contract between individuals and that constitutions precede governments. In spite of his minimalist view of government, he advocates some redistribution of wealth for those who have lost the fruits of their labour because of unjust property arrangements. Paine is not an originator but certainly a populariser of Locke's ideas. The Burke-Paine debate points to the problem of the source of rights. Burke insists that the English have rights that are a product of their history, which is unique to England. Other people with different historical experiences would have their own distinct set of rights. For Paine, rights are derived from nature and are universal irrespective of men, their country and history. This argument has significance in the context of the eighteenth century when universality of right is linked to the idea of democratic forms of government as against traditional authority. Jefferson, the author of the *American Declaration of Independence* (1776) and the *Bill of Rights* restates Locke's conception of natural rights as those that protect the individual from the governmental intrusion by securing life, liberty and property. He considers rights of free speech and free press not as goods in themselves but the essential precondition for deliberation in small republics. He also stresses on the importance of right to an education in consonance with one's capacities, a fair amount of economic independence and an opportunity to mould one's social life by participating in the community's affairs as necessary for cultivating a person's moral sense.

Rights for women

Feminism arises as a middle class movement during the eighteenth century, demanding a re-examination of the theories of natural rights and citizenship. Just as the failure of early liberalism to fulfil its own promise give rise to Marxism, similarly, the silence on the part of the natural rights theorists on the status, role and position of women gives rise to feminism. This neglect prompts Olympe de Gouges in France to proclaim a manifesto of her own *Proclamation of the Rights of Woman and Female Citizens* and **Wollstonecraft** in England writes her *A Vindication of the Rights of the Woman* (1792) dedicating the book to the French Minister Talleyrand in the hope that he would include women's rights under the new French constitution. Embedded in the natural rights theory is a duality. It accepts the principles of reason, equality and freedom but restricts it to men—all rational and dismissing women as the 'other'—all emotion denied legal and public existence.

Wollstonecraft, like Paine, is critical of Burke for his support of the tradition and hereditary rights since these impede progress. She asserts that human beings by birth are rational creatures with certain rights especially the equal rights of liberty compatible with that of the others. Like Paine, she welcomes the French Revolution, for it represents the first expression of humankind towards general emancipation and hopes that the liberal beliefs of liberty, equality and fraternity are translated in reality. She regards sexual distinction as arbitrary, a product of the patriarchal society and pleads for women's education along rational lines. Using Locke's arguments, she appeals that women are included in universal rights. If women appear deficient in reason, it is due to a combination of poor education, patriarchal culture and the dull domestic chores. She defends equality of civil rights, wealth and opportunities within a vibrant commercial market society and opposes the law of primogeniture, for all children in a family are to receive an equal share in parental property. She does not press for political rights for women in view of the hostile reaction it would elicit and does not specify but insists that women have their representatives and a share in the deliberations of the government rather than being arbitrarily governed. Like Paine, she is critical of inadequate parliamentary representation, primogeniture, and aristocracy and state religion and denies reverence to the 1688 English settlement and its 'Bill of Wrongs' that a non-elected House of Commons enacted. She defends property rights but insists that large estates should be divided. She draws attention to the discrepancy between attack on aristocratic privileges in public and support for husband's authority in the home.

Legal Theory

Hume rejects the natural rights theory on the grounds that rights, justice, obligation and property arise out of convention and the common experiences of humankind. **Bentham** rejects the idea of natural rights as 'nonsense upon stilts', for rights abstracted from positive law retain no relevance or meaning. He proposes the principle of utility as the basis of the greatest happiness of the greatest number providing an objective moral standard unlike other theories, which supply a purely subjective criterion. Like Burke, he is particularly scathing in his criticisms of the concepts of natural law and natural rights. Like Hume, he criticises these notions on pragmatic and conceptual levels. However, unlike Hume, he has immense faith in the power of reason regarding it as a guardian and director of morals. On normative grounds, Bentham points out that natural rights impel an individual to rise up in arms against anything or anyone, whatever that one does not like. Talk of natural rights and natural law is like using a 'terrorist language'. It incites a 'spirit of resistance to all laws—a spirit of resistance against all governments' encouraging chaos and disorder.

On a conceptual plane, he dismisses the notion of natural rights as mischievous as, 'there is no such thing as natural rights opposed to, in contradiction to legal', thus arguing for a legal basis to the theory of rights. Bentham dismisses natural rights as meaningless for two reasons—first, they do not mean anything, similar to a stance which the Vienna Circle adopts in the 1920s that theology and metaphysics lack meaning and second, the sentences of the natural rights text guarantee their falsity. Like Hobbes, Bentham is insistent that words have to be defined precisely and clearly to avoid ambiguity, for that is the source of most conflicts in politics.

Bentham regards the principles of the *Declaration of the Rights of Man* as fallacious but not pernicious as Burke does. Interestingly, like Burke who sympathises with the cause of the American colonies, Bentham is also less harsh on the *American Declaration of Independence*. Both favour changes without undermining security, continuity and order. Neither is Bentham enamoured of Paine's logical defense of the French Revolution. He rejects natural rights and natural laws because of his conviction that every aspect of social phenomena could be calculated and measured mathematically by an expert and skillful legislator, becoming an instrument of happiness. Like Burke, Bentham believes that rights are to be protected by existing laws but he differs from Burke in his perception of English law. Unlike Burke, he is not so reverential about the English law just because it is an 'ancient collection of unwritten maxims and customs'. Law, according to Bentham, has to be codified in a simple, systematic and logical manner and based on the principle of the 'greatest happiness of the greatest number'.

Interestingly, though Bentham does not consider natural rights to be sacrosanct, he still recognises the importance of rights as being crucial for the security of the individual. He defines rights and duty in the context of positive law. Without a law-giver, there could be no law, no right and no duty. Law, as rational human contrivance, is needed for social and political life. Rights exist only within the framework of law and are anterior to law. Real law leads to real rights but imaginary laws lead only to imaginary rights. Hence, rights and legal duties are normally correlative. He applies his celebrated distinction between the 'descriptive' and 'censorial' jurisprudence, namely what the law 'ought to be' or whether a particular law is bad or good, to establish the validity of moral propositions about legal rights. It makes sense if one contends that an individual shall have a particular legal right. It becomes nonsensical when it is claimed that an individual already has some natural rights by virtue of which the legal rights are called for. Moreover, there is no absolute claim to rights and duties. There is need for some constraints, so at best one can speak of a clearly qualified commitment to liberty, property, democracy and so on. For Bentham, positive law makes human life tolerable, secure and prosperous and that, if law is attacked, it results in chaos and insecurity, similar to the Terror of early 1790s.[2] He considers the arguments for natural rights distasteful, for they encourage rebellion and are associated with anarchy, terror and insecurity.

He is equally critical of the notion of equality of rights, since that ignores the distinctions, which a society may find useful to make. He also points out that the absolutism inherent in the doctrine of natural rights is based on the presumption that government shall fulfil all the aspirations. The final reason for his indictment of natural rights is that these threaten social solidarity and attenuate selfishness in society.

Bentham distinguishes between liberty rights and rights to services with the latter sub-divided into forbearance services and active ones. He subscribes to what has subsequently been termed as the benefit theory of rights, a theory that Hart derives using Bentham's observations. A right is the legal expectation of the performance of a legal duty, intended to benefit the bearer since a right bearer is a beneficiary of an obligation under a system of law. A right is complementary to legal duty and it gives its bearer a power over the potential benefactor. Bentham's assertion that a right has to be determinate and intelligible gave the legal view an advantage over the theory of natural rights. Bentham, unlike Burke and Marx, identifies self-interest as the core of human nature but like them visualises the possibility of human society depending on people pursuing interests other than those that are narrowly self-centred.

Idealist View

Hegel accepts Locke's conception of rights but transforms it by insisting that rights belong to societies and communities and not individuals. He argues that human needs and desires are social needs, a point that Marx borrows and develops subsequently in his critique of capitalism, and that the relationship between individuals and society is reciprocal and organic with both needing one another. There can be no conflict between individual interests and that of the community for freedom consists in acting rationally and harmoniously in accordance with universal principles which the rationally organised organic community embodies. The rational state has to be a constitutional monarchy with a legislature that mirrors public opinion. He accepts freedom of expression and trial by jury but opposes the right to vote as is evident from an essay that he wrote against the Reform Bill of 1832.[3] The influence of Hegel is evident from the *Declaration of Rights* proclaimed by the liberal nationalist Germans in 1848, for it spoke of the '*Rights of the German People*'.

Green incorporates elements of Hegelian theory and integrates it with English liberal theory. He rejects the natural rights doctrine for three reasons—first, it assumes that individuals enjoy certain rights which society does not grant, second, it argues that certain rights can be held against society and third, rights are de-linked from duties that individuals owe to their society. He emphatically argues that individuals have rights as members of a society, for they attain their ends only through social cooperation with each working towards common good with which their good is inextricably linked. Green is willing to use the term natural to mean the moral capacity in each individual, which the society recognises as the necessary end. The free development and exercise of these capacities enable the rational individuals to act thereby providing a link between autonomy and rights. Any right contains two aspects—it is the claim of the individual that arises out of his rational nature because of the free exercise of some faculty and it is a concession society made to that claim, a power it gave to the individual. Green categorically emphasises that morality is a result of spontaneous and voluntary action and that human beings have the capacity for freely fulfilling some function as members of a society. Rights were moral claims made by the individual for self-development and recognised for their contribution to common good.

Marxist Critique

Marx dubs these rights as bourgeois claims, for it promotes class interests under the cover of universal categories. In *On the Jewish Question* (1844) while dealing with the claims of the Jews to political emancipation, he proclaims that human rights separate one human being from the other. 'Human rights' represent the rights of an egoistic and acquisitive individual. Scrutinising the French declarations, he observes the right to property in effect means that the arbitrary disposal of private possessions and the right to security are basically a guarantee to maintain and safeguard existing capitalist arrangements. The right to resist government is there to prevent curtailment or encroachment of bourgeois activity. Taking a cue from Babeuf, Marx points out that freedom in the absence of economic equality leads to enslavement of the masses and lack of human dignity. Babeuf emphatically highlights the contradictions within the French revolutionary slogans of liberty and equality. Freedom means not only legal and civil liberties, namely physical protection against arbitrary power, but also freedom from slavery, exploitation, misery and inequality, which is possible only with universal right to work, equal natural right to earth and its goods and ensuring a rough parity for human happiness. Marx reiterates these arguments and contends that a society that recognises innate individual rights and bases itself on selfishness, gain and private interest on the premise, that this would promote common welfare, fails to recognise the inequality among individuals, reducing the all-round human development to one dimensionality. Such a conception of rights represents a selfish and false view of human nature each isolated and separated from the rest of the community. Like Aristotle, Marx believes that an individual develops only within a society and becomes 'species being' through social activity and social enjoyment. On this premise, he dismisses political emancipation as nothing but a chimera and thus, criticises both the natural rights theory and legal theory.

In face of the critiques developed by Burke, Bentham and Marx theories of natural rights of the individuals declined during the nineteenth and early twentieth centuries. This process was underlined by the growing importance of **utilitarianism** in Britain. The central tenet of utilitarianism—principle of utility—rather than the theory of natural rights provided the theoretical justification for the gradual development of mass democracy in Britain after 1832. Furthermore, the writings of **Weber** and **Durkheim** weakened the claims of the natural rights doctrine for they perceived society not as an artificial creation of rights-bearing individuals, but rather as an evolving natural process shaped by the interaction between individuals and cultural, social and economic forces. In the 1920s and 1930s, logical positivism as developed in the writings of Russell, Moore and Ayer gave a further blow when they asserted that all propositions should consist of statements that could be verified by experience or observation. As a consequence, it was rejected as meaningless, in a manner identical to Bentham's critique, any statement about natural rights. However, in the 1940s, the doctrine of natural rights regained its influence, although in the form of '**human rights**' when the *Universal Declaration of Human Rights* was adopted by the United Nations General Assembly. Philosophically, the doctrine found a central place in Nozick's theory.

Libertarian View

Nozick (1974) updating Locke's arguments on natural rights declare individuals in the pre-political state 'have rights and these are things no person or group may do to them' (1974: p. ix). These rights are absolute, 'negative side constraints', but unlike Locke's natural rights, they are derived from god's natural law and are understood as conditions for a conception of the person as free and equal subject. Nozick does not adequately explain or defend these rights. While Locke argues for one's duty to preserve oneself as the rational basis for political obligations, Nozick contends that one's rights create no duties other than those that one freely assumes. He argues that no new rights emerge at the group level and that individuals collectively do not create new rights, nor are they the sum of pre-existing ones. He rejects general rights and acknowledges only, 'particular rights over particular things held by particular persons and the particular right to reach agreement with each other' (1974: 238).

Rights and Community

Historically, the development of rights is closely associated with the rise of individualism. With changes in the notion of individualism, the rights associated with the individual also underwent simultaneous change. The individual as a unit of analysis has remained but acquired greater sophistication, namely the developmental view of human nature. The credit for this goes to **Ritchie** who points out that the development of natural gifts of an individual is the end of the state, which he defines as a rational community. Besides the individual, groups are increasingly acknowledged in rights based theory, in recent years and analogously of the term, collective rights as belonging to the family, ethnic communities and trade unions. This brings into focus the idea of the community that attenuates human sociability. In its mild version, the emphasis is on mutual sympathy and interdependence that propel individuals to seek cooperation from others for self-development and fulfillment. In its stronger sense, it emphasises that the essence of human beings is in their group membership. This may diminish the importance of rights, for traditional libertarian negative-rights theorists speak of the need to protect the free action of a person from the interference of others whereas that may be beneficial, desirable and perhaps necessary for the functioning of the individuals. However, one needs to be cautious, for overemphasis on human sociability could cut at the very roots of individual rights. While Green and recent communitarians like Sandel espouse a mild version of community that accepts individuals as inseparable from their communities, yet the interests of the community are not exactly alike to the interests of its members in totality. It involves two types of interests—one, where the interests of the members depend on cooperative communal action or are moulded by the concerted behaviour and second, individual interests that benefit the community at large. The stronger version of community views society as an actor, as a bearer of rights. The earliest exponents of this view were the Levellers.

Ritchie continuing with Green's analysis argues that there are certain mutual claims that could be termed as fundamental or natural rights that can be ignored without being destructive to the well-being and in the final analysis, to the very being of the community. Ritchie is not only a virulent critic of natural rights theory but also tries to synthesise the rights based theory and utilitarianism. **J.S. Mill's** revision of utilitarianism is significant but Ritchie's was pivotal, for he underlines morality as the 'conscious and deliberate adoption of those feelings, acts and habits which are advantageous to the welfare of the community', helped by the process of natural selection. As a result, he forwards the idea of social utility, that society has identifiable ends, interests and capacities to which rights relate. For instance, Hobson argues that just as there is the right to property similarly even society can claim one on the basis that it too is a worker set and a consumer. Hobhouse in a different vein contends that, if private property is of value to the fulfillment of personality, common property is equally valuable for the development and expression of social life. Non-Marxist socialists concur with this view of society as bearers of property rights. The rights of the community are different from social rights that apply to the individuals, such as, right of leisure or financial assistance.

Liberal communitarianism does not see individual rights as less secure or more important than community rights. However, some communitarians like MacIntyre, dismiss the idea of natural rights by alleging that to believe in it is like believing in 'witches and unicorns' (1981: 67). MacIntyre objects to the liberal individualism, since it abstracts persons from their social situations treating them as socially disconnected beings and unjustifiably tries to arrange the political system to suit their preferences. Since the communitarians perceive good to be prior to right, they consider the idea of abstract rights as ignoring shared values. There is a fear that overlooking shared values may result in social disintegration and moral disaster, a process that has started to occur in liberal states, evidenced by the high incidence of drug abuse, crime and violence and breakdown of family in these societies. Taylor points out that human agency, freedom and rights exist in a social context and that modern political theory does not satisfactorily account for the reciprocity of relations among individuals and between individuals and society. Human agency may be understood only from the premise that persons exist, as embodied individuals engaged both in self-interpretation and in constant interaction with others. Understanding the modern self then requires a sense of history, and the social and linguistic context within which human actions of crucial importance. Communitarians are skeptical of the deontological liberal commitment to universal rights and individuals particular ends restricting the pursuit of collective good. Sandel points out that the shared life of a community permits the emergence of common self-understandings among people and with these, goals that are truly common and not imposed. He observes that liberals devalued the good by leaving its definition to individuals who calculate to maximise their self-interest, while a community normally works towards a morally-worthy common good. Feminists too develop the same theme that it is possible to create real communities out of an aggregate of freely choosing adults.

Social Welfare Theory

This conception establishes a co-relationship between rights and social welfare and is akin to the views of social liberals like Green, Hobhouse and Hobson. It also shares an affinity with those who champion the idea of welfare rights. Laski's conception has been a lucid exposition of the social welfare perspective on rights. He considers rights, 'as the conditions of social life without which no man can seek, in general, to be himself at the best' (1979: 91). The end of the state is to maintain them, for rights are useful since they serve the ends of the state. He defines a right as a claim of an individual, which is recognised by society and that rights have a meaning only in society. The state has to create the conditions that enable the individual to achieve his best self, in consonance with that of others. There is an intimate link between individual happiness and public welfare, for one could be pursued without the other. Since social welfare entails certain economic and social rights, like right to work, adequate wages, reasonable hours of work, limited right to property, participation in the industry and right to education, these have to be guaranteed. Cole considered the individual as a social creature, thus, implying that the distinction was not between individual and society but between individual acts that were personal to ones that were social and therefore, liberty associated to an individual *qua individual* was different from liberty associated to institutions and groups with which the individual is concerned. He insists that both the conceptions have to be preserved within a society, for they are complementary and that one cannot exist without the other.

Choice Theory

This theory states that *a* may have a right only if *b*'s duty is owed to him, in the sense that he has the power to waive it, if he pleases. For instance, if a person has been promised something then surely he has a right not merely because the one who promises has a duty to execute his promise but because the person who has been promised is in a position to release him from that duty. On this account, rights can be relinquished. An individual has the option to exercise or not to do so any right he may have. The difference is important though a simple one—between a right to exercising the specific capacity to choose; and a choice over whether or not to exercise any right. Hart points out that a right bearing a correlative duty is a power that right-bearer *a* exercises on right-upholder *b*. The decision of the latter will decide the options the former has and relinquishing means that the right-bearer has temporarily decided from claiming a right in a particular case. The idea of forgoing confers ultimate sovereignty on the choice-exercising individual, irrespective of the consequences of such waiving and develops an idea of rights derived from private agreements or quasi-contracts. This depletes Hohfeld's distinction between powers and liberties, as even liberty-rights assume that individuals exercise powers. For Hart, this conception is consistent with *laissez faire* social relationships. Hence, he exempts some fundamental freedoms and benefits relating to the security, development and dignity of the individual from those rights whose performance, even existence is determined by individual choice. Golding (1984: 44–45) differentiated between option rights related to freedom and choice from welfare rights that concern entitlement to some good, necessary for human well-being. There is considerable diversity with regard to welfare right, which is generally understood as satisfaction of needs, of desires or of interests. However, a right to what persons need is not the same as to what they desire or want. One can conclude that a person has a right to have his needs satisfied but that need not apply with regard to desire. Furthermore, one can argue that a person needs to have some of his wants satisfied, even if they are not necessary for his functioning. Generally, the idea of welfare means providing material assistance to individuals in need, which is promoted through public assistance programmes, ensuring a fair redistribution of the resources available in a society. However, it is one thing to argue that securing a fair share of available resources is a human right and quite another to secure the broad needs of people. Regarding the former, most liberal-reformist and socialists concede that people have a fundamental claim on the resources that nature and society provides, for that enables them to fully enjoy their human potential. As far as the fulfillment of needs is concerned, it runs into rough weather, for it evokes the image of an insatiable and all-consuming individual. A broader view of welfare rights has to be defined by acknowledging that these—health, education, physical requirements—are necessary for a person's rational choice and purposive action. It is important to bear in mind that not all restrictions of liberty-as-choice mean reduction of autonomy, as some choices—to sell oneself into slavery or consume a dreaded drug—may be harmful to autonomy as well as welfare. This is the focus of the socialist critique of laissez faire capitalism that the latter not only leads to inequality but also constrains the consequences of liberty of the worst off. The choice and welfare rights theories accept that the human being is a composite of physical, psychological, emotional, mental and moral attributes.

Interest Theory

This theory stipulates that a person is said to have a right whenever, an interest of his is regarded as sufficiently important in itself to justify holding others to have a duty to promote that interest in some way. According to this view, rights and duties are not correlative rather rights are perceived to generate duty. This view remains formal and needs to be joined to a substantive theory that indicates what interests are sufficiently important to be regarded as a basis for producing a duty and which are not. The function of a theory of rights as indicated by Dworkin (1977) is to identify and justify certain pivotal individual interests and accord them priority over common interest. Benefit theory of rights stipulates that to have a right is to be the intended beneficiary of someone else's duty.

Human Rights

These are those rights that have been traditionally called natural or fundamental rights. They are 'moral rights which are owed to each man and woman solely by reason of being a human being' (Macfarlane 1985: 3). They have five distinguishing features—universality, individuality, paramountcy, practicability and enforceability. Universality implies that these rights belong to all people. These are individualistic since it accepts the notions of free individual, human dignity and individual moral choice. They are paramount as a denial of these rights is an affront to justice. Practicability suggests the feasibility of attaining these rights. These rights are enforceable by the state through its elaborate legal and constitutional machinery.

The *Universal Declaration of Human Rights* (UDHR) adopted by the United Nations General Assembly in 1948, guarantees rights to life, liberty, property, equality before the law, privacy, fair trial, safeguards against torture, slavery and other forms of degrading practices, protection of family and minorities, free expression, information, association, assembly, movement, religion, conscience and culture, to participate in government, to political asylum. These are to be safeguarded through institutions and practices, like constitutional government, democratic institutions, rule of law, independent judiciary, free press, trade union rights, innocent till proved guilty, and protection from arrests, detention and exile. Most constitutions of the world today enshrine these precepts and most political and social systems accept these as a basic minimum of civilised existence. Largely due to the insistence from the erstwhile Soviet bloc, various social and economic rights were included, like the right to work, to equal pay, to an adequate standard of living, and paid holidays, representing a diplomatic gain.

Since 1960s, there has been a special focus on women's rights. From the nineteenth to twentieth centuries, the feminists focused on the need for equal civil rights—right to vote, right to property—for women, who have been denied all along these rights that other individual citizens enjoyed. The focus of this debate shifted in the 1980s to advocate special rights for women to enable them to cope with their distinctive needs and characteristics and to overcome past inequalities and disadvantages, built into various social institutions and practices (Carter 1988). The demand for a quota law to ensure rough parity with regard to women's representation is a case in point. Besides women's rights, animal rights and children's rights have become slowly part of the political agenda in many democracies.

BASES OF RIGHTS

Recent theories attempt to identify the profound moral values and principles that underlie the notion of rights rather than to find natural foundations for them. These theories base moral rights on the considerations of freedom, autonomy and equality.

Freedom and Rights

Historically, rights have been defined as absence of non-intervention. **Hobbes'** formulation belongs to this category. Subsequently, there is a change, drawn from Kant's philosophy in the perception of the person from bearers of liberty-rights to one of autonomy and choice implying that an individual can make rules for himself and can choose from wide ranging possibilities of one's preferences. As a result, the individual guaranteed a space by negative rights is now a holder of special endowments, namely the capacity for an intelligent and creative exercise of rights. Thus, negative rights are the basis for these faculties. The salience of this argument is clear in **Hart's** (1955: 175–191) exposition that argues that if there is one natural right then it is the right of all people to be free. The import of the argument is that the essence of being human is to be moral. Morality is achieved through autonomy and choice and hence to be human and express one's nature one has to be free. For Hart and others, rights are important, for they protect and promote the distinct human interest in freedom. Many of those who associate rights with freedom espouse some version of choice-theory: the right-bearer is an active agent rather than a mere beneficiary of another's duty. So, animals and unborns could have rights as they are incapable of exercising choice and the freedom. Gewirth

(1982: 1–38) adds the right to well-being to the right to freedom as both try to ensure the attainment of rational autonomy, for a human being to realise himself. Furthermore, since each individual as a rational agent is entitled to the liberty to pursue his good, all human beings are entitled to do the same for themselves. **Rawls** (1972) also considers rights understood as civil liberties to be a primary good that rational/moral individual regard it as necessary for a just society. All these three arguments accept purposive action, self-control and self-development to be the essence of human nature with autonomy and agency as the culmination of human existence and seeing other characteristics as secondary to them. All individuals are equal in their potential rationality and in the right to action emanating from it (Freeden 1998: 45).

Equality and Rights

Some are critical of the incorporation of socio-economic rights in the UDHR, for these represent utopian aspirations and many Third World countries do not have the resources to provide the goods concerned. **Cranston** (1967, 1973) argues that only the traditional negative rights are the genuine universal human rights and the UDHR has made a mistake by incorporating economic rights for they are ideals, not universally realisable. He uses two grounds to explain his reasoning. The first is 'ought implies can' argument which holds that for any action to be morally obligatory it must be possible for the agent to perform it. Since most poor countries do not have the wherewithal to realise these economic rights, it is absurd to suggest that all citizens of the world have social and economic rights. This is not the case with traditional civil rights, for all it needs is inaction on part of the government. The second argument is that negative rights are more crucial for individual autonomy in the moral sense than economic rights. There is considerable intellectual merit in Cranston's argument, though he does not analyse the consequences of implementing economic rights in affluent societies. Since the 1980s, the New Right, the Neo liberals and libertarians have objected to the idea of welfare rights. Plant (1991: Ch. 7) denies the distinction that Cranston invokes on the grounds that even negative rights, for its implementation, require positive action on part of the government. Instead of this distinction, perhaps it is better to agree with Gewirth (1982) that for well-being an autonomous person requires both negative and positive rights.

Autonomy and Rights

Some have tried to derive rights from the idea of autonomy associated with the moral philosophy of **Kant**. Accordingly, rights are viewed as necessary preconditions for moral thinking and are not the fundamental principles of our moral system. Though autonomy and respect for human agency are freedom-related values, they regard moral autonomy in a more positive light, as something to be nurtured and attained rather than being taken for granted in human life. Theories like that of **Rawls** and **Dworkin** claim to revive Kantian liberalism and reject utilitarianism in its description of a just society. They advocate a moral theory that stresses the equal worth and moral autonomy of all human beings and then use this theory to justify a political society that recognises rights of autonomy and equality. This is called **rights-based liberalism**, for it invokes the moral idea of rights in order to define and legitimatise political authority and power. It uses rights as a theoretical medium for expressing and requiring respect for each individual's freedom and equality. Many of these theories also link liberty with equality as is clearly discernible in Rawls' theory. Dworkin recommends that if utilitarian calculations accommodate the principle of equal concern then it has to leave out what he calls 'external preferences', i.e., preferences that some people have about the treatment that others should receive. He described rights as 'moral trumps'. This conception of liberalism explicitly incorporates moral ideas in its foundations and welcomes the idea that the liberal state has a certain kind of moral role to play in the community, insofar as it must respect and promote individual rights while simultaneously remaining committed to toleration.

IS THE WESTERN TRADITION INDIVIDUALISTIC?

In recent times, the newly industrialised countries of the Asia-Pacific region have offered an Asian perspective to the issue of human rights. They challenge the *UDHR* on a matter of principle by attributing a Western bias to the charter and claiming that Western values are basically incompatible and, at times, detrimental to Asian societies. This is because the Western intellectual tradition is characterised as individualistic, while the Asian societies are community oriented and tradition bound. Kishore Mahbubani, a Singaporean diplomat and writer describes attachment to family as an institution and advocates deference to interests of society, respect for authority, thrift and conservatism in social mores, consensus rather than confrontation in decision-making process as representing Asian values. Furthermore, the proponents of Asian view allege that basic rights of the people to housing, health, education, employment are more important than civil liberties or political freedom. Some like **Dr Mahathir Mohammed** the Prime Minister of Malaysia have even questioned the relevance of human rights and democracy to developing countries. These countries do not deny human rights; they accept its universality. However, they desire a different set of rights from the ones accepted by the West and the fact that the West is numerically in the minority. It is in this context that they articulate an Asian perspective, thereby, raising two questions that need to be addressed: (a) Are these rights Western? (b) Is the Western tradition individualistic?

It needs to be emphasised, as evident from the foregoing paragraphs, that within the Western tradition libertarian theories coalesce with those that are communitarian. In fact, no tradition whether Western or Eastern, is wholly individualistic or wholly communitarian. This is clear in the non-Western tradition as amplified in the writings of Gandhi who absorbed the best from the major ideologies of the West even though he rejected Western civilisation for its materialism and technology. Though a philosophical anarchist Gandhi has been interpreted as a liberal, socialist and a conservative. Like Green, he sought to make life morally relevant for the majority of people, for the relationship between the individual and the community is held together by common interest and good. He cherished individual freedom but reminded that the human being was a social being. Society has to provide opportunities for the maximum growth of the individual but the final decision as to what constituted that growth lied with the individual. He clearly desired to limit the state and strengthen the civil society and the individual, for as he wrote on 1 February 1942 in *Harijan*,

> If the individual ceases to count, what is left of society? Individual freedom alone can make a man voluntarily surrender himself completely to the service of society. If it is wrested from him, he becomes an automation and society is ruined. No society can possibly be built on a denial of individual freedom.

Gandhi as a conservative emphasised performance of duties for enjoyment of rights but did not subscribe to the conservative idea of natural human inequality. He insisted that individual should not look to their rights alone, but in conjunction with his duties. Nonetheless, he also conceded to the individuals to judge the state and its authority in light of moral law and duty.

CONCLUSION

After the collapse of the totalitarian communism and other forms of authoritarianism, the world has been moving towards a liberalised market economy and constitutional democracy. Even within the developing world these are accepted as guarantees for sustained economic development and social justice. The important fact is that democracy with its attendant values like constitutionalism, rule of law, individual rights, impartial judiciary and multi-party system are perceived to be important for guaranteeing and protecting of rights and liberties worldwide. Rights are increasingly used as touchstones of political evaluation. Both, with regard to the conduct of domestic politics and in international affairs, rights are perceived to be the new criterion of political legitimacy. With increasing prospects towards globalisation, serious attempts have to be made to bring about universality, in concepts and paradigms taking into account the Western and the non-Western experiences. Cultural plurality is to be respected but it should not be particularistic so as to become divisive. Issues like human rights are beyond partisan and culture specific politics. They are indeed universal in the sense that Sakharov argued, 'We have a universal responsibility to use a single standard in judging human misfortune and injustice whereever they may occur' (1989: Preface).

Further Reading

Beetham, D. (Ed.), *Politics and Human Rights*, Blackwell, Oxford, 1995.

Flathman, R.E., *The Practice of Rights*, Cambridge University Press, Cambridge, 1991.

Jones, P., *Rights*, Macmillan, London, 1994.

Macpherson, C.B., *The Rise and Fall of Economic Justice and Other Essays*, Oxford University Press, Oxford, 1982.

Martin, R., *A System of Rights*, Clarendon Press, Oxford, 1993.

Pennock, J.R. and Chapman, J.W. (Eds.), *NOMOS XXIII: Human Rights*, New York University Press, New York, 1981. D.D. Raphael (Ed.), *Political Theory and the Rights of Man*, Macmillan, London, 1967.

Ritchie, D.G., *Natural Rights*, Allen and Unwin, London, 1952. H. Steiner, *An Essay on Rights*, Blackwell, Oxford, 1985.

Waldron, J. (Ed.), *Theories of Rights*, Oxford University Press, Oxford, 1984. C.E. Welch Jr., and V.A. Leary, *Asian Perspectives on Human Rights*, Westview Press, Boulder, 1990.

Endnotes

1. Self-preservation is a supreme right, according to Hobbes. Like Grotius, Hobbes regards it as a sufficient basis for morality. If self-preservation is the most basic right then an individual would not be aggressive towards others, unless provoked or threatened. However, he differs from Grotius, for he believes that an individual who pursued the right of self-preservation would still be unpredictable and dangerous towards others and that explained his gloomy description of life in the state of nature. For Hobbes, all rights including that of self-preservation included the option of forbearance, though at the same time self-preservation did not appear to be optional.
2. The period June 1793 to July 1794, was the phase known as the Reign of Terror in France. It began with the overthrow of the Girondins and the ascendancy of the Jacobins under Robiespierre. Against the background of foreign invasion and civil war, opponents were ruthlessly persecuted and about 1400 were executed by the guillotine. The terror ended with a coup on 27 July 1794 when Robiespierre and other leading Jacobins were arrested and executed.
3. This bill redistributed seats in the British House of Commons to include large cities that were previously unrepresented. It also gave the vote to adult males owning premises worth at least £10 a year.

Chapter 11

Liberty

Liberty and freedom are used synonymously and inter-changeably, though for many, freedom refers to a situation, while liberty symbolises a state of mind. Berlin declares that the two words 'mean the same' (1979: 121). Cranston concurs with Berlin but clarifies that 'liberty tends to be used in legal and political contexts, freedom in philosophical and more general ones' (1967: 32). The most succinct difference is provided by Pitkin (1988: 542–543), who drawing on Arendt's view, points out that *liberty* implies protection from state interference while *freedom* implies active involvement in politics. Pitkin suggests that *liberty* is more plural and piecemeal whereas *freedom* is more likely to be holistic, to mean a total condition or state of being.

> Freedom, when applied to persons and their actions, refers to the *ability* of a person in a given set of circumstances to act in some particular way. 'Liberty' refers to authoritative *permission* to act in some particular way. The contrast is a basis for the grammatical distinction between 'can' and 'may', between *de facto* and the *de jure* perspectives, or between (overall) ability and permission (Feinberg 1998: 753).

Freedom is a complex concept that contains within it two basic ideas, both independent and yet interdependent. One meaning of freedom is autonomy or rightful self-government or independence in the sense of sovereign free nation states. The other meaning is the overall ability to do, choose or achieve things that can be called 'optionality'. It is the freedom to do what one desires and wills (Feinberg 1998: 753).

DIFFERENT CONCEPTIONS

Henri Benjamin Constant (1767–1830) contrasts between **ancient and modern liberty** by pointing out that ancients equate liberty with citizenship—that is the right to participate in the assembly that debates and makes public decisions. The moderns define liberty as pursuit and protection of private rights. The ancients stress on cohesiveness and solidarity, viewing liberty as being compatible with the authority of the community so long as this authority is exercised in accordance to the law rather than according to the will of a despot. Liberty connotes advantages to the community rather than importance to the individual.

The moderns emphasise on personal independence and freedom made possible by the notion of equality before law. This change in the idea of freedom is due to the growth of the nation state as a centralised power and to the proclamation of the *American Declaration of Independence* that individuals 'are endowed by their Creator with certain inalienable rights' among which the most sacred is liberty. Through this distinction, Constant warns against the dire consequences of any attempt, that are being made during the French Revolution, to revive the ancient conception of liberty in which the individual is subordinated to the whole. This is best exemplified by Rousseau's ideal of freedom.

Miller identifies three main traditions of thought on liberty. The first and oldest family is **republican**, the most direct 'political conception of freedom since it defines freedom by reference to a certain set of political arrangements' (1991: 2–3). Machiavelli, Rousseau and Arendt are the exponents of republican notion of freedom. A person, according to this view, is free if he is a citizen of a free political community that is independent and self-governing and plays an active role in the government, which means that the laws enacted reflect the wishes of the people. Freedom is realisable through public service and political activity. This provides the basis of civic humanist tradition. This conception existed in ancient Athens but Miller does not regard it as strict democracy, for the Greek philosophers with whom the tradition is associated disqualified a large number of people—women, slaves, manual labourers from citizenship considering them as incapable of achieving freedom. Machiavelli's and Rousseau's conception of liberty is republican in nature. Machiavelli focusses on the question of public interest versus private ends and the importance republican institutions have on realising civic *virtú* (Skinner 1981). When the public space is used for furthering private concerns by individuals, then such people become corrupt and corrupt people can never sustain republics. Freedom, for Machiavelli, means independence from external aggression and internal tyranny and the effective exercise of political rights, which is possible only by a public-spirited person. The threat to liberty comes from human selfishness when citizens evade their civic obligations and redesign institutions to maximise their personal gain. By doing so, common good, civic institutions and even personal liberty are subverted. Machiavelli sees devotion to the public cause as a necessary precondition for claiming and enjoying private freedom. Machiavelli, notes Skinner, is the intellectual godfather of seventeenth century neo-Romanists like Marchamont, Nedham, Milton, Sidney and much later Price. In a recent study of *Liberty before Liberalism*, Skinner (1997) points out that the neo-Roman republican political theory, which develops in England during the Civil War defines liberty as the autonomous will of the state or non-domination. The neo-Roman writers object to Hobbes' negative liberty, which they contend is secured at the cost of political subjugation. They defend the ideal polity as an expression of natural freedom and object to the constitutional monarchical state, for it poses a threat to the lives, liberties and possessions of its subjects.

Rousseau's concern is with the creation of the *right* and not the *first* society through the social contract, a society that maximises individual liberty. This is the crux of his famous paradox that 'man was born free but is everywhere in chains'. He tries to reconcile individual liberty with political authority, whereby the individual enjoys the liberty that he has in the state of nature. He distinguishes between liberty and independence. Liberty consists in acting according to one's wishes. It means not being subject to the wills of other people. Anyone who is a master over another is not free himself. Rousseau regards liberty and equality as being interdependent. Unless people are equal they will never be free. This, he is convinced, is only possible if human selfishness and their particular interests are transformed allowing the essential goodness in individuals to come to the forefront. His ideal republic is a community vested with the 'General Will' in the nature of 'Common Me', consisting of the will of all individuals thinking of general and public interest. For Rousseau, only virtuous individuals are truly free and this also means that each is his own lawmaker without being represented. This also makes Rousseau the first major critic of representative democracy based on majority rule. He desires, instead, a direct participatory democracy close to what the ancient Greeks practised.

Arendt, by contrasting the Greek *polis* and the Roman republic with the modern states, points out that the rise of society, i.e., the nation-wide organisation of individuals' private interests, has eclipsed the distinction between the private and public domains. This is due to the developments in science and economy and an introspective philosophy that denies people the experience of a stable world rendering them 'worldless', resulting in a high premium on sheer survival. She considers freedom to be the focal point of politics and, like Aristotle, regards political activity to be original and supreme. Freedom is the right to take part in the political process of one's polity and human affairs assume significance only if they fulfil the public dimension of life. It does not mean absence of restraints on rights of life, liberty and property—civil rights—and liberation from arbitrary rule. She equates freedom with a republic and emphasises the distinction between liberation and freedom. Liberation is the desire to be free from oppression which is possible in a monarchial though not a despotic form of government, but freedom demands the establishment of the republic.

The second category of views is the **liberal**, which defines freedom as a property of individuals and precludes interference or restraint by others. According to the liberal view, while the government secures freedom by protecting each person from the interference of others, it also threatens freedom by itself imposing laws and directives with the help of force. 'While a republican views freedom as being realised through a certain kind of politics, the liberal tends to see freedom as beginning where politics ends, especially in various forms of private life' (Miller 1991: 3). J.S. Mill's classic *On Liberty* represents the quintessence of the liberal view. An extreme position of the liberal standpoint is the anarchist view, which considers freedom as perfectly realisable only with the destruction of the coercive power of political authority. Liberals differ about what each considers as a proper role of government activity but all liberals agree that, 'freedom is a matter of the scope or extent of government rather than of its forms or character' (Miller 1991: 4). The third view is the **idealist** view, where the focus shifts from the social arrangements to the way a person actually lives and acts. A person is free when he is autonomous. Freedom is no longer the struggle to be free from external constraints but 'with elements within the person himself which thwart his desire to realise his own true nature—weaknesses, compulsions, irrational beliefs and so forth' (Miller 1991: 4). This conception becomes political the moment certain political conditions are identified as being necessary for freedom. The exponents of the idealist view are Hegel and Green.

NOTION OF FREE WILL

The notion of individual liberty is closely linked with the theological doctrine that a human being has 'free will, with which to choose good or evil, and that this is the defining characteristic of his God-given nature' (Goodwin 1992: 275). Though the question whether an individual is free or determined is more pertinent to moral rather than political philosophy but any notion that is advocated has consequences for the adoption of political ideals. Since the eighteenth century, rationalist philosophers have argued that it is possible to provide causal explanations of human behaviour, of events in the natural world leading to the emergence of determinism as the general doctrine. Its affiliated axiom that social environment makes human character, gives rise to a new generation of utopias on the premise that perfect social institutions made perfect people. Marx's materialist analysis is based on this premise. Many philosophers (Berlin 1969, Strawson 1968) contend that an important aspect in social life is the assumption that we are all responsible for our actions, an assumption that is only possible in the context of a theory of free will. This is central to the liberal theory, which accepts that individuals are capable of free and rational choice. Consequently, the notion of free will and freedom forms the bedrock of Western political theory and society. It needs to be emphasised that most philosophers do not assume that one is totally determined or undetermined. Many espouse a 'compatibilist' position that explains individuals as partly free and partly determined the fact that certain factors like conditioning determine human choices but within that one still has the space for choice. The question pertaining to free will as the basis of human action in political theory is very important in deciding how to explain political behaviour and the choice of political values that is made. The theoretical assumptions about free will define the parameters of an ideology. In recent times, the communitarians contend that adult human beings are simply not capable of the kind of autonomous choice of life plan that liberals believe a state must respect. They point out that even highly intelligent and mature persons use their freedom to make bad choices and consider autonomy to be less important than the other values like stability, preservation of social bonds, the preservation of culture and the safety of its citizens.

There is another view of **freedom as obedience** to a higher authority espoused by collectivist thinkers of both left and right. The earliest proponent of this view is Rousseau for whom true freedom consists in obeying the general will that is devoid of particularistic and selfish elements and expressed in a democratic assembly of equals. A deviant is compelled to obey the law, 'forced to be free'. An important pre-requisite is a substantive measure of social and economic equality. The other exponent is **Hegel**, for whom freedom is obedience to self-prescribed laws, as political power of the state is the 'externalisation' of individual's will. The state is 'absolutely rational' and represents universal altruism. Hegel does not see law as a hindrance to freedom: it is a characteristic of freedom. A liberal speaks of submission to self-prescribed laws since freedom is not antithetical to law but he is skeptical of abstract mystical notions like general will or the state as a divine institution. A liberal defends the process whereby the majority rule is consensually arrived at and the need for the individual to accept it, though liberals since J.S. Mill also places considerable stress on the rights of the minority. Those who articulate the idea of freedom as obedience proceed on the assumption that there is a certainty about what is right and who is to be obeyed. Normally, such a view is accompanied by the idea that the whole is greater and wiser than the constituent parts (Goodwin 1992: 279–280).

DIFFERENT IDEOLOGIES AND FREEDOM

In spite of claims by anarchists and libertarians, there is nothing like absolute liberty unrestrained by law, morals or actions of others. Liberty to be meaningful and worthwhile is possible only within a framework of law and that law and liberty are compatible giving credence to the old saying that 'my liberty ends where the other person's nose begins'. For a liberal, liberty is closely linked with law. The idea that all are subject to a law that has been freely consented to, all are equal under the law so that none is subject to the arbitrary will of another person and, therefore, all are equally free is central to liberalism. This is clearly explicit in Locke's famous, phrase, 'the end of the law is, not to abolish or restrain, but to preserve and enlarge freedom' (1960: 348). Locke, the founder of **liberalism**, explains the pre-political state of nature as based on the laws of nature comprehensible to every individual through the power of his reason. He defends religious toleration and considers any attempt to interfere with religious beliefs as unjust, for each person has a right to seek for his own personal salvation. He rejects religious persecution as futile, for the inner-most thoughts of a person can never be known and most often people confess under stress. Locke gives an economic dimension to liberty when he explains labour as the unquestioned property of the labourer and that each person has the right to property by virtue of this labour. He considers the relationship of individuals with political authority as moral and deriving from god who has created them and to whom they owe a duty to preserve one's self, thus, explicitly excluding the freedom to kill oneself or others, or enslave others. However, he grants the right to inflict penalties, including the death sentence on those who violate the laws generally, and particularly if another person's life is threatened. In personal relationships, he points out that parents and husbands do not have absolute power over their children and wives, respectively. Mothers have an equal title with fathers to authority over their children. A wife accepts husband's authority, which is limited to things in common interest and to property and explicitly has a right over her life and fortune. A wife has the right to divorce to end an unhappy marriage. Personal independence—the right to live with dignity within reasonable economic comfort—is a fundamental human right. Locke demarcates the private from the public spheres, a division at the heart of a liberal society. He emphasises on consent as the basis of legitimate political authority, thereby, specifying the limits of political power and the ambit of personal liberty in a liberal society. The liberal state is a minimal and a constitutional state based on the rule of law, providing the later liberals a framework to work with. Montesquieu underlines the importance of safeguards like written constitution, separation of powers, checks and balances, precise legal procedures, clear specification of crimes and independence of judiciary for preservation of liberty. He emphasises correctly that liberty is possible only within fixed legal procedures and institutions. He desires limits to the use of corporal punishment since it is cruel and destructive to human dignity.

Montesquieu's ideas influenced the authors of the *Federalist Papers* and the US Constitution is modelled along his suggestions. **Smith** links freedom with opulence regarding the two 'as the greatest blessings' that human beings can possess. He holds that true freedom is possible through commerce. He considers dependency to be degrading—a view crucial to the civic humanist equation of freedom with independence. He insists that commerce was a preventive to the occurrence of dependency. When the broad principles recommended by Locke become constitutionally established in most European countries, later liberals like J.S. Mill look into specific political liberties. The recent communitarian critique of liberalism takes exception to the latter's attachment for freedom and autonomy on the grounds that some individuals because of illness, mental impairment or immaturity are simply incapable of autonomy and often even mature individuals use their freedom to make bad and wrong choices. Both these criticisms are off the mark and fail to take into account the subtle nuances of the theory, particularly, as it develops in the writings of Mill and Berlin.

While the liberal view of freedom is essentially freedom from interference, the Marxist view drawing from the philosophies of Spinoza, Rousseau, Kant and Hegel, defines freedom as self-determination and self-realisation. It sees freedom as the removal of obstacles to human emancipation allowing the full flowing of the human powers. It emphasises the close link between liberty and equality. Gerrard Winstanley (1609–1660) is the first to establish the link between unequal distribution of land and the oppression of the poor landless and thereby becomes the basis of the socialist critiques of bourgeois rights as being meaningless. For most socialists, only when class divisions and wage labour based on private property leading to competitiveness and selfishness are abolished, that a truly human society based on fellowship, love and cooperative instinct is created. Only collective effort can overcome such hurdles and freedom, as self-determination is collective in the sense that there is an organised human effort over both nature and the social conditions of production. This means the destruction of capitalism and the creation of a communist society that embodies collective control, collective individuality and personal freedom but **Marx** and **Engels** remain reticent about the form of this future society. In the process, they leave unresolved the possible conflicts among these values or between them and others. They presume rather naively that with the abolition of classes there will be harmony or absence of conflicts.

Marxism's concern with a wider and richer view of freedom also leads the Marxists to underestimate the nature and extent of civic and economic freedoms that individuals enjoy in liberal-capitalist societies. In spite of his commitment to human emancipation, Marx has very little faith in mechanisms like constitution, rule of law or charter of rights. He dismisses these as a facade to conceal bourgeois exploitation and oppression and does not acknowledge the protection, even if it is in a limited sense, where they lend to individual against arbitrary rule and physical harm. As a result of these theoretical limitations and shortsightedness, the former Communist States were most brutal in stifling civic freedoms. The Marxists forgot that 'the civic freedoms which, however inadequately and precariously, form part of bourgeois democracy are a product of centuries of unremitting popular struggle. The task of Marxist politics is to defend these freedoms; and to make possible their extension and enlargement by the removal of their class boundaries (Miliband 1977: 189–190). Furthermore, in *On the Jewish Question* Marx cherishes personal liberty but links it to egoism and private property not realizing that personal liberty and private property need not always be inimical to one another.

> For the Marxists civil society is a fraud. The idea of plurality of institutions—both opposing and balancing the state and in turn controlled and protected by the 'state'—is, in the Marxist view, merely the provision of a facade for a hidden and maleficent domination (Gellner 1994: 1).

In spite of the individual variations, socialists of all shades regard economic freedom as primary and consider political and civil liberties to be formal in the presence of economic inequalities. However, many Western socialists argue like J.S. Mill that political freedom is valuable and ought to be coalesced with welfare measures. For the socialists, it is not the state that poses a threat to individual liberty, rather it is economic exploitation that prevents self-realisation and material sufficiency. The socialists have a more deterministic view of human nature than the liberals, for they deny a direct co-relationship between choice and freedom.

The extreme left wing ideology, anarchism desires to do away with all authority, whether that of a state, church or the parent, since an authority and discipline that is imposed from the outside always curtails freedom. Like the Marxists, anarchists too desire the abolition of state power after the destruction of capitalism and describe the post-capitalist anarchist society as being truly free. **Bakunin** holds that freedom in Rousseau's sense is possible only in a community of equals. However, anarchism remains untested in practice. Many of the criticisms levelled against the Marxist theory—like the absence of mechanisms to resolve conflicts, constitutional safeguards as a necessary requirement in any society—can also be made against anarchism. Closely resembling anarchism is **libertarianism** that regards subjective freedom as the highest social and political value. It believes in freeing people not merely from the shackles of traditional, political institutions but also from the inner constraints imposed by the importance they attach and the power that they attribute to ineffectual practices and institutions namely religion, family and social customs especially sexual conformity. Conservatism does not understand freedom as being left alone but as performance of one's duty attached to one's roles. It understands liberties and rights as derived from specific institutional and legal arrangements giving specific benefits, protections and claims to individuals and groups and from history and tradition and not from rational arrangements or from natural law.

Feminism accepts an intrinsic link between freedom and equality, for the Enlightenment feminists like Wollstonecraft and Mary Astell (1666–1731) use the idea of equality to demand recognition of women as human subjects with agency and intellect, an aspect, which J.S. Mill subsequently reinforces. Contemporary feminism defines freedom as empowerment, needing both the negative liberty of absence of restraints and positive liberty's community assistance. This community is non-hierarchical and accepts equality as a vital component of relationships. However, it is an equality among individuals that is based on difference, one that accepts the 'individuals' unique and particular ways of manifesting and living out the commonly shared and similarly encoded aspects of experience' (Hirschman 1996: 70). It emphasises on agency not in the abstract sense but as 'selfless, collective agency of the general will' (1996: 70).

NEGATIVE AND POSITIVE LIBERTY

Negative liberty connotes freedom as the absence of restraints and non-interference while positive liberty means self-mastery and the right of autonomy. Negative liberty asks the question what is the area within which the subject is or should be left to do or what he is able to be without interference by others. Positive liberty asks the question what or who is the source of control or interference that determines someone to do, or be this rather than that. Certain positive accounts stress on the need to subordinate the lesser element within an agent by higher elements. Others emphasise the fact that a person can lead an autonomous life only as a member of a free political community. Negative liberty accepts the postulate that the individual knows and is the best judge of his own interest. It thrived at a time when the individual was struggling to free himself from the arbitrary power of the state and was trying to carve out a private space, both economic and political. Hobbes, Locke, Montesquieu, Bentham, Henry Sidgwick (1838–1900), Herbert Spencer (1820–1903), J.S. Mill, Hayek and classical and neo-classical economists are all negative liberty theorists while Rousseau, Kant, Hegel and Marx are positive liberty theorists.

Hobbes defines freedom as the private pursuit of the individual, which implies that each can create his own conception of freedom within a framework of state authority. In spite of his emphasis on total order, he defines liberty as whatever the law permits and wherever the law is silent, it signifies the absence of restraints and coercion. He accepts the right of private beliefs, for conscience is beyond the reach of the Leviathan. However, the Leviathan can command the individual to perform ceremonies that are necessary for public worship. **Bentham** defines liberty in the same way as Hobbes but crucial to his understanding of civil and political liberty is security that the legislator secures through the law, making it possible for the individual to enjoy liberty. At the level of civil law, a legislator secures the right to property, prevents interference, simplifies judicial proceedings and encourages healthy commercial competitiveness. In the realm of criminal law, a legislator protects the individual against crime through a system of a rational criminal code, a strong effective police force and a judiciary. In the domain of constitutional law, a legislator guarantees against misrule, abuse and arbitrary exercise of power. He regards liberty and law to be antithetical and holds that social utility can provide the necessary balance between freedom and restraint. There is a justification for legal restraint if a net increase in utility for the community as a whole takes place. In Sidgwick's view, the sanctity of the contract becomes clear, for he contends that a person, who negotiates a contract, even if its terms are burdensome, demonstrates his individual choice. The state has the duty to enforce the contract(s). A person's liberty is the realm in which he is left alone without pondering over the quality of his action.

Popper defines freedom as non-interference and considers the aim of public policy to mitigate avoidable suffering of people rather than promote happiness. Hayek uses the term freedom and liberty interchangeably and insists on the priority of freedom over other ideals both in his philosophy of social science and his system of morality. In his social science, liberty is a necessary postulate in a proper explanation of social affairs. An abstract science of society is concerned with the spontaneous evolution of undesigned and unplanned institutions like the *catallaxy*. Therefore, appropriate disciplines theorise about the consequences of free actions of individuals. For instance, an economist is confined to analysing the market order that emerges from uncoerced transactions of individuals. In a perfectly planned economy, there can be no proper explanatory science but only a collection of 'facts'. Hayek holds that there can never be an abstract, deductive science of economics under socialism. In the context of morality, not only is liberty a supreme value but also the condition for other values. This means a society has to be evaluated in accordance with freedom and not in conformity with some trade-off between, for example, freedom and social justice, or by a criterion of economic efficiency. The other values that the individuals wish to promote depend on the institutions of a free society. He insists that genuine altruism is only possible in a free society and cannot be brought about by coercive law. He is critical of the welfare state, for that undermines the sense of personal responsibility, which is so crucial to liberty. He defines freedom in the *Constitution of Liberty* (1960: 11) as that 'state in which a man is not subject to coercion by the arbitrary will of another'. This is slightly different from the traditional formulations of negative liberty that defines liberty as absence of restraints. Hayek considers law and liberty as consistent and contrasts his view with that of political liberty, liberty as power and inner freedom, and regards the private world as a necessary feature of a civilised society. He holds political liberty—the freedom to participate in government, the right to vote and to form political parties—as an illegitimate extension of freedom from the individual to the collective realm. Contrary to this, Hayek suggests that as long as each individual is guaranteed equality under the law, freedom from arbitrary arrest, the right to own property, freedom of movement and free choice of occupation, conditions of free society exist. Hayek criticises the fact that much of the economic and social life that is decided by individual choice is now decided by collective decision. He rejects the idea of freedom as power, as the ability to do certain things and associates this view as a normal feature of socialism which perceives a person as free in the formal but not in the substantive sense. This fallacious view, according to Hayek, identifies freedom with wealth, which it is not and on that basis allows limitless intrusion by centralised authorities, in the mistaken belief that freedom is being increased. Neither is freedom to be understood as inner freedom, associated with conceptions of positive liberty. He argues that the extent to which a person acts as he ought to act is a different question from that of whether he is being coerced by another person, emphasising the importance of the private world as one that preserves genuine individualism. The public-private distinction is crucial for Hayek, for it brings out the difference between two concepts of law—the law of an organisation with specific purposes and the rules of a purposeless spontaneous society. The private world does not mean absence of rule but rules that do not direct the individual towards centrally determined ends and a framework of reasonable security within which one can pursue one's ends. However, the public world functions through commands addressed to officials for the fulfillment of specific collective purposes. The private world is for Hayek the 'protected domain', the essential pre-requisite of a liberal social order that included property. He regards law, liberty and property as inseparable and points out in the *Constitution of Liberty* that a liberal social order minimises coercion and deliberate interference and guarantees material benefit to its citizens through safety nets outside the market.

> His most important objective is to defeat the belief that a person's freedom depends on the material resources available to him—a belief that might justify economic redistribution as a mean of increasing the freedom of the poor. He defines freedom as the absence of coercion and coercion as a state of affairs in which one person is made into the instrument of another's will. For Hayek this implies the rules of law—general, abstract rules laid down in advance of the particular activities they are meant to regulate—are not coercive, for such laws do not direct behaviour but are merely conditions that a person takes into account when deciding how to act. Thus in Hayek's view a liberal political order, composed entirely of such rules, imposes no limits at all on negative liberty in the proper sense of the term (Miller 1991: 14).

Hayek equally insists on the importance of freedom to choose one's own moral standards in personal matters within the protected domain, which has to be free from any specific content being assigned to it. Freedom does not mean doing any particular thing. He contrasts rationalist conceptions of freedom that mistakenly associate liberty with design and social institutions with deliberation, with the empirical tradition, that link freedom with tradition. In the empirical tradition, free institutions emerge accidentally from individual interaction and are designed to bring specific benefits to individuals but once it becomes clear that limitations on government are to the advantage of people there is a reason in maintaining them. The important thing in Hayek's analysis is the link between liberty and individualism, between law and liberty. In view of these linkages, Hayek rejects not only collectivism but also *laissez faire* by pointing out that a truly free society spontaneously develops those rules that liberty requires.

Among the positive liberty theorists, Rousseau and Hegel have been discussed in detail. The other important theorists within this tradition are Kant, Green and Marcuse. **Kant** belongs to the tradition of positive liberty that goes back to the time of Plato. According to this view, a person acts voluntarily only when he acts rightly. All individuals aim to do good and when they do not do so it is because they are ignorant or under the sway of passions. Therefore, no action other than a virtuous one is fully voluntary. Plato rests this argument on the teleological view of the cosmos, which means that each person has a proper aim that he can pursue only if he is fully rational and has a good understanding of the universe. For Kant, a person is free when his 'noumenal' self controls his 'phenomenal' self. Green introduces the notion of positive liberty in English political thought with his famous essay '*Liberal legislation and Freedom of Contract*' (1888) by arguing that state intervention even if it is tantamount to a breach of contract, actually expands positive liberty. He considers negative liberty to be ineffective if there is no positive freedom to pursue worthwhile ends. It is the 'capacity of doing or enjoying something worth doing or enjoying, and that too, something that we do or enjoy in common with others' (1888: 371). However, Green remains committed to liberal ends in spite of championing positive liberty. **Gandhi** reiterates Green's idea of collective well-being or common good as underlying any claim to private right and accepts that the individual's fullest potential was possible only within the society. Both believe that the community is held together not by force but by the idea of common good.

Marcuse advances an influential modern version of positive liberty that Berlin has not taken into consideration (Barry, N.P. 1995: 218). In '*Repressive Tolerance*' (1969), he contends that though the Western capitalist democracies have removed the traditional obstacles to liberty they have managed to stifle freedom and rationality by new forms of domination and repression. The masses do not enjoy true liberty since their tastes and wants are manipulated. Their revolutionary spirit has become dull due to a constant supply of consumer goods. The formal provision of civil liberties does not indicate the presence of genuine freedom of expression since most of the opinion that the majority believe is successfully controlled and shaped by the system. Dissent is tolerated since it is ineffective and poses no threat to the system. True freedom lies in pursuit of rational end that is desirable and not in making mere choices restricted to the present. Modern liberal democracy has created the one dimensional man who subverts the creative critical dimension of man.

MILL'S ANALYSIS

J.S. Mill is perhaps the only theorist who advances both a negative and a positive view of liberty. His defense of freedom of thought and expression is one of the most powerful and eloquent expositions in the Western intellectual tradition. *On Liberty* (1859) constitutes the most persuasive and convincing defense of the principle of individual liberty ever written. Mill defends the right of the individual to freedom. In its negative sense, it means that society has no right to coerce an unwilling individual except for self-defense. 'It is being left to oneself; all restraints *qua* restraints, is an evil'. In its positive sense it means the grant of the largest and the greatest amount of freedom for the pursuit of the individual's creative impulses and energies, and for self-development. In case of a clash between an individual's opinion with that of the community, the individual will be the ultimate judge unless the community can convince him without resorting to threat and coercion. Mill lays down the grounds for justifiable interference. An activity that pertains to the individual alone represents the space over which no coercive interference either from the government or from other people is permissible. The realm, which pertains to the society or others, is the space in which coercion can be exercised for ensuring conformity with an acceptable standard of conduct. The differentiation between the two areas is made clear by the distinction between **self-regarding** and **other-regarding actions**, labels that **Bentham** originally uses.

> The only part of the conduct of any one, for which is amenable to society, is that which concerns others. In the part, which merely concerns himself, his independence is, of right, absolute. Over him-self, over his own body and mind, the individual is sovereign (Mill 1976: 76).

Mill defends individuality or the right of choice. As far as self-regarding actions are concerned, he offers four reasons as to why coercion is detrimental to self-development—first, the evils of coercion far outweigh the good achieved; second, individuals are diverse in their needs and capacities for happiness and that any coercive effort will be futile, since a person is the best judge of his own interests he has the information and the incentive to achieve them; third, on other things being equal, diversity is intrinsically good and shall be encouraged and finally, freedom is the most important requirement for a rational person. Mill contends that autonomy and self mastery are something inherently desirable and that are possible only if there is a great deal of negative liberty, meaning that individuals ought to be allowed the freedom to develop their own talents and invent their own life-styles. Hence, he makes a strong case for negative liberty regarding a liberal society and liberal state to be complimentary. However, he accepts reasonable interference on the part of a society to circumscribe individual liberty in order to prevent harm to other people. He regards liberty of conscience, liberty to express and publish one's opinions, liberty to live as one pleases and freedom of association as essential for a meaningful life and for the pursuit of one's good.

> If all mankind minus one were of one opinion, mankind would be no more justified in silencing that one person than he, if he had the power, would be justified in silencing mankind (Mill 1976: 79).

Mill's defense of freedom of thought and discussion is linked to the persecution of error. Even if an opinion is incorrect, it shall be allowed free expression, for only through active interaction and dialogue can it evolve, otherwise it will lose its vitality and become dead dogmas. Ideas are to be subjected to a critical scrutiny from other points of view for arriving at truth. He supports individuality on the grounds that creative individuals contribute to the great advances in the society and this is possible only if they are allowed to function freely. The early liberals defend liberty for the sake of efficient government, whereas for Mill, liberty is good for its intrinsic worth. It not only helps in the development of a humane, civilised and moral person but also benefits society thereby emphasising the larger societal context within which political institutions and individuals function.

Mill accepts **Tocqueville's** observations that the modern industrial societies are becoming more egalitarian and socially conformistic, bringing about uniformity in opinion and practice, which threatens individuality and creativity. Mill was disturbed by the fact that Victorian Britain had become a nation of dull conformists due to pressures of public opinion and thus, realised the inadequacy of early liberalism. He considered tyranny and intolerance by the majority as the singular threat to individual liberty.

> Protection, therefore, against the tyranny of the magistrate is not enough; there needs protection also against the tyranny of the prevailing opinion and feeling; against the tendency of society to impose, by other means than civil penalties, its own ideas and practices as rules of conduct on those who dissent from them; to fetter the development, and if possible, prevent the formation, of any individuality not in harmony with its ways and compels all characters to fashion themselves upon the model of its own. There is a limit to the legitimate interference of collective opinion with individual independence: and to find that limit, and maintain it against encroachment, is as indispensable to a good condition of human affairs, as protection against political despotism (Mill 1976: 68).

Mill laments the moral timidity of an active and inquiring mind, which disguises its true opinion when discussed in public. This is because the majority projects itself as the controller of social opinion, as the 'moral police' and exercises social tyranny in subtle forms like customs, conventions, mass opinion preventing the individual from stopping to think as to where and how one comes to acquire these. As a result, individuality ceases to exist. Individuality for Mill is not merely being non-conformistic but in exercising the right to choose and in possessing an inquiring mind, for that leads to self-development and the expression of free will. He stresses on absolute liberty of conscience, belief and expression as being crucial to human progress. Mill offers two arguments for liberty of expression in the service of truth—first, the dissenting opinion can be true and its suppression robs humankind of useful knowledge and second, even if the opinion is false, it strengthens the correct view by challenging it.

> But the peculiar evil of silencing the expression of an opinion is, that it is robbing the human race, posterity as well as the existing generation; those who dissent from the opinion, still more than those who hold it. If the opinion is right, they are deprived of the opportunity of exchanging error for truth: if wrong, they lose, what is almost as great a benefit, the clearer perception and livelier impression of truth, produced by its collision with error (Mill 1976: 79).

Its extreme version, individuality, is eccentricity which refuses 'to bend the knee to custom' in the face of an exceptionally assertive mass opinion. However, if the pressure to socially conform is not that strong then there is no need to encourage eccentricity. Furthermore, Mill distinguishes between desirability of difference with desirability of independence of character and concedes the need for plurality of thought and behaviour with moral and mental autonomy. For Mill, all creative faculties and the great goods of life develop only through freedom and 'experiments in living'. Like his father, James Mill, he believes in the individual's capacity for education by which he means not only intellectual training or cultivation of critical inquiry but also the training of moral character. Happiness for J.S. Mill is the ability to discover one's innate powers and develop these while exercising one's human abilities of autonomous thought and action. Liberty and individuality are possible only in a free society. Mill applies the principle of liberty to mature individuals and excludes children, invalids, mentally handicapped and barbarian societies in which race are considered 'nonage'. Liberty can be withheld where individuals are not educated. He considers liberty as belonging to higher and advanced civilisations and prescribes despotism or paternalism with severe restrictions as far as the lower ones are concerned. Mill cautions against sacrifice or infringement of liberty for the sake of making a state strong, for that is inherently counter-productive since states are constituted of human beings. His concluding paragraph is a good testimony of his liberal temper and outlook.

> A state which dwarfs me, in order that they may be more docile instruments in its hands even for beneficial purposes—will find that with small men no great thing can really be accomplished; and that the perfection of machinery to which it has sacrificed everything, will in the end avail it nothing, for want of the vital power which, in order that the machine might work smoothly, it has preferred to banish (Mill 1976: 120).

Though Mill advances two notions of liberty, it is the idea of negative liberty that is predominant (Berlin 1969). This reading of Mill is questioned by Norman P. Barry (1995: 216, 227), for whom Mill defines liberty as not only involving absence of restraints but also as self-mastery meaning exercise of choice. It is true that Mill defends positive liberty, which he links to choice and individuality as end values and not because they promote general happiness. He does not propose a single overarching principle or values, which normally accompany theories of positive liberty. Furthermore, the subject matter of Mill's tract is not the control of negative liberty by legal coercion but the bridling individual autonomy by the 'moral coercion' of an invasive public opinion (Berlin 1969). Mill desires to protect the individual's private space after being made conscious by Tocqueville of the power society and majority wields. He rightly observes that the threat to individual liberty is not just from a government but also from society or to be precise from a tyrannical majority. The theme in *On Liberty* is not just the absence of restraints but the possibility of a denial of individual autonomy through a coercive majority or/and an intrusive public opinion (Berlin 1969). For Mill, individuality signifies a property in human beings that make the scrutiny of prevailing ideas and conventions possible by subjection of them to the litmus test of reason. In this context, freedom not only means absence of restraints but also an ability to cultivate some desirable qualities that enable choice, since human beings pride themselves as being different from apes.

However, Mill's linkage between individuality and liberty leads him to conclude that liberty is possible only for a small number of people, for most others remain enslaved to customs and are not free. This is indeed an elitist perception but that does not dilute his position as an uncompromising liberal, for he repudiates paternalism or the idea that law and society can intervene for individual's good. He explicitly rejects interference with regard to self-regarding actions differing from Bentham who allows the pleasure of malevolence, namely, if the majority abhors a particular kind of private conduct then it is similar to the pain it will cause to the individual if such a conduct is prohibited. Mill disagreeing, explicitly states that the right of liberty can be sacrificed only for some 'other right'. Rawls inverts this logic by asserting that liberty can be curtailed only if it results in less but equal liberty for all. Furthermore, Mill like Bentham contends that social influence abridges liberty. He also accepts liberty and law are compatible and that liberty is possible only in an advanced civilisation. Mill fails to specify the proper limits of legislation and is ambiguous with regard to actual cases. For instance, he supports compulsory education, regulations of business and industry in the interest of public welfare and good but regards prohibition as an intrusion on liberty. He accepts restraint in self-regarding actions if it harms others, for instance, punishment of a habitual alcoholic or an idle man who fails to carry out his obligations towards his family but Mill rejects interference if the agent inflicts harm on himself only. He does not recommend compulsory cure for the alcoholic nor does he see a need for a law against suicide.

Sir Ernest Barker (1915) makes an interesting observation when he considers Mill to be in reality a prophet of an empty liberty and an abstract individual. This observation follows from the interpretation that absolutist statements on liberty like the rights of one individual against the rest cannot be substantiated if one assesses Mill's writings in its totality. Mill qualifies his statements circumscribing his original intent on liberty. For instance, the demarcation he made between self regarding and other regarding actions and his tilt towards welfare conflicting with the larger notion of individualism indicate this incompleteness. However, the point Barker ignores is the fact that the tension that emerges in Mill is an inevitable consequence of attempting to create a realistic political theory, which attempts to extend the frontiers of liberty as much as possible.

Liberty and self-determination the two themes that figure prominently in Mill's writings are extended to the woman's question. *The Subjection of Women* (1869) makes a strong claim for equal status in three key areas that women do not enjoy, namely the right to vote, right to equal opportunities in education and employment. He rejects the prevailing prejudice that marriage is the ultimate choice for a woman. According to him whether a woman desires to marry or not should depend on the woman herself and not on society. The status of an uneducated woman is like that of a slave, since marriage is like Hobson's choice, marry and face abuses and loss of dignity, that subjugation entails or else one could remain single and get deprived of all educational and professional opportunities. Mill deplores women's lack of freedom of choice and the ability to lead a life of a free and rational being. He is convinced that proper education, marriage on equal terms and the life of choice would improve women's position, for he believes that women are as gifted as men are. He also desires the reform of the traditional family, which he describes as a 'school of despotism', since it places 'undue premium on men. All the relationships including the marital one are based on equality, which is a genuine moral sentiment, then both individuals and the society benefit.

BERLIN'S ANALYSIS: FREEDOM AND PLURALISM

I may not deserve to be remembered as a poet, but surely as a soldier in the battle for human freedom.

This is a statement by Heine that Isaiah Berlin quotes in the memory of Boris Pasternak is an apt description of Berlin and his work *Two Concepts of Liberty*, an inaugural lecture that he delivers as the Chichele Professor of Social and Political Theory, in 1958. The *Two Concepts of Liberty* can be described as the finest defense of the liberal theory of freedom since J.S. Mill's *On Liberty*. Berlin derives the value of freedom from the limits of rational choice, advances two concepts of liberty and shows how positive liberty can be developed systematically to defend and justify brutal suppression of the individual. He acknowledges his indebtedness to Constant. In Berlin's scheme of things, freedom is linked to the values of individuality and human diversity or plurality. **Pluralism** suggests that there is no single master idea and that there are many conceptions of good life, good society and these goods are often, at least incommensurable and incompatible. He convincingly argues that human goods are combinable and incommensurable with application at three levels—first within any morality or code of conduct, conflicts will arise among ultimate values of that morality which cannot be resolved through theoretical or practical reasoning. For example, liberty and equality, fairness and welfare are recognised as intrinsic goods, are rivalrous by nature, collide in practice and cannot be explained by any overarching standard. Second, each of these goods is internally complex and inherently pluralistic consisting of incommensurable elements. Negative liberty contains within it rivalrous and incommensurable liberties. For example, liberties of information and of privacy are often competitive and may embody incommensurable values. So is the case with equality, which consists of rivalrous components like equality of opportunity and equality of outcome. Such goods are not harmonious wholes but are in themselves arenas of conflict and incommensurability. Third, different cultural forms will generate different moralities and values. Berlin is not only a value pluralist but also a cultural pluralist. His pluralism differs from that of J.S. Mill's who does not confront the realities of conflict and even contradiction within individual natures though he speaks of human diversity. Berlin comes to terms with the radical choices that complex and conflicting needs of individual natures threw up (Gray 1995).

Opposed to pluralism, for Berlin, is monism that ranks values on a single scheme of things. Consequently, the search for a perfect society that will achieve all genuine goods and ideals is not only utopian but also incoherent. He suspects any project that suggests human improvement or perfection by ignoring local history, culture or social conditions, as an attempt towards enforced conformity and tyranny. He insists on the need to respect national differences, for each individual, each culture, each nation, and each historical period will have its own goals, aspirations and conceptions of good life. It is impossible to knit these together within both individual and society into an overarching single theoretical system in which all ends will be realised without any clashes and conflict. This is because of the incompleteness of any human scheme for all values are unrealisable in one life or in a single social order at any one given time in history. Values, ultimate they may be, exclude one another and their incompatibility has to be reconciled through a constant process of compromise and trade off, rather than a false synthesis that enlightenment rationalism with its belief in the idea of uninterrupted progress of history advocates. However, he remains committed, like Hume to the central idea of the enlightenment project namely the illumination of the human world by rational enquiry. He views human being as an incomplete, unfinished and self-transforming person partly determinate, partly the author of oneself and not subject comprehensively to any natural order. He, like Popper, rejects determinism and a science of history, for if determinism is true and if human beings are links in a universal chain of natural causation then their desire to amend their character is itself causally necessitated. However, unlike Popper and other positivists, Berlin rejects methodological monism or the idea of a unified science embracing all natural and social phenomena on the grounds that the positivists try to reduce all propositions to a single type. Instead he opts for **methodological pluralism** to insist that different subjects require different methods. He also rejects the doctrine of self-determinism that states that human beings are born free insofar as one can deliberately alter one's personality and nature if one so desires. This leads him to reject a conception of common or constant human nature, as found in the philosophies of Sophists, Hobbes, Locke, Rousseau and Hume though he insists that there is some conception of human nature in every developed moral and political theory. For Berlin, certain categories are needed to define human nature from non-human, but these are not substantive claims about human motivations or interests. Similar to the Romantics of the Counter-Enlightenment, he regards human capacity to carve for itself a plurality of divergent natures as supreme. Berlin concludes that activity of choice is the very essence of human nature. This capacity for a self-chosen form of life distinguished human beings from animal species. In the process, he introduces an element of indeterminancy into human nature and conduct which is obliterated only with the abolition of the capacity for choice itself. It needs to be clarified that Berlin is no relativist, which indicates the arbitrary creations of a person's subjective fancies whereas he articulates the idea of multiple values as being objective, part of the essence of humanity. He categorically rules out certain beliefs, attitudes, practices and ways of life, like Nazism, Communism and other forms of despotism, as these deny humanity's common basis. Berlin believes in the existence of an indefinite number of competing and irreconcilable ultimate values from which one makes a choice without coercion. This human capacity for choice underpins his concepts of negative and positive liberty. Freedom is the freedom to choose from an indefinite number of ultimate values competing and irreconcilable.

Berlin defines negative liberty, unlike Hobbes and Bentham, for whom it means unimpeded motion and unobstructed pursuit of one's desires, respectively, as choice among alternatives or options that are unimpeded by others. According to Berlin, a person who does not reflect on his desires nor evaluate or deliberate them lacks basic freedom. A person lacking the capacity for choice among alternatives cannot enjoy negative freedom nor can he be denied negative freedom. Negative liberty has **three** characteristics. **First** it implies freedom from interference with one's capacity to choose and absence of restraints, actual or projected, especially by those who think they know better and can choose for others. This is because an individual as the best judge of his interests has to have the freedom to develop, and execute his projects without any hindrance or coercion. Berlin distinguishes between **non-interference** and **absence of coercion** conceding that these are liberal views but they are not identical, though there is a connection between the two. This is the **first** characteristic of negative liberty. Berlin rejects manipulation, coercion, suffering and sacrifice by real people for a vague utopian bliss, which may eventually be chimerical. He repudiates violence as a means of solving issues and affirmed his commitment to non-violence after personally witnessing brutality during both the Kerensky and the Leninist revolutions in Russia.

Negative liberty can be understood with reference to the question *freedom from what or whom.* The capacity for choice also underpins positive liberty. While negative freedom is freedom from interference, positive liberty is an activity or a series of activities with the idea of self-mastery and rational control of life. As with negative liberty, positive liberty can be curtailed or decreased in different ways. An individual may be free to choose and yet lack the ability or the power to act due to negative factors, lack of knowledge, paucity of money or other resources or because of internal constraints within the individual himself that prevents him from conceiving alternatives as such or having perceived, is unable to act upon them. While the individual has negative freedom he may be positively un-free. Implicit in both the conceptions is the idea that to be free is to face no obstacles. Both involve a measure of self-control except that in negative liberty there is no temptation to press for what controls the self and how to control others. Berlin defines the two concepts in its political sense. Historically, the two concepts have so developed that they now stand for distinct values, goods or conditions. They appear so distinct that they are often perceived to be rivals in practice.

The conception of negative freedom is distinctly modern. Its second characteristic, though not distinctively liberal is autonomy. Two of the most uncompromising exponents of negative liberty—Hobbes and Bentham—are not liberals and many liberals like Kant and J.S. Mill espouse a positive conception of liberty as autonomy. Berlin describes the liberal tradition as complex and pluralistic in nature containing many conceptions of freedom of which negative liberty is the most defensible and most agreeable to liberal concerns of diversity and toleration. Furthermore, a conception of negative liberty does not rest upon the rationalist and monist view associated with the positive conception. For Berlin, there can be no theory or principle of negative liberty that determines how conflicts between often conflicting and sometimes incommensurable liberties that is embedded in the notion of negative liberty are to be resolved. Since there is no theory that tells one how to maximise or treat negative liberty as absolute, he does not advocate an unconditional priority of liberty over other political values in a manner that Rawls does by regarding liberty as being lexically prior to equality. He insists that a trade-off between liberty and other values are often legitimate and unavoidable. Besides force and coercion, negative liberty is lessened by acts of omission and deliberate interventions. Berlin contends that judgements about negative liberty are neither value neutral nor theory neutral. These are value judgements often involving incommensurabilities and these depend on theoretical claims. Negative freedom is the choice among options, which others do not hinder. It is a matter of dispute as what constitutes a hindrance.

The **third** characteristic of negative liberty is of paramount importance that it is not incompatible with some kinds of autocracy or that it is not linked with democracy or self-government. Berlin accepts freedom to be better protected and guaranteed by democracy than other regimes but there is no nexus—rather the link is tenuous—between individual rule and democracy. The issue of 'who governs me?' is logically different from the idea 'how far does government interfere with me?' He regards positive liberty as an unimpeachable human value, necessary for a decent existence but condemns the way it has been misused and to its hideously negative consequences. It is based on a rationalist and monist view of good. Embedded in the positive view whether Socratic or Stoic, Spinozistic or Kantian, Hegelian or Fichtean is the idea of obedience to rational will and not choice. Rational will suggests the presence of one good whereas choice presupposes genuine rivalry among conflicting goods. Theorists of positive liberty presume that the rational will for one is the same for others as well and that all persons will have the same object. Autonomy and self-mastery are good as long as it does not get perverted into 'freedom' to achieve 'self realisation' according to a criteria, that is laid down and often imposed coercively by the self-appointed moral guardians of human society. Berlin outlines the five stages by which positive liberty is usually distorted into an instrument of collective oppression on the individual. Inherent in positive liberty is the idea of control. The five stages are as follows:

1. the idea of control over the self;
2. identification as separate selves of what controls and what is controlled;
3. further identification (a) of the controlling part of the group to which the individual is a member and (b) of the individual as to what is controlled;
4. claim that society as a whole or its representatives might know better what the individual requires and
5. what the individual truly wants is quite opposite of what he is conscious of wanting.

The political implication of positive liberty is dangerous. If genuine freedom means the chance to pursue the good, if all goods are compatible with one another and are the same for all persons, then a community of truly free persons will be one without important conflict of values, ideals or interest. It will be a community of harmonious and identical rational wills. The metaphysical content behind positive liberty suggests that everything can be explained with reference to a single homogenous principle and discoverable laws, and this leads to determinism and totalitarianism. Berlin insists that philosophy cannot offer a set of principles or a theory that would solve all the dilemmas of moral and political life or straightened the 'crooked timber of humanity', his favourite phrase that he borrows from Kant. Philosophy cannot propose radical social reforms. He is hostile to totalitarianism, Marxism and authoritarianism but not to nationalism, even though, it uses the vehicle of positive liberty. He supports the claims of independence of different nationalities, oppressed religious and national groups. However, he opposes ethnic cleansing, transfer of population or religious persecution. He supports Israel because of its long history of persecution and the need for a Jewish national identity, though he was critical of orthodox Jews and the right-wing nationalists.

Berlin rejects the philosophies of Kant, Fichte, Hegel and Marx, for they define freedom as obedience to a rational will and prefers Locke, Hume and Mill for whom choice is the essence of freedom. Choice implies conflict among rivalrous goods whereas rational will suggests one way of life and one plan for most people. Negative liberty or the freedom to choose is an inalienable trait of a person if he has to qualify being human and self-creative. Berlin, an agnostic liberal (Gray 1995), rejects reason as an arbiter among inherently rivalrous and incommensurable goods. This liberal world-view denies a structure of liberties appropriate to a liberal society that derives from a theory, or is stated in a set of principles, since the choice among the conflicting liberties is often a choice among incommensurable. Berlin's pluralism leads him to defend a liberal society with a commitment to tolerance, respect and freedom of choice. He is a libertarian since he considers protection of negative freedom as a basic precondition of a just society, yet he simultaneously realises this to be insufficient thereby supporting positive interference like taxation, the British welfare state and the American New Deal.

Berlin does not deny the intrinsic good in the notion of autonomy but rejects that the worth of negative liberty is derived from that of autonomy. Negative liberty is valuable because it allows self-creation and not autonomy. This is the major difference in the analyses of Berlin and Raz. For Berlin, the pluralism that negative liberty allows is not only the pluralism of good alone but a pluralism of bad and worthless, in that it approves the freedom to choose that which is not worthy of end choice. Negative liberty has this innate value not because it leads to autonomy or choice of good but it is a condition of self-creation. It is possible that the self, who is created, may well not be that of an autonomous person. To expect of self-creation that it corresponds to an ideal of rational autonomy is, according to Berlin, an unacceptable and unnecessary limiting prerequisite. Unlike Raz, Berlin claims negative liberty and not autonomy as the basic idea of freedom. Furthermore, Berlin also argues that a single individual may not be able to harmonise his valued goods and projects, that he will have to forsake some for the sake of others and that no principle can be summoned that settles the conflict within one's life by practical reasoning. *From Hope and Fear Set Free*, a neglected but important paper he speculates, through the example of Vincent Willem von Gogh (1853–1890) that great artistic qualities may be contingent on blemishes in self-knowledge and may be destroyed by an enhancement of self-knowledge. The quest for autonomy through self-knowledge by a person diminishes his potential and ability, keys to his self-creation. Berlin's liberalism is not based on the ideal of autonomy though he admits autonomy to be good.

Berlin affirms the importance of common cultural forms to individual well-being but differs from the civic humanist or the republican view that accepts the primacy of the political. This is because he is convinced that no single activity including political participation could be considered as the supreme end of human life. Nor can activities be graded in hierarchical manner in terms of their importance. This belief in plural inheritances also precludes him from advancing a notion of a single moral community with one dominant end as divisive and dangerous. His is a notion of collective individuality. Berlin's liberal communitarianism differs from the recent communitarian critics of liberalism for whom the community is an ideal form representing common humanity and not a historic practice and not the one, in which individuals have lived, with its distinct linguistic and cultural uniqueness.

Berlin's defense of negative liberty entailing freedom of choice finds resonance in the writings of others, like Popper and Hayek. Gellner and Miliband, in their individual criticisms of totalitarian communism reiterated his proposition of negative liberty as a necessary precondition for substantive freedom. 'It took a long time for British Marxists to realise that bourgeois liberties are liberties and that social problems and conflict of values have neither unique nor complete solutions' (Crick 1997: 20). Berlin is criticised for being neither clear nor consistent in what he says about the meaning of interference or constraint. Equally, he is ambiguous as to whether economic obstacles—lack of resources—shall count as limitations on negative freedom, or whether only laws, coercive threats and other such actively imposed obstacles will qualify (Miller 1991: 13). Norman P. Barry (1995: 220) is appreciative of Berlin's efforts to show how some political theorists misuse the concept of liberty and diffuse the distinction between restraint and autonomy but wonders whether Berlin has sufficiently distinguished between the two concepts.

RECENT CONCEPTIONS: RAZ AND RAWLS

Raz's Conception

To define liberty in the negative sense as the absence of restraint does not tell one what it is that a person can do and why it is necessary to define liberty as autonomy. **Raz** (1986: 207) criticises negative liberty on the premise that the priority of right over the good in traditional liberal theory misleads the morality of freedom by suggesting that rights against coercion are the only important precondition of liberty. The necessary feature of freedom is the pursuit of value, which cannot be restricted to mere subjective desire. He proposes the chief value of negative freedom because of its contribution to the positive freedom of autonomy. This does not mean that negative freedom of non-interference is a necessary precondition of autonomy, in the sense of being a useful means to it, rather it is a constitutive ingredient of autonomous agency that one must not be subject to the will of others. For Raz, non-interference is only one aspect of autonomy, which comprehends much else, including capacities for rational deliberation, the possession of adequate resources for meaningful action, and an array of worthwhile options from which to choose. It is autonomy and not negative freedom, which has, for Raz the status of an intrinsic good, and all or most of, the value of negative freedom is in its enhancement of autonomy. Raz's perfectionist liberalism accepts that the liberal state shall have a moral foundation and a moral role but this does not begin from the idea that the liberal state must enforce rights. According to this view, the liberal state has a duty to work on policies that aim, in certain ways, to improve the moral quality of the lives of its citizenry. A perfectionist liberal agrees with Plato about the role of the state but unlike Plato, believes that human perfection is basically concerned with autonomy thus combining Platonic and Kantian ideas. Raz, thus, questions the proposition that autonomy requires governments to abstain from encouraging a 'good life' for its citizens and rejects the notion that pluralism in modern society can be safeguarded only by a government that substantially limits its political action. Instead, he believes that human autonomy requires a certain kind of community life, the creation of which is the major task of liberal government. That life must be one that allows and promotes what Raz calls 'value pluralism' so that citizens can choose from a number of options and opportunities while creating their lives. It must consist and promote moral behaviour because the moral quality of a person's life is intimately connected with a person's nature as an autonomous being. The one way the state can promote the moral quality of its citizens' lives is to legislate according to the harm principle. He clarifies that in common conception. governments in order to promote morality curtail freedom. However, that is not so if the principle 'is derivable from a morality which regards personal autonomy as an essential ingredient of the good life and regards the principle of autonomy, which imposes duties on people to secure all the conditions of autonomy, as one of the most important moral principles' (1986: 415). Interestingly, Raz says that a liberal state promotes a conception of good but refuses to tell what that good is. Can the Razian state truly promote good by leaving people alone in the way traditional liberalism has done is controversial? Some liberals feel that Raz gives away too much by even admitting that a liberal state ought to be concerned with the moral quality of its citizens' lives. Non-liberal critics distrust whether a state can truly promote the moral quality of its citizens' lives by relying primarily on the harm principle to conduct its legislation.

Gray (1992: 23) reiterates Raz and dismisses negative liberty as lacking in intrinsic value and being a mere introduction to a portrayal of what is valuable in life. Liberty as autonomy does not, as in extreme theories of positive liberty, demand the complete annihilation of individual subjective choice by the state. However, it demands the existence of facilities to convert abstract choices into real opportunities. Gray rejects the idea of human flourishing as being fulfillment of subjective desire, for there are collective goods with an inherent value different from public goods. Raz strongly prefers the idea that persons can express liberty and morality only as members of particular social groupings that embody the idea of the good. Both Raz and Gray accept liberty as the freedom to choose from a variety of ends and to that extent they accept pluralism but Gray, unlike Raz, concedes that the market encourages freedom and autonomy. Raz's argument is subtle and profound but one that Berlin rejects, for he regards the inherent value of freedom especially negative freedom is in its epitome of the 'basic freedom' of choice itself and not the rational choice among genuine goods and worthwhile options that autonomy indicates. Choice for Berlin is the source of negative freedom and in the authentic conceptions of positive freedom. He would perceive Raz's account as one that restricts the value of freedom to the rational adoption of worthwhile ends. Raz considers freedom to be valuable only insofar as it contributes to good life understood as rational pursuit of choice worthy options, a deadly defect that Berlin finds with most conceptions of positive freedom.

Berlin's liberalism differs from Raz's perfectionist liberalism. Berlin rejects perfectionism and his anti-perfectionist liberalism is important because of its rejection of the Kantian idea of the priority of right over the good that exists in theories of Rawls and Dworkin. He rejects any Kantian view in which deontic considerations are basis of morality. Like Raz, he believes that political morality is not and cannot be rights-based, for the basis and content of human rights can be connoted only with reference to their contribution to human good. He differs from Raz, for he does not subscribe to any Aristotelian view of flourishing as the bottom line in ethics and nor does he attach any importance to autonomy. Both Berlin and Raz accept an irreducible diversity of incommensurable goods. Both affirm that the goods of human life are rivalrous and uncombinable and in many cases difficult to harmonise within a single human life. Berlin differs from Raz for he holds that good depends upon, or presupposes evils, and right actions contain or evoke wrongs. It is due to this dismal version that Gray characterises Berlin's liberalism agonistic, enabling him to remain irresolute towards his opposition to ideals of rational autonomy. He, like the later Rawls (1993), refuses to root liberal practice in a comprehensive ideal like autonomy.

Many political theorists reject the division of freedom into negative liberty and positive liberty (MacCallum 1967; Feinberg 1973 and Rawls 1972). They contend that freedom is a single concept. MacCallum points out that freedom is one concept best understood as triadic where the individual *x* is free from constraint *y* in order to perform an action *z* whereas, for Berlin, an agent may wish to be without a constraint and yet has no specific action he wishes to perform. Disagreements about negative and positive concepts, according to MacCallum, are really disputes over the proper range of one or more of the three variables in a single analytical model—what the term 'person' means, what constitutes to be a hindrance or coercive interference and what can be regarded as a wanted or intended action.

Rawls' Conception

Berlin's defense of liberty as part of his overall scheme of pluralism is both formidable and appealing but it gives rise to a practical problem as to how the different values may be operational when it comes to pragmatic social and political policy. The question is one of choosing between values. He needs to distinguish between privately pursued ends and publicly enforced rules. Liberalism means leaving people free, within limits, to pursue their individual conceptions of goods, whose limits are defined by certain publicly enforced rules of right. This distinction between right and good is attempted by Rawls (Lessnoff 1999: 223). Rawls accepts plurality of ends but, unlike Berlin, considers liberty to have a lexical priority over claims of social and economic equality in well-ordered society. In Rawls' rights-based theory the liberal state tries to bind together people with divergent views, together with the help of shared political conceptions and public ways of reasoning, that even if they are moral they are generated by any particular partisan moral theory. He places liberty at the centre of his theory of justice by regarding a list of liberties as basic. He endorses Constant's assertion of liberty of the moderns to be of greater value than the liberty of the ancients. 'While both sorts of freedom are deeply rooted in human aspirations, freedom of thought and liberty of conscience, freedom of person and the civil liberties, ought not to be sacrificed to political liberty, to the freedom to participate equally in political affairs' (Rawls 1972: 202–203). He considers this question to be a substantive political philosophy requiring a theory of rights and justice to answer it and defining liberty as therefore, secondary. Reiterating MacCallum, he explains liberty with reference to three aspects—the agents who are free the restrictions or limitations from which one is free and their ambit of freedom. He distinguishes between 'a concept of justice as meaning a proper balance between competing claims from a conception of justice as a set of related principles for identifying the relevant considerations which determines this balance' (1972: 10). On this basis, he distinguishes between liberty and its worth. The first principle recognises and grants equal liberty to all, compatible with the like liberty for everyone. He concedes that inequalities in wealth and power affect the worth of liberty while leaving the equality of liberty intact.

> Liberty is represented by the complete system of the liberties of equal citizenship, while the worth of liberties to persons and groups is proportional to their capacity to advance their ends within the framework the system defines. Freedom as equal liberty is same for all ... but the worth of liberty is not the same for everyone. ... The lesser worth of liberty is however compensated, for, since the capacity of the less fortunate members of society to achieve their aims would be even less were they not to accept the existing inequalities whenever the difference principle is satisfied (1972: 204).

The principle of equal liberty when applied to the political procedure defined by the constitution is the principle of equal participation, which can be realised within a constitutional democracy. The representative body, which is the legislature with law-making functions, determines the basic policies and is accountable to the electorate. It shall be elected for a limited term and is more than an advisory or registering body endorsing the decisions of the executive. Rawls reiterates Locke's idea of the supremacy of the legislature. Elections are to be held regularly and are to be fair and free, based on universal adult franchise. The principle of loyal opposition has to be recognised if democratic government is to succeed. Freedom of speech, freedom of association and freedom of assembly have to be recognised and guaranteed. To ensure that liberties are not formal, Rawls offers the second principle, fair value of political liberties and fair political procedures whereby citizens are roughly equal in political power. He recommends freeing the dependence of political parties on big business and monopolies through sufficient tax revenues and public finance of election costs. Plural voting, public monies and abolition of gerrymandering[1] guarantees participation and that ensure the self-worth of a person and the worth of liberty. The principle of participation also recognises that each citizen is eligible to join political parties, run for elections and hold places of authority. The traditional devices of constitutionalism namely bicameral legislature, separation of powers, checks and balances, bill of rights with judicial review are consistent with equal political liberty provided it applies to everyone. Furthermore, in society with private ownership of the means of production property and wealth has to be distributed widely. Rawls accepts that the two principles secure the integrity of religious and moral freedom. Equal liberty of conscience is the only principle that the person in the original position acknowledges. They cannot take chances with their liberty by permitting the dominant religious or moral doctrines to persecute or suppress others. The state cannot favour any particular religion nor could it attach penalties to any particular religious affiliation. Liberty of conscience is limited by the common interest in public order and security on the assumption that it is not superior to moral and religious interests nor does the government have any right to suppress philosophical beliefs on the pretext that it conflicts with the interests of the state. Given the principles of justice the state is viewed as an association of equal citizens. It has to try to regulate individuals' pursuit of their moral and spiritual interests in accordance with the principles agreed to in the original position of equality. In this way the government acts as an agent of the public by helping them to satisfy their demands of their public conception of justice. Further, liberty of conscience has to be limited only on grounds of reasonable expectations, that by not doing so, it can damage the public order which the government has to maintain. Toleration is derived from common sense and not from the practical necessities or reasons of the state. All religious views are to receive full and equal tolerance as toleration leads to stability of the system.

Daniels (1975) and Hart (1975) argue that historical experience demonstrates that inequalities of wealth lead to inequalities of power resulting in inequalities of liberties. Economic factors play as much an important role in constraining liberties as legal restrictions and public opinion. In response to this criticism, Rawls replaces 'the most extensive total system' with 'a fully adequate scheme' taking into account the exercise of moral powers in the social circumstances what he calls the 'two fundamental cases' (1982: 41). The first fundamental case connected with the capacity for a sense of justice concerns, 'the application of the principles of justice to the basic structure of society and its social policies'. The second relates to the capacity for a conception of good, 'concerns the application of the principles of deliberative reason in guiding our conduct over a complete life' (1982: 47). Certain liberties like freedom of thought and political liberties are necessary for the exercise of sense of justice in the first case. Liberty of conscience and freedom of association would apply in case of the second. The remainder can be combined with the two cases. The amended first principle now reads as follows:

> Each person has an equal right to a fully adequate scheme of equal basic liberties, which is compatible with a similar scheme of liberties for all (1982: 5).

He clarifies that no particular liberty has a priority. The scheme of basic liberties, which he calls a family of liberties, is distributed equally among citizens. The various liberties are adjusted to one another to ensure the availability of the most adequate scheme for the exercise of the two moral powers.

> The worth of the political liberties to all citizens, whatever their social or economic position must be approximately equal, or at least sufficiently equal, in the sense that everyone has a fair opportunity to hold public office and to influence the outcome of political decision (1982: 42).

The constitution protects the basic liberties as well as the fair value of the political parties. It also specifies a just political procedure and incorporates restrictions that protect basic liberties and secure their priority thereby safeguarding them from the vagaries of legislative policy making. The rest—non-basic rights and matters of economic policy—are, left to the legislative stage. Hart (1975) and Daniels (1975) point out that the criterion 'most extensive scheme' is quantitative and simplistic. Rawls responds by pointing out that basic liberties shall be the same for everyone as one can obtain greater liberty for oneself only if others are granted the same greater liberty (1982: 56). Basic liberties as a family have priority. Liberty anchored to the primary good of equal right to self-respect implies that the self esteem of an individual can be enhanced only by interacting with others as a full-fledged member of an egalitarian political society. Rawls' belief in the moral equality of persons makes him view the individual who enjoys counting blades of grass as fulfilling his nature just as Berlin accepts that there is not just one indicator of either contentment or excellence.

In conclusion, the intense debate about what constitutes the ingredients of liberty in contemporary political theory demonstrates the prime importance of the concept in political theory. The fact remains that a doctrine of freedom ensuring the basic liberties to everyone has become the prerequisite of any viable political theory in our times. In highlighting the paramount importance of negative liberty or freedom as choice as the lynchpin of all other liberties is stated by J.S. Mill and elaborated by Berlin, till date remains the most elegant and formidable theory of liberty. It has become a reference and a starting point for any analysis on the subject. The harm principle that negative liberty enshrines is defended eloquently by both Mill and Berlin, and is the basis for other liberties and that is universal to all cultures and countries.

Further Readings

Bauman, Z., *Freedom*, World View, Delhi, 1997.

Brenkert, G.C., *Political Freedom*, Routledge, London, 1985.

Gray, J. and Smith, G.W. (Eds.), *J.S. Mill: On Liberty in Focus*, Routledge, London, 1991.

Gray, T., *Freedom*, Macmillan, London, 1991.

Hart, H.L.A., *Law, Liberty and Morality*, Oxford University Press, Oxford, 1963.

Kymlicka, W. (Ed.), *Justice in Political Philosophy*, Edward Elgar, England, 1992.

Paul, J. (Ed.), *Reading Nozick: Essays on Anarchy, State and Utopia*, Oxford, Basil Blackwell, 1982.

Pelczynski, Z. and Gray, J. (Eds.), *Conceptions of Liberty in Political Philosophy*, Athlone Press, London, 1984.

Petit, P., *Judging Justice*, Routledge, London, 1984.

Runciman, W., *Relative Deprivation and Social Justice*, Routledge and Kegan Paul, London, 1972.

Ryan, A. (Ed.), *The Idea of Freedom: Essays in Honour of Isaiah Berlin*, Oxford University Press, Oxford, 1979.

Sir, Berlin I., *Four Essays of Liberty*, Oxford University Press, London, 1969.

Sterba, J., *Justice: Alternative Political Perspectives*, Belmont, Wadworth Publishing Company, California, 1980.

Endnote

1. This is a practice prevalent in the US whereby political parties draw boundaries of their constituencies.

Chapter 12
Justice

Ever since Socrates asked the question 'what is justice?' in Plato's *Republic*, this has been a leading question in moral, political and legal philosophy, and a primary virtue of political institutions. Since then justice is regarded as an all-encompassing political virtue so that the good society and the just society are normally regarded as synonymous though one ought to be careful in making such a presumption. Justice, however, is the most 'political' or institutional of the virtues. 'The legitimacy of a state rests upon its claim to do justice' (Ryan 1994: 1).

A feature of justice is that it is considered fundamental or basic. Rawls describes justice as the first virtue of social institutions. This means individuals accept social regulation or cooperation unless the conditions on which society functions are reasonably just. For Plato and Aristotle, justice is a matter of the terms of social and political cooperation allocating basic tasks and of situating people in the social roles they have to fulfil. Of course, there is considerable disagreement about the conditions relating to social and political cooperation. Aristotle pays a great deal of attention to the principle of allocating advantages according to desert or merit, while Rawls totally ignores desert. This difference demonstrates that, like other concepts of political theory, the attributes of justice change over time. For instance, Aristotle justifies slavery. The exclusion of women from political participation was considered valid during the Enlightenment. Even in today's world, there are different yardsticks in judging societies and systems.

NOTIONS OF JUSTICE

A distinction is made between legal and social justice. Legal justice is the punishment of wrongdoing and the compensation of injury through the creation and enforcement of public set of rules (the law). There are two aspects to it. One, it states the conditions under which punishment is imposed, it prescribes punishment according to the nature of the crime, and in the sphere of civil law adjusts the amount of restitution that is made for injuries. Two, it establishes procedures for applying the law, namely the principles of a fair trial, rights of appeal and the like. Social justice is about distribution of benefits and burdens throughout a society. It deals with matters like regulation of wages and profits, the protection of individuals rights through the legal system, the allocation of housing, medicines, welfare benefits and the like. Since punishments are included in legal justice, burdens in the context of social justice mean disadvantages other than 'punishments'. Benefits mean intangible ones, such as, prestige and self-respect along with material goods, especially wealth (Miller 1976: 22). Social justice invokes criteria such as desert, need, merit or sometimes merely more equality for its own sake. Defenders of social justice emphasise on different and at times conflicting criteria but they do concede a positive role for the state.

Desert refers to what is fitting for each person to have and justifies differential treatment. It is expressed as follows '*A* deserves *X*' and that '*X* is due to *A*'. The more industrious, intelligent or skillful should receive more than the less industrious, intelligent and skillful. Social justice does not usually consider desert to be moral. Desert is moral when based upon qualities or actions of the individual, which have an intrinsic moral value—courage, honesty, sincerity and the like. It is non-moral when based on morally neutral qualities like intelligence or ability. Desert signifies a relationship between an individual and his behaviour, and the manner of treatment that are admired and abhorred. A judgement of desert involves evaluating the suitability of this specific person, with his qualities and past behaviour, receiving a given benefit or harm—a suitability that is made clear by considering and evaluating the attitudes that we may take up towards the person. Desert judgements are with reference to past and present facts about a person, never on the basis of a situation that future may create. Desert involves not only an assessment of one's effort but depends on the value of a product. An individual, because of some rare talent, can produce something of a value with little effort and yet one cannot say that the person does not deserve the differential reward his talent has been able to earn him. Economic desert consists of three factors—*Contribution* (a person's reward should take into consideration the value of the contribution that he makes to social welfare in his work activity); *Effort* (a person's reward should depend on the effort he employs in his work activity); and *Compensation* (a person's reward should depend on the costs which he incurs in his work activity) (Miller 1976: 103). What is the role of desert in social justice? It is generally understood that justice consists of rewarding people according to their relative contributions to society. Desert figures prominently in classical liberalism, for it stresses on personal responsibility and autonomy for actions and favours rewards for efforts. However, in modern liberal theories like that of Rawls, desert finds little place. Even libertarian theories of Hayek and Nozick reject desert, for it is inherently an interventionist principle and unlike the classical liberals do not see it as supporting a free market economy but sustaining programmes of social democratic and even socialist reform.

To some need alone is the basis for a just distribution of resources. Barry in *Political Argument* (1965) contends that statements like '*A* needs *B*' are incomplete and should read as follows: '*A* needs *B* in order to do *C*. This implies that need alone cannot be an independent justification for any policy since their whole justificatory force evolves from whatever end' *C* is invoked when the concept is used. Benn and Peters (1959) suggest that 'need' has to be understood in relation to a standard of living that is conventional and changes over time. Miller (1976: 135, 149) points out that need is to be understood as comprising whatever is necessary by one to carry out his plan of life. Justice consists in a distribution of resources according to need so that each person achieves the same level of well-being as others. An egalitarian regards this as the basic part of their conception of equality. It is correct to say that the concept of need has virtually replaced desert in recent egalitarian social welfare theories (Barry, 1995: 155). Welfare goods like housing aid, health care and the like are defended as items of need. It has been argued that if a person experiences distress for no fault of his, then he deserves welfare as an entitlement and not need or benevolence (Campbell 1988: 158). Some, like Spencer, reject the idea of need completely, for it involves depriving some of the deserving of a part of their rewards in order to supply the undeserving with benefits. He argues that need as a principle is applicable only within a family where benefits are inversely proportional to merit—most is given where least is deserved but in society at large benefits are directly proportioned to merit. He accuses the socialists and communists of extending the rule of the family to society at large. Furthermore, those who are superior are to be allowed to gain from whatever their superiority accrues, for that encourages them to perform better. Conversely, the inferior has to suffer the lack or less of talent, so as to discourage them from perpetuating their inferiority. This gradually leads to the improvement in the quality of human race, in accordance with natural laws, which is stifled if distribution is allowed on the basis of need.

Many like Barry (1967: 193) regard desert and need as an integral part of the meaning of justice and consider conceptions, like that of Hume, who used 'rules of justice' to include property rules, as unjust. In contemporary thought, social justice incorporates the idea of welfare, that has traditionally been associated with rights and duties: to act justly is to give each person his 'due' or 'entitlement'. In spite of the differences over what constitute dues and entitlements in specific case justice does not mean an individual's or society's well-being, except in an insignificant sense. The link between justice and welfare originates with utilitarianism, especially Bentham, for he connects every moral idea with aggregate welfare. Utilitarianism is a monist doctrine that subordinates an individual claim to justice to social calculus.

Justice is intimately linked with respect for rights. Greek political theory and Roman law have complex notions about the different dimensions of justice but nothing much about individual rights in the modern sense. Law rather than individual rights defines property and authority. Ownership of property symbolises a person to whom law grants privileges and immunities that locally define property. A legitimate ruler is one whom the law directs to rule. Ancient notion of law, in contrast to modern idea of private property, grants to the family and other groups more power over property (Zimmern 1935: 133). Under the Roman law, ownership is both absolute and sovereign. The law tells the judge to give a person his *ius*, this essentially means that he has to be treated as the law requires. The subjective understanding of rights, whereby the right-holder might stand on his rights or not as he chooses is not a Roman conception (Tuck 1979: 7–13). Neither Plato nor Aristotle regards justice as a subject of individual rights. Hume and Mill discuss justice and rights together but do not raise the question as to whether one is logically or morally prior to the other, for as naturalists, they explain morality as an accepted system of rules of conduct aimed at human welfare (Ryan 1994: 3). For anti-utilitarian non-naturalistic theorists, like Rawls, the principles of justice are basic—dictating the rights that a person has. For Nozick, persons begin with entitlements that one is born with or acquire, and justice inheres when people have what they are entitled to. To understand one's entitlements is the basis of all else.

Justice also shares an intimate link with **equality**. Barry observes, 'In Plato's time as in ours, the central issue in any theory of justice is the defensibility of unequal relations between people' (1989: 3). Certain uses of justice imply equality, for instance, one speaks of equality before the law. Justice does not sanction equality of reward to those whose contributions are varied. If one accepts that some inequalities are defensible, the question then becomes one of determining the criteria of unequal distribution. Conservatives defend existing claims and by reiterating the Roman precept that justice entails rendering to each his own they argue that if someone has acquired the just title to something, he shall keep it. They accept a weak definition of equality, for that will not threaten liberty, rules and social stability. Classical liberals contend that to impose material equality on unequal people destroys the rule of law and gives rise to totalitarianism and consequent injustice towards individuals.

Miller identifies three criteria for applying the idea of justice: to each according to his rights, to each according to his desert and to each according to his need. These three criteria aim to achieve the following. The principle of rights guarantees security of expectation and freedom of choice. The principle of desert recognises the distinctive value of each person's actions and qualities. The principle of need provides the precondition for individual plans of life. These three criteria are conceptually distinct and give rise to conflicting prescriptions for action and that there is no way of choosing between them on purely logical grounds (1976: 151–152).

In the context of common law, when one speaks of an infringement of the rules of **natural justice**, one refers to an arbitrariness that the individual suffers in a rule governed process. **Commutative** justice is that which is understood as a property of individual conduct namely what is owed to a person under a general rule as opposed to **distributive** justice that indicates a desirable state of affairs. A **formal or procedural** conception perceives justice as a characteristic of individual behaviour and not of society. Miller aptly remarks, 'it is impossible to assess the justice of actions without a prior identification of just state of affairs' (1976: 17–18). It insists on meticulous adherence to rules and that like cases must be treated alike. It is described, as a principle of rationality because it holds that some reason must be assigned for treating people differently. It does not comprise of any intuitive or common sense notions of justice because it does not tell of the ways people can be treated differently. Being a purely formal rule it does not assume the idea of basic equality of persons. Critics of this conception say that it focuses on only one aspect of justice and that it is possible even when rules are followed the outcome can be unjust (Sen 1985). Its importance lies in the fact that consistency is a necessary ingredient of moral and political debate.

MacIntrye (1988) contrasts between ancient (Aristotle, Augustine and the philosophers of the Scottish Enlightenment) and modern (Rawls and Nozick) conceptions of justice as a difference between justice defined in terms of what he calls 'the goods of excellence' and 'goods of effectiveness'. In ancient justice, actors aimed for excellence in some specific field of activity which meant the presence of quasi-objective desert judgements. They did not aim directly for material rewards, which were considered secondary and subject to successful performance. In modern justice, individuals directly pursue wealth, social status and power and justice is about formulating rules to avoid destructive competition. Since there are no agreed standards of excellence there is no notion of desert. However, MacIntyre ignores the fact the theorists he discusses have a wider understanding of justice and do not fit so neatly into the excellence/effectiveness divide. For instance, Aristotle was concerned about mundane matters like transactions in the marketplace.

ANCIENT AND MEDIEVAL CONCEPTIONS

There is some dispute as to whether the Greeks have a distinct concept of justice. For Plato and subsequently Aristotle, justice in its most general sense, is the essential virtue, the concise virtue, the virtue most important for the social animals that human beings are, living together in communities whether village, cities or nation-states. In medieval political theory, justice is associated with order. Justice as a judgement upon conflicting acts and claims of individuals is not separate from realms of religion, psychology or virtue, in general.

Plato

In the *Republic*, **Socrates** surveys a whole gamut of the then prevailing definitions of justice before he comes up with a criterion of justice. Socrates tells us what justice is not. In his exchange with the aging Cephalus and his son Polemarchus, he says that justice is about human excellence. In response to Thrasymachus for whom justice is the interests of the strongest, Socrates refutes the view by contending that right has to be properly distinguished from mere might. Glaucon reiterates Thrasymachus' view, in a more modest way, by pointing out that justice ultimately is a matter of self-interest[1] and that people adhere to its conventions only to avoid punishment. It is a convention, a product of a contract between the powerful and the powerless, the strong and the weak. Socrates rejects the idea of justice as mere convention. It is also not a matter of self-interest. The remaining part of the *Republic* is an exposition of what justice is through a long drawn consideration of philosophical issues and human nature. It establishes that justice is a psychic harmony within the individual, the triumph of reason and a bond that cements the individual to the society. Socrates uses the word *dikaiosune* meaning 'righteousness'. Justice is defined as the performance of functions for which one's nature is best fitted. He makes two assumptions—first, every individual is a functional unit and second, society is a harmonised, orderly whole based on the recognition of individual talents and contributions. These diverse human aptitudes need to be accepted and organised for social benefit, cooperation and harmony. The functions of a society are broadly three—ruling, defence and production—and correspondingly there are three kinds of human souls—rational, spirited and appetitive. Every human soul has three qualities—reason, spirit and temperance—but one of these is predominant which justice balances and harmonises with the other two. Justice is, therefore, architectonic in nature. The rational soul rules, the spirited defends and the appetitive soul produces goods and services.

Socrates maintains that a life of justice is preferable to one of injustice. A just person limits his desires, for usually non-satisfaction leads to unhappiness. Second, pleasures that are derived from intellect are more genuine and comforting to those arising from senses. A philosopher understands the difference in pleasures that are derived from the pursuit of reason to those secured from appetite and sensuality. Usually unjust person(s) submit to political and psychological tyranny. An unjust person lacks psychological peace and such a person lacks true friends. The motivation for leading ethical lives devoted to good has nothing to do with god's punishment and reward or from our peers but with inner peace and power of friendship. Socrates is concerned with 'what I ought to do?' and 'how I should do?' Throughout the exposition one does not get a proper and clear description of Good (Bluhm 1965: 77). He does not disprove the concept but only its application. Nor does one get an adequate criterion concerning what sorts of considerations one has to use in evaluating this or that social arrangement or rule. Plato observes that distribution of responsibility is in accordance with ability but ignored the distribution of wealth in society. This is in spite of his acceptance that every city is a city of two, the rich and the poor and in spite of his instruction to his philosophical ruler to avoid extremes in wealth. Plato also deliberately ignores the view of justice as equality, which leads Popper to accuse him of supporting a totalitarian ethic and disregarding democracy, individualism and equality. Furthermore, Popper accuses Plato for 'arresting all social change' by establishing a society that is regimented, hierarchical, static and unequal, where an individual counts only as long as he contributes to the social whole. However, Plato's credit lay in identifying justice as merit, rewarding each person in terms of what is due to them and expecting from them their due to the society.

Aristotle for whom justice is the true subject matter of political philosophy and of its execution as a major purpose of the *polis* divides justice into two categories. In doing so, he criticises Plato for conflating justice with virtue in general and for not showing that justice is invariably better than injustice. A general concept of justice is 'the lawful', which does not mean obedience to the laws of any specific state, while a *particular concept* refers to what is 'the fair and equal'. He divides particular concept into 'distributive' and 'rectificatory' justice. Distributive justice is concerned with what people *deserve* or else what one has a right to receive. Rectificatory or commutative justice referred to justice of transactions—'voluntary matters pertaining to buying, selling or lending' and 'involuntary matters of being a victim of an insult, theft or assassination'. Aristotle links the notion of distributive justice—offices and wealth, rewards and dues—with the idea of proportionate equality, which in turn, is connected to a theory of just rewards, or equal shares according to the merit of its recipients. It means equals deserve equal but unequals deserve unequal, in proportion to their merit defined in accordance with the spirit of the constitution. In an oligarchy, merit means wealth and in an aristocracy it means virtue. Each person is awarded responsibilities as well as financial benefits in proportion to one's just deserts.

> The advantage of Aristotle's doctrine is that it satisfied the demands of social justice in both aspects: the point of proportionate equality is more equitable than the democrats' conception of mere numerical equality. Similarly the idea of special privilege which his doctrine introduces is more justifiable than the oligarch's claim that either wealth or noble birth by itself deserves the highest rewards. ... Proportionate equality is grounded in the principle of fair and reasonable inequality of treatment (von Leyden 1985: 4, 6).

The main idea in Aristotle's overall argument is the notion of justice as a state of character, a cultivated set of dispositions, attitudes and good habits. It is not an abstract scheme or principle. In its specific demonstration, it is concerned with good judgement and a sense of fairness. It is a virtue crucial to those who rule and those who judge. In rectificatory justice, the justice of exchanges, such judgement involves equality, not as proportion, but as straightforward equivalence. It involves equality in the sense that two persons who are before the court for the same crime are to be considered equals 'before the law', even if they are very different otherwise. The notion of equality also enters when matters concerning punishment are taken into consideration. Aristotle said, for example, that a man who has wounded or slain another man should receive a penalty and the 'judge tries to restore the loss to a position of equality, by subtraction from profit'. There is, however, no clear indication whether the penalty is envisioned as retribution or some sort of redress or equalisation. The distinction between rectificatory and retributive justice is ambivalent. Finally, justice is a mean between extremes, between loss and profit. However, the Aristotelian distinction survives in various forms. In contemporary times, social justice uses extensively the distributive conception while the commutative conception—justice as a right or desert—is common in regulating actions between people. **Cicero** observes that justice is the second of the four principal virtues—wisdom, justice, courage and temperance—to constitute moral goodness. It holds society together and allows for the pursuit of common good for which society exists. He considers injustice to be greed and lust for power. Julius Caesar, his political rival was the specific target of his discussion of ambition's role in unjust action but the argument is universally applicable. He also tries to show that justice is generosity, making society kinder and warmer. He instructs us to treat others justly, even if one has not been treated justly. The **Stoics** too believe that morality promotes the common good, implying that relationships that have been violated need to be restored. Cicero and the Stoics are some of the early philosophers to view justice as common good. For **Augustine**, true justice does not exist in a pagan state that denies God his due of worship and obedience. Only a Christian political community can be a true commonwealth, for it fully implements the indispensable requirement of justice. Like Aristotle, he believes justice gives the state its ethical basis. **Giles** of Rome (1246–1316), like Augustine, asserts justice as a quality of a Christian state.

Confucius stresses the importance of 'uprightness' in the prince and obedience and 'gentlemanliness' in his subjects. He introduces two key terms into Chinese thought and ordinary language: the idea of or rules of conduct, and that of *ren*, benevolent love. The ideal of justice is an upright ruler with the devout obedience and praise of the people. However, this ideal is personal—a matter of character of the ruler and his subjects—not merely a matter of law and rules as such. The insistence on obedience and loyalty circumvents the suggestion that an unjust ruler shall be overthrown. **Mencius** develops an elaborate theory of what later in the eighteenth century Europe came to be known as theory of moral sentiments. He emphasises the importance of justice in a ruler and the equal importance of respect and obedience in the ruler's followers. In **ancient Hindu thought** *dharma* meaning what is right, or broadly, duties, is central. An individual's *dharma* is derived from the caste of his birth. It is the king's duty to uphold *dharma*, the spirit of righteousness. By intervening in the affairs of guilds, corporations, new castes, religious organisations, foreign settlements, groups of atheists and heretics, when it contravenes or is ambiguous to public interest otherwise they could conduct themselves in accordance to their customs and usages. The **Buddhists** accept the Hindu view of the king's duty to uphold *dhamma*, akin to *dharma* but reject its caste-based definition and content. Hammurabi's laws recognised three different social groups who received different punishments for the same crime. **Islamic thought** considers justice as the most privileged ethical idea meaning maintenance of things in their proper stations and the regulation of practical life in accordance with the requirements of stability. Justice affirms the maintenance of both religious and rational government, while caprice helps injustice.

EARLY MODERN CONCEPTIONS

Justice, for Hobbes, is whatever free, rational and equal individuals agree to leave out. He says little about what constitutes a just distribution of goods. As long as the distribution is the result of a freely entered agreement the outcome is just. Furthermore, he also asserts 'laws are the rules of just and unjust; nothing being reputed unjust, that is not contrary to some law' (1991: 182). Just and unjust have meaning in relation to law and law is the command of the sovereign. Hobbes' conception can be described as the part of legal positivism, for it contends justice to be a product of positive law and that there is nothing like objective justice. His denial of the possibility of morality by agreement makes it necessary for the sovereign to impose it. Kelsen argues that absolute justice is an illusion. In the abstract sense justice has no application since all statements about justice are relative to positive law which is a product of will and not reason. Since justice is about the conflict of values and since values are subjective, no rational argument can settle conflicts. **Pufendorf**, unlike Hobbes, does not see justice and injustice as being dependent on the sovereign. **Harrington**, a contemporary of Hobbes, observes that justice is to be impartial, and some procedure like a bicameral parliament has to be found that would automatically foil the self-interest and partiality of the parties. **Hume** rejects the idea that rules of justice are laid down by God or written into the nature of things for human intellect to discover. It is not a disposition or an attitude of mind but a set of principles governing individual's actions. He defines the *rules* of justice as conventions whereby material goods (wealth, land, possessions, etc.) are ascribed to particular individuals, and the *virtue* of justice consists in respecting this ascription, by refraining from appropriating the goods of others, and ensuring that wrongly appropriated goods are returned to their owners. For Hume, justice and property are totally interdependent. Where there are no rules of justice, there is no property, only possession, and individuals have no rights to objects, they only have them in their power. Justice is, therefore, an artificial virtue implying that there is no natural motive to perform acts of justice, as there is for acts of benevolence, such as helping an individual in pain. In the absence of conventional rules of justice, what is the basis of this motive. Certainly not in rights for others, for these do not exist. Though justice is an artificial virtue, it is vital to human society, for no society could afford to be lacking in these conventions. The rules of justice—among which are rules concerning private property—have their validity only, if they are conducive to the public good. For Hume, justice is respect for the established rights of others. Though he adheres to a utilitarian moral philosophy he does not share with the utilitarian economists their conception of society as an interaction of competitive egoistic individuals, held together by ties of mutual interest. For him, the need for habit and custom is powerful restraints on destructive passions and he approves of society in which traditional status rather than individual merit is important. He concedes to the distribution of material goods according to desert that takes natural sympathy and abstract reason into consideration as an ideal. However, practical experience suggests that this is totally unworkable, for it destroys the stability of property, which is important for Hume. Individuals would never agree on a standard of merit or on a mode of applying such a standard in a particular case, so a rule based on merit cannot be implemented impartially. As far as an egalitarian system with private property is concerned, he argues it would be impossible to prevent inequalities re-emerging, because individual's unequal capacities and talents would allow some to acquire wealth while others cannot. Hence, he rejects the criteria of equality and merit as principles of justice.

LIBERAL THEORY: THE UTILITARIAN TRADITION

Historically, utilitarianism provides an alternative to the contractual defense of liberal justice by deriving justice from the conceptions of social utility in a manner that results in the maximisation of total happiness in the society but by counting, 'each person as one and as no more than one'. **J.S. Mill** offers the best known classical defense of this utilitarian approach by surveying various types of actions and situations that are ordinarily described as just or unjust and concludes that justice as a set of basic moral rules is derived from the moral ideal of social utility. There are some problems of this conception. For example, consider a society of members equally divided into the Privileged Rich and Alienated Poor and their incomes for two alternative social arrangements are as follows:

	Social Arrangement (A)	*Social Arrangement (B)*
Privileged rich	₹ 10,000,000	₹ 5,000,000
Alienated poor	₹ 10,000	₹ 25,000

From the point of view of social utility, *A* is preferred over *B* but from the perspective of liberal justice that stipulates a high minimum for each person in social arrangement, *B* is preferred to *A*. This casts some doubts over the utilitarian defense of liberal justice. R.M. Hare (1980) attempts to remove some of these doubts by arguing that a theory of justice has to be formulated in accordance with the formal constraints of the concept of justice, meaning one's judgement must be universal and impartial. Besides, one must also take the appropriate empirical considerations into account, for example, people experience a declining marginal utility[2] for money and other social goods over a period of time. This makes the utilitarian approach moderately egalitarian in its precepts. In this case, *B* is preferable to *A*, thus, eliminating the possibility of a conflict between liberal justice and social utility. When declining marginal utility of money and other social goods are taken into consideration, the utility values is as follows:

	Social Arrangement (A)	*Social Arrangement (B)*
Privileged rich	55	40
Alienated poor	10	20

Rawls criticises utilitarianism while developing a contractual liberal conception of justice.

LIBERAL THEORY: THE CONTRACTUAL TRADITION

John Rawls' *A Theory of Justice* (1971) and a score of articles, which constitute the Rawlsian system in the contemporary political philosophy, are classic examples of the contractual approach applied to liberal justice. He weaves an intricate and elaborate pattern of inquiry and provides a coherent, systematic and powerful defense of a new kind of egalitarianism that preserves and extends individual liberty. The first major review by Hampshire (1972: 34) proclaims to be the 'most substantive and most interesting contribution' in the post-Second World War period. Commentaries and critical appraisals have assumed the 'status of a Rawls industry' (Ryan 1985: 103). The impact of his theory can be gauged from the fact that *A Theory of Justice* has been translated into several European languages, Chinese, Japanese and Korean. Rawls' philosophical edifice has elicited responses both immediate and immense, and since 1971 any attempt at moral and political philosophy has to reckon with his conception. It is noteworthy, that one of his severest critics has accepted the fact that '*A Theory of Justice* is a powerful, deep, subtle, wide ranging systematic work in political and moral philosophy. ... Political philosophers now must either work within Rawls' theory or explain why not' (Nozick 1974: 183). Rawls outlines the features of his conception in an article that appeared in 1957, entitled *Justice as Fairness* (also the nomenclature for his theory) culminating in *A Theory of Justice*. The elaboration and clarification of theory continues through a series of book and two more books *Political Liberalism* (1993) and *The Law of Peoples* (1999). He has revived the grand old style of political theory and has restored its grandeur that it commanded in the past, thereby ending the debate about its death and/or decline. During the long gestation period, the Rawlsian theory has undergone subtle alterations and changes, making it difficult to discern some of the arguments that have been revamped (Barry 1973: 1–3). Many of the modifications have been in response to the critical appraisals though in course of revision most of the core doctrines are retained. The model is the result of meticulous and painstaking research, an example of the Socratic Method, reacting to his critics, making the necessary modification and clarification but retaining the core doctrines. Contemporary discussions on Justice—Ackerman, Dworkin, Nozick, Sandel and Walzer—have been in response to Rawls' formulations.

A Theory of Justice coincides with the culmination of various movements in the United States in the 1960s and 1970s. The movements for Civil Rights, liberation of the Blacks, equal rights for the minorities, alleviation of poverty through the Great Society programme and the anti-Vietnam war protests raised questions about individual and minority rights, just and unjust wars and issues of social justice in policy formations and executions. *A Theory of Justice* examines many of these issues while formulating the principles of justice for a well-ordered society. Rawls attempts to deduce a set of permanent principles of justice as congruent with, 'our common sense and firmest convictions' (1972: 19–20) providing the moral basis of a democratic society with which the notion of a just society was inseparably linked.[3] He considers justice as the 'first virtue of social institutions as truth is of systems of thought' and that efficiency and stability were equally important but 'justice has a certain priority being the most important virtue of institutions' (Rawls 1972: 3, 6). Initially, in 1958, he develops the conception for practices,[4] but subsequently applies the conception to the basic structure of the well-ordered society. He acknowledges that existing societies are seldom well-ordered, for there is usually a dispute regarding justice and injustice. Rawls refers to his conception as pure procedural distinguishing it from perfect procedural and imperfect procedural, since there is no independent criterion for the just result:

> There is a correct or fair procedure such that the outcome is likewise correct or fair, whatever it is, provided that the procedure has been properly followed ... the background circumstances define a fair procedure ... what makes the final outcome ... fair or unfair is ... a fair procedure (which) translates its fairness to the outcome only when it is actually carried out (1972: 86).

Rawls tries to demonstrate that justice is about rules that govern a social practice, and not about the evaluation of different situations through criteria such as need and desert. He tackles the main criticism of this approach, which is that, following the rules in an exact manner may produce outcomes that are inconsistent with our common-sense notion of justice. Therefore, he purports to show that under certain carefully specified conditions, rational agents choose a set of principles that are consistent with our intuitive ideas of distributive justice, and that, when followed, yield outcomes which, whatever they might be, are morally acceptable. Notwithstanding its procedural features, Norman P. Barry (1995: 173) regards Rawls' theory as a contribution to the theory of social justice because of his continual stress that there is a need for rational justification of all departures from equality. Furthermore, there is a strong preference for equality in the theory which contrasts it with other renditions of entitlement theory. Rawls makes a clear-cut demarcation between production and distribution. Though he understands the importance of productivity to bring out the natural talents in persons, he realises the importance of controlling the market criteria by principles of social justice. The fundamental needs of all have a moral priority in the distribution of goods and service and that merit and desert does not play a significant role in justice as fairness. He rejects desert and merit on the grounds that skills, talents and endowments are social products. Rawls does not seek to equalise human beings or ignore individual talents and achievements. Rather he believes that inherited advantages and genetic superiority have to serve society and, in particular, the least advantaged.

Critique of Utilitarianism

Rawls develops a concept of justice that is congruent with liberty and reciprocity. Both these concepts are at variance with utilitarianism, a doctrine that has dominated Western moral and political philosophy since the middle of the eighteenth century. Rawls rejects Classical utilitarianism of Bentham and Sidgwick by developing an alternative based on Kantianism, a rival school of utilitarianism. He observes that while utilitarianism is an individualistic theory par excellence, it ignores the distinctions that exist between persons. He accepts its premise that each individual has a view of his good, which the society has to satisfy provided no one is harmed in the process. Though utilitarianism believes in the idea of the 'greatest happiness of the greatest number', Rawls accuses it of ignoring the interests of the least advantaged. He queried about the reasons as to why the greater gain of some should not compensate for the lesser losses of others; or more importantly, why should the violation or liberty of a few should not be made right by the goods shared many (1972: 26, 33). As a result, utilitarianism treats some individuals only as means towards the ends of others, while justice as fairness consider persons as ends and not as means only. Rawls considers the principle of utility as incompatible with the conception of social cooperation among free and equal individuals for mutual advantage and with the idea of reciprocity implicit in a well-ordered society (1972: 13). Furthermore, utilitarianism does not distinguish between the 'claims of liberty and right on one hand and the desirability of increasing aggregate social welfare on the other' (1972: 28). In justice as fairness, basic liberties are taken for granted and rights secured by justice are not 'subject to political bargaining or to the calculus of social interests' (1972: 28). Utilitarianism is a teleological doctrine while justice as fairness is a deontological theory, for it does not specify good independently from the right or interpret right as maximising good. The question of attaining the greatest net balance of satisfactions never arises in justice as fairness. utilitarianism emphasises on the efficient administration of social resources to maximise the satisfaction of the system of desires constructed by the notion of impartial spectator, from which many individual systems of desire are accepted as given. Rawls rejects the notion of the sympathetic spectator, as it is a device of utilitarian theory for thinking of the interests of society, as if they are the interests of a single individual and thus leading 'to impersonality in the conflation of desires into one system of desire' (1972: 188). In utilitarianism, the rational and impartial sympathetic spectator takes up a general perspective, a position where his own interests are not at stake. He is equally responsive to the desires of everyone affected by the social system. In justice, as fairness the parties are mutually disinterested rather than sympathetic.

Rawls points out that his two principles of justice are more congruent than utilitarianism with our common sense convictions and hence closer to **intuitionism**,[5] for it condemns institutions like slavery and serfdom.[6] He also accuses utilitarianism including that of J.S. Mill, in spite of his revisions of the doctrine, for failing to secure individual rights. Mill continues to see right as maximising good without sufficient guarantees of securing equal liberties for all. For Rawls, values like individual liberty and dignity have an independent status and cannot be derived from the maximisation of social good, while for Mill these are derivative. Mill does not show how the distributive ideal could be subsumed under an aggregative one. Like the classical economists, he assumes the greatest good as the maximum total income but fails to devote himself to the question of what happens if maximising total happiness leads to extreme inequality. Sen (1974: 307–308) finds very little difference between Rawls and Bentham, for both,

> captured two different aspects of interpersonal comparison—both necessary and neither sufficient as a basis of ethical judgement. The utilitarian procedure is based on comparing gains and losses of different persons and is insensitive to comparisons of levels of welfare. The Rawlsian procedure does exactly the opposite and is based on comparisons of levels only without making essential use of comparisons of gains and losses.

Sen rightly concludes that the two theories are incomplete and that Rawls' formulations are a corrective of Bentham's prescriptions rather than a complete theory in itself. Rawls retains utilitarianism's aim of maximising social welfare but insists on separateness of persons so that none are viewed as means to the ends of the society at large. Neither the well off nor the worst off are to make undue sacrifices that are disproportionate to the benefits they receive. Recognition of individual distinctiveness enables him to argue a case for equal rights, making it clearly a right-based theory (Dworkin 1977).

Such a theory has long been overdue in the Anglo-American tradition in light of the critiques of natural rights conception. The Rawlsian theory is attractive to the liberals, for it provides an independent basis to the defense of individual rights. Besides utilitarianism, Rawls rejects **perfectionism**[7] since the persons in the original position do not take interest in one another's preferences for they have different conceptions of good. They choose the greatest equal liberty with a similar equal liberty for others, thereby, rejecting perfectionism as a political principle. This does not imply that ends, freedom and well-being of different people are of the same worth but the fact remains that though people's activities and accomplishments differ, all have equal dignity. Rawls' principles are egalitarian, unlike perfectionism, which is a hierarchical doctrine stating its preference for the extraordinary.

Contractual Tradition[8]

Rawls revives the social contract tradition in its Kantian[9] version. This has not only aroused others like Barry (1989 and 1995) and Scanlon (1982) to use the contractual tradition but has also prompted a new tradition of anti-contractualists known as communitarians. The contractual approach exemplifies consent and voluntarism by trying to show how self-interested persons, with legitimate competing claims arrive at mutually acceptable social arrangements. Unlike the social contract theory that uses the device to explain the origins of the state and the nature of sovereignty, Rawls resurrects it to explain principles of justice. These ensure just practices and institutions in a society, viewed as a fair system of social cooperation between individuals fair and equal. A scathing attack by Hume and Bentham put the social contract theory into oblivion till Rawls revived it. Rawls is the not the first to use the idea of contract for outlining what justice is. As explained before, Glaucon also makes use of it. Rawls begins with the assumption that the principles of justice that 'expresses our moral sentiments' (1972: 130) is a product of an original agreement in the original position, a hypothetical situation, and 'a heuristic device' akin to the state of nature of the traditional social contract theory. The persons in the original position are rational, capable of a conception of good and have a sense of justice. They are rational with a capacity for intelligent pursuit of one's own interests, to enter into agreements that they adhere and fulfil. Rational persons do not suffer from envy, for envy tends to make everyone worse off and is collectively disadvantageous. Like Kant, Rawls also believes that envy is one of the vices of humankind. Furthermore, the parties are not in a position to coerce any one, thus, ensuring that agreement is voluntary. The parties are mutually disinterested, are roughly similar in needs and interests, equal in power, and are moral and autonomous, thereby, making it possible for fruitful cooperation. Like Hume, Rawls characterises society as a cooperative venture of mutual advantage, where there is both identity and conflict of interests. Borrowing from Hume, he specifies the circumstances of justice with two background conditions, which give rise to the conception of justice. First are objective circumstances that make human cooperation both possible and necessary. Individuals co-existing together in the same definite territory are similar in physical and mental power and live in conditions of moderate scarcity. The second are the subjective circumstances, where parties with roughly similar needs and interests are willing to cooperate for mutual advantage. They have their own life-plans, which obviously leads them to have different ends and purposes and make conflicting claims on the available natural and social resources. However, the interests advanced by these plans are not in the interest of the self, for the persons are mutually disinterested with the incomplete knowledge and limited powers of reasoning and memory. Rawls concedes plurality of life-styles and the possibilities of diverse philosophical and religious beliefs and social and political doctrines. Among the objective circumstances, he stresses on moderate scarcity and as far as subjective circumstances are concerned, he emphasises mutual disinterestedness (limited altruism). The original position based on pure procedural justice was specified to meet these two conditions. The principles of justice chosen are (Rawls 1972: 131–135):

1. General in form, eliminating both first person dictatorship and free rider forms;
2. Universal in application;
3. Publicly recognised as a final court of appeal for carrying the conflicting claims of moral persons;
4. Conflicting claims ought to be ordered with the help of a conception of right; and
5. Final.

The novelty about the choice situation is the permissible knowledge that is relevant so as to enable the contracting parties to choose principles of justice without prejudice. This is achieved through the device called the veil of ignorance, not mentioned in the 1957 version but introduced in 1958, to nullify the influences of genetic endowments, superior talents and social contingencies that tempt the individuals to exploit and tailor the principles for their own advantage. Rawls assumes that parties do not know certain kinds of particular facts like their class position or social status, their fortune in the distribution of natural assets and abilities, their physical and mental strengths, their conception of good, particulars of their rational plan of life and special features of their psychological framework, like aversion to risk or their ability to be optimistic or pessimistic. They do not know the economic and political situation of their society or its level of civilisation and culture. They have no information as to which generation they belong to but do know they are contemporaries. The parties, however, have general facts about human society, 'understand political affairs and the principle of economic theory; they know the basis of social organisation and the laws of human psychology' (1972: 137). This ensures that all will have an equal say. He assures that the principles chosen are in a state of *reflective equilibrium*. 'It is an equilibrium because at last our principles and judgements coincide; and it is reflective since we know to what principles our judgements conform and the premises of their derivation' (1972: 20). He introduces the technique as a method of testing rival moral theories and gauge which one is to be preferred. This suggests a harmony between conditions that govern rational choice and a person's intuitive and political judgements and that it was not a neutral one. He acknowledges that Aristotle and later

Sidgwick use this method. Taking a cue from Chomsky,[10] he points out that the aim is to formulate principles 'which make the same discriminations as the native speaker' (1972: 47). Rawls uses the original position in two capacities: as an analytic device and as a justificatory device. As an analytical device, it tries to understand the conception of justice with its formal requirements like generality, publicity, finality that apply to the principles. It tries to reduce complex social problems and the choice of principles to simple cognisable problem of individual choice. In its justificatory role, it defends the choice of the two principles through the hypothetical original position. Brian Barry (1973: 10–11) points out that there is no guarantee that the principles chosen in the original position are just and that it is not clear what is deducible and what is not. Goodwin (1992), Lyons (1972), Macpherson (1977), Nagel (1973) and Teitelman (1972) accuse Rawls of writing a liberal individualist bias into the original position, thereby, undermining the claim that it is fair. In his reply, Rawls clarifies that he used the word individualism to mean plurality of human life and the right of each to equal liberty rather than viewing social life as a means to individual ends. Barry (1989) points out that Rawls' theory of justice contains two distinct (and in some respects plainly incompatible) concepts of what it is for a human practice to be just. A just practice is a practice, which is to the advantage of all its human participants; yet a just practice is also practice that treats all its human participants impartially. However, for a practice to be to the advantage of all its participants, it must give each of them a good reason to accept it. He shows that the second of these requirements is a lot more demanding than the first. Rawls also argues that over a wide range of cases the two together are not plausibly compatible with the requirement that a just practice should treat the interests of all its participants impartially. If human agents choose clearly and freely for themselves, they will insist on the best terms they can get and this will reflect their initial inequalities of power. Egoistic rational choice, even under uncertainty, will yield practices that treat real human agents impartially, only if impartiality is directly imposed upon their agency. In addition, if impartiality is to be imposed upon their agency directly, what is the point of presenting them as egoistic choosers in the first place? Barry[11] (1995) shows how poorly the contractual method fares, contrary to its own intentions. Where the theories are internally coherent, the answers are unappealing (except for Hobbesians and the utilitarians) and where the answers are appealing, like that of Rawls' difference principle, it is inconsistent in its reasoning.

Rawls clarifies that the principles of justice are to apply to the **basic structure** of a society that deals with both the economic and social system. The former shapes the aspirations and wants of the citizens, determines what they are and what they want to be while the latter not only specifies the institutional framework for satisfying these wants and needs but also new ones for the future (1972: 259). The role of the basic structure is to 'secure just background conditions against which the actions of individuals and associations take place.

Unless this structure is appropriately regulated and corrected, the social process will cease to be just, however free and fair particular transactions may look when viewed by themselves' (Rawls 1977: 160). The basic structure is procedurally neutral. Its institutions and policies do not exemplify any particular religious, philosophical or moral doctrines, what he terms as comprehensive conception (1988: 263).

The two principles of justice that were chosen through the original position were initially stated as follows:

1. Each person is to have an equal right to the most extensive basic liberty, compatible with a similar liberty for others.
2. Social and economic inequalities are to be arrangement so that they are both (a) reasonably expected to be to everyone's advantage and (b) attached to position and offices open to all (Rawls 1972: 60).

Wolff (1977) accuses Rawls of falling into the same trap as his utilitarian opponents, namely of confusing justice with welfare and the phrases 'everyone's advantage' and 'equally open to all' to be ambiguous. Rawls acknowledges that this part of the second principle could be interpreted in terms of **Pareto criterion**, which states that group welfare is at an optimum when it is impossible to make any one man better off without, at the same time, making at least one other man worse off. In *Distributive Justice* (1969a), Rawls points out the incompleteness of the Pareto criterion, not only vis-à-vis allocation of goods among individuals but also vis-à-vis the many arrangements of an institution and its basic structure. He observes that the Pareto principle can serve as a limited criterion of efficiency, but not as a criterion of justice. The first principle embodies the notion of liberty. The second part of the second principle along with the first principle guaranteed equality. The first part of the second principles embodied the idea of fraternity. The final statement of the second principle read as follows:

> Social and economic inequalities are to be arranged so that they are both (a) to the greatest benefit of the least advantaged and (b) attached to offices and positions open to all under conditions of fair equality of opportunity (1972: 83).

Rawls suggests one measure of determining the least advantaged, namely income and wealth and not the social position, 'All persons with less than median income and wealth may be taken as the least advantaged segment' (1972: 98). Since the two principles are to be applied to the basic structure it 'is to be arranged to maximise the worth of the least advantaged of the complete scheme of equality liberty shared by all' (1972: 205). **2a** is called the **difference principle** or **maximin** and **2b** is **fair equality of opportunity**. The difference principle 'tells us to rank alternatives by their worst possible outcomes: we are to adopt the alternative the worst outcome of which is superior to the worst outcomes of the others' (1972: 153). Rawls taking into cognisance Tawney's criticisms about equality of opportunity acknowledges that it enables only individuals of exceptional ability to overcome the disadvantages which accrue by birth. It is of very little help to individuals of average or ordinary ability. Through fair equality of opportunity, Rawls seeks to mitigate the disadvantages imposed by both natural endowments and social circumstances and in the process, the notion of fairness undercuts a meritocratic society. The first **principle** requires, 'equality in the assignment of basic liberties'. Basic liberties of a citizen are political liberty (right to vote and to be eligible for public office), freedom of speech and assembly, liberty of conscience and freedom of thought, freedom of person along with the right to hold personal property and freedom from arbitrary arrest and seizure, as defined by the rule of law. The second principle applies to the distribution of income and wealth, the design of organisations that regulates differences in authority, responsibility and chains of command (1972: 61). The first principle is *lexically prior to* the second and 2b is *lexically prior* to 2a. This ordering implies that a departure from the institutions of equal liberty required by the first principle cannot be justified or compensated for by the greater social and economic advantages. These principles imply that the social structure is divisible into two or more distinct parts, in which the first principle applies to one and the second to the other. If the parties in the original position feel that their basic liberties can be effectively exercised, they will not exchange a lesser liberty for an improvement in economic well-being. Taking into consideration Lessnoff's (1971) suggestion that restrictions on liberty are unjust unless, either (a) they are necessary to prevent unjust inequalities or (b) they are to the advantage of everyone whose liberty is restricted, Rawls restates the priority rule of liberty. The final statement on first principle and its priority rule is as follows:

> Each person is to have equal right to the most extensive total system of equal basic liberties compatible with a similar system of liberty for all. ... The principles of liberty can be restricted only for the sake of liberty. There are two cases (a) a less extensive liberty must strengthen the total system of liberty shared by all, and (b) a less than equal liberty must be acceptable to those citizens with the lesser liberty (1972: 250).

The superior position is not accorded to liberty as such but rather to the list of liberties described as basic. Rawls does not offer a general definition of liberty from which this list could be deduced. He argues that his difference principle, which he calls democratic equality, is different from liberal equality and the system of natural liberty. The difference principle is a maximising principle and functions within a generation and the just savings principle operates between generations. It tips the balance in the favour of equality by removing the bias of social and natural contingencies. Inequalities arising out of natural endowments and by birth are to be compensated, for they are undeserved. It was not the same as that of redress. It transforms the aims of the basic structure so that the total scheme of institution no longer emphasises social efficiency and technocratic values. It treats natural talents of individuals as social assets whose benefits are to be shared by all individuals. Desert and merit are rejected as the basis of justice.

> The naturally advantaged are not to gain merely because they are more gifted, but only to cover the costs of training and education and for using their endowments in ways that help the less fortunate as well. No one deserves his greater natural capacity nor merit a more favourable starting place in society (Rawls 1972: 101–102).

The reasoning is that natural distribution is neither just nor unjust but simply represents natural facts. The two principles correct this arbitrariness as 'no one deserves his place on the distribution of native endowments any more than one deserves one's initial starting place in society' (1972: 104). Rawls recognises that fortune plays an arbitrary role in the distribution of natural abilities. He does not obliterate natural endowments, but rather gives incentives to the well-off to ensure productivity, which in turn lead to the elevation of the worst off. Unlike the principle of utility that treats some individuals as means to the ends of others the difference principle treated all individuals as both means and ends. Individual assets are social assets, which is why he emphasises the need for reciprocal advantages and benefits, since society recognises mutual respect between individuals. Critics object to the fact that the well-off and the naturally gifted have to make sacrifices for the least favoured. Harsanyi (1975: 605) views the difference principle as a result of an artificial and forced interpretation of the Kantian injunction of 'treating one another not as means but as ends'. Schaefer (1973: 24) observes that the difference principle violates the Kantian dictum of reciprocal freedom and accuses Rawls of 'treating men unequally so as to make them equal'. Nozick (1974) and Sandel (1982) argue that the Kantian dictum that 'no one deserves his natural assets' does not imply that one's assets should be treated as common assets. Arrow (1973: 247–248) concedes the assumption that Rawls makes but observes that it is difficult, however, to convince students that the productivity principle is not completely self-evident. Rawls is not interested in nullifying individual, achievements but insists on its utilisation for the benefit of the least advantaged. He was concerned with majority and minority deprivation. It is the liberalism for the disadvantaged and the underprivileged. The second principle is an acknowledgement of and a tribute to the long socialist critique of liberal equality. Significant assertions of Rawls were his opinion that strict equality was inefficient and his endorsement of Tucker's opinion that Marxism was beyond justice. He rejected trade-off between efficiency and equity and spoke of reciprocal benefits, similar to Gandhi's Trusteeship, for he treated productive capacities as social assets. He accepted social stratification, implicitly rejecting the argument of class divided societies.

Rawls offered two conceptions of justice—**general and special**. The two principles along with their priority rule constitute the special conception, while the general conception permits inequalities in any primary good, which is expressed as follows:

> All social values—liberty and opportunity, income and wealth and the bases of self respect—are to be distributed equally unless distribution of, any or all of these values is to the advantage of the least favoured (1972: 303).

In non-ideal societies, liberty does not enjoy lexical priority over other social values. **Primary goods** are central because they are important to an individual's overall good that is determined 'by what is for him the most rational long-term plan of life given reasonably favourable circumstances ... good is the satisfaction of rational desire' (1972: 92–93). The primary goods—rights and liberties, powers and opportunities, income and wealth and self-respect—are distributed by the basic structure of a society. Primary goods specify the well-being and expectations of the representative person. Rawls counters the criticism that primary goods have an individualistic bias with the help of three observations:

> (a) That income and wealth is the legal command over the material means in general necessary to realise people's needs and interests, whether as individuals or as members of associations and the desire for such goods is not peculiar to a particular type of society, (b) That income and wealth can be held in many forms public and associational as well as private and individual. It is true that the theory of good uses the notion of an individual's plan of life but this does not imply that such plans must be individualistic, (c) That the desire for income and wealth is distinct from the desire to be wealthy and being wealthy is not a primary good (1975: 542).

Rawls describes the **institutional** framework that applies the principles of justice. From the original position the parties move on to a constitutional convention to choose a constitution prescribing the powers of government and the basic rights of the citizen. They then move on to the legislative stage where the justice of laws and policies are to be assessed, from here they move to the stage when rules are applied to particular cases by judges and administrators. The last stage is when the principles of justice are applied and such a society for Rawls is well-ordered with a political system that is a **constitutional democracy**, thus, implicitly rejecting the erstwhile communist societies since these lacked democratic culture and freedoms. Like Arendt, he accepts the importance of constitutionalism as a method of change, as a check against absolute and unaccountable power. A constitution lends stability and durability to the polity and also provides the essential structure for realising freedom and accepts civil disobedience and, within the Gandhian framework, to rectify possible lapses in the political system. Rawls' well-ordered society is a **social union of union** with final ends, which are shared because they value common institutions and activities as good in themselves. It differs from a private society where interests are competing and not complementary. Its institutions lack rationality except for the benefit of the individual's private pursuits and 'everyone prefers the most efficient schemes that give him the largest share of assets' (1972: 521). The societal dimension of an individual's existence is underlined in Rawls' theory.

The economic system combines the market with state regulation. The government has four branches that regulate the free competitive economy. The allocation branch keeps the price system competitive by preventing the formation of an unreasonable market power and change property rights through taxes and subsidies. The stabilisation branch takes care of employment opportunities. The transfer branch is responsible for maintaining a social minimum by way of unemployment and family allowances. The distribution branch preserves an approximate justice in distributive shares by means of taxation and brings about necessary adjustments in the rights of property to rectify unequal distribution rather than merely increasing the revenue. The exchange branch, supposedly the fifth one, looks after the citizens' preferences and various social interests by adhering to Wickshell's unanimity criterion. This suggests that if the public makes an efficient use of social resources there ought to be some scheme for distributing extra taxes among different kinds of tax payers that is unanimously approved. Following the method of avoidance, Rawls remains indeterminate about the type of regime, for he considers his principles as compatible even with the liberal socialist regime (1972: 280). He thereby revives the framework of political speculation that was predominant till the nineteenth century, where the distinction between liberalism and socialism did not exist. This distinction has become redundant before the end of the twentieth century, following the demise of communism. Rawls is the first major political theorist to transcend this ideological categorisation invented within the specificity of the twentieth century. He represents the post-Second World War Keynesian consensus between social democracy and liberal-democratic capitalism.

In *Political Liberalism*, Rawls responds to his Communitarian and Republican critics and wrestles with the problem of cultural heterogeneity within liberal states. He clarifies that the principles of justice are independent of comprehensive philosophical or religious doctrine. He gives us an attractive vision of a social order that every citizen finds legitimate, despite immense variances in their personal values, thus, accepting the public-private divide that liberal theory upholds. Rawls formulates the political as latent in the public political cultures of a democratic society and applies the conception to the basic structure. He builds upon only those ideas that are to be found within the shared political culture of a constitutional democracy—individuals as citizens limited to the political sphere—accepted pluralism as the permanent feature of modern societies. He delinks social justice from diverse moral aspirations and the aims of individuals within the society. Moral ideals, in the sense of conceptions of justice, are one thing and justice is another. By emphasising on the political, Rawls says that his well-ordered society is not a community or an association. A community is governed by comprehensive religious, philosophical and moral doctrines while an association has final ends and aims. Rawls stresses on the political and the fact that society has no final ends and aims. None including a philosopher should be able to identify one form of life as best for all humankind unless he has access to the Creator's intentions. The distinctiveness of human society is in its variety, diversity and unending competition of ideals and languages. His argument is much less universalistic.

Rawls is more explicit by claiming that his principles of justice exemplify the content of a liberal political conception of justice and are not derived from rational choice. He specifies certain basic rights, liberties and opportunities, which are prior to the claims of general good. It expresses an egalitarian form of liberalism in virtue of three elements—(1) a guarantee of the fair value of the political liberties so that these are not purely formal (2) fair equality of opportunity and (3) difference principle. Rawls introduced social minimum rather than maximise the long-term expectations of the least advantaged members of society. He clarified his conception of the individual, which his critics say is a historical and abstract. He pointed out that a person has two sides—the communicative, consensus seeking, politically active, reasonable face and the other a private and autonomous face with his own distinctive good guided by a comprehensive morality. Such a person knows that political justice requires that he should not try to build his private moral ideas into the basic institutions of his society. This is the first commandment of Political Liberalism. Institutions are not individuals and criteria of right and wrong that apply to the institutions are not those applicable to persons. Justice is merely one among the many virtues to which persons for different reasons aspire. It is the great and prime virtue of social institutions and hence of public life.

Rawls says that he is not proposing some general method to resolve problems of public policy and of private conflicts of duty and that he is writing about the basic structure of institutions in a just society and not about choice of policies. A political liberal leaves space for the plurality of moral views to be found in any society but only if they are reasonable. With help of reason one reaches an overlapping consensus regarding diverse views, and an agreement about the political conception, which is not otherwise possible, if each insists on using their metaphysical grounds as foundations of a public agreement on justice. Public endorsement of metaphysical grounds is not possible, given the pluralist nature and the presence of incommensurable visions of human good in modern liberal societies. This means that comprehensive doctrines are excluded from public deliberations on justice. Rawls considers these as central in the private identity of citizens but not in the public sphere, which is the arena where political goals are articulated. However, the public-private that he upholds breaks down when he considers a specific moral issue: abortion. On basis of three arguments—due respect for human life, ordered reproduction of political society including the family and equality of women as equal citizens—he supports abortion. He considers reason as an attribute of all free and autonomous citizens. Contending parties are to sort out rival claims on the basis of certain neutral values like impartiality, consistency and equal opportunity. Justice as fairness remains the main procedural value in an adversarial process where neither side debates and imposes its moral convictions on the rest of society by force.

In *The Law of Peoples: The Idea of Public Reason Revisited* (1999), Rawls extends the argument to the global society. He tries to work out in *The*

Law of Peoples that liberal and non-liberal people can agree upon to govern their international relations. He distinguishes five types of political regime. There are *liberal* peoples whose governments guarantee the familiar set of civil and political rights and the material means to exercise those rights effectively. There are *decent hierarchical* societies that are neither fully liberal nor fully democratic, which protect the human rights of their people, that have a decision-making process that allows political leaders to consult with major social groups and are externally non-aggressive. Then there are the *outlaw states* that are either internally repressive or externally aggressive or both. The fourth category is the *burdened societies* that lack material resources to create the well-ordered society of the first two kinds. Finally, there are *benevolent absolutisms* which respect the human rights of its people but do not contain mechanisms of consultation that make the rulers accountable to the governed. Rawls devotes very little attention to this type of regime.

Rawls underlines the point that there are different kinds of non-liberal regimes, some of which liberals find tolerable and others not. He pays considerable attention to decent hierarchical societies, which he describes as those where a particular religious outlook is widely adhered to and is politically dominant. It is clear that he has the Islamic societies in mind. These societies are governed by what Rawls called 'a common good idea of justice', which can lend legitimacy to the political regime since it is widely shared. Its members consent to follow the same international principles that citizens of liberal societies do, like freedom, protection of human rights, prohibition of war except in self-defense and assistance to peoples of burdened societies. Rawls tries to explain their acceptability among peoples with diverse political cultures with the help of the idea of an Original Position consisting of 'representatives' of different societies.

Rawls characterises peoples as having, in ideal theory, three basic features of decency—institutional, cultural and moral. Institutionally, each people has a 'reasonably just ... government that serves their fundamental interests'. This includes protection of their territory, preservation of their political institutions, culture, independence and self-respect as a corporate body; and a guarantee of their safety, security and well-being (1999: 23–29, 34–35). Culturally, people are united by what J.S. Mill calls 'common sympathies'. For Rawls, like Berlin, this means the idea of nationality based on a 'common language and shared historical memories' (1999: 23–25). Finally, each people has 'a moral nature', in that each is firmly attached to a moral conception of right and justice that is reasonable (1999: 23–24, 61–68). Each, in rationally advancing their fundamental interests, proposes to abide by the fair terms of co-operation, provided other peoples do so as well. Decent people do not mean persons who are free and equal but those under a bona-fide system of law. A law governed scheme of social cooperation differs from a 'scheme of commands imposed by force' because persons recognise, understand and act on the law without being coerced to do so. Rawls develops the notion of decent people with the aim of developing liberal principles of global justice that are tolerant of people with different moral and political traditions. In *Political Liberalism* Rawls has already emphasised that toleration is the key to stability of a well-ordered society.

Rawls reminds his readers that decent non-liberal peoples accept a liberal law of peoples because they are reasonable and do not engage in aggressive wars or pursue expansionist ends or fail to respect the civic order and integrity of other peoples. Decent people accept principles that honour human rights. Their fundamental interests—in security, independence, trade benefits—would lead them to accept and adopt the laws of peace and these, according to Rawls, are nothing less than liberal principles of global justice. Many critics may chasten Rawls for giving a sympathetic description of the decent hierarchical societies, for Rawls tried to convince his readers of the need to tolerate these societies as bona fide members of the world and as consisting of people with a different political culture. Rawls was still willing to describe these societies as decent even though these societies limit the rights of other religions and also those of women but as long as these impositions are not burdensome.

Another significant feature of Rawls' recent book is a highly watered down difference principle, the most distinctive aspect of his theoretical formulation. The procedural elevation of the least advantaged members of the society as stated in *A Theory of Justice* indeed is the result of the years of socialist critique of liberalism. Rawls has always stated that this principle is to apply within the well-ordered society rather than across the world as a whole. In *The Law of Peoples*, he makes it clear that the difference principle applies only among citizens. Among peoples, it will assume the idea of duty to help burdened peoples make their cultural adjustments and achieve the material threshold that leads to decency. Within liberal societies, citizens are assured their requisite primary goods that enable them to use their freedom intelligently and effectively. If they decide to go substantially towards the principle of equality, Rawls would be happy but he no longer thinks that the long-term elevation of the worst off members is a categorical requirement of social justice.

Rawls' significant contribution has been the restoration of the concept of justice at the centre of argument about politics, the place it has occupied since the time of Plato. In his definition of social justice, he detaches the conception from the diverse moral aspirations and aims of individuals within the society. He insists that moral ideals constitute one sphere and justice another, thus adhering to the pluralist faith. Furthermore, he revives the grand old style of political theorising akin to the classical tradition. For the last three decades, the epic theory of Rawls' theoretical construct as delineated in *A Theory of Justice* has dominated political theory like a colossus. No worthwhile political theorising in the contemporary world is possible without a reference to it a fact acknowledged by even his most ardent critic, Nozick. However, the same may not be true of his later two publications, which appear more in the nature of clarifications rather than as fundamental contributions to basic principles. Even in the limited endeavour *Political Liberalism*, he accepts the overall parameter of a liberal framework by guaranteeing the right and choice of abortion to the individual. However, in *The Law of Peoples*, this basic commitment to a minimum liberal constitutional and democratic order with the primacy of the individual is missing.

It is rather disappointing as to why Rawls chooses to isolate non-liberal societies from its liberal critics at a time when the liberal idea has gained credence after the demise of authoritarianism of all shades, both right and left. Rawls himself has travelled a long distance from the universalistic yardstick that he adopted in his landmark book *A Theory of Justice*, which categorically rejected the then prevailing communist regimes, for they lacked the basic human freedoms and a democratic culture. A classic in political theory emerges by transcending the local and focuses on the universal and perennial. Rawls' *A Theory of Justice* is a masterpiece because it contains this intrinsic quality. It transcends the theoretical as well as the practical application of capitalism and socialism and identified freedom, equity, efficiency and stability as common criteria of the well-ordered constitutional democratic society. *The Law of Peoples* lacks this vision and spirit. Had Rawls stopped with *A Theory of Justice* he would have still been assured of immortality as the high priest of liberalism in the second-half of the twentieth century.

LIBERTARIAN THEORIES OF JUSTICE

A libertarian is critical of liberal idea of justice—utilitarian and contractual—and bases his conception of justice on the ideal of liberty. Nozick's entitlement theory of justice provides a powerful philosophical defense of the libertarian position of the minimal state. The entitlement theory is proposed as a critique and an alternate model to Rawls' theory. It is purely a procedural theory of distributive justice which defends 'whatever arises from a just situation by just steps is itself just' (1974: 151). It has three aspects—(a) principles of justice in original justification or acquisition (b) in transfer and (c) of rectification of unjust holdings. The first principle sets the conditions for creation of property, the second, of its passage from one owner to another and the third, for remedies in case any of the other two are violated (1974: 150–153). These principles of distributive justice apply to an ongoing process. The entitlement theory is neither a patterned principle nor an end-state conception. The former (1974: 156) evaluates distribution in accordance with some natural dimension like IQ, need, moral desert, noble blood or labour and requires constant interference from the government for its maintenance, thereby, violating individual liberty. The end-state theories suggest particular goals to which distribution shall conform and are not patterned principles. The Rawlsian paradigm espouses patterned and end-state principles. The argument that individuals are to be rewarded according to desert is a historical principle because it takes into consideration how people acquire and transfer property holdings, whereas Rawls does not explain special entitlements since the parties behind the veil do not know who gets what?

The entitlement theory regards social distribution of goods as just if it is generated by processes that are just, succinctly summed up as 'from each as they choose, to each as they are chosen' (1974: 160). Through the example of Wilt Chamberlain, the famous basketball player in the USA the entitlement theory is explained as follows: In a society of equal incomes, Chamberlain's fans do not mind parting with twenty-five cents extra, in addition to their admission ticket to see Chamberlain play. Chamberlain's team maters do not also object, even though allowing him this extra means as much as $ 250,000, assuming that the attendance at the home games is one million people. This, according to Nozick is perfectly justified because the first action is just and people voluntarily proceed from it to the second making the latter also just (1974: 161). The ultimate result of these actions is a loss of equality but the more important is the preservation and guarantee of individual freedoms including the right to contract. Nozick regards equality of opportunity as unjustified and unjustifiable for that worsens the situation of 'those from whom holdings are taken in order to improve the situation of others' (1974: 233). As long as people have acquired holdings justly, it is theirs, and to take away is a fundamental violation of justice. Furthermore, he argues that the transfer of twenty-five cents by Chamberlain's fans is purely voluntary as money belongs to them. Therefore, none have any right to interfere with it by using governmental power and with the intention of redistribution which in order to maintain equality erodes freedom gradually and steadily, eventually leading to its destruction. The desire for equality arises out of envy, which is an irrational prejudice.

Just as Rawls refines Kantianism, Nozick upgrades Locke's theory by pointing out that appropriation of an un-owned subject shall not worsen the situation of others. This he calls the **Lockean proviso** after Locke's injunction that enough and good must be left for others after one has appropriated for oneself. Nozick clarifies that the proviso is not an end state principle for it reveals the method of how appropriations affect others and has no bearing on the final result (1974: 181). It justifies the natural right to private property on the condition that it is not violated. Appropriations must satisfy the intent behind the 'enough and good' clause or/and if it is necessary for life (1974: 177, 179). This he feels has to be fulfilled within a free market system. Furthermore, if an appropriation and enclosure leaves no further land or resources to be appropriated, the propertyless will loose the right to use the resources appropriated. This is justified if the overall position is not worsened and if the opportunities gained through appropriation of others at least compensate for the liberties lost. Unlike Locke, for whom individual property rights emerge as a result of mixing one's labour with the earth and its fruits Nozick regards it as a result of exclusive domination. Accepting the view of Grotius on acquisition, Nozick views everything in common open to all takers. He is uncomfortable with the labour theory of value (1974: 174–75). However, having rejected the other aspects of Locke's theory of acquisition, he does not explain on what basis he retains the 'enough and good' clause. He presumes the benign effects of distributive functions of the market. The whole idea of justice as acquisition rests on an uncritical acceptance of the operation of the market in capitalism as a sufficient condition for legitimate appropriation and that he accepts it as self-evident.

> I believe that the free operation of the market system will not actually run afoul of the Lockean proviso ... Instead, were it not for the effects of previous illegitimate state action, people would not think the possiblity of the proviso being violated as of more interest than any other logical possibility (1974: 182).

Nozick proposes rectification as a maxim that takes care of violations of the two principles of justice in acquisition and transfer by allowing temporary use of patterned principles of distribution in order to rectify past injustices. Its basic purpose is to restructure society with the intention of maximising the position of the unfortunate group, the least well off. In extraordinary circumstances like these, Nozick deviates from his ideal of the minimal state and prescribes an extensive state, which he justifies as being necessary for a short period of time. Rectification, he believes, is preferable to extreme socialist measures and schemes (1974: 231) but he does not clarify whether rectification is a once and for all a clean state operation or a recurring one. The first one is quite difficult, in fact, an impossible task unless it is brought about by revolution but even this has its limits. What the Lockean proviso leaves unattended, rectification completes it and it is an Achilles' heel of the minimal state. The long-term implication of its application allows for greater governmental interference than even Rawls' difference principle (Plattner 1975: 124).

Nozick like Rawls rejects utilitarianism on the premise that it ignores the distinction between persons. Both base their theories on the Kantian precept of treating individuals as an end and not as means and this is embodied in their principles of justice. Nozick, however, rejects the social nature of individuals by stressing their inviolability. He questions as why the Rawlsian persons should in the original position choose a principle that focus upon groups rather than individuals. Moreover, why should the better off accept and cooperate for the benefit of the least advantaged? The maximin for Nozick rests on an unjustifiable asymmetry between the worst off and the better off in a society, for any major effort of cooperation should be within a particular category rather than between groups. He believes that people in subordinate position shall accept their position as facts of their existence and those with superior talents have a right to give them orders. He objects to the imposition of constraint, in the name of fairness on voluntary social cooperation, for it merely benefits those who are already benefitting from it. He rejects the principle of fairness advocated by Hart and Rawls, for it allows for an expansion of state activities rendering the minimal state as meaningless.

Nozick categorically argues that arbitrariness of assets does not undermine desert, for it depends on not only what the individual deserves but also on the things, which the individual legally has. Even if the individual does not deserve his natural endowments, he is still entitled to it and to whatever follows from it. If this is accepted, then the community has no right to treat individual assets as common assets. Instead, Nozick prefers the view that the individual is a repository of his assets and attributes, accidentally located in him rather than being a caretaker of everything that belongs to God. He considers the conception of need as a form of moral blackmail. He does not differentiate between desert and entitlement but merely assumes that individuals are entitled to their assets and to things that are just and have been acquired legitimately. The entitlement principles are historical process principles rather than end state principles, that is, they specify justice in terms of how holdings come about rather than in terms of how holdings are distributed. He believes, his entitlement principles avoid the continual interference with people's lives as required by the end state conceptions of justice.

Hayek rejects legal positivism as the basis of justice as articulated by Hobbes and Kelsen, for it presumes that there is only one type of law, while for him, legal system as systems of general rules exists independently of legislatures. Just because the officials and legislators can authorise and implement the legal system, it does not indicate that they can determine what the rules shall be. There are rules of evolutionary type in a legal system and decision reached is not a product of the unfettered will of the sovereign but a process of reasoning that constitutes the 'objective' nature of justice. Hayek considers justice in the commutative sense of what is owed to the individual under a general rule. There is no person called society who is just or unjust, or morally evaluated in any way, for social order and a market order are the unintended consequences of individual actions, so the words just and unjust have little meaning for these state of affairs. Only if there has been a violation of some general rule can an act be called unjust but Hayek gives us very little indication of the composition of the rules of just conduct. He uses the term 'protected domain', which means property and the rules of just conduct that protect and preserve property rights extending beyond the notion of property and material goods to include personal liberty, freedom of movement and the like. Beyond this stress on the protected domain and an approving reference to Hume's three fundamental laws of nature (stability of possession, of its transference by consent and of the performance of promises) in *The Mirage of Social Justice* (1976: 80), Hayek does not give us a total explanation of what the rules of just conduct will be. Like Nozick, he thinks there is a case in justice for 'correcting positions which have been determined by earlier unjust acts or institutions' (1976: 31). But he is cautious in stretching this principle very far since all but the most recent acts of injustice will be difficult to correct. His reluctance to detail the content of rules of just conduct is because it is impossible for the human mind to construct all the rules in advance of experience. This means we are in a better position to say what injustice is than what justice is. Through a test of universality it is possible to know which rules are unjust (1976: 35–44). A particular rule is unjust if it cannot be universalised within a general system of rules through a test for its consistency. 'Consistency means that the rules serve the same abstract order of actions and prevent conflict between persons obeying those rules in the kind of circumstance to which they have been adopted' (1976: 24). There are two aspects about these rules of justice. First, they prohibit rather than provide positive directions to individuals. Only in rare circumstances like disasters, famines and catastrophes are individuals directed towards specified ends as a consequence of justice (1976: 36). Second, the rules of justice are consistent with a wide range of liberty in the realm of personal morality.

Hayek argues that social justice is based on a certain moral consensus in society, though he is skeptical of the view that there is a majority view to everything. The idea of social justice presupposed that, of the various values, a single value would be given preference and precedence over others and this for Hayek, is contrary to the idea of diversity of ends inherent in a free and liberal society. Any effort to implement social justice, thus, destroys the market and free society. The ambiguity and indefiniteness regarding the relative merits of these values result in bureaucrats having more power to interpret and exercise it in a discretionary way allowing different interest groups to articulate their own subjective views and get it politically accepted. Too much power leads not only to corruption but also impotence. The word social justice is like the word 'witch', for it means nothing at all. Furthermore, theorists of social justice presuppose a distinction between production and distribution that procedural theories do not make, and which does not exist. Market is merely a device that garners factors of production into those enterprises that have the highest marginal productivity but it does not distribute income on the basis of merit or any other criteria. Market outcomes are ethically neutral. In a free society or market, there is no question of social justice because the distribution of wealth cannot be blamed as an unjust act, in fact, no act can be blamed. It is rather the unplanned and unintended outcome of many separate acts of exchange, as part of the *game of catallaxy*. It does not protect all interests but only guarantees the application of the rules of just conduct to all participants. It does not predict in advance which particular group will benefit from the market process. He concedes that those who come off better due to the market operations do not deserve their advantages, rather they are, as compared to their fellows luckier. He admits that the distribution of wealth in a free market is such that if it were brought about by a design then it will be called unjust but it cannot be so described. Undeserved inequalities of wealth due to free market are no more than unjust than the unequal distribution of natural resources between countries.

No one brings about inequality. It is just that some are luckier than others. The market does not reward individuals for virtue or even hard work but for the economic value of their efforts and contributions. Market rewards are of help to people who make use of their abilities and knowledge to the greatest general advantage but are not indicative of merit, virtue or desert. Hayek points out that since social justice means distribution of wealth according to merit or desert it is brought about only if there is a central authority and if the market and economic freedoms are abolished. To apply social justice is to invite totalitarianism. His rejection of social justice does not mean his support for a minimal state or *laissez faire*. Unlike Nozick and Oakeshott, he advocates state provision for a minimum income[12] for the unfortunate but not as a matter of justice. These recipients do not deserve it any more than the rest who deserve the income that the market enables them to enjoy. They receive it simply because it is right to relieve or prevent suffering. He is not opposed to welfare state but only of the many aspects of the way it has developed. He categorically opposes the idea of any one having a right to a particular share of the total wealth or that the state should use its coercive power to ensure such shares. Interestingly, Hayek attributes the rise of social justice to the rise in the number of salaried employees and commensurate decline in the self-employed. Salaries are determined by merit because it is difficult to measure individual contributions to a large collaborative organisation. Though these organisations will evolve a close relationship with the market, since they compete with one another but its employees will never experience how the market evaluates their services in the same way as the self-employed. Hayek and Nozick are procedural theorists.

EGALITARIAN THEORY

This theory of justice seeks to answer ‘equality’ of what? What is it that the state is supposed to make equal? There are two distinct answers—equality of welfare and equality of resources. Welfare egalitarianism inspired by utilitarianism considers human welfare to be the most important and morally relevant feature of a community to which a state must pay attention. However, the state should pursue welfare not in the aggregate sense but in a manner that ensures the distinctiveness of individuals. Part of the problem stems from the fact that it is difficult to precisely define a person’s welfare. Is it pure pleasure? Or is it preference satisfaction? Furthermore, equalising welfare is impossible and extremely expensive and hard, for example, for the naturally disadvantaged. Though one does not disagree with the view that society has responsibility towards the handicapped and ill, yet there is hesitation to give large amounts of money to the few at the expense of the many. Hence, egalitarians follow Dworkin in advocating ‘resource egalitarianism’ which would have the state equalise resources but not welfare.

Dworkin recommends a way to distribute resources that, while not everyone has exactly the same amount, nevertheless, it leaves each person both satisfied with his lot and able to take responsibility for how his will be satisfied and his welfare secured. He clarifies this conception asking us to imagine a group of people shipwrecked on an island and have to decide how to divide the resources on the island. Knowing who they are, their tastes and so, they decide to follow an 'auction' procedure. Each of them is given an equal amount of purchasing power, the units of which are called 'clam shells'. Now, says Dworkin, 'there is equality'. Of course, everyone does not have the same things, nor will they value one another's share in the same way. Their different tastes convince them that some of them have done better than others. However, the important point is that all of them will have had the same chance as the others, with the same initial resources, to secure the satisfaction of their desires as best as they can and thus feel responsible for how they do. Most important, each will be satisfied with what he receives in the process and as a result none will envy another's share indicating that the distribution is equal and fair. Dworkin makes use of auction, a market device, for it highlights the idea that, 'the true measure of the social resources devoted to the life of one person is fixed by asking how important, in fact, that resource is for others. It insists that the cost, measured in that way, figures in each person's sense of what is rightly his and in each person's judgement of what life he should lead, given that command of justice' (1981: 289). This experiment will translate itself into political practice through varied measures, like taxation policy and the state's arrangement of the environment, giving people roughly equal shares of resources to spend so as to enable them to pursue their life plans. Dworkin admits that the auction does not address the problem of naturally disadvantaged and suggests that some of the island's resources could be given prior to the auction. However, if their disadvantages are severe, then it means more resources are given away with little for distribution of others, resulting in a distribution that may seem unfair to the rest. Hence, he proposes to add to the auction the possibility of buying insurance, meaning that the auction is modified slightly so that each person does not know whether or not he suffers from some severe natural disadvantage. In that situation, Dworkin argues each will want to purchase 'insurance', paying a certain amount if it turns out that they are naturally disadvantaged. In real life political practice, this means compensating the naturally disadvantaged by not affecting adversely the amount of resources available to the other people. In cases of severe handicap, he proposes to allow the simply talented to keep the larger number of resources they get through their greater talents due to their hard work and not because of biological advantages. However, the problem remains as to how one distinguishes between raw talent, effort or ambition. A person's labour is really a combination of both, for talents do not get created without considerable effort, so a person with a developed talent has the choice to work hard at developing it. Most of these questions are left unanswered by Dworkin.

Bruce Ackerman (1980) offers a liberal egalitarian conception of social justice that uses the method of neutral dialogue rather than the hypothetical social contract. With the help of dialogue, he probes into the utilitarian assumptions of justice and rejects conclusively the entitlement theory's ciaim that a commitment to collective property and state regulation of distribution is incompatible with liberalism. Amy Gutrnan (1980) accepts Rawls' contention that liberty and social equality are compatible and added participatory democracy as the framework for realising liberal egalitarianism.

Martha Nussbaum in the *Frontiers of Justice: Disability, Nationality and Species Membership* (2006) points out that the social contract as a general framework for a liberal theory of justice in general and that of Rawls in particular, does not address three important issues, that of disability, global justice and animal rights. Rawls' assumption that the individuals in the original position are equal, free and independent excludes disabled individuals. Rawls does not address the special needs of the disabled in the original position but only at a later stage of legislation. Nussbaum lists four reasons as to why Rawls excludes the disabled. First, he uses wealth and income as an index for social position. Second, as Rawls uses the Kantian conception of the individual that requires a high degree of rationality and that would exclude the mentally disabled. Third, is the assumption that the parties to the social contract are roughly equal in power and abilities and fourth, in the original position, it is postulated that parties pursue the goal of mutual advantage. On all these counts, Nussbaum advocates the capabilities approach which is better as it starts with the Aristotelian conception of individuals as social and political beings. According to this approach, justice and inclusiveness as end of intrinsic value, the good of others is seen as integral to individual good. A drastic change in the design of the public space and massive investment in education of the mentally impaired could bring the mentally disabled above the various thresholds of capabilities.

Sen in his *Idea of Justice* (2009) raises some questions about some of the basic assumptions of Rawls' formulation in *A Theory of Justice*. The book, despite its dedication to the memory of Rawls is a critique of Rawls' formulation. Sen contrasts his conception from that of Rawls which he dismisses as selectively Kantian. He points out that justice is a contested concept. He castigates Rawls' original position as being inherently flawed as there could be many other positions to the one that Rawls proposes. He finds many loopholes in Rawls' theory but is unable to conceptualize a different plausible framework to the one that Rawls proposes. This is evident from the example of the flute with three children trying to acquire ownership to it: with one claiming to be its innovator, the second claiming to be its best consumer and player and third liking it most and hence would like to possess it. Sen points out that these three positions can overlap yet does not accept the fact that by patenting practice and the primacy of innovation it should remain with the first claimant. Rawls would have resolved the same problem by giving primacy to the innovator while ensuring that the other two do not remain disadvantaged by guaranteeing a procedural elevation of the worst off. Furthermore, Sen contends that all the aforesaid three claimants have an equal claim without explaining his assertion as to how all the three are equal.

Sen tries to work out a theory of justice with emphasis on the collective consensus and universal human rationality without taking into account that conflict is endemic in any given situation and individual choices are of an infinite plurality. Sen insists that an acceptable theory of justice can be arrived at with the help of public reason without clarifying the meaning of 'public'. He does not take into account inevitability of conflict, articulation of wants and choices in a complex modern polity nor the resolution of such conflicts within an institutional mechanism that reduces harm as much as possible protecting just meritocracy and just reward. He overlooks the fact Rawls remains committed to the core liberal principles even in his *Political Liberalism* insisting on justice as being political in nature different from comprehensive moral and philosophical doctrines. Sen is also critical of Rawls' proposal for incentive based inequality but does not provide any other scale of measuring and comparing justice. This is a serious flaw when he wants to travel beyond Rawls' scheme in incorporating fairness, justice, institutions and behaviour but unlike Rawls, there is no attempt to discuss them in detail nor does he provide a scheme of making them operational in the complex world of today. The problem becomes more serious when he mentions the plurality of reasons in his critique of rights based liberalism. He insists on the possibility of a definite definition of justice in view of this plurality but does not provide any clue to reaching that definite solution. Unlike Rawls' theory, Sen does not provide for the institutional framework for realizing justice and that makes his theory incomplete.

COMMUNITARIAN THEORIES

These theories of social justice position just claim in particular social value structures and reject the overtly abstract individualism of liberalism. Their emphasis is on the importance of particularistic moral traditions by expressing a preference for the collective pursuit of virtue rather than the defense of individual rights as a principle of social order. It points out that social contract arguments cannot provide a moral motivation unless one is willing to accept the notion of an individual free and equal, separable from his constitutive attachments and if such a view is accepted then the social contract serves no useful purpose in justifying justice.

Sandel (1982) uses the communitarian label to criticise liberalism though subsequently he termed himself a republican. He argues that liberal theory justified an individualism radically unembedded in concrete social institutions and in the wrong thus giving priority to the pursuit of abstract equal justice over a communal, moral good. Pointing to Rawls's conception of the individuals in the original position as disconnected and disembodied he concludes that liberal theories fail to understand our 'embeddedness' in a particular time, place and culture. This is a fact that a political theory has to recognise if it is seeking to generate laws, institutions and practices that are truly good for us and constitutive of an ideal and fully just society. Justice must be theorised not only as the basis of individuals who are independent and separate desiring to profit from one another but from people with attachments that partially constitute their identities, who come to know and relate to one another. **Walzer** (1983), a left communitarian, argues for what he calls 'complex' as opposed to 'simple equality'; that is, a notion of distributive justice based on different rules of distribution for different social goods, rather than one Procrustean rule requiring equal holdings of everything for everyone. Politics, the economy, the family, the workplace, the military are each different spheres having different principles of distribution. Justice requires that the integrity of each sphere should be maintained against transgression from the others. In an implicit critique of Rawls, Walzer points out that the various principles of justice in each sphere are local rather than universal and based only on the communal understandings of a particular people with a historical identity. In other words, there is no single principle of distributive justice, which holds true for all societies, in all places and at all times. Philosophical systems could advance such a principle in view of cultural diversity and pluralistic political choices. 'The principles of justice are themselves pluralistic in form ... different social goods ought to be distributed for different reasons, in accordance with different procedures, by different agents, and ... all these differences derive from understanding of the social goods themselves—the inevitable product of historical and cultural particularism' (1983: 5–6). Walzer believes that questions about justice can only be answered by exploring the 'shared meaning' of a particular society. The problem, however, remains about the objectivity of these shared meanings? Only on this basis it is possible to create a deeper community with shared self-understanding and affection. His critique of justice has some merit but the agenda of communitarianism is beset with problems. The notion of shared common good is not easy to attain. This goes against the grain of pluralism in most modern societies.

Pluralism challenges not only the possibility of gaining consensus on a conception of good but also the possibility of reconciling constitutive communities with the political structures of modern nation states. It is precisely this problem of pluralism which undercuts the force of the communitarian critique and provides the original motivation for contractarian theories such as Rawls. The very attraction of the contractarian device was that it appeared to provide a ground for liberal principles in circumstances where there is no consensus on shared common good. Whereas utilitarian, perfectionist and commmunitarian theories define or identify the good and then try to deduce the political implications of institutionalising that 'good', the contractarian method enables the liberal theory to determine a procedure from which rules of association can be derived which provide each individual with a reason for acknowledging the normative priority of those rules, but without expecting any convergence among individuals on such a common good. This procedural version of liberalism is obviously attractive as a means of realising a liberal polity in a society characterised by pluralism (Kelly 1994: 232).

The communitarians are strongly silent about their economic agenda and in this way they avoid 'the crucial issue of how community can be sustained at all in the face of market-driven economic inequalities' (Miller 2000: 109).

SOCIALIST CONCEPTION

The socialists claim that liberals and libertarians fail to recognise the ultimate moral significance of the ideal of social equality and its intimate link with justice and, thus, provide the most virulent critique from the point of view of equality. This is writ large in the works of the early socialists. **Proudhon** considers justice as the supreme principle of human life and the ways to achieve it in society by using an Aristotelian concept. Justice is same as reciprocity, equality, and equilibrium. Social life, nature itself even, contains irremovable contradictions. Kant's antinomies, and later Hegel's thesis-antithesis are Proudhon's inspiration for the theory that contradiction is the eternal principle in human affairs. Having raised contradiction to this exalted status, Proudhon does not search for the political means of changing social institutions, but for the discovery of the right idea that abolishes contradictions in the abstract. That idea is the concept of justice as equilibrium of opposing forces. Society makes the fullest use of its powers only when the forces of which it is composed are in equilibrium and when it moves away from distributive to commutative justice. The latter is the ideal for an industrial system. The idea of a reconciliation of opposing forces underlies all his theory and his practical proposals and, in particular, his attitude towards property.

Marx and Engels are convinced that with the destruction of capitalism, private property and bourgeois family, it is possible to construct a society based on social equality and realise justice. Capitalism generates inequalities of wealth and welfare because the markets and enterprise work to the advantage of the capitalists and property-owners and Marx explains this with reference to the labour theory of value. Capitalism dehumanises the human being destroying his essence. Furthermore, it produces a profit and not the satisfaction of human needs. His criticisms of wage, labour and his insistence on its destruction with the proletarian revolution have led many to infer that this condemnation represents his passion for justice on the grounds that wage labour rightfully belongs to the worker (Tucker 1961: 18–19). With the abolition of private property and inauguration of common ownership, workers' exploitation ceases and society will be reconstructed to bring forth cooperation and fellow feeling. Nonetheless some inequality and some unpleasant aspect of money, economy will still remain. Initially, the socialist society distributes social goods in accordance with the principle 'from each according to his ability, to each according to his contribution' but with the achievement of communism need becomes the basis of distribution. Beyond these sketchy details, Marx does not offer much as to the working of his ideal. The utopia requires material abundance, which Marx presumes is there because of the technological and scientific revolution and with the bourgeoisie having revolutionised the means of production. It also requires a change in human nature so that people produced goods and services without the incentive of differential reward. If both these are possible, then there is no question of distributive social justice, for problems arise only under circumstances of scarcity and conflict of interests between individuals. The idea of 'justice as rightful balance, a delimitation of mutual claims, settlement' is 'wholly inapplicable to the conflict situation in the world as Marx envisaged it. ... The only possible solution of such a conflict was the ending of it by abolition of forces that made two hostile entities out of one, i.e., labour and capital out of man' (Tucker 1961: 222). As pointed out earlier, Marx argues that socialism will be a perfect society, totally harmonious, without conflict and contradictions. It is for this reason that Rawls reiterating Tucker observes, 'a society in which all can achieve their complete good, or in which there are no conflicting demands and the wants of all fit together without coercion into a harmonious plan of activity, is a society in a certain sense beyond justice' (1972: 281). It is also interesting that none of the thinkers on the Left have responded to this charge that Rawls levels against Marxism, though they described Rawls' theory as a variant of liberalism and an elaborate defense and rationalisation of the twentieth century welfare state capitalism. The most celebrated critique is that of Macpherson who points out the incongruity in Rawls' theory, for it accepts, a class divided society on egalitarian premises, with different and unequal life prospects for the different segments of society. Added to this is the fact that Rawls retains the market system and the bourgeois concept of the individual. He neglects the way exploitation works affecting the transfer of human powers and leading to inequality. Macpherson concludes that Rawls' second principle cannot be achieved by a welfare state mechanism within a broad framework of capitalism (1977: 91) but does not take into account Rawls' claim that his principles are compatible with different types of regimes. Macpherson repeats the familiar left criticism that inequalities of wealth are bound to lead to class domination. This undermines not only equal liberty and equality of opportunity but also diminishes the developmental powers of the non-owners (1977: 92). Rawls does not grasp the link between class and enjoyment of power. Macpherson, however, concedes that in spite of being a liberal theory, Rawls' theory is distinctly different and better than other contemporary liberal theories, for like Green, Rawls tries to develop a harmonious model along with the competitive-conflict model. **Fisk** (1975) points out that only when individual powers are recognised and organised as social powers, is community possible. Furthermore, individuals are equal members of a class rather than a society and judge Tightness of issues from their class perspective. Far from changing institutions and practices, theorists like Rawls only offer to change 'our' perspective on relationships of dominance and subordination through his second principle.

Kropotkin does not search value in the rules of property as such and viewed the existing rules as impositions of a privileged class and not as social necessities. He holds egoism as a perversion of the competitive society rather than as an endemic quality of human beings and is confident that altruism, a natural characteristic of human beings will replace egoistic competitive society. The notion of justice arises when a community concedes equal claim of each of its members to recognition and respect and often remarks to treat others as you will like them to treat you, under similar circumstances. He identifies justice with equality and equity. At the time Kropotkin wrote, collectivist socialists advocated a distribution according to social contribution—hours of work being multiplied by some factor to represent skill, responsibility and the like. This principle, a kind of desert, was found in the writings of **Saint Simon** and his disciples. The second position was that of Proudhon as discussed above.

Kropotkin regards need as the true expression of the demand for human equality. He believes that one has to work for just five hours a day to produce the basic necessities, leaving a good deal of time for pursuing other interests. He is confident that distribution according to need is fully realised with communism. He repudiates Hume's contention for the need of strictly enforced legal rights by maintaining that the self-restraint and security of expectation, which law is supposed to provide, can be achieved without law, by custom and mutual agreement. He rejects the principle of rewarding merit as inappropriate under the new type of social organisation that will be based on common ownership. Assessing individual contribution is possible only under a regime of private property and in simple peasant society but not in modern society where interdependence was the rule. Under the circumstances, it was not possible to argue that any one's contribution was more than some body else's. All available resources are the collective work of human beings and therefore, are to rightfully belong to society as such. Individual appropriation is unjust. Besides this objection on technical grounds, there was a more fundamental reason. The spirit of generosity invigorates common ownership, which was just the opposite of egoism under capitalism. Differential rewards symbolised reassertion of personal selfishness. Distributions by desert separate persons rather than bringing them together.

Unless it is recognised that the needy have a just claim to the resources they require, only then it is possible to attain mutual respect, the essence of true community. For Kropotkin, charity organised by the state is still charity, or condescension on the part of the rich. Kropotkin was reticent about the arrangement of productive work. He assumes that each individual freely chooses the kind of work he has to perform. He also assumes that working day becomes short and that technological and scientific advances eliminate unpleasant jobs. However, these advances never materialised till the middle of the twentieth century. The anarchist idea never really materialised. It was the communist vision that got established but the communist economies never really developed a concept of just meritocracy and reward, and nor did they fulfil the needs of the ordinary people.

FEMINIST THEORIES

For feminism (with some exceptions) like Marxism and communitarianism, an ideal community is based on social solidarity, not needing justice. The feminist critics of political theory focus on distributive justice and point out that the existing theory is unacceptable unless there is a mitigation of the systems of political and social oppression that men exert over women. **Choodorow** (1978) and **Gilligan** (1982) reject the idea of universal moral psychology concerned with justice, rights and principles that are male in code and in its place contrast it with a female 'ethic of care', based on types of empathy, proximity and relatedness. Gilligan observes that attachment rather than autonomy, and caring rather than the abstract principles of justice dictate women's moral sensibilities. According to Gilligan, men/boys tend to engage in a mode of moral reasoning and moral discourse that emphasises rights and justice defined as equal treatment, reciprocity or fairness while women/girls tend to engage in a moral discourse that emphasises relationships, responsibilities and caring.

The private-public distinction is criticised for it not only excludes women from public activities like voting or holding public office but at the same time covers up whatever goes on in the home, including violence against women and children from public scrutiny (Pateman 1988, 1989; Okin 1989; Elshtain 1981). In its place the feminists develop the idea that women have various rights to privacy, from the right to retain custody of their children to the right to choose a life partner to the right to reproductive freedom. The notion of privacy in this context means the need for a workable, humane family and community and for realising female personhood. However, they reject the idea of private central to the liberal feminism, for that reinforces male hegemony and female inequality. **MacKinnon** (1989) condemns women's unequal control of sex and powerlessness to make decisions about matters most closely associated with their own bodies and self-development but concedes that the private sphere is not rejected for this reason. Women, feminists stress, do not just want privacy but something more than that, namely opportunities for affiliation and caring.

Okin (1989) rightly and forcefully argues that the history of male theorising about justice ignores male domination and male privilege as issues of justice, largely because they assume that family relations are within the domestic sphere while principles of justice are to apply to the public space. She broadens the debate on social justice by introducing questions of gender and distribution within the family. She criticises the liberal theories of justice for their failure to address these questions, explains how a gendered society creates injustice between men and women and advances some policy proposals aimed at rectifying this injustice. Okin considers the theories of Rawls, Nozick and Walzer and shows in particular how Rawls having initially included the family as part of the basic structure to which the principles of justice are to apply ignores its internal relations. Having established that domestic relations are part of the subject matter of justice she proceeds to analyse the way in which gender-defined as 'the deeply entrenched institutionalisation of sexual difference' creates a pervasive injustice between men and women. She attributes this to the functionalism, which perceives the man to be the breadwinner and the woman as a rearer of children and performer of domestic chores, and only secondarily as wage earner. She then looks at what happens when such a family is blended into a conventional labour market. A number of consequences follow:

1. Women who share this norm have less incentive than men to acquire marketable skills prior to marrying or taking up a career. So, on an average they will have less human capital than men.
2. When they do marry and have children and then re-enter the labour market they are decisively disadvantaged in comparison to men because they have fewer skills (by 1) and/or their career has been interrupted and/or they need more flexible work. Thus, they will earn less than men of similar age and talent.
3. Given this inequality in earning power it becomes rational for the man to continue full-time work and for the woman not to work or do part-time, an arrangement that a woman agrees to in view of the higher marginal earning power of the man.
4. Owing to this gender norm, a woman continues to do bulk of the domestic chores even when she is doing work outside the home. Okin produced American evidence that shows women performing very much more domestic labour than men in cases where both partners work, and substantially more labour overall, putting domestic and unpaid labour together.
5. The husband's position as the major wage earner gives him greater powers within the family partly because of the norm that the person who brings in the money decides how it is spent but more fundamentally because the costs of quitting the relationship are far greater for the woman than for the man: she is usually given custody of children and, for reason given, her earning power is typically less.

Okin goes beyond the normal liberal case for reforming the public sphere by enacting equal opportunity legislation. She argues for modest reforms to removing injustice pertaining to the sexual division of labour. For instance, for public provision of child care to enable both men and women to combine paid work with raising children; changes in work practices to allow life and family life to harmonise; gender-free education that prepares both the sexes equally for work and political life, alteration to the divorce laws to guarantee equal living standards to both partners in the period following divorce; a requirement on employers that earning should be divided equally between both partners even in cases where one partner chooses not to work. All these proposals are cemented together by the idea that marriage partners should be equal in power, status and living standard and by a general vision of a society in which a person's sex plays no role in determining the kind of life that one wants to enjoy. However, the defect in Okin's analysis is that she presumes equality principle as an appropriate basis of justice in the family but does not provide explicit arguments in its favour. She focuses exclusively between marriage partners and ignores the question of justice between different generations of family members, upwards and downwards. Okin's analysis endorses Walzer's claim and attempts not to formulate a simple monist principle of social justice but instead, think of many different sorts of goods that need to be distributed fairly.

In response to Okin, Rawls makes two claims that are difficult to render consistent (Nussbaum 2000: 271). First, he repeats and defends his initial position that the family is part of the basic structure of the society. Second, he makes a new claim that his two principles while they apply to the basic structure do not directly apply to the internal life of families, for the family is like many other voluntary associations, such as, churches and universities, professional or scientific associations, business firms or labour unions. Justice provides some important constraints but does not regulate its internal governance. He attempts to bring about genuine equality by insisting that law intervene to protect women as citizens and children as future citizens and by excluding gender distinctions limiting rights and liberties (Rawls 1997: 791). In addition, he proposes that the law takes into account a wife's child-rearing work as entitling her to an equal share in the income that a husband earns during marriage and in the increased assets during the time of the marriage, in the case of a divorce (1997: 794). He considers it intolerable that a husband takes with him his earning power while leaving his wife and children disadvantaged than before. On the other hand, he maintains that the traditional division of labour within the families continues 'provided it is voluntary and does not result from or lead to injustice' (1997: 792). He continues to retain the public-private divide and views society as being divided into nuclear family units, pre-political in form, with politics regulating it from outside although he insists that is a space not exempt from justice (1997: 791). However, 'Rawls is clearly torn between the idea that the family is so fundamental to the reproduction of society and to citizens' life chances that it must be rendered just, and the equally powerful idea that we cannot tolerate so much interference with the internal workings of this particular institution' (Nussbaum 2000: 273).

Young (1990) and **Benhabib** (1992) argue that if women are to achieve genuine emancipation from the male dominant power structures of modern society, what is needed is not only gender neutral policies of redistribution but also a rethinking of the goals of political theory. Young points out that the core feminist concerns of sexual liberation, reproductive rights, sexual division of labour, equality in family relations are issues of justice. However, this is not sufficient as normally all issues of justice are reduced to issues of distribution and that is a mistake for two basic reasons. First, issues of justice, which are not understood in distributive sense are either ignored or misconstrued by the distributive paradigm. Second, the distributive paradigm postulates distribution to take place within institutional structures but does not consider the justice of the institutional structures. She alleges that Okin not only ignores issues like sexuality and reproduction but also presumes that much of the distribution of benefits and burdens between the sexes usually take place within marriage and heterosexual relationships without considering the oppressive side of marriage.

Marriage and family are important concerns for the feminists. For some, the demise of the family and the role of women as child-bearers is a requirement. Others have sought a re-evaluation of these roles and institutions. Shulamith Firestone (1945–2012) expounding the first proposition, contends that the source of women's oppression lies in her childbearing capacity (1979). She envisions an androgynous (un-gendered) society free from artificial difference and repression, in the hope that human foetus could be reared outside the body with the advancements in science. Others have stressed the value of reproduction and that women should emphasise the importance of the qualities that childbearing and rearing bring forth. This is a woman's work though not rooted in a woman's nature. However, Adrienne Rich (1977) pays lip-service to shared parenting but her vision of sisterhood is one in which women perform their traditional role finding support from women who are reluctant to share their traditional sphere of fulfillment and maternal power with men. She stresses on the idea that women are different but equal, neglecting the issue of single parenting that is rapidly increasing either by choice or necessity, placing the onus on women by totally excluding men, thereby, resulting in total disadvantage to women (Chapman 1993). These issues of sexuality and childbearing are in themselves political statements, for they point out to the disguised mechanisms of power operations within the private world of the family. Young (1984) concedes that, if shared parenting 'entails monumental changes in all institutions in society then relations of parenting cannot be changed without first changing other structures', thereby, justifying the proposition that 'women's mothering may be less fundamental than other institutions of domination'. Some contemporary feminists categorically insist that gender is not derived from sex but has been imposed on it, 'gender precedes sex' (Delphy 1993).

Young (1990) considers the institution of marriage to be irreparably unjust. She wants social recognition and acceptance of single parenting with supportive policies, like pay-equity schemes to equalise women's wages with men's, expanded welfare support and vastly expanded child care subsidies, including child care services to enable teenage mothers to continue with school. She hopes that the United States emulate some European countries and establish 'mother houses', where single mothers live in private apartments but also have opportunities for shared cooking and child minding. According to Young, dominant theories of justice by focussing on distribution of benefits and burdens within institutions take the institution of marriage as it is which should not be the case. Feminists must question the justice of the institution of marriage itself and conceive of legal frameworks for family relations by deconstructing the series of relations which the present legal framework of marriage and family accepts. Family justice implies social policies that accept plural family norms and provide social support for families, especially those that have special needs. Young insists on recognising differences between different groups of people and for different treatment of those groups in the name of fairness and maintains that justice need not be interpreted as requiring abstraction from the particular circumstances of one's life but a recognition and accommodation of those circumstances. This stress on the need to recognise differences is propounded in view of the fact that men and women differ in important respects and these differences affect women's ability to make full use of their political rights even when such rights are granted. This is in contrast to the positions adopted by **Wollstonecraft** and **J.S. Mill** that since men and women are the same rational beings they are entitled to equal rights. However, recent feminism by stressing the point of difference has rendered the question of gender meaningless. In the modern world of multiple identities, gender is one of the categories and needs to be coalesced with others like race, colour and religion.

SUBALTERNISM

The development of subalternism is out of dissatisfaction with the traditional model of social science enquiry, which focuses more on the mainstream and global events rather than on localised and specific developments. It deconstructs historical narratives by identifying the many little and ignored components, which actually sustain in a diffused and localised manner the mainstream movements and leadership, which traditional social science enquiry has always focused upon. It considers the meta-narratives chronicled by liberal, Marxist and nationalist histories and theories as Eurocentric and rejects, 'those modes of thinking which configure the third world in such irreducible essences as religiosity, underdevelopment, poverty, nationhood, non-Westernness' (Prakash 1990: 384). It makes a bold attempt by its concern for the underprivileged and the wretched of the earth. Its focus is on the 'dispossessed'—the particular forms of agency, subjectivity and modes of sociality (such as customary laws and practices) that the colonial institutions had ignored or suppressed. Like contemporary feminism, it objects to the public-private divide in the colonial situation because with this division the important voices of the subaltern communities are denied their rightful place in a historical account modelled after the European nation state.

Global Justice

One of the important concerns of political theory is to differentiate 'is' from 'ought' and on the basis of that to portray a world that is both desirable and feasible provided humankind makes a serious effort to reach that broadly defined goal of a more equalitarian world ending endemic poverty which takes more life than contemporary wars in world which would move from international relations to intra national relations. Such romantic portrayal begins from the very inception of political theory with Plato's lament that every city is a city of two, one of the rich and the other of the poor, Aristotle's warning that inequality is the cause of revolution. In between the antiquity and the modern terms Lockean projection was also based on such an idealised version of feasibility of human emancipation. The difference between such projections and the contemporary global theorists is that the latter's emphasis is on building a planetary transformation in the thinking process itself leading to the creation of an insurmountable moral pressure to force the important decision makers both at the national and international levels to take up compelling issues like climate change and to end building economic barriers that stifle the lives of millions across the globe.

One of the basic assumptions of global justice theorists is a controversial one that the nation state system created by the Westphalian treaty has become obsolete because of interdependence of nations and emergence of the United Nations and the *Universal Declaration of Human Rights* which has led to a paradigm shift by changing the connotation of the debate from merely war and peace to a higher level of globally implemented minimum treatment to all human beings who may be citizen of any country. This projected scenario is just opposite of Kenneth Waltz's distinction between the national sovereign state with order within and the international system with total disorder, a situation of dog eating dog. One very important omission is this global justice theory is not taking into account the selective way the international organisations and issues of human rights are dealt with by important players in today's world. For instance, the United States accepts the social and political parts of the UDHR but refuses to endorse the economic ones. The second problem is with the assertion that many global and regional organizations perform functions which were performed by national government. However, there is no finality in such arrangements as the states continues to be sovereign and may even withdraw from such agreements as is being reflected in Great Britain's debate about its relationship with European Union. The global justice theorists exaggerate the autonomy of international bodies and supranational agencies.

The idea of global justice started developing since the 1970s when a need to revise the Westphalian world order with the view to enhancing the ethical dimensions of players in the international arena, namely the governments, corporations and individuals. The individual's role is emphasized drawing inspiration from the doctrine of war crimes which was employed against the nations of Germany and Japan retrospectively after the Second World War. It challenges the traditional difference between international and external sovereignties. This has been necessitated by the fact of the emergence of important international players like the UN, WTO, IMF and the NGOs which brought in a new world order transcending the traditional limited interactions and relations between nations.

Rawls' theory of justice and his subsequent work in international relations, the *Law of Peoples* provide important starting points for theorists of global justice. In any ethical framework, Rawls' prescription is applicable to law, practices, social conventions and institutions both within nations and internationally.

A gruesome reality is that roughly 20 percent of the world's population live on less than a dollar a day and more than 45 per cent live on less than two dollars a day and 15 percent live on seventy five dollars a day. The question is how to respond to such a situation (Nagel 2005: 118). The theorists of global justice, such as Pogge, Singer and Beitz take up the issue of world poverty and put forward the cosmopolitan view of justice by pointing out that the governments and people of rich countries have a duty to reform the global order and compensate for its damaging effects but do not tell us how this is to be done? Nagel (2005) accepts that we have moral obligations to prevent people from starving, from being harmed as part of obligations of a universal 'humanitarianism' and concedes the fact that it is possible only if there are coercive institutions to bring about large scale social coordination and cooperation but does not tell us how would this be brought about.

The global justice theory is an important reaction to the process of contemporary globalization and finds the traditional idioms based on national interest and primacy of the individual state as grossly inadequate as global challenges can be met only by joint global action. However, in a world of conflicting interests, different levels of developments and lack of consensus in many of major issues, theorists of global justice are yet to evolve into a philosophical collective action plan on a global scale. In building the edifice it is both empirical and normative but its major failure is that it attempts to theorise from the general to the particular just as Marx did rather than attempting from the particular to the general reminding us what Berlin states that the task of philosophy ought to be limited.

In conclusion, though the concern with justice and injustice is one of the key concerns of political theory, yet there is no unanimity about it even amongst its proponents within the same school of thought like liberalism, socialism, anarchism and feminism. However, in spite the contested nature of the concept there are some broad agreements about the fundamental components of a just society, like commitment to the rule of law, respect for minority rights, state as an instrument for people's welfare, constitutional and legal sanctity of basic human rights and equality of sexes.

Further Readings

Bedau, H.A. (Ed.), *Justice and Equality*, Prentice Hall, Englewood Cliffs, NJ, 1971.

Boucher, D. and Kelly, P. (Eds.), *Social Justice: From Hume to Walzer*, Routledge, London, 1998.

Brandt, R. (Ed.), *Social Justice*, Prentice Hall, Englewood Cliffs, NJ, 1962.

Fishkin, J.S., *Justice, Equal Opportunity and the Family*, Yale University Press, New York and London, 1983.

Fisk, M., *The State and Justice: An Essay in Political Theory*, Cambridge University Press, Cambridge, 1989.

Friedrich, C.J. and Chapman, J.W. (Eds.), *NOMOS VI: Justice*, Atherton Press, New York, 1963.

Endnotes

1. Epicurus also views self-interest as the basis of justice.
2. This law states that, after some point, successive equal increments in the amount of a good yield successively smaller increase in utility, so that marginal utility always diminishes after a certain point.
3. Rawls introduces a brief discussion of the principles of justice in international affairs, like the notion of just war and just conduct of war when he considers the issue of conscientious refusal to fight an unjust war (section 53). He does not, however, consider the possibility of international social and economic cooperation.
4. He defines practices as 'any form of activity specified by a system of rules which defines offices, roles, moves, penalties and defenses. ... The principles of justice are regarded as formulating restrictions as how practices may define positions and offices, assign power and liabilities, rights and duties' (1958: 164).
5. Intuitionism is a doctrine that accepts the existence of an irreducible family of first principles, which are weighed against one another to obtain a just outcome that would match with one's 'considered judgement'. It has two defects—first, it is unable to explain as to why its principles should be followed and second, it gives no guidance for decision when two or more of its principles point to conflicting courses of action in a particular situation. Rawls deals with the first defect by proposing a contractual hypothesis as a method of arriving at principles of justice without having to rely simply on intuitionism. Furthermore, it explains not only what intuitionism leaves unexplained but also resolves a material disagreement regarding the substance of justice. While one may propose distribution based on merit, the other may want it based on need. Rawls points out that the contractual hypothesis leads to the criterion of need, thus, taking care of the second drawback.
6. This assertion is not true. Bentham was a great social reformer who opposed slavery and colonisation of people and demanded a humane treatment for the colonies to maximise their greatest happiness. He believed that no person who is free would wish to be a slave and there is no slave who would not wish to be free. He observed that the system of slavery would disappear in America once its disutility in terms of

general welfare became apparent. He opposed civil inequality in the form of slavery but argued against its immediate abolition, for that would threaten the security of property.

7. Perfectionism is a moral theory, according to which, certain activities or states of human beings such as knowledge, achievement and artistic creation are good, apart from any pleasure or happiness they bring. Furthermore, what is morally right is what most promote these human excellences or perfections. Some versions of perfectionism hold that the good consists in the development of qualities central to human nature so that if knowledge and achievement are good, it is because they realise aspects of human nature. Perfectionist ideas do feature in pluralist morality where they are weighed against other competing moral ideas.

8. Besides Rawls, Gauthier also uses the contract to base moral principles in the creative self-interest of the individuals who adopt controls on their behaviour in order to maximise benefits, not in the sense of aggregate benefit of all or the majority but with the maximin relative benefit of each individual. This has shades of Rawls' difference principle but Gauthier arrives at this conclusion by a different route. Gauthier claims to derive his principle of 'maximin relative benefit' from a hypothetical ideal bargain from rational self-interested individuals without the veil of ignorance but with the idea that a rational self-interested person could not demand of another person, rational and self-interested, anything that is not acceptable to himself. While Rawls' maxim applies to the whole economic product of a society, Gauthier's applies to only what he called the 'cooperative surplus' (1986: 130, 133–134), that is to the increase in economic product brought about by social cooperation. The benefit that is referred to here is the benefit to the individual compared to what he could achieve or acquire in the absence of social cooperation—the latter is the 'starting point' for each individual entering Gauthier's bargaining process. He considers the bargaining process to be Lockean.

9. 'Kantianism, a contemporary but rival school of utilitarianism criticises utilitarianism. It subordinates happiness to duty and declares reason to be a servant of passions. It views the individual, as having a spiritual end and that human relationship is essentially moral. However, both are individualistic doctrines believing in the primacy of the individual and his supreme worth (Individualism as a doctrine explicitly begins with Hobbes. Locke integrates individualism with liberalism by incorporating a doctrine of natural rights and minimal state).

10. Chomsky draws attention to the remarkable and special ability to learn a language in a normal child. The latter has an innate knowledge of the principles of universal grammar which enable him to learn any language. When confronted with the data of a particular language, a child tries to find congruence with the deep grammar of which it has an innate knowledge and in the process succeeds in constructing a coherent grammatical model. This enables him to interpret and produce new sentences of the language in question (See *Language and Mind*, New York, Harcourt Brace Javanovich, 1968 and *The Logical Structure of Linguistic Theory*, New York, Plenum, 1975). He challenges B.F. Skinner's empirical behaviourist model that argues that a child learns a language through stimulus and response, which in turn is reinforced by the habit structure that parents and teachers have set up.

11. He proposes instead impartiality, an idea that principles and rules should be capable of forming the basis of free agreement among people who hold different conceptions of good, seeking agreement on reasonable terms by excluding information that might prejudice the process of deliberation. This is Rawls' aim but he is critical of Rawls' theory on the grounds that there could be no disagreement between people faced with identical information and reasoning in an identical fashion. There is no room for actual bargaining among people who do not know what their ends are. Instead he relies on Scanlon's proposal for an alternative 'original position', one in which well-informed people in a situation of equal power try to reach an agreement with others who are similarly motivated, on terms that could not be reasonably rejected. He instructs that one should act without regard for one's own interests, situation or relation with others in everyday life. However, he does not define reasonable, which plays the role of background constraints on the type of argumentation allowed in Scanlonian original position. He clarifies that reasonable does not include religious dogma (1995: 29, 30, 122–123, 162–163), cultural commmunities that claim special advantage (1995: 8, 115), those who reject the authority of expert opinions, arguments and evidence (1995: 104–06), those who hold false beliefs (1995: 208), those who lack knowledge that other societies do things differently and that their own could feasibly be different in various ways (1995: 107) and those who are impressed by their own experiences than that of the others (1995: 181), thus leaving out a small circle that Barry approves. He concludes by saying that his next volume examines the appropriate role for impartiality and the principles of justice that is supplied by the theory of justice as impartiality (1995: 257). Barry and Scanlon like Rawls justify moral principles as an outcome of a fair agreement.

12. Interestingly, Hayek does not regard Rawls' theory to be egalitarian, for the maximin which looks egalitarian is likely to yield highly inegalitarian outcomes. It permits inequality between the well-off and the worse-off as long as the position of the latter is procedurally elevated.

Chapter 13
Equality

Inequality-equality is a central concern in moral and political philosophy and Aristotle correctly warns of these being the cause for wars and revolutions. Even in our day to day existence when we judge issues using the yardstick of equality and inequality, notions of fairness and unfairness enter our daily language, as much as it is persuasive in our political opinions. While it is easy to accept inequality as part of nature but it is difficult to pursue policies that aim at equality. Richard Henry Tawney (1880–1962), echoing Rousseau, observes that pursuing inequality is like floating along with the current, while that of equality is difficult as it is like swimming against the current (1952: 47). He also points out that inequality has no rational justification and survives only as a matter of prejudice. Inequality is seen as an act of god and equality as a consequence of the conscious human efforts. Sartori (1987: 337) describes equality as a protest ideal par-excellence, for it epitomises and stimulates a revolt against fate and chance, against accidental disparity, which crystallise privilege and unjust power. It is the most quenchless of all our ideals, for the desire to achieve complete equality is an unending quest.

Equality is a complex concept. It means sameness or identity and in another sense justice. The demand for equality does not mean a demand for absolute equality. Rarely has any thinker defined a more equal society to be one of sameness and uniformity, for they accept diversity. The demand for equality is to mitigate large number of existing social and economic inequalities to bring about definite social improvement without obliterating natural differences. The phrase ‘all are created equal’ has a prescriptive rather than a descriptive value of how to promote and achieve equality (Barry 1995: 187). The concern of most political theories is how to create equality while accepting inequality and to what extent can the state apparatus promote equality without violating or infringing liberty and individuality.

TYPES OF EQUALITY

In political philosophy, equality is used in two ways—foundational and distributional. As a **foundational** concept, it is used as a professed description of certain features of human life in society, most significantly the claim that human beings are approximately equal in strength. It is used as a principle of action to the effect that persons shall be treated as having an equal moral worth. There are **four** types of equality. The first is fundamental equality of persons. Second, there is **equality of opportunity** to achieve desirable ends. Thirdly, there is **equality of condition** that attempts to make conditions of life equal for appropriate social groups. Fourthly, there is **equality of outcome** or **equality of result**. As a **distributional** concept, it is used to indicate an apparently desirable set of social conditions, for example, one person one vote, or a more equal distribution of income, social opportunities and/or political powers among people. A crucial issue is the extent of using arguments from the first to evaluate social, economic and political inequalities in the second sense. Egalitarian theories make use of the foundational concept to support questions relating to distributive equality.

Foundational Notion

The idea of human equality is distinctly modern, implying the need to rationally justify discrimination and preferential treatment. All ancient societies, on the contrary, were hierarchical, regarding some as more equal than the others. This thrust on equality does not mean that ability, intelligence, social status, wealth and power are equal in all. It follows from the optimism that inaugurated the modern era that people differ very little, while it is circumstances which make them different and hence all are to be treated equally for the similarities they share and possess. In spite of differences among human beings pertaining to their physical features and mental endowments, it is still claimed that 'all are created equal'. This claim is clearly elucidated by **Hobbes** who advances the proposition of human equality in spite of difference in physical powers and mental faculties, as all are equal in ability and equal in being able to attain the ends they aspire for. The physically weak can achieve by cunning what the strong could accomplish through strength. **Hume** in the eighteenth century and **Hart** in the twentieth century reiterate this argument. This premise of rough equality of strength makes it rational for human beings to accept a common body of rules constituting a system of mutual forbearance and agreement. The **Stoics** and **Cicero** advance a claim to equality on the basis of a common human nature. A **natural rights theorist** advances a case for equal rights on the basis of an equal ability of all to understand their rights and obligations thereby mounting an attack on paternalistic governments. A **utilitarian** believes that all human beings have a similar capacity for experiencing pleasures and pains, which is why in calculating pleasure and pain each is to count for one and no one for more than one. A **Kantian** defends the proposition of equal moral worth of each individual for as moral agents they are capable of formulating and adhering to moral laws lending credence to their claim that individuals are an end in themselves and not as means only. A **Marxist** accepts equality of human essence that is manifest in labour to produce their means of existence and to reproduce their own species. Exponents of equality, like Tawney, underline the need for social institutions to accentuate and reinforce the 'common humanity' that unites persons. Critics of equality contend that it is not possible to 'derive the *value* that all people *should* be treated equally from the *fact* that all people *are* equal. But the foundational claims of equality are not factual in any straightforward sense. To say that people are equal—by virtue of their rationality, passions, or dignity—already entails an evaluation that a shared human characteristic is politically more significant than other apparent differences' (Gutman 1987: 136). Different philosophical works advance the claim for foundational equality on the following grounds.

Proportionate Equality

Aristotle, the most succinct exponent of this view, links equality to the idea of distributive justice. In elaborating this view, he points out that inequality arises when equals are treated unequally and unequals are treated equally. This is because he believes individuals differ in their capacities, interests and achievements. The varied dimensions of human life—social, economic and cultural—differ in importance. It is necessary to distinguish the deserving from the undeserving. He tries to counter the principle of equality by justifying inequalities in two ways. First, the desire for equality is more in the nature of a wish rather than being grounded in reality. Second, even if one accepts the demand of equality as a moral one it still fails to convince. This is because it contradicts 'the spirit of morality with its presupposition of men's different stations and functions, especially their obligations and duties of obedience on the one hand and their rights and positions of authority on the other' (von Leyden 1985: 6).

Equality before the Law or Legal Equality

Equality before the law or legal equality means equality before the law and equal protection under the law. This notion is the lynchpin of the liberal critique against absolutism. It means that the rule of law or the sovereignty of law subordinates everyone, the ruler and ruled alike and it is a guarantee of equal freedom and equality to every citizen. There is never full equality in this respect, for children and lunatics are treated differently from adults with a sound mind. Women as a rule are also treated differently from men. In Britain, the peers are treated differently from ordinary citizens. Therefore, those who fight for equality before the law, try to ascertain which of these distinctions are relevant to legal rights and privilege, and which ones are not. A distinction is also made between *de jure* equality and *de facto* equality: both the wealthy and the poor have equal rights under the law but it is wrong to claim that they have equal power to enforce them.

The idea of equality before the law or *isonomia* was an established feature of Greek democracies. *Isonomia* overlapped with *isopoliteia*, meaning equal citizenship, a citizen distinct and yet opposed to a slave. Greek democracies affirmed the notion of every man as equal to every other in his intrinsic dignity and worth and its modern variant could be found in the statement 'all men have equal and inalienable rights', which was articulated during the French Revolution and is an affirmation of an important egalitarian principle. Initially, equality before law meant equal rights and equal laws, made explicitly clear by the 1795 French Constitution. After the Napoleonic period and the Restoration, the liberal democratic demand for equality includes three specific demands: equal universal suffrage to every adult, social equality understood as equality of status implying that class and wealth distinctions do not carry much weight and equality of opportunity. These were specifically democratic rather than liberal demands, for liberalism is more concerned with political freedom than the problem of class and status (Sartori 1987: 343).

Political Equality

Political equality is equality to vote someone into office and to stand for office oneself. The latter, one of the major aims of the French Revolution, is translated in the Napoleonic idea of the 'career open to the talents'. This resembles equality of opportunity that accords equal recognition to equal merit. Equality of vote takes a long time to be realised. At first, franchise is restricted to men from privileged backgrounds with property. Subsequently, it is extended to the working class and then to women. It was only by the 1950s that women in most of the Western democracies secured the right to vote. In comparison, relatively new independent countries like India granted both men and women political equality simultaneously. Political equality also means equal intrinsic worth of all human beings in making collective decisions and 'the good or interests of each person should be given equal consideration' (Dahl 1996: 639).

Equality of Opportunity

Equality of opportunity is most commonly associated with the liberal democratic tradition. It means, in principle, that access to important social institutions shall be open to all on universalistic grounds especially by achievement and talent. The notion of a career open to talent, an important consequence of the American and French Revolutions, sets aside ascribed status and favoured acquired status, meaning regardless of birth and status, administrative and professional positions are open to persons with talent, willingness to do hard work and capacity. Interestingly, the earliest exponent of this position Plato proposes a meritocracy in the form of philosophic rule, which will be realised through an educational system that allows equal chance for talented children to achieve unequal social positions. The debate on equality of opportunity helps in the development of modern educational institutions and meritocracy, for people are recruited and promoted on the basis of their intelligence and talent regardless of their family connections and wealth.

Equality of Condition

Equality of condition is closely linked to the idea of equality of opportunity, for if the latter is to be effective then a certain degree of equality of condition is necessary. While equality of opportunity implies equal access, equality of condition means equal start. Its aim is equalisation of circumstances to ensure equal initial material conditions for equal access to opportunities. For instance, children from privileged backgrounds normally have an upper hand over those who are decisively disadvantaged. This can be achieved if all competitors in the race start at the same point with appropriate disadvantages. The notion of equal access 'recognised and rewarded actual performance and thereby leads to equality in merit, capacity or talent. The notion of equal start addresses ... how to develop individual potentialities' (Sartori 1987: 347). In the real world, equal access allows, as Tawney points out, persons with exceptional ability to make it, while equal start is akin to Rawls' fair equality of opportunity that undermines the advantages that family and natural endowments give to an individual.

Equality of Outcome or Result

Equality of outcome or result is to ensure an equal result regardless of the starting point and natural ability through social programmes of positive discrimination in favour of the underprivileged groups. For instance, the constitutional reservation for scheduled castes and tribes in India and the affirmative action programme in the United States are examples of such a policy. Economic equality is to ensure a society without economic power, a proposition associated with Marxism and socialism. It supports abolition of private property, a proposition first advanced by **Plato** and reiterated by More, Winstanley and some **Levellers**. Winstanley comprehends that political freedom without economic equality is empty and economic equality is possible only with the abolition of private property and wage labour. Economic equality aims at equal incomes and wealth and equal status but differs from liberal welfare state that narrows the income gaps though rigorous taxation schemes to neutralise the effects of uneven economic possessions without abolishing the institution of private property. The critics of equality as a distributional notion advance three arguments against it. First, the ideal is redundant. Equality adds nothing to the argument of all human beings as equal because they are human beings. Second, it conflicts with other ideals, for instance, any aim towards greater equality leads to a compromise with efficiency and incentives in production. Third, different ideals of equality conflict with one another, for instance, equality of opportunity taken to an extreme may undermine equality of condition and perhaps even freedom (Gutman 1987: 139).

Social Equality

Social equality recognises the equality of persons irrespective of colour, race or gender. The anti-Apartheid struggle in South Africa, the American Civil Rights Movement led by Martin Luther King and the feminists has championed equality of persons irrespective of colour, race and gender, respectively. Rousseau also speaks of the ill-effects of private property but does not demand its abolition. Instead, he conceives of a society of equal lawmakers and property owners. Gutman (1987: 137) calls this **democratic equality**. However, in recent times, some like Macpherson, Pateman and Poulantaz espouse democratic equality within a system of representative institutions by making public officials more responsive to their constituents.

ARGUMENTS FOR AND AGAINST INEQUALITY

Early Liberals

Hobbes and Locke defend human equality as a foundational concept. Hobbes concedes that all human beings not only aspire for the same things but also are equal in the ability to realise it, with the result that there is insecurity. Writing in the overall context of scarcity, he argues for the need for an awesome power to restrain human passions and ambitions by providing total order, which in turn ensures commodious living. Locke, writing in the wake of the discovery of America, conceives of a situation of plenty and thus his depiction of the natural order of things is not so gloomy. He conceives of equal right of everyone to things, which does not remain so with the introduction of money that allows for some the possibility of unlimited appropriation. However, Locke does not, as Macpherson suggests, conceive of a society of property owners and non-property owners. Locke understands rights of life, liberty and estate as indivisible and does not defend possession 'for its own sake or for the sake of unlimited accumulation, let alone 'capital accumulation'. In Locke's time and still for some time, property was not part of chrematistic (money-seeking) economic system' (Sartori 1987: 377). Jefferson reiterates Locke's libertarian conception of equal rights. He criticises extremes of wealth and poverty in pre-Revolutionary France and wants United States to be different by providing equality of opportunity to all and by creating conditions of minimum material independence for all to participate in the process of politics. He considers human beings to be equal and believes that in a just society inequalities among individuals are neither degrading nor injurious. He considers individuals to be equal in the liberal sense of possessing common physical attributes, material needs and the right of self-preservation but he also regards them to be equal in the classical sense of being capable of moral choice and just action. He concedes to the unequal distribution of wisdom and virtue but believes that all are equal in their shared contribution to public good. He accepts the fact that the natural aristocracy is superior to ordinary citizens in virtue and wisdom but the former needs the latter to recognise and elevate them into positions of public trust. Bernard Mandeville (1670–1733), Hume and Kant defend inequality on the grounds that it produces talent, art and leads to progress, though Kant also defends the idea of moral worth of each individual and asserts that no one deserves his natural assets, a point which Rawls lucidly develops. Smith accepts deepening of social inequality as a consequence of capitalism, which he ignores because he is overwhelmed by the notion of economic growth and development. He cites the example of not only an ordinary day-labourer in Britain or Holland who possesses more wealth and goods than the most esteemed and active savage but also the very poor in these countries who lead a more affluent and luxurious life than many North American princes. Nevertheless, he demands that the state maintains public works and public institutions, thus, providing a generous and a compassionate government compatible with a competitive market economy. Social Darwinism with its belief in the survival of the fittest encourages the inegalitarian tendency, for it postulates that some individuals are inferior and any protection or compensation to them weakens the calibre of society as a whole. Fascism borrows from social Darwinism to justify its policies of racial purification and extermination. Joseph-Arthur Gobineau (1816–1882) and Houston Stewart Chamberlain's (1855–1927) argument of Aryan superiority contributes influentially to the development of the notion of racial determination and subsequently lays the basis for the anti-Semitic and racist policies of Nazism. Nazism uses the notion of Aryan superiority to exterminate the Jews and build German military power. Critics of Nazism point out that the concept of race does not have any scientific status. However, this belief that some people are naturally inferior finds resonance in contemporary viewpoints articulated by some Neo-Conservatives and the New Right that direct their arguments against equality and egalitarians. Hernstein and Murray (1994) argue that differences in IQ scores account for much of the variation in a wide range of outcomes, including earnings, and that inequalities pertaining to IQ are to a significant degree inherited from parents. It is inheritance rather than environment that shape an individual.

Rousseau and the Early Socialists

In the eighteenth and nineteenth centuries, a number of thinkers are concerned about the historical foundations of human inequality with significant contributions from Rousseau, Ferguson and Millar. In the *Discourses on Origins of Inequality* (1755), Rousseau virulently attacks the modern society as a highly unequal one. He passionately pleads for equality as a basic moral value and regards natural equality and compassion as the bases of the natural rights. He demonstrates how naturally healthy, good, dumb and roughly equal to one another, human beings become sickly, evil, intelligent and highly unequal when they enter society. For Rousseau, material progress, affluence and wealth only succeed in making human beings miserable, for it multiplies needs and attenuated competitiveness. Civilisation made possible by the discovery of metals and agriculture resulting in division of labour, specialisation of skills and the institution of private property has a corrupting influence on the individuals. Furthermore, modern civilisation is highly unequal, for it does not reflect merely natural but also artificial inequalities.

Rousseau advances two kinds of inequalities. The first is the natural inequality between the young and old, the weak and strong, the intelligent and foolish. The second inequality is the one that results from rewarding those who render special service to the community. He permits natural inequalities and those who make distinguished contributions to society. He sneers at the idea that social inequalities reflect natural inequalities of talents. It is ridiculous to think that the rich are vastly wealthier than the rest of the people because they are infinitely more gifted and talented, rather it is the unscrupulous business practices that their forefathers employed that account for their wealth. It is foolish to think that the powerful are called to occupy their post because of their native genius; they dominate by chicanery and skillful manipulation. Rousseau repudiates differences in ability as the sole justification for social inequalities. Instead, individuals climb over one another to get to the top. Rousseau's position can be summarised in three propositions:

1. The value of equality derives from a hypothetical natural equality.
2. Only that social inequality which is natural or which rewards distinguished citizens is tolerable.
3. Existing social inequalities do not result solely from natural inequalities; they are unnatural and iniquitous.

As far as the first proposition is concerned, it is perhaps not entirely correct to deduce moral values from hypothetical facts but still Rousseau's scathing criticisms of social injustice are essentially right. One shall not be able to buy another. The rich will have the law in their wallets and the poor cannot sell their liberty for a loaf of bread. Furthermore, Rousseau emphasises that every person will enjoy equality of respect as a human being. He goes beyond equality of opportunity and stresses the fact that certain benefits like basic education, medical care and legal services are to be made available as equal claims to all. In a capitalist society, since wealth is the basis of securing benefits, the rich avail of all the opportunities that money can buy while in a communist society it is power that confers privileges. By pleading for fundamental equality, Rousseau rejects both wealth and power as principles of distribution. He rejects the principle of egalitarianism, for it leads to levelling and Rousseau does not want to obliterate distinct individual endowments. He wants society to take these into account and conform to them. His ideal is a society of small independent property owners, thus differing from Marx and Lenin who advocate common ownership as a means for creating an equal society (Colletti 1969: 190, 192). For Rousseau, like **Machiavelli** and **Montesquieu**, there is a direct link between luxury, ever-expanding needs and the rise of arts and science and the decline of true courage and virtue. In a similar vein, Ferguson's *Essay on the History of Civil Society* (1767) argues that the specialisation of professions degrades the lower segments of commercial society threatening to morally corrupt the upper echelons also. **Millar** too shares Ferguson's skepticism about the moral consequences of commerce. **Dahrendorf** (1968) reiterates Rousseau's distinction between natural and social differences and argues the need to make a further distinction between those inequalities that include some form of evaluative rank order and those which do not. Both, with regard to natural features and natural capacities, no two persons are alike. The same is true of also social differences of the non-evaluative kind, namely responsibilities and rights attached to a social position (e.g. father) or of the characteristics assigned to a social type (e.g. woman, man, etc.). In all human societies different positions will enjoy different tasks and different responsibilities but that does not necessarily mean social stratification. Social stratification is social distinction that is evaluative in nature with reference to wealth, status and reputation. It is this form of distinction rather than natural inequality with which political theorists are concerned with when they analyse inequality.

Motivated by a passion for equality the **early socialists** argue for the abolition of property rights since all individuals have an equal right to wealth of the earth. They identify private property, as a source of inequality and, like **Plato**, **More** and **Winstanley** demand its abolition and replacement by common ownership. **Saint Simon** is an exception as he does not recognise equality as an ideal. Since he understands the hierarchic nature of the industrial-scientific society and regards scientists and industrials as persons of special excellence, he is against levelling. He accepts differentiation in terms of distribution of material rewards as a feature of the new society (Giddens 1974: 25; Ionescu 1976: 28), thus, anticipating contemporary arguments on just meritocracy. He desires a system in which merit alone is recognised and rewarded and that means abolition of privileges given by birth and inheritance.

Marx, Bakunin and Weber

Marx regards inequality not as an outcome of personal defects or an attribute, like laziness or thrift, but as a characteristic of a society as whole. He criticises capitalism for its inequalities between the very rich and the very poor and, like Rousseau, believes that inequality arises with the institution of private property. Unlike the early liberal conviction that the overall progress will percolate and raise the standards of living, thereby, making them indifferent to inequality, Marx sees the widening of differences between the rich and poor under capitalism. He considers poverty and affluence as relative, for human needs are social in nature.

> A house may be large or small; as long as the surrounding houses are equally small it satisfies all social demands for a dwelling. But let a palace arise beside the little house, and it shrinks from a little house to a hut ... however high it may shoot up in the course of civilisation,

> if the neighbouring palace grows to an equal or even greater extent, the occupant of the relatively small house will feel more and more uncomfortable, dissatisfied and cramped within its four walls (1977b: 259).

Relying on Lewis Morgan's' *Ancient Society* (1877), Marx and Engels are convinced that primitive society is communal, while the subsequent ones are exploitative because of private property. Therefore, Marx and Engels envision the future communist society to be propertyless and thereby classless and equal. Marxist theory recognises two kinds of equality that correspond with the two phases of the post-revolutionary society. In the first phase, the principle of distribution, 'From each according to his abilities, to each according to the amount of work performed' will prevail. This is because the lower phase of post-revolutionary society will still carry with it the remnants of capitalism and the material basis for full communism are yet to be established. Once done, the second phase will distribute according to the principle 'from each according to his ability to each according to his needs' (Marx 1977c: 18–19). The communist society will treat all human beings—naturally unequal and with unequal needs—equally. With the abolition of division of labour, the distinction between mental and physical labour will also disappear and labour will become not only a means of life but as life's prime want (Marx 1977c: 19) with a guarantee of materially adequate livelihood for all. Each becomes whatever one wishes, allowing a person to hunt in the morning, fish in the afternoon, rear cattle in the evening, criticise after dinner without ever becoming a hunter, fisherman, shepherd, or critic, respectively.

Bakunin considers economic equality as the necessary foundation of justice and liberty. He emphasises on the need for a society that counters egoism and power seeking and 'helps people towards self-determination on the lines of the most complete equality and fullest freedom in every direction, without the least interferences from any sort of domination' (Bakunin cited in Lehning 1973: 193). He realises that even sincere socialists or revolutionaries, if endowed with positions of power, are apt to make full use of the opportunities offered, whether through vanity, ambition or greed. He does not share Hobbes' conception of human nature as being essentially egoistic, aggressive and competitive, for he regards human beings as being endowed with an innate sense of justice and being fundamentally social. The important thing is the need for social equality, for that is the substratum for both justice and morality.

Weber presents an alternative to the Marxist view by accepting social stratification and hierarchy as functionally necessary and inevitable. The social classes are not seen as arising from the underlying modes of production but emphasise distribution, consumption and the market. As a result, he identifies plurality of classes rather than Marx's two-class division. Weber does not consider differences in power and prestige as a result of differences in property and economic wealth. Nor does he consider social inequality and social conflict as arising from economic factors. He accepts inequality as a feature of all human societies since groups and individuals struggles for scarce resources.

Tawney occupies a unique position for his distinctive notion of equality, which he understands with reference to the idea of common good and social function and service derived from a Christian humanist perspective. His socialism addresses human values and their social expression and has nothing to do with class power, economic determinism and historical inevitability. He criticises contemporary capitalism and socialism and observes that, in general, these are sick societies for they lack a moral ideal. He takes the view that the claim of equality is based on the ideas of common humanity between human beings and the equal worth of every person. Common humanity does not mean equal capacity or equal potential but that all persons have a fundamental moral equality that is based on the fact that, under god all human beings have common limitations. Even the greatest do not surpass the moral capacities of the generality of persons; equally, none are so beyond redemption that others cannot see in them the basic characteristics that make human life so worthwhile. Equality for Tawney is a basic value and not a distributive ideal. It does not mean strict arithmetical equality of income or identity of treatment but one that 'enlarged liberty, promoted self development' and 'narrowed the space between the valley and peak' in society. A social organisation based on equality will create the conditions of common culture and his preference for socialism rests upon its ability to establish a moral and integrated society of active citizens pursuing common ends. Such a society is characterised by the quality and nature of its social relationships which it will nourish, a society of fellowship in which citizens will cooperate and try to sustain and develop a true community. The communitarian aspect of socialism is fundamental to the cohesion of a democratic socialist society. Such a society is a functional one as opposed to an acquisitive one, for industry serves social purposes that emerge through the democratic process. He proposes radical democratisation of society and dispersal of power and rejects, like Cole, Webbs' centralising tendencies. The dispersal of power is possible only through greater social and economic equality. He argues that the educated and the privileged shall use their talents in the service of the working class, an idea that Rawls integrates and develops in his theory of justice.

Rawls and His Contemporaries

The Rawlsian paradigm revives the debate on equality and inequality in the modern political theory. Equality for Rawls is an operational concept tied to his procedural theory of justice. He accepts the fact that strict equality is inefficient and that inequality is an inevitable part of society. The innovative feature of his theory is that inequality is justified if it leads to the elevation of the worst-off. Rawls does not lament, like Plato and Aristotle, on inequality as the cause of instability and revolutions in a society. Nor does he, like Rousseau, consider inequality to be the source of human misery, moral degradation and corruption. Neither does he, like Gandhi, accept a poor society, which is equal as compared to a rich society, based on inequalities of wealth and status. His endeavour is to justify the level of morally acceptable inequalities within advanced affluent societies with a pragmatic approach to achieve tangible, substantive and long-term equality. It is certainly not 'an exercise in guilt' (Wolin 1986: 184). The 'difference principle' maximises the minimum and is conceived as a basic right (Martin 1985). It is offered as an alternative to the Pareto principle as a measure of social welfare. Rawls does not accept trade-offs between efficiency and equality. The *maximin* or the difference principle that he advocates does not aim at the fulfillment of needs nor does it merely guarantee that the poor will remain above the social minimum. It advocates procedural elevation of the life prospects of the least well-off. Since risk aversion is an important human motivation, the maximin is a lifesaver, just in case, any one happens to be in the worst-off category. The transfer branch of the government provides allowances in case of unemployment and benefits to the family. He does not merely advocate taxation of the incomes of the rich to subsidise directly or indirectly the incomes of the poor as done by the welfare state. Once transfers ensure elevation of the worst-off, the remainder will be regulated by the price mechanism, which when compared to central planning is efficient in determining production and consumption of goods, both scarce and abundant. The index of identifying the worse-off will be an economic criterion (Rawls 1972: 98).

The whole thrust of Rawls is on reciprocal benefits and advantages where every individual contributes to society and derives benefits in the process. The naturally advantaged gain not because they are more gifted but are only being reimbursed the expenses incurred for their training and education, and for using their assets and skills to the benefit of the naturally disadvantaged. Incentives are given to the well-off in order to secure efficiency and productivity. He considers natural endowments as the outcome of natural lottery and productive capacities as social assets. The individual is not the sole proprietor of his endowments or a privileged recipient of the advantages that it accrues. He argues, like Kant does, that individual talent and aptitudes have a social origin. However, Rawls does not obliterate unequal individual endowments. He takes into account the criticisms against the liberal idea of equality of opportunity, that it applies only to individuals with extraordinary abilities ignoring ordinary human beings. Through the second part of his second principle, he alleviates the disadvantages by birth and social circumstances and undermines a meritocratic society. His idea combines growth with equality, which represented the post-Second World War liberal-social democracy consensus. This is a view that Anthony Crosland (1918–1977) too voices as evident from the following observation:

> The achievement of greater equality without intolerable social stress and a probable curtailment of liberty depends heavily upon economic growth. The better off have been able to accept with reasonable equanimity a decline in their relative standard of living because growth has enabled them (almost) to maintain the absolute standard of living despite redistribution (cited in Plant 1984: 16).

Rawls injects into competitive and private forms of social cooperation attributes of genuine reciprocal relationships and transforms them. He ensures a system that is stable, efficient and just and one not bereft of social responsibility towards the less privileged. While Rawls attempts to construct a theory in which liberty and equality are compatible, Nozick's theory gives primacy to liberty accepting inequalities as they are.

Nozick rejects Rawls' argument that the better off accept and cooperate in the society to elevate the worst-off. He argues that people in subordinate position accept their position as facts of their existence and willingly receive orders from those with superior talents. He opposes imposition of constraints in the name of fairness on voluntary social cooperation, for those who are already its beneficiaries benefit more. Hayek reiterates the classical liberal conviction that inequalities due to upbringing, inheritance and education as permitted by the ideal of liberty, actually benefits society as a whole. Inequality is good, in itself. It is not only inevitable but also desirable in a free society for 'spill over effects' from the existence of private wealth are significant. These private sources of wealth nourish innovation and experiment in science and arts and act as a bulwark against the expansion of the state. Dworkin distinguishes between inequalities that are 'endowment sensitive' from those that are 'ambition sensitive'. The former refers to the advantages that some enjoy as a result of arbitrary distribution of resources while the latter relates to those actions of a person that make him successful. 'By making this distinction, and reserving moral appraisal for the results of ambitions, he is implicitly restoring the idea of desert to distributive questions. The distinction between deserts and entitlements, which is a feature of procedural justice, is abandoned, because in Dworkin's scheme there will be no unjust entitlements' (Barry 1995: 197). This follows from his assertion that every person is entitled to 'equal concern and respect' and a denial of adequate resources to people is a violation of that right.

The foremost critics of Rawlsian egalitarianism emerge in the US from amongst the liberals who style themselves as Neo-Conservatives since the later 1960s. They observe that the US is in the grip of implacable and intense egalitarianism and, Rawls as its representative thinker, shifts the meaning of equality to mean one of opportunities to one of outcomes (Bell 1979: 5). The concept of equality has been enlarged beyond its traditional scope of political rights and political power to include equity in economic power, social status and authority. The moral fervour with which equality is projected, results in a new despotism, which poses a singular threat to liberty (Nisbet 1974a and 1974b) and if ignored, will destroy the fabric of the liberal society (Kristol 1979). Contemporary populism, in its desire for wholesale egalitarianism insists in the end on complete levelling. It is not for fairness but against elitism: its impulse is not justice but resentment. The populists are for power but against authority represented in the superior competence of individuals. Since they lack authority they want power (Bell 1973: 453).

The neo-conservatives regard the clamour for equity warily, since it is difficult to fulfil such a desire. Kristol, Nisbet and to some extent Frankel assert that it is the intellectuals who cherish such an aspiration with the objective of extending their power through the state. They are skeptical of extensive governmental intervention and accept the ethics of liberal capitalism and decision-making through the free market, buttressed by traditions, customs and historical norms. They defend the classic liberal principle of equality of opportunity and admit that an overzealous government with the aim of promoting equity threatens merit advancement, with the aim of promoting equity. Increase in the government activity encroaches on the spontaneity of the individuals and voluntary organisations. The neo-conservatives see the shift from equality of opportunity to equality of condition as a mood towards populist levelling, resentment against authority represented in the superior competence of the individual. As a result, excellence, professional authority and technical expertise are compromised with. They reject Rawlsian theory for its undue stress on egalitarianism. Nisbet (1974b) compares Rawls with the eighteenth century philosophers and in particular to Rousseau, for his emphasis on the notion of an absolute individual and the idea of an absolute moral community which are seen as complementary and compatible. The first principle that Rawls offers does not have so much liberty as equals shared in a vast homogenised structure called liberty. It is utterly outweighed in mass and used by the second principle. Rawls, like Rousseau, expresses liberty in the language of equality and makes the two virtually synonymous. The fair equality of opportunity coupled with the difference principle tips the scale in the favour of an egalitarian society. The conception of justice will be better, if Rawls abandons his first principle. Much of the difficulty lay in the fact that he repeatedly presents liberty as an overall system in which individuals are to have 'equal shares' rather than in the nature of liberty itself. *A Theory of Justice* is 'consecrated to as radical a form of egalitarianism as may be found anywhere outside the pages of social contract' (Nisbet 1974a: 117). For Kristol, the concept of equality lacks a clear and precise meaning. It is not equality of incomes that is at stake. Rather the professional classes raise the banner of equality against the business community to gain power and status, for they regard the bourgeois society as deficient in its conception of common good.

Just Meritocracy

Bell stresses on equality among and for groups. When one speaks of the disadvantaged, it is normally understood in the sense of a group. He points out that it is difficult to measure fairness and it is all the more difficult to state whether the criterion will be subjective or objective. He castigates Rawls for not making it clear as to whether 'we are to accept the subjective evaluation of individuals as the moral norm, or an objective standard, and on what basis' (Bell 1973: 446). Reiterating an oft-repeated assertion, Bell observes that usually people evaluate unfairness or deprivation by comparing with their peers rather than by an absolute standard. People tolerate disparities in income and wealth provided they are justly earned. A social policy has to be such, to be able to determine as to the genuinely disadvantaged from those who out of choice like to remain disadvantaged. Any classification of the disadvantaged has to take precaution, for they may face social stigmatisation because of such a classification. A principle of equality has to be necessarily universal to guarantee impartiality of treatment to persons while simultaneously minimising administrative arbitrariness. Bell points out that Rawls, like Jencks, does not discuss either 'work' or 'effort' or merit, though he considers meritocracy. The fact is that there are different kinds of inequalities relating to income, wealth, status, power, opportunity (occupational and social) and education, 'There is not one scale but many, and the inequalities in one scale are not coupled completely with inequality in every other' (Bell 1973: 452). In this context, Bell formulates an alternate conception of a just meritocracy, which means social equality and respect for each person. Each person is entitled to a basic set of services and income, which will ensure his security and dignity. Meritocracy is defined as 'those who have earned status or have achieved positions of rational authority by competence. ... They are men who are the best in their field, as judged by their fellows' (1973: 454). He reiterates a distinction that **Runciman** makes between respect and praise, and points out that while every individual deserves respect, prestige or esteem, only some deserve praise. A society is just where inequalities are those of praise. It is important to acknowledge differences in achievements between individuals, for the very best in any field must reach the top and this does not contradict the principle of fairness. Nevertheless, a social policy has to take note of the problems of disadvantaged without limiting opportunities for the meritorious to rise to the top. The three principles of merit, achievement and universalism are the essential bedrock, 'for production and a cultivated society' (Bell 1973: 454). The important point to note is that society must be truly an open one. Defenders of meritocracy argue that while genetic endowments are inviolable, social and cultural advantages are not. A person's natural endowments are deeply and intimately his, constitutive of his personality and identity more than the socially conditioned attributes. This assertion is true but it is equally right to suppose, as Rawls does, that a person's characteristics and values are conditioned by the social and cultural environment in which he lives, which for Bell makes the person disappear with only his attributes remaining. (1973: 419). Both Kristol and Bell believe that conflict between competing claims can be resolved by ensuring a meritocracy, in which status and income are allocated on the basis of education and skill rather than on the basis of inheritance, private property or political power, with a guarantee of social minimum to assure every individual of a certain minimum standard of living. They reject equality of condition because it will lead to social instability. Furthermore, Bell points out that the income disparities over the years have been mitigated, not by distribution through policies and judgements about fairness but by technology, which assures increased productivity at affordable prices for all. He points out that meritocracy is a logical outcome of the post-industrial society, which creates technical elites, reshapes the existing class structure of society with differential status and differential incomes based on technical skills and educational qualifications, thus, ensuring a process for the competent and the qualified to make it. **Kristol** defends meritocracy by arguing that human talents and abilities distribute along a bell-shaped curve and the distribution of income and political power also follow the same pattern. To this, **Walzer** observes that there is no reason to assume only a single curve and that 'most people (different in each case) cluster around the middle of whatever we can construct with smaller numbers at the lower and higher ends' (Walzer 1973: 399). Walzer (1983) conceives a **post-liberal state** that accepts moral membership in a community as the greatest good and has a concern for the issue of complex equality. The underlying notion of the idea of complex equality is that each resource must be distributed according to a principle appropriate to its own sphere. The critics on the Left criticise Rawls for not narrowing the gap between the advantaged and disadvantaged and in not abolishing the category of the worst-off. **Macpherson** (1977) points out that for Rawls a classless society is 'unthinkable' and in principle 'impossible' and accuses Rawls for neglecting the way exploitation works, affecting the transfer of human powers leading to inequality in a capitalist society.

However, Rawls' critics misunderstand the clear and precise relationship that Rawls establishes between individual performance, not on desert but with reference to one's contributions to society viewed as a reciprocal exchange of services. His two principles of justice ensures moral equal among individuals by attenuating uncompassionate selfishness and 'deprives men of threat advantages against one another' (Chapman 1975: 590). The distinctiveness of the individual is preserved and recognised within a societal context. Neither the well-off nor the worse-off are required to make undue sacrifices, which are disproportionate to the benefits they receive. He synthesises liberalism with economic egalitarianism by taking into account the notions of just reward and human needs. Crick (1972: 602) concedes that 'he is profoundly wrong but almost perfectly relevant'. For Rawls, like Weber, society is composed of disparate income groups. Rawls represents the Keynesian consensus as outlined by Crosland in *The Future of Socialism* (1956) to which Galbraith and Schumpeter agrees.

> Marx had little or nothing to offer the contemporary socialist, either in respect of practical policy, or of the correct analysis of our society, or even of the right conceptual tools or framework (Crosland 1956: 2).

Post Industrial Society

The Keynesian revolution, the welfare state, institutionalised working of democracy and independent trade union movements have ensured alleviation of mass miseries, controlled inflation, guaranteed economic growth and an overall unprecedented rise in the standards of living, not only in the developed countries but even in the developing ones. These defend equality through diffusion of incomes and wealth, broad consumption base and economic expansion. Structurally, capitalism had undergone what **Burnham** calls the **managerial revolution** and an important indicator of this is the fact that twentieth century has not been able to produce a Carnegie or a Rockefeller. Furthermore, 'the proletarian class also no longer exists in its previous shape. Workers have rights, in developed countries they are proprietors' (Djilas 1990: 7). These changes are characterised as 'post economic' or 'post capitalist' (Dahrendorf 1959); 'post bourgeois' (Lichtheim 1963; Brezezinski 1979), 'trans-industrial' and 'super-industrial society' (Tofler 1979) and as 'post business' (Drucker 1939). The indicators of developments within advanced societies by the mid-twentieth century were (a) importance of authority rather than ownership; (b) spread of public ownership creating a new balance between public and private sectors transcending the bourgeois characteristics of capitalism; (c) a significant role for science; (d) a change in the composition of the ruling class as consisting of heads of bureaucratic hierarchies, cabinet ministers, administrative staff and judges. The new society is a service economy rather than goods producing one, reflecting a change in the occupational structure. In comparison to the total population, the low-skilled workers are less than ten percent. The demand for those with greater education and qualifications is on the increase. The pyramidical shape of occupational distribution of the working population has given way to a diamond shaped one because of rapid expansion in educational opportunities allowing persons from the poor and deprived families to avail of higher university degrees. There is an end to family capitalism, made possible by the growth of large scale bureaucracies and increase in the size and functions of government (Lipset 1979: 9). Professionals and technical class have become influential in decision making, thus, creating a new 'intellectual rather than machine technology' (Bell 1990: 188).

Fallacy in Marxism

Marxism visualises society as being divided into two classes, which in due course polarise and rupture societal fabric, paving the way for a new society that will be classless. This prediction did not sustain for long. **Bernstein** points out that far from polarising into a vast majority of proletariat and a bourgeois minority there is the growth of the middle class. In the Erfurt Programme, he mentions that the peasantry and middle class are not disappearing; small business organisations are not getting eliminated, nor are the industrial working class the overwhelming majority of the population. He observes 'peasants do not sink, middle class does not disappear, crises do not grow ever larger, misery and serfdom do not increase' (1961: 56). These, he substantiates with help of evidence of property ownership and income tax returns filed by people in the industrialised societies of Europe in the late nineteenth century.

> The number of propertied has not diminished but become larger. The enormous increase in social wealth is accompanied not by shrinking number of capitalist magnates but by a growing number of capitalists of all ranges of wealth. The middle classes change their character but they do not disappear from the social scale ... the number of propertied is growing absolutely and relatively (1961: 88).

Bernstein points out that the new middle class consists of technical personnel, white-collar workers, office and sales clerks and government employees. These categories are increasing along with mounting bureaucratisation of monopoly capitalism. Their incomes are not only higher than the wage labourers but their social standing is also closer to the bourgeoisie. He recognises that the working class by itself is not homogenous, anticipating Poulantaz's differentiation between the working class consisting of productive labourers who are separate from the white-collar supervisory workers. He could also see capitalism stabilising itself through the creation of monopolies and cartels, through the credit system, through the growth of world market coupled with tremendous improvements in communications and transportation, and increased wealth of industrialised states in Western Europe. The ownership in the joint stock companies was spreading widely. The real wages of the workers were rising with trade unions safeguarding their rights and the middle class was expanding. Workers were steadily growing in size, power and social importance with citizenship rights and power to seize them, if denied or withdrawn. All these changes were making modern capitalism adaptable and immune to depressions and growing misery. Bernstein's analysis establishes the point that Dahl (1986: 69) makes about the relevance of 'Marx's economics as a reaction to specific evils of early nineteenth century capitalism'.

The idea of the communist society being classless and equal remained a myth. Djilas in the *New Class* (1959) pointed to the presence of the *nomenklatura* in the former communist societies. The nomenklatura enjoyed privileges and special status because of their position within the hierarchy of the Communist Party. This confirms Rousseau's objections that communism uses power as the basis of privilege and **Bakunin's** fear that the dictatorship of the proletariat would create fresh inequities and new forms of oppression and domination. Perhaps no one has captured the myth of a classless society better than **George Orwell** (1903–1950) in his satire *Animal Farm* (1945) and *Nineteen Eight Four* (1949) with memorable phrases as 'all animals are equal but some are more equal than others' and 'big brother is watching'. The Marxist regimes and theory naively assume that anything collective is fulfilling and morally better than private ones. They ignore the age-old wisdom of Aristotle's criticism of Plato's regime of common wives and common property on the grounds that altruism is possible only if it is an extension of self-love. The good of the many has to be based on the good of the self. If personal love, dignity and esteem are ignored, there would be general indifference and feeling of neglect, as was the case with the erstwhile communist societies. The latter's failure to develop the notion of just reward and just meritocracy only led to a situation where the self-worth and self esteem of the ordinary citizen was not respected.

Vaclav Havel, the former President of the Czech Republic condemns these societies for undermining and humiliating the ordinary person's moral character and dignity and their belief in their own capacity to act as moral agents. **Rabindranath Tagore** (1861–1941), as early as 1930s, compares Bolshevism as a medical treatment for a sick society and comments 'indeed the day on which the doctor's regime comes to an end must be hailed as a red letter day for the patient' (1960: 111) This also had an economic dimension. By failing to reward people according to their contribution and work these societies failed to evolve standards of efficiency and productivity to sustain their visions of overtaking the West as Khurshchev or Mao promised to their respective countries.

EQUALITY, FAMILY AND WOMEN

Feminist political theory from its inception stresses on the value of equality between men and women and demands a justification for their different legal and political treatment. In the nineteenth century, it questions laws that allowed men but not women the right to vote and laws that prevented married women from inheriting property and having custody of their children. Liberal and socialist feminism demand equal political rights and access to resources to women within the liberal capitalist state. Their concern is more with women's oppression than sexual inequality as they understand inequality as non-citizenship and exploitation of women. The **liberal feminists** seek to reform the traditional family and accord women their dignity, self-respect and independence by demanding rights of marriage, property, inheritance and custody. **Hobbes** explicitly recognises women's right to equality, repudiating the claim that in the state of nature, dominion over the children belongs to the father alone. He claims that the mother is the original lord of her children in the state of nature. The natural domination of mother is accepted for it is she who can declare the father of her child. Women do not need the protection from men as they have the same strength and capability that men have. However, he later endorses the dominion of men over women in civil society and theoretically moves away from gender equality in the state of nature to sexual inequality in the civil society. The woman becomes subservient to the man within the family for there can be only one decision-making authority and that shall go to the man, since he was physically strong and able. Locke (1960: 345–346) also guarantees women an equal title to power over their children to refute the derivation of political from parental authority, for if the father dies, the children will naturally owe obedience only to their mother. He treats husbands and wives as equal in his critique of absolute government but, like Hobbes, he too argues that the wife shall accept her subordination through the marriage contract to the husband who is physically by nature stronger and abler. However, he considers women contributing to civic culture though he does not elaborate nor suggest ways and means of their political activity.

Wollstonecraft demands equal opportunities for education, civil rights and employment as they establish the dignity and independence of women. **J.S. Mill** reiterates these demands and adds political rights to vote and to be represented. Both confidently argue that women will not sacrifice their primary responsibilities of being wives and mothers, thus, retaining but reforming the private home along the principles of equality and justice. Pateman (1988) accuses liberal feminists of harbouring a masculine bias and not being gender neutral in their conception of individuality. The **socialist** and **Marxist feminists** accept the arguments of liberal feminists but propose abolition of nuclear family along with capitalism, as it is wasteful, inefficient, oppressive and exploitative. Women will be relieved of domestic chores through communal households, common kitchens, dining and child rearing. However, neither the liberals nor the socialist Marxist feminists question the sexual division of labour. They continue to support separate but equal spheres of work. Liberal and socialist feminism glorify motherhood as the most important and fulfilling of women's social functions considering child rearing as the most important task but never got men to shoulder domestic responsibilities. However, the liberals unlike the socialists do not denigrate household work and thereby respect the work that majority of women do.

The **Radical feminists** note that even where laws are gender-neutral women remain at a disadvantage. In most Western liberal democracies, though there are no more laws that prohibit women from being politically active yet there are very few women than men, in positions of political power and influence. This suggests that attaining full, as distinct from formal, political equality requires something more than legal change and law, which are gender-neutral. As a result, feminists have been concerned to defend a concept of equality that goes beyond the formal equality of gender-neutral laws. They stress the notion of difference, meaning that an argument for equality implies uniformity of treatment, while interests in society are in fact plural. Therefore, instead of basing public decision-making on the principle of one person, one vote, the notion of difference allows some groups to be given a special say in the matters of public policy. For example, women should have a veto over changes pertaining to the law on abortion. The radical feminists confront the dilemma as to whether women and men are equal because they are the same, or are they equal but different? 'The project of women's equal inclusion meant that only women's sameness to men, only women's humanity and not their womanliness could be discussed' (Gross 1986: 191). An early voice of caution against gender equality is that of Rousseau who argues for the need to acknowledge sexual differences between men and women by providing different types of education. Only then, can there be meaningful equality.

Interestingly, the equality-difference debate on the woman's question goes back to the time of **Plato** and **Aristotle**. Plato insists that men and women are the same and equal and deserving equal treatment in public life, while Aristotle points to their difference and on that basis justifies their exclusion from public space. The modern socialists reiterate Plato's vision and like Plato, obliterate the public-private divide, while Aristotle's view has resulted in **two** broad developments—a direct legacy in Rousseau and Hegel who on the basis of women's difference consider them to be a source of public disorder and the other, the **liberal** view, retains Aristotle's public-private divide but, unlike Aristotle, tries to argue a case for equal rights.

These two schools—liberal and socialist/Marxist feminists—represent two distinct approaches in feminist political philosophy. In the first case, political theory's concern for equality is shown as incompatible with laws that give women fewer political rights than men. In the second case, political theory's formalistic interpretation is questioned. At times, they press for a consistent application of the core concepts of political theory, while at other times, they demand a reconsideration of some concepts and, in particular, concepts like justice and equality. Explanation is sought as to what are the grounds for excluding domestic affairs considered to be part of the private sphere from the principles of justice and equality and treating it outside the political. Their claim that 'the personal is political' meaning the decision as to what will and what will not count as the proper business of the state is a decision that has a political dimension. They contend that in private life it is compassion and concern that is more important than justice and equality. If the distinction between the private and the public is done away with, then concern and compassion will be more important than justice and equality.

The slogan 'the personal is political' is well-known but the key point is that it has had very little relevance for the ordinary woman and lacks popular backing, which explains the dead-end that contemporary feminist theory and movement finds itself in. This is because radical feminism renounces the libertarian presuppositions of early liberalism. **Okin** (1989) is correct in insisting that a guarantee of equality within the home and family will secure and safeguard the social and economic rights of women and children and to that extent the vision of the early feminists—Wollstonecraft and J.S. Mill—still retains value for contemporary times. For, it is within this framework that a larger equality for women in other aspects of life can be worked out. A meaningful feminist discourse within the complexities of our increasingly technological and democratic society calls for a re-introduction of the liberal premise of a public-private divide as an essential pre-requisite of feminism as well. There is also a growing realisation against the false universality of the gender question. The crux of the matter is that though gender is the most important social division it is not the sole basis of mass political identities that structure political debate and establish political parties. Besides gender, a person has multiple identities that include social class, ethnicity, religion and region. These multiple roles prevent the perpetuation of any single identity as decisive. Within this multiplicity of identities, the gender question has to be discussed and accommodated. This applies not only to gender but all other mega categories of religion, ethnicity and class. Like radical feminism some of these too have questioned the private-public divide of the liberal state. However, the intermingling of the public and private only leads to unmitigated disaster, as has been seen with the collapse of communism and Khomeini-style fundamentalism.

The working of a complex and diverse global economy based on sophisticated technology has also fractured the single agency of women into multiplicity of diverse groups, individuals and split subjects. Women are increasingly occupying elite economic, political, administrative and scientific positions rendering obsolete the male centricism in these areas of human endeavour. Furthermore, there is a general realisation that meta-theories (patriarchy) group identities ('all women' versus 'all men') and visions (women's liberation) or grand narratives (feminism) are no longer feasible and sustainable. This is not only true of feminism but also of any other theory, like Marxism, that claims to be universally applicable without being specific to any particular situation. The survival of feminism like Marxism, in this period of universalisation of democracy depends on its capacity to offer something positive to all categories of women while taking into consideration specific requirements like class, level of development and societal expectation.

For the past two decades, with the end of the Cold War, the political agenda in most of the well-established democracies has been dominated by social issues replacing security concerns. Issues like women's rights and empowerment, rights for ethnic minorities, disabled and environmental protection are being vigorously debated. As a result, all the important political parties are casting-off their traditional image and trying to emerge as 'catch them all parties'. This they have done by extending the traditional democratic argument for equity and formulating an agenda that represents all segments of society. The women's movement too has to adjust with multiple identities and get meaningfully integrated with other concerns, like environmental protection, human rights, safety nets and basic economic rights within a larger democratic structure.

In the context of the developing world, feminism and the women's movement is to identify itself with the realisation of social and economic rights for the disadvantaged and under-represented, which will automatically include poor women. With regard to nutritional, child rearing and educative functions, the upliftment of majority is the basic precondition for raising the standard of women, as the consideration between a baby or a car ultimately depends on the total and shared societal prosperity. The success of the Chipko movement in the Himalayan foothills proves the point that basic economic issues cannot be separated from the purely abstract political rights. They are to co-exist, intermingle and reinforce each other, which also means that human deprivation and the gulf between the rich and the poor is as much a concern for the women's movement as it is for other radical initiatives. Simon de Beauvoir

(1908–1986) justifiably comments that women coming from relatively affluent section, side more with their father, brother and husband rather than identifying themselves with women of lower classes. Gender does not exist in a vacuum. It survives and develops within a larger social and economic context and the larger questions ultimately determine the status, expectation or retardation or fulfillment of the particular segment. This calls for a delicate balancing between the different segments of life and activity. A democratic solution to a problem means more democracy in social, economic and political sense and with a commitment to equality. The achievement of the Scandinavian countries in ensuring economic and political equality of women and the spectacular breakthrough made by Mandela's African National Congress, Blair's New Labour or Clinton's Presidency in increasing women's representation and participation proves that enormous advancement of women is possible within the existing liberal democratic structure. Zweighaft and Domoff (1998) in their interesting study of the power elite in the United States, in the 1990s, have concluded that the power elite has become multicultural and that more women are clearly and steadily visible in the corporate world and cabinets. In corporate boards, the percentage of women has crossed ten percent. The Clinton cabinets (1993–2000) had the highest percentage of women till date with twenty-one percent in the first cabinet and thirty-one percent in the second cabinet, serving key posts like Secretary of State and Attorney General.

What the feminists can seek to do is to plead for the acceptance of special rights for women like maternity leave, child care, taking into consideration that women require these not as privileges but to give effect to the realisation of their basic human rights. Interpreted this way, such rights will be akin to the fulfilling of other societal obligations like consideration of the poor, elderly, children and the handicapped which will mean integration with the larger societal objectives. Evolving ways and means of this integration and not continuing with separateness with inevitable marginality is the challenge that the women's movement faces today. Contemporary feminist writing as pointed out is trying to satisfactorily theorise about racial or class difference by turning to notions of coalition-building of integrating women's experience and women's interests into a shared notion of oppression. At the same time, there is a significant calling back to politics in contemporary feminism.

Furthermore, there is a need for feminists to rethink their attack on patriarchy and on the traditional family structures that suited women as well as men. Since most women yearn for long-term bonding that ensures care and support for themselves and their offspring, patriarchal structures provided that by binding men with long-term obligations. Women use their power to control sexual access in return for long-term support, a fact which feminists overlook by projecting women as the victims of male exploitation. As a consequence, women have lost out as men have been licensed to be free and irresponsible. The corrosion of patriarchy means less fidelity and greater sexual competition and inequality with more middle-aged women being abandoned and left alone to fend for themselves. The loss of patriarchy has also lead to heightened violence and anti-social behaviour among men, since women alone have to shoulder the burden of responsibility for authority and discipline within the family. Feminists also ignore the fact that women also inflict harm just as men within the family and therefore what needs to be protested against is not male or female authority but abuses of power by both men and women. Instead of a crusade against abuses of power, the feminists have waged a self-defeating sex war in which both men and women still continue to abuse power while the idea of authority has nose-dived with disastrous consequences. Children need both the parents for their emotional and practical needs and that's how interdependence between men and women started within the families. Though women have made impressive strides in most walks of life, most of them still continue to emphasise the importance of homemaking and child rearing as their primary role. Women can continue to do both by getting men involved in domestic work just as they play a larger role in the public sphere. The gender question cannot be meaningful if it does not address the needs of the whole families by seeing women and men as complimentary and not as two separate halves. This will ensure equilibrium resulting in independence and affinity that characterise a settled and cohesive family. The family needs to regain its once privileged position reformed and reinvented that stresses complimentary roles for both men and women.

RELATIONSHIP WITH JUSTICE

Equality is closely linked with justice since the eighteenth century at least when doctrines of human equality and 'rights of man' were firmly established in political thought. All individuals deserve equal treatment unless it can be proven to the contrary. Equality before law replaces the feudal system of different grades of citizens and their different courts and their different legal rights. However, a belief in equality does not lead to an egalitarian theory of social justice, for the faith in basic human equality can co-exist with the principle that people differ in certain ways and therefore, shall be treated differently. Fairness requires that equal cases are treated equally. Definitely a notion of equal treatment is a part of the theory of justice for one does have an intuitive idea of fair and unfairness. Equality may play an important part in a substantive theory of justice in two ways—first, ensuring an egalitarian distribution of goods and second, as an ordering principle at a lesser level as a part of due process, requires equal cases to be treated alike and with regard to distribution of goods. Generally, justice is understood in the sense of 'fair and non-arbitrary treatment of equals' although it does not necessarily require a substantive equality between individuals. Theories of justice need to identify the types of inequalities that make unequal treatment inappropriate—inequalities of ability, need and merit for instance.

Procedural theories of justice have a feeble sense of justice that implies, irrespective of differences, all human beings are entitled to be treated equally by the rules of a social practice. This view is not necessarily egalitarian and it accepts the fact that all inequalities have to be justified. This is clearly evident in Rawls' theory. Classical liberals argue that a tendency to equality is baseless for that may cause paying the same income to individuals whose contributions to the output of an economy may be widely different. Equality can, therefore, conflict with principles of justice, especially, desert-based theories of justice even though it is a fundamental ingredient of social justice. An appeal to equality is not a camouflaged demand for the removal of some unjustified inequalities so that all economic and social differences have some rational basis rather it is an argument for equality itself (Barry 1965: 120). Political and constitutional rights like the equal right to vote in a democracy, laws prohibiting sexual and racial discrimination are examples of the application of equality. However, to reduce all arguments for egalitarianism to policies that remove arbitrary privileges is to misunderstand the prescriptive meaning of equality. This point is made clear by Berlin when he says of equality, that 'like all human ends it cannot be rationally justified for it is itself that which justifies other acts ...' (1955–1956: 326). As a pluralist, Berlin (1961) believes that equality has to be traded off against other values.

The emphasis on equality as an important aspect of social justice means that egalitarians do not have to invoke the concept of moral desert to justify particular income distributions and in that they have something in common with *laissez faire* liberals. An egalitarian who also values liberty will distrust centralised institutions deciding a person's worth subject to political controls. The principle of need is more complex, since the satisfaction of needs is a basic matter in the egalitarian's social programme. Yet, there are serious problems in deciding what needs are and linking these to equality. While it is correct that people need food, clothing and shelter, it is obvious that they do not need equal shares of these things. Theories of social justice try to justify the satisfaction of quite different needs. Egalitarianism is a relational doctrine that makes comparative judgements about people's positions on a particular scale and tries to equalise them.

RELATIONSHIP WITH LIBERTY

Is liberty and equality antithetical? For a long time, liberty implied 'equality in liberty' and that is not the case in contemporary times. At present, liberty and equality are recognised as distinct and separate and efforts to advance equality may not achieve liberty and even perhaps destroy liberty, a claim that needs to be re-examined. How valid is the argument that equality presupposes liberty?

We must recognise the fact that liberty has to exist first to be able to demand equality in the sense that one who is un-free cannot claim equality. Just as freedom *from* is the basis for all other liberties, freedom *to* is similarly the precondition for equality. 'Deprive equals of the liberty to "voice for" and they become equal in being voiceless and abused' (Sartori 1987: 358). Once liberty is securely granted the clamour for equality becomes stronger since the ideal of equality seems tangible with material benefits while liberty and its benefits are intangible. This also explains as to why economic equality among all equalities rally people around. Equal distribution of wealth and incomes though desirable can be realised within and without liberal democracy bringing one to the question—When does equality implement liberty, and what kind of equality becomes inimical to liberty? If equality is understood as sameness, it involves minimal intrusion into liberty. However, if equality is understood as equalisation of circumstances, then it involves considerable measures of redistribution, which means intervention by the state in the functioning of the economy and the market. In this sense, efforts to maximise equality is at the expense of liberty. 'So long as the equalisation of circumstances is sought in equal starting points, the pursuit of equality and the requirements of liberty can find a balance and do, if uneasily rebalance one another, Up to this point we remain within liberal democracy' (Sartori 1987: 359–360). This gets offset the moment the state becomes the sole employer and controller of all the means of production and then an enormous disparity between the rulers and ruled comes about. In liberal democracies, economic and political powers are in separate hands and even if they connive they also conflict, whereas, who can control an all-owning and all-controlling state? It is in this situation that equality destroys freedom and even liberal democracy.

> Equality is *only* (nothing more than) a condition of freedom. In particular, it is a condition of freedom but by no means a *sufficient condition* of freedom. A dictatorial polity may enforce participation (everybody must vote) and simultaneously deny freedom of participation (nobody can vote for an alternative). Clearly, equal participation does not entail free participation. It may also be doubted whether equality is a *necessary condition* of freedom (Sartori 1987: 361).

Exponents of economic equality argue as to what is the use of freedom to a starving person? Sartori replies by pointing out that in 'the illiberal systems the problem is not solved by giving more bread away but taking away the right to ask for it' (1981: 361). This clearly reveals that there cannot be any trade off between liberal constitutional authority and an authoritarian one under the guise of equality. What is crucial is the importance of political freedom and 'that a very "unreal" freedom follows for those who call for equality confusing it with freedom. ... Who will equalise the equalisers is not an equality issue—it is a liberty issue' (Sartori 1987: 362). A familiar refrain is that liberty benefits only a few while equality is to the advantage of the many. However, what is ignored is that with liberty neither the few nor the many will be successful in abusing one another whereas with equality both the few and the many may find themselves in bondage. The fact is that the principle of liberty cannot be reversed—in actual practice—into its very opposite which, however, is possible with the principle of equality. The important thing to be realised is that liberal democracy, in comparison to its rivals—fascism and communism—has safeguarded and guaranteed both liberty and equality by maintaining the conditions of equality. There may be tensions between equality and liberty but they are not inimical to one another.

Affirmative Action and Equality

In India the question of reservation has created considerable controversy in recent times. A major defense in favour of reservation is of past deprivation and systematic discrimination. To rectify it, privileges are generally suggested like reservation in jobs and educational courses including coveted ones like medicine and engineering. The two important defenses of this practice are (a) compensatory justice to rectify unjustified discrimination against certain sections and (b) the argument of bringing in equality by state intervention in the form of reservation for the deprived.

A significant criticism of the theory, however, emanates from a procedural presumption that grant of such privileges is both discriminatory and unjust to the persons who are denied this access. This criticism is vindicated by the fact that it is the rich and the socially favoured sections that corner all the advantages rather than the poor and the underprivileged. An added dimension to it is that the worst off do not really get anything out of it because reservation calls for certain educational qualifications which many in these category do not have.

The controversy centres on whether the benefit of reservation should have an individualistic economic basis or a collective one? Any theory of equality will have to be based on some criteria of both needs and rewards. The case against collective reservation is that of disincentive as it may not result in excellence. Apart from this, there is also a psychological dimension to the issue of reservation as it grossly violates the principles of self respect and human dignity. Narrating from his personal experience, Charles Murray points out that the welfare measures broke down the dividing line between the economically independent and being on welfare.

The capacity of reservation either to lead towards more equality or just meritocracy is very limited. The major reason for this is that the people who get benefits like to perpetuate the advantages though it distances the beneficiaries further from the disadvantaged within their own community. The process leads to further alienation of the majority within the reserved categories. An interesting offshoot of the reservation debate in the mid 1960s in the United States, at a time when the question of Black deprivation became a major issue in American politics, the views of some of the Black leaders were in sharp contrast to the ones articulated by the pro-Reservations in India in the mid 1990s. Jesse Jackson points out to the historic economic discrimination by way of two examples against the Blacks—one, a soft drink franchise which did not have a single Black and second, in the automobile industry where the Blacks' share was negligible, leading to a trade deficit of five billion dollars. The net result of it is that the Blacks are disproportionately large on 'public aid or in desperation'. The solution to the problem is not an introduction of a quota but an opportunity with all its risks or reward or loss. He also encourages the Blacks to take up more challenging openings. He points out that if Blacks could be excellent in baseball and basketball they could be excellent in math also but for that to happen they ought to spend more time with their home work and not watch television. Martin Luther King Jr. wanted the furtherance of the civil rights movement by granting Blacks preferential treatment not because of the abuses of the past but because 'the back wheels of a car can never be the front wheels of a car while they are travelling at the same rate of speed'.

Professor Sowell rejects the popular notion that the female headed the Black family is an outcome of slavery. He links it to the welfare state period when government started to subsidise desertion and teenage pregnancy. He contends that as a result of preferential treatment, the Blacks have fallen further behind as only the well-offs have benefitted, marginalising the poor and worst-off. The inadequacy of preferential treatment in elevation is voiced by all these three Black leaders. Their view is supported by the Moynihan Report of 1973 which argues that the basic structural inadequacy of the present system is the large Black female employment which leads to a familiar co-relation between Black poverty and female headed households. Moynihan asserts that it is important to provide opportunities to the Black families and not be concerned with how these families 'run their affairs, take advantage of its opportunities, or their failure to do so'.

The American experience tells us that mere quotas and preferences can never lead to the reduction of inequality among the deprived. Constitutional quotas, like the ones in India, usually create a new class that develops an interest in perpetuating the quota system. The Indian Supreme Court rejects the idea of creamy layer.

CONCLUSION

Cole argues that if there is a choice between poverty and slavery, he will choose the first one. This brings to the surface the problem which comes up while dealing with the concept of equality. A plausible theory of equality may not be formulated in isolation without taking note of other problems of politics and society at large. For instance, Rawls places high premium on efficiency in the well-ordered society committed to the elevation of the least advantaged. Sen (1990) also demonstrates that human misery can best be tackled by accepting democracy as the foundation. Equality mostly means the equality of condition and not the outcome. In fact, more is the equality of condition, more is the inequality of outcome, exemplified by the existence of the richest families in countries well-known for providing the equality of condition. The worldwide spread of the market economy today has enhanced inequality further, which means as Dahl acknowledges 'unequal economic resources will mean unequal political resources' (1996: 647). To change the scenario, the need is for 'sweeping government policies and actions, far more extensive than now exists or are now on the political agenda in any democratic country' (Dahl 1996: 648). However, the important point to note is that the debate about equality is far from over and the intensity of it may increase in the future if more inequality manifests both within and amongst nations.

Further Readings

Beitz, C.R., *Political Equality: An Essay in Democratic Theory*, Princeton University Press, Princeton, NJ, 1981.

Beteille, A. (Ed.), *Equality and Inequality: Theory and Practice*, Oxford University Press, Delhi, 1983.

Charvet, J., *A Critique of Freedom and Equality*, Cambridge University Press, London, 1981.

Dixon, K., *Freedom and Equality: The Moral Basis of Democratic Socialism*, Routledge, London, 1981.

Friedrich, C.J. and Chapman, J.W. (Eds.), *NOMOS VI: Equality*, Atherton Press, New York, 1963.

Nielsen, K., *Equality and Liberty: A Defense of Radical Egalitarianism*, Rowman and Allan held Publishers, New York, 1985.

Nussbaum, M. and Sen, A., *The Quality of Life*, Clarendon Press, Oxford, 1993.

Okun, A.M., *Equality and Efficiency: The Big Trade Off*, The Brookings Institute, Washington DC, 1975.

Rae, D., *Equalities*, Harvard University Press, Cambridge Massachusetts, 1981.

Rees, J., *Equality*, Macmillan, London, 1981.

Turner, B., *Equality*, Macmillan, London, 1986.

Chapter 14
Property

The question of property has elicited wide-ranging debate and controversies in political theory. Thinkers from different philosophical persuasions assume that it is one of the most important components of the conditions of life, liberty and the pursuit of happiness. At one end of the spectrum property is considered as a natural right necessary for human dignity, freedom and decent life. On the other end, it is denounced as an evil as the single most important cause for the rise of inequality and a tool for oppressing and exploiting the many by the few. There is considerable debate about the extent of property rights in a society; while some consider private ownership to be sacrosanct, others demand common ownership arguing that, it symbolises the natural human condition. Property is more than a relationship to things or possessions. It is an essentially social and political concept for it determines 'the relations of the various groups of owners and non-owners to the system of production, and prescribe what each groups' share of the social product shall be' (Schlatter 1951: 273). The arguments for and against private property invoke criteria like need, justice, freedom and utility. Furthermore, debates on private property also involve issues concerning, how free or regulated trade and market should be, and the rationale for division of labour. Much of the controversy surrounding property arises from contradictory claims about the role of the market and, for those who oppose it, alternative mechanisms of allocation. Since time immemorial the close link between property and power has been recognised. This dimension is clearly evident in the struggle for ending slavery and the extension of franchise to the working class and women. The notion of private property involves three features. (1) The right to exclude, namely the right of the owner to exclude other(s) from using or accessing his property, though exclusiveness is a matter of degree. For instance, the owner can refuse a police officer if the latter does not have a warrant to search his premises. (2) The right of the owner to use as he wills but with conditions like one cannot destroy one's house or alter without authorised permission. (3) The right to transfer with the freedom to alienate which classical liberal theory considers important. Some forms of transfer may be forbidden or penalised by taxation, like gift tax or capital transfer tax. It is this third feature that creates the possibility of accumulation and leads to inequalities of wealth. Property rights are rights of control that is a pre-condition to social order. Therefore, maintenance of property right is an important function of the state and law (Benn and Peters 1959: 157, 158).

Macpherson distinguishes private from common property. The former is a right to exclude others and the latter is a right not to be excluded (1973: 124). Ryan suggests a distinction that can be drawn between theorists who take an 'instrumental' view of property from those who articulate a 'self-developmental' view. The instrumental view 'regards work or labour as a cost incurred by men who want to consume the goods thus made available to them' (1984: 7). The self-developmental view is that work 'is, or can be and certainly should be, intrinsically satisfying' and 'that the relationship between a man and what he owns is intrinsically significant; there is a substantial bond between a man and his property, a bond which repays philosophical analysis' (1984: 11). A distinction which is made between natural and legal rights with regard to rights in general is also made in the case of property.

HISTORICAL ORIGINS OF THE DEBATE

The dispute over property is not new. It begins with Plato and Aristotle over common ownership and is repeated in the medieval natural law theory. **Plato** proposes **common property** for the ruling Guardian class, for he grasps the negative effects of the nexus between political power and economic power and desires a government that will promote common good rather than the personal interests of the rulers. **Aristotle** criticising Plato's conception points out that it is wrong to attribute all the troubles in the world to the institution of property. He argues that most evils stem from human nature, which common ownership cannot remedy. Instead, a moral change is required through education and training under good laws that will enable property owners to work towards common good. While common ownership may liberate individuals from the ugly consequences of **private property**, it also denies them the benefits that accrue from possessing something. Rather than abolishing private property altogether, Aristotle proposes the principle of Golden Mean or moderation that steers clear of wealth and poverty, opulence and squalor and helps in maintaining property within limits as prescribed by nature. 'With the partial exception of the Levellers from Aristotle to the late eighteenth century, it was generally agreed that it is the greatest blessing for a state that its members should possess a moderate and adequate property' (Heater 1990: 168–169). Aristotle mentions the virtues of benevolence and generosity that private possessions endow reducing selfishness and envy. He is convinced that a well-regulated institution of property will be socially beneficial.

Like Plato, Aristotle considers economic activity to be highly significant for the purpose of political analysis. Economic activity, he recognises has to be subordinated to the political, since the former is concerned with a single good while the latter's concern is with good life as a whole in its multi-dimensional sense. He distinguishes **natural** and **unnatural** form of acquisition, with the former needed for subsistence, while the latter sanctions unlimited accumulation, which Aristotle objects. Instead, he prefers accumulation that results in the right amount of wealth though he did not specify what that right amount will be. He points out that the intermediate stage between natural and unnatural forms of acquisition is barter, which in due course, because of the inconveniences, will give way to the introduction of money. In the course of time, the natural purpose of exchange, the abundant satisfaction of wants is lost sight of with accumulation of money becoming an end in itself. Following this Greek prejudice, he rejects retail trade on moral grounds, for the end of wealth, whether household income or that of a state has to be good life. He desires to limit the scope of commerce and give it an ethical basis, thus, remaining within the Platonic tradition. He also points out that economic activities like fishing, shoemaking and farming are those that fulfil the needs of the producer and his family and thus have a use-value. However, as society becomes more complex with increase in trade and specialisation of labour, production will take place for the purpose of exchange, thus giving a product its exchange value, a distinction subsequently invoked by Marx. Aristotle is also the first to pay attention to the economic basis of political institutions by focusing on the character and distribution of wealth and its influence on the government.

The most outstanding development of the concept of property happens in the Roman law that grants property owners unlimited right to use and abuse their property. Economic ideas are part of the moral teachings of Christianity. Medieval society combines the teachings of the Gospels and of the early Christian Fathers with those of Aristotle who moderates his economic views with ethical postulates. The Canonists accepts Aristotle's distinction between the natural economy of the household and the unnatural art of money-making. They understand economics as a body of laws, not in the sense of scientific laws but as moral precepts that would ensure the good administration of economic activity. Avarice, covetousness and worldly goods are condemned and made secondary to the material advancement of the individual and his fellow-beings. The Church condemns practices that increases exploitation and inequality and at times preaches indifference to miseries of this world. St. Augustine fears that trade would turn human beings away from the search for god.

Medieval society defines property in terms of the human person as the steward responsible to god and hence not entitled to absolute and unrestricted ownership rights of the earth. Moreover, private property is considered to be a product of a person's sin. According to this conception, the earth and its fruits belong to all human beings in common and private property arises out of human greed. The medieval times roots property rights in a cluster of social and political relationships encompassed in one word *dominium*, referring to property and political authority, while in modern usage dominion means political authority. The lack of any absolute right of ownership along with the idea of common ownership is the natural condition and this means that property rights do not assume primacy. In the later Middle ages, these views of property and trade are at variance with the firmly entrenched economic system that rests on private property which the increase in trade, growth of towns and the expansion of markets brought about. Aquinas tries to reconcile theological dogma with the existing conditions of economic life. With regard to property, he does not reiterate the Roman practice of unrestricted rights that is beginning to come back into its own again. He retains the Aristotelian distinction between the power of acquisition and administration and that of use, an important separation of two aspects of property. The former bestows rights on the individual and Aquinas' defense of it is similar to those criticisms that Aristotle levels against Plato. He restricts property rights to justify theft by the needy and argues that in times of famine the starving have a right to take goods either openly or secretly and this cannot be considered theft. This conception survives well into the modern period and changes only gradually. While the medieval notion grants the poor a right to the means of subsistence, the modern conception accepts the need of the poor but sought to meet it in a different way by claiming that the rich have a moral obligation to act charitably in times of famine. The claim of the poor is changed into the unenforceable legal obligation of the rich.

Aquinas shares with Aristotle the view that trade is unnatural and along with wealth an evil inevitable in an imperfect world. It is justified only if the trader can maintain his household and if the intention of trade is to benefit the country. However, Aquinas concedes that the profit from trade is the reward for labour. The justification of trade depends also on whether the exchange, which is affected is just, whether that which is given and that which was received was of equal value. In developing this argument, Aquinas also falls back on Aristotle. The early Christian Fathers, in spite of their aversion to trade, come to terms with regulation of practices, which they denounce but could not eradicate. They try to specify the principle of 'just price' as an objective, for deviation means violation of the moral code. The passage from feudal conception of property is a protracted process that occurs sometime by the end of the thirteenth century. In many areas of Europe, tenants acquire rights to alienate (sell) land and to bequeath it as they see fit, thereby, acquiring these as the two basic rights with which the right to property is now understood.

DEFENSE OF PRIVATE PROPERTY

The modern debates on property start around the sixteenth and seventeenth centuries. The major figure in initiating the debate is Locke, whose justification of private property forms a part of the argument that human beings have rights derived from natural law prior to the establishment of society and formation of governments. Government is created to secure and protect these rights. Locke's theory categorically rejects the conception that property rights are derived from political society and hence are artificial, and that right to private property is justified only when others consent to it. Locke assumes that the earth and its fruits are originally held in common. Like **Grotius** and **Pufendorf**, he points out that both revelation and human reason make it clear that the earth and its fruits belong to God, who in turn, has given it to the human inhabitants in common to enjoy. He answers Filmer's critique of Grotius as to how could an individual have a private right to any part of a common heritage. He dismisses Filmer's argument by saying that private property is justified when an individual mixes the labour of his hands and that of his body with gifts of nature. Labour is the unquestioned property of the labourer helping to distinguish what is commonly held to what can be privately owned. An individual has a legitimate right to his labour but he must not waste or spoil the common heritage, rather he, through his labour and entrepreneurship makes it a better place, one of conveniences and comfort. It is interesting that, unlike Locke, the modern Greens value wastelands as an integral part of the ecosystem, which preserves and sustains different kinds of life forms. Locke emphasises that the human being is a trustee and a steward of the earth who, through his industriousness, appropriates and consumes but cannot destroy, waste, squander or spoil, affirming the essential teachings of Puritan ethics. Furthermore, he confines himself to use-value of labour and shows the importance of labour in production but avoids the issue of origin of exchange-value (Roll 1992: 98).

In the state of nature, individuals have an initial right that grants appropriation but it is limited by three things—need, leave enough and good for others—and only to that much for which one has mixed the labour of his body with the work of his hands. The last precondition is the most distinctive idea in Locke's theory. Labour not only creates property but also determines its value. These three limitations are transcended with the introduction of money and the equal right to property and appropriation paves the way for inequality of unlimited accumulation. This distinction is similar to one that Aristotle upholds except, unlike Aristotle, Locke is not averse to commerce and trade, since he considers property as crucial to preserving individual life and freedom. 'By making labour the title to property and the source of value, Locke translates the rise of a new class to power into terms of a new political economy. In relation to the age that precedes him, Locke's economic philosophy—the liberation of the enterprising individual form paralysing restrictions of force and custom was altogether progressive' (Ebenstein 1974: 488). Macpherson (1973: 221), however, understands this distinction as one that supports separation between appropriating and labouring, justification of class differentials in rights, rationality and wage contracts and a society from equal individuals evolving into a society with two classes, those with and those without property. Macpherson interprets Locke as defending a market society and providing the moral basis for capitalism. Since money is not perishable, something which Locke also concedes, it removes the limits on accumulation, thereby, allowing ownership beyond one's needs. This makes great inequalities in property possible though there still remains one limit to the amount that may legitimately be held, namely the amount of the individual's own labour that enables him to acquire profit. For Locke, money has a 'double value'. One is the ability of money to supply an yearly income (similar to rent) and the other, the 'Necessaries or Conveniences of Life' that money can obtain in exchange thereby making the same mercantilist error of identifying money and capital (Roll 1992: 98).

It is labour that accounts for the conveniences and increases productivity, which Locke explains with reference to America as a case in point. America, a land of plenty, does not have the conveniences made possible by human labour that the seventeenth century England enjoys. Optimism and a feeling of buoyancy made possible by the discovery of America and the rising mercantilist society permeates Locke's analysis, for it is no longer the vexing question of unlimited human desires and limited means that Machiavelli and Hobbes grapple with. Scarcity becomes a thing of the past. Locke exhibits a feeling of optimism that there is enough for everyone's satisfaction. He describes human entitlements as property, 'the great and chief end of men's uniting into commonwealth and putting themselves under government is the preservation of property.' The purpose of the government is to secure human entitlements, ensure lives, liberties and material possessions. A commonwealth based on freely elected representatives cannot dispose of the property of its subject arbitrarily. Even taxes that are imposed will require the consent of the government. It gives credence to the protest made by the Enclosure movement of the 1660s in England that land cannot be confiscated without the owner's consent. Enclosure means fencing-in by landlords of common land. Enclosure usually leads to increase in agricultural productivity, though it deprives people of free grasing and firewood. Complaints against this practice dated back to the thirteenth century, though in the sixteenth century in particular, enclosure is responsible for popular rebellions. The agrarian revolution of the eighteenth century leads to a spurt in enclosures.

The Americans take a leaf out of Locke, and coin the slogan 'no taxation without representation' during the Boston Tea Party of 1773.[1] The connection between property and the supportive role of society lies in Locke's identification of property with society rather than with the political order' (Wolin 1960: 309). The social character of property enables Locke to defend a limited constitutional state based on the rule of law and consent. Locke assumes the existence of a vibrant economy and civil society prior to the creation of government to emphasise the fact, which becomes a cornerstone of the liberal argument, namely the concern of the political authority is with the political alone. Economic activity is separate and independent of the political, thus initiating 'a way of thinking in which society, rather than the political order, is the predominant influence. Instead of asking the traditional question: what type of political order is required if society is to be maintained? Locke turns the question around to read what social arrangements would insure the continuity of government? Locke launches his attack on the traditional model of society, wherein ordered social relationships and institutions are sustained by the direction imparted from a political centre, by substituting a conception of society as a self-activating unity capable of generating a common will (Wolin 1960: 308).

Locke tries to help in the creation of private property per se, as an institution of capitalism but does not grant special status to landed property. Furthermore, his demand for limiting the rate of interest is to the disadvantage of the landowners to whom low rate of interest means a high rate of capitalisation of their rents, i.e., high land values. Wood (1984: 101–105) rightly interprets, Locke as a spokesman of agrarian capitalism. Sartori (1987: 377) dismisses Macpherson's critique in particular and the Marxist view, in general, of reading back into history a concept of private property that did not actually exist. He points out that 'from Roman times until the end of the eighteenth century property meant, all in one and indivisibly, 'life, liberty and estate'; it did not mean 'possession' for its own sake or for the sake of unlimited accumulation, let alone 'capital accumulation'. In Locke's time, and still for some time, property was not part of a chrematistic (money-seeking) economic system. Capitalism becomes 'capital accumulation' only in unison with the Industrial Revolution. Sartori asserts that both with regard to timing and conceptualisation Macpherson's interpretation appeared to be wrong (1987: 398).

The mercantilist notion profoundly influences Locke's thought for he insists that a country grew rich by exporting more than it imports. In *Discourses upon Trade* (1691), Locke makes a scathing critique of protection and in particular on the prohibition of trade with France thus exhibiting a doctrinaire free-trade attitude. It is Locke who, for the first time, expresses the view that the whole world is as much an economic unit as is a single nation. He regards all trades as profitable, for no unprofitable one is likely to continue and identifies public good with private good, similar to the view expressed by nineteenth century utilitarians. His pamphlet is not received well, since restrictions on foreign trade was still the rule. However, it contains views that are in consonance with the trend of economic development and for this reason its influence is enormous.

Locke's theory of property of labour as the title to property and the source of economic value is developed fully by Smith and Ricardo. For Smith, labour supplies every nation 'with all the necessaries and conveniences of life which it annually consumes'. He enquires into the social rather than the technical appearance of wealth. The wealth of a nation, he says, will depend upon two conditions—first, the degree of productivity of wealth to which it is due and secondly, the amount of useful labour, namely the labour productive of wealth, which is employed. Smith begins with a discussion division of labour to tackle the first aspect. He wishes to find a principle and in that context analyses division of labour, which transforms particular and concrete forms of labour that produces good (use-values) which become the source of wealth in the abstract (exchange-value). Division of labour for Smith is the fundamental cause of the increasing productivity of labour. It depends upon the propensity to exchange, which he regards as one of the basic motives of human conduct. For Smith, exchange cannot exist without division of labour at least in theory, while division of labour also requires the existence of private exchange. He emphasises the influence of market on productivity in order to demonstrate that trade has to be made free as a precondition to develop productive power, and not merely to make full use of the existing powers of production.

There are others who champions free trade. For instance, Bodin while exploring the dangers of unrestricted authority emphasises on the rights of private property since he believes free trade to be beneficial. He anticipates a growing schism between state and society and gropes for a theory that gives 'some place for the consent of subjects to the actions of authority' (Laski 1936: 46–48). Bodin is thus a precursor of liberalism in a more direct sense than the natural law philosophers of the seventeenth century (Roll 1992: 74). Hobbes, a great defender of the absolute state, also accepts individuals' right to private property.

Reiterating a point made by Xenophon and later by Petty, Smith shows that when division of labour and circle of exchange reach a certain stage of development, that increases the dependence of the individual on the rest of the community, then every person becomes, in some sense, a merchant and society develops properly into a commercial society. Smith's great faith lay in freeing the state from the evil spirit of individual and class influence. Once emancipation is attained, then natural harmony will become possible for all. This social harmony is compatible with the institution of private property. He knows very well the relation between property and the evolution of government. Civil government, according to him, is primarily necessary to protect property. It is not needed in primitive societies, which hardly had any property to provoke the envy of poor and make the rich feel insecure. However, once property increases, government becomes necessary to safeguard it. 'Civil government, so far as it is instituted for the security of property, is in reality instituted for the defence of the rich against the poor, or of those who have some property against those who have none at all' (1925: Vol. ii: 233). Smith also believes that property is the chief cause of authority and subordination. He does not worry about the disturbance which private property causes to natural harmony, but he does not favour great inequalities in its distribution. If the state in an opulent and civilised society, in his view, devotes itself to avoidance of privileges and great fortunes, it can prevent oppression and exploitation. None will depend on the benevolence of others, for everything that one gets from anybody one gives an equivalent in exchange. Moreover, the free play of natural forces will bring ruin to all positions that are not built upon continued contributions to the common good.

Smith confronts the dualism between determination of value by labour (the actual time of labour used to produce a commodity) and its determination by the **value of labour**, a point that does not matter in pre-capitalist production. This is because two factors can be shown as being identical—the value of an amount of labour embodied in a commodity is equal to the value of command over the same amount of labour. However, in capitalism the value of the labour that the capitalist buys is greater than the amount of labour embodied in the wages which he is paid for. Thus, a surplus will appear which the capitalist can appropriate. One could argue that, in capitalist production, the identity vanishes and in an exchange of capital and wage-labour, capital gets more value than it gives. This point is developed by Marx in detail. However, for Smith, this does not signify exploitation but an explanation that recognises other factors, additional to labour, as productive of value. The same problem confronts Ricardo but his answer refines Smith's explanation thereby avoiding Marx's conclusion. Ricardo refuses to limit the validity of the labour theory of value to the pre-capitalist period and intentionally considers it as the basic and universal principle by trying to explain how far the different aspects of capitalist economy are compatible with it. He accepts that utility is necessary for a commodity if it has to have exchange value but rejects it as a measure of that value. The exchange value is derived from scarcity of labour. He concludes that it is, 'the comparative quantity of commodities which labour will produce that determines their present or past relative value, and not the comparative quantities of commodities which are given to the labourer in exchange for his labour' (Ricardo 1926: 6). Ricardo regards labour as a commodity whose value must be determined the same way as that of any other commodity. Its 'natural price' is that which was necessary for the labour to subsist and that in turn depended on 'the quantity of food, necessaries, and conveniences which become essential to him from habit' (1926: 52). The market price of the labour depends on supply and demand which will approximate the natural price, as determined by the customary level of subsistence.

The labour theory of value derives its roots from the theory of property. Labour constitutes the source and the title to property in the natural state, which demands freedom from any interference that may disturb the natural property relations. The classical school applies the requirements of the natural world to the facts of the real world. This is because in the real world, property relations, which have been established as a result of a long historical evolution, do not resemble those of the natural world and thus it becomes possible to arrive at different political conclusions to those offered by the classical economists. One trend became conservative and the other critical. After the appearance of **utilitarianism**, not only freedom but also the idea of social harmony is subjected to conflicting conservative and radical interpretations. Bentham considers it as desirable to have an equal distribution of income and while in calculating a maximum of social advantage the poor counted as much as the rich. He believes the government to be an undeniable evil, which could be minimised if it can be used for the production of happiness, understood as security, abundance, subsistence and equality. Of these four ends, security and subsistence are the most important. An assurance that property will be protected encourages individuals to create new wealth, which he defends as idea of expectation. To expect is a distinctive quality that human beings have and the purpose of law was to secure expectations, for that is a precondition not only for peace of mind and for the pleasure of anticipation but also for economic enterprise and investment. Thus, security of expectations rather than equality in distribution led Bentham to favour private property. Nevertheless, he criticises the English law of property of his day. **Hume** explicitly rejects Locke's theory as a figurative expression for he insists that human convention and not the state of nature was the sole origin of justice, rights and property. Property is needed to restrain the most pernicious of human passions, that of acquisitiveness, which can be contained when people are reminded that it is in their self-interest to respect other people's property. In view of scarcity of goods, property is needed, for it guarantees security.

Burke emphasises strongly the rights of property that classical political economy implicitly safeguards and establishes a close link between property, family and inheritance as indispensable for social order. He considers property alone as the basis of government and gives pride of place to landed property though he does not consider the lower classes as capable of governing. For sake of expediency, he favours a wealthy and financially independent Church. He champions the power and importance of state finance though espouses non-interventionism and free trade. There is a liberal and an aristocratic-conservative side to Burke to which Paine and Wollstonecraft direct their response. Wollstonecraft accuses Burke for championing unequal property and argues that inequalities undermine sociability. Paine reiterates Locke's views on natural rights and insists on alleviating the appalling conditions of the poor by taxing the rich, whereas Wollstonecraft suggests the need to divide into small farms as a means of improving the condition of the poor (Dickinson 1977: 267). The conservatives criticise capitalism for its ethic of individualism, which they regard as the main reason that contributes to the disintegration of the social fabric. It is for this reason that they reject the natural rights' doctrine. Later conservatives like Disraeli in England emphasise on the obligation of the rich to help the poor and Bismarck, in Germany, introduces welfare measures, like social insurance in the 1880s. In fact, the detailed critique of factory legislation and conditions by the conservatives provide the arsenal with which the socialists criticise early capitalism (Lipset 1988).

CRITIQUE OF PRIVATE PROPERTY

The progress of capitalism in the nineteenth century elicits **two** types of theoretical criticisms. The **first** reactionary and essentially backward-looking is articulated by a section of the romantics. The second is revolutionary associated primarily with the socialist criticisms of capitalism. The socialist concern is not so much the justification of property as with vast disparities in wealth. They acquiesce that one has a right to what one produces but this right belongs to the labourer and not to the capitalist and the landlord who profit and rent what the labourer produces. They desire to abolish, along with private property, market and division of labour, for each independently and together resulted in inequalities, oppression and misery. The idea of common property has been articulated since the Greeks in general and Plato in particular. More reiterates it followed by the socialists and communists in the nineteenth and twentieth centuries. Most of the advocates of common ownership support it on the grounds that there is a need to separate political and economic power and minimise the effect the latter has on the former. The other reasons are to temper avarice, covetousness and moderate one's needs. All these reasons exist even in the socialist-communist demand for equal property but the most striking addition is the link that they establish between its abolition and the creation of a more just society. Private property breeds and nourishes sentiments of self interest, egoism and competitiveness while a higher and better society—communism—based on cooperation, sociability and fellowship will be possible only with the destruction of capitalism and *laissez faire*.

During the sixteenth century, Winstanley, whom Bernstein considers as a precursor to Marx, wishes to alter the existing property arrangements by advocating the right of every person to have unrestrained access to use the earth for subsistence. True freedom would be possible only when productive land would be restored to its original status of a common treasury. He inspires the Diggers who demand the abolition of private property since it is the root cause of all social evils like greed, covetousness and reduces many to the position of wage earners. While Winstanley comprehends that political freedom without economic equality is empty and economic equality is possible only with the abolition of wage labour and private property, Harrington is the first to establish a link between political change and economic factors. Harrington, like Aristotle is convinced that if property is widely distributed, it would ensure the stability of the government. He attributes the English Civil War (1640) to the tendency to concentrate land ownership through the law of primogeniture. A key influence in the development of socialism is Rousseau whose trenchant criticisms of the modern society as unequal resonate in most socialist works. His *Discourses* (1755) analyses in detail the rise of private property that leads to inequality. The state of nature which is one of bliss and happiness comes to an abrupt end the moment 'the First man, who having enclosed a piece of ground, he thought himself of saying "This is mine" and found people simple enough to believe him as the real founder of civil society' (1958: 192). In this way, the selfish interests of a few but powerful people create civil society. Private property, a right of the few is an artificial privilege, ending the self-sufficiency that exists in the state of nature inflicting misery on the majority.

> But from the moment one man began to stand in need of the help of another; from the moment it appeared advantageous to any one man to have enough provisions for two, equality too disappeared, property was introduced, for work became indispensable, and vast forests became smiling fields, which man had to water with the sweat of his brow and where slavery and misery were soon seem to germinate and grow up with crops (1958: 199).

For Rousseau, not only does property create social dissension but it also brings new kinds of mutual dependence between the rich and the poor. The rich became richer and the poor, poorer. The rich need the services of the poor, and the poor require the help of the rich. The distinctions increase and become sharper with the rich cornering power and in a position to dominate while the poor descend into slavery. More laws are enacted to property rights. The poor covet the property of the rich and the rich fear losing it, which lead to a state of war. Rousseau's ideal is an economic system based on small farmers owning tracts of land. Since dependence makes people vain and contemptuous, he desires the abolition of division of labour, a demand similar to the one Marx makes. He opposes sharp distinctions that property entail namely misery and inequality. However, he does not advocate common ownership, as property is the most sacred of all citizens' rights. He desires a society based on rough equality that takes into account natural endowments but rejects egalitarianism, as that leads to levelling. He considers both capitalism, and socialism to be unequal, for in capitalism, wealth creates benefits while in socialism power confers privileges (Colletti 1969: 190, 192). Rousseau influences the socialists by his emphasis on the idea that 'all rights, including those of property are rights within the community and not against it' (Sabine 1973: 556). Many socialists reiterate his view that property leads to inequality and loss of human sociability and accept his belief that a human being is born good but corrupted by society. Babuef, writing in the immediate aftermath of the French Revolution and inspired by Rousseau, advocates socialisation of industry and land, equal natural right to earth and its goods, rough parity and universal right to work. He argues that freedom means not only civil and legal liberties but also an unhindered pursuit of economic activities. This means not just physical protection against arbitrary power but also an end to slavery, exploitation, misery and inequality which is possible only if capitalism can be destroyed and replaced by socialism. Inspired by Rousseau, Godwin proposes an end to unequal economic system but insists on the need to recognise private property as essential for the exercise of private judgement and independence. He objects to anyone accumulating unearned property produced by the labour of others. He insists that each should perform manual labour for about half an hour a day and spend the rest of his day in enjoying life and in learning.

Among the early socialists it is **Saint Simon** who understands the dynamics of the modern industrial society and the key to its success is organisation and technology, unhindered by private property and the laws of inheritance. He desires a system in which merit alone is rewarded and that means abolition of privileges which occur through birth and inheritance. Each has a right to property according to the services rendered, an idea that Marx later borrows. Since the industrial society is based on talent, intelligence and capacity, there is no need for class and power conflicts. Since the organisational society is based on the rule of law, political power and government slowly disappears, making administration important. Owen demands the abolition of private property and regards it as a part of an irrational trinity, the other two being marriage and religion, as being oppressive and exploitative. Fourier does not demand the abolition of private property but is confident that it loses its antagonistic character once the ideal society 'Harmony' is formed. **Sismondi** (1773–1842), the first to develop a socialist critique of classical economics, opposes landed estates and primogeniture, and monopolies, and favours state intervention to guarantee the worker a minimum standard of living and social security. He is also one of the earliest to speak of the existence of two classes, the rich and the poor, the capitalists and the workers, constantly in conflict with one another. He speaks of class polarisation and the separation of property and labour. **Proudhon**, known for his famous statement 'property is theft', does not attack private property as such. In fact, he regards property as an essential condition of liberty. He accepts the view that labour is the sole source and wealth and constitutes the only title to property and hence considers it vital that everyone should enjoy and own the fruits of his labour. What he objects to is the abuse of property, the power to extract an unearned tribute which capitalism and its law gives to the capitalists. He demands the abolition of rent, interest and profit but seeks the preservation of property. He suggests various reforms but never proposes common ownership of property, for the fear that communism may result in a coercive state. He realises that large-scale industry could never wholly be abolished and wants it to be integrated with small peasants and artisans. He criticises the early socialists, like Saint Simon, for ignoring the laws of economic process and rejects communism because it is based on a false analysis of property. In his *Theories of Property* published posthumously in 1866, he even goes to the extent of proposing the retention of private property in the existing form with its power to use and destroy mitigated only by 'equilibrating' guarantees. He proposes the establishment of exchange bank for giving out free credit in the hope that once interest is abolished, exploitation through property will stand abolished. Since all workers are to have access to the credit bank to buy the means of production, the division of classes disappears. The need to separate property and labour which Sismondi proposes will thus be reunited paving the way to the ideal commonwealth of free and equal producers, to justice and to the abolition of oppressive governments. Proudhon conceives of socialism through the abolition of interest and fails to take into account the principles of capitalist production, the quality of capital and the function of money-making his practical proposals ineffective and his ideal retrograde. While Proudhon is against property abuses but not the institution of property as such, **Bakunin** rejects private property along with the laws of inheritance altogether, as it is responsible for the rise of the state, the chief violator of individual freedom. Other early socialists like John Francis Bray (1809–1895), John Gray (1799–1850), William Thompson (1783–1833) and Thomas Hodgskin (1787–1869) all begin from the Ricardian formulation of the labour theory of value. They accept the account that the amount of labour consisting in a commodity is the substance and measure of its exchange-value. They depend on the distinction between productive and unproductive labour. All of them develop some kind of a concept of surplus value, which is the reason for oppression, exploitation and misery. All of them interpret utilitarianism in a revolutionary way by accepting that the greatest happiness of the greatest number is realisable in a society without private property, egoistic and selfishness. Of the aforesaid pre-Marxian thinkers, **Hodgskin** is the most determined socialist economist. He makes the distinction, later developed by Marx, between the material aids to production or capital and capital as expressive of a certain form of property relation that makes steam engines, raw materials and the labourer's means of subsistence into capital.

Engels provides the first exposition of the Marxist view of property, in 1844. In a moralistic criticism of British capitalism, under the influence of Owen and Carlyle, he criticises the market economy for being responsible for dissolving the affection and bond of a family, social solidarity, morality and untold miseries of the people. The two pillars of liberalism, private property and free competition are identified as the major reasons for the present malady, namely class antagonism, which threatens the very foundation of society. The pessimists, like **Malthus**, are castigated for failing to see that the market subordinates birth and death by its philosophy of fierce competition. To check the catastrophic consequences of the market, an alternative model of organisation becomes essential.

Marx elaborates this thesis in the *Economic and Philosophical Manuscripts* (1844), popularly known as the *Paris Manuscripts*. Instead of concentrating on the market as Engels does, he focuses on the way the capitalistic system turns labour into a commodity and detaches it from its true human essence. He realises the importance of the market for capitalism. Marx also demolishes Proudhon's theory of equal exchange amongst individual producers in 1847 and the *Manifesto* decries the prevalence of self-interest in human relationship. In the *Wage*, *Labour and Capital* (1849), he affirms that market competition keeps wages at the level of subsistence. The rise of profits is in proportion to the decline of labour's share in the total product, yet the quick growth of capital creates the most favourable condition for 'wage labour'. The young Marx till 1850 is, as Licthheim (1975) comments, a Ricardian socialist. In this phase, he denounces institution of private property and the private ownership of the means of production in capitalistic industrialisation. It is a moral criticism of the unequal bourgeois society and a rejection of the theory popularised by Smith that the motivation of self-interest cumulatively does a lot of good to society. He regards private property as unjust and desires its abolition. This sets him apart from the social democrats who seek reform of the existing property arrangements to the workers class. However, he is conscious of the need for reform of the existing capitalistic society and welcomes the introduction of ten-hour working day. However, his theoretical position is for total abolition of private property. After 1850, Marx tries to provide a more rigorous and scientific analysis of the origin, evolution of different kinds of property contrasting with the system under capitalism.

Marx points out that private property originates with the division of labour and the consequent unequal distribution in the family. Wives and children as slaves of the husband and father are the first signs of property. This rudimentary form of property provides the basis of private property even now as 'even at this stage it corresponds perfectly to the definition of modern economists, who call it the power of disposing of the labour power of others' (Marx 1989: 26). For Marx, surplus value exists as the basis of private appropriation and creates private property from the beginning. Division of labour and property are the two sides of the same coin. Out of this, division of labour emerges. The most important division between material and mental labour is reflected in the separation of the cities and the countryside. This contradiction between the city and the village reflects the change from 'barbarism to civilisation, from tribe to state, from locality to nation, and runs through the whole history of civilisation to the present day' (Marx 1989: 26). The establishment of cities necessitates administrative machinery with police and taxes. The first manifestation of the two classes becomes apparent based on the division of labour and instruments of production. The cities reflect concentration of people, different instruments of production and many other manifestations of pleasures and needs, whereas the village reflects the opposite, desolation and separation. This is because 'the contradiction between town and country can exist only within the framework of private property' (1989: 27). It demonstrates the suppression of the individual by division of labour with a forced activity making one either 'a restricted town-animal' or 'a restricted country-animal' (Marx 1989: 27). Labour manifests here as 'power over individuals, and as long as their power exists, private property must exist' (Marx 1989: 27). The separation between the urban and rural also means detachment of capital and landed property. This growth of capital, independent of landed property makes a new beginning of a new kind of property-based labour and exchange.

Marx is categorical that before the origin of private property, communal property exists for a very long time. The existence of such communal property negates a popular notion that without property there cannot be any production. This also proves that each historical epoch develops different kinds of property relationships reflecting different social relations. For instance, the bourgeois property relations reflect the social relations of bourgeois production system. As such there cannot be an abstract category of private property as it is based on concrete reality and changes with changes in reality. For instance, the Glorious Revolution of 1688 in Britain brought a new category of landlords and capitalists as beneficiaries of the surplus value. In fact, the rise of modern private property is a consequence of 'reckless terrorism' (Marx 1989: 85). The appropriation of the property by the Church and the common lands (not state lands) by a few leads to the foundation of modern property. Marx, like Rousseau, is silent on revealing the facts that lead the minority to befool the majority. Capitalistic agriculture begins when the land becomes an integral part of capital and creates the surplus proletariat for urban industries. Regarding the evolutionary details of the rise of private property, Marx describes tribal ownership as the original kind of property existing in a situation of an extended family rule, which existed above and controlled the slaves. The family slavery spills over to the society with the rise of population, other necessities, commerce and war. This is followed by the communal property of antiquity, which took place with amalgamation of several tribes and is still based on slavery. Along with communal property, mobile and immobile private property slowly consolidates but remains subordinated to communal property. Slaves were still commonly owned. The third form of property is feudal property, which develops in the European Middle Ages. Its origin is linked to historical antecedents, like the fall of the Roman Empire and the property is still communal but based not on slavery as in antiquity but on directly producing class of peasant serfs. After 1850, oriental societies also start to receive his attention in which he follows a long tradition of Eurocentricism. The underlying assumption among many post-Renaissance European thinkers who take interest in the non-European world is that there is a marked and qualitative distinction between the advanced European cultures and other backward civilisations. Montesquieu is the pioneer of this perception. Using climatic conditions as the yardstick, he notes that tropical climates are unsuited for democracies and freedom. Smith clubs China, Egypt and India together for the special attention irrigation received in these societies. James Mill observes the difference between European feudalism and governmental arrangements in Asiatic societies. Richard Jones uses the phrase 'Asiatic society' and J.S. Mill uses the term 'Eastern society' in 1848. Others like Spencer, Pareto and Durkheim analyse the Asiatic societies from a comparative perspective. Hegel is the most influential among these thinkers whose philosophy of history not only concurs with this prevailing European perception of the East, but also influences, to a very large extent, the left Hegelians with respect to perceiving colonisation as a modernising force. Hegel with his clear Eurocentricism takes note of the lack of history in India and China as they were stationary and fixed. This he considers true of all Asiatic societies. Hegel points that the East lacks history influences Marx. Marx's novelty lay in working out a non-dialectical and therefore, non-historical account of the non-European mode of production called the Asiatic Mode of Production, which is the key to the understanding all the developments of the East 'in the absence of private property in land' (cited in Lichtheim 1961: 145).

Marx, in evolving his theory of private property is a child of his times. He follows the pattern of Smith in distinguishing productive and unproductive labour, the first providing the output of physical goods and the second the non-economic socially important services. In Marx's time with labour being overwhelmingly manual and unskilled, he concludes that it is practically impossible for a general equal platform in view of the wide differentiation between the skilled and the unskilled. His labour theory of value does not intend to provide for a theory of prices, as his purpose is to discover the distribution of income between different social classes. His analysis of wage labour is not mainly linked to a theory of exploitation, which he considers a 'pernicious nonsense' but an important ingredient in a larger model. The source of material wealth is a combination of nature and labour, but the former is not the possession of the workers under capitalism. The worker has only 'naked labour power' as the other instrument of production, nature, is taken away from him. The vulnerability of the wage labour is because of this lack of control. Here, there is a striking resemblance between Marx's arguments and the economic philosophy of early liberalism reflected in the period between Locke and Jefferson.

In the context of the working of capitalism, apart from this lack of control of nature by wage labour, Marx also argues that surplus value is a basic necessity for its survival. It is not linked to the upward or downward movement of wages but to a natural quality of human beings to produce a surplus. The labour power is a unique quality to produce surplus much above the consumption level in the process of production itself. This is extremely significant for Marx, as unlike other contemporaries who condemn profit arising out of overcharging the consumer, cheating or under payment to the worker this surplus value is Marx's theory of profit. Capitalism survives on the full value of labour while keeping the worker at the subsistence and reproduction cost level. For Marx, the producers maintain unity by greater exchange value of distant markets. However, the internal antagonism persists as the labour tries to recover his control of the means of production. In the monopoly situation, there exists a link between exchange value of commodity production for markets and in the exchange of capital and labour leading to surplus value. This control of capitalism is transient. However, in this way, the capitalist class captures a new source of energy by which it could create material affluence through surplus value. This is Marx's theory of exploitation. The important motivation for this appropriation is accumulation, which is made possible by an unequal social system based on private property that conceals it by projecting a false formal equality. By controlling the apparatus of production, the capitalist class controls the state.

This appropriation of labour has a long history and inheritance flow from it, creates a class of entrepreneurs and later banks and corporations. It leads to a capitalist system in which 'the worker is engaged in building a world which does not belong to him' (Lichtheim 1975: 110). The entire superstructure of law and culture is under the sway of the possessing class. This basic principle gets manifested in all kinds of private property and that is the materialistic conception of history. The division of world history into stages—primitive communism, slavery, feudalism, capitalism and communism—each with its own socio-economic mode of production succeeding one another in a logical sequence is a legacy of the eighteenth century perception. The **Scottish Enlightenment philosophers**—Hutcheson, Ferguson, Hume, Smith, Millar and Lord Kames—

speak of four modes of subsistence—hunting, pastoralism, agriculture and commerce—as constituting a single sequence. The existing property relation is a reflection of the existing production relations, corresponding to the material forces of production. However, there is no technological determinism in Marx as he emphasises the social organisation, which is reflected in surplus value and labour theory. Marx is confident that capitalism based on the institution of private property is inevitably self-destructive, because of the increased accumulation and concentration which happens by doing away with small scale property owners. As a result, there will be polarisation between a few rich and a mass of poor people.[2]

REVISIONS IN CLASSICAL THEORY

J.S. Mill's *Principles of Political Economy* (1848) published in the same year as the *Communist Manifesto* changes liberal theory without renouncing its fundamentals. In view of the Irish famine of 1870s, he proposes the curtailment of the normal right of inheritance and compulsory redistribution of large holdings from absentee landlords to local peasants. He rejects the hereditary class system since it is inherently inefficient and obstructs progress. He does not attack the landowning class for receiving a steady increase in rent but sympathises with the capitalists who face diminishing returns and the labourer who survives at the bare level of subsistence. This is a point that George Bernard Shaw (1856–1950) picks up to furnish the economic basis of Fabian socialism. Shaw's basic thrust is that unearned income in any form is immoral. Mill praises the small landed proprietors and shares Tocqueville's belief that they are the best preservers of democracy. He advocates taxation on inheritance at a modest level rather than taxing industry and economy and equally opposes taxing investments, savings and incomes. This is because he desires to preserve entrepreneurship and is against the idleness and opulence of the landed aristocracy and primogeniture. He believes that while increased production was important for poor countries it is better distribution of the existing wealth that matters in advanced countries. Mill incorporates the idea of human cooperation from socialism but desires its application within capitalism that preserves individuality and freedom. He does not advocate socialisation of the means of production. He also supports limiting of working hours, state control of monopolies, factory legislation for children, workers participation in industry and management (a point that G.D.H. Cole elaborates later) and rights for trade unions.

Green rejects the doctrine of *laissez faire* in economic and social policy, for he advocates substantive state intervention to remove the obstacles to secure and protect rights. It is against this background that he discusses the right to private property the basis of which is 'that everybody should be secure by society in the power of getting and keeping the means of realising a will which in possibility is a will directed to social good'. By getting and keeping he means owning what one acquires through work. Regarding 'a will directed towards social good', Green observes

> … whether anyone's will is actually and positively so directed does not affect his claim to the power. This power should be secured to the individual irrespective of the use which he actually makes of it, so long as he does not use it in a way that interferes with the exercise of a like power by another, on the ground that its uncontrolled exercise is the condition of the attainment by man of that free morality which is his highest good (1888: 248).

This concurs with his general theory of rights. Rights provide the conditions under which the moral agent can achieve the highest level of rationality of which he is capable but there is no guarantee that this achievement will take place. A person's right to acquire and own property is not influenced by the fact that he is wasteful or careless with it. However, the right to property, like every other right, is conditional. There is an obligation to use the property in a way that allows others to become property-owners. For Green, 'when the possession of property by one man interferes with the possession of property by another, when one set of men are secured in the power of getting and keeping the means of realising their will in such a way that others are practically denied the power; in that case it may truly be said that property is theft' (1888: 250). Green does not consider anything wrong with private property. Rather it is a right, a morally justified claim so as the correlative responsibility is fulfilled. It is a power that a person must have if he has to be a moral agent and make a rational life for himself. Like Hegel, he considers property as crucial for developing a healthy moral character. Though Green does support *laissez faire*, he is no socialist either. Inequality in the distribution of private property does not constitute an injustice, according to Green, provided nobody's right to own property has been violated. He regards inequality as inevitable. Regarding the question of producing and distributing property there are two possibilities. One, society provides for the individual and that means total regulation of life, which is incompatible with free morality, the highest kind of human attainment. The individual will have no responsibility to take care of himself and in his workplace; he is no longer a rational agent capable of taking decisions but a cog in a machine with no effective voice. A person who is responsible for looking after himself is unlikely to achieve much as a citizen or husband or father. The other can be through individual effort, which will imply inequality between the properties of different persons. Its abuses can be prevented if the obligation correlative to the right of private property is legally enforced.

For Hayek, the fact that property precedes civilisation and is a precondition of a rule governed society is scientific truth. Property for him does not only mean possession of physical goods alone. Quoting Locke, he maintains that a person possesses property in his person to the extent that he is free to exchange his labour with another and to move without hindrance within a system of general rules. Property guarantees freedom though a person can still be free even if he possesses very little property in the material sense. As long as the means which enables him to pursue a course of action are not in the exclusive control of another then he may enjoy liberty. The important point is that it is not the amount of property that the individuals possess that determines their freedom but its dispersal throughout society at large. He rejects the idea that free market produces social injustice while distributing income and wealth. It cannot do so because only intentional acts cause injustice whereas market outcomes, a product of individual actions of buying and selling produces outcomes that were not intended by anyone. They are product of human action and human design and as such unintended and therefore cannot be described as unjust. Market cannot restrict liberty, for it is not controlled by any specific individual(s). Coercion and injustice can only occur as a result of deliberate action. The sufferings in the market are due to misfortune, which cannot be rectified by claims of rights, justice and equality but only through voluntary action and charity. He stresses that the market cannot and does not distribute according to any particular set of moral principles and to think it can do so is a mirage. Any restrictions or regulation of the market impairs efficiency and personal self help.

Rawls accepts private ownership of property, when it is personal as a basic liberty but not when it is a means of production. The role of the right to personal property is to furnish the material basis for the development and exercise of moral powers in individuals and a sense of independence and self-respect which are its requirement. He restricts certain rights of acquisition and bequest and the right to own means of production and natural resources. He accepts a system of wide dispersion of property, even its public ownership to anchor the difference principle. Property will be regulated through inheritance and gift taxes in order to gradually and continually correct the distribution of wealth and prevent concentration of power detrimental to the fair value of political liberty and fair value equality of opportunity. He recommends management of firms by workers or their councils making decisions collectively and democratically through a constitutional process. He answers to his Left critics by pointing out that the unequal value of these equal property rights is reduced to a point where inequality can be acceptable only if they worked to the elevation of the least advantaged. He distinguishes between two aspects of public sector in order to draw a distinction between an economy based on private property and socialism. He clarifies the nature of the ownership of the means of production and the proportion of total social resources devoted to public goods. Public goods are characterised by their indivisibility, publicness and externality and are to be arranged through the political process and not through the market. A problem be avoided is that of free riders or shirkers which is why the state arranges and finances these goods and ensures that all pay for them. Rawls observes that there is no essential nexus between the free market and the private ownership of the means of production. Its major advantage is efficiency. It plays a crucial role in ensuring decentralisation of economic power and freedom of choice of occupation. It checks monopolies, determined the rate of savings and corrected external economies and diseconomies (Rawls 1972: 272). The vagaries of the market are to be corrected and regulated by the state to prevent its worst inequities. He distinguishes what the market could allocate from its distributive powers. He claims that market institutions and the two principles of justice are common to property owning democracy and socialist regime though the distribution under socialism is greatly restricted since the means of production and natural resources are publicly owned. He is outright in his rejection of the command economy that existed in the erstwhile communist societies because he qualifies that freedom can be restricted only for the sake of freedom and nothing else including material well-being. Command economy depends on complete repression and force to succeed. The Rawlsian position is similar to the distinction that Sen (1990) makes between democracy as a foundation and market as an instrument. He shows how disastrous it could be if the market is operationalised without democracy through the Chinese example that provides good agricultural production but simultaneously removes the organisational support and the financial security of rural health service. Sen observes that radical marketisation of the rural Chinese economy without providing a minimum welfare to the people is possible only because there is no democracy. Democracy as the foundation means multiparty system, fair and free elections, alert and active opposition parties and a free and vibrant press. He points out that the existence of such institutions normally compels ruling parties to check mass miseries or face the prospect of losing the next election. Where democracy has been absent, as in parts of Africa, there have been starvation deaths in the 1950s. Nozick, updating Locke, justifies a natural right to property, as a part of his entitlement theory of justice, which he considers, is perfectly realisable by the market.

FREE MARKET—A MYTH?

The collapse of communism and the rediscovery of market among the scholars and statesman on the left have vindicated the liberal belief that the market, with reasonable and wide ownership of property rights as opposed to centralised planning guarantees growth, productivity, competitiveness, self-help and efficiency, while simultaneously ensuring equity. The hierarchical command economies that existed in the former communist societies were an economic dinosaur—inefficient, stagnant, technologically backward, with low standards of living, self-denial, and lack of motivation—and were slow and cumbersome. Its worldwide failure has been attributed to a fallacious and erroneous conception of the market, broadly classified into two—anthropological and economic (Roos 1990: 6).

The anthropological mistake is to presume as Marx does that 'law of history' dictates fundamental antagonism between capital and labour, which subsequent historical development, since the late nineteenth century, does not vindicate. The operationalisation of democracy, extensive social security schemes and labour welfare laws has improved the working conditions and the position of the proletarian class. The economic mistake has been not to perceive structural changes within capitalism thereby making most, if not all Marx's predictions as redundant not only the affluent societies of the West, but by the 1970s, to most parts of the developing world also. A decisive reason for this shift has been the East Asian miracle. Furthermore, the idea of a free market geared solely to maximise profits is a powerful myth even in the West (Denitch 1990: 178). The presence of the Church, democratic politics, trade unions, social democratic parties and welfare measures has mitigated the consequences of market. The fact is that democratic capitalism with its welfare state apparatus is not *laissez faire*, for there are safety nets, consumer protection, and anti-trust laws that ensure justice, fair play and a social minimum. 'Capitalism in its original or pristine form could not have survived. But under pressure it did adapt. Socialism in its original form and for its first tasks did succeed. But it failed to adapt' (Galbraith cited in Hague et al. 1994: 417). The critics and even those who unabashedly praise capitalism fail to see that self-interest alone cannot be the motivating factor for the success of capitalism. There are other requirements like responsibility, trustworthiness and social norms. This is evident in Smith's extensive discussion of values like sympathy, generosity and public-spiritedness.

CONCLUSION

The cumulative effect of all these factors has led to the splendid success of property-owning democratic capitalism. As Luttwak (1999) remarks, except for the nuclear weapons, capitalism has been the most potent invention of the human mind. As a system, it has spread worldwide that one can speak of a world capitalist system neutralising all other competitors like traditional economics and bureaucratic communism.

> Nothing can equal the unique ability of capitalism to convert simple human greed into infinitely varied production energies. No purposeful central administration can pursue both efficiency and innovation as successfully as the relentless competition for profit and wealth unleashed by capitalism. No disciplined scheme can coordinate tasks and apportion supplies as harmoniously as the utterly spontaneous workings of capitalist markets, which need no scheme or discipline at all (1999: Preface).

The success and attractiveness of capitalism is mainly due to the institution of private property and free market mechanism.

However, in spite of its many virtues it is generally agreed that there is a need for some measures to control the working of capitalism. The counter force of political power can successfully regulate its strong economic forces. This has become all the more important because of the forces of privatisation, deregulation and globalisation. The defense of private property began when the early liberals, led by Locke conceived that a rough parity in ownership pattern would ensure the long-term success of the modern society. This vision will find its fulfillment only if most countries become property-owning democracies.

Further Readings

Becker, L.C., *Property Rights*, Routledge and Kegan Paul, London, 1977.

Chapman, J.W. and Pennock, R. (Eds.), *NOMOS XXII: Property*, Atherton Press, New York, 1980.

Harris, J.W., *Property and Justice*, Clarendon Press, Oxford, 1996.

Munzer, S.R., *A Theory of Property*, Cambridge University Press, Cambridge, 1990.

Reeve, A., *Property*, Macmillan, London, 1986.

Tully, J., *A Discourse on Property: John Locke and his Adversaries*, Cambridge University Press, Cambridge, 1980.

Tully, J., *The Right to Private Property*, Clarendon Press, Oxford, 1988.

Endnotes

1. A protest by a group of Massachussetts colonists against the Tea Act of 1773 that the British Parliament enacted withdrawing duty on tea exported to the colonies, enabling the East India Company to sell directly to the colonies without first going to Britain. This resulted in underselling of colonial merchandise. The protestors boared three British ships and their cargo of tea into Boston harbour to which the British retaliated by closing the harbour.

2. The subsequent social democratic criticism of Marx, beginning with Bernstein that questions many of these arguments, has been discussed in the chapter on Equality.

Chapter 15

Democracy

The ideals of democracy and freedom have their origins at the very beginning of civilisation though their partial realisation and importance as the first and universal principles of governance became a reality only in the twentieth century. Democracy means rule by the people as contrasted with the rule by a person or a group. It is the people who are both rulers and ruled unlike other systems like monarchy, dictatorship or oligarchy where a distinction between the ruler and ruled exists. It is a system of government in which everyone who belongs to the political organisation that makes decisions, is actually or potentially involved. They all have equal power. How are people understood? Even in Greek the term 'demos' is ambiguous, though the overriding meaning of demos means community assembled in the Ecclesia. Sartori (1987: 22) points out that people mean six things—everybody, a great many, lower class, an organic whole, absolute majority and limited majority. Lively (1975: 30) summarises the range of possible positions about the rule by the people:

1. That all should govern, in the sense, that all should be involved in legislating, in deciding on general policy, in applying laws and in governmental legislation.
2. That all should be personally involved in crucial decision making, that is to say, in deciding general laws and matters of general policy.
3. That rulers should be accountable to the ruled; they should, in other words, be obliged to justify their actions to the ruled and be removable by the ruled.
4. That rulers should be accountable to the representatives of the ruled.
5. That rulers should be chosen by the ruled.
6. That rulers should be chosen by the representatives of the ruled.
7. That rulers should act in the interests of the ruled.

Democracy for Sartori is one in which no one enjoys unconditional and unlimited power. The difference between democracy and its opposite lay precisely in the fact that in a democracy 'power is scattered, limited, controlled and exercised in rotation, whereas in an autocracy power is concentrated, uncontrolled, indefinite and unlimited'. In a democracy, no one can declare himself the ruler and no one can hold power irrevocably in his own name. 'No one can choose himself, no one can invest himself with power to rule and, therefore, no one can arrogate to himself unconditional and unlimited power' (1987: 207). Democracy is precisely non-autocracy just the opposite of autocracy. While democracy is at one end of the spectrum, at the other extreme is totalitarianism and in between lies tyranny, despotism, autocracy, absolutism, dictatorship and authoritarianism.

Democracy also means government by consent that can be elicited through elections that register voters' decision. Election is the mechanical process through which democracy functions but what is more important is the condition under which a citizen gets the information, for 'the opinion of the governed is the real foundation of all government' (Dicey 1905: 3). Election is the means to an end—the end being a 'government of opinion', a government responsive and responsible to public opinion. Democracy also uses techniques such as referendum to elicit people's opinion. There is also a clamour to insert techniques such as recall in representative democracies to make it more responsive.[2] Election must be free but this is not enough, for opinion must also be free otherwise 'free elections with unfree opinion express nothing ... an empty sovereign who has nothing to say, without opinions of his own, is a mere ratifier a sovereign of nothing' (Sartori 1987: 87). The ways in which opinions are formed relate to the notion of consensus, which does not merely refer to actual consent, but a 'sharing' that somehow binds. Sharing refers to what Easton (1965) calls three levels of consensus—(a) consensus at the *community level*, or basis consensus; (b) consensus at the *regime level* or procedural consensus; (c) consensus at the *policy level* or policy consensus. The first refers to the same value beliefs and value goals that a given society shares in its entirety. This is a facilitating condition of democracy. The second, are the rules of the game of which the most important is the way conflicts are resolved. Usually, a democracy resolves conflict through majority rule. If majority rule is not acceptable, then there must be an agreement (a) on the rules for disagreeing and for processing disagreements and (b) disagreements within such rules are those that democracy protects and extends (Sartori 1987: 91). The third or the level of consensus over policies emerges through discussion which is 'the basis and essence of all democracy' (Barker 1942: 67). The second and third are necessary conditions of democracy and its presence signals the beginning of democracy.

Democracy is the majority rule-cum-minority rights. Thus, democracy, according to Gallie (1955–1956), is a contested concept, for it is difficult to resolve its meaning since its exponents and practitioners attribute to it values that they favour. For instance, during the Cold War era, both the United States and the former Soviet Union declared themselves democracies though their political systems substantially differed. For the ancients and in Athens, where it originated, democracy meant rule by the people—*demos*—while, in the modern sense, democracy signifies popular sovereignty, representative government as well as direct participatory government also including, though not appropriately, constitutional rule.

Sartori observes that the difference between the two—ancient and modern democracy—is not merely one 'of geographic and demographic dimensions ... but also one of ends and values' (1987: 279). In Athens, democracy was a system of government in which decisions were made collectively. It was a co-extension of community with the individual having no independence and no space that was his, for the community absorbed the individual wholly. In the modern sense, a person other than being a citizen of a state also has his private domain. Modern democracy protects the freedom of the individual as a person, something that the collectivity cannot be entrusted to ensure. Democracy is about political freedom that protects with the help of law and allows the individuals to choose and without it the idea of democracy is a farce (Sartori 1987: 286, 301). The classical democratic theory is based on the following ideas—(a) supremacy of the people, (b) the consent of the governed as the basis of legitimacy, (c) the rule of law as a peaceful method of conflict resolution, (d) the existence of a common good or public interest, (e) the value of the individual as a rational, moral active citizen and (f) equal rights for all individuals (Goodwin 1992: 220).

TYPES OF DEMOCRACY

Sartori (1987: 8–12) contrasts **political democracy** from other types of democracy that are understood in a non-political or sub-political sense and mentions social democracy, industrial democracy and economic democracy. The notion of social democracy is associated with Tocqueville who was impressed with the societal premises—equality of status, manners and customs of American democracy. He attributes this ideal of equality to the absence of a feudal past and finds its spirit permeate the whole of American society. Thus, Tocqueville, contrasts democracy with aristocracy, considers democracy as a state of society rather than a political form. After Tocqueville, it is Bryce who best explains the idea of democracy as a way of life and a type of society. A social democracy is a society that considers its members as socially equal. It also refers to a web of small communities and voluntary organisations that prosper throughout a society arising spontaneously and endogenously and acting as the foundation of the political superstructure. This distinguishes it from **socialist democracy**, which is superimposed by the state as a way of governing and is a way of life as social democracy is. It should not be confused with **social democracy**, an ideological posture adopted by some socialist parties from the late nineteenth century highlighting the importance of gradual reforms as a way of attaining socialism.

Industrial democracy is a term coined by Sidney and Beatrice Webb but G.D.H. Cole was its most influential exponent. Cole believes that realisation of democracy at the grassroots, at the workplace, ultimately paves the way for efficiency, harmony and unity of purpose. Active participation leads to the creation of a community of interest synthesising individual and collective good. A genuine democracy has to be based on a system of coordinated functional representation. Representation has to be specific and functional rather than general and inclusive. This theory of representing functions is similar to Burke's proposal to institutionalise an anti-democratic oligarchic power structure with a natural aristocracy at the helm. Cole desires to make democracy a living reality in every sphere of social, economic and political activity. He observes the failure of self-governed industries due to the overall capitalistic environment in which they functioned. The workers' urge for participation and social plurality are the essential conditions for a vibrant industrial democracy. Economic democracy concerns itself with equalisation of wealth through redistribution of wealth and equalisation of economic opportunities and conditions. Unlike social democracy and industrial democracy that 'address clearly identifiable structures and connote a nonpolitical democracy ... economic democracy ... merely signifies a policy ... enacted by political democracy within its structures and via its procedures' (Sartori 1987: 11).

DEMOCRACY AS AN IDEAL

Evolution of the Idea

In ancient Athens, democracy started as the direct participation of all adult male citizens and differed from the representative democracies of the nineteenth and twentieth centuries. However, the prominent theorists of the ancient world—Plato, Aristotle, Polybius, Cicero and Augustine—considered mixed constitutions, one that combined democratic and oligarchic principles to be the most enduring. They included democracy in the standard classification of constitutions on the basis of the numbers wielding power. Their suspicion of democracy derived from the distrust that they entertained about the many that included non-propertied, the poor and the illiterate—the mob. Plato was highly critical of democracy for its lack of expertise in government, indiscipline and selfishness. Aristotle considered it politically unstable due to the polarisation between the rich and the poor. The Renaissance theorists like Machiavelli incorporated democratic ideal as one of the components of a mixed republican constitution. He conceived of political participation not merely in terms of the involvement of the wealthy and/or noble but also of artisans and small traders (Held 1987: 47). The social contract used the democratic ideal to challenge the traditional absolutism and the divine right of kings. Its conception of the state as a mechanistic artifice assumed prominence, setting aside the organic conception. The contract tradition established the true foundations for later democratic governments by arguing that individuals endowed with natural rights and liberties were the creators and judge of governments. Once and for all it demolished and de-legitimised the idea of hereditary and divine kingly rule as natural. Since the eighteenth century, democracy became the yardstick to measure governments and regimes. The Helvetic Republic of 1798 proclaimed itself to be a democracy. In the nineteenth century, democracy was equated with representative government in which representatives were chosen by free competitive elections with male citizens exercising their franchise. This was the case in the US during the 1830s and 1840s. In Britain, franchise was successively broadened in 1832, 1867 and 1884. Women in most parts of the world, except for New Zealand, where they were enfranchised in 1895 received the right to vote only in the first quarter of the twentieth century. This extension of the franchise by guaranteeing universal suffrage and reform of electoral systems in the West, by the second half of the twentieth century, made democracy the established system of government. Universal suffrage and public education, made it possible for the informed public to participate in the electoral system. This spread to the colonised world where people aspiring for independence demanded the right to collective self-determination rather than mere self-government. Once independent, many of them declared themselves democracies or peoples' republics. There was also a shift from the political meaning of democracy to social and economic ones involving issues of production, distribution, class and property-ownership. The relationship between the legal and political aspect considered as formal, with social and economic aspect regarded as substantive, came under rigorous and intense scholarly scrutiny. The older democracies of the West emphasised on traditional civil and political rights, parliamentary institutions and multi- or two-party system, while the newer ones placed greater premium on egalitarianism, public planning, economic freedom and one-party system. However, with the collapse of communism and the retreat of authoritarianism, both right and left, liberal democracy has become universal. In this long chequered history of democracy, there have been three models—(a) participatory or direct democracy as in ancient Athens, (b) liberal representative democracy and (c) one party democracy that existed in the erstwhile communist systems and in certain parts of Africa. Every ideology has used democracy in its own way to describe its ideal as the most democratic of all systems.

Ancient Direct Democracy

It was more than 2500 years ago, in 508–07 BC, in the Greek city-state of Athens that the first major effort to realise democracy and freedom was attempted, with the establishment of a vibrant, direct and participatory democracy that remains unparalleled till date, both in the ancient and the modern world. This unique achievement was made possible with the creation of the *polis* that provided a way of life for the individual to attain fulfillment and excellence. An important reason for the spectacular success of the Athenian democracy was the overall moderateness and reasonableness among all sections of the people, facts still considered important for the success of democracy today. Unlike Rome, the changes in Athens were peaceful and non-violent. The first manifestation of this democratic temper was evident in the formation of the Union of Attica (the area surrounding Athens was called Attica and the city-state of Athens included both Athens city and Attica) in the fifth century BC. The most distinctive aspect about ancient democracy was that it was stateless since the *polis* was a *koinonia*, a community (Sartori 1987: 279).

Solon's wise and judicious rule witnessed a number of important reforms that resulted in the creation of an exclusive 'citizen elite' devoting time to political debates and duties of citizenship. These reforms checked the growth of noble estates and allowed the creation of small and medium farms. It is noteworthy that Rousseau, an admirer of the Greek *polis*, conceived his ideal as consisting of individuals—small and independent property owners—as equal lawmakers in a direct assembly. In the year 508–07 BC, **Cleithenes** with a view to preventing tyranny and diminishing the strength of the nobility, divided the whole city into demes each having its own assembly, magistrates and administration. Democracy reached its peak under the stewardship of **Pericles** (493–29 BC) for whom it meant a form of government as a cooperative-enterprise of all citizens, rich and poor, high and low. He extended the authority and voice of the people within the free institutions of Athens and introduced remuneration for the performance of public duties and military services. **Plato** and Socrates criticised these measures accusing Pericles of instilling in the Athenian the love for money in exchange of their performance of public duties and for doing what people thought to be good rather than doing what is good for the people. His Funeral Oration Speech outlined the political ideals and values of the Athenian institution in view of the challenge that Sparta posed both militarily and ideologically, similar to the Cold War tussle between the US and the former USSR in the twentieth century. Pericles characterised the Athenian government as a democracy, for it attended to the welfare of the many rather than few. It provided equal justice and equal rights to all irrespective of distinctions. Equality, the distinguishing feature of Athenian democracy inspired Rousseau, Macpherson and Pateman. Merit over-ridded class considerations and public officers were filled according to individual's capacity. Democracy meant citizens' self rule and direct participation in public affairs. Public service was not considered a matter of privilege by a reward for merit. This ideal of common public participation excluded none because of their wealth, rank or status in society. None was born to an office and none could buy an office. The natural political capacity of the average person was accepted. Pericles remarked on this happy versatility in the average Athenian with pride:

> An Athenian citizen does not neglect the state because he takes care of his own household; and even those of us who are engaged in business have a very fair idea of politics. We alone regard a man who takes no interest in public affairs, not as harmless, but as useless characters and if few of us are originators, we are all sound judges of policy (cited in Finley 1951: 106).

Plato criticised this Athenian practice as amatuerism in politics. The citizens voluntarily performed their public duties and cooperated with one another through a free and full discussion of policy in all respects. Freedom of the citizen lay in his power to convince and get convinced in a free public discourse with his fellow beings. Democracy was crucial to the Athenian in order to live in freedom both individually and collectively. Freedom meant respect for the rule of law and customs. Tyranny was considered as the worst form of government, for it exercised power unlawfully and even if beneficent destroyed self-government. A good government respects freedom and the rule of law. The Athenian valued freedom in both private and in public pursuits and that rights and duties realisable within the community. These rights and obligations were not for the maintenance of a framework to protect his own private ends (Sabine 1973: 16–17).

It could be argued that the Athenian democracy was essentially incomplete, for it excluded women, resident aliens and slaves from the democratic process and treated few alone as free. Hegel contended that the Greek realised freedom only partially for they did not develop the idea of free individuality, individual conscience and could not conceive of themselves as separate entities from the community. Durant (1939: 266) described it as 'the narrowest and fullest in history: narrowest in the number of those who share its privileges, fullest in the directness and equality with which all the citizens control legislation and administer public affair'. This glorious experiment came to an end with the defeat of Athens in the Peloponnesian War. With the rise of Macedonia under Philip II (359–36 BC) and Alexander (336–32 BC), the city-states and democracy in Athens went in oblivion. This, however, did not mean the end of the ideals of Athenian democracy, for these have become an integral part of democratic theory.

Liberal Democracy

The term 'liberal democracy' contains two interdependent and complex ideas. Liberalism stands for 'freeing the people' and democracy for 'empowering the people'. Liberal democracy in effect 'consists of "demo-protection", meaning protection of a people from tyranny, and "demo-power", meaning the implementation of popular rule' (Sartori 1995: 102). A liberal state did not begin as a democratic one but with the widening of suffrage and improved techniques of participation, has emerged as a democratic state.

> Liberal ideas and democratic procedures have gradually become interwoven. While it is true that rights to liberty have from the beginning been a necessary condition for the proper application of the rules of the democratic game, it is equally true that the development of democracy has over time become the principal tool for the defence of rights to liberty. Today, the only democratic states are those who were born out of the liberal revolution and only in democratic states are the rights

of man protected: every authoritarian state in the world is at one anti-liberal and anti-democratic (Bobbio 1990: 39).

There can be democratic states like the post-Revolutionary Iran, according to Fukuyama (1992: 44), without being liberal, meaning that citizens have the right to vote but without other individual rights. Liberal democracy has developed from protective to developmental notions of democracy (Held 1987).

Locke conceives of a liberal state through majority rule principle, supremacy of the legislature, consent—direct and indirect—and representative institutions. His definition of political authority as a trust that respects individual rights helps him to work out the basis for a responsive, responsible and accountable government. His conception of the individual as a moral and rational person capable of knowing and deciding his interests makes him reject paternalism as both unsuitable and oppressive. He also gives the people the right to judge and assess the performance of their government and seek redress for their grievance. However, 'most of these ideas were in rudimentary form but stimulate the development of liberal democratic ideas' (Dunn 1980: 53–77). The later liberals focus on how to make governments free and representative, as people's participation and representative institutions are crucial to a liberal state. Locke's suggestion of separation of powers is developed by Montesquieu who prescribes it as the necessary institutional requirement of a representative democracy in order to curtail the highly centralised authority and ensure a virtuous government through checks and balances. His importance lies in his realisation of the pivotal role that institutions play in ensuring effective and good government, particularly in view of the tendency among human beings to place their own particular interests over that of others (Krouse 1983: 61–62). For both Locke and Montesquieu the legally sanctioned political power must have limits. Paine, a century later, affirms Locke's principles with a new emphasis that democratic theory no longer represents people's collective rights against the king but individual rights that guarantee and safeguard one's independence against the state or government. The Bill of Rights of 1789 of the United States Constitution exemplified this shift.

The drafting of the US constitution, the world's first written constitution helps to apply democratic theory in practice. In the US there was a debate between the Federalists and Anti Federalists. with the latter making a populist case for direct democracy with citizens participating actively which, for the Federalists considered as naïve and dangerous. Hamilton's fear of mob rule, a democratic phantom since Plato's times is reflected in the provisions of indirect elections of the Senate and the Presidency, and for allowing state legislatures to stipulate restrictions in franchise. Madison assimilates the views of Hobbes, Locke and Montesquieu and develops them into a cogent political theory and strategy. From Hobbes he accepts the fact that self-interest has to be the basis of politics. From Locke he realises the importance of protecting individual freedom through the institution of public power that is legally limited and accountable ultimately to the people. From Montesquieu, he appreciates that the principle of separation of powers is crucial to the formation of a legitimate state. He considers factions to be inevitable, a fact that politics has to effectively deal with, since dissent, argument, conflicts of interest and clashes of judgment are inescapable because their roots lie in human nature. He also regards every nation as being divided into classes based on property but does not consider the elimination of private property as a way of resolving class conflict. He tries to find the mechanism that regulates the diverse and intruding interests in a manner that they become part of the necessary and ordinary operation of government. His remedy was a powerful American state that acts as bulwark against tyranny and as a means to control the violence that factions unleash. This republican state will periodically face the judgement of the citizens and the ballot box will overcome the political difficulties caused by minority interest groups. In order to counter the tyranny of the majority, he proposes certain measures. First, the number of representatives must be raised to a certain level 'to guard against the cabals of a few'. Social diversity creates political fragmentation that prohibits disproportionate accumulation of power, a view that has exerted considerable influence on the pluralist tradition after the Second World War. Madison advocates representation of different groups and interests, favours cooperation, deliberation and bargaining as a method of decision-making, as opposed to majority rule and voting in English Parliament. This is the difference between the American and British versions of democratic ideal though Locke is the common factor to both. To offset the possibility of representatives becoming remote and impersonal in a large state, Madison proposes federal constitution with separation of powers. The federal representative state will protect individual interests and their rights and sustain security of persons and their property and make politics compatible with the complex modern state due to its trade, commerce and international relations. Madison champions popular governments as long as the majority does not try to run roughshod on minority's privilege with the help of the state. According to Madison there should be representation but in the House of Representative and the Senate filtering it along with the other two branches of the government, to 'cool' House legislation as a saucer cools hot tea', a comment that Washington makes to Jefferson. Paine's close friend, Jefferson favours the rule by a natural aristocracy that combines virtue and talent and not wealth and birth for its effects on society are negative. This natural aristocracy provides the political leadership for the well-ordered and just participatory political model. Burke too supports the rule by a few of the enlightened and aristocratic elite with limited citizenship confined to a segment of adults who own property and have the leisure for discussions and information, and mentally independent. Burke also questions the doctrines of natural rights and the social contract as an appropriate criterion of establishing the state. The masses lack the capacity to rule. Rousseau and Burke attack the individualist basis of liberal democracy, a theme that continues in Marx subsequently.

By the late eighteenth century, liberalism becomes a national philosophy in England with utilitarianism playing an important role. It clearly insists that the government has to be responsive to human needs and in view of that, initiates a series of legal and economic reforms to undermine the monopoly of the land-owning class and freeing commerce from tariffs and other regulatory laws. This forms the basis for their defense of democratic procedures as it generates and safeguards public interests and checks governmental abuse of that interest. Bentham, influenced by James Mill, is convinced that universal suffrage makes governments accountable and less whimsical. A good government makes possible what he calls democratic ascendancy. He grants to the people the power to select and dismiss their rulers. He drafts a complete scheme of parliamentary democracy in his *Constitutional Code* (1830) that pleads for secret ballot, annual elections, equal electoral districts, annual parliaments, a scheme for elementary, secondary and technical public education, election of the prime minister by the parliament, abolition of monarchy, the British House of Lords and unicameralism, checks on legislative authority and rejects plural voting. He also recommends the need for central inspection, a public prosecutor, recruitment of the young in the government and competitive civil service examinations. Annual elections maximise aptitude and minimise expenses and ensure high quality officials and representatives. The threat of dismissal ensures accountability and responsibility. Unlike James Mill (1773–1836), Bentham insists on a code of penal sanctions and attaches considerable importance to public opinion. He accepts that even within democracies an oligarchy exists and tries to control the system but there is nothing negative about this, as there is an assurance both expertise and representation. He views representative government as a solution to the problem raised by Plato, namely finding experts to rule. He accepts that all individuals will be corrupt and the only precaution is to give power to the people, for that ensures the greatest happiness of the greatest number. Like Plato, he accepts, that governing is a skill and that all are not capable of ruling, which is why representatives are needed. Democracy ensures good rule and control of rulers. He rejects the idea of mixed constitution and representing interests, for interests change as Burke proposes and with it representation would also change. The utilitarians defend representation of people, for each individual has a right to be represented and therefore should have the right to vote. In a *Fragment on Government* (1776), Bentham uses the criterion of circumstances to distinguish a free and a despotic government. Free government depends, on the manner in which that whole mass of power, which taken together, is supreme, is in a free state, distributed among the several ranks of persons that are sharers in it; on the source from whence their titles to it are successively derived; on the frequent and easy changes of condition between governors and governed; whereby the interests of one class are more or less indistinguishably blended with those of the other; on the responsibility of the governors; or the right which a subject has of having the reasons publicly assigned and canvassed of every act of power that is exerted over him; on the liberty of press; or the security with which every man, be he of the one class or the other, may make known his complaints and remonstrances to the whole community: on the liberty of public association; or the security with which malcontents may communicate their sentiments, construct their plans, and practice every mode of opposition short of actual revolt, before the executive power can be legally justified in disturbing them (Bentham 1977: 485).

The concern for minority rights and rights of individuality makes J.S. Mill adopt measures against tyranny of the majority thus emphasising on the need for individual rights, tolerance and a liberal society for the proper functioning of democracy. He, like Rousseau, regards democracy as necessary for progress, as it permits citizens to use and develop their faculties fully. It promotes virtue, intelligence and excellence (Macpherson 1977: Ch. 3, Dunn 1979: 51–53). It allows education of the citizens by providing 'an efficient forum for conducting the collective affairs of the community' (Mill 1976: 193–195, 196), a point that theorists like Macpherson and Pateman find inspiring to reiterate in their models of participatory democracy. However, unlike Rousseau, J.S. Mill considers representative democracy as capable of ensuring freedom and right of self-determination. Interaction between individuals in a democracy ensures the possibility of the emergence of the wisest and recognition of the best leaders. It encourages free discussion, which is necessary for the emergence of the truth. He accepts all citizens regardless of their status as equal and that only popular sovereignty gives legitimacy to the government thus attempting to reconcile the principle of political equality with individual freedom (Hacker 1961: 573).

Mill lays down several conditions for the success of representative government such as 'active, self-helping character' citizenry. Backward civilisations where citizens are primarily passive can hardly be able to run a representative democracy. Second, citizens have to show their ability and willingness to preserve institutions of representative democracy. Influenced by Tocqueville's thesis on majority tyranny, Mill advocates a liberal democracy which specifies and limits the powers of legally elected majorities by cataloguing and protecting individual rights against the majority. He pleads for balancing the numerical majority in a democracy by adjusting franchise. Even though he advocates universal adult franchise in 1859 he concedes in 1861 as to whether 'any person should participate in the suffrage without being able to read, write, and I will add, perform the operations of arithmetic' (Mill 1976: 280). He prescribes registration tests for checking performances, universal education for all children and plurality of votes to the better educated in order to balance the lack of voting rights to the uneducated. He also recommends disqualification of three other categories of dependants: those unable to pay local taxes, legally bankrupts and moral deviants like habitual drunkards and those dependent on public welfare will be excluded for five years from the last day of receipt for 'by becoming dependent on the remaining members of the community for actual subsistence, he abdicates his claim to equal rights with them in other respects' (1976: 282). He, however, champions equal voting rights for all irrespective of their sex or colour. Mill regards equal voting rights, universal suffrage, democracy and liberty as conditional good and conferred only on those who have the character for self-control and the ability and the interest in using them for public good. The policy of a government in franchise reform should be 'to make participation in political rights the reward for mental improvement ... I do not look upon equal voting as among the things, which are good in themselves, provided they can be guarded against inconveniences. I look upon it as only relatively good, less objectionable than inequality of privilege' (1976: 288). Mill also recommends 'open' rather than secret ballot. Voting is public trust which 'should be performed under the eye and criticism of the public' (1976: 286). Open voting is less dangerous for the voter is less influenced by the 'sinister interests and discreditable feelings, which belong to himself, either individually or as a member of a class' (1976: 289).

Mill believes that citizens develop intellectual qualities of reason, judgement and moral maturity only through political participation. He worries about the consequences of absolute equality—the trampling of a wise and educated minority by the masses—that universal adult franchise entails, for he recommends compulsory elementary education that makes individual citizens wise, competent and independent judges (Mill 1902: 575–576). He considers representative democracy to succeed only in small and homogenous states, which has been negated by experiences of plural democracies like India. He rules out the Athenian model for modern complex societies in view of vast numbers, physical and geographical constraints. A government in which all participate faces the constant danger of the wisest and the ablest, being overshadowed by those who lack knowledge, skill and expertise. The majority can gain experience in public affairs through jury service and extensive involvement in local government but that ought to be limited. The ideal is people 'exercise through deputies whom they periodically elect as the ultimate controlling power' (Mill 1976: 228). A representative government along with freedom of speech, the press and assembly provides the mechanism that watch and control central powers, established a forum (parliament) to act as a watchdog of liberty and centre for reason and debate. It 'harnesses through electoral competition leadership qualities with intellect for the maximum benefit of all' (1976: 195, 239–240). Mill argues that there is no alternative to representative democracy though it has its costs like inflexibility, rigid routines and loss of individuality and limiting innovation. However, it guarantees accountability with professionalism and expertise. He values both democracy and skilled government and considered one as guaranteeing the other and that neither can be attained all by itself (Held 1987: 95).

Tocqueville in *Democracy in America* (1835) emphasises on the moral rightness of democracy, though he is cautious about its implications. An aristocrat by instinct he fears and despises the masses but is prepared to accept the defeat of his class. He understands democracy to mean not only increased political participation but also civic and social equality. He categorically states that democracy does not rest on either constitutional arrangements or laws but on mores of society, which embrace both habits and opinions that religion makes possible by inculcating moral habits, with respect to all human beings. This is necessary in a free society in the absence of political control. This constitutes the essence of the success of American religion.

In contrast, in Europe, the champions of human freedom having attacked religious opinions do not realise that without religious faith despotism is inevitable and liberty unrealisable. The lack of self-restraint due to destruction of faith, according to Tocqueville, leads to the reign of terror after the French Revolution. In the absence of religion, atheism and tyranny is the fate of all modern democracies. A liberal-conservative, he considers religion as a 'political institution' and vital to the preservation of freedom in a democratic society particularly from the despotic tendencies that equality of conditions unleashes. He observes while 'despotism may govern without religion ... liberty cannot'. This extraordinary emphasis on religion is because of its crucial role in establishing democracy in France and other Christian states of Europe. He concludes that due to the variance between 'the spirit of religion' and 'the spirit of freedom' democracy fails in Europe. The alliance between the Catholic Church and the French monarchy, although injurious to religion in itself, is characteristic of a more calamitous alliance between Christianity and the moribund aristocracy. The Church considers democracy to be antithetical to religion and consequently an enemy. In America the two remains closely linked explaining the success of democracy there. America, the nascent Puritan commonwealth rejects Europe's aristocratic heritage, bringing to the New World a Christianity that is democratic, constitutional and republican and introduces principles like the participation by the people in rule, the free voting of taxes, the responsibility of political representatives, personal liberty and trial by jury. They instill a love of freedom anchored in religious conviction teaching the Americans that their freedom is a gift from God and therefore has to be taken seriously and used wisely.

Religion according to Tocqueville teaches human beings to strive for eternal happiness by resisting 'the selfish passions of the hour' and thus democratic individuals learn that only through persistence and hard work something permanent can be attained in both private and public spheres. Tocqueville, though himself a practicing Catholic, acknowledges like Weber later that the Protestant ethic encourages individualism and freedom but with proper respect for political authority. This increases with greater social equality and the support that the middle class extend to democracy. The combination of all these factors led to the American success with a harmonious evolution of both Christianity and democracy in America. Interestingly, this unique achievement of America is made possible by realising the principle of separation of the Church and the state preventing the consolidation of vested religious interests' in particular political parties and groups as has happened in Europe.

In America, religion has no fear of democracy and democracy has no fear from religion. In fact, democracy facilitates the spread of religion by guaranteeing the right of religious beliefs. All religious faiths gain by political liberty and, consequently, religion also supports the separation of the state and the Church.

Besides religion, the second important factor conducive for democracy in America is equality of conditions. Interestingly, this attribute by itself does not lead to freedom and is compatible with a new kind of despotism made possible by the forces of individualism and materialism that democracy unleashes. While old aristocracies with their hierarchical class structures allow people to forge firm and lasting political ties, democracies with their doctrine of equality loosen those bonds. A large number of human beings becomes economically independent and as a result wrongly assumes that they have complete control of their destinies. This false sense of independence changes the sentiments of obligation that aristocracy fosters into radical self-interest. Religion emerges as the saviour of democracy by checking this degeneration. Tocqueville concedes that religion may be unable to contain the entire urge of individualism and the pursuit of well-being, but it is the only mechanism of moderation and education. He sees religion sustaining moderate individualism with drive for material prosperity, both of which are essential for the success of democracy. Instead of seeing religion as an antithesis of human liberation as Marx does, Tocqueville acknowledges a happy blending of democracy and religion as possible and desirable.

Against the onslaught faced by totalitarian regimes of communism and fascism in the 1930s, philosophers like Berlin, Hayek and Popper defend liberal values. **Berlin's** pluralism defends the multiplicity and variety of human ends. He rejects the possibility of a single pattern of values or a social order. Monism, the opposite of pluralism, only leads to fanaticism and totalitarianism. Hayek upholds moral individualism and values pluralism as exemplified by the spontaneous social order based on market operations. He considers democracy as the best means to secure and safeguard liberty, the highest political end. **Popper** understands democracy to mean changing power without violence, so the question is not how we can get good rulers but how to minimise the damages of misrule, possibilities of its occurring and if it occurs how to deal with its consequences. He highlights the paradox of democracy—the fact that democracy can commit suicide by electing tyranny as it did at the sad end of the Weimar Republic in 1933.

In the late 1960s, the neo-conservatives desire to restore the American pluralist and representative democracy by strengthening mediating institutions that anchor individual firmly and securely in his community and by rejecting participatory and egalitarian variants of democracy. They affirm their faith in the constitutional processes and believe that power ought to be limited through checks and balances. They consider wider participation and economic equality as a product of heightened expectations among the new class and its culture. They do not define the composition of this new class. It includes professionals and journalists and at times graduates and undergraduates, technicians and service workers. As a result, they observed that the political system is overloaded and the citizenry unmanageable and ungovernable. Huntington (1968) characterises this situation as 'democratic distemper' which can be reduced through moderation at all levels and by apathy and non-involvement on the part of some individuals and groups.

DEMOCRACY AS A PROCEDURE

Elitism

The classical elitists—Pareto, Mosca and Michels—dismiss the idea of popular representation as a fiction and argue that there is no such thing as majority rule. In most societies—liberal and Marxist, it is an elite that rules, controls key resources and takes major decisions. **Pareto** (1935) distinguishes the governing and non-governing elite from the masses. **Michels** points out to the iron law of oligarchy in one of the most democratically organised political parties—the German SPD. Many see this as ominous with exceptions like Jose Ortega y Gasset (1883–1955) who in *The Revolt of the Masses* (1961) praise elitism and deplore mass mediocrity of democratic society. He maintains that it is the duty of the masses to follow the elite and that a properly constituted mass and elite is the key to a nation's well-being. These propositions are empirically tested during the behavioural persuasion in politics in the 1950s and 1960s and a general conclusion is that elite groups dominate local politics.

Joseph Alios Schumpeter (1883–1950) tries to make democracy and elitism compatible. He defines democracy as a political method to arrive at political, legislative and administrative decisions by placing in certain individuals the power to decide on all matters as a consequence of their successful pursuit of people's vote (1976: 269). His account is known as democratic elitism (Bachrach 1962) because he reasons that free elections introduce an element of competition among elite groups. He believes that powerful social forces limit participation in politics and that liberal democracy at the very best is a restrictive endeavour for selecting decision-makers and ensuring their legitimacy through elections. He shares Marx's view of the inevitability of the collapse of capitalism due to its own internal contradictions and argues, like Marx, that large corporations dominate production and distribution of goods but rejects Marxist class analysis and class conflict. He considers it appropriate for socialists to develop a suitable model of democracy to fulfil the requirements of big government in context of the importance of planning. He rejects the idea of common good in classical theory as both misleading and dangerous, for people have different wants and different values. Rarely there exists an agreement among individuals and groups about ends and even if there is one there will be disagreements about the means to be employed for the realisation of a given end. In modern societies that are economically and culturally diverse, there are bound to be different notions of common good. He declares the notion of common good as an unacceptable element of democratic theory. In modern complex societies, people's wills are conflicting and divergent (1976: 252 ff). As opposed to the classical democratic theory, he believes that decisions of non-democratic agencies may sometimes prove more acceptable to people than democratic decisions. In this context, he cites the example of the religious settlement, which Napoleon Bonaparte imposed on France at the beginning of the nineteenth century. He observes that this example is far from isolated, 'If results that prove in the long run satisfactory to the people at large are made the test of government *for* the people, then government *by* the people, as conceived by the classical doctrine of democracy, would often fail to meet it' (1976: 256). He rejects explicitly the tenet of classical theory democracy and held that people are and can be nothing more than 'producers of governments' a mechanism to select 'the men who are able to do the deciding (1976: 296). Hence, he disproves the notion of the 'popular will' as a social construct that had no rational basis, as a 'manufactured' rather than a genuine popular will. 'Popular will' is therefore the 'product and not the motive power for the political process' (1976: 263). Democracy, for Schumpeter, merely legitimises competition among governing elites, for he accepts the inevitability of hierarchy and considers the democratic process as a procedure as 'simply an institutional arrangement for reaching political decisions not an end in itself (1976: 126). He draws an analogy between political behaviour and market behaviour where leaders compete for people's votes, the vote having the same importance as money in the market. He perceives a division between political activists and a passive electorate as the key to a strong, efficient government and defense of liberty. Viewed in this perspective democracy and socialism are compatible provided the conditions for its successful functioning are met. These are:

1. The calibre of politician must be high.
2. Competition between rival leaders (and parties) must take place within a relatively restricted range of political questions, bounded by consensus on the overall direction of national policy, on what constitutes a reasonable parliamentary programme and on general constitutional matters.
3. A well-trained independent bureaucracy of 'good standing and tradition' must exist to aid politicians on all aspects of policy formulation and administration.
4. There must be 'democratic self-control', i.e., broad agreement about the undesirability of, for instance, voters and politicians confusing their respective roles, excessive criticism of government on all issues, and unpredictable and violent behaviour.
5. There must be a culture capable of tolerating differences of opinion (1976: 296).

Schumpeter cautions against the collapse of democracy when ideologies and interests are held resolutely, for then people are unwilling to compromise and such a situation would indicate an end to democratic politics. He contends that his account of democracy has some definitive advantages over other theories. It provides an efficient criterion for distinguishing democratic governments from others, acknowledges fully the centrality of leadership and establishes the importance of competition, in politics and, even if imperfect, shows how governments are created and destroyed. The theory clarifies the nature of popular wishes without exaggerating their significance. Schumpeter points out that his theory explains the relationship between democracy and freedom. If freedom means 'the existence of a sphere of individual self-government' (1976: 270–271), then the democracy method requires that everyone is in principle, free to compete for political leadership. This is possible only if there is considerable amount of freedom of discussion *for all* and that entails both freedom of speech and freedom of press.

Schumpeter's theory of democracy highlights many recognising features of modern Western liberal democracies—the competitive struggle between parties for political power; the important role of public bureaucracies; the significance of political leadership; the way in which modern politics deploys many of the techniques of advertising; the way voters are subject to a constant barrage of information, written materials and discussion; and the way, despite these barrage, many voters remain poorly informed about contemporary political issues and express marked uncertainty about them (Held J. 987: 178).

There are some fallacious assumptions in Schumpeter's analyses. He seems to suggest that there is one well-developed classical theory of democracy, which is not the case, for there are a number of models within it (Held 1987: 179). Schumpeter defines democracy with reference to procedures, practices and goals that are prevalent at the time of his writing in the West. He does not take into consideration theories that criticise reality—vision of human nature and of social arrangements that explicitly reject the status quo and propose alternatives (Duncan and Lukes 1963). This criticism would have been more substantive if it has been invalidated by empirical evidence or through a well-argued logical construction. Schumpeter's basic contention is that the tall claims of classical democratic theory are inoperative in the actual functioning of liberal democracies. His argument that his theory of democratic elitism is akin to a competitive market economy providing legitimacy can be questioned on two grounds—(a) That the motivation of each individual voter differs like tradition, apathy, coercion, pragmatic acquiescence, conditional agreement, normative agreement or ideas normative agreement and (b) the manipulation and distortion of political will by holders of political power point to the complexities of the close relationship between legitimacy and power, which Schumpeter overlooks. However, with regard to both these criticisms, Schumpeter is on a firm ground. As regards the first one, his theory emphasises on the atomisation of individual behaviour and regarding the second, his procedural theory seeks to provide a functioning model of competitive party system where these larger normative questions are of little relevance. Macpherson (1977: 89) observes that it is appropriate to describe Schumpeter's model as 'oligopolistic' for 'there are only a few sellers, a few suppliers of political goods ... where there are so few sellers, they need not and do not respond to the buyers' demands as they must do in a fully competitive system. They can set prices and set in range of goods that will, be offered. More than that, they can, to a considerable extent, create ... (their own) demand.

C. Wright Mills' famous gloss of Schumpeter's argument reveals the workings of an industrial-military-political complex in American national politics. The power elite is far more powerful than the other elites and that explains the promotion of arms race, though Mills insists that power elite submit to the control of the intellectuals. This, however, questions Schumpeter's belief that elites are periodically responsible to the people through elections. Bachrach reacting to the elite perception of treating people passively, incapable of making judgment or exercising power points out that 20 per cent of the 'apathetic voters' in the US in the 1950s and 1960s were the poorest strata of society. Instead of revising the democratic ideal, Bachrach considers it necessary to reform social conditions.

Pluralism

The pluralists accept diversity and contend that the modern liberal state is too complex for any single group, class or organisation to dominate society. Pluralism affirms the separation of state and civil society and distinguish economic from political power. It considers the political system to be all-inclusive operating on the basis of consensus by taking into account everyone's interests and ensuring satisfaction of everyone. It differs from the elite theory that establishes a dichotomy between the rulers and ruled. The classical theory of democracy posits the existence of common good that the democratic system throws up, while the pluralists accept that the existence of groups of particular interests does not necessarily indicate the absence of general interest. The classical theory of democracy perceives individuals as isolated and discrete persons and not as members of a group(s) that overlap. This is unrealistic in view of the multiple identities of a person in a modern society. Pluralism, like Madison's, is preoccupied with factions and pressure groups, for it considers society to be essentially heterogeneous and pluralistic with diverse aspirations, interests and wills. It accepts Madison's concern for factions and its modern counterpart—interest groups and pressure groups—as a natural counterpart of free association in a world where most desired goods are scarce and where the complex industrial system fragments social interests and creates a multiplicity of demands. Like Madison, the pluralists accept that the basic function of government is to protect the freedom of factions to advance their political interests, while preventing any individual faction from encroaching on the freedom of others.

However, they differ from Madison in not regarding factions as a major threat to democratic associations or as a source of instability or as undemocratic in nature. They consider the existence of diverse competitive interests as the basis of democratic equilibrium and for a favourable development of public policy. The pluralists combine Locke's individualism, Dewey's participatory ethic with Burke's concern for continuity and stability.

Dahl specifies the exact nature of pluralist democracies and argues—(a) That if competitive electoral systems are characterised by a multiplicity of groups who have strong views on different subjects, then democratic rights will be protected and extreme political inequalities will be certainly avoided other than those guaranteed by law and constitution, (b) there is empirical evidence to suggest that at least certain polities, for example, the USA and Britain, fulfil these conditions. Dahl is convinced that power is distributed and shared by many groups in society representing diverse interests and they defend their particular interests through government, creating a proclivity towards 'competitive equilibrium' that benefits the citizens in the long run and that at the minimum, 'democratic theory is concerned with processes by which ordinary citizens exert a relatively high degree of control over leaders' (1965: 3). This control is maintained by two methods—regular elections and political competition among parties, groups and individuals. He dismisses the concerns of Madison, Mill and Tocqueville about the tyranny of the majority as misplaced, for a tyrannous majority is impossible because elections express the preferences of divergent competitive groups rather than the wishes of a strong majority. Polyarchy or pluralist democracy is a rule by a series of minorities—some self-interested and others disinterested—within the boundaries stipulated by consensus with none being able to dominate but all having a space for their manoeuvre and bargaining. This emphasis on consensus is in contrast to Schumpeter's view of democratic politics as managed ultimately by competing elites. The pluralist system is a decentralised one aiming to arrive at compromise rather than truth. The competition among groups is a safeguard of democracy. Democracy does not establish the sovereignty of the majority but a rule by 'multiple minority oppositions'. The competition among groups establishes the democratic nature of the system. Dahl points out that the change in size from the city-states to modern nation states inevitably moves from monist to a pluralist democracy. This change in scale is crucial to understanding present-day democracies. In the modern context, the very essence of democracy is realised by polyarchy that stipulates the presence of a large number of organisations and associations which enjoy relative autonomy both in relationship to one another as also with regard to governmental power and jurisdiction. The institution of polyarchy distinguishes a democratic regime from an authoritarian one.

The preconditions for a functioning polyarchy are consensus on the rules of procedure, consensus on the range of policy options and consensus on the legitimate scope of political activity, which act as a buffer against oppressive rule. The greater the level of consensus, the more secure is democracy. A society enjoys protection from tyranny in non-constitutional provisions. It is not as if Dahl does not accord importance to principles like separation of powers and system of checks and balances, for it is pivotal in deciding the importance of benefits and burdens that groups face in a political system, which is why they are so bitterly fought over. However, the importance of constitutional rules to the successful development of democracy is less compared to non-constitutional ones. Dahl is convinced that democracy is safe, for it brings about moderation, agreement and maintains social peace if the social preconditions are secure (1965: 134–135, 151). He does not consider equal distribution of control over political decisions or that all individuals and groups have equal political weight as necessary (1965: 145–146).

EGALITARIAN AND RADICAL VARIANTS

Plebscitarian Democracy

Rousseau rejects Locke's prescription as inadequate in preserving freedom, self-rule, equality and virtue. He dismisses the English parliamentary system for it gave people the illusion of freedom whereas in reality the English people are free once in five years, for people lose their freedom once representatives are chosen. Freedom becomes a reality only when people actually govern and take part in the law-making process. He writes:

> Sovereignty cannot be represented for the same reason that it cannot be alienated ... the people's deputies are not, and could not be, its representatives; they are merely its agents; and they cannot decide anything faintly. And law which the people have not ratified in person is void; it is not law at all. The English people believes itself to be free; it is gravely mistaken; it is free only during the election of Members of Parliament; as soon as the Members are election, the people is enslaved; it is nothing (Rousseau 1958: 141).

Rousseau conceives of a free society that presupposes virtue. He describes a community vested with a 'General Will', the will of all individuals thinking of general interests leaving out particularity. Only when an individual is his own lawmaker can law maximise freedom and hence for this reason he proposes a free state that is a consensual and participatory democracy. He is the first major critic of representative democracy and his admiration for ancient Greece, which he resurrects and emulates, has henceforth fired the imagination of all those, especially the socialists, into proposing participatory or plebscitarian democracy as an alternative to representative democracy. However, he criticises the Athenian model for the fact that it does not distinguish between legislative and executive functions. Interestingly, as both Locke and Rousseau consider the legislature as supreme, being the law-making institution, Locke conceives of legislature as representing the people, while for Rousseau legislature means the people themselves as the body politic.

Communist One-Party Model

The early socialists like the Babouvists, inspired by Rousseau are convinced of the efficacy of the institutions of direct democracy. They believe that with universal education people would be able to govern themselves. Not only the socialists but also liberals like Paine recognise the importance of universal education and in removing illiteracy as a sure means for empowering the ordinary people. For the socialists, removal of class differences and privileges are a necessary step to freedom, equal status and democracy. Marx and Engels continue with this view but envisage an imminent collapse of capitalism and revolutionary transformation of society. In the *Manifesto* they observe:

> We have seen above that the first step in the revolution by the working class is to raise the proletariat to the position of ruling class, to win the battle of democracy. ... The proletariat will use its political supremacy to wrest, by degrees, all capital from the bourgeoisie, to centralize all instruments of production in the hands of the state, i.e. of the proletariat organized as the ruling class; and to increase the total of productive forces as rapidly as possible (Marx 1975: 74).

For Marx, the socialist democracy is a true one since for the first time the proletarian majority will rule the state whereas all along a minority ruled all previous states. Socialism can be realised following the destruction of capitalism through a revolutionary class struggle. Marx doubts the possibility of transition through peaceful parliamentary means in view of the severe limitations on suffrage. Hence the *Manifesto* is convinced that the socialist revolution inaugurates democracy for the first time but Marx does not spell out the meaning, content and nature of that democracy. As with the theory of the state, even with regard to democracy, one has to infer his intent, piecing together various writings but the main sources were the *Civil War in France* and the *Critique of the Gotha Programme*. Marx criticises liberal democracy on the grounds that its guarantee of legal and political rights amidst social and economic inequalities makes democracy the system for the moneybags and the propertied. He categorically asserts that genuine freedom and rights for the majority are possible only if the basic inequalities are eliminated if not narrowed. Furthermore, he has mixed feelings about parliamentary institutions dismissing these as formal concealing the exploitation of the bourgeoisie. He focuses on unprincipled compromises that political parties make and the opportunistic nature of their programme with the sole purpose of coming to power and their narrow authoritarian practices.

The abortive Paris commune provides Marx with lessons, which he considers crucial to democratic politics. These are identified as follows—(a) abolition of the standing army and instituting a citizen's militia, (b) election of all officials subjecting them to recall, (c) removal of political attributes of the police, (d) abolition of monarchy and (e) the role of the majority in directing and performing all functions of the state which were previously executed by a privileged minority. With regard to the last point, Marx emphasised on the following measures—(a) abolition of all representative allowances, all monetary benefits to officials and reducing the remuneration for officials to the level of 'workmen's wages', (b) abolition of the distance between the governed and the governors and erasing the label of 'High' dignitaries, (c) election of judges, (d) universal suffrage exercised freely and frequently. The Commune is regarded as a working and not as a parliamentary body exercising legislative and executive powers simultaneously. It breaks down the power of the modern state and organises the people on the basis of a decentralised federal system by disseminating power at the broadest and to the largest extent. Its real strength lay in the fact that it represents the working class and is 'the product of the struggle of the producing against the appropriating class, the political form at last discovered under which to work out the economic emancipation of labour' (1975: 220–225).

Marx's general statements and lack of specific details about the future society allows his followers to attribute different meanings to his formulations. Had he clearly and precisely formulated his blueprint, it would have led to a debate and reflection but instead when 'men range themselves under the banner as friends and enemies of the 'revolution', the only important question which is just and useful is kept out of sight and measures are judged not by their real worth but by the analogy they seem to have an irrelevant abstraction' (Lasky 1976: 573). In tackling the complexities of the modern state, the general descriptions of the ideal as realising true democracy and communism prove to be simplistic in providing the essential institutions of a democratic state.

Dahl points out to the three basic propositions of democracy that political parties agree and zealously defend—(a) inevitability of conflict of interests and articulation of wants as a matter of choice in a complex society; (b) resolution of such conflicts by majority rule, but with due concern for minority rights; and (c) freedom to form political parties and recognition of free competition (1986: 73) are denied by Marxism and hence cannot be considered as an adequate political theory. The emphasis on harmony in socialist society is inconsistent with the first proposition. Marxism does not offer any clue about the distribution of political power in the socialist society and is equally ambiguous about the principle of majority rule. The introduction of universal adult franchise in Germany in 1866, the electoral reforms in England in 1867 and 1884, and the growth of socialist parties have weakened the essential proposition of the state as an instrument of oppression, controlled by the bourgeois minority exploiting and oppressing the proletarian majority. These reforms have given the workers an opportunity to control the state by winning the majority of votes, and thereby seats in the parliament. Marx's politics, according to Dahl, is 'based on particular qualities of the bourgeois state in the nineteenth century' (1986: 69).

Marx never addresses himself to the issues of rights, political freedom, power, and role of authority in the socialist society. In spite of his commitment to a libertarian vision, Marx is consummated by the idea of having absolute, total, concentrated state power unrestrained and unlimited. He is contemptuous and in fact has very little faith in a constitution or law, dismissing it as a sham, formal and a cover to conceal bourgeois oppression and domination. The attack on formal democracy by promising substantive democracy has resulted in reducing formal democracy to the point of non-existence. Marx overlooks the protection that the constitutional representative democracy and the rule of law give against arbitrary rule and the freedom it ensures against physical harm. He fails to understand the dynamics of democracy in empowering people, which has been more revolutionary than a bloody violent revolution itself, 'The overall sweep of the Marxist historical scheme relegates democracy to a subsidiary role in the drama of human development' (Harding 1981: 157). On this point, the social democrats scored over Marx, as they in general and Bernstein in particular comprehend the importance of realising socialism and democracy simultaneously.

Like Marx, Lenin criticizes the representative parliamentary democracy as being a shell to conceal the exploitation of the working class by the bourgeoisie. It is illusory, for it gives the people the impression that they are free and sovereign, while in reality they are so only during the time of elections. It refines Rousseau's indictment of indirect parliamentary democracy as practised in Britain. The dictatorship of the proletariat will permanently abolish the parliamentary system and the separation of the legislature and the executive. It totally rejects the process of modern constitutional development, which began in the United States after the American Revolution. For Lenin, the dictatorship of the proletariat represents both a *regime* and a *form* of government. He distinguishes bourgeois democracy, which in his opinion is narrow and formal, from the proletarian counterpart, characterised as truly and fully participatory and free, and regards the transitional state as necessary for removing the vestiges of the old order and for creating and ushering in the new society. This means that the proletarian revolution will not destroy the state altogether for some kind of state, a qualitatively different one, continues under the dictatorship of the proletariat.

In his critique of the Leninist state, written at a time of the dissolution of Constituent Assembly and abolition of universal suffrage, believes that the attempt to introduce socialism through violence and undemocratic means betrays the essence of Marxism. It will lead to dictatorship and eventual collapse of the regime. This is precisely what happened in the erstwhile Soviet Union. He understands socialist democracy to mean proletarian majority in parliamentary institutions, political and civil rights of citizens, regime based on popular consent through periodic elections and use of violence only if necessary against counter-revolutionaries. Luxemburg reproached Lenin not with the neglect or contempt of direct, rank and file democracy but for exclusively relying on council democracy and eliminating representative institutions like the Constituent Assembly. She observes that the abolition of democratic institutions paralyses and eventually eliminates public life. The restrictions on the press, on the suffrage and on the right of assembly made the rule of masses a mockery. Her memorable words are as follows:

> Freedom for the supporters of the government, only for the members of one party—however, numerous they may be—is no freedom at all. Freedom is always and exclusively freedom for the one who thinks differently. The only way to rebirth is the school of public life itself, the most unlimited, the broadest democracy and public opinion. It is rule by terror which demoralises (Luxemburg 1961: 69).

Luxemburg points out that Lenin and Trotsky basically err in considering democracy as antithetical to dictatorship. She accepts that the Bolsheviks come to power under circumstances in which full democracy is impossible. However, having seized power they make a virtue of necessity, turning the distortion of an exceptional situation into a universal rule. She considers proletarian dictatorship as a more direct and extensive form of democracy, which involves comprehensive democratic procedures, and freedoms, elections, freedom of press, of opinion and assembly. **Poulantaz** (1980: 233) reiterates this view and castigates Lenin for distrusting the idea of competing power centres in society which eventually led to undermining the autonomy of the Soviets after 1917 and putting the revolution an on anti-democratic road. However, it is Bernstein who stands tall among his contemporaries, for he clearly sees the inextricable link between socialism and democracy understood as representative institutions. He does not waver like others between representative institutions and notion of direct democracy.

Social Democratic Alternative

The 1870s are a watershed for European socialism. Germany's rapid industrialisation brought about unprecedented prosperity. The SPD following the footsteps of **Lassalle** recommended the use of the existing state apparatus contrary to Marx's injunction of capturing it. From the Gotha Congress of 1875 to the Erfurt Programme in 1891, the SPD for all practical purposes settled down to reformism even though it remained theoretically committed to the classical Marxist vision of revolutionary overthrown of capitalism. The introduction of universal suffrage in 1866 was a decisive factor, a fact that **Engels** took note of. While writing the *Preface* to the *History of Class Struggles in France* in 1895, he admitted to the positive and successful effect of universal suffrage describing it as an entirely new strategy for the working class struggle. This meant the abandonment of the French Revolution that had been the model for the proletarian revolution and also in acknowledging that 'history has proved us and all those who thought like us wrong' (Engels 1977: 115). He acknowledged that he and Marx had erred in assuming during the 1848 revolutions that the time was ripe for the elimination of capitalist production and the socialist revolution. He admitted that history had transformed the conditions under which the proletariat would have to fight. He stressed on the need for revising old tactics and adopting new ones. He drew attention to the astonishing growth of membership of the SPD increasing from 1,02,000 in 1871 to 3,52,000 in 1874, 4,93,000 in 1877, 5,50,000 in 1884, 7,63,000 in 1887 and 14,27,000 in 1890. This was made possible by universal suffrage, enabling the SPD to emerge as the strongest, most disciplined and the fastest growing socialist party. Engels also conceded that the right to vote was no longer deceptive but an effective instrument of emancipation. These observations by Engels dispelled the standard Leninist argument of Bernstein as the first revisionist. On the contrary, it was Engels who was the first revisionist or the first social democrat (Elliot 1973: 73).

For **Bernstein** democracy means the absence of class government, minority rights, political equality and the greatest possible freedom for all. Socialism means self-organisation of the people. He emphatically defends democracy as an indispensable condition for realising socialism. 'Democracy is at the same time means and end. It is the means of the struggle for socialism and it is the form that socialism will take once it has been realised' (Bernstein 1961: 244–250). In view of the bright prospects for democracy, he rejects dictatorship of the proletariat. He considers social democracy as the spiritual and legitimate heir of liberalism and insists that it cannot renounce its liberal roots. He also stresses that democracy can be realised only democratically and argues that the lesson of the Paris Commune was the workers' need for democracy. Universal suffrage has made workers equal partners in a democratic society and thus Bernstein conceives of a proletarian society as one of universal citizenship, representative, democratic and equal. The remedy for parliamentary excesses is self-government, which can be self-regulatory, federal and decentralised in nature, with maximum power to the local communities. He accuses the Bolsheviks for brutalising Marxism. Bernstein's unflinching commitment to socialism and democracy within a liberal framework are reiterated by Miliband (1977) when he acknowledges that civil liberties are not given but have to be earned after centuries of unremitting struggle and that a socialist society ought to incorporate these and extend them further.

The end of the First World War brought about a schism between communism and social democracy. Having broken away from communism, social democracy began to identify with liberal democracy. They were antagonistic to capitalism but did not have clear-cut alternatives to offer but the post-Second World War period renewed the hopes for social democracy. The Great Depression discredited *laissez faire* capitalism and in view of the enormous devastation that the war caused state intervention and regulation of the economy became the guiding principle. Keynes prepared the ideological base forth state-aided post-war reconstruction with which social democracy identified. Within the former Soviet Union, **Stalin** obliterated the remnants of the libertarianism and voluntarism of the Bolshevik Revolution. One party rule degenerated into the personalised rule of one person. The Leninist-Stalinist state became omnipotent with scant regard for the rule of law, democratic procedures, constitutionalism and respect for individual rights. Khurshchev attempted to politically liberalise in the wake of de-Stalinisation. He succeeded to the extent that he went out through a vote in the *polit buro*, which he considered to be the finest honour. His successor Brezhnev did very little to continue with the reforms that Khurshchev initiated. The ruthless suppression of the **Dubcek** in Czechoslovakia in 1968, who tried to reform socialism by making it humane, represented the highpoint of the Soviet repression in its satellite states. Many others in East Europe rejected Leninism and desired to go back to the democratic and humanistic outlook of Marxism. However, the totalitarian and alienated Soviet state had become ossified and could not reform from within. The communist systems in reality did not encourage discussions, debate and competition among diverse groups. The party straddled both the state and civil society into one centralised bureaucratic monolith.

Meanwhile in Western Europe, the French, Italian and Spanish communist parties inspired by **Palmiro Togaliatti's** idea of progressive democracy and polycentrism, rejected Leninism, and insisted on the need for multi-party system within conditions of pluralist competition. This development known as **Euro-communism** conceived of socialism within a democratic polity and a pluralistic society. It rejected insurrectionist politics, dictatorship of the proletariat, one party state and stressed on the need for multi-parties, parliamentary and representative institutions, trade unions, human rights, freedom of opposition and universal suffrage. It differed from social democracy, for it aimed to transcend and not administer the capitalist system and work out the socialist alternative without a dictatorship of the proletariat.

African One-Party System

The Solidarist philosophy propounded by **Julius Nyerere**, former President of Tanzania was a model of democracy, in Rousseau's sense, applicable for a society, relatively homogenous and which lacked conventional parliamentary system. Nyerere was not a Marxist nor did he believe in one-party state of the Leninist type. However, he was conscious of the situation of the newly independent countries where multi-party system could not work (Machperson 1966). The Solidarist one-party state, according to Nyerere, was democratic with open membership and no restrictions on personal freedom. He understood the importance of a legitimate opposition in a political system but pointed out that this could not work in countries like Tanzania. He asserted that the notion that democracy required organised opposition was not exactly correct, as what it demanded was not the actual existence but a theoretical acceptance of the idea. The central fact that he emphasised was the internal backwardness of the newly emerging nations. Since classes were not well-developed, class politics had to be ruled out. Added to this was an important fact, namely the common aspiration among the entire population. With the absence of differentiated industrial society like Europe and America, the introduction of a pluralist political system was not possible. There was no organised group that exercises its hegemony over others. The challenge of development needed a firm, strong and centralised control from above, a fact that the Western society did not have to contend with. In the African context, the task was to democratise society from the top. The backwardness of traditional societies did not allow for the western type of parliamentary democracy. However, this did not mean the absence of democracy. The absence of viable class divisions ensured equality and since the traditional society was democratic with a tradition of free discussions, governments were established with the approval of people and participation. Unlike the erstwhile Soviet system that had a low level of discussion which was compatible with its totalitarian political structure Africa had an indigenous democratic experience. However, economic difficulties like low productivity and limited output and the dual strategy consisting of public sector and private enterprise created tension in the implementation of the democratic and socialist principles. Nyerere's call for a multi-party democracy in the early 1990s acknowledges that the specific conditions faced by the newly independent countries in the post-independence phase were over and that the one-party state reflected this extraordinary circumstance and is not the general rule.

PARTICIPATORY DEMOCRACY

Theorists of participatory democracy try to assimilate and realise the ideals of direct democracy—responsive arid active citizenry, participation and equality in the modern complex world of nation—states. The idea of participatory democracy is manifest in the works of Poulantaz, Pateman and Macpherson for they draw insights from both liberal and Marxist traditions thus moving the 'political debate away from the seemingly endless and fruitless juxtaposition of liberalism with Marxism' (Held 1987: 263). **Poulantaz** (1980) recommends 'socialist pluralism' by which he means democratising the state, that is making parliament, state bureaucracies and political parties more accountable and simultaneously incorporating new forms of struggle at the local level—the women's groups, ecological groups and factory-based politics. He stresses that there are 'no easy recipes' of how to do these. He prescribes these in view of the rise of the mammoth state both in size and power and also by way of realising that self-management or institutions of direct democracy cannot replace the state. **Pateman** (1970 and 1985) is unique in synthesising the conceptual problems of liberal democratic theory with the theory of the patriarchal basis of sexual politics. By exploring the components of contractarian and liberal theories, she establishes contradictions in concepts like participation, consent and obligation and concludes that this is because the social contract presupposes a sexual contract. She points out that the idea of a free and equal individual that the liberal democratic theory espouses hardly exists, for it was hindered by the inequalities of class, sex and race. Pateman points out to the inconsistency between universal formal rights and class inequality in participation which she feels can be resolved only through institutions that encourage self-management. Here, the imprint of Rousseau is visible. This is because the state inevitably sustains and duplicates the inequalities of everyday life and therefore its claim to distinct allegiance is suspect. However, she concedes like Poulantaz and Macpherson, that institution of direct democracy cannot be extended to all political, social and economic spheres by setting aside institutions of representative democracy. She does not think complete freedom and equality can be created in the management of all spheres. Democracy at the workplace has to deal with complex problems like market instabilities, coordination of resources and availability of different types of labour and skills, for any of these can limit democratic procedures and choice. Democracy has to be reconciled with efficiency and leadership. She concedes to Schumpeter's views on the highly restrictive role of the ordinary citizen in national politics for it very likely that is the concerns of ordinary citizens are about those issues that immediately affect their lives. She accepts the core institutions of liberal democracy—competitive parties, political representatives, periodic elections—as unavoidable in a participatory society. However, she favours direct participation and control over immediate local bodies complemented by party and interest group competition in governmental affairs which can realistically advance the principles of participatory democracy. She points out that if individuals have an opportunity to directly participate in decision-making at the local level they can achieve real control over the course of their everyday life. Opportunity for extensive participation at the workplace radically alters the context of national politics. This is because individuals learn about key issues in resource creation and control, thus, being better able to assess the performance of their political representatives, judge national questions and when the need arises, participate in national decisions. The local and national institutions shall be kept open and flexible for people to experiment with new political forms and reform rigid structures imposed by private capital, class relations and other asymmetries of power.

Crawford Borough Macpherson (1911–1987) champions participatory democracy, deriving his theoretical inspiration from some aspects of the liberal democratic tradition particularly from the writings of J.S. Mill that interprets the individual as a doer and a creator rather than as consumer (1977). This is contrary to the other elements in Western democratic theory that were concerned with utility maximisation. He criticises the possessive individualism of liberalism in general and of Hobbes and Locke in particular, for perceiving the individual as a possessor of his own capacities and potentially of other things as well. This makes them self-interested in possession of faculties or resources that are up for sale, making market relations the fundamental relations of society. A state is seen as 'a human contrivance for the protection of the individual's property in his person and goods' (1973: 264). This narrow possessive individualism, according to Macpherson, determines and limits the particular form of democracy that developed in liberal states. The extension of franchise was accommodated within the competitive market society depriving the liberal state of communal and participatory potentialities. Macpherson argues that a truly democratic society promotes powers of social cooperation and creativity rather than maximise aggregate satisfactions. He argues for transformation based upon a system combining competitive parties and institutions of direct democracy. He concedes that there will always be issues and major differences of interest that give rise to political parties and only competition between parties will ensure that government remains responsive to the people. The parties, however, need to be reorganised on non-hierarchical principles, that is, the principles and procedures of participatory democracy making political administrators and manager more accountable to the persons within the organisations they represent. These genuinely participatory parties can function within a parliamentary system complemented and checked by fully self-managed organisations in the workplace and local community. Only such a political system realises the liberal democratic value of 'the equal right of self-development'. The utility-maximising model is ethically deficient, for it accepts transfer of powers. With the market being unequal when the worker sells his labour power to the capitalists, his powers of creativity and free choice are reduced.

Macpherson concedes that existing liberal democratic systems have preserved civil and political liberties more effectively than the socialist regimes but this does not mean that the socialist system of ownership failed to end the transfer of power under capitalism and preserve liberty. He observes that the attempt of the welfare state to provide goods and services on the basis of need does not fundamentally alter the features of a liberal democratic society. His critique that western capitalist countries with their economic inequalities, absence of real opportunities for its citizen to participate in the decision-making process and remote bureaucracies do not meet the standards of political equality and participation set by the classical democratic theory is unjustified. It is important to make realistic comparisons between them and the former communist systems that denied basic rights and demolished civil society and hardly attained desirable standards of living. Held (1987: 263) points out that all three—Poulantaz, Pateman and Macpherson—"say very little about fundamental factors such as how, for instance, the economy is actually to be organised and related to the political apparatus, how institutions of representative democracy are to be combined with those of direct democracy, how the scope and power of administrative organised are to be checked, how households and childcare facilities are to be related to work, how those who wish to 'opt out' of the political system might do so, or how the problems posed by the ever changing international system of states could be dealt with". They do not, however, tell us how to realise their model.

Macpherson (1966: Ch. 1) points out that other than liberal democracies there are equally valid variants, namely the communist and Third World one-party systems that could claim the label of democracy. The communist systems would have qualified had they granted full intra-party democracy and opened up their closed bureaucratic systems. Even the Solidarist one-party model in Tanzania has moved towards accepting multi-party system. Lively (1975: 45) points out that one-party system is incongruent with responsible government since it does not allow for the possibility of cogent alternatives. A one party to be eclectic both with regard to persons and opinions has to allow factions and unless the party membership is coterminous with a democratic electorate it cannot be responsible to all competent citizens but only to party members. The communist and the elitist models share certain common features. Both require very little of involvement by the people and 'no or very little satisfaction of the claims of equality for a system to be democratic' (1975: 42). This minimal claim is based on the distrust of the masses. The communist model believes the ordinary person to be incapable of knowing his interests correctly while the elitists contend that he cannot competently judge political issues. To separate the term democracy from its political context and apply it in the social domain is to render it meaningless. Democracy has to do with equality and the latter is primarily to be understood in the political sense, meaning equal say in decision-making process. Political equality is not automatically ensured if inequalities in the other spheres are eliminated. Democracy does not merely mean a government that acts in the interests of the ruled.

The Marxists according to Bobbio (1986 and 1987) fail to see that political democracy cannot be reduced to class questions and demands for economic equality. Socialism as practised in the twentieth century means transfer of ownership of the means of production from private hands to that of the state and in that case the abuses by the state were much more than under capitalism. To demand socialism in this sense is undemocratic. As such democracy is subversive, for it questions all forms of despotic power. The participatory variant is unworkable in large-scale complex mass societies. Too much democracy can kill off democracy. The attempt to create full-time political animals and complete politicisation of life are opposed to democracy. Direct democracy requires consensus, which is possible in limited number of policy choices—nuclear power or no nuclear power, and peace or war. Bobbio considers the need to complement existing political democracy with social democracy, which he calls post-liberal democracy the civil sphere where individuals exist as men and women, entrepreneurs and workers, producers and consumers and the like.

DELIBERATIVE DEMOCRACY

It is a theory that concentrates on refining the familiar framework of liberal democracy. Deliberative democracy is a normative theory with an intention to influence the actual political process by improving the popular input into policy by making it as broad based as possible. However, about its popular appeal, feasibility or desirability there are a very large number of unanswered questions. What constitutes public deliberation and how it is to be carried out? The pluralists are clear about a rough parity of groups leading to a large degree of competition between groups, which ultimately leads to a filtering of policy in which all the major groups participate, deliberate, bargain and compromise leading to some kind of a consensual policy framework. But the deliberative democratic theory is silent about the nature and content of public participation in the context of mass democracies of today with all its complexities, diversities, inequalities and technical details, for which an average citizen neither has the inclination, time or expertise to deliberate carefully and judiciously. It is also not very clear about the process of arriving at a consensus in a situation of heterogeneity of interests in the contemporary world. Deliberative democracy has no clear-cut answer to a proper framework of power sharing or to provide a framework to deal with the problem of a permanent majority and a permanent minority in the political order with deep cleavages.

One very important ingredient of a new political theory is rejection of the older theories and dissatisfaction triggered by a crisis. Both these dimensions are there in the origin of deliberative democratic theory. Till the 1970s in the US, the liberal democratic theory emerged out of sociological and economic dimensions. Because of the domination of Dahl's polyarchy and Schumpeter's democratic elitism, under the overall sway of the behavioural revolution, the applied side of democratic theory flourished with emphasis on the nature of the political parties, interest group politics, the role of the media and voting behaviour were the important subject matters of democratic theory.

The Vietnam War, the student revolts of 1968 and the impact of the civil rights movement signaled a shift in the academic perception giving rise to neo conservatism, slowly consolidating the left of centre perception. The focus was not only on the actual political functioning but also raised normative questions of participation, quality of life, post materialist values, a resurrection of Jeffersonian brand of idealized self governing democracy and the desire for a consensual form of democracy inspired by the Swedish model. Rawls' seminal revives interest in the older form of grand theorizing by raising normative questions. The latter Rawls laid the foundations of deliberative democracy. Joseph Basette (1994) coins the phrase 'deliberative democracy' to criticize the elitist or aristocratic interpretation of the US constitution by questioning endemic conflict and competing interests and bargaining, the basis of the popular rational choice theory and the institutional arrangement of a minimal state as articulated by Nozick and the New Right economists like Friedman and Hayek.

In addition the emphasis on negative liberty of atomised individuals, the civic culture projection of dangers of enthusiastic participation and the need for control and balance with dangers of overload also led to the discovery of the virtues of direct democracy like small group initiative, new social movements,[3] democracy at work place thus reviving the spirit of the guild socialists like Cole. The unity of the deliberative democratic theorists lie in a belief that the political process has an autonomy of its own and has to be analyzed much beyond the competitive bargaining of Hobbesian individuals. The rejection of the rational choice paradigm[4] inevitably leads to the key question of the demarcation between the political behaviour of the political man from the economic man of the market. A derivative of the rational choice theory is **Social Choice Theory**, which postulates that a rational individual in desire of collective decision chooses that course of action that is most likely to realise one's goals. Rationality is about the means employed for one's preferred ends. It is the individual who is taken as the basic unit of analysis so even when the focus is on a group.

Social choice theory like classic pluralism accepts conflicts as inevitable among self-interested political actors and democracy with electoral competition but do not share with the pluralist stress on group. Olson sees a serious flaw in pluralist approach: "groups are supposed to act to advance the common interests of the individual who compose them but among these interest is the economic one to minimise costs required to provide resources for the group as a whole, so that each individual will try to avoid incurring these costs and will not voluntarily make any sacrifices to help their attain its political (public or collective) objectives" (1971: 126).

The general framework of deliberative theory emphasizes on civic virtue, which means that political activity is a public act beyond the category of private preferences and gains. The deliberative democratic theorists emphasize on the market (the private sphere) and politics (the public arena) and refer to the ideals of J.S. Mill and Arendt. Elster focuses on two aspects: (a) the capacity and motivation to go beyond one's own market or economic interest and (b) from this civic standpoint deliberation is defensible only if political decision-making helps to achieve common ends. The first pre-requisite is validated by the second proposition that an act of this kind can be propagated and defended only if it helps in achieving common purposes.

Harbermas desires to combine the spirit of civic republicanism with liberalism emphasizing on the participatory characteristics of democracy with due emphasis on institutions and legality. He tries to link political power with the rule of law. In an attempt to incorporate the radical democratic ideals of the French Revolution with the mass democracies of today he resurrects the notion of popular sovereignty by a network of broad and widely dispersed 'subject-less communication' which would reflect an autonomous public sphere with the constitutional decision-making process. Joshua Cohen links political legitimacy to an ideal consensus that would emerge out of free and reasoned deliberation and agreement among equals centring on common good within the specificity of procedural standards like freedom and lack of coercion, both formal and substantive equality of participants with preservation of individual autonomy but with enough safeguards against objectionable outcomes. This suitable procedure will lead to outcomes, which will be broadly acceptable, enduring, just and feasible, institutionally with mediating offshoots of a constitutional democracy like voting and a competitive party system. Procedure is of great importance as it standardises the nature and content of deliberation, eliminating the possibility of a realistic or metaphysical notion of common good dominating the discourse. A decision-making process for Cohen must exhibit sufficient evidence for ensuring correct political judgement and the need for a proper coordinated machinery to synchronise deliberation and democratic decision-making. However, there is considerable disagreement among the theorist of deliberative democracy about the ideal procedure. Some emphasise on linkage between deliberative democratic theory and rational choice theory whereas other resurrect Condercet's jury theorem,[5] which coordinates voting analysis with deliberative theory.

Rawls dissects the relationship between deliberation and common good, which subordinates individual preferences and proposals. For Rawls the major obstacle to deliberation does not lie in pursuance of private interest but in the wide divergence between what constitutes common good and a just world. Relying on plain truth and 'duty of civility' Rawls emphasizes on consensus based on shared values, which in spite of alternative views will be acceptable to all. He also emphasizes on the formal democratic mechanism. Public reason depends on mutual reciprocity in a pluralistic world.

The main thrust of deliberative democratic theory is an emphasis on reason and equal citizens in an ideal order. The emphasis is on public deliberation even when the non-deliberative order may be both fair and democratic. Deliberative democracy emphasises on four essential attributes: (1) aim full deliberation with a specified target of consensus and to a lesser degree co-operation and compromise, (2) the process of deliberation is of vital importance and will consist of three aspects—forums of public discussion, formal institutional structure and the process of decision-making, (3) the essential conditions for deliberation is freedom and equality of citizens, (4) the framework of deliberation must include cultural plurality and social complexities of modern mass democracies (Bohman and Rehg 1997: xviii).

Deliberative democracy is a democratic system that deliberates to the extent 'that the decisions it reaches reflect open discussion among the participants, with people ready to listen to the views and consider the interests of others, and modify their own opinions accordingly' (Miller 2000: 3). In deliberative democracy decisions are taken wholly by consensus. It accepts the premise that there will be conflict regarding political preferences, which the democratic institutions have to resolve though an open and non-coercive discussion. Unlike liberal democracy that gives importance to individuals' distinct preferences, deliberative democracy maintains that a person is rational enough to set aside particular interests and opinions to aspire for fairness and the common interests of the collectivity. It values the manner of open discussion that hears all points of view and reaches a decision, which differs from the procedure of majority rule of liberal democracy. For deliberative democracy to work well, people must exercise democratic self-restraint: 'they must think it more important that the decision reached should be a genuinely democratic one than that it is the decision that they themselves favour' (2000: 22).

Some deliberative theorists accept that procedural equality, which ensures equality of opportunity and participation in political decision-making are of crucial significance for legitimising democracy. But they equally emphasise on substantive aspects of political equality. For instance Knight and Johnson emphasise on the need for equity of opportunity in accessing political influence. Bohman's equality demands an assurance for equal opportunity in speaking. Both these theories derive their inspiration from Sen's theory of 'capability equality', better known than the Rawlsian approach as a resource based formulation for it is practically relevant since uncertainties and inequalities restrict political participation and deliberation. However, Bohman and Rehg comment that Sen's theory not only highlights "the weaknesses of procedural equality of opportunity and equality of resources, but also the possible elitism of deliberative theories" (Ibid: xxiv). This elitism springs from the fact that deliberative democratic theorists demand political equality as a pre-condition so that the better educated, the more virtuous or just the better off do not get favoured. It must ensure all citizens have equal opportunity to influence political decisions. Richardson and Young try to bridge the gulf between epistemic and fair proceduralism by emphasising on truth or fairness as the result of deliberation by arriving at 'partially joint intentions'. Cohen argues that reasonable pluralism concretises the deliberative mechanism of free and equal citizens. It is based both on a procedural and a substantive conception of politics elucidating equalitarian and liberal values of rights and liberties. Reasonable pluralism ensures that none would be excluded because of practicing a particular religion or moral doctrine. Equality envisages capacity to participate in a process, which authorises the exercise of power. Like Rawls, Cohen claims that public reasonableness and consensus is possible in spite of wide disagreements in moral and political belief structure. Cohen is categorical that reasonable pluralism and deliberative democracy guarantees religious, moral and other liberties. The purpose is to provide genuine membership to all citizens in ensuring participation in the filtering and exercise of power. Freedom and equality are intrinsic to such an order and since the process accepts disagreement as part of democracy liberties of conscience, religion and expression are the essential requirements coupled with the idea of reasonableness. He considers the notion of deliberative democracy as "rooted in the intuitive ideal of a democratic association in which the justification of the terms and conditions of association proceeds through public argument and reasoning among equal citizens" (1997: 72).

> Benhabib another exponent of deliberative democracy points out that conflicts over values and visions of good cannot be resolved 'by establishing a strong unified moral and religious code without forsaking fundamental values thus distinguishing the conception from civic republicanism'. She points out that agreement has to be reached not over substantive beliefs but on procedures, processes and practices

> that attain and revise these beliefs (1996: 73). Habermas (1996 and 1998) too insists that institutionalising conditions for deliberative communication is the crux of the matter. It differs from liberalism that sees politics as the administration of competing private interests among citizens and considers democracy as legitimising the exercise of political power and from republicanism that structures law and government to reach positive consensus on moral values and create solidarity among citizens as a republican democracy is supposed to constitute a society as a political community. Unlike the liberals who see popular sovereignty as the exercise of duly authorised state authority and the republicans for whom popular sovereignty resides in a popular general will the deliberative approach sees sovereignty a an ongoing process of "interaction between legally institutionalised will formation and culturally mobilised publics" (Habermas 1998: 295–302).

The deliberative democratic theory tries to resurrect the Periclean principles of popular participation and refines it with the Jeffersonian ideal of harmony by making a balance between liberty, equality and democracy in the modern mass democracies. However it wants to re-inculcate the spirit of Jeffersonian radical individualism without his commitment to rough parity and equality, an integral part of the libertarian tradition of liberalism. But in resurrecting these ideals any democratic theory for our times is to take note of Dahl's (1986) four-fold categorisation: (1) what constitutes people in democracy, (2) problem of size or scale, (3) problem of pluralism and (4) consequences for democracy, liberty and equality in the context of an alternative scheme of change or scale in economy. The theorists of deliberative democracy do not deliberate on any of these issues at length and that makes their account sketchy and impractical. Any critical alternative model to polyarchy in the contemporary world has to provide a coherent and practical primer to aforesaid four-fold categorisation of Dahl. As long as it is unable to do this, the theory will merely remain abroad critic without emerging as an alternative.

OTHER CRITIQUES OF LIBERAL DEMOCRACY

The feminist concern with democracy dates back to Wollstonecraft as she establishes the inter-relationship between social and political processes thereby leading to a new appreciation of the conditions of democracy. Until the twentieth century very few, hardly none perceptively spoke of the connection between the private and the public and the ways in which unequal gender relations cut across both to the detriment of the quality of life in both. Wollstonecraft does not prescribe any model of democracy as an alternative but she draws attention to the fact that no democratic theory could assume individuals to be men. J.Ş. Mill is unique among liberal democrats for his insistence on realising human freedom, happiness and democracy as a possibility only when there is equality of sexes. The *Subjection of Women* argues not only a case for enfranchisement of women but also to remove all legal, political and social hindrances that thwart complete equality between sexes. Wollstonecraft and Mill argue that since women and men are essentially same, women must be given equal rights. However, recent feminist thinking no longer stresses on equality understood as sameness and on the contrary they contend that since in many important respect women and men differ, these differences affect women's ability to make full use of their political rights even when such rights are granted. Attention is given to the ways in which equality and justice between women and men may be guaranteed through recognition of differences rather than through its removal and denial.

> Specifically it indicates that the pursuit of equality via the elimination of difference is not the route to a democratic society, but the route to an oppressive and exclusive society. Historically societies which have claimed to 'represent the people' have in fact represented only that portion of the people which displays homogeneity. In modern theory 'representing the people' must not be interpreted as representing that portion of the people who can forced into the appropriate mould. If there is to be any hope for democracy, it must therefore cease to pursue equality by trying to eliminate difference and instead concentrate on pursuing it by recognising difference more adequately (Mendus 1992: 218).

This stress on difference cannot be carried to a point that it ceases to have relevance to contemporary issues and problems. Feminists need to understand that gender is just one, though important criterion in what is considered as the multiple identity of a person.

The feminist concern with difference finds resonance among **post-modernists** who seek to reorient the institutions of liberal democracy to make it more hospitable to otherness. This means to reconsider the prevailing notion of popular sovereignty and community, resting with the people in whom final, unquestionable authority resides, thus suggesting homogeneity and is not realistic, for in reality it is segments of people who express their will on political matters. Postmodernists desire to re-imagine the democratic community in a radically open way to include those who are left out. The ties of such a community are tenuous as it distinctly recognises difference, sustained by as Connolly (1991) describes mutual 'agonistic respect'. This means that each individual or group accepts that the formation of its identity is always simultaneously the formation of that which is not—the others and since its consequence is tensions, democracy is the most suitable regime. **Communitarianism** moralises about existing representative systems by assailing the corruption of legislators by special interest groups (Etzioni 1995) rather than advance a case for changing political structures to enhance democracy.

In conclusion after the collapse of communism and defeat of both right-wing and leftwing authoritarianism, Huntington (1992) rightly observes that the globalisation of democracy is the most significant political development in the late twentieth century. This is the third wave that dates back to 1974, that began in Latin Europe and in the Portuguese revolutionary upheaval. The other waves were between 1828 and 1926 and between 1943 and 1962. He accepts Schumpeter's procedural theory and describes the core of the democratic process as selection of leaders through competitive elections by the people whom these leaders govern. Free and fair periodic elections sustain such democracies where the leaders wield real power. Reiterating arguments from his earlier works, he asserts that the form of government is not the most important category in deciding the desirability of a good order as the distinction between democracy and dictatorship is much less important than of order and anarchy. However, he still distinguishes democracy from non-democracy for three reasons. First, political democracy assures individual freedom and if one is concerned with liberty then one has to be concerned about the fate of democracy also. Second, there is no close connection between the form of government and stability in the modern world and that a democratic system is less likely to face less civil violence than non-democracy. In a similar vein, Sen (1990) points that in a democracy where the rulers have to face the electorate periodically they try to earnestly mitigate mass inhuman miseries like famines and abject poverty. Third, as democracy permits both dissent and opposition, there is less likelihood of revolutionary change. Change is effected more peacefully through a ballot box than coups and armed uprising.

The challenges before democracy today are 'the diverse sites of social and economic power and the dense networks of regional and global interconnectedness' (Held 1995: ix) that now extend over the globe, threatening the organisational forms of the nation-state and the ideological foundations of its autonomy. Till date the nation-state has remained central to the organisation and conduct of democratic practices, and citizenship rights are still understood largely within the confines of the territorial state but this state of affairs does not necessarily mean a permanent feature. Held considers the possibility of establishing a 'cosmopolitan democracy' that recognises the nation-state level of competence but adds a layer of governance that limits national sovereignty. Cosmopolitan institutions can co-exist with states but can override them in certain defined areas like human rights. It presupposes the creation of regional parliaments, throwing open international governmental organisations to public scrutiny and the democratisation of international functional bodies. Held also insists on the need for a charter of civil, economic, political and social rights enshrined within the constitutions of parliaments and assemblies to develop and restrain democratic decision-making. The ambit of international courts has to be extended so that individuals and groups can seek redress, if necessary, for the effective enactment and enforcement of their rights both within and beyond political associations. Finally, there is a need to establish an authoritative assembly based on the principles of democratic representation of all and only democratic states and societies with the power to make and enforce laws with the help of nation's state police and military. This has to exist within a framework of an international civil society, with individuals and peoples having a right of self-determination while preserving democratic good. Production, distribution and use of resources will be in accordance with principles of social justice and within a democratic process.

With democracy becoming a global phenomenon, Sartori tries to separate the necessary from contingent elements to make a case for its universality. He points to the twin notions within liberal democracy—demo-protection and demo-power and states that the former, as a necessary and defining element, is a global element. This rests on the idea of the harm-avoidance rule, for nobody likes to be imprisoned, tortured or killed. Liberal constitutionalism, 'aims to ensure that no one can be harmed by the coercive instruments of politics without due process and in violation of *habeas corpus*' (1995: 103). It is this idea that is desirable, universal and exportable.

The collapse of communism has led to the triumph of the liberal idea (Fukuyama 1992). The choice is no longer between capitalism and socialism but constitutionalism, rule of law and independence of judiciary versus authoritarianism (Ash 1990: 21). It is about the ability of democratic regimes to manage their economies so as to provide growth, protect their environments, safeguard the welfare of the disadvantaged and help other struggling countries to feed their people and find some viable path of development (Bell 1990a: 187). The strength of liberal democracy in comparison to its rivals—communism and fascism—becomes apparent because it has created a better mechanism for proper recognition of ordinary people (Fukuyama 1992). Furthermore, as Medvedev (1982: 22) rightly observes, democracy today has become as much a necessity for economics as it has been for politics and that implies issues of development, economic equality, civil and political rights have to be guaranteed by any government. The experience of last five decades in the developing world also demonstrates that an acceptance of constitutional democratic order is *a priori* to both development and social justice (Kothari 1971 and 1988). It is in providing proper machinery for governing the complex mass societies of our times that democracy has become more and more universalised, to the extent that the other variants have been exceptions and transient. It is wise to recall Churchill's remark that democracy is a bad form of government, only others are worse and it is because of this relative strength that the critics of liberal democracy remain mere critics. They have been unable to provide a better working formula to the one that liberal democracy provides, with its commitment to the rule of law, accountability and limited authority with a flourishing vibrant civil society.

Further Readings

Arblaster, A., *Democracy*, World View, Delhi, 1997.

Bachrach, P., *The Theory of Democratic Elitism*, London University Press, London, 1968.

Barber, B., *Strong Democracy*, University of California Press, Berkeley, CA, 1984.

Copp, D., Hampton, J. and Roemer, J.E. (Eds.), *The Idea of Democracy*, Cambridge University Press, Cambridge, 1993.

Dahl, R., *Democracy and its Critics*, Yale University Press, Yale, 1989.

Duncan, G. (Ed.), *Democratic Theory and Practice*, Cambridge University Press, Cambridge, 1983.

Dunn, J. (Ed.), *Democracy: An Unfinished Journey*, Oxford University Press, Oxford, 1992.

Finley, M.L., *Democracy: Ancient and Modern*, Chatto and Windus, London, 1973. R. Harrison, Democracy, Routledge, London, 1993.

Hunt, A., *Marxism and Democracy*, Lawrence and Wishart, London, 1980.

Lindsay, A.D., *Essentials of Democracy*, Oxford University Press, London, 1929.

Lucas, J.R., *Democracy and Participation*, Penguin, Harmondsworth, 1976 C.B.

Mukherjee, Subrata and Ramaswamy, Sushila, *Democracy in Theory and Practice*, Macmillan, New Delhi, 2005.

Endnotes

1. *The Life and Times of Liberal Democracy*, Oxford University Press, Oxford, 1977. A. Phillips, *Engendering Democracy*, Oxford University Press, Oxford, 1991.
2. Recall is another measure to secure greater accountability of elected representatives by providing a method wherein the electorate may vote to terminate the appointment before the normal date on which re-election would occur for having breached certain rules or on account of misdemeanor. It is a measure that is normally associated with direct/plebiscitory democracies. The Paris Commune of 1871 had the principle of the workers' right to recall their elected representatives at any time, emulated subsequently by the 1905 and 1917 revolutions in Russia. Marx took note of this feature while writing about it seeing it as intrinsic to majoritarian workers democracy as opposed to formal bourgeois democracy.
3. New social movements are loosely organised popular protest groups, which thrive at a time when conventional political participation as measured by membership in political parties, and trade unions and even voting is on the decline in most Western democracies. Social movements have always existed and have been the source for many political parties and trade unions but in its new incarnation it displays some key differences. The new social movements enlist those—predominantly from the educated and affluent segments, the middle class, who are expressly disenchanted with ordinary politics and aspire for more participatory activities, wanting to get rid of bureaucratic elites within their own organisations, espouse radical actions with preference for street demonstrations, sit-ins,

some degree of violence rather than the routine pressure group tactics for realising their aims. They try to pressurise the state to adopt their specific policies rather than assume power, reinforcing the perception that there is a link between the new social movement and post materialist culture of the West. Their aim is usually to promote and achieve one single specific issue rather than elaborate an overall ideology or programme.

4. Rational choice theory maintains that the primary explanation for an action is that the actor has calculated the said action to be the most efficient way of acquiring a desired goal. Voting behaviour is the first area in which political scientists have applied rational choice theory, as it is relatively easy to see the act of voting as akin to making a purchase.

5. The Condercet jury theorem, in its standard form, says this: suppose each member of a jury is more likely to be right than wrong. Then the majority of the jury too, is more likely to be right than wrong. Furthermore, the probability that the majority of the jury might support the right outcome is a rapidly increasing function of the size of the jury, converging to one as the size of the jury tends to infinity. Extrapolating from juries to electorate more generally, that results constitutes the jewel in the crown of epistemic democrats, many of whom offer it as powerful evidence of the truth-tracking merits of majority rule. What drives the Condercet jury theorem is just the 'law of large numbers'. As the number of voters increases the actual proportion of the vote won by the correct opinion comes increasingly to approximate the antecedent possibility of each individual's voting for the correct opinion. Among a small group of 100, the actual distribution of votes might turn out to be 48:52 and the correct option might therefore lose. But the larger the group, the more likely it will be that the proportion of people voting correctly approximates the same 51% as the probability of each individual voter's voting correctly. And that of course is just to say that it is more likely among a large number of voters that the correct option will win the election (and indeed, will do so by the same majority as represented by the individual's probability of voting correctly in the first place). Hence, if each individual is more likely to be right than wrong and increasingly so, thanks to the law of large numbers as the number of voters increases.

Chapter 16
Development

The term development has many meanings. A distinction is made between development as a process (pace of change) and development as a condition (or level) (Riggs 1984: 133). Either it describes some rate of change like economic growth or indicates a general level of socio-economic welfare or social equality.

MEANING OF DEVELOPMENT

Development as Economic Growth

Development within mainstream economics denotes the process of economic growth in per capita income and the fundamental changes in the economy to facilitate and generate that growth. Commonly, these include industrialisation, the migration of labour to industrial areas, division of labour, changes in productive relations, and steady increase in investments. Political theory and economics are concerned with economic growth because of the assumption that growth ensures well-being. Since the 1980s, the link between economic development and growth of national income per head has been questioned.

Development as Human Development

A criticism of development as economic growth is that it only captures the economic aspect. Development is something more than economic growth and that it is a complex term that ought to relate to the quality of life of humankind. A large number of paradigms measuring the complex nature of human well-being has been devised. A major innovator in this area is Morris (1979), who invents a physical quality of life (PQL) index that takes into account life expectancy and infant mortality. In 1990, the United Nations Development Programme (UNDP) Report defines the idea of human development as not just a higher income and concomitantly a nation's well-being could not be measured by its per capita income alone. It presents a human development index (HDI) that combines an adjusted GDP/per capita estimate, life expectancy, infant mortality and levels of literacy. It takes into account productivity through income generation and remunerative employment, equity through equal political and economic opportunities, sustainability by ensuring that all forms of capital—physical, human, environmental—are replenished for the present and future generations and empowerment wherein people participate fully in the decisions and processes that mould their lives. In 1995, the Human Development Report introduces the idea of gender-related development index (GDI) that reflects gender inequality in basic human abilities. For instance, among the 1.3 billion poor people 70 per cent are women. In the labour force, women's participation has arisen only by four percentage points in twenty years, from 36 per cent in 1970 to 40 per cent in 1990. Among the 900 million illiterate people, women outnumber men two to one. Women receive much lower average wage than men, constitute still less than a seventh of managers and administrators and occupy only 10 per cent of parliamentary seats and 6 per cent of cabinet positions.

THEORIES OF DEVELOPMENT

In the immediate aftermath the Second World War, as a consequence of decolonisation, many new nations emerge and become full-fledged sovereign members of the world community. Their utmost consideration is economic development, of eradicating poverty and raising the standards of living of their people. They understand that political independence alone is not enough unless they could achieve economic power and self-reliance. They carve out a distinct place in the world and style themselves as the Third World with a definitive ideology of Third Worldism that provides a radical critique of the existing world order, one marked by sharp inequities and disparities. They question the rationale for their poverty and backwardness, which is in sharp contrast to the affluence and glitter of Europe, North America and Japan. Their emphasis is on the role of governments and controlling markets to bring about accelerated national economic growth. In view of finding a solution to this problem of poverty eradication, many intellectuals begin to question the proposition of classical economists, like Smith and Ricardo, that growth in free world trading will abolish poverty and backwardness. The basis of this proposition is the assumption that if the world market works freely without restrictions and by encouraging competition, then each country or region specialises in areas in which it has decisive natural advantage. If managed efficiently, it will lead to comparative advantage resulting in gradual equalisation of income. Furthermore, consumers pay much more for the protected product than they would if the market is open to potentially cheaper imports. Free markets and free trade are supposed to be the panacea of all ills. There are two basic objections to this proposition—first, many argue that poverty is not inevitable and second, the world market in itself is not adequate to tackle it. It is pointed out that governments in the developed countries play a central role by regularly intervening and regulating the market through armed forces, prison camps, legal systems, investments and tax policies. The underdeveloped countries are not willing to wait indefinitely for the possible long-term effects of free trade. They regard structural changes in the national economy and indigenous industrialisation rather than a relationship with the world economy as being crucial to economic development and prosperity. They desire a fully diversified home economy that is capable of generating growth on the basis of an expanding home market, regardless of what happens in the world at large.

Prebisch's Thesis

Raul Prebisch (1901–1986) understands that the nineteenth century paradigm of free trade is inoperative and disadvantageous to these new raw materials exporting nations in the middle of twentieth century. He is the first to highlight the weaknesses of the raw materials exporting countries of Latin America vis-á-vis the manufactured goods exporting advanced countries. He divides the world into a centre (developed) and periphery (underdeveloped). A major difference between the nineteenth and the twentieth century is the emergence of the United States, after the Second World War, with its vast resources, strong agricultural base and essentially self-sufficient economy, as the controller of the world economy replacing Great Britain that perennially depended on foreign trade. In the nineteenth century, Great Britain and other European powers depended on imported raw materials for sustaining their domestic manufacturing. Imports from Latin America, which saw enormous investments by European Powers, led to an augmentation of their economies. This enabled them to import manufactured goods and pay for their borrowings from Europe. The division of labour based on exchange of agricultural and industrial goods was mutually beneficial. This got altered in the twentieth century and worked to the benefit of the manufactured goods exporting countries. When the United States replaced Britain as the dominant economic power its necessity for imports from Latin America gradually declined and the Latin American countries found themselves unable to pay for the import of manufactured goods. As a result, they used up their limited gold reserves for payment.

Prebisch attributes it to the 'inner-directed development' of the United States and warns in 1944 of long-term disequilibrium in the world economy. Paralleling this argument Prebisch also develops another one that has serious implications. During the Great Depression, the prices of agricultural exports declined much more than manufactured goods. Raw materials exporting countries specialising in one or more commodities faced the severest impact of the slump. As a result, the exchange between the two categories of producers widened. This happens when the exporters of manufactured goods, which Prebisch identifies as centre(s) commands a monopoly over the supply of these goods and effectively controls their prices. On the other hand, exporters of agricultural goods, the periphery are numerically large and competition among them keeps the prices down. Furthermore, the fast pace of technical development in manufacturing and monopoly controls of the prices of manufactured exports keep the costs of production down benefitting the manufacturers and not the buyers. The reverse is the case with agricultural goods, 'While the centres kept the whole benefit of technical development of their industries, the peripheral countries transferred to them a share of the fruits of their own technical progress' (Prebisch 1950: 65). He adds that along with this monopoly on the supply of manufactured foods, there also operates a monopoly in the supply of labour among trade unions in Europe and America to ensure that wages do not fall during a slump, thereby, keeping the price of manufactured goods high. Even here the reverse operates with regard to agricultural goods, 'the less that income can contract at the centre, the more it must do so at the periphery' (Prebisch 1950). In the periphery, capital investment helps to sustain industrial control over the factors of production by ensuring that all the local production units are geared towards export trade. Local savings and investments remain meagre due to two reasons—(1) the inability of the workers to raise their share of surplus and (2) the incapacity of the government to tax areas that has surplus like multinational businesses and from traditional local groups like traders and landowners. The rigidities of supply rather than excesses of demand led to inflation, a persistent structural problem in the periphery.

Prebisch stresses on solutions that have both national and international ramifications. Internationally, the centre tries to help the peripheries through foreign aid and technical assistance. It gives special treatment to raw materials exporting countries and aids the Third World governments that try to reform domestic industry till a point when the nation begins to consume its own locally produced manufactured goods irrespective of the costs. In other words, it must assist capital accumulation and industrialisation within the periphery through protection. Such an effort at import substitution lessens dependence on imports and reduces the need to export, simultaneously, increasing domestic employment and income, resulting in an expanded domestic market accelerating the process of industrialisation. This policy of 'Import substitution industrialisation' enables the concerned country to retain the benefits of technological progress in manufacturing sector.

The dependency theory is Marxist in orientation but intellectually draws its sustenance from non-Marxist analysis of Prebisch. It originates among the radical social scientists of Latin America and is most popular there. Using the Latin American experiences, they develop their formulations. By giving a twist in the neo-Marxist direction to Prebisch's formulations dependency theory becomes a critique of the modernisation theory.

Modernisation Theory

Modernisation theory combining economic, psychological and sociological factors understands modernity to include value systems, individual motivation and capital accumulation. It emphasises considerably on the values, norms and belief-structures that play a pivotal role in the transformation of a traditional society into a modern one. While Western societies evolve due to internal factors, the developing ones can modernise by their exposure to outside forces, ideas, technology, education, literacy, increased political consciousness and participation, capital investment, greater economic opportunities, emergence of rational-legal system replacing the traditional one, development of mass media, emergence of nuclear family and emergence of representative government.

Western Europe experiences a linear path towards modern development and this finds expression in the theories of evolution that reign in the nineteenth century. Embedded in the view of progress is the premise that Europe can civilise the other parts of the world and spread European values. Weber distinguishes traditional societies from modern ones. **Parsons** observes that traditional society stands for ascriptive status, diffused roles and particularistic values, while modern society accepts achievement statuses, specific roles and universalistic values. **Eisenstadt** (1964) identifies the major structural characteristics of modernisation along the lines that Weber and Parsons suggest. Modernisation, according to Eisenstadt, means a highly differentiated political structure and the dispersion of political power and authority in all facets of society. **Walt Rostow** in the *Stages of Economic Growth* (1960) indicates the universal stages of economic development that all societies pass through before they become fully modernised. There are traditional or agricultural societies, the stage that prepares the preconditions for economic 'take-off, actual take-off, where full commercial and industrial systems are established, sustained economic growth and, finally, the mature high mass-consumption society that represents the completion of social evolution. **Huntington** (1968) stresses on stability that accompanies modernisation as a consequence of rapid social and economic changes. Modernisation means industrialisation, economic growth, increasing social mobility and political participation. In contrast to stability is political decay that signifies instability, corruption, authoritarianism and violence, which are indicators of the failure of modernisation. **Apter** (1965) draws a distinction between development and modernisation.

> Development, the most general, results from the proliferation and integration of functional roles in a community. Modernization is a particular case of development. Modernization implies three conditions—a social system that can constantly innovate without falling apart ...; differentiated, flexible social structures; and a social framework to provide the skills and knowledge necessary for living in a technologically advanced world. Industrialization, a special aspect of modernization, may be defined as the period in a society in which the strategic functional roles are related to manufacturing (1965: 67).

Apter identifies two models—'secular-libertarian' or pluralistic system and 'sacred-collectivity' or mobilising systems. In the former, there is diversified power and leadership, bargaining and compromise as it is in a liberal democracy like the United States. Personalised and charismatic leadership, political religiosity and the organisation of a mass party characterise the 'sacred-collectivity'. China under Mao, Egypt under Nasser and Ghana under Nkrumah are examples of this type.

Dependency Theory

Dependency theory rejects the modernisation theories both with regard to analysis and prediction. It links underdevelopment to the linkage underdeveloped countries has with the developed countries. Unlike Prebisch who suggests remedies both national and international, the dependency theorists analyse the problem of underdevelopment within the framework of international structures and processes. Following the Leninist legacy of Marxism, they connect the continued impoverishment and underdevelopment of the periphery to the sustained unequal exchange with the developed West. While Lenin regards imperialism as the last stage of capitalism, the dependency theorists gloomily consider imperialism as the basis of perpetuating inequality and dependency. Nkrumah's famous word 'neocolonialism' and Huntington's well-known phrase 'invisible empire' explains the sentiment in a nutshell. Bodenheimer defines dependency as a 'reflection of the expansion of the dominant nations and is geared towards the needs of the dominant economics, for example, foreign rather than national needs' (1974: 158). For Caporaso and Behrour, 'dependency refers to a structural condition in which a healthy integrated system cannot complete its economic cycle except by an exclusive (or limited) reliance on an external complement' (1981: 48).

Unlike the development theorists for whom domestic factors are crucial to explaining poverty and backwardness, the dependency theorists attribute the poverty of the poor countries to the affluence of and exploitation by the rich ones. They point to historical antecedents when the colonial powers deliberately dwarfed the indigenous developments of their colonies. They regard dependency and imperialism as two sides of the same coin with the difference that imperialism is the view from the top while dependency the perspective from the bottom. For most of the newly independent countries, political freedom remains meaningless since advanced countries through multinational corporations, foreign aid and technological and cultural dependence economically dominate them. This is established and perpetuated through a policy of collaboration between foreign and local capital with the help of the support base of a new class.

Andre Gunder Frank develops the dependency theory into a grand one by emphasising the intrinsic link between underdevelopment and dependency with globalisation of capitalism. The dependency theorists contend that the distinction between non-development and underdevelopment exists due to the mercantilist and capitalist expansion of the European powers. What follows is a unity of interests among the developed countries while the underdeveloped regions remain disunited. Since then, the unequal relationship between the developed and underdeveloped regions continues with calamitous consequences for the latter. Frank regards contemporary underdevelopment as the consequence of a number of interrelated factors. First, that underdevelopment is due to effects of mercantilism and industrial capitalism and not due to traditionalism of these countries. Second, these societies reflect 'dualism', one urban and modern and, the other, rural and backward. Third, contrary to the presumption that industrialisation needs inflow of capital and culture, Frank argues that the peak of industrial development within the satellites has occurred when the link with the metropolis is at the weakest. He also rejects the claim that there exists a pre-capitalist sector in Latin America, since this is only possible if there is an overall capitalist state. Moreover, the task is to change the capitalist underdevelopment with the socialist development. Frank rejects Marx and Lenin's suggestion of a two-stage theory of revolution and recommends just one revolution, similar to M.N. Roy's proposition. Finally, Frank rejects the idea of import substitution being a stimulus to economic development as it leads to long-term dependence on the international system and permanent underdevelopment. In *Capitalism and Underdevelopment in Latin America* (1967), Frank argues that underdevelopment is not the result of modern capitalism, but in America, was as old as European colonisation.

> My thesis is that these capitalist contradictions and the historical development of the capitalist system have generated underdevelopment in the peripheral satellites whose economic surplus was appropriated, while generating economic development in the metropolitan centres which appropriate that surplus—and, further, that this process still continues ... economic development and underdevelopment are not just relative and quantitative ... (They) are relative and qualitative, in that each is structurally different from, yet caused by its relation with the other (Frank 1967: 3, 8).

These arguments have been widely accepted and developed by many radical social scientists. T. Dos Santos (1973) extends the notion of 'dependence' to mean domestic rather than the external condition of a Third World country. Economic development in Latin America differs from that of Europe because the dual nature of its economy neither allows nor encourages full development of capitalist relations of production but rather bases itself upon slavish forms of work. Dependence, therefore, continues with the transitional colonial stage of economic development *a conditioning situation* in which the economies of one group of countries are conditioned by the development and expansion of others. Dependence is based on an international division of labour, which permits industrial development in some countries while restricting it in others, whose growth is conditioned by and subjugated to the power centres of the world. Under these circumstances no genuine development is possible and the peripheral countries' only hope is to break-off relations with the capitalist world altogether as China did and chart out their own course. Domination becomes possible only because internally influential local group leaders hope to gain by it. External domination is not conducive to proper development. The only solution, therefore, is to change the internal structure, which may lead to confrontation with the international structure.

Since 1960s, dependency theory develops generalisation from the Latin American experience applying it to the rest of the world. **Wallerstein** (1974, 1980 and 1989) advocates his theory of a world economic system in which there are concentric rings—the 'core' countries of the West, a 'semi-periphery' and 'periphery', a differentiation made possible by history. The core states industrialised first and acquires a decisive advantage over the rest of the world. The peripheral states are those that cater to the needs of the core and are willfully prevented from developing higher industrial skills. The semi-periphery is the middle category of states that can move in either direction, and may include one-time core states that have lost their status now. The whole system reflects an international division of labour and the course of transferring surplus from periphery to the core is the basic nature of this system.

P.P. Rey (1971, 1973), a French sociologist refines the idea of dualism by advancing a more refined notion of the 'articulation of modes of production'. He argues that the reason for underdevelopment in certain areas of the world, though not in the developed countries, is largely due to the nature of the indigenous society. In the West, feudalism leads to capitalism because of the attitude of the feudal upper class. In the rest of the world where feudalism in the European sense has not existed, the consequence of a society being integrated into the world economy through trade and investment is by strengthening the control of the existing governing classes and reinforcing their resistance to the extension of capitalism.

Arghiri Emmanuel's Unequal Exchange

A Study of the Imperialism of Trade (1969), Samir Amin's *Accumulation and Underdevelopment* (1970) and Andre Gunder Frank's *Dependent Accumulation and Underdevelopment* (1978) take off from the arguments of Rosa Luxemburg. Emmanuel and Amin, like **Luxemburg**, regard trade rather than the export of capital as the main locomotive of European imperialism and the instrument whereby the West has exploited other countries and produce hurdles to Third World's growth. Both accept the Wallerstein model of a progressive establishment of a single world capitalist economy, with a core and a periphery. They point out to different specialisations in the centre and the periphery, which perpetuates inequality. They reject the Ricardian model of comparative advantage as impossible in this world of basic inequity between the developed and the underdeveloped nations.

Emmanuel rejects the Ricardian principle that differentiation and specialisation of production between more and less developed countries will be to their mutual advantage, even if one country is more developed and affluent than the other. Ricardo's contention hinges on the assumption that the subsistence wages of the labour will remain uniform worldwide but that capital is relatively stationery and that profit varies from one country to another. Thus, a commodity will have a duplicate labour makeup wherever it is produced, but will differ in costs according to its capital component. Since he believes that the value of a commodity is in its labour composition, it follows that international exchange amounts to inequality of exploitation, that is, trade could not bring about transfer of real values unless compelled to do so ignoring market values. Profits vary due to differences in capital component and environmental factors. Emmanuel argues that unlike the early nineteenth century money wages are no longer uniform internationally. In reality, wages vary by a factor of thirty per cent or more internationally. On the contrary, a great reduction in international transport costs means that prices of identical goods tend to equalise everywhere. The rise of multinational companies has made capital mobile and its return is much the same globally. If the prices and profits remain the same internationally, the main variable in exchange has to be money wages since workers are not mobile. Exchange becomes 'unequal' when a low-wage country has to pay more for the goods it imports than it receives for the goods it exports. The world is divided into two spheres—the high-wage, high-value economies, and the low-wage, low-value economies. The former exploits the latter not through capital investment but through the terms of trade resulting in unequal development and a gradual widening of the gap between the two. The solutions for unequal exchange, according to Emmanuel, are autarchy whereby poor countries stop international trading and exchange among themselves and second, form cartels in order to raise traded prices artificially by export duties or by monopoly pricing. From a different perspective, **P.A. Samuelson** (1976) takes up the same Ricardian formula for the England-Portugal trade relationship which Emmanuel uses to prove the fact of unequal exchange and shows that by adding profit rates, both countries in fact benefit in the manner that Ricardo claims. He holds that a poor country benefits absolutely from specialisation and trade, even if it benefits less relatively from these things than a richer country with higher levels of technology and labour productivity.

The major thrust of the dependency and unequal exchange theorists is on the need to bring about structural transformation and greater interdependence between the bourgeoisie of the centre and the periphery. They caution that growth does not lead to development. Frank regards the Latin American middle class as being a major hurdle to reform. He also blames the bureaucracy for playing a conservative role in both administration and politics (Frank 1972: 3–17). He rejects the basic assumptions of developmental approaches of theorists like Rostow. He dismisses the latter's proposition of two stages as fictional and 'incorrect primarily because they do not correspond at all to the past or present reality of the underdeveloped countries whose development they are supposed to guide' (1972: 346). The dependency theorists locate the problem of underdevelopment in the very nature of contemporary capitalism and recommend the erstwhile Soviet model of industrialisation, in which the state rather than the consumer decides priorities as the only way out of the limitations of bourgeois reforms. A leap towards socialism guarantees both a balanced growth and total national control over production and allocation of its resultant surplus. However, they ignore one important historical fact that the socialist countries in the developing world have suffered as much from the phenomenon of dependency as their own non-socialist counterparts. A good example is Cuba whose economy remained paralysed and dependent on subsidy from the former Soviet Union to the tune of four billion dollars a year, half of Cuba's national income. Both Ethiopia and Vietnam in the early 1980s faced virtual famines and had to be helped by the West to tide over the crisis. The communist nations in the developing world were as much dependent on the developed socialist countries, just as the non-communist ones on advanced capitalist countries.

Furthermore, the raw materials exporting countries by their merger into the world capitalist system deviate from the path of self-reliance. The loss of self-sufficiency means their total dependence on exports. Since they supply specific raw materials at a price established by the buyers, they can neither diversify nor increase their economic productivity. This is one of the contributing factors to the severe balance of payments difficulties indicating the contradictions that dependency creates. Another indicator of the contradiction is the stress on increased unemployment and widening inequalities. As a result, the domestic market shrinks inevitably undermining the local bourgeoisie. All theorists of dependency agree on certain points in spite of individual variations in their frameworks. They agree that the centre-periphery relationship leaves very little possibility for a proper economic development of the periphery. This is because capital investment in the periphery, the very organisation of the world market and the pattern of the world demand, all contribute to the benefit of the centre at the cost of the periphery. As a consequence, the dependent countries face negative growth rates, resource drain, excessive rates of capital repatriation, enormous foreign debts and unstable boom and bust cycles mainly because local economies, instead of being directed to solving local problems, are geared towards the world capitalist markets dominated by affluent capitalist countries.

The crux of the argument is that countries with a high degree of dependency have very low rates of economic growth. The growth rate in the satellites is highest when their link with the centre is at the weakest. For instance, Frank cites the examples of the two World Wars and the period of the Great Depression when the Latin American economies did very well. Another caveat of the argument is that within the dual economy an augmented foreign investment can lead to greater inequality in incomes and attenuate foreign indebtedness. Dependency theorists dismiss the argument of the conventional economists that foreign trade and capital is beneficial. However, they do not satisfactorily deal with the problem of isolationism. The erstwhile socialist society pursued an isolationist economic policy with the aim of self-sufficiency and independent development as demonstrated by the fact that they produced little less than 25 per cent of world GNP yet their share of world exports were merely 14 per cent. This also meant that they remained out of the prevailing trend towards internationalisation of the production process and membership of the financial institutions. This exclusiveness meant that the three important components of modern business organisation, increased efficiency, and product quality and consumer choice never became a part of their economic processes. In not dealing with these important issues, the dependency theory ignores some of the very key issues of modern organisational structure and the role of scientific and technological innovations and in that sense is pre-modern.

In the course of testing the hypothesis of the dependency theory, in the context of Latin America, Kaufman, Cheronosky and Geller (1979) take into account the relationship between the dependency economies and economic growth. They incorporate variables like degree of trade partner concentration, degree of concentration of commodities and flow of foreign capital and investment and find gross fallacies in the dependency theory. The majority of indicators point to the fact that the more dependent countries grew faster rather than slowly as contended by the dependency theorists. This is important, for it falsifies one of their core assumptions about dependency and economic growth. Furthermore, Kaufman, Cheronosky and Geller also establish the fact that though dependency produces income inequality yet there is a strong negative link between dependency and land inequality, disproving another major contention of the dependency theorists.

Miracle in East and Southeast Asia: Challenge to the Dependency Theory

The Newly Industrialised Countries (NICs) of East and Southeast Asia have negated the basic assumptions of the dependency theory. By achieving a high standard of living and coming out of the dependency syndrome they have got integrated with the developed nations. With the exception of Thailand, all the new states in this region were colonies. Taiwan (Formosa) and Korea were Japanese colonies from 1895 and 1910, respectively, till 1945. Malaya became independent in 1957, expanding into Malaysia to include Singapore (for two years only) in 1963. Indonesia, Sabah and Sarawak were Dutch colonies till 1949. Hong Kong was a British Colony till 1997, when it was handed over to China.

Most of them were under long years of foreign rule. At independence they faced the same problems as the new states of Black Africa and South Asia. Yet by 1970s and 1980s, they became the most dynamic economies in the world, originating the concept of East Asian miracle. They challenged the assumption that it is impossible for the ex-colonies to join the ranks of affluent industrialised countries. Since their success is due to the export of manufactured goods, it proves that it is possible for countries with predominantly agricultural economies to discover their comparative advantage in manufacturing and exploit it. Within these countries, there are two groups. The first, consisting of Hong Kong, Taiwan, South Korea and Singapore who became pioneers in rapid manufacturing growth and exports. The others followed in and after 1970s. Of these four, Singapore and Hong Kong are city-states but in spite of the limitations of geography, they have become successful exporting countries.

The reasons for East Asian miracle as summed up by the World Bank are high rates of investment, averaging 20 per cent of GDP between 1960 and 1990, and rising endowment of human capital due to universal primary and secondary education. The governments in these countries are interventionists yet market oriented. They pursue sound open market macroeconomic policies but are prepared to intervene when the market appeared to fail. Intervention took many forms. Except for Hong Kong, the others in the early post-war years followed a highly protectionist policy aiming at import substitution, a fact common in almost all the Third World countries. However, what makes the East Asian tigers, except Hong Kong, exceptional, is the fact that they combine protectionism with export promotion. In that way, they are able to gradually move from highly protectionist import-substitution industrialisation to moderately open competitive economies, thereby, maintaining the momentum of industrialisation. Furthermore, the state maintained close ties with the business and technological elite. Their governments were competent and least corrupt with a bureaucracy that was exceptionally efficient at economic management. This enabled them to judiciously combine interventionist with free market strategies. They were also open to foreign technology, which they welcomed via licencing, training and import of capital goods. Taiwan and South Korea restricted their direct foreign investment, mainly because they were able to raise capital at home or by foreign borrowing, and because they rapidly acquired the necessary know-how and operational skills. With the exception of Hong Kong, all the others shifted from import substituting industrialisation to export orienting industrialisation and slowly opened their domestic markets to foreign competition. In short, the success of East Asia is due to 'getting the fundamentals right' in macro-economic policy—high rates of capital accumulation, limited price distortions and broadly based human capital. The private enterprises grew very well. The state also intervened whenever private firms were cautious and whenever business strategies failed. The most important was the adoption of export-push strategies. The distinguishing feature between the successful ones from the others was the quality of governments and wisdom of their economic and social policies. The less successful ones were 'soft' states, weak in their ability to govern and devise complex development policies. Their planning was unrealistic and its execution unproductive. The state imposed and decided the type of economic activity with varying degree of competence. The Gang of Four and their integration into the world economy have become trailblazers for others to emulate. This, however, is unimportant, given the structural changes in the world economy, one or the other will sooner or later have led the way. The changes in world economy have enabled the governments in the NICs to develop spectacularly through policy and management. Johnson (1982) labels the governmental system that Japan pioneers from the mid-1920s and later emulated by other East Asian economies as developmental state. These states consider national security to be the topmost concern, which is possible only through rapid industrialisation. Towards this end, the state assumes responsibility for deciding the national growth priorities with the help of a powerful economic bureaucracy that is insular from democratic/parliamentary and other political interests. An elite-core of technically trained members supports the bureaucracy. The state also aims to bring about consensus and cooperation between public sector, private entrepreneurs and other domestic interests.

Assessment

It is difficult to prove that the Third World has been made poorer, backward and underdeveloped by the creation of a single world economy and market though there have been unattractive consequences, particularly in cultures and lifestyles. The notion of 'dependence' has little explanatory power and that all countries are dependent on one another for exports and sources of imports.

> The concept of a 'self generating' economy is a myth, except for the most backward countries at a very low and vulnerable levels of income. On the contrary, the more advanced an economy, the less self-reliant it becomes. If 'dependency' indicated the economic relationship between a country and the world, the more developed the country, the more dependent it was, that is, the more domestic activity was determined by external relationships (Harris 1986: 123–124).

Trade is a necessary though not a sufficient condition for sustained growth or development. This depends on how well a particular society takes advantage of the gains of trade. In practice, this means ploughing back profits from trade to transform the society as a whole. 'The domestic consumer would benefit by having access to goods, whether produced at home or imported, at the lowest prices in the world system' (Harris 1986: 119).

The development economists rightly argue that commodity production and export lead to industrialisation since these alone counter the Malthusian prediction of limited land and the hurdle of fragile and unanticipated world commodity market. The first step towards industrialisation is through import-substitution. However, this does lead to an economic dead-end, for highly protected markets will soon have to contend with limited domestic markets. If competition is limited by excluding imports it leads to not only monopoly pricing and poor quality of the local output but also stagnation in local technology.

In the long run, industrialisation will lead to sustained growth only if substantial part of the manufacturing industries becomes internationally competitive. Exporting is as crucial for manufacturers as for commodities. Trade, specialisation and comparative advantage as the classical economists have visualised would always lead to growth and not to underdevelopment and misery. This depends on the ability of a society to augment and invest the benefits of trade with each stage of specialised production leading to higher technical levels and to the ability to compete globally.

A basic assumption of the dependency theory that the periphery will always remain raw materials exporting has been negated even before the collapse of communism. By the end of 1970s, the 'less developed countries' exported more manufactured goods than raw materials. By 1980, the more developed countries exported 36 per cent primary commodities than the less developed countries. From the perceptions of the 1950s, it is a world turned upside down. The exports of the NICs, forerunner of a new manufacturing world order, are not assets of intruders, but a complete part of the emerging new structure, the global industrial system. Added to this is the impressive performance in some Latin American countries, like Chile and Mexico. China has had a steady growth rate of 10 per cent for more than two decades. India's growth rate since liberalization in 1991 has been between 5–8 per cent. The steady growth rate in China hovering around 8 per cent, a much better growth rate than India's which is of 5.8 per cent since 1991 when the liberalisation programme began. All these suggest that a greater integration with the world market helps and, in this context, the dependency theory is inadequate to the understanding of not only the NICs but other post-colonial societies as well which have shown the will to change its own fortunes.

Even Wallerstein is not sure if a radical change of the present world economic system which he calls geo-culture can be changed by anti-systemic forces like environmentalism, feminism, political movements of the indigenous people and new kinds of organised labour or student activism. He admits that the core and the periphery are not a static structure and one can move from the core to the periphery and vice-versa. The South Korean success is the example of the movement from periphery to the core and Wallerstein cites the example of Argentina for the core becoming a periphery. This makes the present world system not only unassailable but also just, in the sense, that there is an in-built mechanism of just reward with the possibilities of upward or downward movement. Amongst the available models till date, the present system seems the best possible invented by the humankind so far as rapid economic growth, alleviation of poverty and enjoyment of human rights are concerned. 'Modernisation theory predicted that such developments as economic growth, the spread of science and technology, the acceleration and spread of communications and the establishment of educational systems would all contribute to political change' (Pye 1990: 7). History has vindicated this optimism rejecting the pessimism of the dependency theory.

GANDHIAN CONCEPT

One of the basic principles of Gandhi's analysis of the contemporary Indian reality is the acceptance of the prevalence of acute conflicts in a number of areas and institutions, which he analyses within a scientific framework. He concludes that conflicts are manifest prominently in three sectors—conflict of labour and capital in industry, conflict of tenant and landlord in agriculture and conflict of village and city. In pointing to the last one, he rejects Marx's utter contempt for village life. Gandhi observes that India lives in its villages and the cities do not represent India and are alien to it. He remarks in 1921 that cities are 'brokers and commission agents for the big houses of Europe, America and Japan. The cities have cooperated with the latter in the bleeding process that has gone on for two hundred years' and he accuses the cities as conniving with imperialism and plundering the villages. He was concerned about the enormous gap that exists between villages and cities with regard to education, culture, medicine, and recreation and employment opportunities. This gulf continuously widened. Though Gandhi criticises the cities, he does not want to eliminate them but reform them and place them in their natural setting. He desires to develop a new partnership between the two so that the cities do not become islands of prosperity at the cost of the villages. He was convinced that the prosperity of the village is the key to create a new balanced India, for checking the uncontrollable migration to cities that are increasingly becoming unmanageable in India and to creating a balance between agriculture and industry. It is no accident that in the prosperous states of Punjab, Haryana and Maharashtra the problem of rural to urban migration is not that serious. Delhi and Bombay attract millions not from their immediate neighbourhoods. Gandhi is also aware of the enormous differences between countries and emphasises that India's mission is different from that of the others. Gandhi impresses on the fact that India with abundant labour and large-scale unemployment and underemployment should restrict the use of machinery. He clarifies that his prescriptions are not for all the countries but for India alone, being an ancient country shrouded in superstition and error. However, he argues that India has the ability to solve her economic problems and the inherent capacity to become free from British imperialism and gain *swaraj*.

Rejection of the West

Gandhi criticises contemporary society and denounces Western materialism and modern technology, like the railways, the telegraph, the telephone and heavy industries. He rejects the Western civilisation for two reasons. First, its basis is extreme inequality and second, it dehumanises and depersonalises the individual. Like Rousseau, he rejects modern technology and industrialisation because these lead to misery and inequality. He focuses on this relative fall apparent from the Italian example in the *Hind Swaraj*.

In this example, he specifically mentions the working class and the common people whose aspirations were ignored by the ruling class and that Mazzini's Italy was still in slavery. For Gandhi, the content of independence is important, for true freedom lay in the freedom of the working class and the poorest. Western technology and its concomitant way of life are alien to Indian traditions and also inadequate in fulfilling India's requirements. It hinders any meaningful or real development of the individual person. Gandhi differs considerably from other non-Western revolutionaries like Mao, Ho Chi Minh, Che Guevara and Fanon who not only 'rejected the Western political and economic domination but also their traditional ways of life of their own people and especially the religious elements that provided the foundation for the ancient cultures of Asia and Africa, replacing them by Western political forms and by Western technologies' (Woodcock 1971: 12). Fanon's perception shows some interesting contradictions into the dilemma of the Third World revolutionaries. While forcefully pleading for decolonisation in *The Wretched of the Earth* (1961), he remains utterly contemptuous of the imperialists. He denounces the Europeans virtually as war criminals. He regards European opulence as scandalous, for it was based on slavery but ironically in spite of this severe indictment, he conceives of change only with the indispensable help of the Europeans and by rejecting indigenous ways.

Gandhi, on the other hand, wants to keep the windows of his mind open while his feet firmly entrenched in his own culture. Gandhi desires a free India that would not emulate the Western path. This means giving up machinery, modern methods of transportation, modern medicines and machine-spun cloth. Though he modifies some of his ideas subsequently, like accepting small-scale industries and those industries where labour is not useful or desirable, he adheres to the overall thrust of his initial arguments as articulated in the *Hind Swaraj*. The solution to the Indian problem has to come from within India rather than importing foreign ideas and institutions. Gandhi's free India is one where the economy and polity would be different from that of the other modern industrialised nations. His conception of *Swaraj* is different to the one articulated by the Western Marxists, socialists or even the liberals though he assimilates their ideas. Gandhi is an ardent individualist like the liberals but his ideal is similar to Green, as he tries to maximise individual freedom by promoting common good. Philosophically, like the anarchists, his ideal remains a society where the state plays a minimal role but he shuns their stress on revolutionary violence. Like the Marxists and socialists, he desires an egalitarian society but opposes their deterministic view of history and human nature. It is this synthetic outlook, retaining the best of the Western traditions and integrating it with indigenous roots of the Indian traditions that make Gandhi unique.

Rejection of Industrialisation

Gandhi focuses on the ill-effects of industrialisation and grasps its horrifying aspects. In this resonates the views of Marx, Dickens, Green and the Fabian socialists, who spoke of the lifelessness, exploitation and dehumanisation that industrialisation brought about (Ashe 1968). He concedes that in some vital areas like housing, industrialisation has enabled people to live better than what their ancestors did. He points out that technology has enormously enhanced productive power and the human capacity to accumulate wealth and also drew attention to the other side, namely poverty and inequality. With a remarkable similarity to Marx's criticism of Smith, he rejects the notion of progress and advancement since it is based on inequality. His remedy lay in abolishing the industrial civilisation and to go back to a more simple life. He understands freedom to mean political and economic independence, since the former without the latter is meaningless and hollow.

Constructive Programme and Trusteeship

Gandhi's prescription for social progress and transformation is contained in what he describes as the **constructive programme**. It gives content to the concept of *satyagraha* and takes into account the Indian social and economic milieu. The programme is considered to be the key to the attainment of *Swaraj* and consists of the following proposals—communal harmony, removal of untouchability, prohibition, *khadi*, village industries, village sanitation, basic education, adult education, upliftment of women, education in health and hygiene and propagation of national language. Of these the most important is the production of *khadi*, for it offers a salvation to India's economic, political and psychological problems. Gandhi emphasises the capacity of the *Khaddar* programme to organise the community. Decentralisation of industry is crucial to preserving the purity and cohesiveness of domestic life, of harnessing artistic and creative talents of individuals and more importantly 'people's sense of freedom, ownership, dignity'. He wants to develop what he calls a *khadi* mentality by which he means decentralisation of production and distribution of the necessities of life ensuring economic and political freedom and, thereby, reducing the dependence on the state and government. He believes that spinning had a moral dimension, for it purifies the mind and leads to spiritual progress. He stresses on the need to impart vocational training to the students, preferably the traditional family skill. The aim is to make the individual self-supporting by the sale of the products, and thus, giving an assured occupation to the students. The material reward could be in turn diverted for further education and self-development. This is the practical expression of his belief in the idea of bread labour. Gandhi stresses on the importance of dignity of labour in a society that defines work with reference to one's caste reinforcing inequality and indignity. He makes Indians sensitive to the urgent need for questions relating to social justice and emphasises the importance of punctuality, health, hygiene, sanitation and cleanliness.

To resolve the conflicts that exist in the Indian situation, Gandhi proposes the **trusteeship** system in which the rich use their property and wealth as a trust for the community. Though he regards property as a sin against humanity, he opposes its violent confiscation for that impoverishes society, which loses out of the talent of those who know how to create wealth. The deeper meaning of his theory of trusteeship is very akin to Weber's characterisation of puritan ethics, which does not decry increase in production but prohibits conspicuous consumption. Gandhi's trusteeship has this Calvinistic overtone, for trusteeship shows respect to the person who creates wealth, while simultaneously highlighting the need for self-restraint and charity. Accumulation of wealth accompanied by benevolence reduces envy and animosity among the non-creators of wealth. Property has to be limited so as to prevent exploitation, sensual indulgence and contempt for one's fellow-beings. Interestingly, in spite of his minimalist attitude towards the state he proposes a greater role for the state in economic affairs with limitations on the right of inheritance, state ownership of land and heavy industries, heavy taxes and nationalisation without compensation.

Gandhi understands the causes of disparity in the Indian society due to imperialistic exploitation and the imitation of the capitalist industrial civilisation. Perhaps he misses the point while denouncing technology and machinery that these could be used for bringing about the welfare of the people which has been the case. What he impresses upon is the need to bring out majoritarian welfare and the need to mitigate minority deprivation. It is a vision of development that is people-oriented, a welfare that is holistic and empowering.

SUSTAINABLE DEVELOPMENT AND ENVIRONMENTALISM

Environmentalism is specifically a modern doctrine though many argue that two centuries ago. **Thomas Robert Malthus** (1766–1834) draws attention to the fact that population, if unchecked grows at a geometrical ratio while food supply increases only in arithmetic proportion. Godwin and Condercet realise that population increase will cancel the economic gains made possible by science and technology but see it as a distant threat. In the 1960s and 1970s with growing concerns about pollution, there is a strong realisation that environmental problems are due to a complex interrelationship between humankind, global resources and the social and physical and environments (Turner 1988). This has led to a public debate about conventional growth objectives, strategies and policies. In response, some have given a call for zero-growth strategies (Daly 1977) deriving inspiration from the publication of the Club of Rome report *Limits to Growth* in 1972 (Meadows, Randers and Behrens 1972). The conclusion of the report is similar to the one reached by Malthus and provides the foundations for modern environmentalism.

Campaigning organisations such as Friends of the Earth and Greenpeace are both established in 1969. The first recognised Green political party was formed in New Zealand in 1972. The most famous of them all, the German Greens first gained parliamentary representation in 1983. The rise of this movement is attributed to the growth of a generation of 'post-materialists' born in the prosperous welfare states of post-Second World War Western Europe (Inglehart 1977). Though human beings have for long interacted with nature, the pressing concerns caused by modern industrial age are acute and global. When the greens argue that the long-term human survival and the biosphere's integrity are in doubt, this is because the biosphere's capacity to cushion and support is dwindling, thus, making the environmental issue universal and urgent, something that did not exist in the past. Issues like global warming, ozone depletion, acid rain, deforestation are among the foremost concerns of environmentalists. It is the scale and intensity of the issue that characterises modern environmentalism and in this science has helped to substantiate many of its claims. Green politics usually stress on no-growth, for they contend that infinite growth in a finite system, such as the planet earth is impossible because resources are finite and the capacity of the planet to absorb the waste released by human activity is limited. The Greens propose a 'steady-state' economy by either imposition of a selective taxation to encourage thrifty resource use and discourage waste or political imposition of resource-use quotas.

The wide criticism of the limits to growth argument has led to its partial replacement by view that environmental safety and continuing economic growth need not be mutually incompatible and not necessarily have conflicting aims. The term '**sustainable development**' is used to refer to this new perspective. It becomes a part of public discussion in 1980 with the presentation of the *World Conservation Strategy* that aims to achieve sustainable development through conservation of living resources by the International Union for the Conservation of Nature and Natural Resources. However, this aim is limited since its purpose is ecological sustainability rather than defining sustainability in the context of social and economic issues. The United Nations Environment Programme employs a broader meaning to the term in the report *Our Common Future* published by the World Commission on Environment and Development (WCED) in 1987. It is also known as the Brundtland Report after its president. The WCED is established with the aim of promoting economic development and environmental safety simultaneously in 1983 by the United Nations General Assembly following a decision taken at the United Nations Conference in Stockholm in 1972 that drew attention to the issue of global environment.

The report supports the idea of assimilating environmental policies with development strategies, thus doing away with the common perception that environmental protection can be achieved only at the cost of economic development. Its main belief is that the pursuit of economic development is perfectly congruous with environmental protection. This link is for two fundamental reasons—first, since the developing world is concerned with eliminating degrading national poverty, its cooperation is possible only if there is a clear commitment to goals of development and second, since poverty is perceived to be a major cause for environmental degeneration, its reduction through economic development helps the environment. The WCED report insists on following these three principles:

1. All economic decision making procedures whether of the states, companies or household must be committed to better environment management. This implies two things—first, to refrain from dumping waste into rivers, seas and the atmosphere and second, to develop new technologies that will reduce the amount of energy and materials used in every sphere of economic life.
2. Refrain from wasting or squandering of environmental resources and leaving the planet a better place for living for succeeding generations. The rich countries should assist the poor to achieve economic development with minimum damage to the environment.
3. Sustainability means to give more importance to quality of life rather than higher material standards of living.

The report defines the concept of sustainable development with reference to two key concepts—**needs** and **limitations**. With regard to the first, it accepts the importance of giving overall priority to the essential needs of the world's poor. Since needs are socially and culturally determined, the report argues that sustainable development should promote those values that encourage consumption patterns that are ecologically feasible. There is a need to change consumption pattern, particularly, in the developed societies of the North. The argument regarding limitation refers to the environment's ability to meet the present and future needs depending on the state of technology and social organisation. The report stipulates a number of social and political changes to achieve sustainable development at the global level—elimination of poverty and exploitation, equal distribution of global resources, an end to the current pattern of military expenditure, new methods of ensuring just population control, lifestyle changes, appropriate technology and institutionalised changes including democratisation achieved through effective citizen participation in decision-making. It also implies a concern for both inter-generational (meaning needs of future generation in the formulation and execution of the present policy) and intra-generational (meaning the basic needs of the present generation) equity in resource use. Sustainable development in short aims to remove the disparities in economic and political relationships between the rich North and the poor South.

The report argues that there is no single blueprint of sustainable development since the economic and social systems and environmental conditions vary between countries. It acknowledges the fact that despite sustainable development being a global concern individual countries are to work out its own concrete policy options. The report adopts anthropocentric position with respect to sustainable development regarding human beings and their well-being as the ultimate goal of all environment and development policies. In 1989, the General Assembly decided to convene a meeting of the United Nations Conference on Environment and Development (UNCED) at Rio de Janiero in 1992 (Earth Summit) to discuss the implementation of sustainable development, thus, marking the beginning of environment as an object of public policy. It considers issues such as climate change and bio-diversity. The Kyoto Summit of 1997 agrees to cut greenhouse gas emissions by an overall 5.5 per cent (on 1990 levels) by the year 2012 with varying targets for different countries.

Strategies

Sustainable development can be achieved through broadly four different policy options—the treadmill approach, weak sustainable development, strong sustainable development and the ideal model. The treadmill approach hinges on the belief that if human ingenuity is given the freedom to innovate new technology it can successfully manipulate the environmental systems. In other words, it supports the idea of sustained growth that is assessed solely in terms of gross national product (GNP). The weak sustainable development tries to integrate capitalist growth with environmental concerns, a position adopted by David Pearce and the highly influential Pearce Report (1989). It accepts sustainable development through economic growth by taking into consideration environmental costs. Pearce argues that there are two dimensions to sustainability—first is sustainable development that 'implies some reasonably constant rate of growth in per capita real incomes, without depleting the nation's capital stock' and the second is sustainable use of resources and environment which implies 'some rate of use of the environment which does not deplete its capital value' (1985: 9). This is the approach that is favoured by the World Bank and the United Nations and is associated with environmental management. This view has been criticised for regarding environment in monetary terms and not for its cultural and spiritual worth. Advocates like O'Riordan (1981) and Weale (1992) of strong sustainable development emphasise environmental protection as an essential precondition of economic development: This is the position that the WCED report highlighted. The Ideal Model is associated with Naess (1989), Echlin (1993, 1996) and Goldsmith (1992). It offers a vision at structural changes in society, the economy and the political systems by radically altering the attitude of humankind towards nature. It measures overall growth not in quantitative terms meaning standard of living but in qualitative sense, namely the quality of life, which can be achieved by radically altering the nature of economic activity. Sustainable development requires not only the role of national government but also the local ones, just as it also needs the involvement of international agencies. More so the importance of grassroot organisations with high levels of participation is crucial. This is because radical alteration in lifestyles cannot be imposed from above in an authoritarian manner. To succeed, it has to be bottom-up involvement, for that interweaves citizenship and educational aspects of development with the fusion of material and environmental wealth creation (O'Riordan 1981).

Political Arrangements

There is considerable disagreement about the political organisation in a sustainable society. Some Greens urge the need to 'act local but think global' and emphasise on localised production and consumption on the grounds that it uses less resource in comparison to a global economy. Other argue that decentralised polity is a disorganised one and points to the continuing relevance of traditional political arrangements associated with the state since even in a sustainable society decisions about resource use and distribution will have to be made. Still others stress that many of the environmental problems are global in nature and call for global organisations to solve them.

Criticisms

Lele (1991: 613) points out that the main problem with the idea of sustainable development is its effort to unite everybody from green activists, conservationists and poor farmers in the developing South but fails to provide concrete measures for anyone. Lele questions the main tenet of the idea that economic growth will reduce poverty and inequality when it has never been the case and wonders how can economic growth can contribute to environmental protection. Furthermore, to alleviate poverty, there has to be concerted effort to redistribute incomes in favour of deprived groups (1991: 614). Sachs expresses fears of the creation of a new type of elite, global 'eco-crats' (1993: xviii) which has hijacked the environmental agenda from the more radical groups. The eco-crats unlike the Green activists do not consider the biosphere as a brittle legacy that needs to be safeguarded for successors, but consider it as a 'commercial asset in danger' (Lele 1991: xvii) that needs to be managed globally by and on behalf of the rich and powerful.

Community Based Sustainable Development: Elinor Ostrom Prescriptions

Elinor Ostrom's (1933–2012) lifelong quest has been to find a balance between human interactions and the eco-systems by evolving a mechanism of sustainable development rejecting both the models of privately-owned markets and the rigid and remote state control of scarce and life sustaining resources like fisheries, forests, oil fields, grazing fields, biodiversity, oceans and water bodies and the atmosphere which are common pool resources. In this search for a third way, in her seminal work *Governing the Commons: The Evolution of Institutions* (1990), her research is monumental and path-breaking in development economics. She was a co-recipient of the Nobel Prize in Economics in 2009 and the only woman to have received the award till now. She is not a trained economist as her major discipline is Political Science. She has demonstrated with meticulous care, with the help of extensive fieldwork that societies have evolved collectively by developing diverse institutions to manage scarce resources and by evolving a collective consciousness without leading to a collapse of the eco-system by overuse.

Ostrom admits that not all the collective arrangements have succeeded in preventing resource exhaustion by overuse. Her only point is that human interaction with nature is multi-faceted and diverse underlining the fact that no single model can be touted as the panacea for solving the problems that individuals and society face in their relationship with nature. She argues that it is impossible for a single governmental or an international agency at the global level to address problems of environmental degradation as the issue itself is complex and diverse. She stresses on the need to adopt a polycentric approach that emphasises decision by people, the real stakeholders and that local problems, issues and concerns need local solutions involving local people. As a realist, she also rejects the theories of Deep Greens and argues that by maintaining the eco-system, creation and perpetuation of prosperity is feasible.

With reference to Buchanan-Tollock Programme and inspiration from Hayekean attention to importance of local knowledge, Ostrom argues convincingly that private groups, though not always, but quite often, have been able to avoid the tragedy of the commons. She points out the dangers of grand generalised theories of group and collective action that are referred to as pillars of public policy. She criticises three influential models—Garrett Hardin's *Tragedy of the Commons* (1968), the prisoner's dilemma game and Mancur Olson's *Logic of Collective Action* (1965) based on the problem of the free riders and individual rational users of resources which inherently act against the best interests of the users collectively. Such an assertion is based on the universal acceptance of particular conditions like (a) when individual actors possess high discount rates; (b) absence of mutual trust; (c) lack of capacity to communicate or have effective and binding agreements and even if it is arrived at (d) the absence of full proof mechanism to arrange for monitoring and enforcement leading to over investment and overuse.

According to Ostrom, Hardin's thesis is an attempt to create and introduce markets into traditional arrangements that have been enduring and sustainable for centuries. Hardin demonstrates the conflict between individual interests and common good. The commons is a shared plot of grassland used by all livestock farmers in a village. Each farmer continues to add more livestock to graze on the commons, because it costs him nothing to do so and as a result, in a few years the soil gets depleted by overgrazing making the commons unusable and with it the village perishes. The cause for any *tragedy of the commons* is that when individuals use a public good, they do not bear the entire cost of their actions. Each individual seeks to maximise his utility and ignores the costs that other bear. This is an example of externality. Common land as opposed to public land is land, usually held in private ownership that has rights of common over it. These lands are generally open, unfenced and remote. These lands are for those locals who are 'commoners' with rights for grazing, gathering fuel wood non-destructively. Hardin's thesis is based on individual rational action based on self interest, which leads to depletion of shared limited resources like fishing. To this, he suggests two ways to deal with the problem—one, governmental regulation and second, division of resources between the users and to privatise.

Ostrom rejects this solution for a number of reasons—(1) fencing would mean that many farmers would be left with no grazing grounds; (2) overexploitation can be checked by a scheme of ensuring fairness in the use of common resources; (3) the tragedy takes place when one or a handful of stakeholders who do not belong to the community's social economic system impose their own will exerting political power by changing the observed rules to gain advantage for themselves for immediate profit. Ostrom's data and examples, unlike that of Hardin's, are drawn from history and experiences of real people and communities worldwide.

A commonly held critical resource can both be well-governed and efficiently managed by close community engagement. She gives the example of a government protected forest which the local inhabitants do not consider to be legitimate resulting in a failure of the government to protect the forest. Legislation is not same as law. Without trying to bring such counter-productive legislation, a better way of preservation is to put attention to the ways and means of common law evolution of protecting and perpetuating common resources. Legislation in conformity with such laws, according to Ostrom, is the safest and time tested solution.

Both in the contemporary theories and practice of public choice movement and participatory democracy, Ostrom's views are of seminal importance. With regard to collective management of shared resources and environmental resource management, enduring cooperative institution organised, governed and shared by the resource users themselves is the best possible mechanism. The attraction of collective benefit can check the problem of free riders. Opportunism is negated by the viability of long-term benefits of common property regime. To give it a proper shape, she offers eight principles for governing the commons sustainably and equitably in a community. These are (1) define clear group boundaries; (2) match the rules governing the use of common goods to local needs and conditions; (3) ensure that those affected by the rules can participate in modifying the rules; (4) make sure the rule making rights of community members are respected by outside authorities; (5) develop a system, carried out by the community members, for monitoring members' behaviour; (6) use graduated sanctions for rule violators; (7) provide accessible, low-cost means for dispute resolution and (8) build responsibility for governing the common resource in nested tiers from the lowest level up to the entire interconnected system.

Ostrom also asserts that rules and principles are not only applicable to common resources but also to arenas of common services like communal property management, community policing and money systems. She asserts that top down approach to climate change must be discarded. The international initiatives to reduce green house effects would be counter-productive unless such initiatives have local basis and supported by local communities. She remarks 'what we have ignored is what citizens can do and the importance of real involvement of the people, versus just having somebody, in Washington, making a rule'. This is the recipe to avert big change, destabilisation and chaos.

Ostrom acknowledges that the impressions of her childhood in the background of the Depression taught her usefulness of self-help cooperatives and barter labour. Local unity is a basic ingredient in such economic arrangements. Forcefully speaking for a polycentric and a pluralistic world, she insists that a wide variety of solutions are to be there to solve the contemporary social and ecological problems. The world needs today a network of social connections and interactions. Ostrom does not reject the role of government but rejects only the over-centralised prescriptive action and top-down planning. Acknowledging her indebtedness to Lasswell and Kaplan in formulating her ideas, she comments that *Power and Society* (1952) 'broadened my perspective on individual choice and behaviour in a way that was instrumental'.

Ostrom accepts a world of diversities and existence of multiple values and possibility of multiple outcomes. She rejects Hardin's conclusion that 'freedom is a Commons brings ruin to all'. For Hardin, the Commons is comparable to a bank robbery. She rejects theories of environmental degradation and arguments about private ownership. She finds no such evidence and argues that human beings are not just self interested but have the capacity of considering the larger ramifications of their actions, both for those around them and for the larger environment in which they operate. Difficulties can be overcome democratically, and with local participation growth can be both equitable and sustainable. As she rightly states, 'what we need are universal sustainable development goals on issues such as energy, food security, sanitation, urban planning, and poverty eradication, while reducing inequality within the planet's limits'.

Beyond the two paradigms of Hobbes' sovereign and Smith's invisible hand, Ostrom finds and defends a third way to prove that the 'tragedy of the Commons' is an 'opportunity of the Commons'. It is not in the state or in the market but in the people that she places hope to solve social dilemmas which they confront and find solutions through various means of self governance. Ostrom addresses her arguments primarily to policy makers and not to scholars. The task now is to take her findings seriously as her way matters for entire humanity.

CONCLUSION

Economic arrangements are mainly made in the context of command and demand politics, which clearly flows, from the developmental perspective. Command politics postpones immediate benefits of development to future. The Prebisch thesis and our own Mahalanobis Model is a reflection of this perspective, 'a social version of this worldly asceticism that Weber associates with the Protestant ethic and the rise of capitalism in the West' (Rudolph and Rudolph 1998: 215). One may add that Gandhi's idea of trusteeship is quite compatible with the theory of Protestant ethic as Gandhi, unlike most of the other contemporary leaders of the liberation struggle, pronounces productionist view and not merely a distributionist one. The demand politics emphasises more on the quality of life in the contemporary world rather than emphasising on the uncertain promises of the future.

Recently, the developmental theories which emphasise more on the future rather than on the present have met with stiff challenges from advocates of goals who just do not concentrate on GNP as the index of development. The major reason for this change comes with an increasing realisation that the poor are neither benefitting nor contributing to development. This is reflected by the fact that the economic condition of the people who live under the poverty line remains virtually static. The poor lack the resources, educational skills, health and medical care to lead a better life and contribute to economic development. The proposition of 'basic human needs' employments generation, the physical quality of life index, literacy, life expectation, empowerment of the poor and women, have drawn the attention of the World Bank in the past few years. In response, the World Bank has started to champion broad issues like environment, health care, gender, political decentralisation and local accountability.

Owens (1987) criticises the trickle-down theory that is implicit in the argument for economic growth and points out that development not only means broad-based economic growth but must also be linked with one's own improvement and productivity. Furthermore, development is just not economic and social but also political, meaning the proper kind of freedom and democracy. By his definition, most democracies in the developing world are false because they are top-down, centralised and externally imposed. True democracy, on the contrary, is indigenously derived and provides ordinary people to access the system and its resources and public organisation, establishes the rule of law and realise political freedom. The basic malady with most development strategies lies in the fact that the focus is limited to economic and social aspects of life. Local institutions that are absolutely essential to sustain proper development by securing participation of the common people are generally ignored. A notable distinction between the industrialised and the developing countries does not lie in the capability to generate GNP but the fact that in the former the governments have at least been partially reformed. In contrast, in the developing world, only a handful of government have treated economic development as a part of the political reform process and it is ironic that all such unreformed governments are authoritarian. This proves that certain essential reforms that are needed to involve the poor and the underprivileged in the development process are fundamentally non-ideological and are feasible in any kind of political system, democratic, fascist, communist and non-ideological authoritarian. Owens also insists that development involves decentralised structures, for that ensures accountability of members, provides access to law, brings integrity in public affairs and secure rule of law. He is of course surprised that none of these reforms exist in false democracies and this demonstrates that social and economic rights can be created without creating political rights and the presence of just formal political rights is no guarantee for the realisation of social and economic rights. He considers the ideal situation as one that combines political rights with social and economic rights as the first ceases to be important without the second. He observes that those countries, which are securing social and economic rights, are on the right side of history and the others, which are not on the wrong side. He laments that most of the governments in the developing world are unreformed and underdeveloped.

Sen (1990) argues that inhuman miseries like abject poverty and periodic famines can be alleviated by resolving of the leaders and by following the right kind of policies. For Sen, this means acceptance of democracy with fair and free elections, multi-party systems, alert and active opposition political parties and groups and a free and vibrant press as part of the foundational arrangement. He demonstrates by giving examples from Sri Lanka and Kerala that just a rise in GNP and production is not enough, as true development means enrichment of the life of an average person according to the values that one cherishes.

The development theory now accepts that human capital is as important a component as physical capital. Schumpeter differentiates between political economy and economics arguing that the former has value and ideological preferences whereas the latter is value free. The development debate of the last several decades clearly reveals that a meaningful discourse is possible only within the framework of political economy, with a value shift within the developmental paradigm, from narrow basis of a GNP growth to concerns of the quality of life.

Further Readings

Almond, G., *Political Development: Essays in Heuristic Theory*, Little Brown, Boston, 1970.

Avery, J., *Progress, Poverty and Population: Re-reading of Condercet, Godwin and Malthus*, Frank Cass, London, 1993.

Bagchi, A.K., *The Political Economy of Underdevelopment*, Cambridge University Press, Cambridge, 1982.

Baran, P., *The Political Economy of Growth*, Monthly Review Press, New York, 1957.

Eisenstadt, S., *Modernization: Protest and Change*, Prentice-Hall, Englewood Cliffs, NJ, 1966.

Goldthrope, J.E., *The Sociology of Post-Colonial Societies: Economic Disparity, Cultural Diversity and Development*, Cambridge University Press, Cambridge, 1996.

Goodin, R.E., *Green Political Theory*, Polity Press, Cambridge, 1992.

Harris, N., *The End of the Third World*, Penguin, London, 1987.

Heilbroner, R.L., *An Inquiry into the Human Prospect*, W.W. Norton, New York, 1975.

Johnson, L.E., *A Morally Deep World: An Essay on Moral Significance and Environmental Ethics*, Cambridge University Press, Cambridge, 1991.

Kothari, R., *Political Economy of Development*, Orient Longman, Bombay, 1971.

Randall, V. and Theobald, R., *Political Change and Underdevelopment: A Critical Introduction to Third World Politics*, London, 1985.

Chapter 17
Welfare State

Since the Second World War, the term 'welfare state' has been increasingly used not only in political theory but also in political practice. The idea of institutionalising state welfare crystallises by implementing **Keynesianism** to combat the effects of the depression and subsequently as a blueprint for social reconstruction of Western Europe after the Second World War. The momentum towards welfare legislation and poor laws picks up in the last two decades of the nineteenth century, in particular with Bismarck's social welfare legislations of 1883–1889 and the model for the West European states to emulate in the post Second World State. Archbishop William **Temple** (1881–1944) introduces the term welfare state in *Citizen and Churchmen* (1941) to describe a state that makes substantial provision through law and administration for those in need, namely the sick, poor, elderly, disabled and indigent.

The underlying ideas of the welfare state come from varied sources—from the French Revolution comes the notion of liberty, equality and fraternity. While **Bentham** and his utilitarian disciples emphasise the importance of the greatest happiness of the greatest number as the aim of state policy, **Bismarck** and **Beveridge** stress on the importance of social security and social insurance as the basis of state policies. The **Atlantic Charter of 1941** mentions four freedoms that include freedom from fear and want that would ensure a more peaceful world. The **social liberals—Green**, John Atkinson **Hobson** (1858–1940) and **Hobhouse**—speak of the need for a state to remove obstacles to human self-development. This is in contrast to the classical liberals for whom the state is primarily needed to guarantee security governed by the principle of the greatest happiness of the greatest number. The social liberals do not accept the socialist contention to do away with the institution of private property, as they do not consider capitalism as the root cause of poverty and misery. Mill's revision manifest in Green's philosophy is the desire to create a middle class that would dutifully help the poor and convert the workers into small property owners. This balance between individual liberty and social security is reflected in the **Beveridge Report** (1942) that forms the original charter for British welfare state. The rise of Fabian **collectivism** and its influence on the Labour Party is an increasing indication of the force of collectivism in the early twentieth century. The Fabians champion public ownership of basic industries and essential services. The Webbs draw elaborate plans for eradicating poverty and creating better opportunities for the less privileged. The Minority Report of the Poor Law Commission of 1909 felt the need to encourage the poor, the habits of providence, thrift and self-help and to assist the poor to meet their special and elementary needs. The Commission proposed scrutiny of each application on the basis of eligibility for self-support and to consider whether the relief granted was really necessary. **Keynes** questioning the faith of the classical economic theory in the free market, provides state intervention to ensure full employment and control of trade cycles. The acceptance of Keynesianism was first reflected in the New Deal in the United States and then subsequently by the planners of Western Europe in the post-Second World War period leading to its ascendancy and dominance till the 1980s when the New Right led by US President Ronald Reagan and the British Prime Minister Margaret Thatcher dislodged it. The British fought the Second World War largely under a command economy. The resources for the war machine were determined in a centralised manner by the National Government in which the Conservative Party and the Labour Party participated and the private consumption was mostly regulated by a universal ration system. Non-rationed items were heavily taxed and production was streamlined to 'the patriotic war effort'. A promise of post-war reconstruction that would be greatly advantageous to the masses won the support of the trade unions. Socialist intellectuals within the Labour Party strengthened this process further, and the collectivistic thinking unleashed by the war was further reinforced by thousands of returning soldiers.

HISTORICAL ANTECEDENTS

In the nineteenth century Britain, the state intervenes in a number of areas in social and economic affairs with the purpose of alleviating mass poverty. Queen Elizabeth I's parliament in 1601, which stipulates that provision for the poor is a duty incumbent on every parish, enacts the First Poor Law. In 1834, the system of poor relief was rationalised and placed under state control. Since then, social welfare becomes a national concern rather than remaining a local one. Factory inspection and work safety regulations led to increased government intervention concerning the working conditions. In 1870, the Education Act brought primary education under the purview of state's overall responsibility. The 1880s saw economic hardships and misery, with rising unemployment leading to violent riots in London between February 1886 and November 1887. These disturbances have a profound impact on the middle class who apprehend the incalculable effect that mass poverty would have on the safety of their property and fear that the 'dregs of humanity'—the casual workers, alcoholics and the work-shy would pull down the decent workers among the working class. This change in middle class thinking leads to the questioning of *laissez faire* liberalism. In this the findings of social science research also helps. Charles Booth's famous study on the *Life and Labour of the People in*

London published as two volumes in 1889 and 1891, respectively, makes a significant contribution towards this end. Booth discovers that 30.7 per cent of London's total population and about 35.2 of the city's East-End area live in conditions of abysmal poverty. Booth's work highlights the causes of chronic poverty such as the effects of economic cycle, seasonal unemployment, old age, sickness and disablement. This study brings about a change in local poor law administration, which is managed by local authorities with the centre interfering only in case the poor relief is inadequate. Their duties were taken up by County Borough Councils in 1929 and then by the Unemployment Assistance in 1934 and finally by the National Assistance Board in 1948. This leads the Webbs to argue against dole-outs and charities to the working poor and the need for a state guarantee of the minimum living standard. The demand for reforming the British system picked up momentum and, between 1906 and 1914, successive liberal governments initiated changes with the help of the social liberals. School inspection and free school meal for poor children was introduced between 1906 and 1907. In 1908, state pensions were introduced for the old people in need, above the age of seventy, thus, acknowledging the responsibility of the state to support a segment of the society other than the poor. The 1909 budget by Prime Minister Lloyd George introduces progressive income tax, increases death duties and imposes a tax on unearned wealth resulting from rises in the value of landed property, thus endorsing the arguments of Ricardo, J.S. Mill, Henry George and Shaw. Alongside old age pensions, Lloyd George also introduces sickness and disablement insurance similar to Bismarck's social insurance of 1888 that includes social insurance against sickness, old age and disability and unemployment insurance for the workers paving way for the National Insurance Act of 1911. The Labour government reforms, extends and simplify these provisions between 1945 and 1948 and put into practice a comprehensive social insurance scheme conceived by Beveridge in 1942.

The **Beveridge Report** (1942) is a product of these war years, a blueprint for the post-War reconstruction of England's welfare state. The popular acclaim and interest that the report generates can be gauged by the fact that the content of the report is second in importance to the war news in the British media. The dominant ideology of the post-Second World War period is Social Democracy. *Laissez faire* capitalism is discredited by the Great Depression. It is difficult to visualise a market-led recovery to overcome the devastation to industries and economy by the war. The central themes of the post-War ideology of social democracy are socialisation of the means of production, planning, social citizenship and equality. Socialisation of the means of production is a third way between communism and capitalism because the community would have economic power without the rigid centralisation characteristic of the former Soviet model. The overall coordination and planning by the state is complemented with decentralised planning initiatives, which mean worker participation and private enterprise. Planning is the second key element. In case of the British Labour Party, planned economic development means guarantee of full employment and high standard of living with the state directing the policies of main industries, services and financial institutions. The Socialist Party of Austria understands it to mean a crisis-free expanding economy. It does not advocate socialisation of the means of production nor planning but accepts the necessity of economic security by increasing national productivity. In Norway, there is a shift towards accommodating market forces and liberalisation following large-scale planning and regulation in the 1940s. The Socialist Labour Party in Sweden undertakes a grand plan of transforming the economic organisation of the bourgeois society by giving the people the control over production. The idea of social citizenship is the third key idea. This means extending the liberal principles of political equality into the social and economic spheres. In Scandinavia, Western Europe and New Zealand, there are provisions for comprehensive universal coverage in health, housing, unemployment benefits, educational aid and grants to the poor and equal benefits to all the individuals giving them the right to basic security and welfare.

In the US, the New Deal initiated by Franklin D. Roosevelt in response to the Great Depression of 1930s ensures regulation of business, encourages workers to organise unions to bargain collectively for better wages and benefits, equitable distribution of wealth to alleviate individual suffering. The US government introduces programmes, like social security, government price supports for agriculture, unemployment and workers' compensation, federal guarantees for housing, public health care for the elderly, job training, federal aid to education and public funding for small business. This continues after the War. The Truman Administration offers a ten-point programme with government aid that includes price support, a minimum wage of seventy five cents per hour, the development of natural resources, adequate housing, and aid to education, medical care and protection of loss of income through sickness, accident, unemployment and old age. The Kennedy Administration envisions a 'New Frontier' and the Johnson Administration calls for a 'War on Poverty' which the Congress endorses in the Economic Opportunity Act of 1964. This is in response to an influential book *The Other America* (1962) by Michael **Harrington** (1928–1989) that highlights poverty among the ethnic minorities within the world's most affluent society and the fact that the poor are trapped in a 'culture of poverty'. Harrington observes that unlike the Third World poverty, which is general and extreme, in the US it is at the fringe among marginalised groups—the presence of inner city and the underclass. Johnson's **Great Society** emphasises equity where none live in poverty and all would have sufficient money incomes, public services and civil rights to enable them to participate with dignity as full citizens. Measures such as medicare, mediaid, aid for elementary and secondary education, stipend for college students, cash assistance to senior citizens and handicapped would ensure a compassionate society that cared for its disadvantaged. In Canada, the Liberal Party campaigned for the adoption of universal welfare policies.

In Britain, the chief architect of the welfare state, Beveridge considered the state as pivotal to abolish social evils and guarantee full employment, social security from cradle to grave, a National Health Service, public housing, old-age pension and a war against ignorance and squalor. He assumes full employment as a basic proposition and designs a social security system that would protect every citizen during his lifetime. He envisions a society in which none are denied the basic necessities of education, health care, work and decent housing because of poverty. It would be a society without fear, one in which all has an opportunity to develop their full potential made possible by the new economics of Keynesianism. Keynes observes that the political problem of humankind has to combine three things—economic efficiency, social justice and individual liberty. The first one is a bitter lesson learnt from the First World War and the Great Depression. As a result of the Depression, the second one emphasises that the social liberals cannot relinquish the humane concerns of the Hobson, Hobhouse and Dewey generation. The third one, the more enduring one, is the legacy of J.S. Mill's idea even after half a century of social liberalism. By the middle of 1920s, Keynes realises that Leninism is out to historically destroy capitalism that fascism sacrifices democracy to save capitalism and the option before him is to save democracy by adapting capitalism. He recommends a control of expenditure and demand (amount people have to spend by means of taxation, government spending and credit control) rather than ownership and supply by the state. Focusing on aggregate demand defuses class struggle since vigorous demand leads to high profits and full employment with rising wages. The key issue is employment. Since the market by itself fails to provide full utilisation of resources, the state should step in to manage the economy. If the economy grows too fast, then the total amount of people's spending can be reduced by higher taxes, cutting public spending and making it harder to borrow money, thereby slowing down the boom. In case of recession with goods unsold, factories closing and people losing their jobs, the remedies are cutting taxes, increase government spending and make acquiring credit easier. This will increase demand for goods, needing more factories and workers to make them. By these measures, it is possible to break out of the cycle of boom and slump and replace it with steady economic growth and permanent full employment. Keynes is convinced that these measures civilise and humanise the free market. Thus, the social liberals favour welfarism for enhancing equality of opportunity by getting the state to remove disadvantages due to social circumstances.

Titmuss points out that the post-war enactments by the British Government—the National Health Service Act, the Education Act of 1944, the National Insurance Act and the Family Allowances Act—embodied the principle of universalism with the aim to 'make services available and accessible to the whole population in such ways as would not involve users in any humiliating loss of status, dignity or self-respect. There should be no sense of inferiority, pauperism, shame or stigma in the use of a publicly provided service; no attribution that one was being or becoming a "public burden"

(1976: 150). The other reasons for ensuring universal social rights of all citizens are to prevent turmoil, revolution, war and change, illiteracy, poverty, disease, neglect and destitution. Many of the services are not necessarily benefits or increments but represent partial compensations for disservices, for social costs and social insecurities that are outcomes of a rapidly changing industrial-urban society. It takes care of factors like obsolescence of skills, premature retirements, accidents and the like.

Tawney and Titmuss oppose marketing of education, health and the like and desire to encourage these in the form of a 'gift relationship'. Even if incomes are equalised, it will create social ill-will and hostility. They contend that reformed individualistic market dominated competitive society may improve the lot of the worse off but the continuous inequality demoralises and perverts all social relationships. Titmuss (1956: 243) observes that 'to grow in affluence then does not mean that we should abandon the quest for equality ... It is simply a mark of an irresponsible society'. Marshall (1950: 246) considers intense individualism and collectivism as the defining characteristics of the welfare state. The former bestows on the individual an absolute right to receive welfare and the latter imposes a duty on the state to promote and safeguard the whole community, which may transcend the aggregation of individual claims. According to Marshall, the welfare state does not reject the capitalist market economy but circumscribes it since there are certain aspects of civilised life that can be attained only if the market is restricted or replaced.

In the context of the prevailing climate of opinion and with Labour Party under Clement Attlee, winning the General Elections in 1945, the inauguration of the welfare state, did not come as a surprise. A comprehensive welfare state comes into existence after the War, though the liberal government before the First World War laid down its foundations. The Labour Party is instrumental in establishing the welfare state whose architects are two liberals—Keynes and Beveridge. The Labour government (1945–1951) tries to combine its socialist ideals with Keynesian economic management by nationalising a number of key industries and by creating a mixed economy. The Conservatives, who regained its power in the 1952 elections and governed for thirteen long years at a stretch, do not reverse the changes either. It works within the framework of the welfare state that the Labour Party devises continuing with the basic statist structure and only tinkers with minor liberalisation policies at the fringe during a brief interlude of Heath's Conservative government in 1970, by pledging to restore free markets. However, this policy is reversed within a year.

The post-War Keynesian consensus continues for more than three decades. In the midst of an acute financial crisis, the creation of the welfare state in Britain is an impressive achievement. Within a period of six years, a fantastic transformation, a revolution by consent occurs when a predominantly private economy is transformed to a state-controlled economy with the state at the commanding height of the economy. Labour Party's most famous policy is nationalisation and by a remarkable extension of governmental control it represents almost one-fifth of British GDP. One very important reason for its acceptance and success in economic terms is the Marshall Aid. Kostrzewa, Nunnenkamp and Schmieding (1990) convincingly argue that the Marshall Aid led to the buttressing and subsidising the policies of the Attlee government, which prevented its collapse and this success led to the subsequent conservative acceptance of the pragmatic intervention. The consequences of these policies lead to the narrowing of the inequality gap, reduction in the levels of poverty and unprecedented economic growth, captured in the British Prime Minister Harold Macmillan's slogan that 'one never had it so good'.

Reversal

By the end of the 1970s, however, in economic terms Britain becomes the sick man of Europe, and the final months of the Labour Government in 1978–1979 are described as the 'winter of discontent' with economic collapse visible everywhere. A comparison with Germany for the same period clearly brings out the relative failure of Britain. Unlike Britain, Germany adopts a more aggressive free market model with radical liberalisation. In the post-War period up to 1979, Germany overwhelmingly outstrips Britain. However, the reversal takes place in 1979, which is the beginning of the large-scale reform process initiated by the Margaret Thatcher's New Right Conservative Government. This implies that Germany with its free market policy prospers more than Britain, which follows an interventionist policy. In 1979, Britain abandoned intervention and opted for a free market. It started to perform better whereas the German economy which had by now embraced the earlier British practice saw its growth rate and competitiveness decline. Interestingly, in a comparative perspective, both Britain and Germany received Marshall Aid but Germany opted for the free market mechanism and progresses while Britain with its interventionist policy stagnated. The 1980s, Britain adopted monetarist policies to control inflation to improve the working of markets and placed greater emphasis on the supply-side policies intended to enhance the economy's supply of goods and services. The consequence is remarkable—impressive productivity growth, substantially greater participation of the working age population and reduction in unemployment—confirming the thesis that free markets have a strong effect in increasing the economic performance. In broad comparison, the continental Europe is dominated by social democracy whereas the Anglo-Saxon countries, by different variants of Puritan ethics and Calvinism.

The continental model is based on a high degree of social insurance, which means high taxes and social transfers. The economy is highly regulated with extensive rights and security of workers with a high degree of invisible taxes and transfers. Market is not abolished as in the case of communism, but both price and income are controlled, taxed and supplemented to reach a satisfactory social outcome with social insurance. Though there are important variations within the various countries of continental Western Europe, yet there is a general similarity in providing extensive social insurance in contrast to the limited social insurance in the Anglo Saxon countries. The argument for extensive social insurance is that it makes people more contended and happy which increases workers' efficiency. Security is an important consideration but the question centres on the linkage between security and efficiency, the extra that is added to either. It is also linked to poverty alleviation and the problem of inequality. Extreme security does not lead to efficiency and innovation but to alienation, discontent and retards just reward. In the continental Western Europe with the practice of state initiated social insurance, unemployment and taxes increases but growth rate declines. However, the countries with relatively free market system perform better in all these indicators. In fact, Europe ought to emulate the East Asia mode of welfare in which there is least state intervention and spending, the individual and the family within a Confucian tradition support themselves through savings, insurance and mutual support. As a consequence, tax rates in East Asia are even lower than the Western free market economies, where there is little intervention in the labour market, but a great deal in tax and transfer system for benefiting the poor.

HAYEK'S CRITIQUE OF THE WELFARE STATE

The most formidable free market theoretician who remains outside the post-Second World War consensus is Hayek. His prophetic vision has been the starting point for the dismantling of the extensive welfare state system by Thatcher's New Right government and one that is accepted by both the major political parties in Britain in the 1990s. Hayek's credit and achievement lay in the fact that he furnishes both a critique of collectivism and socialism that subsequent history vindicates and in providing a blueprint for a minimal state with free market relations as being efficient and just. His works fill the intellectual and moral vacuum that economic liberals, New Rights theorists like Milton Friedman are looking for since the middle of the twentieth century. Thatcher who introduces privatisation and monetarism and alters the post-Second World War consensus on the welfare state rightly acknowledges the inspiration she has drawn from Hayek's works. She writes on his ninetieth birthday in 1989, 'none of what her government had achieved would have been possible without the values and beliefs to set us on the right road and provide the right sense of direction. The leadership and inspiration that your work and thinking gave us were absolutely crucial and we owe you a great debt' (Thatcher cited in Lessnoff 1999: 148).

The Road to Serfdom (1944) sets the tone of Hayek's formulations against collectivism, state planning and socialism. It is written at a time when collectivism receives impetus world-wide. Inspired by Ludwig von Mises' critical work on *Socialism* (1922), Hayek considers socialism, planning and collectivism as being co-extensive resulting in the loss of individual freedom. He reiterates Lord Acton and Tocqueville's warning that socialism means slavery. Interestingly, G.D.H. Cole a libertarian socialist echoes this sentiment when he considers slavery and not poverty as the malady of modern times. Hayek contends that collectivism and totalitarianism are two sides of the same coin for they subvert individual ends, totally disregard individual freedom and autonomy. In a nutshell, Hayek's economic and political order called *catallaxy* is spontaneously organised and plural in nature. The business of government is to maintain law and order and to provide public works that require huge capital outlays. It does not impose its views on moral questions on the individual rather it allows the individual to search for his own answers. For Hayek, independence, self-reliance, risk-taking, defiance of majority opinion, voluntary cooperation were the virtues for organising a free and individualist society.

It is not true that liberals in general and Hayek in particular oppose the welfare state. This has nothing to do with Social Darwinism or the contention that the state and its officials need not be responsible for those unable to eke out an adequate living in the *catallaxy*. Hayek criticises the welfare state as it exists in Britain and not by the idea of welfare state. In his opinion, division of labour and division of knowledge enable the market economy to function at a reasonably high level of productivity. In *The Constitution of Liberty*, his concern is with the threats liberty faces when governments pursue aims of welfare. The problem is the belief that some aims are legitimate leading governments to pursue them by means that will destroy freedom. Many believe that the welfare state may be the cover to push for a more comprehensive socialism not intended by the original formulators of the welfare state.

When Hayek writes *The Constitution of Liberty*, he is not so much concerned about the threat of overt socialism but he knows that the same ends could be pursued through other means. The difficulty with welfare ideology is that its aims are diffused and hard to precisely categorise, making it more difficult to conclusively reject by comparison with the more traditional socialist doctrines. The one aim that Hayek consistently opposes is the attempt by the state to ensure some absolute level of security against deprivation for its citizens as the basis for a more egalitarian distribution of incomes.

Hayek objects to a welfare state on the grounds that it deprives individuals the opportunity of making arrangements for old-age pensions, health, housing and the like. He does not object to some form of compulsory insurance against unemployment, sickness and other aspects of social security and even considers the role of the state towards establishing these schemes but he constantly warns against the tendency towards a state monopoly. He laments on the slow reduction of the principle of insurance in the field of social security for the latter's finances do not come from contributions but from taxation. Instead of the individuals receiving what they are entitled to in accordance to their contributions, there is an inclination to give what they need as if there is an objective criterion of need. Furthermore, it is not possible to identify and measure need and it is even more difficult to presume that the state could do so. As a result, there is great power in the hands of the officials who administer the system and the politicians who decide about its ends. The problem of poverty can be dealt with by cash transfers rather than collective uniform consumption of welfare goods, as that allows the individuals the freedom to expand as they desire. Another effect of the state playing a pivotal role in welfare is the emergence of a vast bureaucracy with officials having tremendous discretionary powers over individuals. They also make up a group of persons whose careers depend on the continued expansion of the services of the state. Against the socialist claim that a comprehensive health service by the state is superior to private provision based on insurance principles. Hayek points out the absence of an objective standard of health care. When the state decides the level of health care, it is making a political and arbitrary decision about how their money has to be spent. Hayek basically contends that democratic methods are not as effective as market choice in expressing information about what the individuals want in the way of welfare services.

Hayek's objections to the welfare state also proceed from his considerations about the rule of law and efficiency. When officials have the power to discriminate between individuals, quite often on subjective grounds of need, the rule of law is violated. Regarding efficiency, he argues that the welfare state does not really help of the people for whom it is originally designed, namely the poor. Instead it only helps in proliferation of administration. Even the redistribution argument is rejected on the grounds that the progressive income tax exploits the rich for the benefit of the middle class rather than the poor. The idea of progressive taxation violates the concept of 'equal pay for equal work' for those who produce most are penalised more than those who produce the least, enabling the majority to dictate to the minority. Moreover, it diverts resources into nonproductive areas slowing down capital formation and preventing newcomers from entering the market. The most powerful argument Hayek makes against the welfare state is that it may bring in a socialist society through stealth. He even goes to the extent of suggesting that the public relations exercises that the welfare state agencies employ are similar to the measures employed by the totalitarian state with its monopoly over information. Hayek believes that indiscriminate implementation of material equality destroys a free society and the rule of law.

Hayek succinctly distinguishes between misfortune and injustice and considers injustice as the outcome of intentional actions of individuals. Given his preference for a minimal society, he characterises society as spontaneous, purpose-independent with none being able to predict or foresee the consequences or the outcomes of individuals pursuing their own conceptions of good. Hence social outcomes are unintended. On this basis, he rejects the criticisms of the free market as being unjust since it makes some poor. He argues that in a free economy governed by the rule of law and justice, poverty is not injustice for there is nobody to monitor the outcome and nor are its operations to be understood as distribution of income and wealth. Free market unlike social justice does not presuppose a distributor who could provide the actual needs of the people as they arise and such an act is an unintentional one. The poor suffer out of misfortune and not injustice unless they have been deliberately deprived which is not the case in a free market. Hayek advocates state provision of a minimum income for the unfortunate but not out of considerations of justice. The recipients of minimum income receive it not because they deserve it but rather it is to relieve their suffering. Here, Hayek argues like Popper that the role of a state is to mitigate unhappiness and avoidable suffering. Social justice, according to Hayek, is based on a certain moral consensus in society since he doubted the existence of a majority view to everything. The idea of social justice presupposes that among the various values it should receive precedence over others which for Hayek contravenes the idea of diversity of ends that a free and liberal society stands for. Secondly, because of the ambiguity and indefiniteness regarding the relative merits of these values, the officials will have more power and exercise it in a discretionary way. This allows different interest groups to articulate their own subjective views and get them politically accepted. Too much power leads not only to corruption but also impotence. Hayek criticises the welfare state, since under the garb of guaranteeing a minimum standard of living it only leads to the entrenchment of a certain specific group in a privileged position. It removes the spirit of independence from the individuals who begin to value jobs that guaranteed security and permanence rather than self-reliance, independence and innovation.

Hayek's economic model is similar to the one advanced by the Classical Liberals and has wielded considerable influence. The criticisms levelled against it are similar to the one that are made of the classical model. Basically, the market system is perceived as being imperfect and incapable of solving many human needs, a lacuna that the welfare state and government intervention rectifies. Arrow shows that individual preferences cannot aggregate to provide the best possible scheme of social welfare and the method of moving from individual preference to the social one is to be either imposed or dictated. Olson in the logic of collective action also points out this inevitable coercion to ensure fair contribution for the cost of collective or public good. However, Hayek dismisses these arguments on both ethical and practical grounds. He considers state planning, welfare schemes and excessive taxation as inimical to freedom by rightly pointing out to the need for a delicately balanced trade off.

Hayek's ideas find resonance elsewhere too. In India, defying the overwhelming influence of the British Labour Party in general and Fabian collectivism in particular, C. Rajagopalachari, Minoo Masani and their associates, way back in the 1950s, rejected the Nehruvian state-centric planning and considered a free market mechanism as the best possible economic arrangement for a democratic India. Rajagopalachari, in 1965, dismissed Nehru's plan to achieve industrialisation 'by short cut of heavy borrowing and central planning and a permit license regime' as a fatal mistake. In 1959, he established the *Swantantra Party* to fight Nehruvian socialism. Emphasising Gandhi's doctrine of trusteeship and rejecting cooperative farming, he points out that the same had caused acute shortages in the former Soviet Union, compelling it to import lot of food grains from the US and Canada. The ideologue of the party, Masani asserts that socialism is a failed doctrine and reminded about the dangers of increased state control, echoing Hayek. He also emphasises on the fundamental values of liberty and free enterprise. Though the party has impressive electoral successes at the beginning but subsequently it fades out in the early 1970s. However, the ideology it proclaimes has been vindicated by history when India moves away from Nehruvian plank from 1991 onwards, towards free enterprise and economic liberalisation ironically under the stewardship of Nehru's own party, the Congress.

NEO-CONSERVATIVE RESPONSE

It is the failure of the Great Society Programme in the United States in the 1960s that leads to a reappraisal of the welfare state and liberalism by the Neo-conservatives. The failures are identified as lack of resources, a cumbersome political system, lack of proper understanding of the underlying causes of poverty and overconfidence of the government to implement its various schemes. Though huge sums of money are spent, it does not solve social problems. Instead it creates social dependency and simulates social divisions and social unrest like race riots, inflation, and workers alienation and exaggerates increase in the individuals' expectations. The Neo-conservatives critically dismiss the Great Society as a legacy of that 'decade of rubbish', namely the sixties. Wildavsky points out that the Great Society undoes whatever the New Deal attempts. The New Deal serves 'temporarily depressed but relatively stable lower and middle classes, people who were on the whole willing and able to work but who had been restrained by the economic situation'. The Great Society tried to assist 'the severely deprived, those who actually needed not merely an opportunity but continuing long-term assistance—those whom Marx had called the lumpen proletariat'(cited in Steinfels 1979: 221). Since the government did not know how to go about its task 'an awful lot of money was invested without accomplishing very much' (Steinfels 1979).

Though the Neo-conservatives are hostile to the Great Society, in principle, they support the idea of the welfare state. In light of the Great Society they reject big governments, and centralised administration, for big governments imply greater bureaucratisation and less individual autonomy. The bureaucrats become irresponsible and insensitive to popular will and expectations. They favour decentralisation, local governments and a mixed economy with the market as the mechanism to achieve their ideal of the welfare state. Their ideal, on the contrary, is mutual aid or a 'social insurance state' which provides security, comfort and elevation of its citizens without being paternalistic. The market sustains economic growth, assure material abundance, distribute goods and services, redistribute income to the poorest, protect individual liberties and initiatives, and stabilise society and the polity. They reject free markets and unrestrained capitalism, as unfettered by tradition and authority it leads to social instability and indiscipline. They distrust collectivist planning, nationalisation and centralisation of the economy. They support the welfare state that Disreali and Bismarck pioneered in Britain and Germany, respectively, with the purpose of reconciling the masses to the vicissitudes and hazards of a dynamic hierarchical industrial economy (Gottfried and Fleming 1988: 66). It is this belief in the idea of the welfare state as a permanent and an enduring system that set them apart from the paleo-conservatives or the Old Right.[1]

The neo-conservatives want a welfare state that functions within the framework of capitalism for the latter in comparison to other economic systems delivers goods and satisfies the material aspirations of the people. Its income distribution is also right because it reflects a general belief that 'it is better for society to be shaped by the interplay of people's free opinions and free preferences than by the enforcement of any one set of values by government' (Kristol 1978: 178). It also ensures widespread and rapid upward economic and social mobility. It provides the best available protection for individual liberty and the strongest base for democracy. Its reliance on the market rather than government prevents overload, guarantees individual responsibility and provides a powerful incentive persuading people to do what they should do. However, capitalism lacks a legitimate theory of distributive justice and needs a stronger ethic of self-restraint, hard work and social goals. Kristol calls for the establishment of a 'conservative welfare state by which he means the present American model of mixed economy and a bureaucratically managed democracy. He distinguishes it from the libertarian plea for a minimal state and the democratic and non-democratic brands of socialism' (1978: 126). He points out that the liberal conservative ideal of free society as advocated by Hayek and Friedman will never appeal to the masses of modern society because it defends inequality as a necessary condition for progress under the capitalist economic order (Kristol 1979). Instead there is a need for a theory of distributive justice, which will promote social cohesion by stating who gets what. However, he rules out Rawls' abstract egalitarian principle because its failure to provide a moral justification of capitalism. Kristol also points out the destructive side of welfare on the American poor family by 'making the child fatherless, the wife husbandless, the husband useless' (Kristol 1972: 143).

Moynihan in his report on guaranteed income establishes a nexus between black poverty, male unemployment and female headed households as a cause of structural deficiency in the existing system. He proposes greater recruitment of blacks in the military, creation of more jobs in postal services, increase in family allowances and assistance. This corrects the earlier scheme, 'Aid for Family and Dependent Children' (AFDC), where the amount of money was higher but it encouraged the recipients to avail of the benefits without having to work for it. At the same time, it was anti-poor and anti-black, for coincidentally the majority of the poor were blacks. The basic presumption of Moynihan is to provide for support systems to black families to enable them to provide adequately to their children and avail of opportunities. Beyond this, the nation is not responsible for whether they make use of these opportunities or not. Bell proposes that the state must aim at a social minimum, 'a basic set of services and income which provides ... adequate medical care, housing and the like. These are matters of security and dignity, which must necessarily be the prior concerns of a civilised society' (1976: 453–454).

Neo-conservatism thus rejects the redistributive ethic of the welfare state and the interventionist role of the government. It supports individualism as against collectivism and rejects claims of equality of conditions. It defends capitalism but within a framework of common good. It pleads for the corrected market as a mechanism to ensure social goals, revival of mediating structures, and restoration of pluralist political democracy. It emphasises the importance of individual self-reliance and the role of voluntary associations in realising welfare and thus pioneered an anti-state welfare model. Neo-conservatism like Hayek's critique has to be understood as a corrective to welfare state and capitalism. Unlike the conservatives, the neo-conservatives support social security, collective bargaining laws, voting rights guarantees and a basic social minimum distributed through the state. In all this, they share the liberal vision but, unlike the liberals, they do not desire wholesale income distribution but restrict it to basic social goods. While the liberals are ready to use state power to achieve social justice, neo-conservatives see this as a concealed form of socialism and a direct threat to individual liberty. In the background of the Great Society and the War on poverty, they observe that government policies in the United States have become too ambitious, redistributive and anti-meritocracy. Increase in government activity not only denies, but also encroaches on individual initiative and spontaneity. They endorse liberal capitalism and decision-making through the market. The neo-conservative critiques of welfare state and big governments is more pragmatic. They do not oppose state regulation of the economy but feel that existing regulations in the United States strangle private resourcefulness and serve vested interests. Similarly, the social security programmes have been the main reason for the breaking up of families contributing to unemployment, reducing capital investment and generally make life difficult for the successive generations. They demand the provision of a basic social minimum but reject the culture of dependency and the loss of dignity that existing welfarism entails. They realise that the market may seem heartless but it is a better form of organising people's lives than the other available options. They fear politicisation of society by the general growth in government. They generally desire that the government get off people's back. Thus, neo-conservatives defend the status quo of corporate capitalism, the marginal state, civic religion and liberal democracy (Gottfried and Fleming 1988: 107).

The neo-conservative critiques can not to be dismissed as merely a reaction to the policies and the system in the United States. Many of their arguments have resonance elsewhere, for instance, Singapore has a welfare state that is just the opposite of the Beveridge model. The architect of modern Singapore the former Prime Minister and now a Senior Minister Lee Kuan Yew dismisses the British model as entailing unlimited liability with a devastating effect on the Singapore economy. Singapore has a system of health, education, housing and welfare organised around compulsory saving and the principle of personal responsibility. Singapore shares the neo-conservative outlook and stresses the importance of family values in sustaining a vibrant caring society.

The neo-conservative critique has led to the downsizing of the welfare state and rolling back of government. It has exposed the crisis within capitalism, and the crisis within Keynesianism and social democracy. It has put forward an anti-statist version of the welfare with a firm commitment to a vibrant civil society and individual liberty. As a result of the neo-conservative and the new right critique, liberal and social democratic agenda in both United States and Britain haves undergone a dramatic shift. An indication of this shift is the promise that US President Bill Clinton made in 1996 to 'end welfare as we know it' by signing a law, the Personal Responsibility and Work Opportunity Reconciliation Act, also known as the welfare reform. This put an end to the culture of dependency and welfare as an entitlement available to all parents who qualified, and required recipients—mostly single mothers—to look for work. Many attribute its success due to then booming US economy but also point out to its the positive side—revival of nuclear family and rewards to couple for staying married—for its success.

FEMINIST CRITIQUE

Pateman (1989) argues that welfare state theorists ignore the fact that it is sexually divisive and patriarchal in nature, for it incorporates men and women differently as citizens. The central notion of citizenship is independence, which has three attributes—the capacity to bear arms, the capacity to own property and the capacity for self-government (1988: 185). These characteristics have a gender bias as when the modern democracy began to evolve in the initial years, only property owning males could be full citizens and its legacy continues even today, in the form of domestic subjection of women at home. The welfare provisions have been established within the two-tier system of husband/wife and worker/housewife. There are benefits that are available to individual workers and it is men who usually claim these benefits. There are benefits that are available to dependents of the individuals in the first category, which mostly women claim either as wives or mothers. Rarely do men, even poor men make claims for benefit solely as husbands or fathers. Women are the majority of recipients of many welfare benefits for they are most likely to be poor and single mothers and the reason that they are poor is because most women find it difficult to secure a job that will give them a decent salary. This is because the occupational structure is sexually segregated in spite of equal-pay legislation,

> Capitalist economies are patriarchal, divided into men's and women's occupations; the sexes do not usually work together, nor are they paid at the same rates for similar work... Most women's jobs are unskilled and of low status; even in the professions women are clustered at the lower end of the occupational hierarchy (1988: 191).

For instance, in medicine, women are normally gynaecologists and paediatricians. Women by and large lack the means to be recognised as worthy citizens for they are considered as men's dependents by the welfare state as in case of the National Insurance Act of 1946. Pateman mournfully observes that men and single women are entitled to the pension if they could not engage in paid employment; the criterion of married women is the ability to perform 'normal household duties' (1988: 195). She laments at the fact that household work that constitutes the major chore for most women has no value for citizenship and in order to achieve this, the patriarchal dichotomy between women and independence-work-citizenship has to be eliminated. It is only then can a welfare state become a welfare society (1988: 204).

CONCLUSION

The idea of the welfare state is a brilliant blueprint for alleviating human misery within parameters of liberal democracy. Tawney appreciates the great advancement that welfare states in Western Europe have made in alleviating human misery. It vindicates the view of the democratic left that a decent and dignified life is an essential precondition for enjoying freedom. Tawney, however, criticises soullessness of the welfare state as he finds it mechanical and bureaucratic. However, as it happens with many well-intentioned projects, the original vision of the pioneers did not match the subsequent decline of the welfare state. The idea of the welfare state originally set out by Beveridge was a safety net providing a real sense of security in a situation of exceptional circumstances where it was expected that the individual would normally pursue his normal activities. In such circumstances, a person could live, bring up his family and even retire at the expense of the state. This 'cradle to grave' social security would be used in rare cases and in utmost emergency. However, what has actually happened is the extensive use resulting in high inflation, lack of competitiveness and innovation, and relative fall in growth rate with other comparable nations. The extreme example of the collapse of the former Soviet Union is writ large. But what is forgotten that Sweden, the most popular example of the success of the welfare state with a tax rate of 70 per cent and cradle to grave social security system has become non-viable and has been forced to initiate far-reaching capitalist reforms in the 1970s. Similarly, Germany under the sway of social charterism since the 1980s has been facing an unemployment crisis at 11.6 per cent and underemployment of women and youngsters, with many manufacturing concerns moving out of Germany. A very important reason for the weakness of the Euro is the social security network including pensions in Germany and France.

The notion of welfare state is essentially Western European with the long tradition of social democracy. It is alien in the United States where most people believe in the virtues of capitalism but also accept the need for some amount of monitoring over its working. The reason that sustains such a belief structure for an uninterrupted two centuries, a unique feature in the evolution of the American outlook, lie in essentially a legal framework that keeps a check on the growth of monopolies which hamper fair competition. The American system has evolved a mechanism to check the tendency of successful business to threaten the very dynamics of a free market by monopoly control. The ethical support to capitalism emerges out of puritan ethics, which means acceptance of competitiveness, hard work, and wide economic inequalities in societies. The desire to become rich is admired and praised. The philosophy of self-restraint imposes a moral restraint not to bypass the entire wealth to children, descendants and other near relations. The important societal code explains the existence of forty thousand well-endowed foundations in the US. The society gains without the pitfalls of social ownership of the means of production. The working of American capitalism teaches us that unrivalled economic power of capitalism can be controlled by the will and the force of legal and political institutions and by a societal sanction of capitalism.

In such a situation the argument of Hayek and the New Right criticism are timely and inevitable. They remind us the dangers of what Berlin (1961) calls the positive liberty that allows abuse of state power and in extreme cases to fascism and communism. The New Right points out the economic gain of free society along with its political attraction. It proves that higher tax leads to loss of efficiency as also redistribution measures reducing incentive. The cumulative effect of all these is a net loss for the entire society, for both the taxpayer and the poor.

The Welfare state concept, which emerges in the Western Europe creates unprecedented prosperity and social security for every single individual maintaining simultaneously a democratic framework and personal freedom. However, the subsequent breakdown of the Keynesian consensus leads to serious modifications in both the theory and practice of the welfare state. One off-shoot of the welfare state theory is reflected in the anti-utilitarian theory of Rawls that accepts that the welfare of society increases only if the welfare of the poorest is enhanced. This implies that the theory and practice of the welfare state is an important component of contemporary political theory. It is for this positive aspect of the welfare state that one can agree with Norman P. Barry's (1995: 259) comment 'for those critics of the welfare state who claim that it creates dependency rather than individual responsibility are challenging, often in a regrettably vulgar way, basic tenet of welfare philosophy; that is, that welfare institutions help to foster a less acquisitive agent than that which inhabits the apparently amoral world of competitive markets.'

Further Readings

Bruce, M., *The Coming of the Welfare State*, Batsford, London, 1961.

Pigou, A.C., *The Economics of Welfare*, Macmillan, London, 1920.

Robson, W.A., *Welfare State and Welfare Society: Illusion and Reality*, Allen and Unwin, London, 1976.

Sen, A., *Collective Choice and Social Welfare*, Holden Day, San Francisco, 1970.

Timms, N. (Ed.), *Social Welfare: Why and How*? Routledge and Kegan Paul, London, 1980.

Titmuss, R.M., *The Gift Relationship: From Human Blood to Social Policy*, Allen and Unwin, London, 1970.

Wilensky, H., *The Welfare State and Equality*, University of California Press, Berkeley, 1975.

Wilson, T. and Wilson, Dorothy J., *The Political Economy of the Welfare State*, Allen and, London, 1982.

Endnote

1. Traditionally, European conservatives are as critical of capitalism as the radicals and the Marxists for they dislike its selfish ethic. Not only do they believe in hierarchy but insist that the elite take responsibility for the less privileged. Like the Marxists, they are outraged by the way the capitalists treat the workers. In fact, Marx and Engels rely on the reports written by the conservatives about the oppression that the workers face under British capitalism, the most advanced economy of its times.

Chapter 18

Theories of Social Change

A defining characteristic of modernity is the belief that things change and change is for the better. It is during the era of the Enlightenment that this perception emerges in the minds of significant numbers of opinion makers. Change is considered to be a pivotal concept in social sciences and terms like evolution, development, movement, variation, transition, transformation and decline indicate the criterion by which one evaluates the relative performance of regions and nations. Change varies in scope—world historical change, societal change, economic change and particular facets of social change, like electoral behaviour or development of new political parties and new social movements. Some change is short-term while others are long-term. Change could be incremental, evolutionary or revolutionary. As individuals, one may prefer stability to change, equilibrium and not chaos but as Heraclitus (544–484 BC), the Greek philosopher, succinctly states, 'you cannot step twice into the same river, for other waters are continually flowing on'. This means that 'all is flux, nothing stays still' or remains static. Everything is constantly in a state of flux and carries within it perpetuity and change, stability and instability, order and disorder. An important change between our times and the earlier ones is that we live in a world of quick and unprecedented global change.

Theories of political and social change help us in understanding the connection between agency and structures. Since the nineteenth century, explaining and predicting social change have become a major preoccupation due to two reasons—first is the awareness of the social impact of industrialisation on European societies and the second is the basic gap between European industrial societies and the relatively backward ones. Theories of social change have focused on the nature of capitalist or industrial development and the evident absence of social development in regions that Europe colonised. They concentrate on the long-term and large-scale development. Theories of social change especially the nineteenth century ones are categorised into theories of revolution and theories of social evolution.

Theories of social change require a causal analysis giving us reasons as what makes something happen over time, but this has always been a contentious issue in social sciences. To say that '*x* causes *y*' suggests a sense of determinism. Furthermore, any sequence of social causation, if it happens, is likely to be complex and immeasurable. Even a rigid theory of change like that of Marx is heavily dependent on human consciousness which is hard to determine. Moreover, there is also a problem of deciding as to whether or when causation refers to a causal relationship between one thing and another. Is there a more indirect link whereby the causal factors have contributed or is there a situation in which outcomes occur *necessarily* because of the characteristics of the objects involved but *contingently* due to the circumstances in which they are found? Most often social scientists tend to be cautious when making statements about relationships between variables preferring to talk about 'tendencies' or 'probabilities' or 'degrees of association', especially the nature of the relationship involves the use of statistical analysis. Two other factors need to be considered when political and social change is discussed—first is to clarify which variable is independent and which one is dependent. Nordlinger (1981) stipulates what he calls 'societalist' factors like the degree of class conflict or the power of interest groups, or the ethnic composition of a country to explain the choices governments make. Wallerstein (1974, 1980, 1989) in his study on the making of the modern world diminishes political aspects—the role of nation states, war and ideological conflicts between government—to the fundamental effects of economic forces operating on a world scale. While Marx consigned most, if not all, political forms to the periphery of economic and structural explanatory analysis there are enduring attempts, of late, to reintroduce a more politically centred analysis of historical change. This attempt infers from insights of theorists like Weber, Durkheim and Hegel to construct an alternative theoretical model to the one that Marx offers. The second is the question of whether change is due to internal or external factors. For instance, studies of social change and especially of modernisation of Third World have often assumed that factors internal to a society play a crucial role in the level of that society's development.

Theories of social change, besides being revolutionary and evolutionary, are divided—(1) by their level of analysis, namely micro and macro; (2) whether change is caused by factors internal or external to society, institution or social group; (3) the cause of social change—demographic pressure, mass migration, class conflict, changes in the mode of production, technological innovation or the development of new systems of belief; (4) agents of change; (5) nature of change (whether a gradual dissemination of new values or institutions or a radical departure of the social system. Embedded in the notion of change is both stability and change. Nonetheless, most of social theory emphasise either of the two. Marxism broadly propounds a theory of revolutionary conflict as the locomotive of change while functionalists stress on norms and values that promote social and political stability. Stable societies are seen as those that perform their basic functional imperatives—socialisation, reproduction, education—necessary for their survival while effectively adjusting to technological, economic, societal and cultural changes peacefully. A functionalist is concerned with factors that ensure order explaining the normal process of change as evolutionary and regarding revolutionary change as dysfunctional or abnormal. The purpose of analysis is to establish the means by which societies can regain equilibrium (Parsons 1967).

WHAT IS REVOLUTION?

Revolution signifies drastic and fundamental transformation. Hence, it is customary to refer to Industrial Revolution, French Revolution of 1789, Russian Revolution of 1917, Chinese Revolution of 1948, Cuban Revolution of 1959, Iranian Revolution of 1979 and the present Info-tech revolution since these basically have altered the nature of the social and political systems in which they occurred. 'Revolutions are a form of massive, violent and rapid social change. They are also attempts to embody a set of values in a new or at least a renovated social order' (Dunn 1989: 12). Revolutions are complex events essentially involving three aspects—state breakdown, competition among claimants for central authority and building new institutions which need not occur, 'clearly separated stages or in a consistent order'. These three factors coalesce with one another to differentiate revolution from forms of political violence (Goldstone 1987: 437). The complexity of the revolutions makes it difficult to explain them though theories attempt to dissect them in terms of causes, the various forms of struggle and the possible outcomes.

Plato points out that all governments inevitably would go through a sequence of change and degenerate into timocracy, oligarchy, democracy and tyranny. He is convinced that a chain of creation, decay and dissolution grips the world firmly and only at rare intervals, individuals snatch, a brief moment of seeming immortality. Aristotle counters Plato by pointing to change as inevitable. Things change because they have the potential to move towards perfection. Change is teleological, meaning movement towards a predetermined end. Unlike Plato, Aristotle perceives multiple reasons for revolutions, other than a regime's prominent deficiency like extreme inequality. He analyses both the general and particular causes of revolutions along with preventive measures as remedies from revolutions. He perceives order as being more important than disorder.[1] Following Aristotle, Machiavelli discusses social dissension and their causes. He identifies (a) rivalries among the great, namely the rich and the socially superior and (b) the endemic and natural enmity between the great and the people, or the rich and the poor as the two main causes of disturbances. He accepts conflict as permanent and universal, seeing it as natural unlike his predecessors who viewed social conflict as unnatural and curable by certain kinds of social systems. The basis of social conflict is the permanent struggle between the common man and the powerful and the money though he does not explain the struggle in economic terms. From Polybius he learns that conflict is not only widely prevalent but transformed into an instrument to promote socially useful ends. During the Roman period, theorists were preoccupied with justification rather the causes of revolution. Polybius views revolutions as a corrective tool for restoring a just and properly ordered society that has been disturbed by tyranny. Nicholas of Cusa and Locke justify revolutions if the monarchs and rulers violate people's trust. Locke is categorical that governments can be altered, amended, changed or dissolved legitimately and lists five occasions when this is possible. These are as follows:

1. Whenever such a prince or single person establishes his own arbitrary will in place of laws.
2. When the prince hinders the legislature from assembling in its due time or from acting freely, pursuant to those ends for which it is constituted.
3. When by the arbitrary power of the prince, the elections and the ways of elections are altered without the consent, and contrary to the common interests of the people.
4. The delivery of the people into the subjection of foreign power, either by the prince or by the legislature.
5. The person who has the supreme executive power neglects laws already enacted, and could not be executed (Locke 1960: 454–459).

Locke clarifies that people can use force against unjust and unlawful authority and that authority has to be transparent and accountable. He emphatically stresses that government based on consent coupled with the right of the people to rebel is the best fence against rebellion. On the contrary, Filmer and Bodin maintain that the king derives his powers and authority from god which is irrevocable and absolute. The Glorious Revolution of 1688 and the American War of Independence were understood in the sense that Polybius explained revolutions. Burke, reiterating Polybius, points out that tyranny usually leads to a revolution. On the other hand, some theorists like Hobbes never justify revolutions for the chaos and bloodshed it leads to.

The meaning of revolution undergoes a change with the French Revolution, which was no longer seen as a means to get rid of a tyranny but as a way of establishing a new society. It elicits diverse reactions from the Conservatives, Liberals and the Marxists. Conservatism as an ideology crystallises in response to the French Revolution. Burke's *Reflections on the Revolution in France and on the proceedings of certain societies in England relating to that event* (1790) contains the quintessence of the conservative position. Using the two principles of conservation and correction, he contrasts the English with the French Revolution, for in the former the two principles allowed rectification of the deficiencies of the existing deficiencies within the existing framework. This balances the old with the new. In France, wholesale attack on established religion, traditional constitutional arrangements and the institution of property disturbs the sources of political wisdom that provide a bulwark against sweeping changes. He rejects the French effort to make a clean slate operation by making a complete break with the past. In response to Burke, Paine defends the French Revolution and Enlightenment Liberalism and supports representative government, rule of law and universal suffrage. He rejects Burke's idealisation of the hereditary system of government. Interestingly, Burke supports the American Revolution, as it did not redress its grievances by resorting to a doctrine of natural rights. It merely represented freedom of the colonies from British rule whereas the French Revolution made equality and nationalism the two dominant values and both these are possible means of tyranny that eventually erodes the social and moral conditions of the liberty of citizens. Burke also champions the cause of Ireland and speaks against the oppression, exploitation and misrule in India by the English East India Company. **Tocqueville** is alarmed at the attack on ideas of equality of persons before law and democracy that the French Revolution unleashes as that destroys all class privileges and removes all hindrances to the authority of the state. The Revolution leads to a centralised state, for prior to the Revolution, the powerful and privileged groups stood alongside the state but after the Revolution, the state gets isolated garnering all the power. Marx and Engels view the French Revolution as a symbol of the demise of feudalism, inauguration of a bourgeois society which eventually would be dislodged by the socialist revolution. The idea of total apocalyptic change, central to Marxism comes from the French Revolution.

The theories of revolutionary social change particularly deriving from Marx emphasise the importance of class conflict, political struggle and imperialism as the principal instruments of fundamental structural changes. For Marx, history and historical change represent the unfolding of exploitative relationships between social classes in which clash of great social forces is of paramount interest than the individual. The unavoidable strife between social classes determined by whether they own the means of production or whether they are mere agents of production. For Marx, political change is an important aspect of social change determined by economic factors. Writing in the background of the optimism of the Victorian age he provided a blueprint for wholesale revolutionary change.

Marx comprehends the courses of human history to contain a series of major conflicts that he calls social revolutions, which originate out of objective contradictions or because of strain and disorder that exists in all class divided societies. These contradictions are general to all modes of production but assume particular forms according to historical circumstances. Contradictions ensue within modes of production because of the inevitable tensions between the forces of production (types of technology) and relations of production (ownership of property and social class division whereby one extracts the economic productivity from the other). The exploitative nature of relationships intensifies class conflicts making social revolutions imminent as exploited classes acquire a consciousness and unity, which are then visible in struggles against the dominant class. Conditions for social revolution mature when the structures of a new mode of production—capitalism within feudalism or socialism within capitalism—produce strain that solidifies the revolutionary potential of the young classes. Revolution for Marx represents a cataclysmic leap from one stage to another and stops with the attainment of communism, the perfect society. In the *Manifesto*, Marx and Engels prophesise the inevitable destruction of capitalism in the advanced industrialised areas through a world-wide proletarian revolution. The majority of the working class will spearhead this consciously. However, following the abortive revolutions in Europe in 1848, Marx concludes that as a prelude to a long-drawn one that would come. Engels writes many significant articles on *The Peasant War in Germany* (1850) drawing parallels between the role of nobles and burghers in the sixteenth century to crush the peasants' revolt and the alliance between the bourgeoisie and the aristocracy in 1848 against a newly emerging proletariat. He claims that behind religious struggles lay different interest, demands and requirements of the various classes. Similarly, the French Revolution of 1789 is more than an intense debate on the advantages of constitutional monarchy over royal absolutism as economic concerns of social classes are the key issue.

Taking a cue from Engels' demand for a new mode of struggle as elucidated in the 1895 *Preface to the Class Struggles,* Bernstein insists on the need for a revision of the Marxist doctrine. His close association with the English Fabians during his exile in England reinforces his views. The Fabians emphasise on gradualism, permeation and constitutional democratic procedures as a means to usher in socialism, Bernstein insists on the need for a revision of the Marxist doctrine. While paying tributes to Marx's genius, he points out to the open cleavage between the Marxist theory and the social, economic and political realities within the late nineteenth century capitalism. Contrary to Marx's predictions, the rate of profit has not fallen, the wages have not gone down and there are no signs of an imminent collapse of capitalism. Most important of all, the working class has not shown any desire or inclination to make a revolution in countries with advanced capitalism. Instead of concentration, there is diffusion of wealth making peaceful transition to socialism desireable. Impressed by the progress of the democratic state, Bernstein insists that the workers could use the ballot box effectively to press forward their cause. In this changed situation, Marx's clarion call for revolutionary overthrow of capitalism is neither practicable nor desirable. He also rejects mass strike including Georges Sorel's (1847–1972) idea of a general strike as being outmoded in a full-fledged democracy. Bernstein's vision of socialism realisable through non-violent, evolutionary, gradualist and democratic method becomes the guiding force for not only the advanced capitalist countries of the West but even for the developing world in the latter half of the twentieth century. His success, most impressive and crucial lay in promising 'socialism without the tears of revolution' (Dunn 1989: 25).

Within the socialist doctrine one can see support for both revolution and reform. Babeuf's stress on insurrection and revolution is kept alive by Blanqui 'thus providing a link between the Jacobin Left and the nineteenth century radicals' (Kolakowski 1981a: 214). Blanqui's rejection of parliamentarism and majority rule principle and defense of the need for a small organised disciplined party to foment a revolution is echoed by **Marx**, **Tkachev** and **Lenin**. On the other hand, the earliest advocate of gradual peaceful reform by the state with the purpose of transforming society is **Blanc**. **Lassalle** and **Bernstein** also echo Blanc.

RESTATEMENT OF MARXIST ORTHODOXY

Lenin reads Bernstein's *Evolutionary Socialism* (1899) while in exile from 1895 to 1900. Fearing Bernstein's observations on trade unionism or economism of the working class to be true he chooses to insist on the need for voluntary and decisive individual action with the help of a highly disciplined and organised party that acts as a vanguard of the working class. The party will be based on the principles of secrecy, democratic-centralism, specialisation and exclusivity. This all-encompassing and powerful role of the party is the most important post-Marx development within Marxism. Lenin combines Marx's majoritarian perspective with that of Nicholas Gavrilovich Chernyshevsky's (1828–1889) elite revolutionism, for he insists on the need for a conscious party leadership acting in unison with the masses on the outside. Marx and Engels make contradictory observations despite Russia being predominantly an agrarian country. In 1875, Engels thinks that the revolution in Russia is imminent. In 1882, Marx and Engels express the possibility that if there is an outbreak of a revolution in Russia it might set into motion similar movements in the West. Lenin too hopes in his analysis of imperialism that if Russia, the weakest link in the imperial chain snaps then it would trigger off revolutions elsewhere. In 1885, Engels tells a Russian correspondent and in a letter to Vera Zasulich (1852–1919) that if there is a possibility of a Blanquist kind of revolutionary change engineered by a band of conspirators then it could be in Tsarist Russia that is so highly unstable.

Georgii Valentinovich **Plekhanov** (1856–1918) who popularises Marxism in Russia proposes revolutionary seizure and exercise of power though he cautions against premature socialism. Lenin an already committed Jacobin-Blanquist in the 1880s reads Plekhanov to secure the necessary introduction to Marxism but he never wavers from his conviction that terror and violence are the means for realising the dictatorship of the proletariat. Interestingly, Plekhanov censures Bernstein during the revisionist controversy though subsequently during the debate on Lenin's proposals within the Russian Social Democratic Labour Party (RSDLP) he insists that a true revolution would have to be a democratic one. It is, therefore, not surprising that in 1918 Plekhanov feels responsibility for Lenin's action. With profound anguish and regret, he tells an old colleague as a dying confession that perhaps he has not done the right thing by beginning the Marxist propaganda too early in a country that is pre-modern and backward. This sums up the dilemma and the subsequent distortion of Soviet Marxism both at the level of theory and practice.

Sorel concurs with Bernstein that most of Marx's predictions have not materialised for developments within capitalism and the consolidation of trade unions has raised the standard of living of the workers, thereby blunting class war. While Bernstein denounces violent revolution in an age of democracy, Sorel endorses it as the surest way to recapture the essence of Marxism. Its guiding force is the dream of a new civilisation and heroic morality, which replaces the decadent bourgeois one. He insists on the need for a myth for the masses to revolt for that inspires militant consciousness, forges group solidarity and instills the spirit of heroism and self-sacrifice. He equates revolutionary myths to religious myths and proposes the myth of general strike as the supreme and final aim that subordinated all other actions. His hope is in non-political syndicates that builds and sustains consciousness and solidarity among the workers and rejected political parties and trade union for these normally frustrate the workers' aspiration for liberation. Sorel supports the use of military and not political violence for that is free of cruelty since the wealth of the propertied is left intact. The idea behind the general strike is not to attain political power but to destroy the existing order without setting up a new authority or a master. It is not conspiratorial, for force and repression are not the means to realise it.

Luxemburg criticises Lenin for his rejection of spontaneity of the working class movement and desires a dialectical reciprocity between the spontaneity of the masses, the intellectuals and the political leaders, a point found in Gramsci and Fanon. She criticises Lenin's extraordinary faith in ultra centralism, his implicit contempt for the creativity of the working class and his distrust of spontaneity. She also criticises Bernstein for equating reform with revolutionary class struggle and digressing from the main essence of socialism by positing social reform as the sole and final aim. She, like Sorel impresses upon the need for a myth to create proletarian consciousness.

Mao reiterates the Marxist-Leninist view of revolution as the means of actualising socialism except, unlike Marx and Lenin, he considers the peasantry to be revolutionary by insisting that the Chinese Revolution has to be conducted under the hegemony of the proletariat. He reiterates the idea of permanent revolution that Marx and Engels first enunciated and which is then restated by Plekhanov and Trotsky. He contends that the proletariat brings a permanence of revolution after the bourgeois-democratic revolution with the purpose of overthrowing the bourgeoisie and establishing their transitional state—the dictatorship of proletariat—to create the material basis of true communism. Unlike Lenin, he insists on mass mobilisation of peasants and workers to realise revolutionary goals.

ARENDT'S ANALYSIS

For Arendt, a revolution aims at freedom by establishing the political realm which is the realm of republican freedom and therefore has to preclude violence as it is strictly part of politics. She insists that political freedom must not be confused with liberation. Liberation is the aim of a revolution. However, freeing people from tyranny does not establish freedom. She understands revolution in the sense of establishing a new political order, a body politic that provides the framework for the realisation of freedom and not social and economic transformation. She compares the American and the French revolutions, for it is during these two revolutions that the idea of freedom emerges. The French Revolution is hailed as an important event but the American one remains inconspicuous and its immediate influence marginal. However, both these revolutions illustrate two different aspects of revolutionary phenomena. Their individual revolutionary experience provides the clue to the structure of the body politic and society ushered in by the revolution. The French Revolution with its slogans of liberty, equality and fraternity could not fulfil its own promise of ensuring, freedom, for it degenerates into violence and tyranny. The American Revolution in contrast succeeded for it establishes a constitutional structure for realising freedom. She calls it a clean revolution, for it does 'not break out but was made by men in common deliberation and on the strength of mutual pledges' (Arendt 1969: 280). For Arendt, the French Revolution is a tale of necessity while the American one is a tale of freedom. The efforts of the French Revolutionaries fail because of the social basis of the revolution, its 'sense of pity' to solve the social question by political means. As a result, they justify tyranny and terror in the interest of social betterment. They overthrow absolute monarchy but fail to give their republic a stable footing. The power of the state and its police grows while the freedom of the individual, of press, of speech, of association and of free enterprise steadily diminishes. On the contrary, the founding fathers in America are not moved by any messianic dream of solving the social question and this coupled with their training in town meetings during the colonial period has a sobering influence. The result is a constitutional republic that becomes the basis of freedom and a polity based on free contract with no need for terror and violence. She describes this achievement as 'perhaps the greatest enterprise of European mankind' (1969: 55). Furthermore, the American Revolution also demonstrates the importance of moderation and bringing about far-reaching changes in an evolutionary manner without resorting to violence and messianic zeal.

Arendt admits that issues like mass poverty cannot be ignored by revolutionary leaders but if they got carried away by a sense of 'pity' to end mass misery and poverty then the consequences are fatal, similar to that of the French Revolution. If the goal of survival replaces the goal of freedom, then freedom becomes a mere shibboleth that is invoked more as a routine mechanical symbol and important concerns like public happiness, public freedom and public spirit become a thing of the past. While it is important to take care of human wants, it is equally necessary to restrain men, their passions and their liberties. She sees certain continuity between the French and Russian Revolutions. **Hegel's** 'revolutionary' idea that the 'absolute of the philosophers' as revealed in history is, she suggests, due to the influence of the

French Revolution on his thought (1969: 51–52). Marx inherits this idea and transmits it to Lenin and his successor Stalin. She sees Hegel introducing and restated by Marx the 'most terrible and least bearable paradox in the whole history of modern thought—the paradox that freedom is the fruit of necessity'. Revolutionary freedom comes to be seen, paradoxically, as the child of 'historical necessity'. 'Instead of freedom, necessity became the chief category of political and revolutionary thought' (ibid: 53–54, 58). The French Revolution's change of aim from freedom to happiness infects and corrupts the entire revolutionary tradition. A similar confusion exists in Marx's thought. Despite Marx's concern with freedom, he 'finally strengthened more than anybody else the politically more pernicious doctrine of the modern age, namely that life is the highest good' (ibid: 64). The *raison d'etre* of revolution becomes economic progress. Unlike Fanon who justifies violence since it cleanses like fire, necessary to regenerate human nature and create a new community, Arendt is moderate. She nevertheless permits violence for short-term goals or if it has a chance to succeed or helped to 'dramatise grievances'.

RECENT THEORIES OF REVOLUTION

Skocpol offers the most incisive analysis of revolution by comparing historically what she calls the 'social revolutions' in France, Russia and China. Social revolutions occur due to two variables. First, there must be a *crisis of state* often provoked by international factors such as increasing economic or security competition from abroad. This results in divisions within the elites and the army, about what to do, weakening the loyalty to the regime creating the revolutionary situation. Second, *patterns of class dominance* determine which group will rise up to exploit the revolutionary situation. Skocpol's approach has three distinguishing features—one, structuralist, the objective conditions necessary for the emergence of revolutionary situations; second, internationalist, the influence of transnational economic relations and the international structure of competing states on domestic developments and third, statist, the analysis of emergence of revolutionary situations depends on the relationship of the state with its administrative and coercive powers, to military competitors abroad, and to dominant classes at home.

According to Skocpol, social revolution is one that involves 'rapid, basic transformations of a society's state and class structures, often accompanied by class based revolts from below' (1978: 26). She calls this kind of change as 'structural change' to differentiate it from other sorts of conflicts and processes that may bring about radical but not comprehensive change. It is the coincidence of political and social transformation that characterises a revolution. By this criterion, the Chinese Revolution and the end of the Khmer Rouge in Cambodia between 1975 and 1979 are social revolutions. However, the Puritan Revolution in England in the seventeenth century and the Portuguese Revolution of 1974 that overthrew Salazar's dictatorship are not revolutions, for these do not undermine the class structures of these societies. The industrial revolution brought about changes in the social structures but without resulting in or leading to political upheaval. Skocpol says that revolutionary events share some characteristics with other transformative phenomena, like coups or riots but it is the powerful combination of social and political change that distinguishes them.

Tilly (1975 and 1991) is more cosmopolitan in defining revolution as involving political discontinuity arising from challenges to the control of a government over a single independent political system. It is important to distinguish between political discontinuities on the grounds (1) of how far they change the structure of the polity in question, (2) the make-up of the contending forces and (3) the extent of (social) structural changes that results from the revolution. By this definition Tilly labels accession of Mustapha Kemal to power in Turkey in 1923 and the restoration of the Meiji dynasty in Japan in 1868 after two centuries of rule by the Shogun Gate (military warlords) as revolution. Skocpol, however, characterises these as rebellions or coups, for she is interested only in the structural aspects of revolutionary change and not the manner in which people view change or contribute to it. She is not concerned with cultural and ideological factors. Gurr (1980) recommends that political instability is likely to develop when individuals experience a sense of relative deprivation that is a psychological state which occurs when people perceive a gap between what they have and what they feel they should have—be it in politics, welfare benefits or consumer goods. This perception need not be related to an objective or measurable criteria of deprivation. When there is a feeling of intense and widespread sense of relative deprivation the conditions for violence are present. Davis (1962) describes the dangers for rules when the gap between people's rising expectations and the declining capacity of the government to deliver it widens in course of time for it is during these two that a potentially revolutionary situation emerges. However, these accounts leave unanswered questions pertaining to which segment of the population is likely to rebel? Can collective violence trigger discontent? Why do some discontent people revolt while others do not? Will revolutionary gaps occur where there is an opportunity to express discontent through available political channels? Does the type of value system that is dominant in society matter?

Functionalist accounts of revolution, like those of **Johnson** (1966) and Smelser (1963), place premium over values as the basis of collective action or else to examine more closely at the conditions in which revolutionary action occurs. These accounts are basically interested in causes of what Smelser calls disturbance and strain in societies and in how, as Johnson claims 'synchronous changes' cause shifts in values and the modifications in the environments of communities and societies that accelerate revolutionary activity and disturb social equilibrium. Henceforth, during a period of change caused by factors, like progress in technology or migration or conquest, a system may not be able to endure its equilibrium whether culturally, economically or otherwise. If the changes are sufficiently rapid or intense there will be greater pressure on political elites to respond and if that does not happen it may result in an enormous loss of trust in the system and reduce the perception of the legitimacy of rulers. This 'power deflation' that Johnson calls it, in turn, makes it more difficult for the elites to introduce effective measures to stabilise the system. Augmented violence and other forms of coercion, which the state elites exercise to keep an appearance of control only, lead to further legitimacy deficiency. What is then required is an immediate trigger or accelerator—like a chance event, a massacre of protestors, or an attempted coup by the military to accompany a full insurrection. Functionalist explanations of revolutionary change suffer from the same problems as functionalist explanations in general as they are overly concerned with equilibrium and have a built-in tendency to interpret all change as causing disequilibrium. They overlook psychological factors relating to the motivations of actors or treat them in a rather cursory fashion.

THEORIES OF SOCIAL EVOLUTION

Theories of social evolution perceive social change to connote basic stages of development by which society proceed from simple, rural, agrarian forms to more complex and differentiated, industrial-urban ones. In the eighteenth and nineteenth centuries, there are efforts to explore 'the true foundation of society' without using the social contract theory and its attendant idea that society is a mere collection of individuals whose psychological ends conclude in social institutions. There are two types of evolutionary theory—(1) that which assumes the unilinear, ordered or progressive nature of social change (Comte, Spencer and Durkheim develop this type of evolutionary theory) (2) and that, which is based on an analogy with evolution in plant and animal populations, following Darwin's theory.

1. **Evolutionary viewpoints** are primary to the nineteenth century approach to the study of society emphasising on ordered and directional nature of change. Saint Simon pioneers the idea of viewing society as an organic equilibrium—conventional in the late eighteenth and nineteenth century conservatism—inherently stable because individuals and social classes depend on the success of the whole for their survival. To this he adds an evolutionary idea of social development, a continual progression of organic societies representing increasing levels of advancement. Each society is appropriate in its own time but supersedes by higher forms. He sees growth of knowledge as playing a decisive role in evolution which Comte later develops as three stages—primitive, intermediary and scientific with corresponding forms of human knowledge organised on an identical continuum of theological, metaphysical and positive reasoning. All humankind inevitably passes through these stages as it develops implying unilinear direction and progress. For Comte, society is an organic entity whose parts are interdependent, each balancing the other and in the process creating an integrated whole. He views evolution as the growth of functional specialisation of structures and better adaptation

of parts. Human thought advances by a process of increasing complexity and decreasing generality. Society through division of labour becomes more complex, differentiated and specialised. The division of labour along with language and religion creates social solidarity but also produces social divisions between classes and between the private and public spheres. Spencer maintains that social systems like organisms adjust to their environment by a process of internal differentiation and integration. Societies evolve from simple homogenous and undifferentiated units as in militant society to complex and heterogeneous ones, where the parts of the whole become more specialised by remaining integrated as in industrial society. He uses the organic analogy but does not subscribe to the view of society as an organism. From this Spencer concludes that social planning, social welfare and state intervention interfere with the natural process of social evolution and progress that guarantees personal freedom in industrial society. Spencer is generally regarded as one who subscribes to the idea of the survival of the fittest, but he clearly points out that this is dominant only in militant societies. But as societies progress, they will depend more on co-operation, persuasion and altruism rather than aggression and conflict.

Durkheim is concerned with change and stages of development though he does not subscribe to the organic view of society. It is noteworthy that Marx and Engels also speak of change and stages of development without viewing society as an organism and without understanding change as evolutionary. Marx stresses on social revolutions to explain the transition from one stage to another with conflict rather than order as the mechanism for change. Durkheim points out that as societies industrialise and urbanise, they become more complex. The increasing division of labour erodes moral integration and mechanical solidarity that one finds in primitive societies based on the common beliefs and consensus embodied in the collective conscience. Social order becomes increasingly problematic. However, a new social order arises in advanced societies on the basis of organic solidarity comprising of interdependence of economic ties. Thus, arising out of differentiation and specialisation within the modern economy, a new system of occupational associations such as guilds that connect the individual to the state emerges and once this happens they collectively create moral restrains on individualism.

2. Twentieth century anthropologists and sociologists have been less interested in evolution except for the revival of interest among American functionalists in the 1950s and 1960s. This revival is sometimes referred to a neo-evolutionism, for it tries to utilise the principles of natural selection and adaptation drawn from evolutionary theory of the biological sciences. Functionalism use an organic conception of society and finds in Darwin's evolutionary theory an explanation of how organisms change and survive that have a semblance of being incompatible with their own assumptions. The starting point is the adaptation of societies to their environment that includes both natural world and other social systems. Change

from whatever source is the fundamental ingredient of evolution. Those changes that enhance the adaptive capacity of the society measured by its long-run survival are selected and institutionalised following the principle of the survival of the fittest. Sociological functionalism identify differentiation, the process whereby the main social functions are dissociated and comes to be performed by specialised collectivities in autonomous institutional spheres, as the main source of adaptation and selection. Functional differentiation and the parallel structural differentiation enable the effective performance of each function. Anthropological theories often focus on specific evolution of an individual society to its particular environment whereas sociologists concentrate on general evolution, the evolution of superior forms within the total development of human society. This general viewpoint implies a unilinear direction of change and that some societies are higher than others on a scale of progress assumptions absent in theory of specific evolution.

Functionalism continues to analyse social change within the framework of evolutionary theory regarding change as the adaptation of a social system to its environment by the process of internal differentiation and increasing structural complexity. It explains a social activity by referring to its consequences for the execution of some other social activity, institution or society as a whole. From the varied meanings three are crucial. (1) A social activity or institution may have latent functions by some other activity. For example, the change from an extended to nuclear family benefits the process of industrialisation for people are freed of their family ties and become geographically more mobile. This explains the change in the family structure. (2) A social activity may contribute to the maintenance of the stability of a social system. For example, **Durkheim** argues that religious practices promote social stability. (3) A social activity that fulfils the basic social needs or functional prerequisites, an argument that Parsons advocates. Societies have certain needs that must be fulfilled if they are to survive and institutions have to meet these needs.

Functionalism has been criticised on the grounds that it cannot explain social conflict or other forms of instability because it considers all social activities as interacting smoothly to stabilise society. Functionalists have responded to this assertion by suggesting that social conflict may, in fact have positive functions for social order or, in the notion of dysfunction conceding that not all social activities will have positive functions for all other activities. Furthermore, critics point out within functionalism there are no methods that will disturb existing functional relationships. Functionalists respond by invoking concepts such as differentiation. Functionalism has been described as a form of teleology in that it explains the existence of a social activity by its consequences or effects.

Modernisation theory combining economic, psychological and sociological factors understood modernity to include value systems, individual motivation and capital accumulation. It emphasises that values, norms and belief-structures play a significant role in the transformation of a traditional society into a modern one. Western societies evolved due to internal factors from within. Developing ones conversely modernise by their exposure to outside forces, which can be ideas, technology, education, literacy, increased political consciousness and participation, capital investment, greater economic opportunities, emergence of rational-legal system replacing the traditional one, development of mass media, emergence of nuclear family and representative government. These changes bring about social and structural differentiation. Modernisation theory has been criticised on two grounds—first, it is based on an idea of development that is Western, and is therefore, ethnocentric in nature and second, modernisation need not necessarily lead to industrial growth and equal distribution of social benefits since it is an essentially uneven process that may result in underdevelopment and dependency. Rostow speaks of the universal stages of economic development that all societies pass through before they become fully modernised. These are traditional or agricultural societies, the stage that prepares the preconditions for economic 'take-off, actual take-off, where full commercial and industrial systems are established, sustained economic growth and, finally, the mature high mass-consumption society that represents the completion of social evolution.

POPPER'S PIECEMEAL SOCIAL CHANGE

Popper (1945 and 1957) advocates **piecemeal social change** that is gradual and evolutionary in contrast to holistic revolutionary change by linking piecemeal change to the idea of an open society. An open society, a term used Bergson, connotes two sources of religion and morality, one source of ethics which is tribal and other universal. The first one gives rise to a closed society and the second one, to an open society. Popper borrows the idea from Bergson and develops it as one that is democratic and liberal in character committed to the rule of law and a constitution. It will allow the full play of the market but with the state regulating and intervening to mitigate avoidable suffering that the market may unleash. It values individual merit, places premium on education rather than indoctrination and accepts that society changes not on the basis of some grand design. An open society implicitly rejects **utopianism** and **historicism**, which for Popper means trying to obtain first-hand knowledge with the help of certain laws that govern human societies and individuals. On this basis, Popper rejects theories of Plato, Hegel and Marx because their theories attempt to provide total and scientific explanations of society with the help of discoverable laws of history. Popper is sceptical of such claims, for he argues that a scientific theory cannot and need not try and explain everything. If a theory tries to explain all sorts of possibilities without paying attention to actual state of affairs substantiated by observation and experimental results as evidence, then it cannot contain scientific information. An open society maximises the freedom of the individual and mitigates his avoidable suffering and unhappiness guaranteeing to the individual a wide range of freedom of choice by making education, arts, housing, health and other facets of social life available.

Popper understands the notion of change in the context of **Historicism**, a term that he uses for describing inexorable laws of historical development—the assertion that if natural sciences can predict eclipses then social sciences ought to be able to predict political revolutions. In a highly systematic manner, he shows how both, those who think that social sciences are not at all like natural sciences (anti-naturalists) and those who think social sciences are like natural sciences (the naturalists) have a common aim—that of predicting history. Both advocate the methodology of historicism, which he sees as bankrupt, for they tend to consider societies as whole responding to the pressures of rudimentary social forces. Instead, Popper, like Hayek, prescribes **methodological individualism**—rules to the effect that the behaviour and actions of collectives should be explained by the behaviour of individuals acting appropriately to the logic of their social situation as best they can and as best as they see it. Holistic phenomena are to be described as the unintended consequences of such individual actions resonating through the social system. Social theories are to be tested not by historical predictions that are more in the nature of prophecies but by its efforts to invent institutions that correct social mistakes by social engineering. Historicism is a form of determinism, which Popper rejects for he believes that evolution produces genuine unpredictable creativity and novelty. Hence, he advocates piecemeal change rather than utopian social change. Popper considers universal ideologies, like Marxism, with its claim to the ultimate truth a threat to open society. Believing in the idea of relative truth, Popper believes that those who claim to have the ultimate truth can impose it on the rest only through force and compulsion and that is contrary to the spirit of the open society.

Popper accepts not only the inevitability of change but also the fact that the pace of change gets faster with each year. He rightly points out that a theory that accepts the idea of quick change could never offer a blueprint of an ideal or perfect society. In fact, the idea of a perfect society itself becomes incomprehensible if one accepts that change is not going to stop. Therefore, ideal societies are not only unfeasible because they are perfect, but also static if these societies are to conform or remain close to a blueprint, for embedded in the notion of a perfect society is the idea of a fixed and unchanging order. Accepting the idea of quick change, Popper advises that it is important to learn how to maximise one's control over actual events that occur in a process of change that is never ending and to use that control wisely. Popper's advocacy of piecemeal social engineering is a middle path to conservatism and holistic utopian change. He rejects social revolution as a political method for the following reasons. To abolish all institutions and traditions, what he often calls canvas cleaning, leaves the utopian engineers confused and at a loss as to how to act. The other reason is fallibility of our scientific knowledge as well as social science knowledge. Therefore, it is rational to resort to piecemeal changes that can be executed all the time by private individuals, groups as well as governments. There is a constant process of learning from the inevitable errors and adjusting expectations accordingly. In the absence of any finality, it is wise to adopt a wait and watch policy and go by the trial and error method that allows us to rectify mistakes and wrongs as and when they occur, for it is not possible to anticipate all contingencies. Reforms through this method are modest but democratic, for it tries to accommodate differing points of view, publicly discuss and make open its conclusions and consequences.

On the contrary, holistic revolutionary change proceeds with the assumption that it is possible to anticipate all eventualities and the person who makes the master plan can never go wrong. Popper rebuts by asking, 'who plans the planner?' The larger the scale of social experiment, the more difficult it is to learn from it. Holistic utopian change is contrary to the spirit of scientific theory and is also irrational. For Popper, change would have to be modest and gradual since there is nothing like an absolute truth and he doubted anyone who claims to have found it. Truth at best is relative, depending on the perception of the one who perceives it. He is convinced that utopian change erodes human freedom, for it is simplistic in its understanding the scope of independent individual choices. Opinions about what constitutes an ideal society differs while utopian social engineers would not tolerate deviations, for that frustrates their favoured blueprints. Thus, even if human liberation is the original aim of the utopian engineers, they find themselves compelled to resort to more and more coercive methods to actualise their ideal. Popper's non-determinism and belief in relative truth makes him an advocate of non-violent piecemeal change. He echoes Gandhi who too shuns determinism and deterministic ideologies like Marxism. Gandhi never overlooks the human factor in any social transformation and believes in the efficiency of non-violent revolutionary changes to bring about total transformation of the individual and society.

EVOLUTIONARY THEORY BY CONTEMPORARY WRITERS

In the recent times, some authors have resorted to using cyclical pattern of historical change—a variation of evolutionary theme. **Paul Kennedy** (1988) discusses the decline of the American power in the last few decades of the twentieth century as part of the cyclical pattern of growth and decline largely as a result of economic and technological factors. According to his assessment, global and regional domination always goes to the strongest nation-state. However, domination is not permanent. Strong states prosper and may become more powerful than any rivals but would be replaced by other more resourceful and stronger states. Cyclical models of change underlie Wallerstein's (1974, 1980 and 1989) world-systems analysis. Like Kennedy, **Wallerstein** sees history of the modern world as one of ascending and descending hegemonies—

those of the United Provinces (now called the Netherlands), Britain twice and, most recently, the United States. He admits that the core and the periphery are not a static structure and one can move from the core to the periphery and vice-versa. He cites the example of Argentina for the core becoming a periphery and the example of South Korea as one moving from a periphery to the core. Some evolutionary theory go beyond perceiving history as cyclical in nature by offering a universal history as evident in Fukuyama's (1992) work that announces the worldwide triumph of liberalism following the collapse of communism. Using Hegel's framework, he announces the end of ideological evolution with liberal democracy becoming a universal phenomenon since both fascism and communism have failed. He understands historical change, just as modernisation theory, as the unfolding of the features of Western modernity across the world. Historical stages represent the progressive unfolding of the human potential and human spirit. The end of history, however, need not signify the end of conflict but only that such conflicts can be resolved peacefully.

In conclusion, Laski while writing at the centenary of the *Communist Manifesto* in 1948, propounds the doctrine of 'revolution by consent,' signalling the arrival of the democratic age. Not many today echo Fanon's eulogy of violence as a cleansing force, as the track record of violent revolutions has shown that they inevitably lead to terror, suppression of democratic freedom and institutions and untold human sufferings. It is generally agreed that the ballot box is much more revolutionary and effective as a mode of change than the barrel of a gun. Owing to the universal acceptance of liberal democracy and the spectacular progress of East Asian countries, without having to resort to repression and sacrifices by the ordinary person, the revolutionary theories of social change have ceased to cast their magic spell as they did earlier on. On the contrary, theories that advocate peaceful change, emphasising new social and economic issues have cyrstallised in the form of new social movements like feminism, environmentalism, and the movement of the indigenous people and marginalised groups and individuals. The potentiality of all these movements to effect peaceful social change is much more than the yesteryears' insurrections and violent movements for capturing of state power. It is for this reason that **Havel** proclaims 'violence is not radical enough'.

Further Readings

Brinton, C., *The Anatomy of Revolution*, Vintage Books, New York, 1952.

Calvert, P., *Revolution and Counter-Revolution*, World View Press, Delhi, 1997.

Kumar, K., *Revolution: The Theory and Practice of a European Idea*, Weidenfeld and Nicolson, London, 1971.

Lasky, M.J., *Utopia and Revolution*, Macmillan, London, 1976.

Mazlish, B., Kaledin, A.D. and Ralston, D.B. (Eds.), *Revolution: A Reader*, Macmillan, New York, 1971.

Miller, D. (Ed.), *A Pocket Popper*, Fontana, Great Britain, 1983.

Moore, B., *Social Origins of Dictatorship and Democracy: Lord and Peasant in the Making of the Modern World*, Penguin, Harmondsworth, 1969.

Popper, Sir K., *The Open Society and Its Enemies*, Routledge and Kegan Paul, London, 1945.

Popper, Sir K., *The Poverty of Historicism*, Routledge and Paul, London, 1957.

Endnote

1. Huntington analyses societies along the same lines suggested by Aristotle.

Chapter 19
Recent Developments

Since the seventies, political theory has revived largely due to the efforts of Habermas, Nozick and Rawls. The themes that figure prominently since its revival are broadly the social justice and welfare rights theory within a deontological perspective, utilitarianism, democratic theory and pluralism, feminism, post modernism, new social movements and civil society, and the liberalism-communitarian debate (Young 1996: 481–500, Glaser 1995: 23). In fact, communitarianism tries to fill the void left by the declining popularity of Marxism (Barry, N.P. 1995). However, this unprecedented lease of life that political theory receives is restricted to the academy and as a result it is 'a kind of alienated politics, an enterprise carried on at some distance from the activities to which it refers' (Walzer 1989: 337). This resurgence suggests that earlier pronouncements about its decline and/or demise are premature and academically shortsighted. However, care is to be maintained in distinguishing contemporary political theory from the classical tradition as the former derives its inspiration from the latter and in this sense, attempts are to refine rather than being original, adjusting the broad frameworks of the classical tradition to the contemporary complexities.

This new found enthusiasm is confined to liberal political discourse mainly due to the seminal work of Rawls fulfilling Germino's wish of a need to strengthen the open society. Recent liberal theory, in its revived sense, focuses on the idea of impartiality and fairness in the belief that 'discrimination must be grounded on relevant differences' (Benn and Peters 1959: 133). It is no coincidence that a well formulated and detailed analysis of the concept of justice, long over-due since the time of Plato, emerges in Rawls for whom justice means fairness. Rawls in the classical tradition deals with what ought to be, for he confronts the vexed problem of distribution of liberties, opportunities, income, wealth and bases of self-respect. Among the competing ideologies which usher in the twentieth century, only liberalism, unlike fascism and communism, permits free exchange of ideas. It synchronises, and adapts, if necessary, theory in light of practice and identifies the elements that constitute a just political and social order without being doctrinaire and dogmatic. However, much of this new liberal political theory is in the nature of refining and clarifying the earlier theoretical postures. Moreover, the loss of challenge by both fascism and communism, the first, because of its defeat in the Second World War, and the second, which collapses due to its own internal contradictions, also prove that utopian and radical schemes are no longer theoretically and practically desirable and feasible alternatives. Nonetheless, liberalism faces challenges in recent times from communitarianism, postmodernism and feminism.

COMMUNITARIANISM

Communitarianism rejects the universalistic foundations for political values based, for example, on a theory of human nature. Instead it takes communities and the social meanings embodied in communities and other ways of life as basic and seek to interpret them. It criticises the liberal concept of the individual self that seeks to characterise the individual without any reference to inherited traditions and shared goals. The liberal self is endowed with rights and duties specified in purely abstract and universal terms that leave out the claims and obligations arising from one's personal and social bonds. Normatively, they consider such an individualism as undesirable, an indication of something wrong. Instead the communitarians speak of a 'situated' self—one that is grounded in a community and defined by the attachments and shared self-understandings that encompass community life. Communitarians believe that it is from one's community that one derives specific rights and obligations while simultaneously being embroiled in the purposes and ends of one's community (MacIntyre 1981, Sandel 1984, Taylor 1985). Liberals, according to communitarians, undervalue the political space viewing citizen participation in the community as a mere instrumental good for attaining private ends. Communitarians are suspicious of rights-based liberalism but do not offer any common political alternative. Unlike the liberal emphasis on liberty and equality, which the state must facilitate without actually interfering, they speak of the values of the community, which the state must actively promote. Furthermore, while critiquing liberalism, they do not safeguard themselves against objections that they offer very little protection to individual liberty against the tyranny of the majority or that of tradition. Their stress on moral conformity does not allow for individual dissent. Their vision of a democracy based on consensus as an alternative to majoritarianism is impracticable in a world of culturally individuated people or one in which it is impossible to eliminate scarcity and conflicts of interests. They do not clarify the meaning or the origins of shared common good and how can it be realised in the modern world that is essentially pluralistic with multiple identities. The communitarians do not specify the form that common life should take and how one can get out from the present situation of decline and attain this new moral ideal. They attempt to modernise Rousseau's vision of a plebiscitarian type of participatory democracy without providing for a mechanism to balance the individual self with the social self.

There are three kinds of communitarianism—liberal-communitarianism, right-communitarianism and left-communitarianism. Liberal communitarians, such as, Berlin, Raz and Kymlicka, share two concerns of liberalism: the irreducible plurality of individual values or conceptions of the good, namely there are many valuable ways of life from which people can choose and these cannot be derived from any single model or fundamental principle. The other is the importance of autonomous choice. It considers the political society as being made of plurality of communities that is as far as possible voluntary in nature. It diverges from liberalism with regard to the role of the state vis-á-vis cultural groups. Right-communitarianism, as exemplified in Roger Scrunton's writings, argues that the chief deficiency of liberalism is the failure to address the problem of social unity and considers the community as a source of social union. Second, it is the source of authority manifest through customs and conventions. Left-communitarianism seeks to create or preserve community on the basis of equality and the community should be actively self-determining rather than subject to the authority of tradition.

Communitarianism, like Marxism, provides a well-argued critique of liberal theory, but not a viable alternative. The communitarians claim that it is not possible to engage in constructive moral argument about our shared moral inheritance but simply make an appeal to these undefined values. The task of moral and political theory is not only to identify our common inheritance but also develop the best explanation of that inheritance and in this the arguments must appeal to the criteria of validity that are themselves the outcome of substantive philosophical argument. The inadequacy in communitarian reasoning is that either the argument stops with an appeal to community, as in the case of Sandel, as if this concept does not need explanation and justification; or else there is an appeal to a conception of community as a moral source significantly different from the liberal notion of the community which is difficult to sustain in the modern world, as is the case with Maclntyre. In both the cases, ethical arguments about the nature of community as a moral source or the nature of good life are needed. It will have an abstract philosophical character that most communitarians wish to reject. The communitarians fail to address the key problems of (a) 'how to generate a strong but inclusive political community, (b) how to defend equal citizenship in face of economic inequality and (c) how to ensure that the self-governing is genuinely democratic' (Miller 2000: 109).

The communitarian critique of the liberal theory in general is much less damaging than is often claimed. Liberals like Rawls also emphasise the community and do not consider individual autonomy as the sole end that needs protection and as such their theory is based on far stronger grounds than what is articulated by the communitarians. Nonetheless, communitarianism offers some forceful arguments. It makes us conscious of the way our reason is shaped by our inherited tradition. It reminds us that we are born with moral obligations as a community of which we must be sensitive. It stresses on our moral obligations to people immediately around us—our family, friends or the community. Its ideal of social solidarity draws attention to the genuine deficiency of the atomised modern life, one that many supporters of individual rights share.

REPUBLICANISM

Republicanism criticises liberalism in general and Rawls in particular. Republicanism is a term defined by contrast with monarchy, meaning that the government in a republic is in principle the common business (*respublica*) of the citizens who conduct it for common good, thus differing from a traditional king who exercises personal authority over his subjects. The republican tradition is associated with Cicero, Machiavelli, Harrington, Algernon Sidney and some of the lesser known figures during the English Civil War and many theorists in the eighteenth century Britain, US and France. It considers Locke and Montesquieu as its inspiration. Freedom and virtue are core republican ideas. Freedom means liberty from the arbitrary power of the tyrants along with the right of citizens to manage their common affairs by participating in government. Virtue means patriotism and public spirit, a heroic willingness to give precedence to common good above one's own or one's family's interests. Republican ideas originate in the city-states of Greece, but become central in ancient Rome. The greatness and freedom of Rome is attributed to the virtue of her citizens but some also stress on the institutional arrangement by pointing to its mixed constitution for its success. The idea of mixed constitution that first appears in Plato's *Laws* is fully elaborated by Aristotle and implemented by Polybius. The latter claims that the endless cycle of instability could be halted if there is a balance between the monarchical, aristocratic and democratic elements and thus becomes a basic component of classical republicanism.

During the Renaissance, republicanism receives impetus in the writings of Machiavelli and Francesco Guicciardini (1433–1540), for they maintain that a stable republic is only possible with patriotic virtue, with citizens devoted to public good, refrain from factional quarrels and continuously participate in civic affairs. The decline of Florentine Republic sees the demise of republican ideas, only to be revived partly by Harrington for he emphasises on institutional arrangements to secure liberty and adapts the classical mixed constitution to the contemporary times. Sidney, following Machiavelli, argues that European republics produce better soldiers with greater virtue than the governments of Africa and Asia. The American and then the French Revolutionaries by adopting a republic representing people's will alter perceptibly the view that republics succeeds only in self-governing city-states. Its success makes republics a universal challenge to kings and churches. To some extent, republicanism during the revolutionary era like its classical counterpart stresses on virtue or on institutional arrangements in preserving liberty, but Rousseau's republicanism is moralistic in tone. Tocqueville views self-absorption in private life as a threat to liberty and stresses on the importance of religion, particularly Protestant values, in preserving democracy and freedom in the USA. While Machiavelli understands that religion as socially useful but he could not comprehend its intrinsic link with liberty, a theme that Tocqueville succinctly develops in opposition to the Enlightenment credo that sought to uphold reason and liberty by being anti-religion. During the nineteenth century, republicanism remains an ideal to be fought for against traditional monarchies.

In the twentieth century, Republicanism virtually disappears from the political, program, partly because there are no more monarchies to fight against and partly because of the liberal conception of the primacy of the individual. The latter places premium on the negative and individualistic liberty relegating the ancient conception of citizens' participation in public life as more important than private life, to the background till Arendt revives the idea of freedom as a public rather than private activity. More recently there is pessimism about politics and a renewed emphasis on the pivotal role that political culture play in sustaining free public life as evident in Rawls' *Political Liberalism* (1993). Pocock (1971) and Skinner's (1978, 1981 and 1997) writings show how republican way gives us a new perspective on contemporary politics. Skinner, in particular, also gives a new understanding of freedom. As opposed to the liberal idea of freedom as non-interference, a republican defines freedom as non-domination—absence of a capacity on the part of anyone else to interfere arbitrarily in some or all of other's choices. Linked to the republican ideal of liberty is the notion of civic virtue that emphasises public good and citizens' participation. It is a body of ideas distinct from liberalism, which favours rights over community, liberty over duty, representation over participation and interest over virtue.

POSTMODERNISM

Postmodernism is a movement that originates in France in 1960s and its most influential exponents are Gilles Deleuze (1925–1950, Jacques Derrida (1930–2004), Michel Foucault (1926–1984) and Jean Francois Lyotard (1924–1998). It is an off shoot of a movement more precisely called post-structuralism, for postmodernists accept structuralism's rejection of the self but not its scientific pretensions. Structuralism, as developed by the linguist Ferdinand de Saussure and defended by Claude Levi-Strauss, is concerned not with structures but with such structures as can be held to underlie and generate the phenomena under observation. In other words, the focus is on language, ritual and kinship that makes the individual, for it is not self that creates the culture but the other way round. The postmodernists see the attempt of human beings to be objective about the self beset with profound self-reflexive philosophical problems.

> They applied the structural-cultural analysis of human phenomena to the human sciences themselves, which are, after all human cultural constructions. Hence, they are best named poststructuralists. They

> seemed to announce the end of rational inquiry into truth, the illusory nature of any unified self, the impossibility of clear and unequivocal meaning, the illegitimacy of Western civilisation, and the oppressive nature of all modern institutions (Cahoone 1996: 5–6).

It is a general reaction against modern rationalism, utopianism and foundationalism or the effort to establish the foundations of knowledge and judgement, a preoccupation of philosophy since Descartes, though in reality it can be traced to Plato. It rejects the possibility of the realisation of the perfect set of laws, which can lead to domination and non-freedom of some, 'the other'. In social sciences, it signifies a new method in view of postindustrialism, as the industrial societies have been radically changing since the Second World War. The rise of postmodernism is to be understood in the context of the 1980s, which witnesses the ascendancy of political conservatism and the need for moral regeneration and the return to community. The basis of modernism was industrialization and class solidarity wherein social identity was shaped by one's position within the productive system. Postmodern societies are fragmented and pluralistic. Individuals are seen as consumers rather than as producers as in modern societies. Unlike the latter which is marked by class, religious and ethnic loyalties, postmodern societies are individualistic. Communitarianism and varieties of feminism accuse liberal individualism for undermining the social fabric. At the same time, the modern legacy of rationalism and liberal individualism are defended through re-interpretation. The postmodernists by stressing on the need to circumscribe traditional philosophy's quest for ultimate certainty have stimulated the modern tradition. There is no desire to return to a premodern past or leap forward to a postmodern future. Modernity is not rejected but only its exceeding ambitions are being scaled down. Another crucial factor in the development of postmodernism is the decline of Marxism following the disenchantment with the turn of events in the wake of de-Stalinisation.

Postmodernism recognises pluralism and in-determinacy in the world repudiated by modernism. It considers modernity's faith in reason as a means to ensure and preserve humanity's freedom—particularly after what happened at Auschwitz—to be misplaced. Modernism is derived from the enlightenment ideas and theories and believes that it is possible to establish objective truths and universal values, associated with a strong faith in progress. Postmodernism on the contrary rejects the existence of absolute and universal truth as it posits that all knowledge are local and partial, and in this it is similar to communitarianism. There are three broad themes in postmodernism. First, is the critique of what Lytord calls modernity's 'meta-narratives' or 'grand narratives of emancipation'. It questions the modernist tendency to provide universal and all-embracing narratives, as in Marxism, that delete other narratives resulting in the triumph of consensus, uniformity and scientific reason over conflict, diversity and different forms of knowledge. Second is Richard Rorty's (1931–) anti-foundationalist posture that tries to show that there are no objective perspectives that guarantee truth or knowledge about the world and the philosophical systems from Plato to Kant to Habermas. They assume that it is possible to have a completely detached view of the social processes, consider knowledge minus its historicity or changing character and theorise about a person discounting the traditions and practices of which he is a part. Third, Derrida's de-constructionism[1] demonstrates the impossibility of deciding the essential characteristics of concepts and objects. Derrida contends that it is difficult to establish the essence of something for there are ambiguities and 'undecidables'. The postmodernist alternative is as follows. Lyotard (1984: 75) emphasises on the need for dissent and tolerance of those narratives that modern forms of knowledge neglects or ignores. Rorty insists on the need to accept everything as a product of time and place and not determined by an overarching principle. Derrida points out that fullness is never realised if one denies or expels differences from identity. Postmodernism attempts to expose the construction of political identity in modern liberal democracies through conceptual binaries like we/them, responsible/irresponsible, rational/irrational, legitimate/illegitimate, normal/abnormal and the like. Rather than focusing on the first term of each pair postmodernism highlights the manner in which the demarcation between the two terms are socially produced and policed. This arises out of the misconceived conception of modernity that it is possible to enhance one's mastery of the self, society and nature thereby dividing those who fall on the correct side of the division and the ones that are dismissed as the 'others'. The latter may include racial, ethnic, sexual, national or those without any identifiable external characteristics.

Postmodernism differs from deconstruction with which it is often identified. Deconstruction is a belief that all identities are socially constructed, in terms of a discourse that reflects the perspective and interests of the dominant group and subordinates the rest. Deconstruction's methodology is similar to that of postmodernism but with much limited capability. Deconstruction attempts to look at what is not present rather than what is present, the points of crisis and breakdown in a system than its more obvious positive side. Postmodernism finds its natural allies in multiculturalism and feminism and these reject the traditional liberal notion of equality of opportunity. They highlight the privileged position of upper class men, race and dominant economic groups inherent in exploitative capitalism. The traditional elite, educational systems and political legitimisation are also seen as sophisticated instruments of domination as these are the tools by which the privileged continue to maintain its power and deny the same to the disenfranchised groups like women, minorities and the underprivileged in western capitalist democracies. The political implication of postmodernism is an attempt to admit and confirm 'difference' and 'otherness' under the names of feminism and multiculturalism, movements that overlap with postmodernism. However, postmodernism is only a critique without much prospect of providing a viable alternative. It is accused of relativism regarding different modes of knowing to be equally valid thus rejecting the idea of making a distinction between truth and false. Its attraction lies in its rejection of accepted beliefs and solid realities. Its impact has been more pronounced in architecture where it originates and literature rather than in social sciences in general and political theory in particular.

FEMINISM

In the 1970s, women's movement and feminist studies begin to seriously consider the ideology and theory of women's emancipation and in doing so, began to resurrect from the past, ideas that are pro-woman or at least 'woman friendly'. It reclaims from the pages of history the name 'feminism' and begins to identify a continuous ideological theme through time and across different cultures linking the subordination of women within their homes and families to their denial of political and economic power publicly. The idea that gender could be the focal point in discussing not only the private sphere but also the public arena emerged as a sub-field in most social science disciplines.

Since the 1970s, there has been an enormous amount of work that questions the age old beliefs about women's nature, their subservience to men and their exclusion from political life. Feminists agree that the inequities between the sexes seen as immutable and natural have to be reduced, if not totally eliminated. Women, they contend, suffer and have suffered discrimination and injustices because of their sex and this is something that has gone on since the dawn of recorded history and in every culture and every society. There is a need to recognise women as human beings and as citizens and treated on equal terms with men. Beyond this agreement, there is considerable debate as to the causes of women's subordination, namely whether there exists enormous differences between women themselves, if there is something like a woman's nature which is different from that of a man and above all, whether men and women are fundamentally different which the feminists would have to sought out before they could aspire and demand genuine and complete equality between sexes.

In the process of trying to provide a feminist perspective, the classics within the Western intellectual tradition have been interpreted from the vantage point of women with the purpose of examining the position, role and status that is assigned to them. Initially, the focus had been on why women are excluded from the political process. Subsequently, the feminists begin to subject the entire tradition of political theorising to a general critique for their masculine bias and prejudice. In this context, some of the tracts which discuss the women's question exclusively and objectively are resurrected and given the status as pioneering texts, as classics in feminism. These texts raise questions pertaining to woman's nature, their right to equal educational opportunities, employment and liberties, women's political equality, citizenship rights and enfranchisement, female labour and consequences of industrialisation on sexual division of labour within the family, their role and responsibilities within the family and home, and the importance of restructuring filial and sexual relationships along the lines of equality, independence and self worth of both men and women. In a re-examination of the history of political philosophy from the perspective of a feminist, one can notice that the mainstream theorists and philosophers, barring a few but extraordinary exceptions, have generally ignored the political, social and legal status of women. The tracts written since the eighteenth century on the woman's question raise issues. These issues not only serve the cause of women in their fight for a compassionate and dignified world but also impress upon society at large that any effort or plan to promote human well-being would have to address itself equally to both men and women.

There are several different feminist responses to the perceived short-comings of mainstream political thought. The first response espoused by Wollstonecraft—inclusion/addition—involves the view that Western political theory has omitted women and women theorists and that there is a need to incorporate them. There is a pragmatic concern about reforming Western thought by taking into account what is politically feasible. The second view—criticise and reject and start again—points to the bankruptcy of the whole of Western thought in light of the contemporary feminist concerns. The third—deconstruct and transform—attempts to 'understand the sexual politics of our cultural and intellectual heritage' with a view to 'comment and transform it' (Beasley 1999: 4–5). First-wave feminism was the first concerted movement working for the reform of women's social and legal inequalities in the nineteenth century. It was about women as women, glorifying motherhood, accepting the basic aspects of the division of labour between the sexes; women were responsible for the home and bringing up of children, men were responsible for the public world of paid work. On this basis, the arguments for women's suffrage were articulated. Second-wave feminism is about women as persons, celebrating personhood, and calling for breaking down of the division of labour between the sexes, perceived to be the cause for women's oppression. It demands that women play an equal part in the world of paid work and that men play an equal part in the home. The second wave is shaped and dominated by what came to be known as radical feminism.

Feminism tries to deconstruct the public-private dichotomy in classical and contemporary political theory and has called for a rethinking of this distinction and its meaning for politics (Okin 1979; Elshtain 1981; Young 1987; Shanley and Pateman 1991). It contends that patriarchal family relations, sexuality, and workplace discriminations are properly political relations. It questions the male bias in mainstream political theory and subjects most of the important concepts like equality, justice, liberty, power, citizenship and democracy in political theory to a critical analysis. The third-wave feminism questions the core of the second-wave feminism, namely the sex-gender differences. The experiences associated with the female body—reproduction, motherhood and sexual violence—could be the universal basis for a unified feminist politics (Butler 1990, 1992; Nicholson 1995). Nicholson's 'coat rack' theory of gender identity treats the female body as universal and common, a base for a sense of community in view of the enormous cultural diversity and multiple social identification.

Ecofeminism

Ecofeminism is a term coined by the French feminist Francoise d' Eaubonne in 1974 synthesises feminism with ecology. It is an outgrowth of radical feminism and cultural feminism with a direct thrust on ecology. It stresses on how patriarchy treats women and the natural world. The core of ecofeminism is the integral nature of domination of women and domination of nature. "The fact that man does not consider himself a part of nature, but indeed considers himself superior to matter, seemed to me to gain significance when placed against man's attitude that woman is both inferior to him and closer to nature" (Griffin 1978: xv). There is also a stress on the inter-relatedness and inter-connectedness of women in various movements—ecology, peace, feminist and especially health—all of which are described as the spiritual dimension of life (Mies and Shiva 1997, 500). Ynestra King (1983) emphasises on the need to use the woman-nature connection to create a different kind of culture and politics. It recognises the interdependence among all living beings and the right of all to exist.

The 1990s sees the emergence of 'identity politics' in feminism premised on the assumption, espoused by most of the first-wave feminism and second-wave feminism alike, that women qua women have shared interests based on shared experience (Cott 1987, Riley 1988). Phillips (1995)[2] advances an essentialist assumption of what she calls "the politics of presence", namely representation of the under-represented (in her example-women) by reserving places in governmental bodies for people from marginalised groups and 'politics of ideas' of ensuring that at least some political party platforms feature marginalised group interests. The second one is complementary to the first one and that will ensure representation of the un-represented segments in government. But it is possible that the representatives would not pursue the specific interest of the group that they represent. Party discipline may lead to some accountability but even proportional representation may not lead to electoral success. One solution is by including group list in the list of political party candidates ensuring representation of marginalised groups. Phillips (1991) conceptualises the public and private spheres as interdependent but distinct. She thinks it is necessary to integrate the private sphere into analysis and focus on gendered nature of power relations within the family, and not ignore it as traditional political science has done. The inequities within the family are as relevant to issues of social justice as inequalities in the public sphere. Democratisation of the public sphere understood in terms of higher participation of women is possible only if there is prior democratisation of the private sphere. This, she desires by maintaining the public-private distinction, like Okin (1991a) and Young (1987), so as to preserve areas for individual decision and privacy. Critics point out that race, class, and sexuality are other identities that ought to be taken into consideration in feminist accounts of political community (Collins 2000; Grant 1993; Haraway 1991; Hartsock 1983; Phelan 2001; Rich 1980; Rubin 1984; Spelman 1988).

CULTURAL PLURALISM AND LIBERAL THEORY

In recent years, in many well-established Western democracies, identity politics driven by considerations of nationality, ethnicity, religion, gender, and language has come to the forefront of public debate. It focuses on questions of recognising cultural diversity, the status and rights of immigrants, and in specific cases, of the rights of indigenous people, and underlines the need for group representation and rights. These issues form the subject matter of identity politics with its variants-multiculturalism, politics of recognition of difference and, to the notions of differentiated citizenship and theory of group rights. Classical political theory examined questions concerning justice or democracy in a society which according to J.S. Mill had a shared identity. However, in the twentieth century, demographic and political changes have set aside these traditional assumptions about the relationship between culture and politics. Most of the larger countries today have substantial number of minorities from more than one culture and this has altered the debate on ideals of democracy, justice or citizenship, from those when they were first proposed in a situation of relative homogeneity.

The advocates of identity politics question the liberal individualist[3] conception of citizenship as equal rights to all under the law which differed from the feudal perception that decided people's political status by their group identity of guilds. When this well-established social practice of group identity, behaviour and social balancing was challenged by the theory of Divine Right of Kings, then the theory of natural rights that provides the individualist basis to liberalism emerged. Cultural pluralists argue that on the contrary citizenship must reflect the distinct socio-cultural identity of groups like African American, indigenous peoples, ethnic and religious minorities, gays and lesbians who feel excluded and marginalised because of their 'difference'[4] from the mainstream of society.

MULTICULTURALISM

Multiculturalism stresses on the need to accommodate cultural diversity fairly, as there are different consequences and impact that public policies have for persons of different cultural groups within multinational states. For instance, given the importance of language to culture and the role of the modern states in so many facets of life, the choice of official language will affect different people differently. Similarly, the content of education, personal laws or choice of public holidays, national symbols such as the choice of national anthem, immigration and naturalisation policy, religious freedom, special privileges for minorities or mechanisms for representing minorities have increasingly captured attention of theorists and policy makers in order to avoid policies that entail unfair burdens (Kymlicka 1995b: 1).

ORIGINS AND MEANING OF MULTICULTURALISM

The term 'Multiculturalism' was first used in Canada in 1971 and then, in Australia in 1978, to describe a new public policy that moved away from assimilation of ethnic minorities, and immigrants in particular, towards policies of acceptance and integration of diverse cultures (Lopez 2000: 2–3). It entered the American and British political lexicon in the 1980s (Glazer 1997: 8). In the US, when it entered the public debate, in the first instance, it was about the need for reform of public school curriculum, in disciplines like history, literature and social sciences as its contents reflected a euro-centric bias. Glazer observed that initially, it was about 'how American society, particularly American education should respond to diversity' (1997: 8). Since then, multiculturalism has questioned the traditional conception of the US as a 'melting pot' of diverse people bonded in a common culture of the New World. The metaphor 'melting pot'[5] is seen as a cover for oppressive assimilation to the dominant or hegemonic white culture. As the American society, from the very beginning has, in fact been, multiracial and diverse, there is a need to underline the separate characteristics and virtues of the different cultural groups. Instead of 'melting pot', terms such as 'salad bowl' and 'glorious mosaic' are preferred as they convey more a sense of separateness and distinctiveness in describing a nation of immigrants (ibid: 10).

Like many other concepts in political theory, there is no unanimity about what constitutes multiculturalism and it continues to be a contested concept. For some, multiculturalism requires reasonable changes in social and political institutions to enable cultural minorities to preserve their language and their distinctive customs. For others, multiculturalism is about eliminating racism and nurturing rather than repudiating or tolerating 'difference', as differences spring from a universally shared attachment of importance to cultures, and this implies greater social transformation. A unifying theme amongst the multiculturalists is their resistance to homogenisation or assimilation which is evident in the conception of citizenship implicit in the contemporary liberal theories of justice that conceptualises justice as equal rights for all citizens irrespective of their gender, religion and ethnicity. Kymlicka points out that the logical conclusion of liberal principles of justice 'seems to be a colour-blind' constitution—the removal of all legislation differentiating people in terms of their race or ethnicity (except for temporary measures, like affirmative action, which are believed necessary to reach a 'colour blind' society (1989: 141). Multiculturalists see this attempt towards a 'colour blind' society as ill founded, for it is not possible to separate the state and ethnicity and when the liberal state attempts to do this, it unfairly privileges certain ways of life over others. They allege that liberals do not take diversity seriously. This is despite the fact that liberals value pluralism, with Rawls stressing on 'reasonable pluralism', which is why liberals defend a neutral public philosophy that entails equal rights for all citizens. Kymlicka (1995a) argues that liberals, like Rawls and Dworkin, have falsely assumed that members of a political community are members of the same cultural community. He regards a culture as a civilisation, self-sufficient and with its own social institutions. Parekh observes that Rawls, like many liberals, "is sensitive to moral but not cultural plurality, and thus takes little account of the cultural aspirations of such communities as the indigenous peoples, national minorities, subnational groups, and the immigrants" (2000: 89). A culture has a claim to rights if it is vital to the basic interests of its members and contributes to the wider society (ibid: 217–218). Multiculturalism is not merely 'about difference and identity per se but about those that are embedded in and sustained by culture, that is, a body of beliefs and practices in terms of which a group of people understand themselves and the world and organise their individual and collective lives' (Parekh ibid: 2–3).

It was in the 1990s that political theorists began to furnish the theoretical basis of a multicultural society. The first systematic theory of multiculturalism was elaborated by Will Kymlicka in his two major works—*Liberalism, Community and Culture* (1989) and *Multicultural Citizenship* (1995a). Kymlicka criticises the earlier models of unitary republican citizenship in which all the citizens enjoy common citizenship rights on the grounds, that in its assumption of a more homogenous political community, it ignores cultural and ethnic diversity. He observes that liberalism with its stress on individual rights has not paid adequate attention to group rights. Following J.S. Mill, Kymlicka points out that the distinctive feature of liberalism is that it ascribes to the individual the freedom to choose and revise their conception of good life. The capacity of an individual to make meaningful life choices depends on one's access to a culture because one is shaped by one's culture. According to him, the institutions of liberal democratic societies embody the culture of the major national group. If members of minority cultural groups are to have autonomy, freedom and identity as those of the majority community, then justice and fairness requires that their culture be secure. This would entail granting demands of minority groups for rights of self government within the polity, of guaranteed representation or veto rights over certain decisions, measures like education arrangements in the form of protection of minority languages through special radio or television channels. These measures can be claimed as a matter of just and equal treatment and not as a matter of special treatment: in this way Kymlicka argues that multiculturalism and liberalism are compatible. He argues that in a multicultural state, a comprehensive theory of justice would have to include both universal rights and certain group differentiated rights or special status for minority cultures (1995a: 6).

Kymlicka is dissatisfied with the post-war liberal political theory, which in his view, wrongly assumes that provision of basic individual rights could resolve the problem of national minorities. He contends that minority rights could not be subsumed under human rights because "human rights standards are simply unable to resolve some of the most important and controversial questions relating to cultural minorities" (ibid: 4). These included questions about which languages should be recognised in parliaments, bureaucracies and courts; whether any ethnic or national groups should have publicly funded educations in their mother tongues; whether internal boundaries should be drawn so that cultural minorities form majorities in local regions; whether traditional homelands of indigenous people should be reserved for their benefit; and to what degree of cultural integration might be required of immigrants seeking citizenship (ibid: 4–5). As traditional human rights doctrines offer no guidance on these questions, Kymlicka recommends the need for a theory of minority rights to supplement human rights theory. This would enable us to confront burning issues that raged in places like Eastern Europe which was mired in disputes over local autonomy, language and naturalisation. He proposes to develop a liberal theory of minority rights which would explain 'how minority rights could coexist with human rights and how minority rights are limited by principles of individual liberty, democracy and social justice' (ibid: 6).

Kymlicka, in course of elaborating his theory, distinguishes three kinds of minority or group differentiated rights that are to be assured to ethnic and national groups—self-government rights, poly-ethnic rights and special representation rights. Self-government rights require the delegation of powers to national minorities, such as indigenous people, but are not available to other cultural minorities who had immigrated into the country. Instead, their claim is for rights of fair recognition since immigrant groups choose to immigrate into a host society, they must bear some of the burdens of integration. Poly-ethnic rights are for cultural minorities as it guarantees financial support and legal and political protection from the state for certain practices associated with particular ethnic or religious groups and in particular to aboriginal people as to enable them to maintain their culture and autonomy. Poly-ethnic rights might include legislation to prevent suppression or marginalisation of cultural and identity concern of minority ethnic groups by the deliberate, or unthinking, discrimination of the majority ethnic population within a country. Special state support for media policies and funding to address the media interests of minority ethnic groups are one particular expression of poly-ethnic rights. Both indigenous people and immigrant minorities might also be eligible for special representation rights which guarantee places for minority representatives on state bodies or institutions.

Of pivotal importance in Kymlicka's account of group-differentiated citizenship is the distinction that he makes between two kinds of minorities—national minorities and ethnic minorities. The former are people whose previously self-governing, territorially concentrated cultures have been incorporated into a large state. These are 'American Indians', Puerto Ricans, Chicanos and native Hawaiians in the United States; the Quebecois and various aboriginal communities in Canada and the Aborigines in Australia. Ethnic minorities are people who have immigrated to a new society and do not wish to govern themselves, but nonetheless wished to retain their ethnic identities and traditions.

But Kymlicka also strongly believes that group-based protection should not violate rights fundamental to individual well being. He acknowledges the fact that individuals might need protection from the abusive power of their own ethnic communities. He endorses group-differentiated rights which provide for external protection for groups, but does not permit 'internal restrictions' except in cases of systematic and gross human violations like slavery or genocide, in which case state intervention is warranted. For Kymlicka, culture is important because it is the context within which individuals learn how to choose, but its value reduces when it disallows individuals to choose their lives for themselves, thus retaining the overall spirit of liberalism that it permits individual's capacity for autonomous choice. Cultural membership and cultural diversity is to sustain those options within which autonomous persons can exercise choice. Devoid of autonomy, cultural diversity is neither morally or aesthetically valuable (1995a: 121–123).

Parekh insists that members of cultural minorities must be treated as equal and valued members with the rest, as equal respect is central to individual's sense of dignity going beyond conventional notions of nondiscrimination and equal opportunity, and not be given unintended discrimination in employment, housing, education, promotion, appointment to public offices. Minority communities may be allowed to run their internal affairs themselves so long as they are not internally oppressive. They should also be free to set up their own cultural, educational and other institutions, organise literary, artistic, sports and other events and to institute museums and academies, with the help of the state if they need or ask for. Cultural differences should also be taken into account in the formulation and enforcement of public policies and laws. Parekh points out that multiculturalism is not about difference and identity per se but about those that are embedded in and substantiated by culture, namely a body of beliefs and practices in terms of which a group of people understand themselves and the world and organise their individual and collective lives. Parekh also points out that multiculturalism occupies a middle position between naturalism or monism and culturalism or pluralism. Culturalists like Vico, Montesquieu, Herder and the German Romanticists insist that human beings are culturally constituted and varied from culture to culture while thinkers like Hobbes, Locke and Rawls speak of human nature as unrelated to culture and society.

MULTICULTURALISM AND COMMUNITARIAN CRITIQUE OF LIBERALISM

Multiculturalism coalesces with the communitarian critique of liberalism. The liberal perspective of free and equal disembodied individual, each pursuing their own conception of good life with the primacy of rights and liberties over community life and collective goods is viewed as fallacious as it fails to take into account the fact that individual identities are social constructs. Communitarians reject the idea of the individual as prior to the community and that the value of social goods can be reduced to their contribution to individual well-being. The traditional liberal emphasis on identical liberties and opportunities for all individuals are replaced by a scheme of special rights for minority cultural groups. Theorists like Will Kymlicka, however, have justified the claims of multiculturalism within liberalism based on values of autonomy and equality. Kymlicka argues that individuals choose but within a cultural context and derive a self-respect as there is an intimate connection between a person's self-respect and the respect accorded to the cultural group of which one is part. Kymlicka also argues inequality arising from membership in a minority culture is unchosen and need redress. To the query as to whether anti-discrimination laws can address the disadvantage or the serious inequality that cultural groups suffer, Kymlicka and other liberal theorists of multiculturalism point out that anti-discrimination laws fall short of treating members of minority groups as equals and that states are not neutral with respect to culture. In culturally diverse societies, there exist patterns of state support for some cultural groups over others. Furthermore, Kymlicka defends self-government rights to indigenous people and national minorities who have been coercively incorporated into the larger state while immigrants are voluntary economic migrants who have given up their native culture while migrating. There are multiculturalists who writing from a post colonial perspective defend tribal sovereignty argue that in liberal societies if diversity is to be taken seriously there is a need to recognise liberal as one of the many substantive outlooks. Bhiku Parekh observes that liberal theory cannot provide an impartial framework of governing relations between different cultural communities. Multiculturalism is in sharp contrast to classical liberal theory that emphasises on shared identity within a society that is democratic and just, as evident in the writings of John Stuart Mill. With the changes in politics and demography since the 1980s, the traditional perception of culture in general and in societies that consist of substantial minorities in particular has undergone a change altering the debate on ideals of democracy, justice and citizenship.

Politics of recognition is an alternative theory offered by Charles Taylor in his book entitled *The Politics of Recognition* (1994) by rejecting as inadequate the liberal theory of multiculturalism. Liberalism, which in his view, is incapable of giving culture the recognition it requires. He suggests that the liberal ideal of public neutrality is inapplicable in culturally diverse societies and should be replaced with the idea of equal worth of cultures. Liberalism emphasises on sameness, viewing individuals as bearers of rights and possessors of dignity as equal citizens, but cultural groups desire recognition of their distinctness and not sameness. He wants to recognise cultures that have fairly large number of members, have survived for some time and articulate a language of moral evaluations. He contends that democracies need to take the claims of indigenous people, linguistic minorities and other kinds of social groups seriously. He rejects Kymlicka's efforts to develop a liberalism that might accommodate difference by granting individuals differentiated rights to enable them to pursue their particular ends. According to Taylor, this solution works only 'for existing people who find themselves trapped within a culture under pressure, and can flourish within it or not at all. But it does justify measures designed to ensure survival through indefinite future generations' (1994: 62). In this context, he cites the example of Quebecois whose aim is the long-term survival of the French speaking community in Canada.

One of the main foundations for Taylor's theory of recognition is the assertion that our sense of our own well-being and moral goals depends critically on how we see ourselves reflected in the eyes of others. Being in a group whose culture is reviled and devalued leads to moral harm of its members and hence there is a need for revaluation and public acknowledgement of the despised group as a legitimate presence in the body politic. While acknowledging the need for 'difference-blind procedures for interpreting and redeeming individual rights' within a liberal polity, there is also a need for a substantive sense of common moral purpose forged out of the interaction of the different cultures subsisting within it. He also proposed strongly the need for a multiculturalist education to enhance mutual cultural understanding. For Taylor a multicultural liberal society is one in which individuals are given respect insofar as they are followers of a particular cultural heritage, as well as a distinctive kind of legal-constitutional regime in which the basic structure of rights and liberties is preserved.

Defenders of the **politics of difference** desire an extension of the democratic processes to give greater scope to the participation of cultural minorities in the shaping and governing of the polity (Young 1990, 2000; Phillips 1995; Williams 1998; Tully 2003). In *Strange Multiplicity* (1995), Tully recommends a reconstruction of modern constitutionalism as to accommodate the wide variety of cultural traditions to enhance the quality of liberal constitutional arrangements. Williams (1998) proposes measures like proportional representation, holding reserved seats in legislative bodies for members of underrepresented marginalised groups, redrawing of electoral boundaries when underrepresented groups are concentrated in geographically determined ridings or providing for multimember districts when appropriate and providing for quotas for underrepresented groups in political party candidate lists.

Young demands guaranteed representation only of oppressed disadvantaged groups and veto power over policies that affect them. These groups can only be fully integrated through what she calls differentiated citizenship. It means that members of certain groups should be incorporated into the political community, not only as individuals, but also through their group, and their rights should depend in part on their group membership: "group veto power regarding specific policies that affect a group directly, such as reproductive rights policy for women, or land use policy for Indian reservations" (1990: 184).

Young does not consider protection of minority cultures as a state responsibility, a notion advanced by some liberal multiculturalists like Kymlicka and Raz (1986; 1994), as adequate, as this is tantamount to confining groups to the private sphere. It fails to give public endorsement to their distinct identities. The public sphere is dominated by norms which appear to be universal and culturally neutral but in reality reflects cultural values of the dominant social categories—middle class white males. Young (1992), picking up on the model of 'associative democracy' of Cohen and Rogers (1992) proposes that the state ought to be an organisation of oppressed minorities with the view that they could exercise real power. Arguing within the US context, she (2000) also points out exclusive emphasis on rational argument further disadvantages minorities who are well-versed in its niceties. She supports forms of communication like rhetoric, story-telling (or testimony, or narrative) and an oral tradition argument, which are more accessible to disadvantaged minorities.

Phillips (1995)[6] puts forward an essentialist assumption of what she calls 'the politics of presence' namely representation for the under-represented (in her example—women) by reserving places in governmental bodies for people from marginalised groups or 'the politics of ideas' of ensuring that at least some political party platforms feature marginalised group interests. The second one is complementary to the first one and that will ensure representation of the un-represented segments in government. But it is possible that the representatives would not pursue the specific interest of the group that they represent. Party discipline may lead to some accountability but even proportional representation may not lead to electoral success. One solution is by including group list in the list of political party candidates ensuring representation of marginalised groups.

Phillips (1991) conceptualises the public and private spheres as interdependent but distinct. She thinks it is necessary to integrate the private sphere into analysis and focus on gendered nature of power relations within the family, and not ignore it as traditional political science has done. The inequities within the family are as relevant to issues of social justice as inequalities in the public sphere. Democratisation of the public sphere understood in terms of higher participation of women is possible only if there is prior democratisation of the private sphere. This, she desires by maintaining the public-private distinction, like Okin (1991) and Young (1987), so as to preserve areas for individual decision and privacy. In this context, she mentions the right of abortion. She also argues for the need to detach the two spheres of gender differences and base it instead on the criterion of the right to privacy.

CRITICISMS OF MULTICULTURALISM

Critics raise a number of objections to many of the aforesaid basic formulations. For some, it is simple that only individuals, and not groups, have rights (Narveson 1991; Hartney: 1991). Graf (1994: 194) observes that groups are fictitious entities and fictitious entities could not be right bearers. The idea of differentiated citizenship is a contradiction in terms. If groups are encouraged to focus on their 'difference' then how citizenship can be a shared identity, a source of commonality and solidarity among the various groups in society. There is another criticism that alleges that it is individual and not group that has rights. Chandran Kukathas points out that there are no group rights and the state by granting special protection and rights to cultural groups is overstepping its role. He insists that states should not pursue 'cultural integration' or 'cultural engineering' but 'politics of indifference' towards minority groups as there are groups that do not themselves value toleration and freedom of association, including the right to dissociate or exit a group may practice internal discrimination group members and that the state has very little authority to interfere in such associations. Kukathas is convinced that such a benign approach would permit the abuse of vulnerable members of groups, tolerating 'communities which bring up children unschooled and illiterate; which enforce arranged marriages; which deny conventional medical care to their members (including children); and which inflict cruel and "unusual" punishment'.

Aboriginal peoples, on whose behalf multiculturalists speak, see multiculturalism as facilitating further marginalisation of their communities and culture in a modern state which is more attuned to the needs of migrants than to the aborigines. Many press for the rights of indigenous minorities and insist that unlike immigrants, what they need is not only recognition of their independent status but also rectification of past injustice. A severe objection to multiculturalism is that in pleading for special rights for cultural groups or religious communities, it may permit these groups to continue with practices that are sexist and highly disadvantageous, if not harmful to women. Okin (1998; 1999a; 1999b; 2002) finds among most exponents of multiculturalism a weak commitment to women's rights and interests.

The non-liberal critics contend that the prevailing theories of liberal multiculturalism are essentially arguments for homogeneity, since the idea that one will support cultural diversity as long as the cultures are liberal. They observe that liberal multiculturalism is narrow: since its base is in a liberal theory of autonomy, it does not give enough support to non-liberal cultures (Deveaux 2000, Parekh 2000). The non-liberal multiculturalists stress on the intrinsic worth of culture.

Mouffe (1992) in response to group-differentiated citizenship points out that the solution is not to make gender or other group characteristics important to the concept of citizenship but to reduce their significance. She proposes a conception of citizenship which is neither gendered nor gender neutral but one based on real equality and liberty for all citizens. She stresses on political issues and claims, and observes that the public-private distinction needs to be redefined from case to case, according to the type of political demands, and not in a fixed and permanent way.

Miller (2000) considers identity politics as dangerous to the groups, which it is supposed to serve as the identities of these groups are much more open and fluid than recognised by the advocates of group identity. Identity politics emphasises on separateness creating a barrier to the politics of inclusion. This political mechanism of inclusion is important to reshape the public space, as an expression of shared national identity in a manner that, it is 'more hospitable to women, ethnic minorities and other groups without emptying them of content and destroying the underpinnings of democratic politics' (ibid: 80). Miller mentions J.S. Mill, who, despite lending support to the independence movements in Poland, Hungary and Italy, is appreciative of the role that national identities play in supporting liberal institutions (2006: 534). In the *Considerations on Representative Government* (1861), Mill argues that unless the several groups, which compose a society, have mutual sympathy and trust that is derived from a common nationality, it would be difficult to have free institutions. There would be no common interest to prevent government excesses and politics would become a zero-sum game, in which each group could only hope to profit by the exploitation of the others. Rule of law in such a situation usually becomes the first casualty. Miller also cites the example of Mazzini who argued passionately for Italian unity and independence while defending individual rights and republican government. He observes that liberal thinkers by the mid-nineteenth century "forged links between individual freedom, national independence, and representative government in opposing the imperial powers of Europe" (ibid: 534). Miller (1995; 2000; 2001) states that nationality is important and its recognition need not mean suppression of other sources of ethnicity or culture. One major reason as to why nationality is important is because it is the precondition of the pursuit of social justice, which cannot be pursued globally (1999a & b). The pursuit of social justice requires a measure of social solidarity and that would mean that citizens go along with the institutions which perform a redistributive function.

Waldron (1993) questions as to whether there exist distinct cultures as most of us are cultural fragments imbibing from a variety of ethno-cultural sources without feeling any sense of membership in or dependence on a particular culture. Defending the cosmopolitan alternative, he argues that most of the people in the modern world live 'in a kaleidoscope of culture' moving freely from one cultural tradition to another. Cultures can no longer remain monolithic in view of globalisation of trade, the increase in human mobility and the development of international institutions and communications. The only way that a culture could remain authentic is by adopting a wholly inauthentic way of life by denying the 'overwhelming reality of cultural interchange and global interdependence' (Waldron, cited in Kymlicka 1995b: 8). A liberal conception of the self give importance to the ability of individuals to question and revise in inherited ways of life which is in contrast to the communitarian perception of viewing people as embedded in particular cultures. Waldron rightly worries that this process of cultural interchange would be decisively hampered if the notion of protecting the 'authenticity' of minority cultures through minority rights is accepted.

Glazer (1975) and Walzer (1992) point out that expression and perpetuation of cultural identities should be left to the private sphere and, as Glazer observes the response of the state ought to be one of salutary neglect (1975: 25). Protection against discrimination and prejudice is provided to members of ethnic and national groups and they are free to maintain their identity and heritage, consistent with the rights of others but strictly in the private sphere.

Barry (2001) argues that multiculturalism is a fog that blots out recognition of class inequalities and human rights abuses. It is inconsistent with liberalism and disrespectful of liberal values and should be rejected. By replacing the idea of equal citizenship based on equal rights with culturally differentially rights, and in modifying the doctrine of equal citizenship, the multiculturalists are insensitive to the abuse of power which is inevitable in such a policy. Barry considers the concept of uniform citizenship and individual autonomy as an achievement of the Enlightenment. By criticising the Enlightenment and in advocating culturally differentiated rights, these theorists overlook the gross irregularities and inequities that existed prior to the Enlightenment. Barry finds an affinity between the Right and the Left, in their anti-liberal rhetoric as emphasis on special interests is an old policy of divide and rule beneficial to those who gain from the status quo. Such an emphasis denies any unified struggle for the common demand of the disadvantaged. There is a larger arena at the shared disadvantages of all like unemployment, poverty, low quality housing and inadequate public housing which can be tackled only from the point of view of the larger category of the disadvantaged. Particularity of group politics dissipates the political effort for mobilising people on the basis of a broad shared interest. Emphasis on cultural heterogeneity does not lead to either promotion of liberty or equality. Such policies are policies of retreat as group differentiated politics is inimical to the pursuit of a programme of universal material benefit to which all must have access. He insists that politics of multiculturalism undermines the politics of redistribution.

Barry is clear that the conflict between culture and law is over-emphasised as exemptions in the name of culture normally leads to sidetracking or breaking the law in the context of denial of individual rights within the group. He additionally regards multiculturalism and group rights discourses as endangering protections hard won over the centuries, in now liberal polities for individuals' religious freedoms and autonomy of family lives. Arguing within the framework provided by J.S. Mill, Barry writes:

> The defining feature of a liberal is, I suggest, that it is someone who holds that there are certain rights against oppression, exploitation and injury to which every single human being is entitled to lay claim, and that appeals to cultural diversity and pluralism under no circumstances trump the value of basic human rights. For [the multiculturalists] a society is to be conceived as a fictitious body whose real constituents are communities (ibid: 132–133, 300).

Contrary to 'Enlightenment liberalism' which Barry defends is 'reformation liberalism' propounded by Galston (1995) one which takes into account diversity and underlines the importance of 'differences among individuals and groups over such matters as the nature of the good life, sources of moral authority, reason versus faith, and the like' (1995: 521). Barry rejects reformation liberalism on three grounds—(1) liberal theory is based on the primacy of respect for individuals which included the culture as well provided the culture is not illiberal by itself and does not violate equal respect to other cultures; (2) on the question of liberalism's commitment to diversity as enhancing the range of choice, Barry argues that for liberals, individualism is more important than diversity and (3) regarding the question of public-private divide and the liberal commitment to non-intervention in the private sphere, Barry points out that throughout the process of history, liberalism has challenged both parental and paternal authority while protecting the individual from the group to which he belongs. On the question of every group having to conform to liberalism, Barry points that it is a free choice of the individuals to join any group or association with a rider that such groups are to be consistent with the legal protection that exists for all those outside the group. There are, however, two important preconditions—(a) all participants in the group are sane adults and (b) participation should be voluntary (ibid: 148). Groups may then do as they please, provided those who do not like the way the group functions can exist without facing undue costs (ibid: 150).

Barry (2002: 208) castigates multiculturalists for supporting national autonomy as 'they see it as a way of enabling nations within which illiberal values are politically dominant to pursue them in ways that violate the constraints imposed by any standard list of liberal rights, such as those embodied in the *Universal Declaration of Human Rights*, the US Constitution, the Canadian Charter of Rights and Freedoms or the European Convention on Human Rights'. Liberalism guarantees norms and institutional devices to ensure freedom from injustice and oppression and 'these do not (contrary to a popular multiculturalist claim) prevent different societies from expressing their differences politically' (ibid: 209). Barry stresses the need to subject minority cultural rights to democratic deliberation. 'If a cultural or a religious minority failed to gain a concession from the political process' then it 'could not properly claim that it had suffered an injustice' (ibid: 214).

CONCLUDING REMARKS

Ever since Durkheim and Weber paid attention to the cultural dimension of social, economic and political analyses, it has remained an important component of enquiry within liberalism. However, Tawney's critique of Weber on the factors of the rise of capitalism has brought in serious limitations of this approach as well. Multiculturalism is a continuation of this trend reinforced by the present postmodernist assertion of rejection of traditional post Enlightenment liberal intellectual tradition. Habermas gives an effective reply to such postmodernist assertions. Multiculturalism has remained a critique rather than becoming a viable alternative to traditional liberalism which since J.S. Mill has been able to refine and modernise its premises while retaining its core values to withstand the continuous onslaught. Twentieth century liberalism is conscious of the limits of philosophical enquiry and also the need to limit the political, and instead emphasise on building institutions that are accountable, and protect and enhance civil liberties. In the American context, Daniel Bell observes that the mainstay of the civil society is the existence of the Constitution and the Supreme Court. Within the larger framework of liberal politics, which inevitably consolidates a liberal society, much of the fears whether of recognition or participation can be taken care by not merely highlighting cultural differences but pointing out to the larger commonality of the disadvantaged.

Multiculturalism rejects the idea of the liberal state of J.S. Mill, Rawls and Barry as being neutral to differing conceptions of good life. For Kymlicka, liberalism is about autonomy. A perfectionist liberal, he rejects the idea of the liberal state of Mill, Rawls and Barry as being neutral to differing conceptions of good life. Autonomy is good, as long as it is anchored in choice, the quintessence of negative liberty according to Berlin. Dworkin (2006) asserts that liberal principles flow from two principles and these are—(1) each human life is intrinsically and equally valuable and (2) each person has an inalienable personal responsibility for identifying and realising the values in his life.

Multiculturalism's charge that liberalism's championing of individualism intrinsically incapacitates it from explaining some of the inherently collective features of political life are flawed. In the nineteenth century, European liberal thinkers, in contrast with their Enlightenment predecessors and their twentieth century successors with the exception of Berlin and Raz, understood the importance of collective identities to human beings, other than, and more particularistic than, that of the species as a whole. J.S. Mill, for instance, considered the sentiment of nationality an important source of social solidarity, and of political stability of a liberal society. Berlin's own life-long commitment to the idea of a Jewish nationalist homeland or Zionism is within the broader liberal framework of his thought. He also supported a Palestinian state for the Palestinians. He is clear that individual well-being demands common cultural forms, and that individual self-identity and self-esteem require the respectful recognition of these cultural forms by others. However, he does not advocate special rights for the members of minority cultures nor does he insist on the need of the state to extend official recognition ranging from legal exemptions to self-determination to minority cultures within its jurisdiction. He is not advocating assimilation but integration where the members of the group maintain their distinct identity within the family and voluntary associations while accepting the same public rights and duties as other citizens. He subordinates cultural identity and diversity to two values—(1) Freedom, understood as choice which implies that people have a right to choose how to live, a right which is common to all human beings. Cultures also have to promote diversity of goods. (2) A successful liberal politics cannot flourish in situations of chronic instability, like the Weimar Republic. It requires high levels of trust and cooperation and that is possible only if there exists within a society, a common cultural identity. Aggressive cultures which encourage divisiveness in society cannot sustain free institutions.

Both traditional liberalism and multiculturalism are concerned with addressing the problems of the disadvantaged. The former, since Green's revision of the doctrine which paved the way for Keynesian consensus and the inauguration of the welfare state in the post Second World War period and Rawls' theory focusing on the procedural elevation of the worst off, with its stress on non-discrimination and equal opportunity through the mechanism of constitutional guarantees of equal rights within the rule of law, ensures that individuals are not adversely affected because of their beliefs and ways of life in matters pertaining to education and employment. The guarantee and protection of individual rights which is the basis of a liberal state is still an important component of modern democracy. Multiculturalism with its emphasis on cultural exclusivity tries to bring in marginalised and neglected groups and redesigns the political space by accepting larger fragmentation and then, its incorporation. However, in doing so, not only are economic disadvantages relegated to secondary importance but the attempt to stress and highlight difference results in fragmentation of identities thus undermining the benefits which uniform citizenship based on one person one vote, and equal rights for all, after years of protracted struggle, guaranteed. Stressing any one identity to the point of excluding others make it meaningless as modern societies accepts the multiple identities of persons in which no one identity is decisive and that different identities—gender, class, language, religion, region, ethnicity, culture, colour and race—coalesce in a person. It is this spirit of unity in diversity, of the possibilities of co-existence of various identities in a person, which multiculturalism overlooks. Cultural exclusivity and differentiation beyond a point could be both oppressive and coercive. Within the groups, some practices could be discriminatory and oppressive. What is the possibility for redress of grievance available to the individual against such practices? What is the basis of their assumption that the group will protect and advance the rights of its individual members than the constitutional state? On these important questions the multiculturalists do offer satisfactory answers.

As Miller points out that 'by turning their backs on forms of identity, particularly national identities, that can bond citizens together in a single community, advocates of identity politics would destroy the conditions under which disparate groups in a culturally plural society can work together to achieve social justice for all groups. Minority groups are likely to have little bargaining power, so they must rely on appeals to the majority's sense of justice and fairness, and these will be effective only to the extent that majority and minorities sympathise and identify with each other' (2000: 4–5). Multiculturalism prevents the forging of a common public space which sustains democratic life. It questions the idea of shared moral values that exists among human beings despite their differences due to cultural backgrounds. Culture is fundamental as it is an important source of legitimacy and political power. For authority to be effective, it has to be rooted in people's experiences and identity. Only then it would win the loyalty of its people. However, power aims at unity while culture is diverse. By emphasising cultural diversity and overlooking, the mechanisms of promoting cultural consensus multicultural politics would be divisive.

Multiculturalism alleges that democratic procedures in Western democracies are not neutral but biased in favour of white, middle class males and against women and disadvantaged minorities. They maintain that the interests of these groups are best served not through existing forms of rational deliberation but by adopting new forms of political communication—greeting, rhetoric and story-telling. Their call for encouraging the use of native tongues rather than the official language is fraught with dangers as can be seen from the following incident. Sir William Jones, as the judge of Supreme Court of Calcutta from 1783 for the next 11 years, felt the need to have the knowledge of Persian and other Indian languages as he realised that the court orders based on translations from Indian languages which often were wrongly translated and that led to denial of justice. While many see the idea of English as the common lingua franca in colonial and independent India as privileging the elite, but what is overlooked is the continued discrimination and unfairness faced by those who are well-versed only in their mother tongues. A common language is necessary for justice and to ensure minimal mischief, apart from the fact that such knowledge would help in career advancement creating a climate of mutual respect which exclusivity denies and allows greater flowering of talent as the recent Indian writing in English prove. Liberalism accommodates cultural plurality and stresses on the need for shared identity. Multiculturalism by stressing on cultural difference and cultural exclusivity underestimates the safety values that exist within traditional liberal political theory for answering satisfactorily its concerns.

Environmentalism[7] or green political thought deals with matters relating to ecology by placing nature at the centre of debate and focus. It is critical of traditional political philosophy for being anthropocentric or humanist in its bias and considers human beings as one of the many species that exist in nature. Instead it believes that the health and well-being of the biotic community takes precedence over any of its individual members. Some dark green thinkers especially those who call themselves 'deep ecologists' press for a radical shift in our thinking from regarding ourselves at the pinnacle of a hierarchical pyramid to seeing ourselves as part of an interdependent web that consists of other species as well. The greens object to the view, dominant since the eighteenth century, that science and technology will help us to control and harness nature. They reject the idea of using nature only as a 'resource base', as a means to human ends and advocate the concept of sustainable development. The greens demand the need for laws and policies to safeguard and protect the environment. Furthermore, extending Aristotle's definition that the aim of politics is good life they point out that good life is not only for human beings but also for the non-human creatures and the biotic community who inhabit this planet. Extending Burke's idea of partnership between generations, they focus on not only the present generation but also the future and the unborn and stress that the way we live also impinges on posterity. Green political theory attempts to do two things—it is critical of the conventional ways of thinking about human beings and their proper place in the natural world; and secondly, it is constructive for it aims to outline the institutions of a society that values the natural world, practices sustainability and attends to long-term implications of present policies and strategies.

CONCLUSION

Doctrines like clash of civilisations or eurocentricism, and in recent times, a refined version of Said's Orientalism, are particularistic challenges to mainstream political theory that espouses the principle of universality, and is a minimum requirement everywhere. Furthermore, the contention of the Asian values school that the Western tradition is wholly individualistic can also be questioned. It is misleading to describe any tradition as being wholly individualistic or wholly communitarian for most of them is a happy blend of libertarian individualism with a concern for social welfare and common good. Aristotle had rightly established the link between altruism and self-interest and in a similar vein the early liberals also spoke of the link between private good and public good. While there must be respect and recognition for cultural plurality, it cannot become exclusionary and particularistic so as to cause divisions. By acknowledging the different streams of political theory one must not overlook the rich heritage and cumulative knowledge that its masters rightly considered its soul.

Further Readings

Bell, D., *Communitarianism and its Critics*, Clarendon Press, Oxford, 1993.

Connolly, W.E., *The Terms of Political Discourse*, Princeton University Press, NJ, Princeton, 1983.

Eisenstein, Z.A., *The Radical Future of Liberal Feminism*, Longman, New York, 1986.

Goodin, R.E. and Petit, P. (Eds.), *A Companion to Contemporary Political Philosophy*, Basil Blackwell, Oxford, 1993.

Gunnell, J.G., *Between Philosophy and Politics: The Alienation of Political Theory*, Amherst University of Massachusetts Press, Massachusetts, 1986.

Hall, S. and Giben, B. (Eds.), *Formations of Modernity*, Polity Press, Oxford, 1968.

Kymlicka, W., *Liberalism, Community and Culture*, Oxford University Press, Oxford, 1989.

Marsh, D. and Stoker, G., *Theory and Methods in Political Science*, Macmillan, London, 1995.

Mulhall, S. and Swift, A., *Liberals and Communitarians*, Basil Blackwell, Oxford, 1992.

Plant, R., *Community and Ideology*, Routledge and Kegan Paul, London, 1974.

Vincent, A., *Political Theory: Tradition and Diversity*, Cambridge University Press, Cambridge, 1997.

Endnotes

1. Deconstruction is a belief that all identities are socially constructed, in terms of a discourse that reflect the perspective and interests of the dominant group and subordinate the rest. Deconstruction's methodology is similar to that of postmodernism but with much limited capability. Deconstruction attempts to look at what is not present rather than what is present, the points of crisis and breakdown in a system than its more obvious positive side.
2. For Phillips, there is a parallel between the multicultural critique of liberal theory of rights and social justice, and the feminist critique of the distributive paradigm of liberal egalitarianism. She differs from the multiculturalists on the issues of patriarchy and the defence of traditionalism within some religious and cultural groups.
3. At the core of the arguments for recognising cultural diversity is the contention that individual identity is a social construct, taking off from where the communitarians left in their debate with the liberals in the late 1970s and early 1980s within Anglo American political theory. The publications of Rawls *A Theory of Justice* (1971) and Nozick's *Anarchy, State and Utopia* (1974) led Taylor, MacIntyre and Walzer to criticise the individualist underpinnings of their theories. However, by the middle of the 1980s, communitarianism peaked off mainly because its 'main theorists had either failed to come up with persuasive alternative conception of moral and political community (MacIntyre) or had conceded much of the normative terrain to the liberals while turning their attention to other issues of social ontology, history and interpretation (Taylor). Out of this stalemate emerged the sudden growth of interest in multiculturalism' (Kelly 2006: 9–10).
4. Those who claim themselves to be 'different' from the mainstream are broadly of two types. For some groups, the poor, women, ethnic minorities and immigrants, the demand for group rights is a demand for greater inclusion and participation in the mainstream society, as they feel excluded, under-represented or un-represented. Or, they might seek exemption from laws that disadvantage them economically or they want

school curriculum to recognise their contributions to society's culture and history. These groups accept the goal of national integration, for they desire to be part of mainstream society as full and equal members but only insist that recognition and accommodation of their 'difference' is needed to bring about national integration. The other group demanding differentiated citizenship reject the goal of national integration and wish to be self-governing, to freely develop their culture and are usually national minorities or distinct historical communities occupying their own territory with a distinct language and history. They do not want greater representation in the central government but transfer of power from the central government to their communities, often through some kind of federalism or local autonomy. They do not desire greater inclusion into the larger society but autonomy from it.

5. Israel Zangwill, an Anglo Jewish writer coined the term, in his play of the same name produced in 1908 in New York to refer to the manner in which immigrants who came to the US at the end of the nineteenth century were encouraged to think of themselves as Americans, gradually discard their culture of origin until, as in the action of the melting-pot, they become fully a part of the new alloy.

6. See section on Differentiated Citizenship in the Chapter on Citizenship.

7. See section on Elinor Ostrom in chapter on Development.

References

Ackerman, B. (1980), *Social Justice in the Liberal State*, Yale University Press, New Haven.

Allen, J.W. (1941), *Political Thought in the Sixteenth Century*, Methuen, London.

Almond, G.A. and Verba, S. (1963), *The Civic Culture: Political Attitudes and Democracy in Five Nations*, Princeton University Press, Princeton.

Althusser, L. (1969), *For Marx*, Allen Lane, London.

Amin, S. (1970), *Accumulation on a World Scale*, Monthly Review Press, New York.

Anderson, P. (1974), *Passages from Antiquity to Feudalism*, New Left Books, London.

Apter, D.E. (1965), *The Politics of Modernization*, University of Chicago Press, Chicago.

Arendt, H. (1951), *The Origins of Totalitarianism*, Meridian, New York.

____ (1958), *The Human Condition*, University of Chicago Press, Chicago.

____ (1968), 'What is authority?', in, *Between Past and Future: Six Exercises in Political Thought*, Viking Press, New York.

____ (1969), *On Revolution*, Viking Press, New York.

____ (1973), 'On Violence', in, *Crisis of the Republic*, Penguin, Harmondsworth.

Arrow, K. (1973), 'Some ordinalist-utilitarian notes on Rawls' Theory of Justice', *Journal of Philosophy*, **70**, pp. 245–263.

Ashcraft, R. (1986), *Revolutionary Politics and Locke's Two Treatises of Government*, Allen and Unwin, London.

Ash, T.G. (1990), 'Eastern Europe: The year of truth', *New York Review of Books*, pp. 17–22.

Ashe, G. (1968), *Gandhi*, Viking Press, New York.

Austin, J. (1873), *Lectures on Jurisprudence*, Unwin Books, London.

Avineri, S. (1969), *Karl Marx on Colonialism and Modernization: His Despatches and Other Writings on China, India, Mexico, the Middle East and North Africa*, Cambridge University Press, New York.

____ (1976), *Karl Marx: Social and Political Thought*, S. Chand, New Delhi.

Bachrach, P. and Baratz, M.S. (1962), 'The two faces of power', *American Political Science Review*, **56**(4), pp. 942–952.

Barbalet, J.M. (1997), *Citizenship*, World View Press, Delhi.

Barker, E. (1915), *Political Thought in England from Herbert Spencer to the Present Day*, Oxford University Press, Oxford.

____ (1942), *Reflections on Government*, Oxford University Press, Oxford.

____ (1960), *Social Contract: Locke, Hume Rousseau*, Oxford University Press, London.

____ (1976), *Principles of Social and Political Theory*, Oxford University Press, Calcutta.

Barry, B. (1965), *Political Argument*, Routledge and Kegan Paul, London.

____ (1967), 'Justice and Common Good', in, *Political Philosophy*, A. Quinton (Ed.), Oxford University Press, London.

____ (1973), *A Liberal Theory of Justice*, Clarendon Press, Oxford.

____ (1989), *Theories of Justice*, Harvester Wheatshef, London.

____ (1995), *Justice as Impartiality*, Clarendon Press, Oxford.

____ (2001): *Culture and Equality: An Egalitarian Critique of Multiculturalism*, Oxford, Polity.

Barry, N.P. (1995), *Introduction to Modern Political Theory*, Macmillan, London.

Beasley, C. (1999), *What is Feminism: An Introduction to Feminist Theory*, Sage, London.

Beitz, C.R. (1979), *Political Theory and International Relations*, Princeton University Press, Princeton.

____ (1984), 'Difficulties with Flathman's moderation thesis', *Social Philosophy and Policy*, **1**, pp. 172–185.

Bell, D. (1973), *The Coming of Post-Industrial Society*, Penguin, New York.

____ (1976), *On Cultural Contradictions of Capitalism*, Basic Books, New York.

____ (1979), 'Meritocracy and equality', in, *The New Egalitarianism*, D.F. Schaefer (Ed.), Kennikat Press, Washington.

____ (1990), 'On the fate of communism', *Dissent*, Spring, pp. 186–188.

____ (1990a), 'American exceptionalism revisited: The role of civil society', *The American Review*, pp. 9–14.

Benhabib, S. (1992), *Situating the Self*, Polity Press, Cambridge.

____ (1996): *Democracy and Difference: Contesting the Boundaries of the Political*, Princeton University Press, Princeton NJ.

Benn, S. (1978), 'Human rights—for whom and for what?', in, *Human Rights*, E. Kamenka and C. Tay (Eds.), Edward Arnold, London.

Benn, S.I. and Peters, R.S. (1959), *Social Principles and the Democratic State*, George and Allen, London.

Bentham, J. (1977), *A Fragment of Government*, J.H. Burns and H.L.A. Hart (Eds.), Athlone Press, London.

Berki, R.N. (1977): *The History of Political Thought: A Short Introduction*, Dent, London.

Berlin, Sir I. (1939), *Karl Marx*, Time Books, New York.

____ (1955–1956), 'Equality', *Proceedings of the Aristotelian Society*, **LVI**, pp. 301–326.

____ (1961), 'Equality as an ideal', in, *Justice and Social Policy*, F.A. Olafson (Ed.), Prentice Hall, Englewood Cliffs, New Jersey.

Berlin, Sir I. (1969), 'Historical inevitability', in, *Four Essays on Liberty*, Oxford University Press, Oxford.

____ (1979), 'Two concepts of liberty', in, *Four Essays on Liberty*, Oxford University Press, Oxford.

____ (1980), *Concepts and Categories*, B. Williams (Ed.), Hogarth Press, London.

____ (1992), *Conversations with Isaiah Berlin*, R. Jahanbegloo, Peter Halban, London.

Bernstein, E. (1961), *Evolutionary Socialism* (translated by E.C. Harvey), Schoken Books, New York.

Bessette, J. M. (1994): *The Mid Voice of Reason: Deliberative Democracy and American National Government,* University of Chicago Press, Chicago.

Bluhm, W.H. (1965), *Theories of Political System: Classics of Political Thought and Modern Political Analysis*, Prentice Hall, Englewood Cliffs, New Jersey.

Bobbio, N. (1986), *Which Socialism? Marxism and Democracy*, Polity Press, Cambridge.

____ (1987), *The Future of Democracy*, Polity Press, Cambridge.

____ (1990), *Liberalism and Democracy*, Polity Press, Cambridge.

Bodenheimer, S. (1974), 'Dependency and Imperialism: The Roots of Latin American Underdevelopment', in, *Readings in US Imperialism*, S.I. Fann and F. Hodge (Eds.), University Press, Boston.

Bohman, J and Rehg, W. (1997): *Deliberative Democracy: Essays on Reason and Politics*, The MIT Press, Massachusettes, London.

Bondurant, J. (1967), *Conquest of Violence: The Gandhian Philosophy of Conflict*, University of California Press, Berkeley.

Brecht, A. (1965), *Political Theory: The Foundations of Twentieth Century Political Thought*, The Times of India Press, Bombay.

Brezezinski, Z. (1979), *Between Two Ages: American's Role in the Technocratic Era*, John Day, New York.

Bull, H. (1977), *The Anarchical Society*, Macmillan, Cambridge.

Burke, E. (1969), *Reflections on the Revolution in France*, C.C. O'Brien (Ed.), Penguins, Harmondsworth.

Burnham, J. (1941), *The Managerial Revolution: What is Happening in the World*, John Day, New York.

Cahoone, L. (1996), *From Modernism to Postmodernism: An Anthology*, Blackwell, Cambridge.

Campbell, T. (1988), *Justice*, Macmillan, London.

Caporas, J.A. and Behrour, Z. (1981), 'An interpretation and evaluation of dependency theory', in, *Dependency to Development: Strategy to Overcome Underdevelopment and Inequality*, Boulder, Monthly Review Press, New York.

Carnoy, M. (1984), *The State and Political Theory*, Princeton University Press, Princeton, New Jersey.

Carr, E.H. (1979), *The Russian Revolution: Lenin to Stalin*, Penguin, Harmondsworth.

Carter, A. (1988), *The Politics of Women's Rights*, Longman, London.

Cassese, A. (1986), *International Law in a Divided World*, Clarendon Press, Oxford.

____ (1988), *Violence and Law in the Modern Age*, Polity Press, Cambridge.

Catlin, G. (1927), *The Science and Method of Politics*, Routledge, New York and London.

____ (1930), *A Study of the Principles of Politics*, Routledge, London and New York.

Chapman, J. (1993), *Politics, Feminism and the Reformation of Gender*, Routledge, London.

Chapman, J.W. (1975), 'Rawls' a theory of justice', *American Political Science Review*, **69**, pp. 588–593.

Chilcote, R.H. (1981), *Theories of Comparative Politics: The Search for a Paradigm Reconsidered*, Westview Press, Boulder.

Chodorow, N. (1978), *The Reproduction of Mothering: Psychoanalysis and the Sociology of Gender*, University of California Press, Berkeley, California.

Cobban, A. (1953), 'The decline of political theory', *Political Science Quarterly*, **LXVIII**, pp. 321–337.

____ (1960), *In Search of Humanity*, Braziller, New York.

Cohen, J. and Rogers, J. (1992): 'Secondary associations and democratic governance', *Politics and Society*, **20**, pp. 393–472.

Cohen, M. (1972), 'Liberalism and disobedience', *Philosophy and Public Affairs*, **1**(3), pp. 283–314.

____ (1997): 'Procedure and Substance in Deliberative Democracy' and 'Deliberation and Democratic Legitimacy' in *Deliberative Democracy: Essays on Reason and Politics* (Eds.), J. Bohman and W. Rehg, The MIT Press, Cambridge MA.

Coker, F.W. (1966), *Recent Political Thought*, The Words Press, Calcutta.

Colletti, L. (1969), *From Rousseau to Lenin*, Oxford University Press, New Delhi.

Collini, S., Winch, D. and Burrow, J. (1983), *That Noble Science of Politics*, Cambridge University Press, Cambridge.

Connolly, W. (1991), *Identity/Difference: Democratic Negotiations*, Cornell University Press, Ithaca, New York.

Coole, D. (1993), *Women in Political Theory: From Ancient Misogyny to Contemporary Feminism*, Harvester Whestsheaf, New York.

Coole, D. (1994), 'Women, gender and contract', in, *The Social Contract from Hobbes to Rawls*, David Boucher and Paul Kelly (Eds.), Routledge, London and New York.

Cornell, D. (1987), *Feminism as Critique*, Polity Press, Cambridge.

Cranston, M. (1967), *Freedom*, Basic Books, New York.

____ (1973), *What are Human Rights*? The Bodley Head, London.

____ (1986), *Philosophers and Pamphleteers: Political Theorists of the Enlightenment*, Oxford University Press, Oxford.

Crevald, M.V. (1999), *The Rise and Decline of the State*, Cambridge University Press, Cambridge.

Crick, B. (1963), *In Defence of Politics*, Pelican Books, Harmondsworth.

____ (1972), 'A Theory of Justice', *New Statesman*, pp. 591–602.

____ (1973), *Political Theory and Practice*, Basic Books, New York.

Crick, B. (1997), 'Sir Isaiah Berlin: The most intellectual of academics', *The Guardian*, p. 20.

Crosland, A. (1956), *The Future of Socialism*, Cape, London.

Cunningham, F. (2000): *Theories of Democracy: A Critical Introduction*, Routledge, London.

Curtis, M. (1961), *The Great Political Theories*, **2**, Avon, New York.

Dahl, R.A. (1957), 'The concept of power', *Behavioural Science*, pp. 202–203.

____ (1958), 'Political theory today', *World Politics*, **XI**, pp. 89–102.

____ (1963), *Modern Political Analysis*, Prentice Hall, Englewood Cliffs, New Jersey.

____ (1965), *A Preface to Democratic Theory*, University of Chicago Press, Chicago.

____ (1967), *Pluralist Democracy in the United States*, Rand McNally, Chicago.

____ (1985): *A Preface to Economic Democracy*, University of California Press, Berkeley.

____ (1986), *Democracy, Liberty and Equality*, Norwegian University Press, Oslo.

____ (1989): *Democracy and its Critics*, Yale University Press, New Haven, Connecticut.

____ (1996), 'Equality versus inequality', *Political Science and Politics*, Vol. 29, No. 4, December, pp. 639–648.

Dahrendorf, R. (1959), *Class and Class Conflict in Industrial Society*, Routledge and Kegan Paul, London.

____ (1968), *Essays in the Theory of Society*, Routledge and Kegan Paul, London.

Daly, H.E. (1977), *Steady State Economics*, W.H. Freeman, San Francisco.

Daniels, N. (1975), *Reading Rawls*, Basic Books, New York.

Davis, J.C. (1962), 'Towards a theory of revolution', *American Sociological Review*, **43**(1), p. 5.

Delphy, C. (1993), 'Rethinking sex and gender', *Women's Studies International Forum*, **16**(1), pp. 1–19.

Denitch, B. (1990), 'The triumph of capitalism', *Dissent*, Spring, pp. 177–180.

Derathe, R. (1950), *Le Rationalism de Jean-Jacques Rousseau*, Presses Universitaires de France, Paris.

Devaux, M. (2000): *Cultural Pluralism and Dilemmas of Justice*, Cornell University Press, Ithaca, NY.

Dicey, A.V. (1905), *Lectures on the Relation between Law and Public Opinion in England During the Nineteenth Century*, Oxford University Press, London.

Dickinson, H.T. (1977), *Liberty and Property: Political Ideology in the Eighteenth Century*, Holmes and Meier, New York.

Dietz, M. (1985), 'Citizenship with a feminist face: The problem with maternal thinking', *Political Theory*, **13**(1), pp. 19–37.

Djilas, M. (1990), 'Social democracy is a worldwide movement', *Moscow News Weekly*, 12 March, p. 7.

Dolgoff, S. (1973), *Bakunin on Anarchy*, edited, translated and introduced, Vintage, New York.

Dos, S.T. (1973), 'The crisis of development—Theory and the problem of dependence in Latin America', in, *Underdevelopment and Development*, S. Bernstein (Ed.), New Left Books, London.

Draper, H. (1977), *Karl Marx's Theory of Revolution: State and Bureaucracy*, Monthly Review Press, New York.

Drucker, P. (1989), 'The coming of the post industrial society', *New Perspective Quartely*, **6**(1), pp. 44–46.

Dryzek, J.S. (2000): *Deliberative Democracy and Beyond*, Oxford University Press, Oxford.

Duncan, G. and Lukes, S. (1963), 'The new democracy', in, *Essays in Social Theory*, S. Lukes (Ed.), Macmillan, London.

Dunn, J. (1968), *The Political Thought of John Locke—An Historical Account of the Argument of the Two Treaties of Government*, Cambridge University Press, Cambridge.

____ (1979), *Western Political Theory in the Face of the Future*, Cambridge University Press, Cambridge.

____ (1980), *Political Obligation in its Historical Context: Essays in Political Theory*, Cambridge University Press, Cambridge.

____ (1989), *Modern Revolutions*, Clarendon Press, London.

Dunning, W.H. (1902), *A History of Political Theories*, Macmillan, New York.

____ (1966), A *History of Political Theories: From Luther to Montesquieu*, Central Book Depot, Allahabad.

Durant, W. (1939), *The Story of Civilization*, **11**, Simon and Schuster, New York.

Dworkin, R. (1977), *Taking Rights Seriously*, Harvard University Press, Cambridge, Massachusettes.

____ (1981), 'What is equality? Part I: Equality of welfare' and 'What is equality? Part II: Equality of resources', *Philosophy and Public Affairs*, **10**(3 and 4), pp. 185–246 and 283–345.

____ (2006): *Is Democracy Possible Here? Principles for a New Political Debate*

Easton, D. (1953), *The Political System: An Inquiry into the State of Political Science*, Wiley, New York.

____ (1965), *A Systems Analysis of Political Life*, Prentice Hall, Engelwood Cliffs, New Jersey.

____ (1997), 'The future of the postbehavioural phase in political science', in, *Contemporary Empirical Political Theory*, K.R. Monroe (Ed.), University of California Press, Berkeley.

Ebenstein, W. (1974), *Great Political Thinkers*, Oxford and IBH, New Delhi.

Echlin, E.P. (1993), 'Theology and sustainable development after Rio', *The Newman*, **30**, pp. 2–7.

Eckstein, H. (1963), 'A perspective on comparative politics, past and present', in, *Comparative Politics: A Reader*, H. Eckstein and D.E. Apter (Eds.), Free Press of Glencoe, London.

Eisenstadt, S.N. (1964), 'Modernization and conditions of sustained growth', *World Politics*, **16**, pp. 576–594.

Eisenstein, Z. (1996), 'Equalizing privacy and specifying equality', in, *Revisioning the Political: Feminist Reconstructions of Traditional Concepts in Western Political Theory*, N.J. Hirschman and C.D. Stefano (Eds.), Westview Press, Harper Collins, London.

Elliot, C. (1973), 'Problems of Marxist revisionism', *Journal of the History of Ideas*, **28**, pp. 71–89.

Elshtain, J.B. (1981), *Public Man, Private Woman: Women in Social and Political Thought*, Oxford, Martin Robson and Princeton University Press, London & Princeton.

Emmanuel, A. (1969), *Unequal Exchange: A Study of Imperialism of Trade*, New Left Books, London.

Engels, F. (1977), *Selected Writings*, Progress Publishers, Moscow.

Etzioni, A. (1995), *The Spirit of the Community*, Fontana, London.

Falk, R. (1969), 'The interplay of Westphalia and charter conceptions of international law', in, *The Future of the International Legal Order*, Princeton University Press, Princeton.

____ (1995), *On Humane Governance: Towards a New Global Politics*, Polity Press, Cambridge.

Fanon, F. (1961), *The Wretched of the Earth*, Penguin, Harmondworth.

Feinberg, J. (1973), *Social Philosophy*, Prentice Hall, Englewood Cliffs, New Jersey.

____ (1980), *Rights, Justice and the Bounds of Liberty*, Princeton University Press, Princeton.

____ (1998), 'Freedom and liberty', in, *Routledge Encyclopedia of Philosophy*, Craig, E. (Ed.) Routledge, London and New York.

Ferguson, A. (1792): *Principles of Moral and Political Science*, Edinburgh, UK.

Fieldhouse, D.K. (1999), *The West and the Third World Trade, Colonialism, Dependence and Development*, Basil Blackwell, Oxford.

Figgis, J.N. (1913), *Churches in the Modern State*, Allen and Unwin, London.

Filmer, R. (1991), *Patriarcha and Other Writings*, J.P. Sommerville (Ed.), Cambridge University Press, Cambridge.

Finley, M.I. (1951), *The Ancient Greeks*, Penguin, Harmondsworth.

Finnis, J. (1980), *Natural Law and Natural Rights*, Oxford University Press, Oxford.

Firestone, S. (1979), *The Dialectic of Sex*, Virago, London.

Fisk, M. (1975), 'History and reason in Rawls's moral theory', in, *Reading Ratals*, N. Daniels (Ed.), Basic Books, New York.

Focault, M. (1980), *Power/Knowledge*, C. Gordon (Ed.), Harvester, Brighton.

Forsyth, M.G. (1987), 'State', in, *The Blackwell Encyclopaedia of Modern Political Thought*, D. Miller (Ed.), Basil Blackwell, Oxford.

____ (1994), 'Hobbes's contractarianism: A comparative analysis', in, *The Social Contract from Hobbes to Rawls*, D. Boucher and P. Kelly (Eds.), Routledge, London and New York, Routledge.

Fox-Genovese, E. (1991), *Feminism Without Illusions: A Critique of Individualism*, University of North Carolina Press, Chapel Hil.

Frank, A.G. (1967), *Capitalism and Underdevelopment in Latin America*, Fontana, London.

Frank, A.G. (1972), 'The development of underdevelopment and sociology of development and underdevelopment of sociology', in, *Dependence and Underdevelopment—Latin America's Political Economy*, Cockcroft, Frank and Johnson (Eds.), Monthly Review Press, New York.

____ (1978), *Dependent Accumulation and Underdevelopment*, London, Fontana.

Freeden, M. (1998), *Rights*, World View Publications, Delhi.

Friedrich, C.J. (1973), 'Authority, reason and discretion', in, *Concepts in Social and Political Philosophy*, R. Flatham (Ed.), Macmillan, New York.

Friedrich, C.J. and Brzezinski, Z. (1965), *Totalitarian Dictatorship and Autocracy*, Harvard University Press, Cambridge, Massachusettes.

Fukuyama, F. (1992), *The End of History and the Last Man*, Penguin, Harmondsworth.

Galbraith, J.K. (1990), 'Communism failed because it did not adapt', *The Times of India*, 27 February.

Gallie, D. (1955–1956), 'Essentially contested concepts', *Proceedings of the Aristotelian Society*, **56**, pp. 167–198.

____ (1983), *Social Inequality and Class Radicalism in France and Britain*, Cambridge University Press, London.

Galston, W. (1995): 'Two Concepts of Liberalism', *Ethics*, 105(3), pp. 516–534.

Gandhi, M.K. (1908), *Hind Swaraj*, Navjivan, Ahmedabad.

____ (1947), *The India of My Dreams* compiled by R.K. Prabhu, Foreward by Dr. Rajendra Prasad, Hindi Kitabs, Bombay.

Gauthier, D. (1986), *Morals by Agreement*, Oxford University Press, Oxford.

Gellner, E. (1994), *Conditions of Liberty: Civil Society and its Rivals*, Hamish Hamilton, London.

Germino, D. (1967), *Beyond Ideology: The Revival of Political Theory*, Harper and Row, New York.

Gettel, R.G. (1924), *History of Political Thought*, George Allen and Unwin, London.

Gewirth, A. (1982), *Human Rights*, University of Chicago Press, Chicago.

____ (1984), 'A reply to Danto', *Social Philosophy and Policy*, **1**, pp. 31–33.

Giddens, A. (1974), *The Class Structure of the Advanced Societies*, Harmondsworth, London.

____ (1982), 'Class division, class conflict and citizenship rights', in: *His Profiles and Critiques of Social Theory*, Macmillan, London.

____ (1984), *The Constitution of Society*, Polity Press, Cambridge.

____ (1985), *The Nation-State and Violence*, London, Macmillan.

____ (1987), *Social Theory and Modern Society*, Polity Press, Cambridge.

Gilligan, C. (1982), *In a Different Voice*, Harvard University Press, Cambridge Massachusettes.

Glaser, D. (1995), 'Normative theory', in, *Theory and Methods in Political Science*, D. Marsh and G. Stokes (Eds.), Macmillan, London.

Glazer, N. (1975): *Affirmative Discrimination: Ethnic Inequality and Public Policy*, Basic Books, New York.

____ (1997): *We Are All Multiculturalists Now*, Harvard University Press, Cambridge MA.

Golding, M.P. (1984), 'The primacy of welfare rights', *Social Philosophy and Policy*, **1**, pp. 34–48.

Goldsmith, E. (1992), *The Way*, Faber, London.

Goldstone, J.A.G. (1987), 'Theories of Revolution', in, *The Blackwell Encyclopaedia of Modern Political Thought*, D. Miller (Ed.), Basil Blackwell, Oxford.

Goodwin, B. (1992), *Using Political Ideas*, John Wiley and Sons, Chicester.

Gottfried, P. and Fleming, T. (1988), *The Conservative Movement*, Twayne Publishers, Boston.

Graf, James A. (1994): 'Human rights, peoples, and the right of self determination' in J. Baker (Ed.), *Group Rights*, University of Toronto Press, Toronto.

Gray, J. (1992), *The Moral Foundations of Market Institutions*, Institute of Economic Affairs, London.

____ (1995), *Berlin*, Fontana, London.

Green, T.H. (1888), *Lectures on the Principles of Political Obligation*, Cambridge University Press, Cambridge.

Gross, E. (1986), 'Conclusion: What is feminist theory?', in, *Feminist Challenges: Social and Political Theory*, Allen and Unwin, London.

Gunnell, J.G. (1978), 'The myth of the tradition', *American Political Science Review*, **72**, pp. 122–134.

____ (1987), 'Political theory and political science', in, *The Blackwell Encyclopaedia of Political Thought*, D. Miller (Ed.), Blackwell, Oxford.

Gurr, T.R. (1980), *Why Men Rebel*, Princeton University Press, Princeton.

Gutman, A. (1980), *Liberal Equality*, Cambridge University Press, Cambridge.

____ (1987), 'Equality', in, *The Blackwell Encyclopaedia of Political Thought*, D. Miller (Ed.), Blackwell, Oxford.

Habermas, J. (1972), *Knowledge and Human Interests*, J.J. Shapiro (Trans.), Heinemann, London.

____ (1985), 'Civil disobedience: Litmus test for the democratic constitutional state', *Berkeley Journal of Sociology*, **30**, pp. 95–116.

____ (1987), 'The hermeneutic claim to universality', in, *Interpreting Politics*, M.T. Gibbons (Ed.), Basil Blackwell, Oxford.

____ (1996): 'Three Normative Models of Democracy' in *Democracy and Difference: Contesting the Boundaries of the Political*, (Ed.) S. Benhabib, Princeton University Press, Princeton NJ.

____ (1998): *Between Facts and Norms: Contributions to a Discourse Theory of Law and Democracy*, MIT Press, Cambridge MA.

Hacker, A. (1961), *Political Theory: Philosophy, Ideology and Science*, Macmillan, New York.

Hague, R., Harrop, M. and Breslin, W. (1994), *Comparative Government and Politics*, 3rd ed., Macmillan, Basingstoke.

Halsey, A.H. (1984), 'T.H. Marshall: Past and present', *Sociology*, **18**(1).

Hampsher Monk, I.W. (1992): *Modern Political Thought from Hobbes to Marx*, Basil Blackwell, Oxford.

Hamsphire, S. (1972), 'A new philosophy of the just society', *New York Review of Books*, 24 February, pp. 34–39.

Harding, N. (1981), *Lenin's Political Thought*, St. Martin's Press, New York.

Hare, R.M. (1980): Justice and Equality in *Justice: Alternative Political Perspectives* (Ed.) James Sterba, Wadsworth Publishing Company, Belmont California.

Harrington, M. (1962), *The Other America: Poverty in the United States*, Penguin, Baltimore.

Harris, N. (1986), *The End of the Third World—Newly Industrialized Countries and the Decline of Ideology*, Penguin, Harmondsworth.

Harsanyi, J.C. (1975), 'Can the maximin principle serve as a basis for morality', *American Political Science Review*, **69**, pp. 594–606.

Hart, H.L.A. (1955), 'Are there any natural rights?, *Philosophical Review*, **64**, pp. 175–191.

____ (1967), 'Are there any natural rights', in, *Political Philosophy*, A. Quinton (Ed.), Oxford University Press, London.

____ (1968), 'Austin John', in, *Encyclopaedia of Social Sciences*, Macmillan, London.

____ (1975), 'Rawls on liberty and its priority', in, *Reading Rawls*, N. Daniels (Ed.), Basic Books, New York.

Hartney, M. (1991): 'Some Confusions concerning collective rights', *Canadian Journal of Law and Jurisprudence*, **4**, pp. 293–314.

Hayek, F.A. (1944), *The Road to Serfdom*, Routledge and Kegan Paul, London.

____ (1955), *The Counter-Revolution of Science: Studies on the Abuse of Reason*, The Free Press, Glencoe.

____ (1960), *The Constitution of Liberty*, Routledge and Kegan Paul, London.

____ (1976), *The Mirage of Social Justice*, Routledge and Kegan Paul, London.

Heater, D. (1990), *Citizenship: The Civic Ideal in World History, Politics and Education*, Orient Longman, London.

Hearnshaw, F.J. (1924), 'Bodin and the genesis of the doctrine of sovereignty', in, *Tudor Studies*, R.W. Seton-Watson (Ed.), pp. 109–132, Oxford University Press, Oxford.

Hernstein, R. and Murray, C. (1994), *The Bell Curve*, Free Press, New York.

Hegel, G.W.F. (1969), *Philosophy of Right*, T.M. Knox (Trans.), Oxford University Press, Oxford.

____ (1976): *Philosophy of Right*, T.M. Knos (Trans.) Oxford University Press, Oxford.

Held, D. (1983), 'The Frankfurt School', in, *A Dictionary of Marxist Thought*, T. Bottomore (Ed.), Blackwell, Oxford.

____ (1987), *Models of Democracy*, Polity Press, Cambridge.

____ (1989), *Political Theory and the Modern State*, Polity Press, Cambridge.

____ (1991), *Political Theory Today*, Polity Press, Cambridge.

____ (1992), 'The development of the modern state', in, *Formations of Modernity*, S. Hall and B. Gieben (Eds.), Polity Press, Cambridge.

____ (1995), *Democracy and the Global Order*, Polity Press, Cambridge.

Held, D, Archibugi, D and M. Köhler (1998): Re-Imagining Political Community: Studies in Cosmopolitan Democracy, Stanford University Press, Stanford California.

Hempel, G.G. (1966), *Philosophy of Natural Science*, Prentice Hall, Englewood Cliffs, New Jersey.

Heywood, A. (1999): *Political Theory: An Introduction*, 2nd ed., Macmillan, London.

Hindess, B. (1996), *Discourses on Power: From Hobbes to Foucault*, Basil Blackwell, Cambridge.

Hirschman, N.J. (1996), 'Rethinking obligation for feminism', in, *Revisioning the Political: Feminist Reconstructions of Traditional Concepts in Western Political Theory*, N.J. Hirschman and C.D. Stefano (Eds.), Harper Collins, Westview Press.

Hobbes, T. (1991), *Leviathan*, R. Tuck (Ed.), Cambridge University Press, Cambridge.

Hobhouse, L.T. (1911), *Liberalism*, Oxford University Press, New York.

Hohfeld, W. (1919), *Fundamental Legal Conceptions*, Yale University Press, New Haven.

Hunt, R.N. (1975), *The Political Ideas of Marx and Engels*, Yale University Press, New Haven.

Huntington, S.P. (1968), *Political Order in Changing Societies*, Yale University Press, New Haven.

____ (1992), *The Third Wave: Democratization in the Late Twentieth Century*, University of Oklahoma Press, Oklahoma.

Ingelhart, R. (1977), *The Silent Revolution: Changing Values and Political Styles Among Western Publics*, Princeton University Press, Princeton.

Ionescu, G. (1976), *The Political Thought of Saint Simon*, Oxford University Press, Oxford.

Jennings, J. (1994), 'Rousseau, social contract and the modern leviathan', in, *The Social Contract from Hobbes to Rawls*, D. Boucher and P. Kelly (Eds.), Routledge, London and New York.

Johnson, C. (1966), *Revolutionary Change*, Beacon Press, Boston.

____ (1982), *MITI and the Japanese Miracle*, Stanford University Press, Stanford, CA.

Jordan, A.G. and Richardson, J.J. (1987), *Government and Pressure Groups in Britain*, Clarendon Press, Oxford.

Kaufman, R., Cheronsky, H. and Gellar, D. (1979), 'A preliminary test of the theory of dependency', *Comparative Politics*, April, pp. 26–42.

Keane, J. (1998): *Civil Society and the State*, Verso, London.

Kelly, P. (1994), 'Justifying, 'Justice: Contractarianism, communitarianism and the foundations of contemporary liberalism,' in, *The Social Contract from Hobbes to Rawls*, D. Boucher and P. Kelly (Eds.), Routledge, London and New York.

Kelly, P. (Ed.), (2006): *Multiculturalism Reconsidered*, Polity, Cambridge.

Kelsen, H. (1960), *What is Justice*? University of California Press, Berkeley.

Keohane, N. (1980), *Philosophy and the State in France*, Princeton University Press, Princeton, New Jersey.

Kennedy, P. (1988), *The Rise and Fall of the Great Powers: Economic Change and Military Conflict from 1500–2000*, Fontana, London.

King, P. (1987), 'Sovereignty', in, *The Blackwell Encyclopaedia of Political Thought*, D. Miller (Ed.), Blackwell, Oxford.

Kolakowski, L. (1981), *Main Currents of Marxism*, **3**, Oxford University Press, Oxford.

Kostrzewa, W., Nunnenkamp, P. and Schmieding, H. (1990), 'A Marshall Plan for Middle and Eastern Europe', *The World Economy*', Vol. 13(1), March, pp. 27–49.

Kothari, R. (1971), *Political Economy of Development*, Orient Longman, Bombay.

____ (1988), *Rethinking Development: In Search for Humane Alternatives*, Ajantha, Delhi.

Kristol, I. (1972), 'About equality', *Commentary*, pp. 41–47.

____ (1978), *Two Cheers for Capitalism*, Basic Books, New York.

____ (1979), 'About equality', in, *The New Egalitarianism*, D.L. Schaefer (Ed.), Kennikat Press, Washington.

Krouse, R.W. (1983), 'Classical images of democracy in America: Madison and Tocqueville', in, *Democratic Theory and Practice*, G. Duncan (Ed.), Cambridge University Press, Cambridge.

Kuhn, T. (1970), *The Structure of Scientific Revolution*, University of Chicago Press, Chicago.

Kymlicka, W. (1989): *Liberalism, Community and Culture*, Oxford, Oxford University Press.

____ (1995a), *Multicultural Citizenship: A Liberal Theory of Minority Rights*, Oxford University Press, New York.

____ (Ed.), (1995b): *The Rights of Minority Cultures*, Oxford, Oxford University Press.

Laski, H.J. (1936), *The Rise of European Liberalism*, Unwin Books, London.

____ (1979), *A Grammar of Politics*, S. Chand, Delhi.

Lasky, M.J. (1976), *Utopia and Revolution*, Macmillan, London.

Laslett, P. (1957), 'Introduction', in, *Philosophy, Politics and Society*, 1st Series, P. Laslett and W.G. Runciman (Eds.), Blackwell, Oxford.

____ (1960), *John Locke's Two Treaties of Government*, Cambridge University Press, Cambridge.

Lasswell, H.D. (1936), *Politics: Who Gets What, When, How*, McGraw-Hill, New York.

Lasswell, H.D. and Kaplan, A. (1952), *Power and Society: A Framework for Political Inquiry*, Yale University Press, New Haven.

Leftwich, A. (1984), *What is Politics? The Activity and its Study*, Basil Blackwell (Ed.), Cambridge.

Lehning, A. (1973), *Michael Bakunin: Selected Writings*, Jonathan Cape, London.

Lele, S.M. (1991), 'Sustainable development: A critical review', *World Development*, **19**(6), pp. 607–621.

Lenin, V.I. (1977), *The State and Revolution and Proletarian Revolution and Renegade Kautsky*, Progress Publishers, Moscow.

Lessnoff, M.H. (1971), 'John Rawls' theory of justice', *Political Studies*, **19**, pp. 63–80.

____ (Ed.), (1990), *Social Contract Theory*, Basil Blackwell, Oxford.

____ (1999), *Political Philosophers of the Twentieth Century*, Basil Blackwell, Oxford.

Lichtheim, G. (1961), *Marxism, A Historical and Critical Study*, Routledge, London.

____ (1963), *The New Europe: Today and Tomorrow*, Frederick A. Praeger, New York.

____ (1975), *A Short History of Socialism*, Fontana, Glasgow.

Lindbolm, C.E. (1977), *Politics and Markets*, Basic Books, New York.

Lindsay, A.E. (1914), 'The state in recent political theory', *Political Quartely*, **I**, pp. 128–145.

Linklater, A. (1982): Men and Citizens in the theory of International Relations, Macmillan, London.

Lipset, S.M. (1963), *Political Man*, Doubleday, New York.

____ (1964), 'Introduction', In, *Class, Citizenship and Social Development* by Marshall, Westport, Greenwood Press, Connecticut.

____ (Ed.), (1979), *The Third Century: America as a Post-Industrial Society*, Hoover Institute Press, Standford.

____ (1988), 'Neo-conservatives: Myth and reality', *Society*, July/August, pp. 29–37.

Lively, J. (1975), *Democracy*, Basil Blackwell, Oxford.

Locke, J. (1960), *Two Treaties on Civil Government*, P. Laslett (Ed.), Cambridge University Press, Cambridge.

Lopez, M. (2000): *The Origins of Multiculturalism in Australian Politics*, Melbroune, Melbroune University Press.

Lloyd, G. (1984): *The Man of Reason; "Male" and "Female" in Western Philosophy*, University of Minnesota Press, Minneapolis.

Lukes, S. (1974), *Power: A Radical View*, Macmillan, London.

Luttwak, E. (1999), *Trubo Capitalism: Winners and the Losers in the Global Economy*, Harper Collins, New York.

Luxemburg, R. (1961), *Russian Revolution: Leninism or Marxism*, Introduction by B.R. Wolfe, University of Michigan Press, Ann Arbor.

Lyons, D. (1972), 'Rawls versus utilitarianism', *The Journal of Philosophy*, **18**, pp. 535–545.

Lyotard, J.F. (1984), *The Postmodern Condition*, Manchester University Press, Manchester.

MacCallum Jr., G. (1967), 'Negative and positive freedom', *Philosophical Review*, **76**(3), pp. 312–334.

MacCormick, N. (1982), *Legal Right and Social Democracy*, Oxford University Press, Oxford.

____ (1987), 'John Austin', in, *The Blackwell Encyclopaedia of Political Thought*, D. Miller (Ed.), Blackwell, Oxford.

MacFarlane, L.J. (1985), *The Theory and Practice of Human Rights*, Temple Smith, Hounslow.

Maclntyre, A. (1971), A *Short History of Ethics*, Macmillan, New York.

____ (1981), *After Virtue*, Duckworth, London.

____ (1988), *Whose Justice? Which Rationality Justice?*, Duckworth, London.

Maclver, R.M. (1926), *The Modern State*, Oxford University Press, Oxford.

Mack, M.P. (1955), 'The fabians and the utilitarians', *Journal of the History of Ideas*, **16**, pp. 76–88.

____ (1977), *Democratic Theory: Essays in Retrieval*, Clarendon Press, Oxford.

Mack, M.P. and Mackinnon, C. (1989), *Towards a Feminist Theory of the State*, Harvard University Press, Cambridge, Massachusettes.

Mack, M.P. and Macpherson, C.B. (1966), *The Real World of Democracy*, Oxford University Press, Oxford.

Mack, M.P. and Macpherson, C.B. (1973), *The Political Theory of Possessive Individualism—Hobbes to Locke*, Clarendon Press, Oxford.

Magee, B. (1984), *Popper*, Fontana, London.

Mann (1986), *The Sources of Power*, Cambridge University Press, Cambridge.

Marcuse, H. (1969), 'Repressive tolerance' in R.P. Wolff, B. Moore Jr. and H. Barcuse, *A Critique of Pure Tolerance*, Jonathan Cape, London.

____ (1972), *Studies in Critical Philosophy*, New Left Books, London.

Marshall, T.E. (1945), 'Work and wealth', in, *Class, Citizenship and Social Development*, Greenwood Press, Westport, Connecticut.

____ (1950), *Sociology at the Crossroads and Other Essays*, Heinemann, London.

Martin, R. (1985), *Rawls and Rights*, University of Kansas Press, Kansas.

Marx, K.H. (1975), *The Communist Manifesto*, Progress Publishers, Moscow.

____ (1977), *Selected Works*, **3**, Progress Publishers, Moscow.

____ (1989), 'Reproducing the concrete by way of thought and the real history of the relations of production', in, *Readings from Karl Marx*, D. Sayer (Ed.), Routledge, London.

Maximoff, G.P. (Ed.) (1953), *The Political Philosophy of Bakunin: Scientific Anarchism*, Free Press, Glencoe.

McCloskey, H.J. (1976), 'Rights—Some Conceptual Issues', *Australasian Journal of Philosophy*, **54**, pp. 99–115.

McIlwain, C.H. (1932), *Growth of Political Thought in the West*, Macmillan, New York.

Meadows, D.H., Randers, J. and Behrens, W.W. (1972), *The Limits to Growth*, Earth Island, London.

Medvedev, R. (1982), 'USSR after Brezhnev', *Marxism Today*, pp. 15–27.

Mendus, S. (1992), 'Losing the faith: Feminism and democracy', in, *Democracy: The Unfinished Journey 508 BC to AD 1993*, (Ed.), J. Dunn, Oxford University Press, Oxford.

Michels, R. (1962), *Political Parties*, Free Press, New York.

Miliband, R. (1965), 'Marx and the state' the Socialist Regester, pp. 309–319.

____ (1969), *The State in Capitalist Society*, Weidenfeld and Nicholson, London.

____ (1977), *Marxism and Politics*, Oxford University Press, Oxford.

Mill, J.S. (1902), *Principles of Political Economy*, Unwin Books, London.

____ (1976), *Utilitarianism, On Liberty and Considerations on Representative Government*, Fontana, London.

Miller, D. (1976), *Social Justice*, Clarendon Press, Oxford.

____ (Ed.) (1991), *Liberty*, Oxford University Press, Oxford.

____ (1999a): *On Nationality*, Clarendon, Oxford.

____ (1999b): 'Justice and Global Inequality' in A. Hurrell and N. Woods (Ed.), *Inequality, Globalization and World Politics*, Oxford University Press, Oxford.

____ (2000), *Citizenship and National Identities*, Polity Press, Cambridge.

____ (2001): 'Nationality in Divided Societies' in A.G. Gagnon and J. Tully (Eds.), *Multinational Democracies*, Cambridge University Press, Cambridge.

____ (2006): 'Nationalism in J.S. Dryzek, B. Honig and A. Phillips (Eds.), *The Oxford Handbook of Political Theory*, Oxford University Press, Oxford.

Miller, J.D.B. (1962), *The Nature of Politics*, Pelican Books, Harmondsworth.

Mills, C.W. (1956), *The Power Elite*, Oxford University Press, New York.

Mitchell, J. (1974), *Psychoanalysis and Feminism*, Penguin, Harmondsworth.

Modelski, G. (1972), *Principles of World Politics*, Free Press, New York.

Moodie, G.C. (1984), 'Politics is about government', in, *What is Politics? The Activity and its Study*, A. Leftwich (Ed.), Basil Blackwell, Oxford.

Morris, M.D. (1979), *Measuring the Conditions of the World's Poor: The Physical Quality of Life Index*, Pergamon Press, New York.

Morrow, J. (1998): *History of Political Thought: A Thematic Introduction*, Macmillan, London.

Mosca, G. (1939), *The Ruling Class*, McGraw Hill, New York.

Mouffe, C. (1992): 'Feminism, citizenship and radical democratic politics', in J. Butler and J. Scott (Eds.), *Feminists Theorise the Political*, Routledge, New York.

Moynihan, D.P. (1976), *The Politics of Guaranteed Income under Nixon Administration*, Basic Books, New York.

Nagel, T. (1973), 'Rawls on justice', *Philosophical Review*, **82**, pp. 220–234.

____ (2005): The Problem of Global Justice, *Philosophy and Public Affairs*, **33**, No. 2, pp. 113–147.

Naess, A. (1989), *Ecology, Community and Lifestyle*, Cambridge University Press, Cambridge.

Narveson, J. (1991): 'Collective Rights?' *Canadian Journal of Law and Jurisprudence*, **4**, pp. 329–345.

Nicholson, P.P. (1984), 'Politics and force', in, *What is Politics? The Activity and its Study*, A. Leftwich (Ed.), Basil Blackwell, Oxford.

Nisbet, R. (1962), *The Quest for Community*, Oxford University Press, New York.

____ (1974a), 'The pursuit of equality', *The Public Interest*, **35**, pp. 103–120.

____ (1974b), 'Rousseau and equality', *Encounter*, September, pp. 44–48.

____ (1975), *The Twilight of Authority*, Basic Books, New York.

Nordlinger, E. (1981), *The Autonomy of the Democratic State*, Harvard University Press, Cambridge, Massachusettes.

Nozick, R. (1974), *Anarchy, State and Utopia*, Basic Books, New York.

Nussbaum, M.C. (2000), *Women and Human Development: The Capabilities Approach*, Cambridge University Press, Cambridge.

____ (2006): *Frontiers of Justice: Disability, Nationality and Species Membership,* The Belknap Press Harvard University Press, Cambridge, MA.

Oakeshott, M.J. (1933), *Experience and its Modes*, Cambridge University Press, Cambridge.

____ (1956), 'Political education', in, *Philosophy, Politics and Society*, 1st series, P. Laslett and W.G. Runciman (Eds.), Blackwell, Oxford.

____ (1967), *Rationalism in Politics*, Methuen, London.

____ (1975), *Hobbes on Civil Association*, Basil Blackwell, Oxford.

Okin, S.M. (1979), *Women in Western Political Thought*, Princeton University Press, Princeton.

____ (1989), *Justice, Gender and the Family*, Basic Books, New York.

____ (1991), Gender, the public and the private, in, *Political Theory Today*, D. Held (Ed.), Polity Press, Cambridge.

____ (1998): 'Feminism and Multiculturalism: some tensions', *Ethics*, **108**, pp. 661–684.

Okin, S.M. (1999a): 'Is Multiculturalism bad for women?' in J. Cohen, M. Howard and M. Nussbaum (Eds.), *Is Multiculturalism bad for Women*? Princeton, NJ: Princeton University Press.

____ (1999b) 'Reply' in J. Cohen, M. Howard and M. Nussbaum (Eds.), *Is Multiculturalism Bad for Women*? Princeton University Press, Princeton NJ.

____ (2002): 'Mistresses of their own destiny: group rights, gender and realistic rights of exit', *Ethics*, **112**, pp. 205–230.

Olson, M (1971): *The Logic of Collective Action: Public Goods and the Theory of Groups*, Harvard University Press, Cambridge MA.

O'Riordan, T. (1981), *Environmentalism*, Pion Press, London.

Owens, E. (1987), *The Future of Freedom in the Developing World: Economic Development and Political Reform*, Pergamon Press, New York.

Paine, T. (1977): *Common Sense*, Penguins, Harmondsworth.

Parekh, B. (2000), *Rethinking Multiculturalism: Cultural Diversity and Political Theory*, Macmillan Press, London.

Pareto, V. (1935), *The Mind and Society*, Jonathan Cape, London.

Parsons, T. (1967), *Sociological Theory and Modern Society*, Free Press, New York.

____ (1969), *Politics and Social Structure*, Free Press, New York.

Pateman, C. (1970), *Participation and Democratic Theory*, Cambridge University Press, Cambridge.

____ (1983), 'The family and the market: A study of ideology and legal reform', *Harvard Law Review*, **96**(7), pp. 1497–1578.

____ (1985), *The Problem of Political Obligation: A Critique of Liberal Theory*, Polity Press, Oxford.

____ (1988), *The Sexual Contract*, Polity Press, Cambridge.

____ (1989), *The Disorder of Women*, Polity Press, Cambridge.

Pearce, D.W. (1985), 'Sustainable futures: The economic issues: The compatibility of industrial development and care of the environment', *Sustainable Development in an Industrial Economy*, Proceedings of a Conference held at Queen's College, Cambridge, UK, Centre for Economic and Environmental Development.

Pearce, D.W., Markandya, A. and Barber, E.B. (1989), *Blueprint for a Green Economy*, A Report for the UK Department for the Environment, London, Earthscan.

Petchesky, R.P. (1990), *Abortion and Women's Choice: The State, Sexuality and Reproductive Freedom*, Northeastern University Press, Boston.

Phillips, A. (1991): *Engendering Democracy*, Polity, Cambridge.

____ (1993): *Democracy and Difference*, Polity Press, Cambridge, 1993.

____ (1995): *The Politics of Presence*, Clarendon, Oxford, Princeton University Press, Princeton NJ.

Pitkin, H.E (1967), *The Concept of Representation*, University of California Press, Berkeley.

____ (1972), 'Obligation and consent', in, *Philosophy Politics and Society*, 4th series, P. Laslett, W.G. Runciman and Q. Skinner (Eds.), Blackwell, Oxford.

____ (1988), 'Are freedom and liberty twins?', *Political Theory*, **16**(4), pp. 523–552.

____ Polsby, N. (1963), *Community, Power and Democratic Theory*, Yale University Press, New Haven, Connecticut.

____ Poggi, G. (1978), *The Development of the Modern State*, Hutchinson, London.

____ (1990), *The State: Its Nature, Development and Prospects*, Polity Press, Cambridge.

Plamentaz, J.P. (1963), *Man and Society*, **2**, Longman, London.

____ (1966), *The English Utilitarians*, Basil Blackwell, Oxford.

____ (1968), *Consent, Freedom and Political Obligation*, Oxford University Press, Oxford.

____ (1969), *German Marxism and Russian Communism*, Longman, London.

Plant, R. (1984), *Equality, Markets and the State*, Fabian Tract No. 494, Fabian Society Publications, London.

____ (1991), *Modern Political Thought*, Blackwell, Oxford.

Planner, M. (1975), 'The new political theory', *The Public Interest*, pp. 119–128.

Pocock, J.G.A. (1962), 'The history of political thought: A methodological enquiry', in, *Philosophy, Politics and Society*, 2nd series, P. Laslett and W.G. Runciman (Eds.), Blackwell, Oxford.

____ (1971), *The Machiavellian Moment: Florentine Political Theory and the Atlantic Republican Tradition*, Princeton University Press, Princeton, New Jersey.

____ (1980), 'Review of political theory: Tradition and 'interpretation', *Political Theory*, **8**, pp. 563–567.

Popper, Sir K.R. (1945), *The Open Society and its Enemies*, Routledge & Kegan Paul, London.

____ (1957), *The Poverty of Historicism*, Routledge & Kegan Paul, London.

Poulantaz, N. (1973), *Political Power and Social Classes*, New Left Books, London.

____ (1980), *State, Power and Society*, New Left Books, London.

Prakash, G. (1990), 'Writing post-orientalist histories of the third world: Perspectives from Indian historiography', *Comparative Studies in Society and History*, **32**.

Prebisch, R. (1950), *The Economic Development of Latin America and Its Principal Problems*, United Nations, New York.

Pye, L. (1990), Political science and the crisis of authoritarianism', *American Political Science Review*, **84**(1), pp. 3–17.

Randall, V. (1987), *Women and Politics*, Macmillan, London.

Raphael, D.D. (1990): *Problems of Political Philosophy*, rev. ed., Macmillan, London.

Rawls, J. (1957), 'Justice as fairness', *The Journal of Philosophy*, **54**, pp. 653–662.

____ (1958), 'Justice as fairness', *Philosophical Review*, **57**, pp. 164–194.

____ (1969), 'The justification of civil disobedience', in, *Civil Disobedience: Theory and Practice*, H.A. Bedeau (Ed.), Pegasus, New York.

____ (1969a), 'Distributive Justice', in, *Philosophy, Politics and Society*, 3rd series, P. Laslett and W.G. Runciman (Eds.), Blackwell, Oxford.

____ (1972), *A Theory of Justice*, Oxford University Press, Oxford.

____ (1975), 'Fairness to goodness', *Philosophical Review*, **84**, pp. 536–584.

____ (1977), 'The basic structure as subject', *American Philosophical Quarterly*, **14**, pp. 159–165.

____ (1982), 'Basic liberties and their priority', in, *The Tanner Lectures on Human Values*, S. McMurrin (Ed.), Cambridge University Press, Cambridge.

____ (1988), 'The priority of right over good', *Philosophy and Public Affairs*, **18**, pp. 257–276.

____ (1993), *Political Liberalism*, Columbia University Press, New York.

____ (1997), 'The idea of public reason revisited', *University of Chicago Law Review*, **64**, pp. 765–807.

Rawls, J. (1999), *The Law of Peoples: The Idea of Public Reason Revisited*, Cambridge, Mass. Harvard University Press, Cambridge.

Raz, J. (1986), *The Morality of Freedom*, Clarendon Press, Oxford.

____ (1994): 'Multiculturalism: a liberal perspective' in his *Ethics in the Public Domain*, Clarendon, Oxford.

Reimer, N. (1962), *The Revival of Democratic Theory*, Appleton Century Crofts, New York.

Rey, P.P. (1971), *Colonialisme, Neo-colonialisme et Transition au Capitalisme*, Presses Universitaires de France, Paris.

____ (1973), *Alliances de Classes*, Presses Universitaires de France, Paris.

Ricardo, D. (1926), *Principles of Political Economy and Taxation*, Everyman, London.

Rich, A. (1977), *Of Woman Born*, W.W. Norton, New York.

Riggs, F.W. (1984), 'Development', in, *Social Science Concepts: A Systematic Analysis*, Sartori, G. (Ed.), Sage Publications, Beverly Hills, California.

Riley, O. (1982), *Will and Political Legitimacy*, Mass. Harvard University Press, Cambridge.

Roll, E. (1992), *A History of Economic Thought*, 5th ed., Faber and Faber, London.

Roos, L. (1900), 'Two fundamental mistakes that doomed the centrally planned economy', *The German Tribune*, **1408**, p. 6.

Rorty, R. (1994), 'Strangers and liberals', *Political Theory*, **22**, pp. 167–175.

Rosenblum, N. (1981), 'Thoreau's militant conscience', *Political Theory*, **9**(1), pp. 81–110.

Rostow, W. (1960), *The Stages of Economic Growth: A Non-Communist Manifesto*, Cambridge University Press, Cambridge.

Rousseau, J.J. (1958), *A Discourse on the Origins of Inequality in the Social Contract and Discourses*, G.D.H. Cole (Trans.), Dent, London.

Ruddick, S, (1983): "Maternal Thinking", Mothering: Essays in Feminist Theory (Ed.), Treblicot, J, Rowman and Allanheld, Totowa NJ.

Rudolp, L.I. and Rudolp, S.H. (1998), *In Pursuit of Laksmi*, Orient Longman, New Delhi.

Runciman, W.G. (1965), *Social Science and Political Theory*, Cambridge University Press, Cambridge.

Russell, B. (1938), *Power*, George Allen and Unwin, London.

Ryan, A. (1984), *The Political Theory of Property*, Blackwell, Oxford.

____ (1985), 'John Rawls', in, *The Return of the Grand Theory in the Human Sciences*, Q. Skinner (Ed.), Cambridge University Press, Cambridge.

____ (1994), Justice, Clarondon Press, Oxford.

Sabine, G.H. (1939), 'What is political theory?', *Journal of Politics*, **1**(1), pp. 1–16.

____ (1973), *A History of Political Theory*, 4th ed., revised by J.L. Thorson, Oxford and IBH, New Delhi.

Sachs, W. (Ed.), (1993), *Global Ecology: New Areha of Global Conflict*, Feuwood Books and Zed Books, London.

Sakharov, A. (1989), *My Country and the World*, Free Press, New York.

Samuelson, P.A. (1976), 'The illogic of Neo-marxian doctrine of unequal exchange', in, *Inflation, Trade and Taxes*, Belsey, Kane, Samuelson and Slow (Eds.), Ohio University Press, Ohio.

Sandel, M. (1982), *Liberalism and the Limits of Justice*, Cambridge University Press, Cambridge.

____ (1984), 'Morality and the liberal ideal', *New Republic*, **7**, pp. 15–17.

____ (1996): *Democracy's Discontent: America in Search of Public Philosophy*, Harvard University Press, Cambridge MA, 1996.

Sartori, G. (1987), *The Theory of Democracy Revisited*, **I**: *The Contemporary Debate* and **II**: *The Classical Issues*, Chatham, Chatham House Publishers, New Jersey.

____ (1995), 'How far can free government travel', *Journal of Democracy*, **6**(3), pp. 101–111.

____ Scanlon, T.M. (1982), 'Contractualism and utilitarianism', in, *Utilitarianism and Beyond*, A. Sen and B. Williams (Eds.), Cambridge Univesity Press, Cambridge.

Saxonhouse, A W. (1985): *Women in the History of Political Thought: Ancient Greece to Machiavelli*, Praeger, New York.

Schaefer, D.L. (1973), 'The sense and nonseuse of justice, Rawls' A Theory of Justice', *The Political Science Reviewer*, pp. 1–26.

Schlatter, R. (1951), *Private Property*, George Allen and Unwin, London.

Schumpeter, J.A. (1976), *Capitalism, Socialism and Democracy*, George Allen and Unwin, London.

Scrunton, R. (1982), *A Dictionary of Political Thought*, Macmillan, London.

Sen, A. (1974), 'Rawls versus Bentham: An axiomatic examination of the pure distribution problem', *Theory and Decision*, **4**, pp. 301–309.

____ (1985), 'The moral standing of the market', in, *Ethics and Economics*, E. Paul, F. Miller and J. Paul, (Eds.), Blackwell, Oxford.

____ (1990), 'Socialism, markets and democracy', *The Hindu*, 9th January.

____ (1999): *Development as Freedom*, Alfred A. Knopf, New York.

____ (2009): *Idea of Justice,* The Belknap Press Harvard University Press, Cambridge, MA.

Shanley, M.L. and Pateman, C. (Eds.) (1991), *Feminist Interpretations and Political Theory*, Penn State Press, University Park.

Shapiro, I. (1986), *The Evolution of Rights in Liberal Theory*, Cambridge University Press, Cambridge.

Shepard, M.A. (1930), 'Sovereignty at the crossroads: A study of Bodin', *Political Science Quartely*, **XLV**, pp. 580–603.

Skinner, Q. (1969), 'Meaning and understanding in the history of ideas', *History and Theory*, **8**, pp. 3–53.

____ (1978), *The Foundations of Modern Political Thought*, **2**, Cambridge University Press, Cambridge.

____ (1981), *Machiavelli*, Oxford University Press, Oxford.

____ (1997), *Liberty before Liberalism*, Cambridge University Press, Cambridge.

Skocpol, T. (1978), *States and Social Revolutions: A Comparative Analysis of France, Russia and China*, Cambridge University Press, Cambridge.

Smelser, N. (1963), *Theory of Collective Behaviour*, Free Press, New York.

Smith, A. (1925), *An Inquiry into the Nature and Causes of the Wealth of Nations*, Everyman, London.

Smith, M.J. (1990), 'Pluralism, reformed pluralism and Neo-pluralism', *Political Studies*, **38**, pp. 302–322.

Smith, M. (1995), 'Pluralism', in, *Theory and Methods in Political Science*, D. Marsh and G. Stoker (Eds.), Macmillan, Basingstoke.

Squires, J, (1999): *Gender in Political Theory*, Polity Press, UK.

Steinfels, P. (1979), *The Neo Conservatives—The Men Who are Changing Politics*, Simon and Schuster, New York.

Strawson, P. (1968), 'Freedom and resentment', in, *Studies in the Philosophy of Thought and Action*, Oxford University Press, Oxford.

Strauss, L. (1936), *The Political Philosophy of Hobbes: Its Basis and Genesis*, Clarendon Press, Oxford.

____ (1949), 'Political philosophy and history', *Journal of the History of Ideas*, **10**, pp. 30–50.

____ (1952), *Natural Right and History*, Chicago University Press, Chicago.

____ (1959), *What is Political Philosophy and Other Studies?*, The Free Press, Glencoe.

____ (1962), 'Epilogue', in, *Essays on the Scientific Study of Politics*, H. Storing (Ed.), Holt, New York.

Tagore, R. (1960), *Letters from Russia*, Visva Bharathi, Calcutta.

Talmon, J.L. (1960), *The Origins of Totalitarian Democracy*, Praegar, New York.

Tawney, R.H. (1952), *Equality*, Allen and Unwin, London.

Taylor, A.E. (1938), 'The ethical doctrine of Hobbes', *Philosophy*, **13**, pp. 406–424.

Taylor, C. (1985), *Philosophical Papers*, Cambridge University Press, Cambridge.

____ (1994): 'The Politics of Recognition' in A. Gutman, (ed.), *Multiculturalism: Examining the Politics of Recognition*, Princeton University Press, Princeton, NJ.

Teitelman, M. (1972), 'The limits of individualism', *The Journal of Philosophy*, **69**, pp. 545–556.

Thatcher, M. (1982), *The Paths to Power, Fontana, London.*

Thucydides (1954), *The Peloponnesian War*, R. Warner (Trans.), Penguin, Harmondsworth.

Tilly, C. (1975), *The Formation of National States in Western Europe*, Princeton University Press, Princeton.

____ (1990), *Coercion, Capital and European States, AD 990–1990*, Blackwell, Oxford.

____ (1991), 'Does modernization breed revolution', *International Social Science Journal*, **134**, pp. 22–43.

Titmuss, R.M. (1956), *Essays on the Welfare State*, George Allen and Unwin, London.

____ (1976), 'Welfare State and Welfare Society', in, *Talking about Welfare: Readings in Philosophy and Social Policy*, Noel Timms and David Watson (Eds.), Routledge and Kegan Paul, London.

Tocqueville, A. (1981): *Democracy in America*, 2 Vols., J.R. Mayer and M. Lerner (Ed.), Fontana, London.

Toffter, A. (1979), *Fature Shock: A Study of Mass Beurilderment in the Face of Aececorating Change*, Random House, New York.

Truman, D. (1951), *The Governmental Process*, Alfred A, Knopf, New York.

Tuck, J. (1995), *Strange Multiplicity: Constitutionalism in an Age of Diversity*, Cambridge University Press, Cambridge.

Tuck, R. (1979), *Natural Right Theories: Their Origins and Development*, Cambridge University Press, Cambridge.

____ (1993): The Contribution of History in *A Companion to Contemporary Political Philosophy*, R.E. Goodin and P. Petitt (Eds.), Blackwell, Oxford.

Tucker, R. (1961), *Philosophy and Myth in Karl Marx*, Cambridge University Press, Cambridge.

Tully, J. (1988), *Meaning and Context—Quentin Skinner and his Critics*, Cambridge University Press, Cambridge.

____ (1995): *Strange Multiplicity: Constitutionalism in an Age of Diversity*, Cambridge University Press, Cambridge.

____ (2003): 'Ethical Pluralism and Classical Liberalism' in R. Madsen and T.B. Strong, (Eds.), *The Many and the One: Religious and Secular Perspectives on Ethical Pluralism in the Modern World,* Princeton University Press, Princeton, NJ.

Tunick, M. (1998), 'Hegel on justified disobedience', *Political Theory*, **26**(4), pp. 514–535.

Turner, B.S. (1986), *Citizenship and Capitalism*, Allen and Unwin, London.

Turner, R.K. (1988), *Sustainable Environmental Management: Principles and Practice*, Belhaven, London.

Vaughan, C.E. (1962), *The Political Writings of Jean Jacques Rousseau*, **2**, John Wiley, New York.

Vincent, R.J. (1986), *Human Rights and International Relations*, Cambridge University Press, Cambridge.

Vogelin, E. (1952), *The New Science of Politics*, University of Chicago Press, Chicago.

von Leyden, W. (1985), *Aristotle on Equality and Justice: His Political Argument*, Macmillan, London.

Waldron, J. (1987a), *Nonsense Upon Stilts—Bentham, Burke and Marx on the Rights of Man*, Methuen, London.

____ (1987b), 'Rights', in, *The Blackwell Encyclopaedia of Political Thought*, D. Miller (Ed.), Blackwell, Oxford.

____ (1993): *Liberal Rights*, Cambridge, Cambridge University Press).

Wallerstein, I. (1974), *The Modern World System* (**3** Vols., 1974, 1980, 1989), Academic Press, New York.

Wallas, G. (1908), *Human Nature in Politics*, Constable, London.

Walzer, M. (1973), 'In defense of equality', *Dissent*, pp. 339–407.

____ (1983), *Spheres of Justice: A Defense of Pluralism and Equality*, Basic Books, New York.

____ (1989), 'The state of political theory', *Dissent*, **17**, Summer, p. 337.

Walzer, M. (1992): *What it Means to be an American* (New York, Marsilio).

Warrender, H. (1957), *The Political Philosophy of Hobbes: His Theory of Obligation*, Clarendon Press, Oxford.

Wasby, S. (1970), *Political Science: The Discipline and its Dimensions*, Scientific Book Agency, Calcutta.

Wayper, C.L. (1977), *Political Thought*, B.I. Publications, Bombay.

Weale, A. (1984), 'Politics as collective choice', in, *What is Politics? The Activity and its Study*, A. Leftwich (Ed.), Basil Blackwell, Oxford.

Weale, A. (1992), *The New Politics of Pollution*, Manchester University Press, Manchester.

Weber, M. (1958), 'Politics as a vocation', in, Gerth, H.H. and Mills, C.W. (Eds.) *From Max Weber*, Oxford University Press, New York.

Weldon, T.D. (1953), *The Vocabulary of Politics*, Penguins, Harmondsworth.

White, A.R. (1984), *Rights*, Oxford University Press, Oxford.

Williams, H. (1994), 'Kant on social contract', in, *The Social Contract from Hobbes to Rawls*, D. Boucher and P. Kelly (Eds.), Routledge, London.

Williams, M. (1998): *Voice, Trust and Memory: Marginalized Groups and the Failings of Liberal Representation*, Princeton University Press, Princeton, NJ.

Williams, R. (1958): *Culture and Society*, Harmondsworth, Penguins.

Wilson, E. (1941), *To the Finland Station*, Fontana, Glasgow.

Wilson, G. (1977), *Special Interests and Policy Making*, John Wiley, Chilcester.

Wolfe, B. (1969), *Marxism: One Hundred Years in the Life of a Doctrine*, Doubleday, New York.

Wolff, R.P. (1977), *Understanding Rawls*, Princeton University Press, Princeton.

Wolin, S. (1960), *Politics and Vision: Continuity and Innovation in Western Political Thought*, Little Brown, Boston.

____ (1968), 'Political theory: Trends and goals', *International Encyclopaedia of the Social Sciences*, **12**, Macmillan, New York.

____ (1969), 'Political theory as a vocation', *American Political Science Review*, **LXII**, pp. 1062–1082.

____ (1970), *Hobbes and the Epic Tradition of Political Theory*, William Andrews Clark Memorial Library of the University of California, Los Angeles.

____ (1977), 'Hannah Arendt and the ordinance of time', *Social Research*, **44**, Spring, pp. 91–105.

____ (1986), 'Contract and birthright', *Political Theory*, **14**, pp. 179–194.

____ (1987), Democracy and the welfare state, *Political Theory*, **15**, pp. 467–500.

____ (2000), 'Political theory: From vocation to invocation', in, *Vocations of Political Theory*, J.A. Frank and J. Tambornino (Eds.), University of Minnesota Press, Minneapolis, London.

Woodcock, G. (1944), *The Anarchist Reader*, Fontana, Glasgow.

____ (1971), *Gandhi*, Fontana, London.

Wood, Ellen, Meiksins (1983), 'The state and popular sovereignty in French political thought: A genealogy of Rousseau's general will', *History of Political Thought*, **IV**.

Wood, N. (1984), *John Locke and Agrarian Capitalism*, University of California Press, Berkeley.

Wrong, D. (1979), *Power: Its Forms, Bases and Uses*, Blackwell, Oxford.

Young, I.M. (1984), 'Is male gender identity the cause of male domination', in, *Mothering: Essays in Feminist Theory*, J. Trebilcot (Ed.), Ottawa, Rowman and Allanheld.

____ (1987), 'Impartiality and the civic public: Some implications of feminist critiques of moral and political theory', in, *Feminism as Critique*, S. Benhabib and D. Cornell (Eds.), University of Minnesota Press, Minneapolis.

____ (1989), 'Polity and group difference: A critique of the ideal of universal citizenship', *Ethics*, **99**(2), pp. 250–274.

____ (1990), *Justice and the Politics of Difference*, Princeton University Press, Princeton.

____ (1992): 'Social Groups in associative democracy', *Politics and Society*, 20, pp. 529–534.

____ (1996), 'Political theory: An overview', in, *A New Handbook of Political Science*, R.E. Goodin and H.D. Klingemann (Eds.), Oxford University Press, Oxford.

____ (1998): "Polity and Group Difference: A Critique of the Ideal of Universal Citizenship", *Feminism and Difference* (Ed.,) Phillips, A, Oxford University Press, Oxford.

____ (2000): *Inclusion and Democracy*, Oxford University Press, Oxford.

Yuval-Davis, N. and Anthias, F. (Eds.), (1989), *Woman-Nation-State*, Macmillan, Basingstroke.

Zimmern, Sir A. (1935), *The Greek Commonwealth*, Clarendon Press, Oxford.

Zweigenhaft, R.L. and Domoff, W. (1998), *Diversity in the Power Elite: Have Women and Minorities Reached the Top*? Yale University Press, New Haven and London.

General Readings

Appadorai, A., *The Substance of Politics,* Oxford University Press, Delhi, 1971.

Axford, B., Browning, G.K., Huggins, R., Rosamond, B. and Turner, J., *Politics: An Introduction,* London and Routledge, New York, 1997.

Barry, B. (2005): *Why Social Justice Matters*, Polity Press, Cambridge.

Barry, B., *Democracy, Power and Justice, Essays in Political Theory,* Clarendon Press, Oxford, 1989.

Beiner, R. (1995): *Theorizing Citizenship*, State University of New York Press, Albany.

Bellamy, D., *Theories and Concepts of Politics,* Manchester University Press, Manchester, 1993.

Bhargava, R and A. Acharya (Ed.) (2008): *Political Theory: An Introduction*, Pearson, New Delhi.

Blondel, J., *The Discipline of Politics,* Butterworths, London, 1981.

Bowie, N. and Simon, R.L., *The Individual and the Political Order: An Introduction to Social and Political Philosophy,* Prentice-hall, Englewood Cliffs, New Jersey, 1977.

Brock, G. and D. Moellendorf (2005): *Current Debates in Global Justice*, Springer, Netherlands.

Brown, C. (2002): *Sovereignty, Rights and Justice: International Political Theory Today*, Polity Press, Cambridge.

Campbell, T. (2006): *Rights: A Critical Introduction*, Routledge, London.

Carney, S. (2005): *Justice Beyond Borders: A Global Political Theory*, Oxford University Press, Oxford.

Carter, I., Kramer, M.H. and Steiner, H. (2006): *Freedom: A Philosophical Anthology*, Blackwell, Oxford.

Clayton, M. and A. Williams (Eds.) (2000): *The Ideal of Equality*, Macmillan, London.

Coker, F.W., *Readings in Political Philosophy,* Macmillan, New York, 1938.

Cott, N.F., *The Grounding of Modern Feminism,* Yale University Press, New Haven, 1987.

de Crespigny, A. and Minogue, K. (Eds.), *Contemporary Political Thinkers,* Methuen, London, 1975.

Dobson, A. (2000): *Green Political Thought*, Routledge, London.

Dobson, A. and R. Eckersley (Eds.) (2007): *Political Theory and the Ecological Challenge*, Cambridge University Press, Cambridge.

Dryzek, J.S., B. Honig and A. Phillips (2006): *The Oxford Handbook of Political Theory*, Oxford University Press, New York.

Dworkin, R. (2000): *Sovereign Virtue: The Theory and Practice of Equality*, Harvard University Press, Cambridge MA.

Farrelly, C. (2004): *Contemporary Political Theory: A Reader*, Sage Publications, London, Thousand Oaks and New Delhi.

Faulks, K. (2003): *Citizenship*, Routledge, London and New York.

Goodin, R.E. and Klingemann, H.D. (Eds.), *A New Handbook of Political Science*, Oxford University Press, Oxford, 1996.

Goodin, R.E., P. Petitt, and T. Pogge (Eds.), (1993) and (2012): *A Companion to Contemporary Political Philosophy*, First and Second Edition, Blackwell, Oxford.

Hampton, J., *Political Philosophy,* Westview Press, USA, 1997.

Held, D. (2004): *Global Covenant: The Social Democratic Alternative to the Washington Consensus*, Polity Press, Cambridge.

Hoffman, J. and P. Graham (2007): *Introduction to Political Theory*, Pearson Education, Delhi.

Jones, T., *Modern Political Thinkers and Ideas: An Historical Introduction*, Routledge, London and New York, 2002.

Kingsnorth, P. (2003): *One no, Many Yeses: A Journey to the Heart of the Global Resistance Movement*, Free Press, London.

Knowles, D., *Political Philosophy,* Routledge, London and New York, 2001.

Laslett, P. and Runciman, W.G. (Eds.), *Philosophy, Politics and Society,* Series 1–5, Blackwell, Oxford, 1956–1979.

Lerner, M., *Ideas are Weapons,* Macmillan, London, 1932.

McKinnon, C. (2003): *Issues in Political Theory*, Oxford University Press, New York.

Miller, D. (2006): *The Liberty Reader*, Edinburgh University Press, Edinburgh.

Miller, D. (Ed.), *The Blackwell Encyclopaedia of Political Thought,* Basil Blackwell, Oxford, 1987.

Nussbaum. M. (2000): *Woman and Human Development: The Capabilities Approach*, Cambridge University Press, Cambridge.

Ostrom, E. (1990): *Governing the Commons: The Evolution of Institutions for Collective Action*, Cambridge New York: Cambridge University Press.

Parekh, B., *Contemporary Political Thinkers,* Martin Robertson, Oxford, 1982.

Pogge, T.P. (1989): *Realizing Justice*, Cornell University Press, Ithaca New York.

Schochet, G.J., *Patriarchalism in Political Thought,* Basil Blackwell, Oxford, 1975.

Shanley, M.L. and Narayan, U., *Reconstructing Political Theory: Feminist Perspectives,* Polity Press, Cambridge, 1997.

Singer, P. (2002): *One World*, Yale University Press, Connecticut New Haven.

Stirk, P.M.R. and Weigall, D., *An Introduction to Political Ideas,* Printer Publishers, London 1995.

Name Index

Subject Index